Central and East European Politics

Central and East European Politics

From Communism to Democracy

Third Edition

EDITED BY
SHARON L. WOLCHIK
AND JANE LEFTWICH CURRY

ROWMAN & LITTLEFIELD
Lanham • Boulder • New York • London

Published by Rowman & Littlefield
A wholly owned subsidiary of The Rowman & Littlefield Publishing Group, Inc.
4501 Forbes Boulevard, Suite 200, Lanham, Maryland 20706
www.rowman.com

Unit A, Whitacre Mews, 26-34 Stannary Street, London SE11 4AB, United Kingdom

British Library Cataloguing in Publication Information Available

Library of Congress Cataloging-in-Publication Data

Central and East European politics : from communism to democracy / edited by Sharon L. Wolchik
and Jane Leftwich Curry. — Third edition.
     pages cm
  Includes bibliographical references and index.
  ISBN 978-1-4422-2420-9 (cloth : alkaline paper) — ISBN 978-1-4422-2421-6 (paperback :
alkaline paper) — ISBN 978-1-4422-2422-3 (electronic) 1. Europe, Eastern—Politics and
government—1989– 2. Europe, Central—Politics and government—1989– 3. Post-communism—
Europe, Eastern. 4. Post-communism—Europe, Central. 5. Democracy—Europe, Eastern.
6. Democracy—Europe, Central. 7. North Atlantic Treaty Organization—Europe, Eastern. 8.
North Atlantic Treaty Organization—Europe, Central. 9. European Union—Europe, Eastern. 10.
European Union—Europe, Central. I. Wolchik, Sharon L., editor of compilation. II. Curry, Jane
Leftwich, 1948– editor of compilation.
  DJK51.C437 2015
  947.0009'049—dc23
                                                                              2014037276

Printed in the United States of America

We dedicate this edition of this volume to our parents, Olga and Leon Wolchik and Fred and Elizabeth Leftwich. Their love and support have been extraordinary throughout our lifetimes. We thank them for their constant love and for sharing their wisdom, curiosity about the world, pride in their heritage, and understanding with us.

Contents

PART III: CASE STUDIES

PART IV: CONCLUSION

Illustrations

Figures

Maps

Photos

Tables

Acknowledgments

We would like to acknowledge the support of the Institute for European, Russian, and Eurasian Studies at The George Washington University, the Centre for East European Studies at the University of Warsaw, and Santa Clara University.

We thank Nancy Meyers, Bret Barrowman, Amber Footman, Isabelle Chiaradia, Michael Kilbane, Melissa Aten, Christine Cannata, Allison Beresford, and Kallie Knutson for their research assistance for this and previous editions of this volume. Daniel Brett would like to thank Irina Marin for her help with the Romania chapter.

We also thank Alex Mehrtens for his dedication to this edition. Elwood Mills deserves special thanks for his seemingly unending work and patience in preparing maps and illustrations. We are also grateful to Monika Szewczyk, Margarita Assenova, and the Embassy of the Slovak Republic for their help in obtaining photographs.

We thank all of our previous contributors for their patience, persistence, and diligence in preparing their contributions for the first and second editions of this volume. We are especially grateful to them for their willingness to update their chapters for the third edition and to the new contributors to this edition. We would also like to thank several anonymous readers as well as the participants in the twelfth annual "Recovering Forgotten History—the Image of East Central Europe in English Language Textbooks" workshop held in June 2014 for their comments and advice.

We also want to acknowledge the intellectual debts we owe not only to Václav Beneš, to whom the first and second editions of this book were dedicated, but also to others whose mentoring and teaching have shaped our views of Central and East European affairs and comparative politics. Our colleagues and friends in Central and Eastern Europe have challenged and informed us, giving us valuable insights and untold hours of their time. For that, we owe them much. We are also grateful to the generations of students whose interactions with us helped us learn what students want and need to know about the politics of the region.

We are indebted, as always, to our families for their support in this endeavor, as in all others. This book, as our other work in this region, has been a part of their lives as well as ours, and they have shared in its creation and revision through dinner table conversations and e-mail and phone updates. We are gratified by their interest in Central and Eastern Europe, evident in their travel, study, and research in the region.

Finally, the idea for this book grew out of our common difficulty in finding up-to-date, accessible materials about the politics of Central and Eastern Europe after communism. But its origin actually dates to 1970, when we found ourselves beginning the study of what was then termed "Eastern Europe" with Václav Beneš at Indiana University. Our meeting at the reception for new graduate students led to a friendship that has seen us through graduate school, the births and growth of six children between us, and nearly forty years of professional and personal triumphs and tragedies. In addition to all those we have thanked for their role in producing this book, we are grateful for each other and for our friendship.

Part I

INTRODUCTION

CHAPTER 1

Twenty-Five Years after 1989

ISSUES IN POSTCOMMUNIST EUROPE

Sharon L. Wolchik and Jane Leftwich Curry

In 1989, the unthinkable happened: communist rule collapsed, virtually like a house of cards, all over what had been the Soviet bloc. As Timothy Garton Ash said, "In Poland it took ten years, in Hungary ten months, East Germany ten weeks: perhaps in Czechoslovakia it will take ten days!"[1] This statement, although not entirely accurate, captures several crucial aspects of the end of communist rule: it was fast, unexpected, and unplanned.

Slightly more than a year later (October 3, 1990), not only had the Berlin Wall come down, but Germany was no longer divided into the Soviet-occupied communist German Democratic Republic and the richer democratic Federal Republic of Germany. As Germany came together, Czechoslovakia, Yugoslavia, and the Soviet Union came apart, creating, from what had been eight states, twenty-nine states, nineteen of which are geographically in Europe. In the process, the collapse of Yugoslavia brought the first European war since the end of World War II.

A decade and a half after the collapse of communist rule, the Czech Republic, Hungary, and Poland joined the North Atlantic Treaty Organization (NATO)—once the military bulwark of the Americans and those we then called the West Europeans against communism. Five years later, in 2004, NATO took in the Baltic states, Bulgaria, Romania, Slovakia, and Slovenia. That same year, fifteen years after the first roundtable negotiations between the Polish communists and their Solidarity opponents, the European Union (EU) expanded eastward to take in eight of the new democracies. Romania and Bulgaria became members in 2007. In 2013, Croatia became the twenty-eighth member of the EU. Macedonia and Montenegro remained candidate members; Serbia became a candidate in 2014, and Albania was expected to become a candidate member in 2014, pending further progress on issues such as corruption and judicial reform. After the Orange Revolution in 2004, Ukraine pushed to begin negotiations with the EU, only to have this policy reversed under Victor Yanukovych. After Yanukovych fled in the wake of street demonstrations following his refusal to sign, as anticipated, an association agreement with the EU at the Vilnius summit in November 2013, the acting Ukrainian government signed the agreement. In 2014, only Bosnia, Kosovo, and Ukraine remained far from membership.

True, after almost fifty years of communist rule and a Cold War that most had assumed meant a Europe irreversibly divided between East and West, the countries of Central and Eastern Europe were once again free to chart their own courses. But the return to Europe and the transition from communism have not been easy for these states. When communism collapsed, the new leaders and citizens in the region hoped that democracy and capitalism would take root and flourish easily and quickly. The realities, though, proved more complicated. Almost all of these states had to catch up from centuries as the backwaters of Europe, most often as a part of someone else's empire. State economies whose failures had helped bring down communist control had to be unraveled. Political systems in which elites shared power and citizens both had a voice and took responsibility had to be devised, established, and consolidated. Finally, both the leaders and the populations had to come to grips with their communist past.

As we noted in our introduction to the second edition, these states are becoming part of European institutions, but they are not yet totally "European" in their politics or their economic developments. Governments in the region have changed often, and party systems are still fluid in most countries. Populist and far-right parties and movements have made headway in some countries in the region. In all countries, corruption has become far more significant than we anticipated and has had a negative impact on citizens' attitudes toward politics, including political institutions and leaders as well as their own role as participants in politics. Although democracy seems well entrenched in much of the region, the last five years have seen significant backsliding in several countries, most notably in Hungary and in Ukraine under Yanukovych, and governments have been less stable in many of these countries than elsewhere in Europe. Economic reform has brought private ownership and multinational corporations. At the same time, it has brought deep divisions between rich and poor, a decline in social welfare that has impacted the health and lives of much of the population, and, for many, real disappointment in the fruits of capitalism.

In contrast to the first decade after the end of communism, when there was relatively little popular protest, even when the shift to the market made living conditions very difficult for certain groups of people, in the last decade we have seen a significant growth of popular protest. In some cases, protests stemmed from political decisions taken or, as in Ukraine in 2013 and 2014, not taken (in this case, President Yanukovych's decision not to sign an agreement with the EU at the Vilnius summit). Similarly, in Hungary, the Viktor Orbán government's amendment of the Hungarian constitution in March 2013, which the EU criticized, sparked popular protest. In other cases, citizens protested against what they perceived to be very high levels of corruption, as in Bosnia in 2014, or to demand better wages or action on other economic grievances, as in the many short-term strikes and protests by doctors, nurses, teachers, and other state-sector workers in numerous countries. These actions demonstrate that the patience of the population with the privations created by the shift to the market and the actions of initially inexperienced leaders facing very difficult and complex tasks has largely reached its end. No longer satisfied to look toward a better future for their children, many citizens have begun to use protest as a way to articulate their political demands.

Accession to the European Union was the logical outcome of the fall of the Berlin Wall, but inclusion of Central and East European countries has complicated the EU's politics and economics. The postcommunist European countries are poorer than the original members, and their incorporation was costly for earlier members of the EU. Many of their citizens faced far higher unemployment rates. As a result, they were easily tempted by the possibility of working in the West, provoking fears in most of the rest of continental Europe that these job seekers might fill the least well-paid jobs and drag down wages for others. Many citizens in this region proved to be far more skeptical of the EU than those in earlier member states. As a result, some of these states—particularly Poland under the leadership of the Kaczynski twins and the Czech Republic when led by former president Václav Klaus—took stances that complicated EU debates and nearly blocked key changes to EU structures and policies.

EU accession has had a mixed impact on the countries in the region themselves. As Ronald Linden and Shane Killian's chapter on the EU illustrates, there is little doubt that accession to the EU has strengthened European values and norms in the countries that have become members. The good neighbor treaties required as part of the accession process have smoothed relations within the region in many instances. In many of these countries, EU practices concerning the rights of ethnic minorities have had a beneficial influence on the status of these groups, with the exception of the Roma, many of whom continue to face discrimination and violence, despite EU pressure. And, as noted by Vesna Pusic, foreign minister and deputy prime minister of Croatia, the latest country to become a member of the EU, the very process of adopting the *acquis communautaire* and going through the negotiations required to become EU members has helped shift the focus from the "heroic" issues that dominated the politics of the region for some time (i.e., defining national identity and defending the nation) to the more prosaic, mundane issues that are, after all, the bread and butter of decision making in democratic states.[2]

At the same time, as the chapter on Hungary in this volume illustrates, EU membership is no guarantee that backsliding on some dimensions of democracy will not occur. The Hungarian case also illustrates the fact that EU influence and ability to affect policies has been greatest before and during the accession process. Once the major carrot, membership, has been offered, the EU has had fewer and far weaker means to enforce adherence to the values, norms, and behaviors it endorses.

As the transitions progressed, scholars debated whether these transitions would follow the models of democracy building in southern Europe (Spain, Portugal, and Greece) and in Latin America in the 1970s and 1980s or whether Central and East European countries' precommunist histories and the impact of communism made them different enough from each other and from the earlier transformations that they would follow different paths. Although there are similarities in some of the dimensions of the transition from authoritarian rule in the postcommunist and other cases, there are also many differences. As Valerie Bunce noted in her much cited, provocatively titled article "Should Transitologists Be Grounded?," the transition from communist rule involved a number of dimensions that were not present in the other transitions, including the need to re-create market economies and deal with the fact that communist regimes were much more intrusive and affected daily life more profoundly than other forms of authoritarianism.[3] Communist leaders came to power not only to rule but to transform their societies and economies, as well as their political systems. They also sought, particularly in the early period, to transform the values, attitudes, and behaviors of their populations. This legacy, as the chapters to follow illustrate, and the "lived experience" of communism have had an enduring impact on some aspects of life in the region. The role—or, better said, the lack of an independent role—of the military is another factor that has made the transition from authoritarianism in postcommunist states different from that in Latin American and southern Europe. Ethnic issues have also loomed large as political issues in the postcommunist states. The transition from communism, then, has differed in important ways from the transition from other forms of authoritarian rule. At the same time, certain elements of these transitions have been similar. Thus, in certain areas comparison of the transitions has been fruitful. These include the impact of the change on gender issues[4] and transitional justice and dealing with the past.[5]

Controversy over whether the very term "transition" is any longer of use has also influenced study of this region. As perhaps most succinctly set out by Thomas Carothers, some analysts have argued that the term itself implies "directionality" (i.e., that the process will eventually lead to a specific outcome, that is, democracy). They argue that we should instead view these systems as systems that may endure in their current state for some time to come, regress to some form of less democratic or authoritarian rule, or move back and forth between these poles.[6] Other scholars have argued that the term "transition" has outlived its usefulness now that the events of 1989 are receding into the background and a generation now coming of political age in the region has never experienced communism in any form. It is more appropriate, these analysts argue, to consider these countries as European countries, rather than as postcommunist states in transition.[7] This question remains a subject of debate, and we will return to it in our conclusion.

This book lays out the paths—the commonalities and the differences—that have marked the transitions from communism to democracy, from centrally planned economies to the market, and from the Soviet bloc and Iron Curtain to NATO and the European Union. Its chapters also consider how Russia's new assertiveness in foreign policy—particularly its annexation of Crimea, arming, training, and supplying of separatists in southern and eastern Ukraine, and invasion of the country in late August 2014—are influencing individual countries as well as the EU and NATO. As Vladimir Putin's actions in these areas illustrate, the view that prevailed after the dissolution of the Soviet Union in 1991 and for much of the first two decades after the end of communism that there was no credible threat to the security of Central and Eastern Europe is no longer accurate. As a result, leaders and citizens in many countries in the region—particularly the Baltic states, which have Russian minorities, but also in those countries, such as Poland, whose citizens have long memories of conflict with Russia and the Soviet Union—have called for the presence of NATO troops and bases on their land and for a strengthening of NATO in general. At the same time, the high level of dependence on Russian energy supplies of many of the countries in the region, particularly Hungary and Bulgaria, as well as countries outside the region, such as Germany, has led their governments to urge caution in applying sanctions in dealing with Russian aggression in Ukraine.

Scope of This Book

The countries dealt with explicitly in this volume are those from the old European communist world that have been the focus of attention for Europe and have made substantial progress along the path to democracy. These include

- Poland, Hungary, the Czech Republic, Slovakia, and the Baltic states, where there was an early and decisive break with the past and a clear turn toward building democratic institutions and politics in 1989 or, in the case of the Baltic states, with the collapse of the Soviet Union in 1991. Slovenia also falls into this group, since it was the only state that emerged from former Yugoslavia that experienced a transition similar to those of the other states in this group rather than the delayed pattern of change that occurred in the other successor states.

- Romania, Bulgaria, Albania, Croatia, Serbia, Montenegro, Ukraine, and Macedonia, where politics turned toward democracy more slowly. Progress in this regard occurred after war (in the case of successors to the Yugoslav federation) or only after critical elections or "electoral revolutions" replaced the semi-authoritarian or "illiberal democracies"[8] established after the fall of communism.

- Bosnia-Herzegovina and Kosovo, where outside powers sent in troops and peacekeepers in the wake of violent conflict in the first case and Serbian ethnic cleansing in the second and effectively ruled the region for some time. Bosnia is formally independent, even though its elected officials' decisions can be overruled by the international community's High Representative, who can remove, and has removed, elected officials who act against the Dayton Agreement of 1995, which is the basis for the current organization of the country. The independence of Kosovo remains a highly contested issue: Serbia's 2006 constitution claims Kosovo as an integral but autonomous region, and Serbia does not formally recognize Kosovo's independence, despite its recognition by the United States, most (though not all) members of the EU, and many other states. Recent progress in negotiations between the two sides has, however, led to Serbian agreement that Kosovo can seat its representatives in international gatherings, as long as the country's nameplate includes a note to the effect that Serbia does not recognize its independence.

These states, as well as the others that arose from former Yugoslavia, with the exception of Slovenia, had transitions that were marked in important ways—and, in most, delayed—by the impact of the violent wars that accompanied the breakup of the Yugoslav federation. In these cases, elites and citizens faced issues that those in the rest of the region did not have to deal with, including the aftermath of armed conflict, use of rape as a weapon of war, ethnic cleansing, and waves of refugees. These issues complicated both the domestic transitions and the progress of these states in joining the EU and other international organizations, including NATO.

This volume does not deal with East Germany, the former German Democratic Republic, which went through many of the same processes in its shift to democracy but in the context of reunification with West Germany rather than as a separate state. Given the role of West Germany in supporting and directing the incorporation of the east into a common state and the different nature of this process as a result, we have not included eastern Germany in our cases. Nor does this volume deal with Belarus, which, after a brief "democratic moment," returned to authoritarian rule with the victory of Alexander Lukashenko in 1994, after he campaigned against the corruption and impoverishment that came with economic reform. As what has been termed the "last dictatorship in Europe," Belarus is, at best, a tragic outlier.

The remainder of this chapter focuses on several tasks. First, we provide a general overview of some of the factors that influenced the development of the countries we consider in the period before communist systems were established and under communism.

We then examine the way communism ended and the common tasks involved in the transition away from communism. Finally, we highlight the issues that the rest of the volume explores in order to create a comparative context for the thematic and country chapters that follow.

The Rocky Roots of Central and Eastern Europe

History has not always been kind to the peoples in the east of Europe. The landscape of the region is a mosaic of different nationalities that have their own languages, religions, and cultures. For most of their histories, many of the peoples of this region have been under the control of other states for long periods. They were underlings first of each other and then of the empires of Europe: the Ottoman Empire to the south, the Russian Empire to the east, and the Austro-Hungarian and Prussian empires to the west. In those empires, they were not the leaders. Instead, they served the empires' needs by producing food, providing cheap labor, or staffing the bureaucracy. Most often, they struggled to develop or preserve their national identities against attempts to assimilate or control them. Thus, when they became independent states, most after World War I, virtually all except what became Czechoslovakia—more accurately, the Czech Lands, though not Slovakia or Ruthenia—were economically behind and politically troubled.[9]

The division into empires created a second layer of difference in this area. The lines drawn between the empires were more than geopolitical divisions. They resulted in clear differences in the trajectories of these states toward democracy and industrialization. Nearly a century after the empires collapsed, the differences between how these states' democracies do or do not work, with few exceptions, follow the lines of the empires' nineteenth-century divisions. When new states were formed and old states re-created after World War I, the empires' boundaries reappeared in the differences in the economies and infrastructures of the new states. Each empire had made its capital the focus. The train lines went back and forth to Berlin, Vienna, and Moscow, not between Warsaw and Kraków or between Prague and Bratislava.

The areas of southeastern Europe that became Serbia, Montenegro, Bulgaria, Bosnia, Albania, and parts of Romania and Croatia were loosely ruled by the Ottoman Empire. The Ottomans did little to develop this area. Corruption glued the empire together. It also brought the Ottomans down after local nationalism began to increase and the European empires, led by Austria-Hungary, moved in to take the pieces they could of most of these areas. Before World War I, Serbia, Bulgaria, Albania, and Romania were formally independent but internally divided. The battles that emerged over their borders and who belonged where have continued since. Their economies were based largely on subsistence agriculture.

The Russian Empire in Europe encapsulated the Baltic states (Latvia, Lithuania, and Estonia), eastern Poland, and eastern Ukraine. Unlike the Ottomans, the Russians aimed to Russify and hold on tightly to these lands and their populations. Despite Russia's stranglehold, though, these nations retained memories of national glory and religions that were, at best, not Russian and, most often, anti-Russian. Many of their intellectuals

Map 1.1.   Central and Eastern Europe Today

Map 1.2.　Empires in Central and Eastern Europe, 1800

escaped to Western Europe and the United States, creating strong ties with the West that defied Russia's attempts to keep out new democratic ideas and make its subject peoples "Russian." The Poles were the most determined. They fought Russian control with uprisings and underground organizations starting in the 1700s when Russia, Austria, and Prussia partitioned Poland. Under Russian rule, Poland, Ukraine, and the Baltics remained largely agricultural economies with only a few pockets of industry and mining.

Until World War I, Prussia and later united Germany extended into what is now western Poland. The Germans in western Poland and in the Czech Lands of Bohemia and Moravia had a long history of dominance and were also a large part of the population in much of this area. They dominated the economies of both western Poland and the border regions of what came to be Czechoslovakia. These areas were industrialized and their agriculture the most modernized in Central and Eastern Europe.

The Austro-Hungarian Empire encompassed the Czech Lands, Slovakia, Hungary, Croatia, Slovenia, part of Poland, and what is now western Ukraine, as well as Bosnia after 1878. If foreign control can be good, Austrian control was. In parts of the areas ruled from Vienna (the Czech Lands, parts of Poland and Ukraine, and Slovenia), industrial development and local governance were allowed and encouraged. Citizens from these states participated in regional government and the Diet in Vienna. Schooling took place in German and also in the local languages. The Czechs flourished under Austrian rule; Bohemia and Moravia came to account for the majority of the industry in the empire. Citizens in the Hungarian part of the empire (Slovakia and Croatia) had fewer opportunities to develop national movements. In Slovakia, little education in Slovak was available beyond the elementary level, and particularly after the 1870s, Slovaks came under heavy pressure to assimilate and adopt Hungarian as their language. Non-Hungarians had few political rights or opportunities to participate in politics even at the regional level. Opportunities for education and participation in local governance were somewhat greater in Croatia under Hungarian rule. However, given the domination of political life in Hungary by the landed aristocracy, there were few incentives to develop industry. Apart from Budapest, much of the region remained dependent on agriculture.

World War I marked the birth of a new constellation of states in the east of Europe. The war was triggered by the assassination of Austrian archduke Franz Ferdinand in Sarajevo by a Serbian who wanted Bosnia to be part of Serbia, not the Austro-Hungarian Empire. After the war, US president Woodrow Wilson's call for national self-determination for the peoples of Europe was reflected in the carving up of the old empires into nation-states. The boundary lines of the states established at this time were far from perfect. The results of these settlements created serious problems within and between states in the interwar period that persist in political conflicts between ethnic groups even today.

At the end of the war, the Treaty of Versailles drew the borders of the new Europe. Although national self-determination was the call, ethnic groups were intermingled when the borders were drawn. The Allies' desire to punish Germany, Austria, Hungary, and Bulgaria; the establishment of communism in Russia; and the constellation of military forces on the ground instead determined the borders of the new Europe. To punish Germany and Austria, the lands of the German and Austro-Hungarian empires were cut apart. Hungary was most affected: as a result of the Treaty of Trianon of 1920, it lost two-thirds of its territory and roughly 60 percent of its population to its neighbors.[10] Although many of the areas Hungary lost were populated largely by non-Hungarian ethnic groups, the treaty left sizable numbers of Hungarians outside the borders of Hungary proper. Many citizens and leaders in the shrunken Hungary saw this loss as unjust. The popular response to Trianon, "No, no never," was played out in the efforts of Hungarian leaders to reverse the treaty and regain Hungary's "historical lands," an effort that dominated Hungarian politics and poisoned its relations with its neighbors during the interwar period. Bulgaria was also punished; it lost land to Greece, Romania, and Yugoslavia. With the breakup of Austria-Hungary, Germans lost their dominant position in what became Czechoslovakia and the newly re-created Polish state.

The boundaries of the new states of Czechoslovakia and Yugoslavia brought together ethnic groups that were very different in their religions, cultures, economies, and levels of development. These differences were most divisive in Yugoslavia. There the languages and religions, as well as the empires under which the different ethnic groups had developed, varied greatly. The political opportunities and experiences of the main groups in these countries also differed widely in the new states. Instead of being on equal footing, one group dominated the others in each state.

The Polish territories straddled German areas in the west and areas with mixed Lithuanian, Ukrainian, Belorussian, and Polish populations in the east. Like Poland, Romania emerged as a multiethnic state patched together from pieces of very different European empires. As in Czechoslovakia and Yugoslavia, the new leaders of these states had to create unified states from peoples who brought with them very different histories and resources. Very often, states were created from national groups whose historical memories included conflict with or resentment of each other.

The Russian Revolution in 1917 and the attempts to spread the revolution beyond Russia created new ideological pressures and divisions that further complicated the political fortunes of these fragile new states. Ukraine had a brief period of independence that ended when it was conquered by Bolshevik armies in 1921. In Hungary, communist supporters led by Béla Kun established the Hungarian Soviet Republic, a short-lived experiment with communism that discredited Bolshevism in Hungary and contributed to Hungarian antagonism toward the Soviet Union and communism more generally. The communists also tried but failed to spread their revolution to Poland.

The interwar period began with high hopes of building democracy in the new states. But, with the exception of Czechoslovakia, these new democracies disintegrated rapidly into autocracies. Only Czechoslovakia, Hungary, and Poland had more than fleeting moments of democracy. In Hungary and Poland, these ended with authoritarian regimes under military rulers. In Bulgaria, Romania, and Yugoslavia, royal dictatorships replaced parliamentary rule. In Albania, which had maintained its independence at the Paris Peace Conference despite the plans of many of its neighbors and the larger powers to partition it, parliamentary rule was disrupted by a coup and, in 1928, the proclamation of a monarchy by Ahmet Zogu.

Ruled by combinations of bureaucratic and military elites, supplemented in some cases by representatives of the rising industrial class, these governments paid little attention to the needs of citizens, who, after a brief period, had few avenues for effective political participation. As authoritarian governments usurped the powers of parliaments, most of the numerous small political parties that had been active in politics were outlawed.

Citizens were channeled into movements or parties loyal to the government.[11] Communist parties were established in 1921 in all of these states. They, too, were soon outlawed in most cases. Extremist parties and movements, particularly those on the far right, such as the Iron Guard in Romania and the Arrow Cross in Hungary, flourished and were a real threat to political stability. In Bulgaria, the radical Internal Macedonian Revolutionary Organization ruled parts of the country briefly.

With the exception of Czechoslovakia, which was one of the most developed nations in the world during the interwar period because of the concentration of 70 to 90 percent of Austria-Hungary's industry in Bohemia and Moravia, these countries remained largely (Poland and Hungary) or overwhelmingly (the others) agrarian. The new leaders of all these states aggressively tried to industrialize. They achieved some success in the 1920s. Growth rates at this time were higher in Poland and Romania than in France or Germany. However, their economies continued to depend heavily on agriculture. In the fewer than twenty years between the wars, none of the largely agrarian states were strong enough to develop their infrastructures, build up their industry, or compete on the world market. Indeed, economic conflict over land distribution and ownership amplified ethnic conflict. The trauma of the Great Depression derailed early efforts to develop and increased the susceptibility of these economies to foreign penetration and economic and political domination. The degree of development these states did achieve also proved problematic from a political perspective. The bureaucracies and leaders of these new states proved incapable, in most cases, of meeting the increased demands for services and infrastructure that urbanization created. They also were generally unsuccessful in incorporating growing working classes into their national political communities.

In the end it was the actions of outside powers and the advent of World War II that brought about the end of the interwar system in Central and Eastern Europe. The inability of the interwar leaders to resolve old issues, such as ethnic conflict, or to deal with the new demands resulting from the development that did occur, however, played a role by increasing their vulnerability and making them easy targets for outside manipulation.

World War II was the watershed event for the fledgling democracies in Central and Eastern Europe. None of the new states had the time or resources to build real defenses against a German onslaught. The first steps to war occurred when the Germans took the Sudetenland from Czechoslovakia with the approval, in the infamous Munich Agreement, of Italy, France, and Britain in September 1938. After that, the move toward war continued with the Molotov-Ribbentrop Pact for the division of Poland between the Soviets and the Germans and their simultaneous invasion of Poland in 1939. The German invasion triggered French and English declarations of war against Germany, starting World War II. Bulgaria, Hungary, and Romania fought alongside the Germans as part of the Axis. Albania was essentially occupied by the Italians and then the Germans. Only at the end of the war did Romania manage to leave the Axis camp. Slovakia and Croatia emerged as puppet states of the Axis powers, although Croatia was also eventually occupied. Poland, the Czech Republic, the rest of former Yugoslavia, the Baltic states, and Ukraine were occupied by Germany. Two years later, in 1941 (the 149th anniversary of Napoleon's attack on Russia), the German-Soviet nonaggression pact collapsed, and German troops swept across Poland into the Soviet Union.

Map 1.3. Eastern Europe, 1914

World War II would prove devastating for Poland, Ukraine, Yugoslavia, and the Baltic states (as well as Russia and Belarus, which are outside the purview of this volume), all of which suffered great loss of life and physical destruction. In the other Central and East European countries, although the physical damage was less, the destruction of their political and social leadership groups was dramatic. The sizable Jewish and Roma minorities, as well as many intellectuals and others perceived as threats or who fought against the Germans, were decimated by the Holocaust. The complicity of some domestic leaders in the deportation of the Jews to the death camps and the collaboration of some with the Nazis further diminished their moral claims to leadership once the war was over.

The Allied leaders of Britain, the Soviet Union, and the United States began to plan for Germany's defeat and the resurrection of Europe in 1943. At Yalta, the second of three conferences between British, US, and Soviet leaders, Britain and the United States essentially agreed to let the Soviet Union play the dominant role from Berlin eastward. By the end of the war, the slaughter of millions of Jews and Roma, boundary changes, the shift of Poland's borders to the west, the expulsion of Germans from Poland and Czechoslovakia, and population exchanges in border areas made most of these states more homogeneous ethnically than they had been before the war. The Western Allies pushed for free, competitive elections as soon as the war ended. With the partial exception of the 1945 elections in Hungary and the 1946 elections in Czechoslovakia, however, these did not happen. After the war, western Ukraine and the Baltic states were incorporated into the USSR. The other Central and East European states found themselves in the Soviet sphere of influence.

The Imposition of Communist Rule

In many of these states, communist rule came with the Soviet armies. Soviet Ukraine was retaken from the German armies in 1943 as the Soviets moved west, and the western part of Ukraine, which had been part of Poland in the interwar period, was incorporated into the Soviet Union as Poland's borders were pushed west. The Soviet army then conquered the Baltic states and much of Central and Eastern Europe as it fought the Germans and marched to meet the Allied forces in Berlin. As they pushed the German forces out, the Soviets installed "baggage train governments"[12] in countries like Poland led by communist leaders who had spent the war years in the Soviet Union and returned to their home countries with the Red Army; in Czechoslovakia, a coalition government of communist and noncommunist leaders was allowed to rule the reunited country. Hungary and Bulgaria, as Axis powers, were simply occupied by the Soviet Union. Soviet troops also brought handpicked Romanian communists with them when they marched into Romania, which had defected from the Axis to the Allies in 1944.

In Yugoslavia and Albania, the Soviets played a very limited role in establishing communism. Although the Soviet army helped liberate Belgrade, Josip Broz Tito and the Partisans liberated most of Yugoslavia through guerilla warfare against the German occupiers. Most of the aid they received came from the Western Allies. The Partisans thus came to power largely through their own efforts. In the process, they also often fought nationalist Croatian Ustaše forces and Serbian Četniks, who in turn fought each other and the Axis occupiers. The Soviet role in establishing communism was also negligible in Albania, where resistance fighters with Yugoslav and Western support ousted the occupiers and established a provisional communist government in 1944.

In Czechoslovakia and Hungary, a period of modified pluralism followed the end of the war. Soviet forces withdrew from Czechoslovakia after the end of hostilities but remained in Hungary. Although the Communist Party initially had a number of advantages in both countries, other political forces were able to play a role in political life for several years. In Hungary, the Communist Party was far less popular than its main political rival, the Smallholders Party. In the election of 1945, the Smallholders received 57 percent of the vote; the Hungarian Communist Party and the Social Democratic Party each received 17 percent. Over the next two years, the Communist Party's membership increased greatly, and party leaders succeeded in gradually restricting the freedom of action of other political parties and discrediting their leaders. The ultimate step in this process was the manipulated election of 1947 in which the Communist Party emerged as the strongest political force. In Czechoslovakia, where the Communist Party won the largest number of votes in the generally free elections of 1946, decreasing support for the party and changes in the international environment led the communists to orchestrate a government crisis in February 1948. After the democratic ministers in the coalition government resigned, a government dominated solely by the Communist Party took power.

In the Baltic states and western Ukraine, the imposition of communism came about by a fourth method: direct incorporation into the Soviet Union. In Latvia, Lithuania, and Estonia, which had been independent in the interwar period, and in western Ukraine, which had been part of Poland before World War II, Soviet forces liberated the region and, much as occurred in the first pattern discussed above, put communist elites in power. In addition, however, these areas were absorbed into the Soviet Union itself. In the case of the Baltic states, each became a republic of the USSR. Western Ukraine became part of the already existing Ukrainian Soviet Socialist Republic.

When communist governments took over after the war, they installed their men and women at the local level and in the key ministries so that they controlled the economy, military, and police. Far-right parties were tarred as Nazi collaborators and outlawed soon after the end of the war. The timing varied, but in all cases, noncommunist parties were either eliminated or allowed to exist under Communist Party control to mobilize sectors of the population unlikely to join the party. The socialist parties from before the war were forced to merge with the communist parties. Communists who had fought against the Germans in their countries were purged in favor of those who had come from the Soviet Union with the Red Army. This process generated purge trials and attacks on communist and noncommunist intellectuals and workers for their connections with the West, the prewar regime, or criticism of the new socialist state.

In states such as Yugoslavia, where there was a fair degree of domestic support for the Partisans under Tito, the process of establishing communist rule was often very violent. In some cases—for instance, in the Baltics and western Ukraine, where certain segments of the population had sided with the Germans against the Russians in World War II— reprisals were often brutal against individuals who had collaborated against or opposed Soviet rule. In Poland and western Ukraine, armed opposition to communism in the one case and Soviet rule in the other, which existed into the early 1950s, was met with forceful countermeasures by the new regimes. In other cases, the violence was less general, but individuals were sometimes tried and imprisoned or sent to labor camps for real or alleged opposition to the new system.

At the same time, communist rulers had to reconstruct their countries and economies after the destruction of the war. For the Polish communists, this process meant rebuilding most of the major cities and industries. In other countries, this task was less monumental. All of these governments, however, had to deal with population shifts and the need to create functioning economies. This process included the collectivization of all agricultural land into state-owned farms or cooperatives farmed by large groups of farmers. This was a bitter pill for those who, less than a generation before in many cases, had received their own plots. It also meant drawing young people from the farms to the cities to build and run new industries. In the 1950s, propaganda portrayed these developments as the great glory of these new socialist states. The dramatic growth in industry also resulted in a great deal of upward social mobility, as a generation of peasant children became educated workers who went on to leadership positions. The old elites were pushed aside in the process.

Communist Rule and Its Realities

Communist rule was intended to put everything under the supervision and direction of the Communist Party and to insure that the various states in the Soviet bloc were themselves supervised and directed by the Soviet Union. No aspect of life or politics was to be excluded. Everything was owned and controlled by the governments. They, in turn, were led by the Communist Party. Ostensibly, this arrangement was intended to speed up the transformation Karl Marx predicted in which industrialization would bring capitalist exploitation of, then increasing equality and power to, the working class. But since these were not the states or the economic conditions in which Marx had said this transition would occur, Vladimir Lenin's turning of Marx on his head was used to justify establishing communist regimes in places where the Industrial Revolution was delayed. The promise was that the state, rather than capitalists, would develop and own industry and transform the working class into the ruling class.

In reality, the institutions and policies associated with communist rule in Central and Eastern Europe failed both economically and politically. As developments throughout the communist period in the region illustrate, in most cases, the Soviet model was neither welcomed nor implemented by the population; rather it was imposed from above. It also came into conflict with underlying conditions and values in many of these societies.

The irony of communist rule in the east of Europe is that it never worked as it claimed and was never monolithic. As early as 1947, the Soviet bloc had its first breakaway. In the period immediately after he came to power, Tito in fact went faster in implementing the Soviet model (to be detailed below) than Joseph Stalin wanted, given his hope that communist parties would come to power peacefully in Italy and France and his emphasis on "national roads to socialism." Tito refused to accept Soviet interference in Yugoslav affairs and also offended Stalin with his plans for a "Balkan union" under Yugoslav leadership. Disagreement over the speed with which Yugoslavia was moving to establish a communist system and its own control of the secret police led to an open break between the two leaders. Soviet advisors withdrew, and Tito became the icon of evil in Soviet communist rhetoric.

The break, which was formalized when the Tito-Stalin rift was followed by Yugoslavia's expulsion from the Communist International (Comintern) in 1948, meant that the fragile multiethnic state of Yugoslavia was on its own, without access to Soviet bloc supplies or markets and, because it remained communist, without immediate aid from the West either. To explain away the split, Tito charged that Soviet-style communism was ideologically incorrect and proposed real decentralization of decision making in the party and government. In 1952, the party changed its name to the League of Communists of Yugoslavia, a step that symbolized its intention to lead by example rather than force. Over the next two decades, power devolved to the republics and away from the center. The Yugoslav leadership also instituted a system of "workers' self-management" that involved workers in decision making in factories, even though management retained a good deal of power. Tito also became a founder of the nonaligned movement and positioned Yugoslavia between the Western and Eastern blocs.

Ironically, its neighbor, Albania, would isolate itself from both the West and the Soviet Union and its European allies. In response to de-Stalinization in the Soviet Union and Nikita Khrushchev's peacemaking with Yugoslavia in the mid-1950s, Albania turned to China. That alliance grew stronger in the late 1960s when Albanian leader Enver Hoxha followed the Chinese in declaring an Albanian Cultural Revolution. In the 1970s, when China normalized its relations with the United States, Albania isolated itself from the outside, legally banning acceptance of foreign aid.

Although Yugoslavia remained a one-party system in which no organized political dissent was allowed, Tito's innovations permitted a degree of openness in debate within the country and contact with the West that no other communist government in the region tolerated. Many of the institutional innovations the Yugoslavs tried were directed at giving different ethnic groups a stake in maintaining a unified state. The system, in the end, gave each Yugoslav republic a veto over decision making at the federal level. It worked for a decade after Tito's death. But it failed to overcome the divisions that played out in a series of brutal wars between the former republics in the 1990s.

After communist governments were established in the rest of the region, they implemented far-reaching institutional and policy changes. This process, which began in earnest after the Stalin-Tito rift and the February 1948 coup in Czechoslovakia, involved copying Soviet experience in all areas. The early emphasis on the need to find national roads to socialism gave way to efforts to create a uniform system of political and economic organization throughout the region by 1948. The Central and East European leaders emulated the Soviet model that existed in the Soviet Union at the time, which was the Stalinist pattern of political and economic organization, economic development, and social and value change. In 1989 and 1991, when communist rule collapsed, this model left the countries in the region with an elaborate set of institutions and huge bureaucracies involved in coordinating and directing the economy as well as the state apparatus. The fused nature of political and economic power both contributed to the end of communism and complicated the transition away from it.[13]

The Communist Party was charged throughout this period with playing the "leading role" in the system. Its goal as a party was not to win elections. Those victories were guaranteed because there was, in normal circumstances, only one candidate per seat, and whether or not he or she was a party member, that candidate was selected by the Communist Party. Its goal was to serve as the "vanguard of the proletariat" and to lead the state in the name of that proletariat. Membership in the party was selective rather than elective. Joining the 10 to 20 percent of the population in the party required that people apply, serve a long candidacy, and be approved for membership by the party.

The Communist Party was organized hierarchically from the primary party organizations found in every workplace up to the Politburo—or Presidium, as it was sometimes called—led by the first secretary. Its basic rule was "democratic centralism." This organizational principle required that all decisions made at the top be supported and carried out by all party members without question. In reality, though, party membership had very little to do with any commitment to communist ideology. It was, most often, simply a ticket to upward mobility. Decisions were made not by the membership and its elected bodies but by a huge party bureaucracy (*apparat*) that not only managed internal party issues such as organization, ideology, and propaganda but also directed and supervised the work of each state institution. It did this through a system of parallel hierarchies, whereby party leaders supervised and directed the workings of each state institution at every level of government.

At the very top of the Communist Party, Politburo members allocated to themselves the key party and state offices. From their perch, they served as the "interlocking directorate," coordinating the various branches of the party and state. Information came up to them from the various party organizations and bureaucracies, and their directives were translated downward. From the top down, the Communist Party structures were the skeleton of the state. The party selected or approved the managerial or politically significant personnel working at all levels of the state bureaucracy and economy (*nomenklatura*), channeled information between the top and bottom, took ultimate responsibility for all major policies, coordinated the work of different sectors of the state, and provided ideological guidance.

Although the Communist Party controlled and directed all political life, everyone was expected to participate in the system. In contrast to the interwar period, when many different charitable, professional, political, and interest organizations existed in most of the region, those that survived the war were brought almost entirely under the control of the Communist Party. Mass organizations, ranging from trade unions to children's organizations, served as "transition belts" to carry the party's directives to the population and mobilize ordinary people to carry out the party's bidding.

Elections were also regularly held for national, regional, and local government bodies. The candidates for these positions (party and nonparty members), as in the Soviet case, were selected and assigned by the Communist Party, one for each open seat, even if they were not party members. Elections were held to demonstrate support rather than to select. Individuals showed opposition by defying the requirement to vote or, for the daring few, crossing out the name of the single candidate. As the 99 percent turnout rates and the small number of "damaged" ballots (those with crossed-out names) demonstrated, opposition, however meek, was virtually impossible in this system.

The Soviet model also included a system of economic institutions and policies and a strategy of economic transformation that subordinated economic life to the party's direction and control. These economies were centrally planned, with a large, party-directed planning apparatus. Decisions about what would be produced, how much, where, and for whom, as well as what workers of different ranks were to be paid and the cost of each product, were made by the state Planning Commission. All parts of the economy, from agriculture and industry to social welfare and the arts, were owned and run by the state. The Planning Commission's decisions were based on general policy goals set by the Communist Party leadership rather than the market. Often, these policy goals were established for political reasons and were not based on economic rationality.

The establishment of state ownership of most, if not all, economic assets began almost as soon as the communists took power. Communist leaders expanded the process of nationalizing industry that started in most of these countries immediately after the end of the war. In line with Soviet practice, they adopted rapid industrialization as a goal. They also emphasized heavy industry, particularly metallurgy and mining, to the detriment of light industry, agriculture, and the service sector. Collectivization of agriculture was another component of the model. In many cases, peasants who had only recently received land confiscated from expelled Germans or collaborators resisted fiercely. Communist elites also redirected foreign trade away from traditional patterns with the rest of Europe toward the Soviet Union and other communist countries.

The impact of this model on economic performance varied at first by the initial level of development of each economy. Stalinist economic policies worked best, at first, in the least developed countries in the region. There they produced rapid growth and urbanization as well as high rates of social mobility. The inefficiencies of centralized economies and Stalinist strategies of development eventually plagued and doomed all the economies of the region. However, in the economies that began with a higher standard of living and industrialization, these failings became evident more quickly. Shortages of basic goods and a lack of adequate services resulted in poor worker morale and low productivity. There was little incentive to innovate. As a result of these failings, these economies could not compete on the world market. These dismal economic conditions were facts of life everywhere in the region. What the population got from state control of the economy was cradle-to-grave welfare, very low-cost housing, guaranteed employment, little pressure to work hard, and prices that virtually never changed, even as products disappeared from the shelves. To cope with shortages and the disappearance of goods, elaborate personal systems of barter and an entire second economy based on illicit trade emerged and became a prime part of the "marketplace" wherever possible.

Communism, though, involved far more than state ownership and Communist Party elite control of the state and the economy. The system demanded public conformity and loyalty. Direction and control of the media and public discussions blocked criticism of the system, its leaders, and their decisions. It also discouraged support for alternative institutions and beliefs. All the media were organized as party mouthpieces, which ensured that views other than those the party sanctioned did not get reported. Lest the population see how others lived, travel and communications in and out of the country were controlled and restricted.

The Soviet model also involved social change and efforts to change the population's value systems. Elimination of most private property served to undermine the economic base of the old elites and minimize the resources they could use to resist the

Photo 1.1.   Bread lines were infamous in communist Europe due to frequent shortages of food and consumer goods. (Peter Turnley/Corbis)

new system. In the process, it also helped to turn the social hierarchy virtually upside down. Restrictions on upper- and middle-class children's ability to obtain higher education and admissions procedures that gave children of workers and peasants preference also promoted changes in the status of members of different social groups. Wage structures that rewarded manual labor in priority branches of the economy, such as heavy industry, mining, and construction, more than work in the "nonproductive" sectors of the economy, such as education, medicine, public trade and catering, and administration, served the same purpose. Even when these policies faded away in the 1970s and 1980s in some of these countries, the old national elite was disadvantaged in comparison to the men and women who had risen from the peasantry to the working class in the 1950s and then moved up through the Communist Party's ranks. They had the power in the state and party to buy themselves into the new economy in ways many who had fought the system or come out of the intelligentsia did not. Political leaders also used education, art and culture, and leisure activities to try to change popular values. The goal was the creation of "new socialist men" (and women) who put "the collective" above individual interests and who worked tirelessly for the promotion of socialism. In the arts and culture in communism's early years, the doctrine of socialist realism required that all artistic expression be directed toward political ends.

The humanities, the social sciences, and even many of the hard sciences that did not contribute to national defense suffered an infusion of ideology into their content. Certain disciplines, such as sociology, were branded bourgeois sciences and banned outright in many countries. Everywhere but Poland, anti-religion campaigns were used to try to wean the population off religion and to steer people toward a belief in Marxism-Leninism as a worldview. In Poland, Catholicism was so deeply rooted that it was impossible to block the Church. Instead, Church actions were limited but politically important, particularly after the Polish cardinal Karol Wojtyla was elected pope in 1978—inspiring popular action in Poland and giving the opposition an external voice.

Communism was also a system in which leaders placed little trust in those they worked with or in the population as a whole. The Soviet model was not chosen by the population but imposed from above. In most cases, the communist leaders who imposed it were in turn also chosen by outside actors (the Soviet leadership). The changes the model required were far-reaching and affected all areas of life. As a result, these regimes relied heavily on coercion. The secret police were an important tool to control dissent and punish opponents and to provide information to the party leadership about what the population did and thought. The military hierarchy included a political force to make sure soldiers and officers were politically trained. In the end, society was watched and directed from all sides.

This pattern was extended into relations among communist parties and rulers. The central Soviet party in Moscow controlled what the party units—and, through them, the governments—did in the Baltics, Ukraine, and elsewhere in the Soviet Union. Although formally independent, the other states in what came to be the Soviet bloc were not truly so. Their party leaders had to be approved by the Soviet leadership, to consult with them and follow their lead on all aspects of domestic and foreign policy, and to work with their neighbors only under Soviet supervision. As a result, changes in the Soviet Union or elsewhere in the bloc impacted all bloc members.

Formally, all members of the Soviet bloc (which did not include Yugoslavia and, after 1961, Albania) were members of the Warsaw Pact and the Council for Mutual Economic Assistance (Comecon or CMEA). The Warsaw Pact, a response to the formation of the North Atlantic Treaty Organization, organized all the military units of the Soviet Union and the Central and East European states under the command of the Soviet military leadership. It had elaborate plans as to who would do what for both offensive and defensive battles in Europe. Perhaps more importantly, it allowed for a monitoring of the preparedness and attitude of the various nations' troops and also forced bloc states to coordinate their military hardware.

The Council for Mutual Economic Assistance was the economic trade organization that coordinated the economies of these states. It, too, was led by the Soviet Union. Through Comecon, Soviet interests were played out in the distribution of economic specialties to individual Central and East European countries (other than Yugoslavia, Albania, and, after 1961, Romania), the direction of trade within the bloc and with the West and Third World, and the management of all currency exchange, since the currencies of Soviet bloc states could not be exchanged outside the "ruble zone" as currency values were set as much for political reasons as for economic ones. In the process, tasks were divvied up so that no country could become economically independent.

In the early communist period, Soviet control played a critical role in determining the course of events in the region. After the death of Stalin in March 1953, Soviet control shifted from direction to guidance and from prescription to proscription. The leaders of

Map 1.4. Axis and Allies, December 1941

Central and East European countries were urged to come to some sort of accommodation with their populations. The Soviet leadership served more as a watchdog, lest orthodoxy be challenged too vigorously, than as the director of events. However, although the Soviet model could be reformed and adapted, there were limits. The Communist Party had to retain its "leading role." There could be no criticism of the Soviet Union or turn from the Warsaw Pact to the West. Twice, popular demands on the street and disillusionment within the party went beyond these limits. Both times, Soviet (in Hungary in 1956) and Warsaw Pact (in Czechoslovakia in 1968) troops invaded, put down the revolt or effort to reform, removed the leaders who went along with the population, and then installed "safe" leaders.[14] When the recognition of Solidarity as the only independent trade union in the communist world in Poland in 1980 led to challenges to the party's leading role, Poland's communist leaders under General Wojciech Jaruzelski imposed martial law in December 1981 to prevent a Soviet-led invasion.

On a day-to-day basis, though, the whole system worked to prevent things from spinning so far out of control. Individual leaders worked their way up through the ranks. They knew the Soviet leaders well enough to estimate easily what would be tolerated and what would not. What they did not know they were told in meetings with the Soviet leaders. Soviet troops were stationed in every country (except Romania, Yugoslavia, and Albania—all of which were far enough away to be able to have separate foreign policies). Long-established economic ties and dependence on cheap Soviet oil and natural gas further tied the bloc together. The Iron Curtain that divided Berlin snaked between East and West economically, politically, and militarily.

Yet, even with these controls and this grand divide, the Soviet model was modified over time in each country. The "Polish road to socialism," after Stalin's death and the Polish upheavals of 1956, brought in a nationalist leadership that was able to trade its population's tolerance for private agriculture, small-scale private industry, and legal rights for the Catholic Church, to which 98 percent of Poles belonged. As part of its mission in Comecon in the 1970s, Poland actively sought trade with the West. In the late 1980s, Poland's communist leaders were so weak and unpopular that they turned to Solidarity to share power and responsibility for improving Poland's disastrous economic performance, only to lose the first partially free election in communist Europe in 1989.

In the 1960s, Romania took its own road. Its communist leaders imposed a form of communism that was both nationalist and highly repressive. Consumer needs were denied in order to support Romania's international position. Romania withdrew from Comecon because it was pressed to become a purely agricultural state and refused direct participation in the Warsaw Pact's invasion of Czechoslovakia. It deviated from Soviet foreign policy by maintaining relations with Israel and China when the Soviet Union broke them. And it was courted by the West because of its foreign policy independence. The bloc countries both tolerated and used all of this, as it provided them with a channel to two critical international actors, the West and China. At the same time, Romania demonstrated how repressive communist rule could become.

Hungarians also took advantage of the opening created by the death of Stalin and disunity within the Soviet leadership to challenge the communist system in the mid-1950s. In what is now recognized as the Revolution of 1956, Hungarians fought Soviet troops in the streets of Budapest until they withdrew. Then, when Hungarian leaders sided with the population, declaring the country's neutrality and announcing plans to adopt a multiparty system, the Soviets invaded again, executed Imre Nagy, the reformist communist leader, and installed a leadership they trusted. After a period of harsh repression, Hungarian leader János Kádár presided over a process of gradual reform. Adopting the slogan "He who is not against us is with us," Kádár shifted to a more conciliatory posture toward the population that has been described as "goulash communism." In the late 1960s, the Hungarian leadership progressively permitted more market elements in an attempt to stimulate the economy. Private enterprises proliferated, and state-owned firms' earnings were determined more by what they produced than by what the plan ordered. To further improve the economy and regain the support of an alienated population, the

"Kádár Compromise" also came to include the gradual withdrawal of the Communist Party from many areas of life and a corresponding increase in room for debate and independent activity. Hungary also followed Poland in shifting the balance of its trade with the bloc and the West. In the process, Hungary's economy moved further than any other toward the market.

In the late 1960s, Czechoslovakia also experienced a period of reform. A delayed response to de-Stalinization and the failing of the economy, this process of renewal and reform at the elite level gained a mass following in early 1968. When Alexander Dubček and his colleagues proved unable or unwilling to rein in calls for even greater freedom, the Warsaw Pact intervened to "protect" socialism from its enemies. The so-called Brezhnev Doctrine enunciated at this time justified the invasion as a defense of the right of the Soviet Union and other socialist states to ensure that socialism was not threatened in any socialist country and reaffirmed the Soviet Union's role as the arbiter of the limits of reform.

As part of the Soviet Union, the Baltic states and Ukraine experienced shifts in policy and the degree of openness that occurred elsewhere in the USSR as leaders changed after Stalin's death. Although de-Stalinization allowed somewhat more room for the republics to chart their own courses, however, the Soviet system remained highly centralized. Moscow often interfered in a republic's affairs to quell excessive nationalism or particularism on the part of its Communist Party leaders or population. Still, national movements continued to develop in the 1970s and 1980s. These movements were particularly strong in the Baltic states, where the memory of independent statehood in the interwar period was still very much alive.

The Collapse of Communism

Much as Communist Party leaders and their minions tried to claim that communism would create a better world, it did not. The plan failed to encourage or allow for the research and development needed for the economies to be effective or even to replace outdated and failing machinery. After the 1950s, workers no longer worked out of fear; they worked for a better life. But in an economy of shortages, with salaries paid whether or not workers and their factories produced, there was little incentive for productivity. And so, as the machinery failed and workers did less and less, productivity dropped. This pattern created a vicious circle: Lacking the new equipment available in the West, communist economies sank further, and productivity decreased, as did what was obtainable on the market, so workers had even less reason to work. As less and less was available and the wait for apartments remained decades long, the population grew more alienated. At the same time, the continuing shortages meant that those with power claimed as much as they could for themselves. Corruption and connections were decisive in what people got and how they lived.

When Mikhail Gorbachev came to power in the Soviet Union, he tried to deal with the crumbling of the communist system. Soviet reforms moved from mere attempts to "accelerate" production by making people work harder, to revelations of the faults in the system through glasnost and efforts to restructure the economy through perestroika, to widespread changes in how the state and the party worked and the expansion of opportunities for people to organize independently and make their views known. The other countries in the bloc were pressed to follow the direction of the Soviet Union. For hard-liners in Czechoslovakia, East Germany, Bulgaria, and Romania, the reforms were far from welcome. For the Poles and the Hungarians, they justified going even further in reforms already underway. For all of the countries in Central and Eastern Europe, as well as the Soviet Union itself, the reforms were destabilizing. Not only did the once stable limits of reform suddenly seem flexible, but as the Soviet leadership focused on solving its own serious problems, it in effect cut Central and East European communist leaders loose to please their populations while propping up their own economies and paying market prices for once cheap Soviet energy resources.

In the end, the softening of Soviet rule and mounting pressure from young people and others who wanted more, together with systems that were increasingly unable to deal with their failings and the disillusionment of the party faithful, started the tumbling of the Soviet bloc dominoes, and it could not be stopped. Where there was an established opposition, the changes were smoother than where no opposition had been able to form or survive. But the system fell apart everywhere outside the Soviet Union in 1989 and 1990, and in 1991 the Soviet Union itself broke up.

Changes in the Soviet Union under Gorbachev and the Soviet leadership's decision to allow Central and East European countries to go their own ways (the so-called Sinatra Doctrine) clearly were important factors in bringing about the end of communism in the region. Similarly, Boris Yeltsin's decision to recognize the independence of the Baltic states in August 1991, after the abortive hard-line coup, and the dissolution of the Soviet Union in September of that year opened the way for the Baltic states and Ukraine to become independent states again. Developments in countries such as Poland and Hungary, which were at the forefront of the process of change, and the fall of the Berlin Wall also influenced developments elsewhere. But while outside factors facilitated the process and in some cases catalyzed the changes, the collapse of these systems also reflected the deep economic and political crises that communist systems had created in all of these states.

The end of communism in the region varied in terms of the speed of the process, the extent of citizen involvement, and the level of violence involved. If we combine these dimensions, five main patterns emerge. The first occurred in Poland and Hungary, where the end of communist rule most closely resembled the pacted transitions in Latin America and southern Europe. In both, reformist leaders in the Communist Party negotiated the end of communism with representatives of the opposition in roundtable discussions. In Poland, the regime and Solidarity leaders agreed to hold semi-free elections in June 1989. Although the agreement guaranteed the party's candidates certain seats, Solidarity won an overwhelming victory and formed the first government not dominated by the communists since the end of World War II.

In Hungary, where the opposition was much smaller, its leaders used issues connected with the Revolution of 1956 to open roundtable negotiations with reformers in the Communist Party. In what was, in some ways, the most remarkable case, the Hungarian communists negotiated themselves out of power without any significant pressure from mass public action other than the peaceful crowds that gathered in the streets for the reburial of the leaders killed after the 1956 revolt, which gave the process of change a public face. In 1990, presidential and parliamentary elections formalized the change of regime agreed on in 1989. In both the Polish and Hungarian cases, the end of communism reflected a longer-term process of organized opposition and change within the party as well as in the broader society.

A second pattern was evident in East Germany, Czechoslovakia, and Romania, where the collapse of communism came about suddenly as the result of massive citizen protests. The process began in East Germany, where peaceful demonstrations led by activists in several cities gained momentum and became explicitly political once the Hungarians opened their borders and allowed large numbers of East Germans to reach West Germany through Hungary. In November 1989 the fall of the Berlin Wall, the most potent symbol of the division of Germany into two halves, had repercussions around the world and encouraged citizens in other communist states to press for change in their own countries.

In Czechoslovakia, the beating of peaceful protestors in Prague who had gathered on November 17 to commemorate a student killed by the Nazis in 1939 led to mass demonstrations in Prague and Bratislava that quickly spread to other towns and cities. Aware that the Soviet leadership would not come to their aid, Czech and Slovak leaders yielded power in negotiations with the opposition twenty-one days after the beginning of the demonstrations. The election of Václav Havel as president by a parliament still dominated by the Communist Party in December capped the victory of what came to be called the Velvet Revolution for its peaceful nature.

Photo 1.2.   Deputy Prime Minister Mieczysław Rakowski (in photo) meets with the crew of the Gdańsk shipyard, where he criticized the activities of Solidarity. The emergence and tolerance of Solidarity for fifteen months in 1980 and 1981 and the martial law regime that followed were the final protest and repression before 1989, when the authorities gave in. Rakowski went on to become the last communist prime minister and, after the 1989 defeat of communist candidates, the last head of the Polish United Workers' Party. (Stefan Kraszewski/PAP)

Mass demonstrations also brought down the extremely repressive, personalized dictatorship of Nicolae Ceaușescu in Romania. Protests in Transylvania spread to the capital and other cities. In contrast to the above cases, in which Communist Party leaders yielded power peacefully, Ceaușescu's secret police force, the Securitate, fired on the peaceful demonstrators. When this action failed to stop the protests, Ceaușescu's opponents within the Communist Party engineered a coup. Nicolae Ceaușescu and his wife, Elena, who was also very deeply involved in the regime's politics, were convicted in what can only be described as a show trial and executed on Christmas Day.

The third pattern occurred in Bulgaria and Albania, where the transitions occurred in two stages. In the first, less repressive Communist Party leaders took over from the old guard. These leaders were, in turn, replaced by the opposition in later elections. In Bulgaria, the reformed Communist Party won in multiparty parliamentary elections in 1990, although the opposition gained a significant number of seats in parliament. The opposition won the 1991 elections only to lose to the reformed communists, now the Bulgarian Socialist Party, in 1994. Not until the mid-1990s did a coalition of the democratic opposition return to power. In Albania, the Communist Party won the 1990 multiparty elections. The newly formed opposition was able to form a noncommunist government only after the 1992 elections.

The transition in Yugoslavia differed in many important ways from the end of communist rule elsewhere in the region. In Yugoslavia, which is the only case that falls into this, the fourth pattern, the end of communism coincided with the breakup of the country and a series of wars that resulted in a large number of deaths, in addition to large waves of refugees as a result of ethnic cleansing, widespread physical destruction, and economic devastation. With the exception of Slovenia, which succeeded in defending its independence in a three-week war in 1991, the transition to postcommunist rule in the states formed from Yugoslavia followed a very different path, one complicated by the impact of the wars and the need to come to terms with their aftermath.

The fifth pattern resembles the fourth in that communism collapsed in the context of state dissolution, but it did so, however, without widespread violence or war. In the Baltic states, the transformation was torturously close and yet impossible until the whole Soviet Union collapsed. The Lithuanians in 1990 and the Latvians in 1991 tried to declare independence, only to have the Soviets move in. Not until the crisis in Russia that developed after the attempted coup in the summer of 1991 were movements for independence able to succeed in Latvia, Lithuania, and Estonia. In all three, groups that had originally supported cultural autonomy gained adherents within the respective communist parties, which also supported self-determination and later independence.

In Ukraine, activists centered in the western part of the country gained supporters in the late 1980s and early 1990s. After Yeltsin recognized the independence of the Baltic states in August 1991, Ukraine's leaders declared Ukrainian independence. As in a number of postcommunist states, the first free elections in Ukraine resulted in the election of a former Communist Party functionary. Political life in Ukraine moved in a markedly democratic direction only after the Orange Revolution defeated President Leonid Kuchma's handpicked candidate and brought Viktor Yushchenko to power in 2004.

The Transition to Postcommunism: Common Tasks and Different Responses

Despite the many ways in which they differed from each other and the different ways communism developed in each of their countries, the leaders of Central and Eastern Europe had to resolve a number of similar crises after the end of communist rule. The most visible of these were summarized by the election slogans of most political parties in the first free elections in these countries: "Democracy, the market, and a return to Europe." In the first area, the new elites had to create or re-create democratic political institutions, values, and practices. The process involved dealing with the economic and political power of the Communist Party and revising the legal system and constitutional structures to make them compatible with democracy, the establishment of a multiparty system, the repluralization of associational life, and the recruitment and training of new leaders. They also had to counteract the influence of communism on the political values and attitudes of the population and foster new values supportive of democracy.

The economic aspect of the transition was equally daunting. In addition to privatizing state assets and fostering development of new private enterprises, the new leaders in the region also had to devise redistribution policies to restore property confiscated by the state to its rightful owners or heirs. They needed to redirect trade patterns, particularly after the disbanding of the Council for Mutual Economic Assistance and the end of the Soviet Union, and begin to deal with the environmental devastation that communist patterns of development created. They also had to deal with the requirements of international financial institutions and the economic and social consequences of the dramatic drop in production that accompanied the shift to the market.

These policies had their counterparts in the arena of foreign policy. In addition to asserting their independence on the world stage and negotiating the withdrawal of Soviet troops when necessary, the new elites undertook a series of actions to reclaim what they perceived to be their rightful place in Europe. Many of these focused on efforts to join European and Euro-Atlantic institutions, with particular emphasis on the European Union and NATO. As of this writing, most of the postcommunist states of Central and East Europe have achieved these goals. In the remaining countries, political elites continue to push for inclusion. Ukraine is the exception to this rule, as its leaders and citizens have been divided concerning Ukraine's integration into the EU and particularly NATO.

The transition from communist rule has also had social and psychological dimensions. In the first area, there has been a major change in the social structures of these countries. New (or old, previously prohibited) groups, such as entrepreneurs, and numerous occupations associated with the rapid development of the previously neglected service and financial sectors have emerged. The status of different social groups has also changed. With the shift to the market, the restitution of property, and the end of most state subsidies, visible income differentials, which were previously small, increased. Social inequality, poverty, and unemployment also increased substantially. While some people were able to take advantage of the new opportunities available in politics, the economy, and society, many others were not. For the latter group, the end of communist rule largely entailed new hardships, particularly in the early postcommunist period, when production and the standard of living fell dramatically in most countries. The division of society into winners (the young, well educated, and urban) and losers (older, less skilled workers, those living in rural areas, and single parents, as well as many women) in turn had important political repercussions.

The end of tight political control and the opening of borders, coupled with the uncertainty and disruptions created by the transition itself, exacerbated old social pathologies and problems, such as alcoholism, juvenile delinquency, prostitution, violence in the home, drug use, and street crime, and allowed new problems to emerge. Organized crime, human trafficking, smuggling, and the sex trade are among the most visible of these. Certain social issues, such as tensions between various ethnic groups, the widespread discrimination against and marginalization of the Roma, and the xenophobia and anti-Semitism that often poison political discussions, all existed in the communist era but were taboo. Now they are recognized as problems and discussed openly,[15] although they all too often continue to serve as sources of violence and repression. Support for extreme nationalist parties and the development of skinhead movements, particularly in economically depressed regions, further reflect these trends.

The experience of living in a time in which most aspects of life, from political choices to the organization of daycare, were in flux also had predictable psychological consequences in the region. Although these effects were most widespread among those for whom the transition largely brought new hardships, they also affected those who could be seen as winners. As one Czech student put it soon after communism fell in that country, "Under communism, it was a question of whether I was allowed to do things; now it is a question of whether I will prove capable of doing them." Greater uncertainty as well as far greater choices, coupled with new pressure to perform well at work, increased competition, and the specter of unemployment, all contributed to the stress individuals and families experienced, even among those groups fortunate enough to be able to take advantage of new opportunities.

The leaders of these postcommunist states have tried different policies in dealing with the common issues they have faced since the end of communist rule. They have had varying degrees of success in meeting their common challenges and those specific to their societies. As the pages to follow illustrate, the response of the international community to these states has also varied. In the process, many of these countries have gone forward and backward on their roads to democracy. Seeming success has often been followed by failure. Just as underlying realities in the region led to diversity in the way communist institutions, policies, and ideology played themselves out in particular countries, so too has the transition from communism, though it has involved the same tasks for all, reflected the diverse social, economic, and ethnic composition of these countries as well as their individual histories and political traditions. The chapters that follow address these strategies. In our conclusion, we draw a balance sheet of successes and failures—or, more optimistically put, remaining challenges. We also address the question of whether it still makes sense to view these states as postcommunist.

The Role of International
Organizations and Outside Actors

In contrast to the interwar period in which outside actors either largely ignored the region (the United States, Great Britain, France) or had designs on it (Italy, Germany, at times the USSR), the international climate has been far more favorable to the success of efforts to create stable democracies and market economies and engineer a return to Europe in the postcommunist period. All of these countries have received substantial economic and democracy-building assistance from the United States, the EU, and many individual European countries. The postcommunist states have also received economic assistance and loans as well as a great deal of advice from international financial institutions such as the International Monetary Fund (IMF) and World Bank. The latter, as well as the European Union, have exerted significant influence not only on the policies adopted by successive governments in the region but also, in many cases, on the institutional design of these societies and polities.[16] In the case of the successors to former Yugoslavia, the international community intervened with negotiators, military force, and peacekeepers to resolve or prevent conflict. It also provided humanitarian aid and established the International Criminal Tribunal for the Former Yugoslavia at The Hague to try war criminals for acts committed during the wars in the 1990s. Cooperation with this tribunal was one condition for beginning negotiations toward EU accession and NATO membership for several of these countries.

At the same time that joining European and Euro-Atlantic institutions has brought many benefits to the countries involved, the asymmetrical nature of the relationship between these countries and these institutions, as well as powerful Western countries, has also led, predictably, to resentment and skepticism on the part of certain segments of the population in all of these countries.[17] The impact of this backlash on politics in the region should not be underestimated. It is clear in the second-term victory of Viktor Orbán in Hungary and support for his pronouncements against the European Union and support for "illiberal democracy," such as that found in Russia and China, as well as in the growth of small but radical antisystem parties on the far right in a number of these countries since that time.

Membership in these organizations has also facilitated much greater contact with the rest of Europe and introduced new influences, both positive and negative, that go far beyond even the dense web of official contacts that link these states to older members and to each other. Now that many of these states are part of the European Union and others are working to join, their leaders also face new challenges as EU members. These include establishing themselves so that their interests are considered in debate and decision making and balancing the demands of their membership in both European and transatlantic organizations.

As the chapters to follow and our conclusion discuss in greater detail, both attitudes toward these organizations and the salience of membership in them have changed in the recent past as the result of Russia's more aggressive posture toward the region. As the Ukrainian government tries to reassert its authority in parts of the country where Russian forces fomented unrest and in late August 2014 invaded, and as conflict became more deadly, leaders in other countries in the region, like their counterparts in the rest of Europe and in the United States, have searched for ways to help defuse the conflict and prevent it from spreading to other countries with ethnic Russian minorities. Leaders of the EU and the United States have condemned Russian actions in the region, including the forceful annexation of Crimea as well as the recent invasion, as violations of Ukraine's sovereignty and of international law. As of this writing, it is unclear whether the sanctions the European Union and the United States have imposed on Russian banks and industries as well as prominent individuals will be sufficient to end Russian aggression in Ukraine. It is also unclear what additional steps, if any, the EU, NATO, the United States, and individual European countries will take to help Ukraine preserve its sovereignty.

Organization of the Chapters to Follow

The chapters to follow examine the issues we have set out above in two ways. The chapters in part II provide a region-wide overview of the main political, economic, foreign policy, and social issues postcommunist leaders have faced. The chapters in part III then focus on the thematic issues analyzed in part II as they have been dealt with in individual countries. Chapters in this section also discuss questions of particular importance in the countries examined.

In chapter 2, Valerie Bunce examines some of the main developments involved in creating democratic political systems in the region and traces the diversity of original approaches that have led, in her estimation, most of the states considered to a common destination—democracy. Central issues discussed in this chapter include factors that influenced the early success stories, as well as those that contributed to the delay in establishing democracy in other states.

Bunce's chapter is followed by Sharon Fisher's discussion of the tasks and strategies used to transform economies from state control to the market. Noting the different starting points of different countries, Fisher highlights the complex issues involved in this transformation as well as the often unintended consequences of elite policies in this area.

Alfio Cerami's chapter on the social aspects of the transition follows up in greater detail on a number of the issues Fisher raises, focusing on the impact of social welfare policies and the availability or lack of jobs on social issues such as poverty and inequality. Cerami also looks at some of the less desirable by-products of the transformation, related to the decrease in rigid political control and more open borders, including such social pathologies as juvenile delinquency and other crime, drug abuse, trafficking, and other forms of illicit trade.

Zsuzsa Csergő's chapter highlights an issue that has been problematic in this region for much of its history. As she illustrates, ethnicity has become more politically salient in almost all countries of the region after the end of communism. Until recently, ethnic issues, apart from the tragic wars that ended the federal Yugoslav state, have generally been managed by political means. Armed conflict between citizens in eastern and southern Ukraine due to Russian fomenting of separatist unrest and infiltration of Russian troops into those regions after the annexation of Crimea demonstrates the transformation of regional political conflicts into ethnicized physical conflict in that country. Csergő discusses the political ramifications of ethnic issues in other countries in the region, as well as the plight of the Roma throughout the area.

Marilyn Rueschemeyer's chapter deals with another set of issues that continue to be problematic in the postcommunist period: gender issues. After a brief discussion of other aspects of women's status in the region, she focuses on women's role in politics. Noting the shift in policy toward women's issues and the backlash against the goal of gender equality in the early postcommunist period, she discusses more recent trends and highlights both progress and continued problems in the area of women's participation in the exercise of power.

Peter Rožič and Brian Grodsky examine the responses of governments in the region to issues raised by the communist past. Focusing on the mechanisms used to achieve this "transitional justice," they highlight the ways in which this process differed across this region and in the postcommunist region in general compared to cases of democratization in other parts of the world. They also discuss issues related to memory and memorialization of the past, which still remains a point of political contention, although an increasingly less explosive one, in many of the countries considered.

Ronald Linden and Shane Killian's discussion of the relationship of Central and East European countries and the EU analyzes the process of EU accession and the progress countries throughout the region have made in this regard. It then turns to the costs of EU membership, its impact in the region, the economic and Eurozone crisis, and the future of the EU in the Western Balkans and Ukraine.

Joshua Spero's examination of security issues and the role of many of these countries as members of NATO concludes the thematic section of the book. Spero's chapter also discusses the role of NATO in the region, new threats to European security from Russia, and the impact of these on NATO's presence in Central and East European countries and on thinking about NATO's mission.

The chapters in part III of the book share a common framework and also examine issues of particular importance in each country included. After brief summaries of the precommunist and communist periods, authors analyze the end of communism and then turn to a number of common topics. These include the institutional structure of each state, elections and political parties, and civil society as well as citizen's attitudes toward politics. Each chapter also discusses the particular issues the economic transition involved in the country under discussion, as well as the social consequences of the economic changes and major trends in each country's foreign policy. We have asked the authors of country-specific chapters to conclude by identifying issues specific to the countries they discuss, as well as some of the main challenges that leaders and citizens face at present and are likely to face in the near future.

As these chapters illustrate, there are both common and distinctive patterns in each of these areas. There is a large literature on the impact of institutions on democracy.[18] Most of the countries under study are essentially parliamentary systems that also have presidents with a circumscribed role and in which the executive, commonly termed the government, is led by a prime minister who typically leads the party that won the most votes in elections for the legislature. These systems, which may be governed by a variety of electoral rules, may have open lists, in which citizens are free to vote for individuals as well as party lists; closed lists, in which individuals vote only for a party, whose list is determined by party leaders before elections; or a combination of both, such as when citizens vote for a party list but may also enter preference votes for particular candidates, which may alter the positions of candidates on the list. Developments in Hungary, Bosnia-Herzegovina, and Ukraine, as well as in Slovakia under Vladimir Mečiar's rule, all illustrate the impact that changes in electoral laws can have on politics.

In parliamentary systems, the prime minister and his cabinet are the most important political actors. There is frequently also a president, but the functions of this office are generally more ceremonial. At the same time, some of the countries in the region have, or have had, presidents who have exercised a fair amount of power, either formally, in which case the country has a semi-presidential system, or informally, in which case a president's influence exceeds the formal authority of the institution due to the incumbent's character, moral authority, or desire to exercise more power. The relationship between the prime minister and president has been contentious in some cases, as in Poland when Lech Wałęsa was president and, more recently, in Romania, where the prime minister led an effort to impeach the president. Contrary to expectations based on analysis of developments in earlier transitions from authoritarian rule, presidential systems appear to be no less detrimental to democracy worldwide than parliamentary systems, if presidents are constrained by other institutions.[19] In the postcommunist world, however, parliamentary systems or semi-presidential systems have generally proved more democratic than strong presidential systems.[20]

Each chapter also explores the patterns of elections since the end of communist rule and the evolution and role of political parties. Although there is disagreement among scholars about the criteria required to qualify as a democracy[21]—particularly a consolidated as opposed to an emerging or unconsolidated democracy[22]—as well as about the utility of various kinds of "democracy with adjectives,"[23] to quote one prominent analysis, all agree that holding free and fair elections is a minimal, if not sufficient, condition for laying claim to being a democracy.[24] Certain authors also argue that having two successive, peaceful transitions of power is another minimal condition.[25]

Most also agree that political parties are an indispensable part of the political structure of a democratic state. Parties are critical to democracy because they fulfill a number of important functions. Thus, they serve as vehicles for recruiting political leaders and help articulate policy options; they also serve to simplify political choice for citizens and, through the development of stable identification with particular parties, link citizens to the political system and thereby make them less susceptible to mobilization by extreme political forces on the left or the right.[26]

The size and function of political parties in established European democracies, where parties used to be large membership organizations whose auxiliary organizations encompassed much of a citizen's or family's life and where levels of party identification were high and stable, have changed in recent decades. Thus, many of the parties that participated in elections and governments year in and year out disintegrated or were replaced by more loosely organized social movement organizations or new parties. Levels of membership in parties fell in many countries, as did citizens' identification with particular parties, although these trends vary to some extent from country to country.[27]

In the countries under study in this volume, stable party systems have yet to develop. After the end of communism, one-party rule was replaced by the creation or re-creation of a multitude of political parties. But, with very few exceptions, party systems are still fluid. Despite threshold requirements enacted early in the transition to reduce the number of so-called couch parties, all of whose members could allegedly fit on a sofa, new parties take part in most elections, and many win enough votes to seat deputies in the legislature or even form part of the governing coalition, only to disintegrate as their leaders quarrel or the parties fall below the threshold in the next election. Even party systems that seemed to be heading toward greater stability, such as those in the Czech Republic and Hungary, have seen a reversal of this trend in the recent past, as some of the "perennial" parties that were part of the picture since the fall of communism or shortly thereafter have lost a great deal of support, leaving the political field more open to the "annuals," to use Kevin Deegan Krause and Timothy Haughton's terminology.[28] Poland has, in recent years, moved in the opposite direction after more than a decade of "annuals" and radical-right parties. Currently there are essentially two strong moderate parties and very few annuals. Analysts have found that the fluidity of party systems is in fact higher in postcommunist countries than in Latin America or more established European democracies.[29] At the same time, fluid as the party systems are and organizationally weak as most political parties are, they served as vehicles for citizens to "throw the rascals out" with great regularity until the early 2000s in most countries. They therefore have brought about a good deal of turnover of elites and in this way strengthened democracy.[30]

The lack of a stable system of political parties has been one factor leading to another common trend the country-specific chapters in this volume explore: citizen alienation from politics and unwillingness to take part in politics as usual. As the growth of street protest in recent years illustrates, many citizens have very little faith in the political system. Citizen distrust of the political realm, as well as of politicians and political institutions, is evident in the decline in voter turnout in many elections, as well as in public opinion polls that document low levels of political efficacy, interpersonal trust beyond one's narrow circle of family and friends, and willingness to band together with others in voluntary organizations to pressure political leaders, call attention to public problems, or deal with communal issues. Together with intolerance toward minorities and, in some cases, extreme nationalism, these attitudes suggest that it may indeed take a generation or longer for most of these states to develop a political culture supportive of democracy.[31]

These attitudes in turn are reflected in civil society. There is broad agreement among scholars, as well as policy makers, that a large, vibrant civil society is essential for establishing and maintaining democratic rule.[32] Almost immediately after the end of communism, the associational life of the postcommunist countries, which had been stifled almost completely until the Gorbachev years, was repluralized. The plethora of nongovernmental organizations (NGOs), foundations, and other voluntary associations that developed at that time, most with foreign funding, has thinned out considerably in most countries as that funding has dried up. Membership in NGOs and participation in their activities has grown somewhat over the last twenty-five years in many countries, and citizens are generally more willing to participate in the work of NGOs than to join political parties. But the depth of civil society and citizen participation is still lower in Central and East European countries than in more established European democracies.[33]

The country-specific chapters in part III also examine each country's foreign policy. In contrast to earlier studies of the transitions from authoritarianism in other parts of the world, which have seen these transitions as largely domestic affairs, there has been a recognition from the beginning that international actors have played a critical role in the transition away from communism in Central and Eastern Europe.[34] Scholars disagree, however, on how important outside actors have been in fostering democratic values and rule in these countries.[35] In addition to this issue, the authors also discuss each country's role in or efforts to join European and transatlantic organizations, as well as significant issues in relations with neighbors and reactions to change in the international environment in recent years, including the 2008–2009 economic and Eurozone crises and Russian's new assertiveness internationally.

Each chapter concludes with a look at ongoing challenges citizens and leaders face. Although some of these are specific to the country under consideration, many are common. These include energy issues, corruption, and, in many states, the lingering effects of the communist past, as well as ethnic issues.

In part IV of the book, we return to many of the themes set out in this introduction to draw a balance sheet of where these countries are at present. We also discuss the utility of various ways to view these countries and of various approaches to studying political developments in Central and Eastern Europe.

Additional Resources

Each of the chapters in parts II and III includes a set of study questions to guide readers in recognizing the most important points discussed in the chapter. These questions may also be used as discussion questions for in-class debates. Authors have also provided short lists of additional readings that may be useful. Finally, each author has included several websites that may be consulted for additional and up-to-the minute information about the thematic issues and countries discussed.

Notes

1. Timothy Garton Ash, *The Magic Lantern: The Revolution of '89 Witnessed in Warsaw, Budapest, Berlin, and Prague* (New York: Random House, 1990), 78.

2. Vesna Pusic, talk at the Johns Hopkins School of Advanced International Studies, Washington, DC, April 2014.

3. See the debate among Terry Lynn Karl, Philippe C. Schmitter, and Valerie Bunce in the following articles: Philippe C. Schmitter with Terry Lynn Karl, "The Conceptual Travels of Transitologists and Consolidologists: How Far to the East Should They Attempt to Go?" *Slavic Review* 53, no. 1 (spring 1994): 173–85; Valerie Bunce, "Should Transitologists Be Grounded?" *Slavic Review* 54 (spring 1995): 111–27; Terry Lynn Karl and Philippe C. Schmitter, "From an Iron Curtain to a Paper Curtain: Grounding Transitologists or Students of Postcommunism?" *Slavic Review* 54 (winter 1995): 965–78; Valerie Bunce, "Paper Curtains and Paper Tigers," *Slavic Review* 54 (winter 1995): 979–87.

4. Jane S. Jaquette and Sharon L. Wolchik, eds., *Women and Democracy: Latin America and Central and Eastern Europe* (Baltimore: Johns Hopkins University Press, 1998).

5. Alex Barahona de Brito, Carmen Gonzales Enriques, and Palomar Agular, *The Politics of Memory* (Oxford: Oxford University Press, 2001); Jane Curry, "When an Authoritarian State Victimizes the Nation: Transitional Justice, Collective Memory, and Political Divides," *International Journal of Sociology* 37, no. 1 (April 1, 2007): 58–73, doi:10.2753/IJS0020-7659370104; Tricia D. Olsen et al., *Transitional Justice in Balance: Comparing Processes, Weighing Efficacy* (Washington, DC: United States Institute of Peace, 2010); Neil J. Kritz, *Transitional Justice: How Emerging Democracies Reckon with Former Regimes*, vol. 1: *General Considerations* (Washington, DC: United States Institute of Peace, 1995).

6. Thomas Carothers, "The End of the Transition Paradigm," *Journal of Democracy* 13 (January 2002): 5–21; see also Larry Diamond, "Thinking about Hybrid Regimes," *Journal of Democracy* 13 (January 2002): 36–50.

7. See, e.g., Paul Kubicek, *European Politics* (Boston: Longman, 2012).

8. Fareed Zakaria, *The Future of Freedom: Illiberal Democracy at Home and Abroad* (New York: W. W. Norton & Co., 2003).

9. Barbara Jelavich, *History of the Balkans*, vol. 2: *20th Century* (Cambridge: Cambridge University Press, 1983), 128–31.

10. Lonnie R. Johnson, *Central Europe: Enemies, Neighbors, Friends* (Oxford: Oxford University Press, 1996).

11. Andrew Janos, "The One-Party State and Social Mobilization: East Europe between the Wars," in *Authoritarian Politics in Modern Society*, ed. Samuel P. Huntington and Clement Henry Moore (New York: Basic Books, 1970), 204–36.

12. Zbigniew Brzezinski, *The Soviet Bloc, Unity and Conflict* (Cambridge, MA: Harvard University Press, 1960).

13. See Bartlomiej Kaminski, *The Collapse of State Socialism: The Case of Poland* (Princeton, NJ: Princeton University Press, 1991); Valerie Bunce, *Subversive Institutions: The Design and the Destruction of Socialism and the State* (Cambridge: Cambridge University Press, 1999).

14. Brzezinski, *The Soviet Bloc*.

15. See Zoltan D. Barany and Ivan Volgyes, eds., *Legacies of Communism in Eastern Europe* (Baltimore: Johns Hopkins University Press, 1995); James R. Millar and Sharon L. Wolchik, eds., *The Social Legacy of Communism* (Cambridge: Cambridge University Press, 1994).

16. For discussion of the influence of the EU in the region, see Wade Jacoby, *The Enlargement of the European Union and NATO: Ordering from the Menu in Central Europe* (Cambridge: Cambridge University Press, 2004); Jan Zielonka and Alex Pravda, eds., *Democratic Consolidation in Eastern Europe* (New York: Oxford University Press, 2001); Ronald H. Linden, ed., *Norms and Nannies: The Impact of International Organizations on the Central and East European States* (Lanham, MD: Rowman & Littlefield, 2002).

17. Ronald H. Linden and Lisa Pohlman, "Now You See It, Now You Don't: Anti-EU Politics in Central and Southeast Europe," *European Integration* 25 (December 2003): 311–34.

18. See, e.g., Juan J. Linz, "The Perils of Presidentialism," *Journal of Democracy* 1, no. 1 (1990): 51–69; Juan J. Linz and Alfred Stepan, eds., *The Breakdown of Democratic Regimes: Crisis, Breakdown and Reequilibration: An Introduction* (Baltimore: Johns Hopkins University Press, 1978); Matthew Soberg Shugart and John M. Carey, *Presidents and Assemblies: Constitutional Design and Electoral Dynamics* (Cambridge: Cambridge University Press, 1992); Adam Przeworski et al., *Democracy and Development: Political Institutions and Well-Being in the World, 1950–1990*, 1st ed. (Cambridge: Cambridge University Press, 2000); José Antonio Cheibub, *Presidentialism, Parliamentarism, and Democracy* (Cambridge: Cambridge University Press, 2006); John Gerring, Strom C. Thacker, and Carola Moreno, "Centripetal Democratic Governance: A Theory and Global Inquiry," *American Political Science Review* 99, no. 4 (2005): 567–81, doi:10.1017/S0003055405051889; Richard P. Gunther, Nikiforos Diamandouros, and Hans-Jürgen Puhle,

The Politics of Democratic Consolidation: Southern Europe in Comparative Perspective (Baltimore: Johns Hopkins University Press, 1995); Juan J. Linz and Alfred Stepan, *Problems of Democratic Transition and Consolidation: Southern Europe, South America, and Post-communist Europe* (Baltimore: Johns Hopkins University Press, 1996); José Antonio Cheibub and Fernando Limongi, "Democratic Institutions and Regime Survival: Parliamentary and Presidential Democracies Reconsidered," *Annual Review of Political Science* 5, no. 1 (2002): 151–79, doi:10.1146/annurev .polisci.5.102301.084508; Andrew Reynolds and John M. Carey, "Getting Elections Wrong," *Journal of Democracy* 23, no. 1 (2012): 164–68, doi:10.1353/jod.2012.0006; Arend Lijphart, ed., *Parliamentary versus Presidential Government* (New York: Oxford University Press, USA, 1992); Arend Lijphart, *Electoral Systems and Party Systems: A Study of Twenty-Seven Democracies, 1945–1990* (New York: Oxford University Press, USA, 1995); Philip G. Roeder, *Power Dividing as an Alternative to Ethnic Power Sharing* (Ithaca, NY: Cornell University Press, 2005); Christian Houle, "Inequality and Democracy: Why Inequality Harms Consolidation but Does Not Affect Democratization," *World Politics* 61, no. 4 (2009): 589–622, doi:10.1017/S0043887109990074.

19. See Cheibub, *Presidentialism, Parliamentarism, and Democracy*; Cheibub and Limongi, "Democratic Institutions and Regime Survival"; Houle, "Inequality and Democracy"; Lijphart, *Parliamentary versus Presidential Government*; Shugart and Carey, *Presidents and Assemblies*; Ethan B. Kapsten and Nathan Converse, "Why Democracies Fail," *Journal of Democracy* 19, no. 4 (2008): 57–68, doi:10.1353/jod.0.0031.

20. Valerie Bunce, "Rethinking Recent Democratization: Lessons from the Postcommunist Experience," *World Politics* 55, no. 2 (2003): 167–92, doi:10.1353/wp.2003.0010.

21. Carles Boix, *Democracy and Redistribution* (Cambridge: Cambridge University Press, 2003); Carles Boix, "Democracy, Development, and the International System," *American Political Science Review* 105, no. 4 (2011): 809–28, doi:10.1017/S0003055411000402; Robert A. Dahl, *Polyarchy: Participation and Opposition* (New Haven, CT: Yale University Press, 1972); Linz and Stepan, *Problems of Democratic Transition and Consolidation*; Geraldo L. Munck, *Measuring Democracy: A Bridge between Scholarship and Politics* (Baltimore: Johns Hopkins University Press, 2009); Adam Przeworski, *Democracy and the Market: Political and Economic Reforms in Eastern Europe and Latin America* (Cambridge: Cambridge University Press, 1991); Przeworski et al., *Democracy and Development*; Carsten Q. Schneider, *The Consolidation of Democracy: Comparing Europe and Latin America*. Democratization Studies 14 (London: Routledge, 2009).

22. See, e.g., Gunther, Diamandouros, and Puhle, *The Politics of Democratic Consolidation*; Munck, *Measuring Democracy*; Guillermo A. O'Donnell, Philippe C. Schmitter, and Laurence Whitehead, eds., *Transitions from Authoritarian Rule: Comparative Perspectives* (Baltimore: Johns Hopkins University Press, 1986); Przeworski, *Democracy and the Market*; Philippe C. Schmitter, "Twenty-Five Years, Fifteen Findings," *Journal of Democracy* 21, no. 1 (2010): 17–28; Schneider, *The Consolidation of Democracy*; Jay Ulfelder, *Dilemmas of Democratic Consolidation: A Game-Theory Approach* (Boulder, CO: Lynne Rienner Publishers, 2010); Andreas Schedler, "What Is Democratic Consolidation?" *Journal of Democracy* 9, no. 2 (1998): 91–107, doi:10.1353/jod.1998.0030; Boix, *Democracy and Redistribution*; Larry Diamond, "Why Democracies Survive," *Journal of Democracy* 22, no. 1 (2011): 17–30; Valerie J. Bunce and Sharon L. Wolchik, "Democratic Consolidation: Global Pathways and Postcommunist Variations" (unpublished manuscript, March 2013). See Adam Przeworski, *Democracy and the Limits of Self-Government* (Cambridge: Cambridge University Press, 2010), for a detailed review of theories of democracy and sources that have dealt with this question from the time of the Greeks to the present.

23. David Collier and Steven Levitsky, "Democracy with Adjectives: Conceptual Innovation in Comparative Research," *World Politics* 49, no. 3 (1997): 430–51, doi:10.1353/wp.1997.0009.

24. For discussions of different views about the importance of elections to democratization, see Valerie J. Bunce and Sharon L. Wolchik, *Defeating Authoritarian Leaders in Postcommunist*

Countries (Cambridge: Cambridge University Press, 2011); Staffan Lindberg, "The Power of Elections in Africa Revisited," in *Democratization by Elections: A New Mode of Transition?* ed. Staffan Lindberg (Baltimore: Johns Hopkins University Press, 2009).

25. Samuel P. Huntington, *The Third Wave: Democratization in the Late Twentieth Century* (Norman: University of Oklahoma Press, 1991).

26. See Elmer E. Schattschneider, *Party Government* (New York: Rinehart, 1942); Przeworski, *Democracy and the Limits of Self-Government*; Russell J. Dalton, *Democratic Challenges, Democratic Choices: The Erosion of Political Support in Advanced Industrial Democracies* (New York: Oxford University Press, USA, 2004).

27. See, especially, Gunther, Diamandouros, and Puhle, *The Politics of Democratic Consolidation*; Linz and Stepan, *Problems of Democratic Transition and Consolidation*; Frances Hagopian and Scott P. Mainwaring, eds., *The Third Wave of Democratization in Latin America: Advances and Setbacks* (Cambridge: Cambridge University Press, 2005); Cheibub, *Presidentialism, Parliamentarism, and Democracy*; Herbert Kitschelt and Steven I. Wilkinson, eds., *Patrons, Clients and Policies: Patterns of Democratic Accountability and Political Competition* (Cambridge: Cambridge University Press, 2007); Kenneth M. Roberts, "Market Reform, Programmatic (De)alignment, and Party System Stability in Latin America," *Comparative Political Studies* (September 9, 2012), doi:10.1177/0010414012453449; Dalton, *Democratic Challenges, Democratic Choices*; Russell J. Dalton, David M. Farrell, and Ian McAllister, *Political Parties and Democratic Linkage: How Parties Organize Democracy* (Oxford: Oxford University Press, 2011). See also Per Selle and Lars Svåsand, "Membership in Party Organizations and the Problem of Decline of Parties," *Comparative Political Studies* 23, no. 4 (January 1, 1991): 459–77, doi:10.1177/0010414091023004002.

28. Timothy Haughton, "Perennials and Annuals in East Central European Party Systems," lecture at the US Department of State, Foreign Service Institute, April 2012; Tim Haughton and Kevin Deegan-Krause, "'Hardy Perennials': Parties Which Buck the 'Live Fast, Die Young' Norm in Central and Eastern Europe," ECPR Joint Sessions, St. Gallen, Switzerland, 2011, 12–17; Attilagh Agh, *The Politics of Central Europe* (London: SAGE Publications Ltd, 1998); Paul Lewis and Geoffrey Pridham, eds., *Stabilising Fragile Democracies: New Party Systems in Southern and Eastern Europe* (London: Routledge, 1995); Anna Grzymala-Busse, *Redeeming the Communist Past: The Regeneration of Communist Parties in East Central Europe* (Cambridge: Cambridge University Press, 2002); Paul G. Lewis, "Party Systems in Post-communist Central Europe: Patterns of Stability and Consolidation," *Democratization* 13, no. 4 (2006): 562–83, doi:10.1080/13510340600791863; Grigore Pop-Eleches, *From Economic Crisis to Reform: IMF Programs in Latin America and Eastern Europe* (Princeton, NJ: Princeton University Press, 2011); Herbert Kitschelt et al., *Post-communist Party Systems: Competition, Representation, and Inter-Party Cooperation* (Cambridge: Cambridge University Press, 1999).

29. Michael Bernhard and Ekrem Karakoç, "Moving West or Going South? Economic Transformation and Institutionalization in Postcommunist Party Systems," 44, no. 1 (2011): 1–20; see also Brad Epperly, "Institutions and Legacies: Electoral Volatility in the Postcommunist World," *Comparative Political Studies* 44, no. 7 (July 2011): 829–53, doi:10.1177/0010414011401226, for a contrasting argument concerning the causes of this volatility.

30. Bunce and Wolchik, *Defeating Authoritarian Leaders in Postcommunist Countries*.

31. See George Schöpflin, "Obstacles to Liberalism in Post-communist Polities," *East European Politics and Societies* 5, no. 1 (1990): 189–94; Dalton, *Democratic Challenges, Democratic Choices*; World Values Survey Wave 6, 2010–2014, Official Aggregate v.20140429, World Values Survey Association (http://www.worldvaluessurvey.org). Aggregate File Producer: Asep/JDS, Madrid SPAIN; ESS Round 6: European Social Survey Round 6 Data (2012). Data file edition 1.2. Norwegian Social Science Data Services, Norway—Data Archive and distributor of ESS data; see also Russell J. Dalton, *Citizen Politics: Public Opinion and Political Parties in Advanced Industrial Democracies*

(Washington, DC: Congressional Quarterly Press, 2013); see International Idea (http://www.idea .int) for information about elections and voter turnout in Europe as a whole.

32. Robert D. Putnam, Robert Leonardi, and Raffaella Y. Nanetti, *Making Democracy Work: Civic Traditions in Modern Italy* (Princeton, NJ: Princeton University Press, 1993); Bunce and Wolchik, *Defeating Authoritarian Leaders in Postcommunist Countries*; Nancy Bermeo and Philip Nord, eds., *Civil Society before Democracy* (Lanham, MD: Rowman & Littlefield, 2000).

33. Marc Morjé Howard, *The Weakness of Civil Society in Post-communist Europe* (Cambridge: Cambridge University Press, 2003); Sarah L. Henderson, "Selling Civil Society Western Aid and the Nongovernmental Organization Sector in Russia," *Comparative Political Studies* 35, no. 2 (March 1, 2002): 139–67, doi:10.1177/0010414002035002001; Dalton, *Democratic Challenges, Democratic Choices.*

34. See, e.g., Jon C. Pevehouse, "Democracy from the Outside-In? International Organizations and Democratization," *International Organization* 56, no. 3 (2002): 515–49, doi:10.1162/002081802760199872; Milada Anna Vachudova, *Europe Undivided: Democracy, Leverage, and Integration after Communism* (New York: Oxford University Press, USA, 2005); Richard Youngs, *The European Union and the Promotion of Democracy* (New York: Oxford University Press, USA, 2002); Geoffrey Pridham and Tatu Vanhanen, *Democratization in Eastern Europe* (London: Routledge, 1994); Laurence Whitehead, ed., *The International Dimensions of Democratization: Europe and the Americas* (New York: Oxford University Press, USA, 2001); Judith G. Kelley, *Monitoring Democracy: When International Election Observation Works, and Why It Often Fails* (Princeton, NJ: Princeton University Press, 2012); Bunce and Wolchik, *Defeating Authoritarian Leaders in Postcommunist Countries.*

35. See Tim Haughton, *Party Politics in Central and Eastern Europe: Does EU Membership Matter?* (London: Routledge, 2013); Tim Haughton and Marek Rybář, "A Tool in the Toolbox: Assessing the Impact of EU Membership on Party Politics in Slovakia," *Journal of Communist Studies and Transition Politics* 25, no. 4 (2009): 540–63, doi:10.1080/13523270903310928; Wade Jacoby, "Inspiration, Coalition, and Substitution: External Influences on Postcommunist Transformations," *World Politics* 58, no. 4 (2006): 623–51, doi:10.1353/wp.2007.0010; Jacoby, *The Enlargement of the European Union and NATO*; Linden, *Norms and Nannies*; Milada Anna Vachudova, "Democratization in Postcommunist Europe: Illiberal Regimes and the Leverage of the European Union," in *Democracy and Authoritarianism in the Postcommunist World*, ed. Valerie Bunce, Michael McFaul, and Kathryn Stoner-Weiss (Cambridge: Cambridge University Press, 2010), 82–104; Vachudova, *Europe Undivided.*

Part II

POLICIES AND ISSUES

CHAPTER 2

The Political Transition

Valerie Bunce

The collapse of the communist regimes and communist states from 1989 to 1992 has produced a number of remarkable changes in the political and economic landscape of Europe's eastern half. In particular, authoritarian regimes have given way to political orders that are, albeit to quite varying degrees, more competitive and more respectful of civil liberties. In addition, twenty-two new states have arisen from the rubble of the Soviet Union, Czechoslovakia, and Yugoslavia, while one communist state, the German Democratic Republic, has merged with its neighbor, the German Federal Republic, to reconstitute a single Germany. As a result, a region once composed of nine states now consists of twenty-nine—if we include all of the successor states of the former Soviet Union, together with Central and Eastern Europe and the Balkans. At the same time, open market economies, again to varying degrees, have replaced state-owned, centrally planned, and highly protectionist economies. Finally, the post–World War II separation of Europe into two halves has ended, not just because of the economic and political liberalization of the east, but also because of the eastward expansion of three international institutions: the Council of Europe, the North Atlantic Treaty Organization (NATO), and the European Union (EU). In short, over the past twenty-five years we have witnessed a revolution in Central and Eastern Europe—in state boundaries, in the organization and practice of politics and economics at home and abroad, and, finally, in elite and mass identities and political preferences.

This chapter assesses the political side of this revolution. In particular, I compare patterns of regime transition in Central and Eastern Europe since the dramatic events of 1989, draw some generalizations about what has transpired and why, and place these changes in the larger context of the global spread of democratic governance. My discussion is divided into two parts. In the first section, I focus on the short-term political consequences of the collapse of communism, or the forms of governance that came into being during the early years of the transition from 1989 to mid-1996. Of interest here are such questions as the following: Did the end of Communist Party hegemony lead, as many expected, to the immediate rise of democratic politics, or do we in fact see a more complicated political story? To what extent were the early political dynamics of postcommunist Europe typical or distinctive when compared with the collapse of dictatorships and regime change in other parts of the world? Finally, what factors seem to provide the

43

most compelling account of the first stage of the political transition in postcommunist Europe?

In the second part of this chapter, I shift my focus to developments beginning in the latter part of 1996 that continued through 2014. Here, the discussion addresses one notable trend: the expansion of democratic polities since the mid-1990s. This expansion represents two convergent developments: the remarkable ability of virtually all of the first democracies in the region (with Hungary since 2010 as the exception) to stay the political course, coupled with the failure of the remaining and more authoritarian regimes in the area to maintain their political momentum. In this sense, there have in fact been several waves of democratization in postcommunist Europe, with the first occurring immediately after the fall of state socialism and the second occurring roughly a decade later.

Postcommunist Political Diversity

By 1996, one could identify three types of political regimes in postcommunist Central and Eastern Europe.[1] The first, which included Poland, the Czech Republic, Hungary, Slovenia, Lithuania, and less perfectly Estonia and Latvia (because of some political discrimination against their Russian minorities), was a democratic order, characterized by political arrangements that combine free, fair, and competitive elections that are regularly held; representative institutions that convert public preferences as expressed through elections into public policy; rule of law, or rules of the political game that are accepted by both elites and publics and applied consistently across time, space, and circumstances; and extensive civil liberties and political rights guaranteed by law. Because of all these features, democracy in general and in these cases in particular can be understood as a way of organizing politics that rests on accountable government.[2] What is striking about Poland, the Czech Republic, and the other countries listed above at this time, therefore, was that they managed to move quickly to full-scale democracy.

The second type of regime in the region at this time was authoritarian. In authoritarian states political arrangements lack the characteristics noted above, thereby producing governments that have neither the incentives nor the capacity to be accountable to their citizens. Authoritarian regimes, in particular, lack the institutionalized competition, individual rights, and procedural consistency that translate individual preferences into public policy through elections and representative government. This combination of traits describes the politics during the period under discussion in two of the successor states of Yugoslavia (Croatia and Serbia-Montenegro). Here, it is interesting to note that, despite the efforts of their dictators, Franjo Tudjman in Croatia and Slobodan Milošević in Serbia-Montenegro, some political pluralism was in evidence—most notably in the capitals of Zagreb and Belgrade, where oppositions had a presence and where publics, even in the face of fraudulent elections, still managed to deny their dictators decisive electoral support.

Finally, the remaining countries in the region, Albania, Bosnia (but only after the Dayton Peace Accords of 1995 had demilitarized the country and provided a skeletal form of government), Bulgaria, Macedonia, Romania, Slovakia, and Ukraine—a group of countries roughly equal in number to the full-scale democracies at this time—fell between

Photo 2.1.   Václav Havel and Alexander Dubček toast the turnover of power by the communists in Prague in November 1989. (Peter Turnley/Corbis)

the extremes of dictatorship and democracy. They were what can be termed "hybrid regimes," that is, political arrangements that feature some of the formal characteristics of democracy, such as representative institutions and political competition, but fall short of the liberal standard as a result of unfair elections, extensive corruption, irregular recognition of civil liberties, significant biases in the media, opposition parties that are poorly organized in comparison with parties in power led by authoritarians, and weak ties between political representatives and the citizenry. Also common in this category are several other characteristics that undermine the development of accountable government—in particular, rapid turnover in governments (a characteristic that Poland also shared), an inability of citizens to counteract the power of the state through associational ties with each other (or what has been termed "civil society"), and a sharp divide between urban and rural politics, with the latter more consistently supportive of authoritarian rule.[3]

In short, in the first stage of the transition from state socialism, we find three characteristics. The first is political diversity. Put simply, the deregulation of the political, economic, and social monopoly of the Communist Party that occurred throughout Central and Eastern Europe from 1989 to 1991 was not followed necessarily by the rise of democratic politics. In this sense, the Central and Eastern Europe of this period presented an important lesson. There can be a substantial lag, and even no relationship, between two developments that are often assumed to be tightly intertwined: the decline of authoritarian rule and the rise of democratic politics. Second, regime change in this region was largely peaceful but not invariably nonviolent. The Baltic states' attempts to separate themselves from the Soviet Union invited a short-term violent response on the part of the Soviet leadership. The merger in Yugoslavia between two issues—the future of the regime and the future of the state—produced very different political trajectories among the republics that made up the state and a war from 1991 to 1995 that left over two hundred thousand people dead and undermined democratization in those successor states that served as the major site of this conflict, Croatia and Bosnia, while in the process shaping developments in their neighbors, particularly Macedonia and Serbia-Montenegro. The fall of Nicolae Ceauşescu in Romania in 1989 was also violent. These contrasts aside, however, it is striking that where regime transition was accompanied by violence, the result was either a hybrid regime or a dictatorship. Thus, democracy and a peaceful adjudication of conflicts—with the latter often serving as one definition of democratic governance—were closely associated with one another in the Central and East European transitions.

Finally, there were significant differences across the region in the resources, cohesion, and political goals of both the communists and the opposition. For example, while the communists were quick to embrace the liberal political and economic agenda of the opposition in the Baltic countries, Poland, and particularly Hungary and Slovenia, they were more resistant in the remaining cases. Serbian political dynamics under Milošević are the most extreme example of this resistance. At the same time, oppositions varied greatly. Whereas in the Baltic countries, Poland, the Czech Republic, Hungary, and Slovenia, the opposition was large, sophisticated, relatively cohesive, and committed to liberal politics, in the remaining countries the opposition tended to suffer from a number of problems. For example, Bulgaria saw divisions over the best way to build capitalism and democracy and become an effective political force, and in both Serbia and Slovakia elite struggles over political power and manipulation of national tensions in order to maintain authoritarian control and stave off demands for democracy demobilized the liberals.[4]

Comparative Perspectives: The Puzzles of Diversity

Was the diversity of postcommunist political dynamics and political pathways in the first half of the transformation surprising or predictable? The answer is that for many analysts the political patterns of postcommunism, as summarized above, were in fact unexpected. This was the case whether we refer to specialists on comparative democratization or specialists on postcommunist Europe.

At the time that communism collapsed, there had already been a clear trend, in evidence since the mid-1970s, suggesting that the decline of authoritarian rule led invariably to the rapid and peaceful rise of democratic politics. This was precisely what had happened, for example, in one state after another in both Latin America and southern Europe (though the Portuguese case was an exception). In addition, the dichotomous thinking of the Cold War, which had framed political dynamics and therefore political assumptions in the international order for forty-five years, made it easy to presume that there were only two political choices in the world: democracy or dictatorship. Thus, if the hegemony of the Communist Party was challenged and dictatorship rested on this hegemony, and, just as importantly, if the Soviet Union failed to back up communist rule in its client states and at home and, indeed, failed in the more profound sense of being able to continue functioning

Photo 2.2. The Romanian revolution was the only one that was violent. Here, a Romanian at a demonstration cries over those killed by the government forces in December 1989. Until Nicolae Ceauşescu and his wife were executed by a military tribunal after a show trial, there was fighting in the streets of Romanian cities. (David Turnley/Corbis)

as a regime, a state, a regional hegemon, and a superpower, then in the wake of its collapse, it was widely thought, democratic revolutions would follow both within the Soviet Union and throughout the Soviet bloc. As we have seen replayed in US debates about Iraq from 2002 to the present, moreover, many assumed not just that the political world offered only two regime options but also that, if dictators and dictatorships were subtracted from the equation, publics would necessarily rise up to embrace the democratic cause—and be able to translate these preferences in relatively quick order into well-functioning democratic institutions and procedures. Democracy, in short, was natural, and this would be revealed once the distorting effects of dictatorship were removed.[5]

From these perspectives, therefore, the assumption was that the end of dictatorship constituted the beginning of democracy—and full-scale democracy at that. Such an optimistic reading of the future was unusually tempting in the wake of 1989, given the rapid and region-wide character of the collapse of Communist Party control and the dependence of these regimes and their specific economic and political features on that control. This position, however, was as flawed in the postcommunist world as it would be a decade later in Iraq and Afghanistan.[6] Oppositions can be fractious, dictatorships invariably have supporters, constructing democratic institutions in weak states can be difficult, and publics can care as much about their personal circumstances as about governmental forms.

Scholars specializing in the postcommunist region had different expectations—though these were also inaccurate in some respects.[7] For some scholars, the emphasis had long been on the striking similarities among the communist states—similarities that spoke not just to common ideological texts but also to the foundational role of the Soviet Union as the "inventor" and then the "exporter" of state socialism. In all of these cases, communist regimes were governed by a single Communist Party that enjoyed a monopoly on power, money, and social status and was committed to rapid socioeconomic development through control of the allocation of both labor and capital. It is puzzling, therefore, that the structural and ideological similarities across this region—similarities far greater than those found, for example, among dictatorships in Latin America or southern Europe during the 1960s and 1970s—could have translated so quickly into such differences, not just in political regimes, as already noted, but also in economic regimes. Thus, capitalism replaced socialism very quickly in Poland, Hungary, the Czech Republic, the Baltic states, and Slovenia, whereas socialist economics, especially with respect to state control over the economy, remained in place to varying degrees in the other countries in the region. Commonalities, therefore, in the most basic building blocks of politics and economics—for example, state control over politics and the economy—gave way very quickly to diversity.

For other specialists, there was widespread recognition that these countries entered the transition with variable mixtures of assets and liabilities, such that postcommunism would not produce, especially in the early stages, identical political dynamics—the similarities in the institutional "skeletons" of these systems notwithstanding. In this sense, diversity was expected. Not expected, however, was the range of regimes that appeared, with the most improbable group comprising those countries that made a quick and thoroughgoing transition to democratic politics. As some observers were quick to note, of the many countries in Central and Eastern Europe that had experimented with democratic politics during the interwar era, only one—Czechoslovakia—had managed to survive until World War II with democratic institutions and procedures intact. Even in that case, however, the inclusiveness of the polity and the extent of political and certainly economic equality among the nations that shared that state at the time were both in some question.[8] In short, little of the political past could be recycled to support democratic change. As a result, democracy was assumed to be, at best, an uphill struggle—in direct contrast, for example, to the Latin American case, where the norm was redemocratization, not building democracy from scratch.[9]

Many analysts also recognized the considerable costs of the state socialist brand of authoritarian rule due to its unusually penetrative and despotic character. These were dictatorships that, while less and less brutal over time in most cases, were nonetheless extraordinarily ambitious. By owning and planning the economy, monopolizing political power, sealing borders, and atomizing publics, these dictatorships seemed committed to the destruction of some of the most elementary building blocks of democratic life—for example, interpersonal trust; respect for the law; confidence in political institutions, such as political parties; and participation in associations independent of the state, such as labor unions, clubs, professional associations, and the like. The autonomy of individuals and groups, so important for countering the power of the state in a democratic order, therefore, had been severely limited by the communist experience. Economic decline during the last years of state socialism, moreover, would also seem to have constrained the rise of democracy, especially since the political regime transition in question would be tied to an unusually costly economic transition. Indeed, it is not just that Central and Eastern Europe featured—and still features—a much lower level of economic development than Western Europe, which many have read as undermining democratic governance, but also that citizens in Central and Eastern Europe experienced a far greater decline in living standards in the first half of the 1990s than one saw during the Great Depression, when nearly half of Europe's democracies, we must remember, had collapsed.[10]

When we compare the perspectives of specialists in the postcommunist region and those of specialists on recent democratization in other regions, therefore, we find a clear contrast. Whereas the former tended to underpredict democracy, assuming in effect that many more regimes would fall into either the hybrid or authoritarian camp, specialists on comparative democratization had the opposite problem: they overpredicted democratic rule. In both cases, the political diversity of the region—at least halfway into the transition—was puzzling. How then can we explain why some countries in Central and Eastern Europe moved decisively in a democratic direction, others moved less decisively, and still others moved in a decidedly authoritarian direction?

Explaining Early Political Pathways

A number of plausible factors would seem to be helpful in accounting for the differences among postcommunist regimes during the early stages of the transition. One could suggest, for example, that a key consideration would be the age of the state. As a number of studies have suggested, in the West, states were built long before the possibility of democratic politics either entered or could enter the political agenda. State building is a nasty process, wherein political leaders, wanting to secure their access to people and economic resources and to deny that access to their competitors, use their militaries, local allies, and rudimentary bureaucracies to solidify their political and economic control over a spatially defined group. Rather than negotiate each time they need money and troops, they prefer to create more permanent arrangements—or what subsequently became known as states. The essence of state building, therefore, to borrow from Charles Tilly, is that wars make states, and states make wars.[11]

The demand for democracy in the West, therefore, took place after state building. Once people have lived together for some time in a common state and operate within an increasingly integrated and interactive political and economic context, they can learn to define themselves as members of a common political community, or nation. In the process, they can also embrace a common political project that redefines the relationship between citizens and the state by arguing that states cannot just be coercive or just provide citizens with security. Instead, they are expected to do more—by recognizing citizens as equal, by guaranteeing political rights, and by creating accountable government.

The necessary sequencing of these developments—or spatial consolidation of political authority followed by growing pressures for accountable and legitimate governance—would seem to suggest that the key difference in Central and East European political trajectories after communism is whether the state is new—and thereby committed to the draconian politics and economics of state building—or better established and, because of prior integration of the economy and settlement of borders and membership in the nation, more responsive to political demands for equality and rights. Indeed, precisely this contrast led Dankwart Rustow to argue more than thirty years ago that democracy only enters into the realm of political choice when issues involving membership in the nation and the boundaries of the state have been fully resolved.[12]

The problem here, however, is that the variations in postcommunist political trajectories are not predicted by the age of the state. Just as some of the long-standing states in Central and Eastern Europe, such as Bulgaria and Romania, were hybrid regimes in the first half of the 1990s, some of the newest states in that period—Slovenia, the Czech Republic, and the Baltic states—were in the group of early and robust democracies. Even more interestingly, in the cases of Slovenia and the Czech Republic, the states were in fact completely new formations—in contrast to Estonia, Latvia, and Lithuania, which had been independent states during the interwar years.

Might the differences be explained by ethnic and religious diversity? Again, it is logical to assume that democracy is harder to construct when many nations share the same state, when national differences coincide with differences in economic resources and political power, when previous governing arrangements play diverse groups off one another, and when national minorities spill over into neighboring states, thereby generating tensions about the legitimacy of existing boundaries. However, this factor does not distinguish well among the Central and East European countries either. Both Poland and Albania, for example, have national homogeneity despite their very different political pathways immediately after communism, and the robust democracies of Estonia and Latvia have unusually high levels of diversity, defined here as the size of the second largest ethnic community.

This leaves us with two remaining hypotheses. One is that variation in democratization reflects differences in the mode of transition. Put succinctly, transitions engineered by bargaining between opposition and incumbent elites are more likely to produce democratic government than transitions that occur in reaction to mass protests—a contrast that has been used to explain differences in democratizing dynamics in Latin America and southern Europe. The problem here is that most of the transitions in Central and Eastern Europe involved mass—indeed massive—mobilization, and all of the most successful transitions, except in Hungary, took place in response to mass protests. The other hypothesis targets differences in the nature of politics during communism. Here, the argument is that the more liberalized regimes during communism would have laid more of the groundwork for democracy after communism—for example, because their communists were reform minded and because opposition forces had more opportunities to expand their support and develop sophisticated political strategies for winning power. However, the strong democracies within our group are in fact divided between those that experienced more hard-line communist rule—Czechoslovakia and the Baltic countries— and more reformist regimes—Slovenia, Poland, and Hungary.[13]

Explaining Diversity

How, then, can we explain the early patterns of postcommunist politics? We can begin to answer this question by recognizing the importance of the age of the state and the difficulties introduced by what was for many states in this region a simultaneous transition to a new regime and a new state. For states that were already defined at the time of the transition from communism, the key factor that shaped subsequent political pathways seems to have been the outcome of the first competitive election. In particular, where the opposition won handily (Poland and Hungary), we see quick and sustained democratization. By contrast, where power was more equally divided between the communists and the opposition (as in Romania and Bulgaria), the result was a hybrid regime.

But is this argument in fact a tautology, in that when communists win, dictatorships follow; when the opposition wins, democracy follows; and, finally, when they are neck and neck, a synthesis of the two options materializes? Despite the logic of this observation, there are in fact several reasons to be more confident that the argument about initial electoral outcomes is illuminating. One is that this line of explanation also captures variations in economic reform, with rapid reforms following a clear victory of the opposition, resistance to such reforms when the communists win, and a pattern of "fit-and-start" reforms when electoral outcomes are more evenly divided. Another is that there is no particular reason to assume that, if the opposition wins, it will necessarily embrace democratic politics—though in every one of the established states it did. Oppositions, after all, can want many things. Third, it is notable that this argument flies in the face of the generalization in the literature on Latin America and southern Europe that "balanced transitions"—or those in which the opposition and the authoritarians are evenly balanced in their power and form political pacts with each other as a result—lead to the most successful transitions to democracy. With this type of equality, it has been argued, both sides feel secure enough to proceed with regime change. Thus, what seems tautological in Central and Eastern Europe is in fact counterintuitive in other regional contexts.[14]

This leads us to a final point, which helps us deal with the problem of what "causes the cause." Initial electoral outcomes in the contest between authoritarians and opposition forces correlate in turn with patterns of protest during the communist era. To put the matter succinctly, one can conclude that, at least in Central and Eastern Europe, rapid progress toward democracy seems to have depended on a dynamic wherein the development of a strong opposition during communism translated, with the end of the party's monopoly, into an unusually strong political showing in the first elections, which augured well for the future and quality of democratic governance. In this sense, the proximate cause, or variations in electoral outcomes, alerts us to a more distant cause, or variations in opposition development during communism.

We can now turn to the new states in the region—or the Baltic countries, the Czech Republic, Croatia, Macedonia, Serbia-Montenegro, Slovakia, Slovenia, and Ukraine. (Because of the war and its subsequent development as an international protectorate, Bosnia is left out of the comparison.) Here, a key issue seems to be whether the nationalist project connected with a liberal or illiberal political project—or whether defending the nation was understood to require, or at least be consistent with, democracy or dictatorship. For those countries (then republics) that had nationalist demonstrations or movements during communism (Croatia in the early 1970s, Serbia-Montenegro in the early 1980s, and Slovakia in the late 1960s), the resulting dynamics divided the opposition into democrats and nationalists while weakening public support for the communists and pushing them to bear down on nationalism and to resist any political and economic reforms that might expand opportunities for nationalism to reinvigorate itself. As a result, when communism collapsed, either communists became nationalists in order to maintain dictatorial power (as in Serbia-Montenegro and Slovakia), or the nationalists, facing discredited communists, rejected liberal politics in order to take power (as in Croatia). In either case, democracy was poorly served, whether the communists, the nationalists, or some combination of the two emerged triumphant. By contrast, where nationalist mobilization materialized only when communism began to unravel (as in the Baltic countries, Macedonia, and Slovenia), the nationalist ideology was defined in a liberal way such that nationalist and liberal forces came together to form a powerful opposition, and communists, not as politically isolated or as compromised as in the first set of cases, had little choice, in terms of either personal preferences or self-interest, but to defect to the liberal cause. Ukraine is also an example of late mobilization. However, because of the east-west divide in Ukraine with respect to identity, history, and economic interests, there were more obstacles to democratic change in that country than the others.

In short, we find two pathways. In the older states, regime change was a product of the balance of power between the communists and the opposition forces and, to push the causal process further back in time, the development of a capable opposition during the communist era, whereas in the new states the key factor seems to have been varying combinations of nationalism, liberalism, and communism, with the particular combination strongly affected by when nationalist mobilization took place and the effects of this timing on the preferences and popularity of both the communists and the nationalists. Put more simply, one can suggest that patterns of political protest during communism, albeit playing out in different ways in republics versus states and introducing different political options, seemed to play a critical role in either ushering in democratic politics or compromising the democratic political agenda.

Durability of New States and New Democracies

If many observers were surprised by political outcomes in Central and Eastern Europe in the first phase of the transition, they were even more surprised, given these early developments after the fall of communism, by what transpired in the second phase. From 1996 to 2014 we find two political trends, both of which have contributed in distinctive ways to greater stability in the region. First, the number of states in the region and the boundaries of the new states that formed from 1991 to 1992 have remained nearly constant; at the same time there are several important exceptions to the durability of state borders in this region. One is the division of Serbia-Montenegro into two separate states in late spring 2006; another is the rise of Kosovo (once a part of Serbia-Montenegro) as an independent state in 2008 to 2009; a third is the territorial expansion of the Russian Federation at the expense of its neighbor, Ukraine, as a result of the transfer of Crimea (a peninsula in southeastern Ukraine) to Russia in the spring of 2014. While the international community recognizes the new states of Montenegro and Kosovo (though the Russian government and a few others have objected to the latter) and, thus, Serbia's new name and boundaries, it views the sudden boundary changes of Russia and Ukraine as illegitimate. Several aspects of the Crimean case make it very different from the other two. One is that the key international actor involved in the reformulation of boundaries gained territory as a result of its engagement. Russia, in short, was a far more "interested" observer with respect to Crimea than were the United States or the EU in the cases of Montenegro and Kosovo. Second, in contrast to Kosovo, the citizens of Crimea did not need to be protected from attacks launched by their own government. Finally, the hastily held referendum that purportedly legitimated Crimea's secession from Ukraine was not a referendum on independence (as had been the case for Kosovo and Montenegro) but rather a choice about whether to remain in Ukraine or join the Russian Federation. That referendum, moreover, took place with Russian troops already in control of the peninsula and in the absence of any international monitors.

The relative stability of borders in this region since 1992 speaks to several factors. One is that opportunities for redefining boundaries tend to be fleeting, occurring primarily during the unusual circumstances of a conjoined shift in domestic and international regimes, as happened from 1989 to 1992 when communism collapsed, the Soviet Union was dismembered, and the Cold War ended. Another is that state dissolution during the earlier tumultuous period succeeded to some degree in providing a closer alignment of national and state borders and, with that, an expansion in the legitimacy of both the regime and the state. Finally, powerful actors in the international community tend to resist border changes because they see an opening up of the question of borders as highly destabilizing for both domestic and international politics. To question existing borders is to invite minority communities throughout the region—and certainly their leaders—to demand states of their own. Such demands are tempting in many cases, because they empower minority leaders, while allowing them to ignore other, more pressing issues that might challenge their political influence—for example, rising corruption, poor economic performance, and a decline in the quality of democratic life.

Recent developments in both Montenegro and Kosovo, however, remind us that the borders in southeastern Europe, at least, are still in some flux. Indeed, in sharp contrast to their words and deeds in other parts of the world, including the Caucasus and Russia, major players in international politics, such as the United States and the European Union, have been both increasingly unwilling and unable to support the borders of Serbia-Montenegro as established during the wars that accompanied the dissolution of the Yugoslav state from 1991 to 1995. Thus, beginning in 1997, the Montenegrin political leadership began to question the value of its federal relationship with Serbia. In 2003, the EU, eager to keep borders intact, brokered a deal, whereby Montenegro agreed to stay within the larger, but quite decentralized, state until 2006, when a referendum would be held on the question of Montenegrin independence. In the spring of 2006, this referendum did take place, and a majority (though not an overwhelming one) of Montenegrins expressed their desire to establish their own state. Quickly following the referendum, Serbia and Montenegro went their separate ways.

The situation in Kosovo has been different. Following the US-led NATO bombing campaign in 1999 to protect Albanian inhabitants in Kosovo from the increasingly repressive actions of the Milošević regime, the United States, with EU support, defined Kosovo as an international protectorate. When it became increasingly clear that Kosovo could not be reintegrated with Serbia, because of the institutional precedents set by its postwar status, the strong support of the majority within Kosovo for independence, and continuing tensions between the Serbian and Albanian communities co-inhabiting the province, the United States took the lead, with EU support, in providing verbal, economic, and technical support for a gradual transition in Kosovo to sovereign statehood.[15] This culminated in a February 2008 declaration of independence. For Serbian publics and politicians, the departure of Kosovo has been a good deal more controversial than the exit of Montenegro. Moreover, widespread poverty, the dearth of state institutions that could be recycled from the past, and continuing tensions between the Serbian and Albanian communities living in Kosovo have also rendered the state-building project there a more difficult and prolonged venture than in Montenegro. Thus, while the establishment of the Montenegrin state took place relatively smoothly and quickly, the same has not been the case for Kosovo.

The second trend in the region since the mid-1990s is a pronounced contraction in the political diversity in this part of the world and the emergence of a Central and Eastern Europe composed, for the first time in its history, solely of democratic orders (albeit of varying quality). This development reflected two trends: on the one hand, virtually all of the first democracies stuck and indeed deepened, an outcome one cannot necessarily have expected, especially in view of the constraints on democratization, noted earlier, as a result of the authoritarian past and the stresses of economic reform; on the other hand, the hybrid democracies of the first stage managed for the most part to shift to the democratic camp in the second stage, while the regimes that were initially dictatorships all moved in a liberal direction, thereby joining the hybrid category and sometimes moving in an even more liberal direction (see table 2.1). It is safe to conclude, therefore, that

Table 2.1.   Freedom House Rankings for Central and East European States, 2002–2012

Country	2002	2004	2006	2007	2008	2009	2010	2011	2012
Albania	3.5	3	3	3	3	3	3	3	3
Bosnia and Herzegovina	4.5	4	3.5	3	3.5	3.5	3.5	3.5	3
Bulgaria	2	1.5	1.5	1.5	1.5	2	2	2	2
Croatia	2	2	2	2	2	2	1.5	1.5	1.5
Czech Republic	1.5	1.5	1	1	1	1	1	1	1
Estonia	1.5	1.5	1	1	1	1	1	1	1
Hungary	1.5	1.5	1	1	1	1	1	1.5	1.5
Latvia	1.5	1.5	1	1	1.5	1.5	2	2	2
Lithuania	1.5	1.5	1	1	1	1	1	1	1
Montenegro				3	3	3	2.5	2.5	2.5
Poland	1.5	1.5	1	1	1	1	1	1	1
Romania	2	2	2	2	2	2	2	2	2
Serbia	3	2.5	2.5	2.5	2.5	2.5	2	2	2
Slovakia	1.5	1.5	1	1	1	1	1	1	1
Slovenia	1.5	1	1	1	1	1	1	1	1
Ukraine	4	4	2.5	2.5	2.5	2.5	3	3.5	3.5

Source: Freedom House's "Freedom in the World" (http://www.freedomhouse.org/report-types/freedom
-world).
Note: The cumulative average of political rights and civil liberties scores is based on a scale of 1 to 7, with
   1 considered free and 7 considered unfree.

the Baltic states, Poland, the Czech Republic, Slovakia, Slovenia, Bulgaria, Romania, and Croatia, all EU members, are very likely to continue as democratic regimes in the future. At the same time, Albania, Bosnia, Macedonia, Serbia, and Montenegro have all made significant progress since 2000 in building more democratic polities.

There are, however, two important exceptions to this "happy" pattern of democratic progress throughout the region. One is Ukraine, which had made significant strides in building democracy in the aftermath of the Orange Revolution in 2004 but experienced a decline in democratic performance following the election of Viktor Yanukovych as president in 2010. The other is Hungary. While an "early riser" with respect to its transition to democracy (in contrast to Ukraine), Hungary has nonetheless experienced, since its 2010 parliamentary election, a decline in democratic performance. It is not just that an illiberal government formed after the election; it is also that this government has had sufficient support in parliament to enact legislation that has undercut civil liberties and political rights.

The recent developments in Hungary and backsliding under Yanukovych in Ukraine notwithstanding, it is fair to conclude that a democratic Central and Eastern Europe has finally come into being. In this sense, the pessimists have been proven wrong, whereas the optimists seem to have been validated—with one important qualification. As the division of this chapter suggests, democratization in Central and Eastern Europe has come in two stages. The first wave, as already outlined, featured an immediate and sharp break with the communist past, or a process wherein massive demonstrations, a large and unified opposition embracing liberal politics, and communists who were marginalized (as in the Czech Republic), ideologically sympathetic to the goals of the opposition (as in Hungary

and Slovenia), or sufficiently self-interested in the face of a powerful opposition to recognize the logic of defecting from dictatorship (as in the Baltic countries) combined to
end the old order and lay the groundwork for competitive elections, which the forces in
support of democratic politics then won handily. Although this scenario describes what
happened with most of the "early democratizers" in the region, some variations on these
dynamics should be noted. Thus, in both Poland and Hungary—the two countries that
in effect jump-started the collapse of communism in 1989—the critical political turning
point was in fact a roundtable between the communists and the opposition forces (with
the roundtable following significant protests in Poland in the fall of 1988 and the roundtable in Hungary strongly influenced by the surprising political outcome of the Polish
precedent). In both cases, the roundtable set the stage for subsequent elections, which
were semi-competitive in Poland and fully competitive in Hungary. In both cases, noncommunist governments were formed and predictably fueled the democratic momentum.

The second wave, or developments that took place in Albania, Bulgaria, Croatia, Macedonia, Montenegro, Romania, Serbia, Slovakia, and Ukraine from 1996 to 2014, has entailed one overarching similarity. Founding elections in all of these cases had compromised
the transition to democracy—either through the victory of the ex-communists, who were
divided in their commitments to democratic politics, or through the victory of nationalist
oppositions, who were often more illiberal than their ex-communist counterparts. However,
subsequent elections changed the political balance in ways that, in contrast to the earlier
period of transition, better served a democratic outcome. In this sense, a key issue in all of
these countries was the growth of political competition during the transition—a pattern
that we also find in the first democracies and that, because it produced turnover in governing parties and coalitions, contributed to the deepening of democratic politics.

The dynamics of the second round of democratic transitions in Central and Eastern
Europe, however, varied in detail. In Bulgaria, Romania, and Slovakia, the key issue was the
eventual rise of a more effective liberal opposition that was able to win power and, for the
first time, form a durable and effective government. We find a different dynamic in Albania, Croatia, Macedonia, and Montenegro. Here, the key issue was the growing incentives
for the ex-communists, reacting to an opposition that was either liberal or illiberal but in
both instances highly competitive, to embrace the liberal cause as a means of weakening the
incumbents, differentiating themselves, and thereby accumulating political power.

The final dynamic was in Serbia, where we see a replay, in effect, of the first transitions
to democracy in the region, albeit a decade later—a process that also took place, three years
later and informed by the Serbian precedent, in Georgia in 2003 and in Ukraine in 2004.
In Serbia, mass protests in fall 2000 in reaction to an attempt by the increasingly corrupt
and politically repressive ex-communists to steal the election, enabled the opposition—a
coalition as broad as that seen, for example, in Czechoslovakia in 1989—to win power
over the long-governing ex-communists. This sharp break with the past, however, was not
so sharp, as the subsequent instability of Serbian politics indicated—consider, for example,
the continuous squabbling between the Serbian president and the prime minister, the inability of elections to reach the constitutionally required level of turnout, the assassination of
Prime Minister Zoran Djindjić in spring 2003, and the continued popular support for the
antidemocratic Radical Party by a substantial minority of Serbian citizens. The outcome of
the presidential elections held in June 2004 and thereafter; the acceptance of Montenegro's

Photo 2.3.   General and former president Wojciech Jaruzelski and former president Lech Wałęsa at a debate on Poland's past. Jaruzelski was head of Poland's martial law government and leader during the Roundtables and Poland's first year after the fall of communism. Wałęsa, former leader of Solidarity, won the first popular election to the presidency after Jaruzelski resigned. (*Rzeczpospolita*)

declaration of independence in 2006; the use of the International Court of Justice to challenge Kosovo's declaration of independence in 2008; significant progress in both economic reforms and economic performance; the impressive Serbian record since 2000 with respect to civil liberties, political rights, and free and fair elections; and, finally, the commitment of once antidemocratic parties to the democratic project, however, suggest that Serbia is indeed on the road to democracy.

These details aside, all of these "second-wave" democracies are interesting in that the shift from either dictatorship to democracy or from hybrid to full-scale democracy took place in response to elections that brought to power governments with the incentive and the capacity to change the country's political course.[16] But this leaves two obvious questions. Why did the "laggards" in stage one all move in a more democratic direction in stage two? And how can we explain, more generally, the recent convergence in regime types in Central and Eastern Europe?

Explaining the Second Wave: Domestic Factors

In contrast to the explanations offered with respect to the first stage of the transition, the explanations of the second stage are much less parsimonious. Indeed, the importance of both domestic and international factors, both of which pushed in a similar liberalizing direction, is striking. On the domestic side, we can point to two influences. One is suggested by the fact that, if we look at postcommunist Eurasia as a whole (or add to our Central and East European group the remaining twelve Soviet successor states), we find a high correlation between contemporary political arrangements and the duration of Communist Party rule. All of the states of interest in this volume are democratic, and they all became communist after World War II. By contrast, the record of democracy in those Soviet successor states where communism had been in place since World War I is far more mixed, featuring, for example, clear-cut dictatorships, as in Belarus and Uzbekistan; low-quality democracies, as in Ukraine prior to the Orange Revolution in 2004 and after Yanukovych's election as president in 2010; and formerly relatively democratic orders that have moved decisively in a dictatorial direction, such as in Armenia and Russia. The durability, albeit continued fragility, of democracy in Moldova—the only Soviet successor state, aside from the Baltic countries and the western part of Ukraine, to have been added to the Soviet Union after World War II—makes this comparison even more instructive. Just as strikingly, given the Armenian, Russian, and Belarusian cases, there have been no cases of democratic breakdown in Central and Eastern Europe since the end of Communist Party hegemony (though the period of Vladimír Mečiar's rule in Slovakia after the breakup of the Czechoslovak federation certainly compromised Slovak democratic performance in the short term).

Why is the length of Communist Party rule so important? Two plausible factors come to the fore. First, a longer experience with communism means deeper penetration by communist ideology, institutions, and practices—penetration secured in part by the number of generations that lived under communist rule. This could make a transition to democracy more difficult, because of the absence of democracy-supporting institutions and values and because of the constraints on the development of a viable political opposition. The second reason is also historical in nature but asks us to think in broader terms about what this correlation means. The countries of concern in this volume all have a long history of close connections with Western economies, cultures, and political ideas—a history abruptly ended by the rise of communism during and immediately after World War II. The geographical proximity to the West, therefore, may have been important in laying the groundwork, once opportunities for political change presented themselves, for subsequent democratic development. The ability of these countries to withstand the challenge of communism, of course, was aided by the brevity of the communist experience—especially, for example, the unusually brief duration of Stalinization, when the most antidemocratic aspects of state socialism were imposed.[17]

The second domestic factor focuses particularly on those countries where illiberal nationalists came to power after the deregulation of the Communist Party's monopoly: that is, Slovakia, Croatia, and Serbia. In all three cases, the liberal opposition, having been divided and demobilized by the struggle over the national question, finally managed to regroup and remobilize and thereby win elections. The literature on both nationalism and democratic transitions is in fact silent about when and why once successful illiberal nationalists lose power and politicians with a more liberal agenda take their place, focusing far more on the question of why some transitions to democracy feature a central political role for illiberal nationalists. In response to the first and largely unexplored question, we can identify two striking commonalities in our three cases: the opposition was able to focus on the threats and costs of one leader in particular (Mečiar, Tudjman, or Milošević), and international actors, including the EU, the United States, and transnational networks of nongovernmental organizations, played an important role in providing support to the opposition—for example, training them in the art of resistance, providing electoral monitors, and helping them organize campaigns to increase voter registration and electoral turnout. International influences, in short, were critical—a dimension that I will now address more systematically.

International Influences

As noted above, geography played a role in the second wave of democratization. However, its impact was also expressed in international dynamics. If the events of 1989, or the region-wide collapse of Communist Party hegemony, indicated the power of diffusion when neighboring states have similar domestic structures, similar historical experiences, and similar external constraints (such as Soviet control), then diffusion, we might suggest, can still operate after these momentous events. Here, it is important to remember that there was in fact a great deal of interaction among the states of concern in this volume during the communist era. For example, oppositions in Poland, Hungary, and Czechoslovakia were in contact with each other during communism; the rise of the Solidarity movement in Poland in 1980 influenced opposition development in the Baltic states and in Bulgaria before the dramatic developments at the end of the decade; and protests in Central and Eastern Europe during the communist era invariably called for adoption of some features of the Yugoslav alternative model of communism. While this pattern did not guarantee by any means that these countries would all follow identical pathways once the hold of the communists weakened, it did mean that developments in one country had the potential to influence developments elsewhere in the region—for example, demonstrating that democracy was possible in the first stage of the transition and, later, helping weaker opposition forces in, say, Bulgaria, Romania, and Slovakia to acquire the strategies needed to move their less democratic countries in a more liberal direction. Indeed, changes in Slovak politics in the second half of the 1990s influenced subsequent political changes in Croatia and Serbia—and Georgia and Ukraine, for that matter. In this way, over time the region converged in both its political and economic forms—as it had in the past, only in an illiberal way and then with the additional nudge of a hegemon, the Soviet Union, committed for reasons of security and ideology to dictatorship.

The importance of geography, or the spatial side of politics, also alerts us to several other international factors. One is the global wave of democratization. By the turn of the twentieth century, a majority of the world's population lived in democratic orders—an unprecedented situation and one that contributed to developments in Central and Eastern Europe by rendering democracy perhaps the "only game in town." That the countries under discussion are in Europe, of course, also mattered, especially given the role of the Helsinki Process, beginning in the 1970s, in solidifying a European norm of democracy and human rights and, indeed, in providing the opposition in Central and Eastern Europe during the communist era with greater resources to question their regimes' legitimacy and performance.

This leads to a final international variable: the European Union. As numerous scholars have argued, the European Union has had two effects in Central and Eastern Europe.[18] It has provided a clear standard for democratic politics (and capitalist economics) by which both publics and elites in this region can measure regime performance, and it has provided powerful incentives for those countries to meet (and continue to meet) EU standards—for example, by offering advice on the construction of liberal orders and by holding out the promise of markets, financial support, and the legitimacy that comes from being coded as European and, therefore, part of a prosperous, stable, secure, and, to use the language of many Central and East Europeans, "normal" community. Many scholars and Central and East European citizens, of course, debate whether the EU has been such a powerful force for democracy. Does the EU, for example, make democracy both possible and doable, or has it merely courted those countries that were already on the road to democratic government? Does the EU secure sovereignty for the postcommunist countries or undermine their newly won sovereignty by reducing domestic policy control? Do the economic benefits of joining the EU outweigh, especially in the short term, the costs of preparing for membership—which include not just meeting a huge number of expensive conditions but also facing the constraints imposed by EU markets, the protectionism of older members, and the EU's commitment in recent years to austerity measures in the face of the global economic crisis? Has the EU encouraged competition or merely strengthened those already in power, thereby contributing to inequalities in power and money? Finally, does EU membership produce equality among countries through the creation of a single Europe, or has the eastward expansion of the EU effectively created a hierarchy, sundering the rich western members from their poor eastern cousins and dividing the east, in turn, into countries designated as either current or possible future members and those countries that, because of geography, have no hope of joining and may, as a result, be isolated and thereby locked into authoritarian rule?

While insightful in certain respects, these concerns must be placed alongside two incontrovertible facts. First, all of the countries that have recently joined the EU (though Hungary at present is an exception) or applied for candidate status evince clear improvements over time in democratic assets. Second, there is a clear correlation between prospects for joining the EU and the breadth of the domestic political spectrum. Put simply, we have witnessed in Central and Eastern Europe a sharp decline in most countries (though, again, Hungary is a recent exception) of extremist political voices and the convergence of political parties around support for the EU (though public support of the EU, it must be recognized, varies over time within countries as well as among them). For example, after returning to power in 2003, the Croatian Democratic Union (HDZ), a party that had formerly ruled over Croatia as a dictatorship, went further than its more "moderate" predecessor in embracing EU membership as its primary policy goal. Similarly, the new president of Serbia (elected in 2012), Tomislav Nikolić, has done the same, despite a long record of opposition to the EU and support for illiberal Serbian nationalism. We can, of course, debate whether political moderation, as in most of the second-wave democracies, is a consequence of the EU's influence or a function of purely domestic developments. However, the fact remains that political leaders in Central and Eastern Europe, either early in the transition or later, have come to believe that joining the EU is critical for their own political futures and for concerns about identity, money, stability, and security that are critical to voters.

However we construe this dynamic, improvements in democratic performance in such areas as rule of law, state provision of civil liberties and political rights, and moderation in the political values and attitudes of citizens and politicians alike are associated with EU membership. In the rush to embrace the EU, other ways of meeting goals, such as international security and economic growth, as offered by the extreme right and left, have lost political support, either during the accession process or following membership. With respect to the latter dynamic and the second round of democratization in Central and Eastern Europe, extremist parties have either gone into decline or chosen to adapt. Thus, just as political competition increased in all of the countries in Central and Eastern Europe that had lagged in democratization, the structure of competition itself changed through the decline in political polarization. The EU may very well have played a key role in that process.

Conclusion and Some Speculation

In this chapter, I have argued that the transition to democracy in Central and Eastern Europe has proceeded in two stages. In the first stage, from 1989 to the first half of 1996 (with the Romanian presidential elections constituting the turning point), there were variable regime outcomes, with half of the region moving quickly to democracy and the other half either stuck in dictatorship or perched precariously between the two regime extremes. In this period, the key issue was the development of oppositions during communism and the extent to which they embraced liberal politics and were able to win in the first competitive elections. In the second period, 1996 to 2014, the "laggards" in democratization all moved in a liberal direction. In this case, the causes were multiple, including diffusion effects within the region, the role of the European Union, the declining capacity of authoritarian leaders to maintain power through exploitation of cultural differences, and limited constraints on democratization because of what was, from a broader regional standard, a shorter history of Communist Party rule. As a result, the pronounced political diversity of Central and Eastern Europe in the immediate aftermath of the collapse of communism and communist states declined. Just as state boundaries tended to endure, so democratization spread. Indeed, even the exceptional cases of Montenegro and Kosovo and their secession from Serbia could be construed as an investment in a more authentic democratic politics for all three parts of the original Serbian-Montenegrin federation.

The patterns of democratization in Central and Eastern Europe, together with their underlying causes, present us with several important questions that are relevant to this region and, more generally, to the study of recent transitions to democratic rule. What do we mean by regime outcomes? Does it make sense to argue that some countries in Central and Eastern Europe succeeded or failed to become democratic orders after communism, or does it make more sense to argue that the countries in this region were differentially situated to build democratic orders, with the result that democratization took longer in some cases than in others? The analysis presented above suggests that the latter interpretation is more compelling. This implies that there are differences in the assets and obstacles to democratization and that these differences affect how long a transition can take, even after the evident decline of authoritarian rule.

The time horizons we use to evaluate democratization, therefore, are critical in two ways. First, we can draw premature conclusions about political pathways after authoritarianism if we rush to judgment. Second, we may need different explanations for these pathways, depending on when we choose to step back and evaluate political patterns. In this sense, there seems to be no single road to democratic politics, especially if we allow ourselves to recognize faster versus slower transitions.

But does this mean that, given time, democracy is inevitable? Given the region-wide victory of democracy in Central and Eastern Europe by 2004, or fifteen years into the transition, we might be tempted to draw such a conclusion. However, there are ample reasons to be skeptical. One is that there are still significant differences in the quality of democratic governance in Central and Eastern Europe. For example, major protests in Macedonia in 2001 threatened to bring down democracy (but had the opposite effect, given the subsequent construction of a more inclusive polity); political support for conservative nationalist parties and conservative politicians has increased in recent years in Poland, Bulgaria, and especially Hungary; and the shift to the democratic column in Croatia and especially Serbia is of very recent vintage. In addition, other waves of democratization in the past, while admittedly not as global in their reach as the current wave, have been followed by democratic breakdowns. Here, the Hungarian example serves as a cautionary tale of being too quick to generalize about democratic change. This is especially the case since, in the third wave in particular, we have seen few examples of the collapse of democracy but more examples of a subtler deterioration in democratic performance. Moreover, the current global wave reveals a disturbing pattern: the rise of more and more hybrid regimes, which could tip in either political direction and, at the same time, could endure as halfway houses built on political compromises that promote stability at the cost of corruption and checkered economic performance. Still another consideration is that democratization in Central and Eastern Europe, as I have repeatedly emphasized throughout this chapter, is strongly advantaged by the long connection of this area to Western Europe and, more recently, by the influence of international institutions such as the European Union. Finally, Central and Eastern Europe is distinctive in another way that has also invested in democratic political outcomes. This is a region that does not force dominant international powers, such as the United States, NATO, or the EU, to choose between security concerns and democracy promotion—a choice that was evident throughout the Cold War and that undermined, as a result, democratic politics. Even after the Cold War, this choice is being made again with regard to US policy toward Russia, Central Asia, the Caucasus, and Pakistan.

Democratization in Central and Eastern Europe, therefore, as in southern Europe beginning in 1974, while proceeding in stages, has nonetheless been strongly aided in ways that are largely unavailable to many other countries that have participated in the third wave. Unlucky throughout its history, especially in comparison with Western Europe, Central and Eastern Europe at this time—in comparison with other regions undergoing regime change—has become, in these respects, lucky. Domestic and international factors are working together to support democratic rule, whereas both sets of factors in the past had usually pushed these countries in the opposite direction.

These advantages, however, must be judged alongside some constraints on democratization that are likely to become even more apparent in the future, once the "big" issues of the transition, such as the breakthrough to democracy and staying the democratic course, building capitalism, and integrating with the West, give way to other, more concrete concerns. One issue is the declining capacity of the European Union to provide incentives for new members, candidate members, and countries with association agreements to deepen the dynamics of both democratization and economic reform. The problem here is that the EU is very divided from within; it is perceived by many publics, whether inside or outside the EU, as too bureaucratic and too removed from its various citizenries to represent their interests and speak for them; it is facing deep economic problems; and it is unlikely in the near future, precisely because of all these problems, to expand to include such new but precarious democracies as Albania, Bosnia, Macedonia, Montenegro, Serbia, or Ukraine. The EU, in short, is less willing and able to invest in the newest democracies than it was in the case of the first and most robust democracies in the region. In this sense, the north-south divide in Central and Eastern Europe is likely to continue.

In addition, there is the continuing problem in many of these countries of significant corruption and expanding socioeconomic inequality—with the latter often correlated with cultural cleavages. These developments can contribute to political polarization, especially in hard economic times—as we have seen, for example, in Hungary. Moreover, most of the regimes in the region feature weak political parties—as institutions that structure the political preferences of mass publics, serve as the primary linkages between citizens and their governments, and shape, especially through elections and parliaments, the course of public policy. The "party" problem, in combination with a severe economic crisis, helps explain political polarization and deterioration in the quality of democracy in Hungary. Yet another issue for even the well-established democracies in the region is the very high level of political cynicism (whether citizens focus on the performance of democratic institutions or on specific politicians), coupled, not surprisingly, with often low voter turnouts. Throughout the region, therefore, we find both continuing weakness in democratic institutions and public disappointment with the democratic experiment. Democracy, therefore, while region-wide, is flawed, and these deficiencies, while unlikely to be fatal to democracy, will necessarily define the boundaries and the consequences of political competition for many years to come.

Study Questions

1. Is it accurate to say that the end of communism led to an immediate and region-wide transition to democracy in Central and Eastern Europe?
2. What are the key differences between democracy and authoritarianism?
3. What are hybrid regimes?
4. How typical have the experiences with region transition in Central and Eastern Europe been in comparison with such transitions in other parts of the world?
5. What have been the key differences in the political evolution of regimes in Central and Eastern Europe since the fall of communism, and what key factors account for these differences?

Suggested Readings

Bunce, Valerie. "Global Patterns and Postcommunist Dynamics." *Orbis* 50 (autumn 2006): 601–20.

Bunce, Valerie, Michael McFaul, and Kathryn Stoner-Weiss, eds. *Democracy and Authoritarianism in the Postcommunist World.* New York: Cambridge University Press, 2009.

Bunce, Valerie J., and Sharon L. Wolchik. *Defeating Authoritarian Leaders in Postcommunist Countries.* New York: Cambridge University Press, 2011.

Gagnon, Charles P. *Myth of Ethnic War: Serbia and Croatia in the 1990s.* Ithaca, NY: Cornell University Press, 2004.

Mungiu-Pippidi, Alina, and Ivan Krastev, eds. *Nationalism after Communism: Lessons Learned.* Budapest: Central European University, 2004.

Vachudova, Milada Anna. *Europe Undivided: Democracy, Leverage, and Integration after Communism.* Oxford: Oxford University Press, 2005.

Zielonka, Jan, ed. *Democratic Consolidation in Eastern Europe.* Oxford: Oxford University Press, 2001.

Websites

Radio Free Europe/Radio Liberty: http://www.rferl.org

Freedom House, "2014 Nations in Transit Data": http://www.freedomhouse.org/report-types/nations-transit#.VzAizM5Z9ac

World Bank, "Worldwide Governance Indicators": http://www.info.worldbank.org/governance/wgi/index.aspx#home

Notes

1. The tripartite political division of the region in the immediate aftermath of communist regimes has been analyzed by several scholars. See, e.g., Valerie Bunce, "The Political Economy of Postsocialism," *Slavic Review* 58 (winter 1999): 756–93; M. Steven Fish, "The Determinants of Economic Reform in the Postcommunist World," *East European Politics and Societies* 12 (winter 1998): 31–78; Michael McFaul, "The Fourth Wave of Democracy and Dictatorship: Noncooperative Transitions in the Postcommunist World," *World Politics* 54 (January 2002): 214–44.

2. There are many competing definitions of democracy. Perhaps the most helpful summary of these debates can be found in Robert Dahl, *On Democracy* (New Haven, CT: Yale University Press, 1998).

3. Since the early 1990s, hybrid regimes have become the most common outcome of the global wave of democratic change that began in the mid-1970s. See Larry Diamond, "Thinking about Hybrid Regimes," *Journal of Democracy* 13 (April 2002): 3–24; Steven Levitsky and Lucan A. Way, "The Rise of Competitive Authoritarianism," *Journal of Democracy* 13 (April 2002): 51–65. See also Marina Ottaway, *Democracy Challenged: The Rise of Semi-authoritarianism* (Washington, DC: Carnegie Endowment Press, 2003).

4. On the issues of demobilization of the liberals in these two countries, see V. P. Gagnon, *The Myth of Ethnic War: Serbia and Croatia in the 1990s* (Ithaca, NY: Cornell University Press, 2004);

Kevin Deegan-Krause, "Uniting the Enemy: Politics and the Convergence of Nationalisms in Slovakia," *East European Politics and Societies* 18 (fall 2004): 651–96.

5. See, e.g., Samuel P. Huntington, *The Third Wave: Democratization in the Late Twentieth Century* (Norman: University of Oklahoma Press, 1991); Guillermo A. O'Donnell, Philippe C. Schmitter, and Laurence Whitehead, eds., *Transitions from Authoritarian Rule,* vols. 1–4 (Baltimore: Johns Hopkins University Press, 1986); Giuseppe Di Palma, *To Craft Democracy* (Berkeley: University of California Press, 1991).

6. On the unexpected problems encountered after the fall of Saddam Hussein, see Larry Diamond, "What Went Wrong in Iraq?" *Foreign Affairs* 83 (summer/fall 2004): 34–56; Peter Galbraith, "Iraq: Bush's Islamic Republic," *New York Review of Books* 52 (August 11, 2005): 6–9.

7. A useful summary of these arguments can be found in Grzegorz Ekiert and Stephen Hanson, eds., *Capitalism and Democracy in Central and Eastern Europe: Assessing the Legacy of Communist Rule* (Cambridge: Cambridge University Press, 2003).

8. Carol Leff, *National Conflict in Czechoslovakia: The Making and Remaking of a State, 1918–1987* (Princeton, NJ: Princeton University Press, 1988).

9. See, especially, O'Donnell, Schmitter, and Whitehead, *Transitions*; M. Steven Fish, *Democracy from Scratch: Opposition and Regime in the New Russian Revolution* (Princeton, NJ: Princeton University Press, 1995).

10. See Nancy Bermeo, *Ordinary People in Extraordinary Times: The Citizenry and the Breakdown of Democracy* (Princeton, NJ: Princeton University Press, 2003).

11. Charles Tilly, *Coercion, Capital and European States, AD 990–1992* (London: Basil Blackwell, 1992).

12. Dankwart Rustow, "Transitions to Democracy: Toward a Dynamic Model," *Comparative Politics* 2 (April 1970): 18–36.

13. See Terry Lynn Karl, "Dilemmas of Democratization in Latin America," *Comparative Politics* 23 (spring 1990): 28–49; Valerie Bunce, "Rethinking Recent Democratization: Lessons from the Postcommunist Experience," *World Politics* 55, no. 2 (January 2003): 167–92.

14. Bunce, "The Political Economy"; McFaul, "The Fourth Wave"; Valerie J. Bunce and Sharon L. Wolchik, "Favorable Conditions and Electoral Revolutions," *Journal of Democracy* 17, no. 4 (October 2006): 5–22.

15. International Commission on the Balkans, *The Balkans in Europe's Future* (Sofia: Secretariat Center for Liberal Strategies, 2005).

16. For a comparison of these two waves, see Valerie Bunce and Sharon Wolchik, "A Regional Tradition: The Diffusion of Democratic Change under Communism and Postcommunism," in *Democracy and Authoritarianism in the Postcommunist World*, ed. Valerie Bunce, Michael McFaul, and Kathryn Stoner-Weiss (New York: Cambridge University Press, 2009).

17. The importance of geographical proximity to the West has appeared in a number of studies that have attempted to explain variations among postcommunist political and economic trajectories. See, e.g., Jeffrey S. Kopstein and David A. Reilly, "Geographical Diffusion and the Transformation of the Postcommunist World," *World Politics* 53 (October 2000): 1–37.

18. See, e.g., Milada Anna Vachudova, *Europe Undivided: Democracy, Leverage, and Integration after Communism* (Oxford: Oxford University Press, 2005); Wade Jacoby, *The Enlargement of the European Union and NATO: Ordering from the Menu in Central Europe* (Cambridge: Cambridge University Press, 2004); Ronald H. Linden, ed., *Norms and Nannies: The Impact of International Organizations on the Central and East European States* (Lanham, MD: Rowman & Littlefield, 2002).

CHAPTER 3

Re-creating the Market

Sharon Fisher

Transforming the economies of Central and Eastern Europe was probably the most complicated aspect of the transition from communism. At the start of the reform process, there was no single model for how the changes should be carried out. The postcommunist transition was unique. Unlike with the transitions in Latin America and elsewhere in the world, there was no real market economy on which to build, so the old state economy had to be dismantled as a market economy was developed. Thus, reforms happened in a rather haphazard way, and most knowledge of the transition process was formed after the fact.

Defining the "success" of a country's transition can be difficult, as some former communist states gained international recognition for certain reforms (such as privatization) but were laggards in other areas (such as banking reform). Some countries that initially appeared to be on a rapid path toward a market economy eventually slowed down, while the opposite occurred in other cases. In most countries, foreign observers perceived the success of reforms much differently than the domestic population did, and reformist politicians often suffered in elections. Regardless, it is generally agreed that the most successful economic transitions in the region were those of the eight countries that joined the European Union (EU) in May 2004. Still, even among those countries, there have been great variations, and the global economic crisis of 2008 and 2009 and the subsequent Eurozone debt drama had a surprisingly negative impact on several of the new member states.

In retrospect, the two most important factors in determining the economic success of Central and East European countries seem to have been initial conditions and the strength of commitment of successive governments to reforms.[1] The Central and East European countries began the transition from communism from somewhat disparate starting points. Some, such as Hungary and Poland, had a head start: they had begun reforms during the final years of the communist era. Others, such as the Czech Republic, benefited from a strong manufacturing tradition. The more advanced countries in the region were generally those with close proximity to Western markets, whether because of historical traditions or the ease of trade and investment ties with the EU. This situation made it easier to attract foreign direct investment (FDI) and turn from trade with the East (the Soviet Union and Central and Eastern Europe) to the West. For example, despite being substantially behind the Central European countries at the end of the communist era, the three Baltic states benefited in the transition period from cooperation with their

Nordic neighbors. The countries that experienced the bulk of their industrialization during the communist era often had a more difficult economic transition, especially when they were far from Western markets.

The other key factor determining the success or failure of the initial economic reforms was the policy approach of the new governments. While the political developments in each individual country had a substantial impact on the way market-oriented reforms were carried out, the economic situation also had a major effect on politics, as fickle populations frequently shifted their support from government to opposition depending on which side was promising prospects of greater well-being. It is important to keep in mind that frequent changes in government, often brought on by popular dissatisfaction with how the economic reforms worked, contributed to a lack of continuity in the reform process throughout the region.

The way communism ended in the various countries of Central and Eastern Europe also had a significant impact on the approach governments took to economic reforms. According to the European Bank for Reconstruction and Development (EBRD), the presence of a noncommunist government in the initial transition period is strongly correlated with the character of reforms in subsequent years.[2] Communists or former communists initially remained in control in Bulgaria, Romania, Ukraine, and Albania but were ousted in Poland, Hungary, Czechoslovakia, and the three Baltic states. As a result, reforms were faster in the latter countries in the early 1990s. Once the pace was set, successive governments generally continued with the reform process, even when the reformed communists came to power. By the middle to late 1990s, prospects for EU accession also helped push them along.

The Demise of Central Planning

Formally, communist economic policy was based on a protection of workers' interests through a "dictatorship of the proletariat." In practice, however, the Communist Party leadership controlled all social and economic organizations and made all major decisions about the economy. All appointments, including the managers of enterprises, had to be approved by the party, whether by the Central Committee or local organs. Those who formed the party *nomenklatura* (defined as a list of people from which high-level government appointments were selected) were provided with special rights and privileges to motivate them.

A key element of communist economic policy was "collective ownership," or nationalization of the means of production. Private ownership of land and the means of production were abolished without compensation, while lower classes benefited from social promotion. Agriculture was collectivized with the installation of communist rule. Only in Yugoslavia and Poland was private farming allowed. Central planning was another important aspect of communist economic policy, with a focus on quantity rather than on quality or profit. Prices in this system were regulated, and fixed prices at both the wholesale and retail levels meant that open inflation was never a problem. With regard to labor, the communist system offered full employment. Those who did not work were considered "parasites." A balanced budget, on the surface at least, was another element of the communist economic program.

Foreign trade was regulated by the Council for Mutual Economic Assistance (CMEA) trading bloc, established by the Soviet Union, Bulgaria, Czechoslovakia, Hungary, Poland, and Romania in 1949. The CMEA was formed in response to the US Marshall Plan's offer of economic aid to some of these countries (which the Soviet Union insisted they refuse). Within the CMEA (also known as Comecon), a system of international specialization was laid out so that different goods were produced in different parts of the region to meet Soviet needs (and also those of the bloc as a whole), particularly in the military sector. This policy ensured that no state could stand alone economically. It did not work like a common market; instead trade was negotiated and conducted bilaterally, with oversight by the Soviet Union.

The communist economic system was, even at its best, a tragedy of errors. Central planning meant that bankruptcy was not a possibility. State subsidies were used to keep unprofitable firms afloat. Maintaining a balanced budget thus would have been a challenge if there had been open accounting. Even though most countries' budget deficits were quite small, they created substantial imbalances. The only way to cover deficits was through foreign borrowing or printing more money.

Economic plans focused on production rather than personal consumption. There was similarly little investment in health care, transportation, housing, and services. Moreover, there was a complete disregard for the environmental effects of production. The pricing system encouraged an intentional lowering of quality by producers and contributed to shortages. After all, decisions were made at the Central Planning Commission based on political goals. Citizens relied on their personal connections to obtain goods and services, and the gray economy grew steadily. This meant that corruption was rampant, a trend that has continued well into the second decade of the twenty-first century. Although socialism was supposed to create individuals committed to the common good, most people were focused primarily on providing for their families.

Because domestic prices were regulated nationally, there was no link between domestic and foreign prices. As a result, currencies were not convertible. There were official and unofficial exchange rates. An overvalued domestic currency provided little reason to export goods outside the region as long as countries did not have debts they needed to repay to foreign creditors. By the end of the communist era, some 60 to 75 percent of trade was conducted with other CMEA members, and many of the goods produced were not competitive in the West.

Before long, the communist economic system began to show signs of strain. As these economies faltered, some countries implemented limited economic reforms. Hungary launched its so-called goulash communism in 1968. In Poland, after several failed attempts, market reforms were begun a final time in 1982. In Yugoslavia, the communist system was considerably more liberal and the economy less plan oriented and more "self-managing" than in other countries in the region. In the late 1980s, the Yugoslav regime introduced extensive market-oriented reforms. However, most other regimes were reluctant to make any economic reforms. Even after Mikhail Gorbachev launched partial reforms in the USSR during the late 1980s, countries such as Czechoslovakia, East

Germany, Bulgaria, Romania, and Albania maintained a hard-line stance until the fall of communism in 1989.

In those countries that did introduce reforms, there was a clear pattern. The reach of the plan (the number of things it regulated) was cut. Power was delegated from branch ministries to enterprise managers to help decentralize decision making. Economic incentives were promoted. Pricing was made more flexible and market oriented. Inflation was made a fact of life. The establishment of small private enterprises was permitted. Foreign trade was partially liberalized. Since substantial distortions remained, other, new problems emerged. For example, as unemployment was legalized, jobless benefits were introduced, so a higher share of state revenues had to be devoted to social welfare.

By the late 1980s, the communist system was in precarious shape. Most countries experienced severe economic crises with falling output, profound shortages of consumer goods, accelerating inflation rates, widening current-account deficits, and rising foreign debt. Failing to deliver the expected growth, economic reforms instead called into question the legitimacy of the entire communist system with its claim of superiority over capitalism. Countries such as Poland and Hungary were forced to borrow heavily from abroad to spur investment and consumption in an effort to raise growth rates and appease the population. As the debt to foreign lenders increased, debt service also rose, and international credits began to dry up by the end of the decade. Many countries in the region were forced to reschedule their foreign debts.

During the last years of the communist era, the only relative "success stories" were Hungary and Czechoslovakia. Hungary had transformed itself into a socialist market economy while maintaining some degree of economic balance, although foreign debt did rise substantially. Czechoslovakia, on the other hand, managed to steer clear of major imbalances, despite the hard-line approach of its communist system. Both countries avoided the debilitating shortages that plagued other economies in the region.[3]

Macroeconomic Stabilization

As they transformed toward capitalism, most Central and East European countries inherited strong macroeconomic and external disequilibria from the communist system, including budget imbalances based on overarching social welfare systems and high levels of foreign debt. Even countries like Czechoslovakia, which had relatively stable and positive initial macroeconomic conditions at the outset, had to deal with the inflationary impact of price liberalization and the effects of the collapse of trade with the USSR. Across the region, advisors from organizations such as the International Monetary Fund (IMF) gave technical assistance to devise macroeconomic stabilization programs based largely on methods that were applied in developing countries. Even as governments implemented these programs, it was unclear how effective they would be. After all, postcommunist transitions were unprecedented in the scope of the changes required.

Macroeconomic stabilization programs included price liberalization, restrictive monetary and fiscal policies, and foreign trade liberalization, accompanied by a sharp devaluation of the domestic currency, making it weaker against international currencies such as the US dollar. These measures were aimed at stabilizing the economy and allowing for the introduction of structural changes, including enterprise privatization and reforms of the banking sector and social welfare system.

The main debates on the transition focused not on what needed to be done but rather on how to sequence and pace the reforms. Some argued that demonopolization of industry was required before prices were set free to prevent firms from simply hiking prices. In the stabilization package, there was also considerable debate over the extent of the currency devaluation and how much interest rates should be shifted. Devaluation helped to improve external trade balances, allowing for international stabilization. Nonetheless, it also raised the price of imports of consumer and industrial goods, thereby contributing to higher inflation. The small or medium-size open economies in Central and Eastern Europe were particularly vulnerable to these cross pressures.

In terms of speed, reformers were divided into proponents of "shock therapy" versus gradualism. The gradualists argued for relatively lax monetary and fiscal policies and a slower transfer of assets from the state to the private sector, with the aim of protecting the population from the social consequences of reforms. With time, it became clear that none of the countries that consistently advocated a gradual approach were successful reformers.

PRICE LIBERALIZATION

Among the countries that launched reforms before 1989, only Hungary broadly liberalized prices under the communist regime. Elsewhere in Central Europe, the "big-bang" approach to price liberalization was used after the fall of communism. Poland took the lead in January 1990, and Czechoslovakia followed a year later. When "big bangs" happened, market forces set prices for consumer durables and nonfood items, so shortages disappeared since people were less able to purchase goods. But politicians and consumers were often reluctant to give up fixed prices on essentials such as food (particularly bread and meat) and gasoline because such a step would impoverish a population that expected economic gains under the new capitalist system. In the end, many governments dropped price controls only because of their inability to continue providing subsidies. In most Central and East European countries, rents, public transport, and utilities remained under state control throughout the 1990s and even into the first decade of the twenty-first century. Prices were often set below the real costs because price hikes were seen as politically risky. In Slovakia, for example, consumer prices for natural gas did not reach world market levels until 2004; regulated rents in the Czech Republic remained well below market prices through 2006.

Price liberalization caused inflation to surge throughout the Central and East European region in the initial transition years. Most countries experienced triple- or quadruple-digit price growth after the fall of communism. Those increases were largely a result of filling out the imbalances from the previous regime, particularly where countries printed money to cover budgetary expenditures. The former Czechoslovakia, where the state maintained a balanced budget under communism, had the smallest increase in inflation following the launch of price liberalization, and inflation never reached triple digits. In contrast, countries such as Ukraine and rump Yugoslavia, where macroeconomic stabilization programs initially failed, suffered from hyperinflation.

Several key lessons regarding price liberalization can be drawn from the postcommunist transitions in Central and Eastern Europe. First, the initial liberalization had to be as comprehensive as possible. Any additional deregulation of prices proved to be extremely complicated, spurring passionate public debates and broad opposition. Second, greater distortions of initial price levels required more comprehensive deregulations, even as the distortions made price hikes more difficult for the public to stomach due to the large increase over communist-era levels. Third, populations willingly accepted price deregulation when it was accompanied by a change in the system. In fact, nowhere in the region did price liberalizations stir widespread protest.[4] Finally, high levels of inflation are incompatible with economic growth. In contrast, countries that did not experience hyperinflation were able to moderate the declines in gross domestic product (GDP) during the early transition years.

RESTRICTING MONETARY POLICY

The liberalization of prices in Central and Eastern Europe usually involved higher increases in inflation than were initially expected. This inflation resulted in demands for a loosening of control over monetary policy. Many countries in the region, in fact, maintained low interest rates in the initial transition years. This discouraged savings and contributed to a low level of trust in local currencies. Although this negatively affected average citizens, it benefited politically connected individuals because they could obtain loans at low real interest rates.

Eventually, monetary authorities shifted from expanding the money supply to restricting it, with the aim of keeping inflation down. Their policies involved, instead, a slow growth in the money supply, even a negative growth in real terms. These policies were also accompanied by large increases in interest rates to make them higher than the rate of inflation. In Ukraine, for example, real interest rates were set at a high of 200 percent in spring 1996.[5] This policy of high interest rates discouraged domestic borrowing and encouraged saving and investment. Perhaps more important was the impact high interest rates had in reducing risky lending practices. In each country's transition, "success" required that monetary authorities eventually find a balance between the two extremes of high versus low interest rates to support economic growth.

BALANCING FISCAL BUDGETS

Because the main source of financing for budget deficits comes from the printing of money, fiscal policy is closely linked to monetary policy as an important element in stabilizing economies undergoing transformation. The persistence of fiscal imbalances poses serious risks for the sustainability of long-term economic growth because it triggers higher inflation rates. Thus, a first step in the macroeconomic stabilization programs in Central and Eastern Europe was a dramatic reduction of fiscal deficits, so that revenues and expenses in the state budget became more balanced. By reducing state expenditures and increasing revenues, the new elites sought to ensure that the fiscal reforms would provide the necessary funds to sustain a radical stabilization program. Balanced budgets were especially crucial in those countries that were very indebted because the financing of fiscal deficits contributed to sustaining inflation and made it difficult to satisfy creditors. A balanced budget became a main criterion for receiving IMF financing and other credits from international financial markets. Governments in the region struggled to balance the demands of their constituents with the austere fiscal targets required by international financial institutions.

Initially, fiscal deficits were driven largely by the high expenditures associated with the oversized public sector and the collapse of revenues due to production declines in the transition process. On the expenditure side, the first step transitional governments took was to eliminate consumer price subsidies, especially for basic food products. The second step involved cutting subsidies for state enterprises. This step proved much more difficult to implement because it contributed to higher levels of unemployment. As firms sought profitability, they typically laid off workers. Pressures for more state expenditures emerged through public demands for higher social spending in the form of social welfare programs and pensions. Most countries in the region maintained enterprise subsidies throughout the 1990s in at least a few key but inefficient sectors, most notably agriculture, mining, and energy. Eventually, direct subsidies were frequently replaced by indirect subsidies, with state companies getting cheap credits from state-owned banks.

On the revenue side, an entirely new taxation system was necessary. Under the new system, personal income and consumption taxes accounted for a larger share of total tax revenues, thereby taking the burden off enterprises and helping them maintain competitiveness. The first step was to replace the communist-era "turnover tax" with the value-added tax (VAT), a consumption tax levied at each stage of production based on the value added to the product at that stage; the final consumer ultimately bears the tax burden. In contrast, the turnover tax was utilized under the previous system on a discretionary basis. Goods considered socially necessary were subsidized by negative tax rates. In the new system, VAT rates were typically around 20 percent, often with lower rates for necessities such as food and medicines.

The second important element in reforming the revenue side of the budget was the establishment of personal income taxes. Under communism, personal income taxes were insignificant. In the transition period, three alternative models were used: a social democratic approach with high progressive income taxes that went up to more than 50 percent of gross income for the wealthiest citizens (Hungary and Ukraine); a standard model with a progressive system taxing individuals between 12 and 40 percent of their income; and the Baltic model (Estonia, Latvia) with a flat personal income tax—the same percentage for everyone.

The third step involved the establishment of a corporate tax system that was legislated rather than being subject to negotiations between managers and their government supervisors, as it had been during the communist era. Most countries initially chose to impose a flat profit tax of 30 to 35 percent.[6]

Another major concern of the transition countries was the need for an efficient and effective collection system. After all, since "taxes" were not really a part of a state economy, there was no real infrastructure for tax collection and enforcement. Under communism, taxes were automatically transferred to the budget through the state-owned banking system. In the new regimes, there was a need for institutions, people, and funds to manage the new tax system. Most of the Central and East European countries were relatively successful in establishing a strong, relatively unitary revenue service. The countries of the Commonwealth of Independent States (CIS) had more problems. In most cases, the introduction of the VAT proved successful in boosting revenue collection. With regard to personal income tax, the Baltic approach proved by far the most successful in terms of revenue collection because it was simple and easy to enforce. The progressive tax systems found elsewhere merely encouraged underreporting and avoidance.

CURRENCY CONVERTIBILITY AND EXCHANGE RATE REGIMES

Currency convertibility and the unification of exchange rates were important prerequisites for foreign trade liberalization. As already mentioned, communist regimes had no link between domestic and foreign prices, making currencies inconvertible for international payments. Most former communist countries immediately adopted a fully convertible current account, allowing for trade in goods and services. In contrast, convertibility was introduced only gradually on capital accounts, which govern the transfer of financial assets. The Baltic states emerged in the forefront of the reforms aimed at bringing capital-account convertibility.[7]

In regulating the currency, policy makers began the transition with an initial devaluation that accompanied the introduction of a stabilization program. While two or more different exchange rates had existed in communist systems, including the official and black market rates, this could not happen in economies that were joining the world economy. So a single, official exchange rate had to be established. The devaluation was done to improve trade imbalances by making imports more expensive and exports cheaper. After the initial devaluation, governments adopted one of four types of exchange rate regime: floating rates (in which the currency floats freely without intervention from the central bank), pegged rates (where the currency's value is fixed against that of another currency or basket of currencies to provide a nominal anchor), crawling pegs (a pegged exchange rate regime where the reference value is shifted at preestablished times), and currency boards (in which foreign exchange reserves are used to back the currency).

FOREIGN TRADE LIBERALIZATION

Under communism, trade in the Central and East European region was handled through the CMEA. That system was disbanded in January 1991. At that time, the USSR began demanding payment for raw materials in Western currencies and at world market prices. Thus, the USSR signaled that it was no longer willing to subsidize the rest of the region by exporting hard goods and importing soft goods in exchange for political loyalty. Similarly, the Central and East European countries were no longer willing to accept political domination in exchange for Soviet subsidies. While many analysts initially thought that the CMEA's demise would significantly increase trade within the region by removing many of the impediments associated with the old structures, the opposite occurred. The collapse of demand in the Soviet Union caused sharp declines in interregional trade. For the Central and East European countries, the postcommunist transition required a major redirection of trade. These transitional economies needed to find export products that would be competitive on world markets in order to service their debts.

Trade liberalization was carried out through a shift to tariffs, accompanied by reductions in tariff rates. This was reflected in the abolition of the many administrative restrictions on the import and export of industrial products from the old system. That shift had the advantage of making trade regulation more transparent and compatible with the General Agreement on Tariffs and Trade (GATT) and later the World Trade Organization (WTO). Trade liberalization began in manufacturing and gradually shifted to sensitive areas such as services and agricultural trade. The Central European countries and Estonia initially had the most success in the first phase of liberalization, introducing tariffs and reducing tariff rates in 1990 through 1991.

Trade liberalization was important for several reasons. Opening the domestic markets to imported products from the West helped satisfy consumption-starved citizens. Moreover, trade liberalization pushed countries forward in their structural adjustment; given the small size of the domestic markets, competition in most countries could only happen from imports. External economic relationships also contributed to stabilizing the economy by forcing domestic inflation into line with international rates.

In addition to foreign trade liberalization, currency convertibility, and exchange rate policy, there were two other important aspects of external economic relations: developing new market-friendly institutions to promote economic integration within the region and gaining access to preferential trading arrangements in the international economy such as the European Union. The Central European Free Trade Agreement (CEFTA) was established in 1992 by Hungary, Poland, and Czechoslovakia with the aim of testing regional cooperation prior to EU integration. It was soon enlarged to include other countries from the region. In the USSR, all former republics except for the three Baltic states joined the Commonwealth of Independent States in 1991. Most Central European and Baltic countries had signed association agreements with the EU by the mid-1990s. These agreements served to boost exports and consolidate the opening of markets. GATT/ WTO membership also helped to guarantee the maintenance of free trade. In May 2004, eight Central and East European countries took the final step in international economic integration and became full EU members. They were joined in January 2007 by Bulgaria and Romania and in July 2013 by Croatia.

Structural Reforms

The achievement of macroeconomic stabilization paved the way for the launch of structural reforms, creating an investment climate conducive to the entry of new businesses, including small and medium enterprises. In centrally planned economies, all means of production, transportation, and financial intermediation had been owned by the state. As a result, firms had few incentives to produce high-quality goods. Long-term investment was limited. Moreover, in planned economies no consideration was given to profitability. Firms were often grossly overstaffed, with employees working at half capacity because of shortages of inputs for production. The initial path toward transition involved removing barriers to private business. This required the establishment of an institutional framework conducive to the development of a market economy. Governments had to develop commercial, labor, and tax codes that provided the base for the creation of new businesses. Of all the institutions that had to be developed, the establishment of a two-tiered banking system was the most critical.

Fiscal reform played a double role in the transformation process of the former socialist countries. In addition to being a key element in the stabilization efforts, it was also part of the structural adjustment program. Under communism, companies had provided social protection to their employees. The state took over that role in the new regime. This required a transformation of the entire social welfare system through a process referred to as "rightsizing" government.

PRIVATIZATION

Privatization was a crucial aspect of the restructuring process because, most significantly, it improved the efficiency of resource allocation and contributed to stronger budget constraints on enterprises. Private firms divested themselves of unprofitable sectors and laid off excess employees. Privatization also had positive spillover effects throughout the economy. It helped spur the development of entrepreneurial spirit. Moreover, receipts from privatized enterprises improved the state's fiscal position as it struggled with reforms. Finally, although the privatization process itself was often plagued by corruption, the sale of state-owned firms eventually contributed to a reduction in the power of government policy makers by establishing new, private owners.

The privatization process across Central and Eastern Europe began through the sale of small-scale enterprises, typically through auctions, direct sales, or giveaways, or through restitution schemes that returned properties to their precommunist owners. Restitution was also used with respect to land and housing. While Hungary and Poland had allowed for small private businesses in the 1980s, in hard-line regimes such as Czechoslovakia, 99 percent of the economy remained in state hands up until the fall of communism. Despite these very different starting points, small-scale privatization was accomplished with relative ease and was close to completion within one to two years in most countries.

The sale of state-owned companies became more complicated when countries began selling off medium- and large-scale enterprises. Privatization agencies were created to choose which firms should be sold and to establish the rules and regulations for the sales. The main methods used were manager-employee buyouts (MEBOs), voucher schemes, direct sales, initial public offerings (IPOs), and public tenders. The strategies varied between countries. Countries typically chose one main method and combined it with a mix of other approaches.

Privatization through MEBOs involved selling the enterprise to the current management and employees at discounted prices or sometimes simply transferring ownership without a cash payment. That is why the approach is often referred to as an "insider" model. While MEBOs are relatively quick, simple, and popular with the workers, they are also inefficient. Use of the MEBO method slowed the restructuring of the enterprise's management and operations; required continued state support, given the dearth of funds the employees and managers had for investment; failed to bring in the required market expertise; and left the state with little or no monetary compensation for the sale of the enterprise. Slovenia is the only country from the Central and East European region that had real success in using the MEBO approach, probably because its economy was already well integrated with Western Europe when the transition started.

The voucher or coupon method involved the transfer of shares in state-owned companies to citizens. In this method, citizens are given coupons for nominal sums (or sometimes for free). They trade these coupons for shares in firms or investment funds. The main advantages of the coupon method have been its speed, relative ease of administration, and equitability. In Central and East European countries, coupon privatization was presented as a way of garnering public support to continue market reforms by turning citizens into shareholders. Nonetheless, like the MEBOs, coupon programs failed to bring in the funds needed for enterprise restructuring. Another downside was that the diffusion of ownership translated into weak corporate governance, which, narrowly defined, refers to the relationship between a company and its shareholders. Both the coupon and MEBO methods allowed for the transfer of property in capital-starved economies, but state budgets did not benefit from the temporary boost in revenues that privatization can bring. The coupon method was first launched in Czechoslovakia in 1992 and later copied in other countries before eventually falling out of favor.

Many Western market analysts see issuing stock on securities markets at a predetermined price in an IPO as the most transparent way of selling off state corporations. That method can also reap large revenues for the government. However, IPOs were seldom used in the Central and East European region because of the lack of developed financial markets in the transitioning countries.

Direct sales and public tenders were among the most common forms of privatization in Central and Eastern Europe. These were usually managed by the state privatization agency. In theory, direct sales go to the highest bidder. However, in practice, corruption can be rampant in direct sales due to the lack of transparency. Unlike direct sales, public tenders are based not on the level of privatization proceeds but rather on the premise of achieving the highest long-term economic growth potential. Thus, sales are negotiated with buyers who must present a business plan that takes into account such factors as employment issues, investment, and performance guarantees. These schemes require that the enterprises for sale be attractive enough to find investors willing to make a long-term commitment. The tender method is more difficult in the short term because negotiations can take a long time and revenues from the sales are generally not as high as in the case of direct sales. Another downside is that the rules for the tender are set at the discretion of state officials. Nonetheless, the short-term disadvantages are typically more than offset by the long-term benefits. The public tender method has been seen as the most successful privatization method in the Central and East European region.

PRIVATIZATION STRATEGIES IN THE VISEGRAD COUNTRIES

The four countries of the Visegrad Group—so named for the Hungarian town of Visegrad, where the meeting that formed the group was held—are the Czech Republic, Hungary,

Poland, and Slovakia. These countries approached privatization in radically different ways in the early 1990s. Hungary first focused on creating an institutional and legal framework for the new capitalist system and addressed the problem of limited domestic capital by beginning early with sales to foreign investors. That proved a wise approach since the new foreign owners replaced the socialist-era managers and removed what could have become a powerful force with the potential to obstruct market-oriented reforms. In privatizing, the Hungarians stuck to traditional methods such as public tenders and IPOs, largely avoiding experimentation with alternative forms such as voucher schemes, restitution, and employee buyouts. Most of Hungary's lucrative state properties had been sold off by 1997, allowing deep restructuring to take place earlier than in the other three Visegrad countries.

Czech and Slovak privatization began when the two nations were still part of the same country. The Czech-devised voucher scheme was launched in an effort to transfer property to private hands as quickly as possible. The program compensated for the lack of domestic capital by offering shares to the population for a symbolic price. This move was aimed at broadening public support for reforms. There was an element of nationalism in the Czech scheme. The desire to keep firms in domestic hands was greatest for strategic companies such as banks, telecoms, utilities, and other "family jewels." A major flaw of the coupon program was that, unlike the Hungarians, the Czechs failed to first create an adequate legal and institutional framework. Insufficient regulation allowed for high levels of abuse, including insider trading and asset stripping. Moreover, because most shares were put in investment funds—many of which were controlled by banks that remained in state hands—corporate governance was absent, unemployment remained unnaturally low, and the banking system ended up in shambles. Only after an economic crisis in 1997 did the Czech Republic shift its approach and focus on public tenders. Key firms in the banking and energy sectors were sold to foreign investors.

After Slovakia gained independence in 1993, the second wave of voucher privatization was canceled. Privatization initially ground to a halt until political elites had devised ways of benefiting from the sale of state assets. From 1994 to 1998, privatization focused mainly on MEBOs and direct sales, usually to political allies of then prime minister Vladimír Mečiar at rock-bottom prices. That approach appealed to nationalists as the ruling parties stressed their aim of shunning foreign investment and instead creating a domestic entrepreneurial class. As a result, many politically connected but incompetent owners led their empires to ruin, causing great damage to the economy. After the change of government in 1998, Slovakia shifted to an approach similar to that in the Czech Republic with international tenders for key firms in the banking, telecom, and energy sectors. In both cases, the financial sectors were in such poor shape by the late 1990s that there were few protests when the banks were finally sold to foreign investors.

In its approach to privatization, Poland used a mix of different methods, depending on the orientation of the government in power at the time. In the early transition years, privatization was slower in Poland than in Hungary and the Czech Republic. But it accelerated in the latter part of the 1990s after the financial and legal framework had been established. While initially not as open to foreign investors as the Hungarians, the Poles were more welcoming than the Czechs and Slovaks.

Despite the different paths taken in the early 1990s, the approaches of all four countries converged by the end of the decade as they prepared for the competitive pressures of

EU accession. As demonstrated by the Slovak and Czech cases, it was possible to prevent key firms from coming under foreign control for some years. However, the results were often not positive, as domestic owners frequently appeared more concerned with their personal interests than with those of their firms and employees. In contrast, foreign investors generally led the economic recoveries throughout the region, providing improved management techniques and know-how, boosting production and exports, and preparing the economies for the shock of full EU membership.

"RIGHTSIZING" GOVERNMENT

Rightsizing government is a matter of adapting the public sector to the needs of a capitalist economy. While the stabilization programs dealt with such issues as cutting enterprise and price subsidies and introducing a new taxation system, the structural reform programs required that the government take over certain social welfare functions previously performed by state enterprises, including the provision of health care, housing, and kindergartens.

This process involved several dilemmas. First of all, there was no "optimal" size for government in established Western economies. The public sector, after all, accounts for less than 30 percent of the gross domestic product in the United States and over 50 percent in Sweden. Second, the public sector experienced severe shocks during the transition. As declines in GDP and fiscal pressures reduced funding for social welfare programs, issues of poverty and inequality became more urgent. Rightsizing does not necessarily mean cutting the size of the public sector, however. While the state's declining role is crucial with regard to enterprise development, it must expand in other areas, such as regulatory activities (including antitrust, securities, and bankruptcy mechanisms) as well as unemployment insurance and other labor market policies.

Under communism, central government tax revenues averaged about 50 percent of GDP and reached as high as 61 percent in Czechoslovakia in 1989. That was far higher than warranted by the level of economic development.[8] During the transition, states faced the challenge of taking on more social welfare functions while at the same time reducing budget deficits. In practice, that was especially complicated since people were accustomed to relying on the welfare state. In the early transition years, governments set up generous unemployment schemes with long payment periods covering a large share of former salaries. Benefits also applied to new entrants to the labor market. As unemployment rates rose, however, the generosity of the schemes declined. Although public sectors decreased in size substantially in the early years of the transition, they remained large: budget revenues accounted for 42 to 47 percent of GDP in Central Europe by 1995.[9]

Countries adopted a variety of approaches to fiscal reform. Radical reformers such as Czechoslovakia, Estonia, and Latvia started early with balanced budget targets. The record shows this was a wise decision, given that delayed attempts at balancing were unsuccessful in Poland, Hungary, and Lithuania. In the latter cases, the habit of generous social spending was difficult to break for political reasons. Despite a favorable starting point in the Czech Republic and Slovakia, fiscal deficits surged in those countries during the latter part of the 1990s, partly due to the high cost of bailing out the banking sector and also because of the soft-budget constraints related to off-budget funds. The official state budget deficit reached about 1 to 2 percent of GDP in the Czech Republic during 1997 and 1998; however, the hidden deficit was almost three times that size.[10]

Fiscal reforms became especially important as privatization wrapped up. In the early years of the transition period, some governments used privatization revenues to finance more spending, helping to compensate for the gap between domestic savings and private investment needs. As the countries approached the end of the transition, however, the international financial community discouraged such practices and called on countries to use privatization revenues to pay off government debts.

LABOR MARKET REFORMS

Under central planning, unemployment did not exist. Governments introduced identity cards. Each citizen was required to have a place of employment or prove that he or she was legitimately out of the labor force. Factories were built in areas with high levels of joblessness. Collective farms and large enterprises helped to absorb residual unemployment. The maintenance of full employment meant that many workers received wages in excess of their contribution to their firms' revenues. Thus, the full-employment policy functioned as a disguised form of unemployment compensation.

A key aspect of the postcommunist transition was to transfer employment from the public to the private sector. In a market economy, companies locate plants where they can maximize profits, not reduce unemployment. Access to transport, electric power, and raw materials is a crucial factor and often more important than labor costs. Delivery times and transport costs are also key, so manufacturers often prefer to have plants closer to clients and markets. Thus, growth has been concentrated near big cities or Western borders. Large plants in out-of-the-way locations are frequently loss makers.

All of the countries in the region witnessed a rise in unemployment during the early years of the transition. In certain respects, the emergence of unemployment can be seen as a healthy development, a sign of the rationalization of production and employment. Enterprises had incentives to shed redundant workers as they faced firmer budget constraints, particularly in industries with declining competitiveness. Meanwhile, farms shed labor as agricultural subsidies fell. Still, the increase in unemployment was much greater in some countries than in others. In Central and Eastern Europe, layoffs were much more common during the 1990s than in the CIS, where less restructuring took place.

During the 1990s, governments fought the layoffs without much success. They did make it more difficult for companies to cut their workforces, however, by imposing high severance pay requirements along the West European model. Financial pressures forced enterprises to utilize other mechanisms to reduce labor costs, such as early retirement schemes and wage arrears, with the latter especially prevalent in the CIS countries. In an effort to deal with rising unemployment rates, some governments introduced active labor market policies such as public works projects, job retraining programs, and employment subsidies, especially for uneducated groups such as Roma. Active labor market policies were often mixed with passive policies such as changes in taxation laws and regulations governing the hiring and firing of employees.

While active labor market programs are not always effective in the long run, cutting high payroll taxes and approving legislation that makes it easier for companies to hire and fire workers have had a more substantial impact on job growth. Also important are changes in the jobless benefits system aimed at encouraging the unemployed to find work, as benefits are sometimes set too high in relation to minimum wage. Deregulation of rents can help encourage labor mobility, as can improvements in the banking sector that allow for the growth of mortgage lending.

Some countries have tried to use foreign direct investment as a way to bring down unemployment rates. Nonetheless, much of the FDI in the region has been related to privatization. Foreign investors who buy existing firms do not always provide more jobs. Governments often require that investors agree to keep employment at a certain level; however, eventually, the workforce has to be cut to raise productivity. Greenfield investment—which entails the construction of a new plant—is much more beneficial in terms of job creation; however, attracting investors is tough, given the stiff competition among countries. Some investors were attracted by the region's low wages, but there was little to stop those firms from moving further eastward once salaries edged closer to West European levels.

Hungary is the one Central and East European country that achieved substantial success in using FDI as a job-creation policy. After reaching double digits between 1992

Photo 3.1. This wood-processing plant was abandoned in eastern Poland (Ruciana Nida) as a result of the economic transition, leaving hundreds out of work in the area. (Hanna Siudalska)

and 1995, Hungarian unemployment rates fell to around 6 percent from 2000 to 2004. That reduction occurred thanks partly to government incentives for foreign investors, especially those who invested in regions with high levels of unemployment, such as eastern Hungary. By 2000, Hungary was experiencing labor shortages in certain areas, as the country's population has been declining since 1980. Still, those shortages were eventually diminished by the recent crises, which drove Hungary's unemployment rate back up to approximately 10 to 11 percent from 2009 through 2013.

For most countries, the development of small and medium enterprises remains the only real answer to cutting unemployment. Many countries in the region were slow to develop legal frameworks conducive to substantial growth of small business. Moreover, the slow development of the lending market also delayed progress, as banks were hesitant to lend to small enterprises because there was little recourse if they did not pay their debts, as long as courts did not function properly. In contrast, mortgages were a safer bet for banks since property could be used as collateral.

Since the postcommunist transition began, unemployment rates in Central Europe and the Baltic states have rarely reached as high as 20 percent, although divergent demographics have contributed to wide variations in jobless rates among countries (see table 3.1). The younger populations in Poland and Slovakia meant that unemployment rates were considerably higher than in Hungary, for example, particularly among youth. Variations among regions within a given country were also substantial since poorly functioning housing markets limited labor mobility.

In general, Balkan countries have experienced much higher jobless rates than those in Central Europe, often reaching or exceeding 30 percent. That was partly a result of

Table 3.1. Unemployment Rates for Central and East European States, 1998–2013 (Percentage)

	1998	2004	2008	2013
Czech Republic	6.5	8.3	4.4	7.0
Ukraine	5.6	8.6	6.9	7.2
Romania	5.4	8.0	5.8	7.3
Estonia	9.9	9.7	5.5	8.6
Slovenia	7.4	6.3	4.4	10.1
Hungary	8.7	6.1	7.8	10.2
Poland	10.2	19.1	7.1	10.3
Lithuania	13.2	11.6	5.8	11.8
Latvia	14.0	11.7	7.7	11.9
Bulgaria	12.2	12.1	5.6	13.0
Slovakia	12.7	18.4	9.6	14.2
Albania	16.7	14.7	12.8	16.2
Croatia	17.2	13.8	8.4	17.3
Montenegro	18.5	27.7	17.2	19.5
Serbia	12.2	19.5	14.4	23.0
Bosnia	n/a	21.5	23.4	27.5
Macedonia	34.5	37.2	33.8	29.0
Kosovo	n/a	39.7	47.5	30.0

Source: Eurostat, IHS Global Insight.

the wars of the 1990s and low levels of foreign direct investment. Kosovo, which declared independence from Serbia in February 2008, has faced some of the highest unemployment rates of the region, surpassing 50 percent of the labor force in 2001 and 2002 before falling to 30 percent by 2013. While unemployment levels in the Balkans have been unbearably steep, jobless rates are thought to be considerably lower in reality because of the strong informal economy in those countries. Still, long-term unemployment remains a serious challenge for policy makers in the Balkan region, especially given the deterioration since 2009 amid the recent crises.

Macroeconomic Trends

TRANSITION RECESSIONS AND RECOVERIES

Certain elements of the communist economic system had strongly negative implications for the transition process, even for those countries that had already begun reforms. The causes of recession in the transitions can be divided into macro- and microelements. Macroelements include the effects of high inflation; the impact of the stabilization program, with contractionary fiscal and monetary policies spurring reductions in aggregate demand; and the collapse of intraregional trade, which had negative effects on both export demand (reducing aggregate demand) and import supply (reducing aggregate supply). Microelements of the transitional recessions included problems in coordinating production when the collapse of central planning left enterprises unprepared to find new buyers for their outputs and suppliers for their inputs. The communist regime had left managers with poor marketing skills.

The countries that recovered most quickly from the recession generally had favorable initial conditions. It is no accident that the Central European economies were the first to begin recovering, followed by the Baltic states. Other factors helped limit the term of the transition recession, including a rapid reduction in inflation; the implementation of institutional and policy changes at the microlevel to allow for the introduction of competitive market forces; rapid growth in the private sector without excessive restrictions; a geographic redirection of trade away from traditional markets and toward the EU; and sectoral restructuring, allowing for rapid growth in the service sector.

The countries that faced special difficulties with stabilization were those struggling the most with the legacies of the old system. Many of the countries in Central and Eastern Europe were new, established in the early 1990s after the collapse of the USSR, Yugoslavia, and Czechoslovakia. They struggled simultaneously with state- and nation-building concerns and defining and defending their borders. As a result, economic reform was often not their top priority. Many had no previous experience with macroeconomic management. Problems also arose from having been part of dysfunctional currency areas, such as the ruble (former USSR) and dinar (former Yugoslavia) zones. In Ukraine, as in other former Soviet countries, the initial use of the ruble was a major impediment to macroeconomic stabilization and a significant cause of inflation, as each country in the ruble zone had an incentive to pursue expansionary macroeconomic policies because some of the resulting inflation would be exported to other countries in the region.

All Central and East European economies experienced large declines in GDP (15 to 70 percent) between 1989 and 1993. After the onset of the initial postcommunist recession, Poland was the first to begin to recover (1992), followed by the rest of Central Europe in 1993 through 1994. Poland, in 1996, was the first to reach its 1989 level of GDP, with Slovenia and Slovakia not far behind. In contrast, Ukraine experienced one of the most serious transition recessions in the entire Central and East European region. Its economy did not begin to experience GDP growth until 2000.

It is difficult to compare pre- and post-transition GDP given the different ways of using statistics and the deliberate falsification or omission of unfavorable data under the old regime. GDP statistics exaggerated the true decline in economic welfare that occurred during the transition. In the communist system, output levels were often overreported for the sake of plan fulfillment. On the other hand, once the transition began, enterprises faced incentives to underreport in order to avoid taxes and divert output to the gray economy. Another factor was the so-called forced substitution practice: the lack of substitutes gave buyers little choice but to purchase goods available under the old system that were not really desired. After the transition began, better substitutes were often imported, reducing GDP but, at the same time, increasing consumer welfare.

As with GDP data, official measures of inflation exaggerated the declines in economic welfare associated with postcommunist inflation. Price liberalization only made explicit the hidden inflationary pressures that had existed in the previous system. The higher prices that resulted from liberalization reduced households' real income on paper, but they also allowed households to purchase whatever they could afford without having to wait in line or endure forced substitution. This trade-off—higher prices and lower real incomes in exchange for less waiting and forced substitution—benefited some people and rendered others worse off. It did not, however, connote automatic impoverishment. Moreover, the higher prices that occurred after liberalization were a partial reflection of the higher product quality that resulted from price liberalization and the creation of a buyer's market.

SECOND-STAGE STABILIZATION

In the transition process, it is important to distinguish between first- and second-stage macroeconomic stabilization programs. The first stage occurred from 1990 to 1993 during the early part of the postcommunist transition. Some countries that started out well later showed signs of imbalance and had to implement second-stage programs. This happened in Hungary in 1995 with the Bokros Plan, as well as in the Czech Republic (1997–1999), Slovakia (1998–2000), and Poland (2001).

The justification for second-stage stabilization programs differed depending on the country, and a variety of solutions were implemented. For example, in the case of Slovakia, the country was on the verge of an acute economic crisis by the time of the September 1998 parliamentary elections because of poorly designed structural and macroeconomic policies, particularly during the years 1994 to 1998. The government's expansive fiscal policy was among the main causes of the crisis. It involved public financing of large infrastructure projects and state guarantees for bank loans. Another reason for the crisis related to inadequate bank regulation, contributing to serious problems with nonperforming loans. A third cause was the privatization strategy, which favored domestic over foreign buyers and thus generated high current-account deficits financed by foreign borrowing instead of inflows of foreign direct investment. The impact of those policies was exacerbated by the central bank's attempts to maintain a fixed exchange rate regime. This meant that monetary policy had to be tightened, sending interest rates upward and contributing to increased insolvency among Slovak enterprises. A solution to the credit crunch necessitated intervention in macroeconomic management and in the banking and enterprise sectors. That included austerity measures aimed at stabilizing public finances and reducing the current-account deficit, restructuring and privatizing the state-owned banks, and easing and accelerating bankruptcy proceedings.[11] With stabilization largely achieved by 2002, the country was then able to move on to more advanced reforms.

THE GLOBAL CRISIS OF 2008 AND 2009

Thanks to the impact of second-stage stabilization programs, compounded with the positive effects of EU integration, the average GDP in Central Europe and the Balkans surged by some 6 to 7 percent annually between 2004 and 2007. Strong GDP growth was accompanied by a sharp drop in unemployment rates in most of the new EU member states and candidate countries. By 2007, rising labor shortages were seen as one of the main problems facing the more advanced countries of the region.

When the global crisis struck in the United States and Western Europe, Central and Eastern Europe initially seemed relatively immune. However, the first signs of recession emerged in the final months of 2008, as falling demand in Western Europe contributed to sharp declines in industrial output and exports further east. By early 2009 unemployment rates were rising, and many analysts warned of imminent catastrophe across the region. Indeed, the crisis highlighted certain imbalances, particularly regarding high current-account deficits and external debt (see "External Economic Trends" below), which became harder to finance as credit tightened. In addition, the region faced sharply declining inflows of FDI, as global companies scaled back their investments. Another key source of foreign-currency earnings—remittances from citizens working abroad—also became scarcer. Even the new EU member states were not immune to the impact, as the crisis hit Hungary and the three Baltic states especially hard. The IMF and EU stepped in to help remedy the situation, allowing the afflicted countries to avoid default. Nonetheless, most Central and East European countries experienced sharp declines in GDP during 2009, in many cases the largest drops since the early 1990s. Poland, Albania, and Kosovo were the only countries in the region to avoid recession in 2009. Whereas Poland's large domestic market helped to shield the country from troubles elsewhere, Kosovo and Albania avoided recession due to their relative economic isolation.

THE EUROZONE DEBT CRISIS

Just as a recovery from the global crisis was underway in the region, a new set of economic challenges emerged, as a sovereign debt crisis that began in Greece spread through several other Eurozone member states. Slovenia was the only country in the region to experience the Eurozone debt crisis directly, as deteriorating bank assets due to a rapidly rising level of nonperforming loans led to calls for an EU bailout in 2013. Still, the government was reluctant to turn toward the Eurozone for help and instead drew up plans to recapitalize the sector and transfer nonperforming assets to a bad bank, much like in Slovakia and the Czech Republic during the second-stage stabilization process of the late 1990s. In December 2013, three Slovenian banks were bailed out, and a fourth requested recapitalization in April 2014.

Indirect and secondary effects of the Eurozone crisis were felt across Central and Eastern Europe. Countries with strong economic links to Italy and Greece saw reduced revenues from exports, workers' remittances, and investment. By 2012 and 2013 the crisis had widened and deepened, pulling much of Europe into a double-dip recession. In Central and Eastern Europe, a deteriorating export performance was matched by weak consumer confidence and investment. The situation was further exacerbated by the need to cut budget deficits and public debt following the upward surge in 2009. Otherwise healthy economies such as the Czech Republic were punished by the government's enthusiasm for fiscal austerity, pulling the country into a long-running recession. Other countries in the region managed to find a balance between austerity and growth, but even these economies saw a sharp slowdown. By 2013 GDP in most Central and East European countries remained below the levels seen prior to the 2008–2009 crisis. The only exceptions were Kosovo, Albania, Poland, Slovakia, and Macedonia.

External Economic Trends

BALANCE OF PAYMENTS

Current-account balances in Central and Eastern Europe have fluctuated considerably during the transition period (see table 3.2). By the mid-1990s most countries in the region had balances within respectable limits, with deficits of about 5 percent of GDP or less, while some countries even recorded surpluses. However, deficits shot back up between 1996 and 1998, as access to external financing grew. In many countries, current-account gaps narrowed in subsequent years, particularly where second-stage adjustments took place. However, current-account deficits for the region expanded again between 2004 and 2008, as EU enlargement eased access to credit. There were some notable exceptions, though. Excluding the CIS countries, the Czech Republic had the lowest current-account deficit in Central and Eastern Europe in 2008 (at less than 3 percent of GDP), followed by Poland, Slovenia, and Slovakia (all at about 5 to 6 percent of GDP). It is no coincidence that those four countries had the easiest time weathering the global downturn of 2008 and 2009.

The level of the current-account deficit is often closely linked with the gap between exports and imports of goods, particularly in the less developed countries of the region. While foreign trade deficits in the Central European countries have generally remained at reasonable levels, Balkan countries such as Kosovo, Bosnia-Herzegovina, and Albania have been plagued with very low export-to-import ratios. As a result, those countries must rely on high surpluses on the "current transfers" account (which includes foreign grants and

Table 3.2. Current-Account Balances for Central and East European States as a Share of GDP, 1995–2013

Country	1995	2000	2004	2008	2013
Slovenia	−0.6	−3.2	−2.6	−5.4	6.3
Hungary	−3.6	−8.6	−8.6	−7.3	3.1
Slovakia	2.0	−3.5	−7.8	−6.0	2.3
Bulgaria	−0.2	−5.4	−6.6	−22.9	1.8
Lithuania	−9.1	0.3	−7.6	−12.9	1.5
Croatia	−6.5	−2.3	−4.4	−8.7	0.8
Romania	−5.0	−3.6	−8.4	−11.6	0.4
Latvia	−0.3	−4.8	−12.9	−13.1	−0.8
Estonia	−4.2	−5.4	−11.3	−9.2	−1.1
Poland	0.6	−6.0	−5.3	−6.6	−1.4
Czech Republic	−2.4	−4.6	−5.0	−2.1	−1.4
Macedonia	−6.7	−2.0	−8.2	−12.6	−1.9
Bosnia	n/a	−6.8	−15.5	−13.6	−3.1
Serbia	n/a	−1.8	−13.9	−21.9	−6.5
Kosovo	n/a	0.1	−7.2	−11.7	−6.6
Ukraine	−3.1	4.7	10.6	−7.1	−9.0
Albania	−0.5	−4.3	−4.9	−15.5	−10.8
Montenegro	n/a	n/a	−18.0	−49.8	−14.6

Source: IHS Global Insight.

workers' remittances from abroad) to keep overall current-account deficits in line. Even so, current-account deficits in the Balkans have tended to be much higher than those in Central Europe, often reaching well into the double digits. Throughout the broader region, the balance of trade in services, which includes transport, travel, and other services, has generally been in surplus. That is especially true in countries with thriving tourism sectors such as Croatia and Montenegro. One factor that has introduced an element of uncertainty into the level of the current-account gap has been the rising income deficits, as foreign investors send their earnings home. Large income deficits have been especially apparent in Central European countries that have attracted significant levels of FDI.

Generally, a current-account deficit of more than 5 percent of GDP is seen as unsustainable. A negative current-account balance must be compensated for by a positive financial account. This can stem from inflows of foreign direct and portfolio investment as well as long- and short-term foreign loans. If supported by inflows of FDI rather than by foreign borrowing, high current-account deficits were not seen as overly worrying. Indeed, Estonia's current-account gap reached about 10 to 18 percent of GDP between 2002 and 2007, a time when economic growth was strong, inflation was low, and budget balances were in surplus. Nonetheless, large external deficits raise a country's vulnerability amid a global downturn, and Estonia was one of the first countries to be hit during the crisis of 2008 and 2009.

FOREIGN DIRECT INVESTMENT

Privatization deals involving foreign investors were initially unpopular in some Central and East European countries, as people feared that their governments were "selling out." That was particularly true when firms in certain strategic sectors were sold. Nonetheless, experience has shown that all of the Central and East European countries have needed to attract foreign capital in order to provide the investment resources and expertise necessary to fuel growth. FDI brings modern technologies, know-how, new forms of management, and an altogether different corporate culture. Thus, foreign investment is recognized as a way of speeding up the restructuring of companies and helping to improve their overall competitiveness. It also accelerates a country's access to global markets. Foreign-owned companies have often had much stronger export sales than domestic ones, particularly during the early transition years.

Much of the FDI in the Central and East European region was initially concentrated in a few manufacturing branches, such as automobiles and automotive components, electronics, food processing (particularly soft drinks, beer, dairy products, and sweets), tobacco, and construction materials. Investments in retail trade were also significant. From the mid-1990s, states began selling their shares in the strategic utilities, telecom, and banking sectors, with foreign investors often gaining significant stakes. FDI in the banking sector has been especially important, bringing in more competition, a greater variety of products, and higher levels of expertise.

Although there are many advantages to investing in the Central and East European region, transition economies are, in certain respects, risky for foreign investors. Labor regulations and taxes are frequently complex and subject to rapid change, depending on the whims of policy makers. Relatively high levels of corruption and insider trading exist, and many countries in the region have experienced serious problems with corporate governance, as company managers have often felt little responsibility to shareholders. Company registration has also been difficult, with barriers to small business and smaller-scale investors. Privatization negotiations have frequently been long and difficult, with significant political interference. Meanwhile, bankruptcy procedures have been complicated by an inadequate justice system. Finally, exchange rate volatility has added substantial risk.

During the 1990s, most of the FDI in the region went to Poland, Hungary, and the Czech Republic, all of which proved to be good locations for investment due to the rapid liberalization of foreign trade, proximity to Western markets (resulting in low transportation costs), relatively large domestic markets, high levels of technical education, much lower labor costs than in their West European neighbors, and relatively good infrastructures. Moreover, the fact that the three countries were seen as front-runners in the EU accession process made investment especially attractive.

As it became clear that additional countries would be included in the first wave of the EU enlargement process, FDI also rose rapidly elsewhere. Many of the countries that scored high cumulative levels of FDI per capita did so by virtue of their small size, while the opposite was true for Poland. With Croatia and Montenegro the most notable exceptions, FDI inflows were typically greatest in the countries that made the fastest progress in EU integration. Investors in the new EU member states have the advantage of operating in the same legal and regulatory environment as their main markets. Moreover, EU membership is generally seen as a guarantee of a certain degree of political stability as well as the existence of enforceable contracts, should problems occur. More risky countries require higher returns to make the investment worthwhile. While Serbia has achieved considerable success in attracting FDI since the fall of Slobodan Milošević in 2000, most investments have been linked to privatization.

Photo 3.2.   With the demise of communism and the influx of Western capital, there was a rush of construction in the capitals of the former Central and East European states. Here is the main street of Warsaw with the Soviet era Palace of Culture and new high-rises. (Malgorzata Alicja Gudzikowska)

Moving Forward

Some ten to twelve years after the transition began, the more advanced countries in the Central and East European region had completed the vast majority of the postcommunist economic reforms. That was particularly true in the case of the eight states that joined the EU in May 2004. As the postcommunist transition neared completion, the leading economies shifted their focus instead to issues also facing their counterparts in Western Europe and elsewhere in the world, including taxation, pension, and health-care reform. At the same time, the Central and East European countries have to deal with the emergence of poverty, growing disparities in income, and demographic challenges. Other key concerns for the eleven Central and East European countries that joined the EU between 2004 and 2013 are preparation for joining the Eurozone and the convergence of incomes with the wealthier West European economies. By 2014, only four new member states (Slovenia, Slovakia, Estonia, and Latvia) had adopted the euro, but Lithuania is scheduled to join in 2015.

TAXATION REFORM

Accession to the EU spurred a third round of taxation reforms in many of the Central and East European countries, with the aim of raising competitiveness, simplifying the taxation system, and ensuring a reduction in budget deficits. Fiscal policies are carefully scrutinized once countries join the EU, as the Maastricht criteria for Eurozone entry required that budget deficits remain below 3 percent of GDP. The need to meet the Maastricht criteria was a key impetus for fiscal reforms in Slovakia between 2002 and 2006, for example. Nonetheless, the Maastricht budget requirements are also important in providing a basis for healthy medium- and long-term economic growth. If budget deficits are not brought under control, macroeconomic balance could be threatened, particularly once privatization revenues run out.

There are several justifications for introducing more competitive taxation policies. First of all, initial transfers from the EU budget were considerably lower with the 2004 enlargement round than in the case of countries such as Portugal and Greece. Thus, the new member states had to rely on other factors to spur development with the aim of catching up with richer EU countries (see table 3.3). Strong investment inflows are seen as a prerequisite for the more rapid GDP growth needed to help countries reach the income levels in Western Europe. Once in the EU, however, member states are limited in the kinds of incentives they can offer to foreign investors. Many of the perks provided by Hungary in the 1990s are no longer permitted. Moreover, the new EU member states have struggled to attract investments that are not based on low wages alone, given that salaries are rising as the countries become increasingly integrated with the West. Thus, fiscal reform provided a relatively simple way for these countries to bring in more investment. By 2012, three new member states (Slovenia, the Czech Republic, and Slovakia) had met or surpassed the levels of GDP per capita in Greece and Portugal, although that achievement was met partly thanks to the poor economic results in the latter countries.

In the older EU countries, the so-called European social model, characterized by strong labor unions and the need for consensus in social dialogue, makes reforms difficult. In contrast, the new member states have found it easier to implement sweeping changes. Slovakia was the regional leader in introducing a taxation system that was both simple and attractive

Table 3.3.   GDP per Capita, 2001–2013

Country	2001	2005	2008	2013
Slovenia	80	87	91	83
Czech Republic	73	79	81	80
Slovakia	53	60	72	76
Lithuania	42	55	64	74
Estonia	47	62	69	72
Poland	48	51	56	68
Hungary	58	63	64	67
Latvia	39	50	58	67
Croatia	51	59	65	61
Romania	28	35	49	54
Bulgaria	30	37	43	47
Montenegro	n/a	31	43	42
Serbia	n/a	32	36	36
Macedonia	25	29	34	35
Albania	n/a	22	25	30
Bosnia and Herzegovina	n/a	25	26	29

Source: Eurostat, August 2014.
Note: Calculated in purchasing power standard (PPS) terms; EU-28 = 100; PPS calculates GDP by taking into account differences in prices across countries.

to investors, and the reforms met with very little formal protest. Whereas Estonia introduced a flat income tax in the early years of its transition, spurring several other countries to follow suit, Slovakia became the first to adopt that approach at a more advanced stage of reforms. Slovakia's flat tax took effect in January 2004, just months before the country's EU entry. Slovakia's taxation changes applied not only to individuals, but also to corporations, all at a flat rate of 19 percent. Moreover, the country's VAT rate was unified at 19 percent, while the government canceled the inheritance, dividends, real estate transfers, and gift taxes. Although considerable doubts emerged before those changes took effect, the impact on tax collection was surprisingly positive. That was particularly true with regard to the corporate income tax, as the new system helped to reduce tax evasion.

Slovakia's tax changes triggered reform efforts elsewhere in Europe as well. In 2004, Poland's corporate income tax rate was reduced to the same level as in Slovakia, while the rate in Hungary was brought down to just 16 percent. The Czech Republic began to gradually lower its corporate income tax rate starting in 2004, reaching 19 percent by 2010. Initial reactions from countries such as Germany and France to tax reforms in the new member states were not positive, and Slovakia and other so-called neoliberal states were accused of "tax dumping." Some older member states called for the harmonization of taxation rates within the EU to prevent firms from moving eastward to benefit from more advantageous conditions. However, the prospect of harmonization proved challenging, and countries like Austria and Germany were forced to substantially reduce corporate tax rates to maintain competitiveness with their eastern neighbors. The tax changes in Central Europe and the Baltic states also inspired EU hopefuls in the Balkans and elsewhere. Serbia imposed a flat corporate tax rate of just 10 percent in August 2004, which at the time was the lowest rate in Europe. Montenegro went one notch lower in January 2006, with a 9 percent rate. A number of countries in the region adopted a flat tax on personal income as well.

After the surge in budget spending in 2009, Central and East European countries have been under pressure to reduce deficits, leading many to backtrack on earlier reforms and raise taxes. Several countries in the region—including Slovakia, the Czech Republic, and Montenegro—have been forced to abandon the flat tax on personal income, as governments introduced a series of austerity measures including higher tax rates for wealthier residents. Some countries raised the corporate tax and VAT rates as well.

SOCIAL POLICY REFORM

Social policy is one of the most difficult aspects of the reform process, as such changes are extremely unpopular politically. The Visegrad countries inherited very comprehensive social safety nets from the communist period, featuring such perks as free health care, free education through graduate school, extensive paid maternity leave for women, and full pensions, even if no contributions had been made. Many of those policies were maintained during the 1990s. Thus, the Central European countries were considered premature welfare states, with social security benefit levels found in countries with much higher per capita GDPs. By contrast, the CIS countries generally had underdeveloped welfare states during the transition period, given their difficult budgetary constraints.

In carrying out reforms, a key concern was to better target the benefits provided to reach the people who needed them the most. Much of the traditional safety net was regressive, with the bulk of the subsidies going to those who were already relatively well-off. For example, across-the-board subsidies for household electricity and natural gas were especially beneficial for people with large homes, while those with smaller dwellings received less. Thus, one way of addressing that imbalance was to raise household electricity prices to market levels, while providing subsidies for lower-income people.

Another key question relates to which agencies and levels of government should be charged with administering benefits. Two conflicting principles exist in that regard. First, if policies are made by national governments, statewide standards are established. Thus, a country avoids the situation in which regions compete for business by lowering taxation rates and providing fewer benefits. At the same time, however, putting policy making in the hands of regional or local governments may help promote experimentation and provide more accountability. There is no single standard in the EU; France embodies the first option and Germany the latter approach. Several of the new EU member states, including Poland and Slovakia, have implemented administrative reforms aimed at achieving decentralization.

The pension system has been a key concern of policy makers in the realm of social welfare reform, particularly in countries such as Hungary, where the aging population would have resulted in a fiscal meltdown if reforms were not implemented. Pension reforms generally include raising the retirement age, taxing working pensioners, shifting

Photo 3.3. Upscale stores with imported and domestic luxury goods, like this one in a mall in Warsaw, are now common in much of Central and Eastern Europe. (Monika Szewczyk)

the formulas by which pensions are indexed, and moving toward a system based on employee contributions. International organizations such as the World Bank urged Central and East European countries to privatize their pension systems, in line with the models developed by Chile and other Latin American countries. Thus, countries were encouraged to shift from a pay-as-you-go system, where today's workers pay the benefits for current retirees, to one with personal accounts. The new approach is often referred to as a "three-pillar system," with the first pillar consisting of a downsized pay-as-you-go scheme and the second pillar comprising personal accounts. The third pillar is optional and refers to voluntary private savings accounts. The new approach to pensions was intended to encourage savings while at the same time improving the long-term health of state finances.[12]

Hungary and Poland were the first countries in the Central and East European region to pursue pension reform along the Chilean model, transforming their pension systems in 1998 and 1999, respectively. Latvia (2001), Bulgaria, Croatia, and Estonia (all 2002), Macedonia (2003), Lithuania (2004), Slovakia (2005), Romania (2008), and the Czech Republic (2013) followed, with variations from country to country. The costs of switching from one system to another were quite large. Nonetheless, privatization revenues provided a good source of funding, helping to make the reforms socially acceptable by avoiding large hikes in taxation rates. Participation in the new pension system was generally mandatory for new workers but optional for older citizens.

Initially, the personal accounts were more popular than expected among older workers, signaling distrust in the old system and expectations of higher yields from private funds.[13] Nonetheless, the economic uncertainty in Europe that began in 2008 contributed to a changing attitude toward private pension accounts. As was the case with the flat tax, pension reforms frequently fell victim to the fiscal difficulties around the region following the 2008–2009 crisis. In an effort to reduce budget deficits and public debt, several countries introduced a reduction in the level of funds going into personal accounts. The most dramatic backtracking occurred in Hungary, where the pension system was effectively renationalized in 2011. Amid rising fiscal pressures, Poland moved in early 2014 to take control of government bonds that were previously held by private pension funds, transferring them to the state-run system. Moreover, Poles were discouraged from remaining in the private system. Despite the rising skepticism elsewhere, the Czech Republic introduced its own three-tier system in 2013, making participation in the second-tier voluntary. Nevertheless, the center-right government that launched the Czech pension reforms failed to gain a political consensus, and the cabinet that took over in early 2014 dismantled the new system.

ADOPTING THE EURO

The eleven Central and East European countries that acceded to the EU between 2004 and 2013 are all expected eventually to join the Economic and Monetary Union (EMU), meaning that they will use the euro as their national currency. In order to do so, they must first meet the criteria on inflation, interest rates, fiscal deficits, national debt, and exchange rate stability laid out in the EU's 1992 Maastricht Treaty. Inflation must fall below the "reference value," with the rate of consumer price inflation not exceeding the average in the three best-performing EU member states (excluding those countries with negative inflation) by more than 1.5 percentage points. Likewise, average nominal long-term interest rates must be no higher than 2 percentage points above the three best-performing member states. The public finance deficit must be less than 3 percent of GDP, while public debt must be below 60 percent of GDP. Prior to entering the Eurozone, each country must join the Exchange Rate Mechanism–II (ERM-II), which serves as an EMU waiting room. On entry to the ERM-II, a country pegs its currency to the euro, keeping the exchange rate within 15 percent of its central rate. A country must remain in the ERM-II for two years without a currency devaluation before it may adopt the euro.

The EU does not judge these criteria equally. A revaluation of the currency against the euro is more tolerable than a devaluation. One somewhat flexible criterion concerns public debt, as countries with debt over the 60 percent limit have been accepted into the Eurozone in the past, so long as the overall share was declining. Although Hungary and Croatia were the only new member states to exceed the public debt criteria in 2012, Eurostat data published in October 2014 showed that Slovenia joined them in surpassing the 60 percent mark by 2013. In the case of Slovenia, the surge in public debt in 2013 was directly related to the bank bailouts.

Three of the new Central and Eastern Europe member states (Estonia, Slovenia, and Lithuania) entered the ERM-II in June 2004. All three countries initially hoped to adopt the euro in 2007, which was the earliest possible date for the new member states. Nonetheless, only Slovenia was given approval by the European Commission to join the EMU in 2007, as both Estonia and Lithuania were delayed by inflation rates above the Maastricht limit. Having joined the ERM-II almost one year after its Baltic neighbors (in May 2005), Latvia initially expected to join the Eurozone in 2008. However, as in Estonia and Lithuania, stubbornly high inflation delayed EMU membership for Latvia. Inflation was a particular challenge in the Baltic states because the currency pegs do not allow for exchange rate fluctuations, meaning that real appreciation had to occur through inflation.

At the time of EU accession, the four Visegrad countries all had problems that would prevent them from adopting the euro in the near term. Public finances were seen as the biggest obstacle for Poland, Hungary, the Czech Republic, and Slovakia. Rising to the challenge, Slovakia launched major fiscal reforms between 2003 and 2005 and joined the ERM-II in November 2005. Although the change in government following the June 2006 parliamentary elections presented some risks with regard to both fiscal policy and inflation, Slovakia's euro adoption occurred on schedule in January 2009.

Slovakia's Eurozone entry happened just in time, as the global crisis would have set the country off course in 2009, particularly on the fiscal front. As budget deficits surged in 2009, most of the new EU member states outside the Eurozone were expected to experience further delays in EMU entry (see table 3.4). Already in 2008, several of the new member states had deficits that were above the 3-percent-of-GDP Maastricht limit. Estonia was the only new member state to see its deficit fall within the Maastricht limit in 2009, and the country adopted the euro in January 2011. Latvia made great strides in reducing its budget gap after the 2008–2009 crisis and won approval to join the common currency zone in January 2014. Lithuania is also scheduled to adopt the euro in 2015.

Even after the larger Central European countries meet the Maastricht criteria, Eurozone accession may be pushed back even further for political reasons. It makes sense for

Table 3.4. Public Finance Deficit as a Share of GDP, 2009–2013

Country	2008	2009	2011	2012	2013
EU–28	–2.4	–6.9	–4.5	–4.2	–3.2
Estonia	–3.0	–2.0	1.0	–0.3	–0.5
Latvia	–4.0	–8.9	–3.4	–0.8	–0.9
Bulgaria	1.6	–4.2	–2.0	–0.5	–1.2
Czech Republic	–2.1	–5.5	–2.9	–4.0	–1.3
Hungary	–3.7	–4.6	–5.5	–2.3	–2.4
Lithuania	–3.3	–9.3	–9.0	–3.2	–2.6
Romania	–5.6	–8.9	–5.5	–3.0	–2.2
Slovakia	–2.4	–7.9	–4.1	–4.2	–2.6
Poland	–3.7	–7.5	–4.9	–3.7	–4.0
Croatia	–2.7	–5.9	–7.7	–5.6	–5.2
Slovenia	–1.8	–6.1	–6.2	–3.7	–14.6

Source: Eurostat, October 2014.

small countries such as the Baltic states to accede to the Eurozone as soon as possible. Advantages include reduced exchange rate risks, lower interest rates, and the elimination of transaction costs associated with maintaining a national currency. Those factors should help attract investment and contribute to real economic convergence. Nonetheless, some politicians and economic analysts in the larger Central European countries have been more hesitant, preferring to maintain a national currency as long as possible in order to have more control over domestic economic policy. Although the currency instability that was associated with the 2008–2009 global crisis made some skeptics in the larger countries more amenable to rapid EMU entry, sentiment shifted away again during the subsequent Eurozone debt drama.

DEALING WITH POVERTY AND DEMOGRAPHIC CHALLENGES

Countries in the Central and East European region began the transition with among the lowest levels of income inequality in the world; however, that situation has been changing. Eurostat data indicated that by 2013 Bulgaria and Romania had the highest risk-of-poverty or social exclusion rates in the entire EU with Latvia close behind. Still, other new EU member states, such as the Czech Republic, Slovenia, and Slovakia, ranked among the best performers. While high inflation impoverishes society as a whole, stabilization programs can harm certain groups, particularly those living on fixed incomes or reliant on the state for transfers. The incidence of poverty also appears to be associated with high jobless rates, particularly when combined with states' increasing frugality in providing unemployment benefits. The loss of a stable income is the main cause of poverty throughout the region.[14] In terms of demographic groups, poverty is generally found more frequently among citizens with low levels of education and skills, those living in rural areas, those with large families, and women, children, and the elderly.

Although poverty and inequality have emerged as a real problem in some CIS countries, they are generally less severe in Central and Eastern Europe than in other transitional societies. That may be partly due to the high levels of literacy in the postcommunist world, the close proximity to Western Europe, and better-targeted social benefits. Some citizens supplement their incomes with household garden plots and occasional employment; others work in the informal economy. Many urban families depend on relatives in the countryside for certain agricultural goods. Populations in countries such as Albania have survived mainly thanks to foreign assistance and workers' remittances, as citizens move to Greece and Italy in search of work, sending their earnings back home to their families. Despite rising poverty levels in the 1990s, purchases of consumer durables also increased significantly in many countries, partly due to the declining prices of such goods relative to salaries.

Poverty levels may stop growing or even decline once a country's economy strengthens; however, certain groups will likely continue to suffer. The situation is particularly severe among Roma, whose share of the total population varies from less than 1 percent in Poland to nearly 10 percent in Slovakia. In absolute terms Romania has by far the biggest Romani population, at an estimated 1.8 million. Throughout the region Roma generally have lower levels of education than the rest of the population. For example, an estimated 1 million Romanian Roma are illiterate. They frequently face racial discrimination in hiring, resulting in much higher jobless rates than among the rest of the population. Moreover, the housing of Roma is often poor and sometimes lacks electricity and running water.[15] Although efforts have been made by various governments and international institutions to alleviate poverty among Roma, the obstacles are great and progress has been slow.

Another unwelcome consequence of the transition has been a significant brain drain from Central and East European countries to Western countries, especially among young, educated people who speak foreign languages. This trend has intensified since EU accession, which allows for the free movement of labor to richer West European countries. Countries hit especially hard by external migration include Poland and the three Baltic states, contributing to serious demographic challenges for policy makers over the medium to long term. Migration is likely to continue until economic opportunities and wages converge with those in more developed countries.

When Is the Transition Complete?

Despite the challenges still faced throughout the Central and East European region, many countries have managed to emerge from the shadow of communism. In economic terms, the transition is deemed complete when soft-budget constraints are eliminated and formerly state-owned companies begin performing like competitive enterprises. Thus, the end of the transition is defined as the point at which the wide differential in the productivity of labor and capital among new versus old firms that existed at the start of the transition has eroded. It marks a time when there are no more distinctions between old, restructured, and new companies.[16] Policy makers are no longer focused on issues specific to the postcommunist transition and instead face problems shared by more advanced, Western economies.

Whereas most of the new EU member states have reached the end of the postcommunist transition period, at least in economic terms, significant challenges remain in many of the Balkan and CIS countries. Fortunately, the states that are further behind have the advantage of being able to study the various reform models implemented by their counterparts in Central Europe and the Baltics to determine the appropriateness of certain policies in their own countries. That may help the Balkans and CIS to move forward more rapidly, once they adopt a consistent pro-reform course.

Study Questions

1. Which countries in Central and Eastern Europe have had the most successful economic transitions? Have there been any surprises?
2. Which countries in the region remain the most dependent on the Russian market?
3. Privatization took many forms in Central and Eastern Europe. Which methods were the most successful in ensuring stable growth and employment?
4. Why did the global economic crisis hit Central and East European countries so hard? Which countries remain most vulnerable to future crises?
5. Why have some countries in Central and Eastern Europe been eager to adopt the euro as quickly as possible, while others have been hesitant?

Suggested Readings

Aåslund, Anders. *Building Capitalism: The Transformation of the Former Soviet Bloc*. Cambridge: Cambridge University Press, 2002.

Connolly, Richard. "The Determinants of the Economic Crisis in Post-Socialist Europe." *Europe-Asia Studies* 64, no. 1 (2012): 35–67.

Ekiert, Grzegorz, and Stephen E. Hanson, eds. *Capitalism and Democracy in Central and Eastern Europe*. Cambridge: Cambridge University Press, 2006.

European Bank for Reconstruction and Development (EBRD). *Transition Report 2000: Employment, Skills and Transition*. London: EBRD, 2000.

Frydman, Roman, Kenneth Murphy, and Andrzej Rapaczynski. *Capitalism with a Comrade's Face*. Budapest: CEU Press, 1998.

Funck, Bernard, and Lodovico Pizzati, eds. *Labor, Employment, and Social Policies in the EU Enlargement Process: Changing Perspectives and Policy Options*. Washington, DC: World Bank, 2002.

Keereman, Filip, and Istvan Szekely, eds. *Five Years of an Enlarged EU: A Positive Sum Game*. Berlin: Springer, 2010.

Lavigne, Marie. *The Economics of Transition: From Socialist Economy to Market Economy*. 2nd ed. New York: Palgrave Macmillan, 1999.

World Bank. *Transition: The First Ten Years*. Washington, DC: World Bank, 2002.

Websites

Eurostat: http://epp.eurostat.ec.europa.eu (EU statistics)

V4 Revue: http://visegradrevue.eu (analysis from Central Europe)

EUbusiness, "Eastern and Central Europe": http://www.eubusiness.com/regions/east -europe (economic news from Central Europe)

Notes

1. See World Bank, *Transition: The First Ten Years* (Washington, DC: World Bank, 2002), chap. 2.

2. European Bank for Reconstruction and Development (EBRD), *Transition Report 2000: Employment, Skills and Transition* (London: EBRD, 2000), 18–19.

3. For more on the communist economic system and its collapse, see Anders Aåslund, *Building Capitalism: The Transformation of the Former Soviet Bloc* (Cambridge: Cambridge University Press, 2002), chaps. 1 and 2.

4. The first three lessons are noted by Anders Aåslund. See Aåslund, *Building Capitalism*, 167–68.

5. Aåslund, *Building Capitalism*, 238.

6. See Aåslund, *Building Capitalism*, 227–32.

7. Aåslund, *Building Capitalism*, 171.

8. Aåslund, *Building Capitalism*, 222.

9. See EBRD, *Transition Report 2000*, 55, 69.

10. World Bank, *Transition*, 53.

11. Slovakia's second-stage stabilization policies and their causes are discussed in Katarína Mathernová and Juraj Renčko, "'Reformology': The Case of Slovakia," *Orbis* (fall 2006): 629–40.

12. World Bank, *Transition*, 81–83; Aåslund, *Building Capitalism*, 344–45.

13. World Bank, *EU-8 Quarterly Economic Report* (April 2005).

14. EBRD, *Transition Report 2000*, 106.

15. Arno Tanner, "The Roma of Eastern Europe: Still Searching for Inclusion," Migration Policy Institute, May 1, 2005, http://www.migrationpolicy.org/article/roma-eastern-europe-still -searching-inclusion.

16. World Bank, *Transition*, xix.

CHAPTER 4

Social Aspects of Transformation

Alfio Cerami

The fall of the Berlin Wall marked not the end of the transition to democracy but its beginning, with still uncertain outcomes in terms of electoral continuity and change.[1] In order to provide a more comprehensive picture of the regime vulnerabilities and instabilities that stem from the difficult transition from a centrally planned, authoritarian economy to a free market–oriented democracy, this chapter discusses the most important aspects of the transformation that has occurred in Central and Eastern Europe since the end of communism. These aspects include key patterns of social change, social welfare, social problems, and associated social pathologies. Understanding what worked and what went wrong in the social policy domain will improve our understanding of the prospects for future and more successful reforms in this region, as well as in other transitional and developing countries currently on the road to democracy.

The first section of this chapter provides a brief overview of the key patterns of social change, including social welfare, social problems, and social pathologies, as well citizens' adaptation to the new environment. The second section discusses similarities and differences among countries in order to understand what policy options have been more successful and why. The third section complements this analysis by addressing ten areas where we can learn from previous mistakes.

Social Welfare, Social Problems, and Social Pathologies

The economic transformation from a centrally planned to a market-oriented economy put under serious stress the economic capacity and performance of firms and markets in dealing with endogenous and exogenous pressures. The internal and external challenges, discussed more extensively by Sharon Fisher in chapter 3, were linked to the restructuring of the previous economic system and its adaptation to the new global market environment. The result of this difficult process of economic restructuring was job loss for several million workers of ex-state-owned enterprises, which led to important social changes and a temporary decrease in social welfare, as well as to growing social problems and social pathologies.

Especially during the first years of transition, unemployment, once virtually nonexistent in this region, grew exponentially, causing an increase in poverty, crime, and juvenile delinquency, as well as a temporary deterioration of the health status of the population with subsequent worsening of quality of life and overall life chances. Fortunately, the negative results that emerged from the early phase of transition, the period of transition shock (1990–2000), improved in the second stage of reforms (2000–2010), the period of adaptation or recalibration,[2] albeit to different extents in different countries.

After two decades of persistent battles against unemployment, in 2010 the number of unemployed persons reached particularly high levels in southeastern Europe, immediately followed by the Visegrad countries and the Baltic states. Especially in Albania, Bosnia-Herzegovina, Croatia, Hungary, Montenegro, Poland, Serbia, Slovakia, and Slovenia, unemployment has recently become an extremely pressing issue, breaking the psychological threshold of two digits. Significant improvements have been made since the early 2000s in almost all countries, though to a different degree depending on their vulnerabilities to the shock of the 2008–2010 crisis (see table 4.1). Those countries, such as Estonia, Hungary, and Lithuania, where the external vulnerabilities to the crisis were stronger (e.g., monetary weaknesses, unsustainable budget expenses, excessive dependence on foreign investors),[3] have also been the ones where unemployment has grown with a higher intensity. Interesting to note in this context are the extremely low unemployment

Photo 4.1. Homeless man in Budapest. The transition to democracy and difficult economic reforms profoundly affected vulnerable segments of the populations, as the governments often had to cut welfare programs to adjust the economy. (Daniel Nemeth)

Table 4.1. Registered Unemployment Rate (Average Percentage of Labor Force)

	1990	1995	2000	2005	2010
Albania	10.0	12.9	16.8	14.1	13.6
Bosnia and Herzegovina	n/a	n/a	42.2	49.7	42.6
Bulgaria	13.2 (1992)	11.4	18.1	11.5	9.5
Croatia	9.3	14.5	21.1	17.9	17.4
Czech Republic	0.3	3.0	9.0	9.0	9.0
Estonia	n/a	4.1	5.3	4.3	12.3
Hungary	0.8	10.4	8.7	9.2 (2006)	13.5
Latvia	n/a	6.6	7.8	7.4	4.9 (2007)
Lithuania	n/a	6.1	12.6	6.4	12.5 (2009)
Macedonia	23.0	35.6	n/a	n/a	n/a
Montenegro	n/a	n/a	n/a	18.5	12.2
Poland	3.4	15.2	14.0	18.2	12.3
Romania	8.2 (1992)	9.5	10.5	5.9	7.0
Serbia	n/a	n/a	25.6	26.8	26.9
Slovakia	0.6	13.8	18.2	11.6	12.5
Slovenia	4.7	13.9	12.2	10.2	10.7
Ukraine	0.3 (1992)	0.4	4.2	4.4	2.2

Source: UNICEF 2013.

rates in Ukraine, which are paralleled by similarly low rates in several other members of the former Soviet Union, outside the scope of this book; however, the virtual absence of unemployment has not prevented people from falling into poverty. More jobs do not in fact mean better jobs, which are the sole instruments that can prevent people from falling into poverty or engaging in criminal activities. The establishment of inclusive welfare institutions able to protect citizens from a wide range of new social risks, including social disintegration, is the key to success.

Poverty is subsequently an important negative social aspect of the transition, one that, strictly linked to the absence of more and decent jobs,[4] has greatly influenced the emergence of new social problems and social pathologies. After two and a half decades of transition, the poverty headcount ratio measured at $5 a day is higher in the countries of southeastern Europe, particularly in Albania, Bulgaria, Macedonia, and Romania, as well as in Estonia. This situation tends to improve when the poverty threshold is set at $2.50 a day, as the percentages of the population living below the poverty line decrease to less than 20 percent in all the countries under consideration (see figure 4.1). Faster improvements are, in this case, due to better integration into regional and global markets, increasing the welfare for the country's economy and population, even though the positive effects of such convergence must still be fully exploited.

Similar considerations apply with regard to income inequality and, more specifically, with regard to the share of income owned by households. The income share held by the highest 20 percent of the population is greater in Albania, Bosnia-Herzegovina, Croatia, Latvia, Macedonia, and Slovenia (see figure 4.2). These are all countries that have witnessed a more exponential growth in the number of "new rich" with consequently more unequal distributions of income and life risks. The potential redistributive effects of welfare institutions have also been more limited in these countries, and the still inefficient

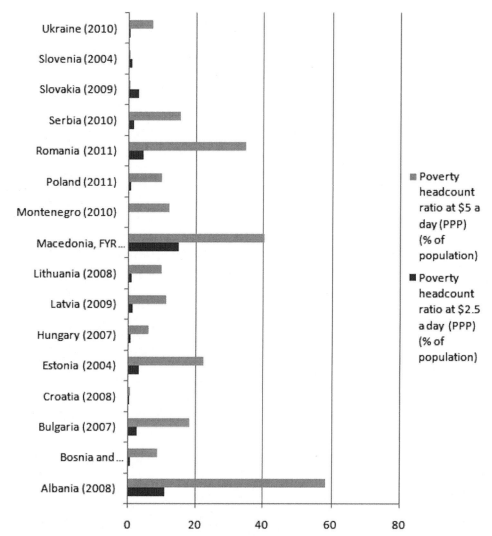

Figure 4.1.   Poverty Headcount Ratio

Note: Comparable data for the Czech Republic are missing.

Source: World Bank Development Indicators 2014, http://data.worldbank.org/data-catalog/world
-development-indicators. Author's calculations.

welfare regimes have not yet succeeded in lowering existing differences (see "Similarities and Differences among Countries" and "Ongoing Issues in Transformation" below).

In order to fully understand the real extent of poverty and income inequality, it is also important to analyze gross domestic product (GDP) per capita (purchasing power parity [PPP] in current international US dollars), as this measure provides a good indicator of the similarities and differences that exist among countries and regions with regard to the real purchasing power of citizens. Here, the Czech Republic, Slovakia, Poland, Hungary, and the Baltic states show a higher percentage of GDP per capita, followed by the countries of southeastern Europe and Ukraine (see table 4.2). In practical terms, this

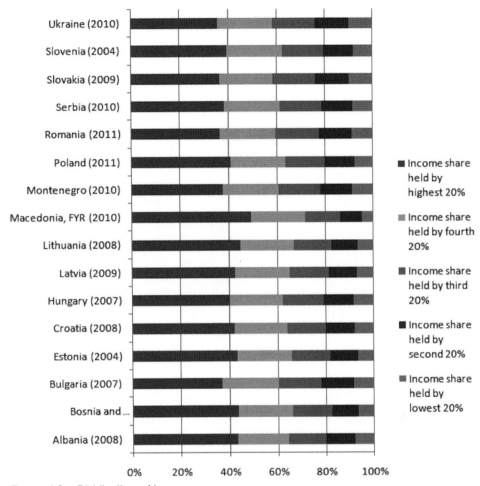

Figure 4.2. Distribution of Income

Note: Comparable data for the Czech Republic are missing.

Source: World Bank Development Indicators 2014, http://data.worldbank.org/data-catalog/world -development-indicators. Author's calculations.

means more money at the population's disposal for its members to access a better life, but such access also requires the availability and obtainability of better welfare services.

Crime and juvenile delinquency are strongly associated with poverty and income inequality, but also, as discussed in the next section, with the absence of well-functioning welfare institutions. The registered total crime rate (per one hundred thousand average population) reaches unexpectedly high levels in Hungary, Poland, and Slovenia, followed by Estonia, Latvia and Lithuania, Bulgaria, Croatia, Romania, Macedonia, and Ukraine (see table 4.3). Differences also exist among countries in terms of crimes committed by the young; Hungary, Poland, Ukraine, and Romania have higher rates of juvenile criminality (see table 4.4). However, these differences in crime rates can, in fact, be the outcome of an increase in criminal activities or of a statistical bias, as these countries have made the reestablishment of "law and security" the keywords of several political

Table 4.2. GDP per Capita, PPP (Current International Dollars)

	1990	1995	2000	2005	2010
Albania	2,824	2,928	4,258	6,102	8,631
Bosnia and Herzegovina	—	1,354	4,521	6,341	8,635
Bulgaria	5,402	5,528	6,225	9,809	13,892
Croatia	—	7,973	10,922	15,332	18,727
Czech Republic	12,314	13,379	15,546	21,264	25,358
Estonia	—	6,315	9,882	16,548	20,092
Hungary	8,931	8,971	11,882	16,975	20,734
Latvia	7,818	5,386	8,039	13,040	15,943
Lithuania	9,311	6,197	8,614	14,197	18,120
Macedonia	5,559	4,799	5,943	7,872	11,083
Montenegro	—	—	6,303	8,238	12,977
Poland	5,967	7,407	10,514	13,784	20,033
Romania	5,186	5,366	5,662	9,361	14,526
Serbia	—	—	5,768	8,517	11,421
Slovakia	7,697	8,299	11,006	16,175	23,149
Slovenia	11,509	13,000	17,556	23,476	26,509
Ukraine	5,823	3,172	3,279	5,583	6,678

Source: UNICEF 2013.

Table 4.3. Registered Total Crime Rate (Per Hundred Thousand Average Population)

	1990	1995	2000	2005	2010
Albania	—	195	161	276	—
Bosnia and Herzegovina	—	—	—	—	—
Bulgaria	772	2,452	1,823	1,780	1,969
Croatia	1,123	1,018	1,081	1,779	1,649
Czech Republic	2,099	3,637	3,818	3,361	2,986
Estonia	1,517	2,754	4,219	4,129	3,607
Hungary	3,288	4,860	4,414	4,328	4,472
Latvia	1,302	1,575	2,120	2,297	2,437
Lithuania	1,002	1,676	2,354	2,404	2,213
Macedonia	784	1,178	978	1,111	1,386
Montenegro	—	—	—	—	1,131
Poland	2,318	2,526	3,311	3,616	2,969
Romania	422	1,309	1,576	963	1,365
Serbia	—	—	1,165	1,391	1,070
Slovakia	1,323	2,137	1,645	2,294	1,761
Slovenia	1,919	1,919	3,395	4,216	4,365
Ukraine	716	1,252	1,124	1,035	1,106

Source: UNICEF 2013.

Table 4.4. Registered Number of Crimes Committed by or with Participation of Children or Juveniles

	1990	1995	2000	2005	2010
Albania	—	—	559	701	—
Bosnia and Herzegovina	747	—	458	633	—
Bulgaria	6,873	15,348	10,006	10,998	7,086
Croatia	2,689	2,174	2,375	2,630	3,270
Czech Republic	—	21,116	13,507	7,614	5,339
Estonia	—	2,433	2,301	3,768	—
Hungary	12,264	14,321	19,988	21,499	17,379
Latvia	2,410	2,591	3,923	2,726	785
Lithuania	2,506	4,551	5,519	4,308	3,260
Macedonia	3,588	4,918	3,120	2,399	1,686
Montenegro	—	—	—	413	422
Poland	60,525	82,551	76,442	71,482	99,187
Romania	9,245	26,511	25,470	18,578	13,531
Serbia	—	—	3,458	2,945	3,747
Slovakia	5,640	9,183	9,724	6,411	4,282
Slovenia	4,300	4,475	4,836	2,847	2,150
Ukraine	28,819	41,648	37,239	26,470	17,342

Source: UNICEF 2013.

campaigns. Consequently, governments have invested more time and effort in the fight against crime, which has often led to a higher number of arrests.

Improvement or deterioration in the health and quality of life of citizens is also an important aspect of social transformation. Overall, the health of the population in this region has drastically improved since the first phase of the transition, as life expectancy for both men and women is substantially higher than in the pre-transition phase. The countries that have witnessed greater improvement, slowly coming closer to most European Union (EU) standards, are the Visegrad countries and the Baltic states, followed by the countries in southeastern Europe. The latter entered the phase of transition with more difficult circumstances, more protracted economic crises, and more accentuated structural weaknesses—a situation that has greatly hindered faster improvements (see tables 4.5 and 4.6). However, with the exception of Bosnia-Herzegovina, Croatia, and Montenegro, the fact that these countries also invested less in health-care expenditures (see table 4.7) also helps explain why the health statuses of their populations remain significantly lower than those of other East or West European populations. The presence of corruption, mismanagement of health-care funds, and inefficiency in the health-care delivery system contribute to explaining the rest of the differences.

Finally, another important aspect to take into account is the quality of life of citizens as this is an important indicator for understanding citizens' satisfaction with national governments. With regard, for example, to the issue of new family composition, the traditional patterns of family formation have dramatically changed. Couples in the region are marrying less and less, and the number of children has decreased. Divorce rates have grown in almost all countries.[5] This situation has entailed not only increasing poverty for

Table 4.5. Male Life Expectancy at Birth (Years)

	1990	1995	2000	2005	2010
Albania	69.3	68.5	71.5	71.7	74.3
Bosnia and Herzegovina	69.7	69.5	71.3	72.1	74.1
Bulgaria	68.1	67.1	68.2	69.0	70.0
Croatia	68.4	67.1	—	71.8	73.5
Czech Republic	67.6	69.7	71.6	72.9	74.4
Estonia	64.6	61.7	65.1	67.3	70.6
Hungary	65.1	65.3	67.1	68.6	70.5
Latvia	64.2	60.8	64.9	65.6	68.8
Lithuania	66.4	63.3	66.7	65.4	68.0
Macedonia	70.3	70.1	70.7	71.6	72.7
Montenegro	—	—	71.1	70.4	—
Poland	66.5	67.6	69.7	70.8	72.1
Romania	66.6	65.7	67.0	68.2	69.8
Serbia	—	—	69.7	70.0	71.4
Slovakia	66.6	68.4	69.1	70.1	71.6
Slovenia	69.4	70.3	71.9	74.1	76.3
Ukraine	66.0	61.8	62.4	62.2	65.3

Source: UNICEF 2013.

Table 4.6. Female Life Expectancy at Birth (Years)

	1990	1995	2000	2005	2010
Albania	75.4	—	78.1	76.9	78.1
Bosnia and Herzegovina	75.2	75.1	76.7	77.5	78.7
Bulgaria	74.8	74.9	75.3	76.3	77.2
Croatia	76.0	75.7	—	78.8	79.6
Czech Republic	75.4	76.6	78.3	79.1	80.6
Estonia	74.6	74.3	76.0	78.1	80.5
Hungary	73.7	74.5	75.6	76.9	78.1
Latvia	74.6	73.1	76.0	77.4	78.4
Lithuania	76.3	75.1	77.4	77.4	78.8
Macedonia	74.5	74.4	75.2	75.9	77.0
Montenegro	—	—	76.3	74.9	—
Poland	75.5	76.4	78.0	79.4	80.6
Romania	72.7	73.4	74.2	75.5	77.3
Serbia	—	—	74.8	75.4	76.6
Slovakia	75.4	76.3	77.2	77.9	78.8
Slovenia	77.3	76.8	79.1	81.3	82.7
Ukraine	75.0	72.7	73.6	74.0	75.5

Source: UNICEF 2013.

Table 4.7. General Government Expenditure on Health as a Percentage of GDP

	1995	2000	2005	2009
Albania	1.6	2.3	2.7	2.8
Bosnia and Herzegovina	5.0	4.1	5.0	6.7
Bulgaria	3.7	3.6	4.3	4.4
Croatia	6.9	6.7	6.0	6.6
Czech Republic	6.4	5.9	6.0	6.1
Estonia	5.7	4.1	3.9	5.3
Hungary	6.1	4.9	5.8	5.1
Latvia	3.8	3.3	3.5	3.9
Lithuania	4.0	4.5	3.8	4.5
Macedonia	5.0	4.9	5.0	4.6
Montenegro	5.5	5.5	6.3	6.7
Poland	4.0	3.9	4.0	4.8
Romania	2.5	3.1	3.4	3.5
Serbia	4.8	4.8	5.8	—
Slovakia	5.4	5.6	5.0	5.7
Slovenia	5.8	6.1	5.8	6.4
Ukraine	4.1	2.9	3.8	3.8

Source: UNICEF 2013.

single-headed households; single parents with children; the young; households with unemployed, part-time, or atypical workers; and households of the Roma minority but also more pronounced social reproduction of inequalities and intergenerational transmission of poverty than existed during communism.[6] It comes, then, as no surprise that, according to the European Bank for Reconstruction and Development's (EBRD) *Life in Transition Report*, in 2007 only 30 percent of people believed (agree or strongly agree) that their household lives were better in 2007 than in 1989.[7] Even more importantly, again according to the EBRD report, in 2007 only about one-third of respondents in Central and Eastern Europe supported "democracy and the market" as their preferred political and economic systems.[8] "Democracy and planned economy," "authoritarianism and market economy," and "authoritarianism and planned economy" also stand out as important feasible options, receiving from 10 to 27 percent of support, depending on the region. In this account, the Visegrad countries and the Baltic states showed greater support for the "market and democracy" option, followed by the southeast European countries and those belonging to the former Soviet Union.[9]

Similarities and Differences among Countries

How do we explain the similarities and differences among countries and these social problems? Differences in unemployment rates can be explained, on the one hand, by structural preconditions, such as the presence of more agricultural societies, as in Bulgaria and Romania versus, for example, the more industrialized Czech and Slovak republics. On the

Photo 4.2. Children playing outside a run-down apartment building in Bulgaria. (*Capital Weekly,* Bulgaria)

other, they also depend on the economic attractiveness of countries to foreign partners and on their capacity to avoid excessive dependence.[10] However, their internal capacity to resist external shocks, such as those that may arise from a sudden withdrawal of foreign investors, is also important, as dependence on FDI in the Visegrad countries, Baltic states, and southeastern Europe or on gas price subsidies in Ukraine has powerfully shown.

The system of protection against unemployment also played a significant role in cushioning the negative effects of transition. Those countries that coupled a system based on unemployment insurance with longer-term universal unemployment benefits and social-assistance measures, such as the Visegrad countries,[11] often obtained better results in reducing poverty and thus the negative effects of transformation. The reasons for poverty lie, in this context, in country-specific structural deficiencies and in the poverty-reduction policies adopted in particular countries. Those countries that invested more in nonpolarized social welfare policies and limited elite capture, as in Central Europe (Czech Republic, Hungary, Poland, Slovakia, and Slovenia) and the Baltic states (Estonia, Latvia, and Lithuania), had lower levels of poverty and were more successful in protecting vulnerable citizens, compared to Albania, Bosnia-Herzegovina, Bulgaria, Croatia, Macedonia, Montenegro, Romania, Serbia, and Ukraine.[12] Thus, the absence of an integrated set of social-assistance measures able to lower the costs of transition was an important reason for failure in the social domain, as was the failure to implement well-established family policies and child-protection provisions that would have lowered the burden of new social risks.[13] In those countries where family policies and child benefits were more extensive, as in the countries of Central Europe (particularly the Czech Republic, Hungary, Poland,

Slovakia, and Slovenia)[14] and in the Baltic states,[15] women and their children had better chances for getting ahead in the new environment than in Albania, Bosnia-Herzegovina, Montenegro, Macedonia, Romania, and Ukraine, where the availability and extent of these benefits continue to be more limited.[16]

The same considerations apply with regard to crime and juvenile delinquency, though, in this case, the absence of well-functioning social services to cover particularly vulnerable groups of citizens through, for example, the establishment of more comprehensive educational policies and vocational-training measures should be mentioned as a primary cause of failure.[17] In those countries that had lower levels of social protection, due to budget constraints or wrong policy decisions, such as Bulgaria, Romania, Albania, Bosnia-Herzegovina, Croatia, Serbia, and Ukraine, crime and juvenile delinquency have a more destructive potential. When money for integration policies was not readily available, repression of crime became the only option.

Differences in health and quality of life reflect, in addition to the already mentioned economic vulnerabilities, policy decisions that did not adequately take into account the importance of investing in citizens' health.[18] Especially with regard to the reforms of the health-care sector, most countries restructured the Soviet-style model based on centralized though inefficient management and delivery of services by introducing a system that depended on health insurance contributions.[19] Unfortunately, as access to health-care services depended on citizens' employment status, increasing unemployment often resulted in a deficit of health funds, which subsequently led to a loss of coverage for most unemployed people, an outcome evident throughout the region.[20]

Finally, increasing social inequality may be traced to inadequate social integration policies that did not succeed in including the unemployed and, more generally, the most vulnerable citizens in the new political, economic, cultural, and social order. A more comprehensive approach toward social integration through more coherent, socially inclusive welfare policies would have, in this context, been the key to success. As D. Acemoglu and J. Robinson have correctly affirmed, inclusive political institutions are a crucial variable to consider in order to understand how societies evolve and react successfully to internal and external threats.[21] This also implies understanding differences in the political and social construction of poverty.[22] The current deficiencies in integrating Russian-speaking communities in the Baltic states,[23] war veterans in the countries of former Yugoslavia (especially Serbia, Montenegro, and Bosnia-Herzegovina),[24] and the Russian community in Ukraine are among the reasons for the current tensions in these countries.

Ongoing Issues in Transformation

In order to improve the prospects for future policy options, this section highlights ten ongoing issues in the transformation. The first issue arose from a mistaken assumption that the transition from communism to democracy would automatically lead to more social welfare and increasing citizen support for the national government and the new democratic system. After the fall of the Berlin Wall, no backsliding toward authoritarian rule was thought to be possible. This point of view was shared by the majority of academics and international observers, who saw, following Francis Fukuyama's famous assumption,[25] the fall of the Berlin Wall as the end of a difficult transition to democracy.[26] Recent surveys of citizens' attitudes toward the government and democracy have painted a different picture. In 2010, only a minority of citizens stated that they were satisfied or very satisfied with the national government. The satisfaction rate corresponded to 19 percent of respondents in Bulgaria, 20 percent in the Czech Republic, 31 percent in Estonia, 9 percent in Croatia, 31 percent in Hungary, 11 percent in Lithuania, 24 percent in Poland, 20 percent in Slovakia, 10 percent in Slovenia, and 5 percent in Ukraine.[27] Similarly, in 2010, only a minority of citizens said that they were satisfied or very satisfied with the way democracy works. The percentages corresponded, in this case, with 7 percent of respondents in Bulgaria, 29 percent in the Czech Republic, 29 percent in Estonia, 12 percent in Croatia, 20 percent in Hungary, 13 percent in Lithuania, 29 percent in Poland, 15 percent in Slovakia, 8 percent in Slovenia, and 7 percent in Ukraine.

The transition from communism to democracy should, in fact, be understood as a long process of economic, political, social, and cultural restructuring, which has implied (and still implies) important economic, political, social, and cultural costs.[28] Improving the social welfare of citizens has required more time than expected, and delay in improving citizens' economic situations has negatively affected citizen support for national governments and the new democratic system. There is little doubt that a "democratic fatigue" has materialized in this region and that the transformative power of external actors (such as the EU), though important,[29] has diminished.[30] As A. Przeworski has correctly affirmed, backsliding toward authoritarian rule is likely to occur if the social costs of transition are too prolonged and the past seems less painful than the unforeseeable future.[31]

The second issue arose from the mistaken belief that economic restructuring would automatically lead to increasing well-being and that social problems would suddenly disappear. This point of view was shared by most proponents of orthodox neoliberal economics (i.e., survivors of the Chicago School and Milton Friedman's understanding of economic development), who saw the primacy of the economic over the social sector as the key to success. In contrast to this view, R. Inglehart's analysis of subjective well-being rankings of eighty-two societies based on combined happiness and life satisfaction scores has demonstrated that all twenty-five postcommunist countries included in the World Values Survey, except Vietnam, Slovenia, and the Czech Republic, have low, medium-low, or negative scores.[32] As a matter of fact, restructuring an obsolete economic architecture implies a long and difficult process of transformation that does not automatically lead to immediate well-being because of the many problems that occur in adapting different socioeconomic, political, and cultural structures to the new environment. Drastic economic change comes at a cost. Rising up from the bottom of an economic depression, as portrayed in the so-called Kuznets curve,[33] also often requires more effort than predicted in terms of cultural adaptation. When this mismatch between expectations and cultural adaptation materializes, new social problems and new social risks are likely to emerge and persist, leaving citizens feeling uncertain about the future.[34] This situation in turn has a negative impact on citizens' subjective well-being, quality of life, and life chances.

The third mistaken expectation concerning the transformation involved the conjecture that drastic austerity measures, as promoted in the so-called Washington Consensus, would lead to increasing fiscal stability and growth, with limited social costs. During the first phase of the transition (1990–2000), the majority of officials with the International

Monetary Fund, Organisation for Economic Co-operation and Development, and World Bank strongly advocated this policy as the best way to ensure long-term sustainable development.[35] Although it is correct that a substantial reduction in state expenses was (and still is) absolutely necessary to ensure the long-term survival of the new economic system, drastic austerity measures did not lead, without intervention in the social sector, to increasing fiscal stability and economic development.[36] As P. C. Schmitter has correctly noted, "Despite the neoliberal enthusiasm for privatization and globalization, democratization continues to rely on a political unit with a capacity for exercising legitimate public coercion and implementing collective decisions within a distinct territory—that is, a state."[37] The policies followed, which were often based on a set of self-sustaining ideas[38] that gave primacy to short-term political objectives rather than to long-term social outcomes. Regardless of a substantial increase in GDP per capita, overall household purchasing power fell during the first decade of transition. This situation has deteriorated as a result of the 2008–2010 economic crisis and has reduced the legitimacy of newly established democratic states. According to the EBRD *Life in Transition Report*, in 2011, almost two-thirds of respondents in the eastern region of Europe stated that they were affected by the crisis, with more than two-fifths affirming that they were hit "a great deal" or "a fair amount."[39] In addition, about 70 percent of households affected by the crisis stated that they were "cutting back on spending on staple foods and health as a result of the crisis." The economic crisis thus also influenced support for democracy and markets, which has decreased compared to 2006 in the majority of countries.[40]

The fourth mistaken hypothesis regarding the transformation was the improbable hope that Central and East European citizens would immediately abandon old mentalities and patterns of behavior and easily adapt to the new social order, rejecting, once and for all, the old one. This hope was widely shared by the majority of political scientists, economists, and policy makers of the time (in both the West and the East), who, by excessively emphasizing the future positive effects of transition, underestimated many precepts widely known in cultural sociology,[41] cultural economy,[42] and economic sociology[43] that emphasized, instead, the importance of path-dependency and historical legacies in policy making.[44] Another widely shared hope during the first phase of the transition was, in this context, that with the dissolution of communism, clientelistic relations and corruption would also suddenly disappear from the scene. In contrast, as W. Sandholtz and R. Taagepera have correctly affirmed, "Communism created structural incentives for engaging in corrupt behaviors, which became such a widespread fact of life that they became rooted in the culture in these societies—that is, the social norms and practices prevailing in communist societies."[45] According to Sandholtz and Taagepera, the transition toward democracy has not removed this culture of corruption yet. The process of privatization, in fact, opened myriad new opportunities for corruption.[46] Although this problem is by no means confined to postcommunist countries, the sad truth is that the present has an ancient heart and that citizens face enormous difficulties in abandoning old mentalities and patterns of behavior. Adaptation to the new social order has not been automatic, as predicted, and the old regime has continued to represent a more tolerable option for several million citizens. It comes, then, as no surprise that clientelistic relations and corruption have survived the collapse of the communist order, since they continued to be part of the acquired way of doing business, which permitted, for several decades, citizens' daily survival. In terms of social welfare and social pathologies, this continuation has resulted in a privileged access to welfare provisions for certain categories of citizens linked to the old and new *nomenklatura*. The persistence, for example, of "gratitude money" in the health-care sector has continued to drastically diminish citizens' access to better services.[47]

The fifth mistaken hypothesis of transformation was based on the assumption that citizens would employ, by default, the democratic liberties associated with the transition from communism to democracy (e.g., freedom of speech, free elections) and that the old lifestyle would be easily forgotten.[48] Unfortunately, the availability of democratic liberties did not coincide with increasing social support for the new democratic system. Institutional[49] and intellectual legacies,[50] as well as more practical material benefits, such as those linked to the absence of poverty and inequality, have, on the contrary, played a more important role in citizens' evaluation of the new social order. There has also been a general deterioration of trust.[51] As Sharon Wolchik and Jane Curry note in the introduction to this volume, the lesson to be learned here is the fact that rapid social change implies a drastic psychological adaptation to the new environment. In the presence of institutional and intellectual constraints and in the absence of tangible benefits, rapid social change has not always resulted in increasing support for the new democratic order.[52]

The sixth mistaken expectation about the transformation was based on the belief that in the presence of continuous economic growth, no anger and resentment among the population would arise or, at least, that the reasons for protest and resentment would be limited. On the basis of a simplistic linear assumption, greater GDP growth was expected to lead to more jobs, and more jobs were expected to create better access to social welfare provisions.[53] Unfortunately, as the restructuring of the systems of social protection was carried out with a limited version of the social insurance principle, and as unemployment emerged, several million citizens found themselves, from one day to the other, with little to no coverage. The history of the transition from communism to democracy has produced, in this context, an extremely complex scenario. Although labor mobilization has been limited compared to that in European countries that were not formerly communist, anger and resentment among citizens has continued to arise.[54] The extent of such resentment has depended primarily on important political realignments,[55] which greatly influenced the real distribution of material benefits among citizens and the extent to which different groups were successfully included in the new democratic order.[56] Because our future has not only a distant but also a relational past,[57] citizens have assessed their current condition in relation to that of their peers, often underestimating the real improvements they have obtained in social welfare. When numerous so-called nouveaux riches (often children of the old *nomenklatura*) invaded shops, pubs, and restaurants, flaunting with no hesitation their newly acquired wealth, it comes as no surprise that the majority of the population felt substantially excluded from the benefits of the new democratic order, despite a significant growth in their real incomes. The unequal distribution of wealth and privileges thus also contributed to anger and resentment. Not surprisingly, in 2010, 87 percent of respondents in Bulgaria, 63 percent in the Czech Republic, 74 percent in Estonia, 85 percent in Croatia, 88 percent in Hungary, 90 percent in Lithuania, 75 percent in Poland, 77 percent in Slovakia, 90 percent in Slovenia, and 88 percent in Ukraine[58] agreed or strongly agreed that the government should do more to reduce differences in income.

The seventh mistaken hypothesis of transformation concerned the notion that new social policies could be implemented easily and aligned with the new economic order. For

Photo 4.3. Solidarity demonstrations in Poland to protest the low salaries and lack of benefits for state employees, such as teachers and doctors, as well as the general lack of government aid for impoverished citizens in 2013. (Adam Dauksza/FORUM)

the majority of policy makers, the mismatch between the current and past systems of social protection was supposed to be automatically resolved by an abrupt institutional transformation.[59] Most international advisors, including several experts in the EU-sponsored Technical Assistance and Information Exchange (TAIEX) and Twinning programs,[60] who saw in a simple policy transfer[61] from west to east the key to the successful restructuring of social policy, were responsible for this misunderstanding. In reality, new social policies have been hard to implement because transformation has taken place by adding new institutions onto old layers that did not always fit with the new economic order as they had been based on a different set of ideas and social policy strategies.[62] The mismatch between current and past systems of social protection has, in this way, continued over the years, despite several important incremental rather than abrupt transformations.[63] Change requires time to adapt to new circumstances, a rule not easily avoided. A notable example is the restructuring of the pension system in Hungary, which, after a first phase of drastic neoliberal transformation, reacquired most of the previous features of a centralized, state-led system of pension insurance.[64] Social pathologies, in this case, implied growing poverty for the elderly and uncovered patients in the health-care sector—all citizens who could not afford not to pay the price of voluntary health or pension insurance contributions.

The eighth mistaken expectation about transformation was the supposition that new ideas, interests, and institutions[65] could be easily implemented, replacing overnight the old ones. Again, international consultants, proponents of a simple policy transfer from west to east, often employed by the most famous financial institutions,[66] were responsible for this misconception. They in fact paid very little attention to the real speed required for cultural adaptation, to the differences among countries, or to different historical experiences and the imprint these left on people's minds, hearts, and patterns of behavior. In real practice, new ideas, interests, and institutions can hardly be established and accepted by a community from one day to the next, since they are often associated with dominant patterns of behavior that have persisted over decades.[67] Incremental adjustment and recombinant transformation[68] have, in this case, been the outcomes of institutional changes that have involved a transformation and democratization not only of institutional structures but also of mentalities and patterns of acquired behavior.[69] Social problems associated with this misconception reflect the difficulties citizens have had in adapting to new life styles (e.g., the increasing number of divorces) and the new labor market, which, necessarily, implied more proactive behavior on the part of workers to ensure their own social protection.

The ninth mistaken hypothesis regarding transformation was the expectation that poverty and inequality would immediately diminish with the fall of the Iron Curtain, leading to a paradisiacal inclusive society. Excessively optimistic Keynesian-oriented social policy experts, who saw in the diminution of poverty and inequality through an unsustainable increase in internal demand the cure for all the ills of human societies, were responsible for this misunderstanding. Poverty and inequality do play a role, but more variables must be taken into account. Not surprisingly, poverty and inequality have not disappeared overnight, since the establishment of a new and a more inclusive society depended on several different variables, with economic variables representing only one part. Innovation and modernization meant, in this context, not only updating an obsolete industrial and technological organization[70] but also "deepening democracy, enhancing collective and individual agency, reducing poverty, achieving greater equality of wealth, power, respect, legal status, or opportunity, and cultivating solidarity in democratic communities."[71] These measures necessarily required a drastic transformation that could not be imposed from one day to the next by simple Keynesian policies or by a coercive change in the main patterns in citizens' behavior. Instead, they require time and the political will to accept and include even the most uncomfortable differences present in the new social order.[72]

The tenth and final mistaken hypothesis of transformation was the view that the presence of a unique "communist" model of political economy and welfare capitalism would soon disappear and that the postcommunist countries would rapidly come to embrace Western models of welfare capitalism and political economy.[73] The peculiar "communist" welfare regime in force for more than forty years has, in reality, not disappeared from one day to the next, while convergence with Western models of political economy and capitalism has required immense sociostructural adaptations.[74] A more careful reading of Max Weber's famous work on economic sociology[75] would have certainly helped several social policy experts of the time.[76] Hybridization of existing welfare institutions has, in this case, been the most common outcome of the capitalist transformation,[77] often associated with the emergence of local welfare capitalism and subregional models of political economy that complemented those at the national level.[78] This process has simultaneously involved path-dependent and path-departing patterns of transformation in the allocation and redistribution of welfare benefits.[79]

Conclusion

This chapter has discussed the main social aspects of the transformations that have occurred in Central and Eastern Europe since the end of communism. It has discussed the main changes in the labor structure and their repercussions in terms of social welfare, with associated social problems and social pathologies. It has also analyzed ten mistaken expectations experts and policy makers have had concerning the transformation, expectations that have greatly hindered full democratic stabilization and consolidation. The lessons that must be learned from this experience show that these views were poorly formulated and that important adjustments are required. Not only should the social aspects of transformations have been considered more carefully, but so should have the timing and sequencing of reforms, with more attention to emerging social problems and their impact on the attitudes of the population toward the new democratic order. Overall, the socioeconomic situation has drastically improved in these countries since the end of communism, but the multiplication of possibilities has also led to a multiplication of risks. As people tend to evaluate their present conditions in relational terms, often looking at the past through rose-tinted lenses, current socioeconomic insecurity has cast a shadow over a possibly brighter future. It would, in this case, be misleading to assume that since the first and most difficult part of the transition has occurred, the future will unquestionably bring peace, prosperity, and stability. In order to avoid past mistakes and increase the prospects for future improvements in this region and in other countries currently on the road to democratization and democratic consolidation, a more careful analysis of future social problems is necessary, as is the adaptation of policies and reforms to the peculiar culture of each nation. Increasing poverty and income inequality represent, in this context, important variables to take into account, as they influence not only individuals' life chances and quality of life but also their prospects for societal success. As discussed elsewhere,[80] poverty and inequality produce locked-in and self-reinforcing mechanisms that constrain the resources available to the individual and thus preclude full integration into society. But poverty and inequality may also lead to anger and feelings of resentment or a desire for revenge that create distrust in the existing social order, potentially motivating actions that could lead to civil conflict or war. Thus, establishing well-functioning welfare institutions is crucial not only to increase the social welfare of citizens and, by so doing, their long-term advancement and full development in society but also to establish long-term trust in and loyalty to the system.

Study Questions

1. What are the main social changes that have occurred in Central and Eastern Europe since the end of communism?
2. What are the main socioeconomic challenges that citizens faced immediately after the fall of the Berlin Wall?
3. What are the most important social problems and social pathologies that have emerged since 1989?
4. What are the most important social achievements of the transition from communism to democracy?
5. How have these social aspects influenced citizens' perceptions and the process of democratization in postcommunist societies?

Suggested Readings

Cook, L. J. "Eastern Europe and Russia." In *The Oxford Handbook of the Welfare State*, edited by F. G. Castles, S. Leibfried, J. Lewis, H. Obinger, and C. Pierson, 671–88. Oxford: Oxford University Press, 2010.

Deacon, B. *The New Eastern Europe: Social Policy, Past, Present and Future.* London: SAGE, 1992.

Frye, T. *Building States and Markets after Communism: The Perils of Polarized Democracy.* New York: Cambridge University Press, 2010.

Kornai, J. *Economics of Shortage.* 2 vols. Amsterdam: North-Holland Publishing Company, 1980.

Orenstein, M. A. *Out of the Red: Building Capitalism and Democracy in Postcommunist Europe.* Ann Arbor: University of Michigan Press, 2001.

Websites

UNICEF TransMonEE Database: http://www.transmonee.org

World Bank World Development Indicators: http://data.worldbank.org/data-catalog/world-development-indicators

World Values Survey: http://www.worldvaluessurvey.org

Notes

Special thanks go to Sharon Wolchik, Nancy Meyers, and two anonymous reviewers for very constructive comments on an earlier version of this chapter.

1. V. J. Bunce and S. L. Wolchik, "Defeating Dictators Electoral Change and Stability in Competitive Authoritarian Regimes," *World Politics* 62, no. 1(2010): 43–86.

2. A. C. Hemerijck, *Changing Welfare States* (Oxford: Oxford University Press, 2012); S. Romano, *The Political and Social Construction of Poverty: Central and Eastern European Countries in Transition* (Bristol: Policy Press, 2014).

3. A. Nölke and A. Vliegenthart, "Enlarging the Varieties of Capitalism: The Emergence of Dependent Market Economies in East Central Europe," *World Politics* 61, no. 4 (2009): 670–702.

4. International Labor Organization (ILO), *The Financial and Economic Crisis: A Decent Work Response* (Geneva: ILO, 2009).

5. UNICEF, TransMonEE Database (Florence: UNICEF Innocenti Research Centre, 2013).

6. Profit, ed., *European Studies on Equalities and Social Cohesion 1/2005 and 2/5* (Lodz: Lodz University Press, 2005).

7. European Bank for Reconstruction and Development (EBRD), *Transition Report 2007: Life in Transition: A Survey of People's Experiences and Attitudes* (London: EBRD, 2007), 7.

8. EBRD, *Transition Report 2007*, 23.

9. For a more detailed discussion, see C. Offe, "The Political Economy of Post-1989 Capitalism in East-Central Europe," in *1989 as a Political World Event: Democracy, Europe and the New International System in the Age of Globalization*, ed. J. Rupnik (London: Routledge, 2013), 152–68.

10. M. Myant and J. Drahokoupil, *Economics of Transition: Russia, Eastern Europe, and Central Asia* (Hoboken, NJ: Wiley-Blackwell, 2010).

11. International Social Security Association (ISSA), *Social Security Programs throughout the World: Czech Republic, Hungary, Poland, Slovakia, Estonia, Latvia, Lithuania, Albania, Bosnia-Herzegovina, Bulgaria, Croatia, Montenegro, Romania, TFYR of Macedonia, Serbia, Armenia, Azerbaijan, Belarus, Georgia, Kazakhstan, Kyrgyzstan, Moldova, Russian Federation, Tajikistan, Turkmenistan, Ukraine, Uzbekistan* (Geneva: ISSA, 2014).

12. For a more detailed discussion, see A. Cerami and P. Stubbs, "Post-communist Welfare Capitalisms: Bringing Institutions and Political Agency Back In," in *Comparative Public Policy*, ed. M. Hill (London: SAGE, 2013), 2:360–64.

13. K. Armingeon and G. Bonoli, eds., *The Politics of Postindustrial Welfare States: Adapting Post-war Social Policies to New Social Risks* (London: Routledge, 2006); G. Esping-Andersen and B. Palier, *Trois leçons sur l'État-providence* (Paris: Seuil, 2008).

14. D. Szelewa and M. P. Polakowski, "Who Cares? Changing Patterns of Childcare in Central and Eastern Europe," *Journal of European Social Policy* 18, no. 2 (2008): 115–31.

15. J. Aidukaite, *Poverty, Urbanity and Social Policy: Central and Eastern Europe Compared* (New York: Nova Science Publishers, 2009).

16. For country comparisons, see ISSA, *Social Security Programs throughout the World*.

17. K. Thelen, *How Institutions Evolve: The Political Economy of Skills in Germany, Britain, the United States, and Japan* (Cambridge: Cambridge University Press, 2004); A. Cerami, "New Social Risks in Central and Eastern Europe: The Need for a New Empowering Politics of the Welfare State," *Czech Sociological Review* 44, no. 6 (2008): 1089–110; M. R. Busemeyer, "Asset Specificity, Institutional Complementarities and the Variety of Skill Regimes in Coordinated Market Economies," *Socio-economic Review* 7, no. 3 (2009): 375–406.

18. P. A. Hall and M. Lamont, *Successful Societies: How Institutions and Culture Matter for Health* (Cambridge: Cambridge University Press, 2009).

19. A. Cerami, *Permanent Emergency Welfare Regimes in Sub-Saharan Africa: The Exclusive Origins of Dictatorship and Democracy* (Basingstoke, UK: Palgrave Macmillan, 2013).

20. M. Stambolieva and S. Dehnert, eds., *Welfare States in Transition: 20 Years after the Yugoslav Welfare Model* (Sofia: Friedrich Ebert Foundation—Office Bulgaria, 2011).

21. D. Acemoglu and J. Robinson, *Why Nations Fail: Historical Origins of Poverty* (New York: Crown Publishing Group, 2012).

22. Romano, *The Political and Social Construction of Poverty*.

23. P. Vanhuysse, "Power, Order and the Politics of Social Policy in Central and Eastern Europe," in *Post-communist Welfare Pathways: Theorizing Social Policy Transformations in Central and Eastern Europe*, ed. A. Cerami and P. Vanhuysse, (Basingstoke, UK: Palgrave Macmillan, 2009), 53–72.

24. P. Stubbs and S. Zrinščak, "Re-scaling Emergent Social Policies in South Eastern Europe," in *Social Policy Review 21: Analysis and Debate in Social Policy, 2009*, ed. K. Rummery, I. Greener, and C. Holden (Bristol: Policy Press, 2009), 285–306.

25. F. Fukuyama, *The End of History and the Last Man* (New York: Avon Book, 1992).

26. Philippe C. Schmitter, "Twenty-Five Years, Fifteen Findings," *Journal of Democracy* 21, no. 1 (2010): 17–28.

27. ESS Round 5, "European Social Survey Round 5 Data" (2010). Data file edition 3.0. Norwegian Social Science Data Services, Norway—Data Archive and distributor of ESS data, http://www.europeansocialsurvey.org/data/download.html?r=5 (accessed October 8, 2013).

28. H.-D. Klingemann, D. Fuchs, and Z. Jan, eds., *Democracy and Political Culture in Eastern Europe* (New York: Routledge, 2006).

29. Schmitter, "Twenty-Five Years, Fifteen Findings."

30. J. Rupnik and J. Zielonka, "Introduction: The State of Democracy 20 Years On: Domestic and External Factors," *East European Politics and Societies and Cultures* 27, no. 1 (2013): 3–25.

31. A. Przeworski, *Democracy and the Market: Political and Economic Reforms in Eastern Europe and Latin America*. Studies in Rationality and Social Change (Cambridge: Cambridge University Press, 1991).

32. R. Inglehart, *Subjective Well-Being Rankings of 82 Societies (Based on Combined Happiness and Life Satisfaction Scores)*, World Values Survey, 2004, http://www.worldvaluessurvey.org/wvs/articles/folder_published/publication_488 (accessed October 8, 2013).

33. The Kuznets curve implies that a necessary degree of inequality must first materialize before citizens can succeed in obtaining a certain level of income.

34. K. Armingeon and G. Bonoli, eds., *The Politics of Postindustrial Welfare States: Adapting Post-war Social Policies to New Social Risks* (London: Routledge, 2006).

35. J. E. Stiglitz, *Globalization and Its Discontents* (London: Penguin Books, 2002).

36. P. Hamm, L. P. King, and D. Stuckler, "Mass Privatization, State Capacity, and Economic Growth in Post-communist Countries," *American Sociological Review* 77, no. 2 (2012): 295–324; M. Blyth, *Austerity: The History of a Dangerous Idea* (New York: Oxford University Press, 2013).

37. Schmitter, "Twenty-Five Years, Fifteen Findings."

38. V. A. Schmidt and M. Thatcher, eds., *Resilient Liberalism in Europe's Political Economy* (Cambridge: Cambridge University Press, 2013).

39. European Bank for Reconstruction and Development (EBRD), *Transition Report 2011: Life in Transition after the Crisis* (London: EBRD, 2011).

40. EBRD, *Transition Report 2011*, 4.

41. J. C. Alexander, R. Jacobs, and P. Smith, eds., *The Oxford Handbook of Cultural Sociology* (Oxford: Oxford University Press, 2012).

42. H. K. Anheier and Y. R. Isar, "Introduction: Introducing the Cultures and Globalization Series and the Cultural Economy," in *The Cultural Economy*, ed. H. K. Anheier and Y. R. Isar (London: SAGE Publications, 2008), 1–13.

43. J. Beckert and M. Zafirovski, eds., *International Encyclopedia of Economic Sociology* (London: Routledge, 2006).

44. P. Pierson, *Politics in Time: History, Institutions and Social Analysis* (Princeton, NJ: Princeton University Press, 2004).

45. W. Sandholtz and R. Taagepera, "Corruption, Culture, and Communism," *International Review of Sociology/Revue international de sociologie* 15, no. 1 (2005): 109.

46. Sandholtz and Taagepera, "Corruption, Culture, and Communism," 109.

47. J. Kornai, B. Rothstein, and S. Rose-Ackerman, eds., *Creating Social Trust in Post-socialist Transition* (Basingstoke, UK: Palgrave Macmillan, 2004).

48. For a review of works by academics that reflect this view, see Schmitter, "Twenty-Five Years, Fifteen Findings."

49. G. Pop-Eleches and J. Tucker, *Communism's Shadow: Historical Legacies, and Political Values and Behavior*, Princeton University, http://www.princeton.edu/~gpop/biography.html (book manuscript in preparation).

50. T. Inglot, "Western Welfare States Watched from the East during the Cold War: Condemnation, Competition and Creative Learning," *Journal of International and Comparative Social Policy* 29, no. 3 (2013): 241–57.

51. C. Offe, *Herausforderungen der Demokratie. Zur Integrations- und Leistungsfähigkeitpolitischer Institutionen* (Frankfurt: Campus Verlag, 2003).

52. Offe, "The Political Economy of Post-1989 Capitalism in East-Central Europe."

53. For a critical review, see Hemerijck, *Changing Welfare States*.

54. D. Ost, *The Defeat of Solidarity: Anger and Politics in Postcommunist Europe* (Ithaca, NY: Cornell University Press, 2005); P. Vanhuysse, *Divide and Pacify: Strategic Social Policies and Political Protests in Post-communist Democracies* (Budapest: CEU Press, 2006); D. Bohle and B. Greskovits, *Capitalist Diversity on Europe's Periphery* (Ithaca, NY: Cornell University Press, 2012).

55. S. Haggard and R. Kaufman, *Development, Democracy, and Welfare States* (Princeton, NJ: Princeton University Press, 2008).

56. Acemoglu and Robinson, *Why Nations Fail.*

57. N. Bandelj, "Relational Work and Economic Sociology," *Politics and Society* 40, no. 2 (2012): 175–201.

58. ESS Round 5, "European Social Survey Round 5 Data (2010). Data file edition 3.0. Norwegian Social Science Data Services, Norway—Data Archive and distributor of ESS data," http://www.europeansocialsurvey.org/data/download.html?r=5 (accessed October 8, 2013).

59. Jon Elster, Claus Offe, and Ulrich K. Preuss, *Institutional Design in Post-communist Societies: Rebuilding the Ship at Sea* (Cambridge: Cambridge University Press, 1998).

60. C. De la Porte and B. Deacon, *Contracting Companies and Consultancies: The EU and the Social Policies of Accession Countries* (Helsinki: Helsinki Stake University, 2002); A. Cerami, *Social Policy in Central and Eastern Europe: The Emergence of a New European Welfare Regime* (Berlin: LIT Verlag, 2006); M. A. Vachudova, "The European Union: The Causal Behemoth of Transnational Influence on Postcommunist Politics," in *Transnational Actors in Central and East European Transitions*, ed. M. A. Orenstein, S. Bloom, and N. Lindstrom (Pittsburgh: University of Pittsburg Press, 2008), 19–37.

61. K. Featherstone and C. M. Radaelli, eds., *The Politics of Europeanization* (Oxford: Oxford University Press, 2003).

62. T. Inglot, *Welfare States in East Central Europe, 1919–2004* (Cambridge: Cambridge University Press, 2008); Inglot, "Western Welfare States Watched from the East."

63. W. Streeck and K. Thelen, eds., *Beyond Continuity: Institutional Change in Advanced Political Economies* (Oxford: Oxford University Press, 2005).

64. J. Drahokoupil and S. Domonkos, "Averting the Funding-Gap Crisis: East European Pension Reforms after 2008," *Global Social Policy* 12, no. 3 (2012): 283–99.

65. P. A. Hall, "Institutions, Interests and Ideas in the Comparative Political Economy of the Industrialized Nations," in *Comparative Politics: Rationality, Culture and Structure*, ed. M. Lichbach and A. Zuckerman (New York: Cambridge University Press, 1997).

66. M. A. Orenstein, *Privatizing Pensions: The Transnational Campaign for Social Security Reforms* (Princeton, NJ: Princeton University Press, 2008); M. A. Orenstein, S. Bloom, and N. Lindstrom, eds., *Transnational Actors in Central and East European Transitions* (Pittsburgh: University of Pittsburg Press, 2008).

67. B. Palier and Y. Surel, "Les 'Trois I' et l'analyse de l'état en action," *Revue française de science politique* 55, no. 1 (2005): 7–32.

68. D. Stark and I. Bruszt, *Postsocialist Pathways: Transforming Politics and Property in East Central Europe* (Cambridge: Cambridge University Press, 1998).

69. G. Ekiert and D. Ziblatt, "Democracy in Central and Eastern Europe One Hundred Years On," *East European Politics and Societies and Cultures* 27, no. 1 (2013): 90–107.

70. U. Dolata, *The Transformative Capacity of New Technologies: A Theory of Sociotechnical Change* (London: Routledge, 2013).

71. M. Goodhart et al., *Democratic Imperatives: Innovations in Rights, Participation, and Economic Citizenship: Report of the Task Force on Democracy, Economic Security, and Social Justice in a Volatile World* (Washington, DC: American Political Science Association, 2012).

72. D. C. North, J. J. Wallis, and B. Weingast, *Violence and Social Orders: A Conceptual Framework for Interpreting Recorded Human History* (Cambridge: Cambridge University Press, 2009).

73. G. Esping-Andersen, *The Three Worlds of Welfare Capitalism* (Cambridge: Polity Press, 1990).

74. I. Szelényi and K. Wilk, "Institutional Transformation in European Post-communist Regimes," in *The Oxford Handbook of Comparative Institutional Analysis*, ed. G. Morgan (New York: Oxford University Press, 2010), 565–87.

75. M. Weber, *Economy and Society*, ed. Günther Roth and Claus Wittich. 3 vols. (New York: Bedminster Press, [1922] 1968); M. Weber, *The Protestant Ethic and the Spirit of Capitalism* (New York: Scribner's Sons, [1904–1905]1958).

76. Cerami, *Social Policy in Central and Eastern Europe*; S. Golinowska, P. Hengstenberg, and M. Żukowski, eds., *Diversity and Commonality in European Social Policies: The Forging of a European Social Model* (Warsaw: Wydawnictwo Naukowe Scholar and Friedrich-Ebert-Stiftung, 2009).

77. D. Szikra and B. Tomka, "Social Policy in East Central Europe: Major Trends in the 20th Century," in *Post-communist Welfare Pathways: Theorizing Social Policy Transformations in Central and Eastern Europe*, ed. A. Cerami and P. Vanhuysse (Basingstoke, UK: Palgrave Macmillan, 2009).

78. B. Hancké, M. Rhodes, and M. Thatcher, eds., *Beyond Varieties of Capitalism: Conflict, Contradictions, and Complementarities in the European Economy* (Oxford: Oxford University Press, 2007); Bohle and Greskovits, *Capitalist Diversity on Europe's Periphery*.

79. A. Cerami and P. Vanhuysse, eds., *Post-communist Welfare Pathways: Theorizing Social Policy Transformations in Central and Eastern Europe* (Basingstoke, UK: Palgrave Macmillan, 2009).

80. Cerami, *Permanent Emergency Welfare Regimes in Sub-Saharan Africa*.

CHAPTER 5

Ethnicity, Nationalism, and the Expansion of Democracy

Zsuzsa Csergő

As Central and East European societies emerged from communism, people throughout the region expressed their preference for democracy, free markets, and the European Union (EU). Many in the West expected the EU to supersede the political ideology of nationalism, which has traditionally pursued the establishment of territorially sovereign, culturally homogeneous nation-states. In earlier centuries, efforts to achieve such congruence between the political and national unit in Europe involved aggressive efforts to change state boundaries, eject or assimilate nonconforming groups to "purify" the nation, or encourage minority populations to repatriate to other countries.[1] By the end of the 1980s, such methods of nation-state creation were no longer acceptable in the western part of the continent. The European Union seemed to offer the best prospect for moving beyond the era of the traditional nation-state.

A lesson that much of the scholarly literature about nationalism drew from West European development in this period was that, if democratization and marketization could progress unhindered, politics grounded in ethnic and national identity would lose its relevance, and more advanced—rational, individualist, and inclusive—notions of citizenship would take its place.[2] These were the thoughts voiced from within the Iron Curtain during the communist decades by dissident Czech, Hungarian, Polish, and other intellectuals who articulated alternative visions of a free society and spoke poignantly about universal human values and inalienable individual rights and freedoms.

Against the backdrop of such expectations, the story of Central and Eastern Europe after the collapse of the communist regimes is filled with reasons for disappointment. Even after the initial euphoria over the end of communism, the voices expressing themselves most forcefully spoke about "nationhood" and, in the overwhelming majority of cases, exalted the supposed inalienable rights of groups rather than individuals. Ethnically conceived national groups all over the postcommunist countries of Central and Eastern Europe viewed democratization as the opportunity finally to achieve or consolidate sovereignty over territories they claimed as their "national homelands." National aspirations contributed to the collapse of all three multinational federations (the Soviet Union, Yugoslavia, and Czechoslovakia). Of the seventeen countries commonly considered to belong to this region, twelve were established or reestablished after 1989 along national lines. Only five countries continued within their existing borders. Conflicts over nation

121

building became significant features of the difficult process of regime change in most of these states.

Nationalism not only remained relevant after the collapse of communism but emerged as the most powerful ideology that most important and popular political elites and parties advanced and that publics in these countries found appealing. At the same time, the desire to "return to Europe" and join Western institutions was also a very significant motivation throughout the region. In some cases, aspirations to strengthen national cultures while joining an integrated Europe seemed fully compatible. For instance, people throughout the West cheered the fall of the Berlin Wall, which led to the subsequent reunification of the German state. Although wary of the disintegration of the Soviet state, Westerners also celebrated the reestablishment of the three Baltic states as examples of forward-looking, Western-oriented nationalism. When mass nationalist violence broke out in former Yugoslavia, however, influential public voices in the West began asking whether Central and East Europeans were returning to their violent past rather than transitioning into a peaceful and prosperous future in a common European home. Some argued that ancient hatreds made the rebirth of nationalism inevitable in such places as the Balkans.[3] Others argued that the process of democratization engendered manipulative elites' interest in employing nationalism.[4] Such arguments are often associated with a debate between "primordialism" and "constructivism" in nationalism scholarship. The first label describes explanations based on the assumption that enduring elements of ethnic kinship serve as "primordial" sources of nationalism. Thew second label describes arguments that emphasize the significance of institutions, particularly the modern state, and the role of political actors in "constructing" nationhood.[5] An increasing number of scholars today question the usefulness of these labels and aim to develop more nuanced explanations for the salience of ethnicity and nationalism in contemporary societies.[6]

Developments in other parts of the world since 1989 have demonstrated that neither the popular appeal of nationalism nor the problems that this ideology poses for democratic governance are specific to the postcommunist region. Wherever political elites design nationalist strategies, the process reveals sources of tension rooted in the "Janus-faced" character of nationalism: as with other political ideologies, nationalism is forward-looking in the sense that it articulates a vision of the future; at the same time, nationalist strategies almost always call for turning to the past for self-definition.[7] When nationalists claim self-government rights for "the nation" on a "national" territory or "homeland," they usually offer a certain interpretation of history to justify these claims. Whether such a historiography relies on historical evidence is less important than the degree to which it can foster a sense of shared history and purpose. To express this idea, "national myth" is the term most often used to describe national stories. Some national myths have been more successful than others in accommodating ethnic diversity. The so-called civic type of nationalism, which builds community on shared political traditions, is potentially more inclusive than "ethnic nationalism," which requires members of the nation to share a common ethnicity. Nonetheless, even countries commonly considered textbook cases of "civic nationalism," such as Britain, France, and the United States, reveal significant similarities to "ethnic nationalism," as schools, churches, the media, the military, and various other state and private or public institutions perpetuate unified national stories and literatures and mental maps of national homelands.[8]

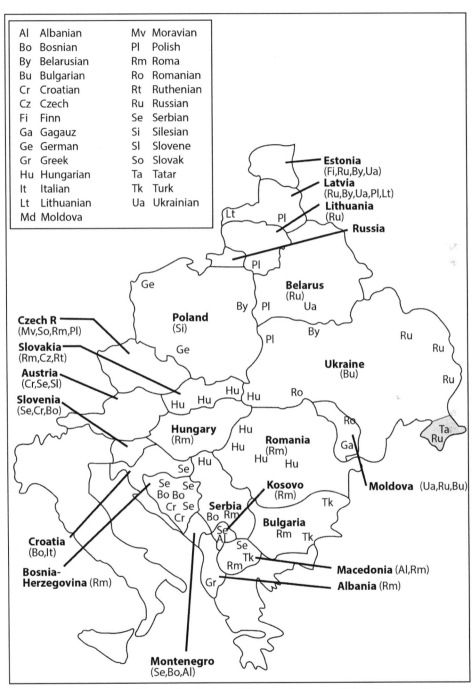

Al	Albanian	Mv	Moravian
Bo	Bosnian	Pl	Polish
By	Belarusian	Rm	Roma
Bu	Bulgarian	Ro	Romanian
Cr	Croatian	Rt	Ruthenian
Cz	Czech	Ru	Russian
Fi	Finn	Se	Serbian
Ga	Gagauz	Si	Silesian
Ge	German	Sl	Slovene
Gr	Greek	So	Slovak
Hu	Hungarian	Ta	Tatar
It	Italian	Tk	Turk
Lt	Lithuanian	Ua	Ukrainian
Md	Moldova		

Estonia
(Fi,Ru,By,Ua)
Latvia
(Ru,By,Ua,Pl,Lt)
Lithuania
(Ru)
Russia

Lt

Pl

Pl

Ge

Belarus
(Ru)

By   Pl   Ua

Czech R ——
(Mv,So,Rm,Pl)
Slovakia
(Rm,Cz,Rt)
Austria
(Cr,Se,Sl)
Slovenia
(Se,Cr,Bo)

Poland
(Si)

Ge

By

Pl

Ru

Ru

Ukraine
(Bu)

Ru

Hu Hu

Hu

Ro

Hu

Ro

Ta
Ru

Hungary
(Rm)

Hu

Se

Hu

Hu

Romania
(Rm)

Hu

Hu

Ga

Moldova (Ua,Ru,Bu)

Se

Se   Se
Bo Bo
Cr Se
Cr

Serbia
Bo   Rm
Se
Al

Kosovo
(Rm)

Tk

Bulgaria
Rm   Tk

Croatia
(Bo,It)

Se
Tk
Rm

Macedonia (Al,Rm)

Bosnia-
Herzegovina (Rm)

Gr

Albania (Rm)

Montenegro
(Se,Bo,Al)

Map 5.1.   Ethnic Minorities in Central and Eastern Europe, 2014. The map includes minorities over 0.2 percent of the population in the latest official census for each state.

In many instances, the national myth contains stories about ethnic competition over territory, invoking memories of past ethnic dominance and subordination, which continue to influence current state- and nation-building processes.[9] Yet not all ethnic groups engage in national competition. A key difference between ethnic and national groups is that, although ethnic groups aim to reproduce particular cultures, only national groups claim self-government rights on a particular territory. In postcommunist Central and Eastern Europe, the majority and minority groups that articulated competing notions of self-government rights were national groups that defined "nation" on the basis of ethnic markers—most commonly language, in some cases religion. Yet significant differences emerged in the way national aspirations were articulated and posed against one another. Before offering explanations for these differences, the following pages provide a brief account of state and nation building in the period that preceded democratization, highlighting processes that created the conditions in which postcommunist democratization and nationalism subsequently took shape.

Nationalism before Democratic Competition

The pursuit of modern nation-states by nationalist political elites and counter-elites within the Hapsburg Empire began in the second part of the nineteenth century, and the dynamics of these efforts revealed the fundamentally competitive character of modern nationalism. Whether in the framework of the multinational Hapsburg state (reconstituted after 1867 as the dualist Austro-Hungarian Empire) or its successor states, the nationalist policies that a dominant ethnic group adopted invariably triggered resentment and engendered conflicting nationalist aspirations from other groups. During this process national literatures emerged in vernacular languages, and national historiographies were written and became justifications for nationalist demands. Czechs and Hungarians defined their national myths and aspirations in opposition to Austria's Germans. After the creation of the dualist state, the same pattern remained characteristic in both parts of the monarchy. In the Austrian part, Czechs and Slovenes challenged German cultural dominance and articulated unsuccessful calls for national sovereignty. In the Hungarian part, the nationalist movements of non-Hungarians (Slovaks, Croats, and Romanians) encountered rejection by Hungarian elites.[10] Besides challenging one another, nationalist political elites also competed for international support and legitimization for their conflicting notions of national power. The complex matrix of these domestic and international interests led Austria-Hungary into World War I and, at the end of the war, resulted in the dissolution of the monarchy into its successor states.

When the victorious powers agreed to establish the successor states at the end of World War I, they relied on the Wilsonian principle of national self-determination. The demographic patterns of the region, however, made the delineation of clear "national" borders impossible. The states created to bring justice to previously subordinate national groups of the monarchy also became multinational, with new "titular" nations attempting to establish political and cultural hegemony over national minorities. Although relations of dominance and subordination were reversed after the dissolution of the Austro-Hungarian state, the same pattern of nation building continued, with multiple groups sharing the same state but holding conflicting notions about legitimate territorial sovereignty.

Incompatible narratives about the "justice" of the post–World War I settlements became part of conflicting national historiographies that have remained significant sources of tension over territorial sovereignty in the region.

Sovereignty is a fundamental principle of political organization and also one of the most contested because it takes different forms, and these forms are at times incompatible with one another.[11] As J. Samuel Barkin and Bruce Cronin observe, "There has been a historical tension between state sovereignty, which stresses the link between sovereign authority and a defined territory, and national sovereignty, which emphasizes a link between sovereign authority and a defined population."[12] This tension had become particularly apparent in Central and Eastern Europe by the mid-nineteenth century and remained salient throughout the region's history. Yugoslavia, created to provide southern Slav peoples with a common state, in reality comprised a diversity of national groups that maintained strong prejudices and reproaches against one another. A famous expression of Slovene prejudices, for instance, is the 1927 statement by Catholic party leader Anton Korošec: "In Yugoslavia it is thus: the Serbs rule, the Croats debate, and the Slovenes work."[13] Even in Czechoslovakia, where the leadership established the strongest democratic institutions in the region, large national minority populations remained discontented with their status and continued to challenge the legitimacy of the new state.

With the political principle of national self-determination internationally legitimized, competing nationalist aspirations crystallized in the interwar period and formed the basis for strategies that later escalated into some of the atrocities committed during World War II. The Hungarian government focused its efforts on regaining lost territories and population. Wary of this Hungarian policy of irredentism, neighboring governments that had gained significant territories from historic Hungary designed aggressive economic and cultural policies to achieve more effective control over those territories and their inhabitants. Greater Romania, for example, based its institutional policies primarily on reordering the ethnic hierarchy in Transylvania in favor of Romanian dominance.[14] Hungarian organizations forcefully challenged these policies. Similarly, in Czechoslovakia many Germans and Hungarians joined political parties that challenged the legitimacy of the state. These groups felt vindicated when Adolf Hitler dismembered Czechoslovakia in 1938, occupied the Czech Lands, and helped to redraw contested political borders throughout the region. The supposed right of the sizable German-speaking population of interwar Czechoslovakia, the Sudeten Germans, to belong to a common German nation-state served as a pretext for Hitler's destruction of the Czechoslovak state. After Germany's show of military might, the governments of Hungary, Romania, and Slovakia (a state that Hitler helped create) each became Hitler's allies at various times of the war, trusting that their participation on the victor's side would help them establish, reclaim, or maintain sovereignty over mutually claimed "national" territories and peoples. As a result of Hitler's policies, the Hungarian government was able to reannex two regions with majority Hungarian populations (the southern region of Czechoslovakia in November 1938 and northern Transylvania between 1940 and 1944). These sudden reversals of fortune were as traumatic to the Slovak and Romanian inhabitants of these territories as they had been for Hungarians after World War I. After the defeat of the Axis powers at the end of World War II, the post–World War I borders were reestablished, and the conditions for nationalist policies changed significantly.

The evolution of Polish state and nation building provides another example of traumatic shifts in territorial and ethnocultural boundaries in the context of great power politics. By the end of the eighteenth century, the territories that had once been part of the medieval Polish kingdom were split among the Russian, German, and Austrian empires. When an independent Polish state was created at the end of World War I, that state incorporated an ethnically diverse population with complex histories of competition that provided significant sources of conflict during the interwar period. This multiethnic society was devastated during World War II. After the division of Poland by the Soviet Union and Germany in 1941, the violence perpetuated on that territory (primarily through state-designed strategies of ethnic cleansing but also through violence committed by social actors) annihilated one-third of the population—including almost the entire population of Polish Jews and large numbers of Poles, Ukrainians, and other ethnicities.[15] The peace agreements at the end of World War II re-created a Polish state but within territorial boundaries that were moved significantly to the west. The boundary shift was coupled with ethnic cleansing ("unmixing") of a different kind: millions of ethnic Germans from the western part of the new Polish state were forced out of their homes and moved to postwar Germany, and large numbers of Poles and Ukrainians were forced to resettle in the west.[16] As a result of these traumatic territorial and demographic changes, the Polish state turned from a long history of ethnic diversity to significant ethnic homogeneity.

Nationalist competition contributed also to the collapse of Yugoslavia in 1941, when Hitler and Benito Mussolini divided the state among Germany, Italy, Hungary, and Bulgaria and established, in the center of the former federation, a Croatian state ruled by the fascist Ustaša. In the bloody civil wars that engulfed Yugoslavia in subsequent years, the Ustaša government led a violent campaign against Jews, Roma, Serbs, and other groups; Yugoslav Partisans fought to defend villagers against terror; and the extreme nationalists among Serbian Četniks engaged in revenge attacks against ethnic Croatians, Muslims, and Partisans. By the end of the war, over 1 million people had been killed, including Serbs, Croats, Bosnian-Herzegovinian Muslims, Danube Swabians (a German-speaking ethnic group), Jews, Slovenes, and Roma.

Against the backdrop of such violence, many communist leaders in the region, among whom ethnic minorities were represented in disproportionately high numbers, viewed internationalism as an appealing alternative to nationalism. Although communism provided leaders with unprecedented power to conduct "social engineering," none of these regimes succeeded in creating homogeneity in societies where multiple groups had earlier competed for national rights. There emerged no sizable "nonnational" Yugoslav population in Yugoslavia or Czechoslovak population in Czechoslovakia, capable of holding these federations together when the communist regimes began collapsing in 1989.[17] The Soviet state was similarly unable to engender nonnational identities and loyalties.

Despite an initial emphasis on internationalism, in practice nationalism remained a key organizing principle during the communist period.[18] In Yugoslavia, communist leader Josip Broz Tito made the eradication of national antagonisms his primary goal in 1945 and suppressed all overt manifestations of ethnic sentiment. Nonetheless, by the end of the 1960s, Slovenian, Croatian, Serbian, and other national identities were reasserting themselves in literature and the arts, and by the mid-1970s these groups had achieved self-government in the constituent republics of the Yugoslav federation. In the

Photo 5.1. Roma refugee camp in Zvecan, north of Kosovo, November 1999. Although the exact figure is unknown, millions of Roma live in often substandard conditions throughout Central and Eastern Europe and often have disproportionately high unemployment rates. (Lubomir Kotek/OSCE)

other part of the region that fell under Moscow's dominance, each of the "brotherly states" of Central and Eastern Europe pursued its own brand of nationalism in domestic politics.[19] The postwar Czechoslovak government, for instance, declared ethnic Germans and Hungarians collectively guilty of having contributed to Hitler's destruction of Czechoslovakia and gained Soviet approval for the expulsion of these ethnic groups from the country. Based on the so-called Beneš Decrees (named for the state's president, Eduard Beneš), Czechoslovakia expelled the overwhelming majority of ethnic Germans to Germany and a large percentage of the Hungarian population, including much of the Hungarian educated class, to Hungary.[20] Those who remained in the state were denied citizenship rights until 1948. Despite such a drastic policy to achieve an ethnic balance favoring the state's two titular groups, the Czechs and the Slovaks, a significant number of Hungarians remained in the Slovak part of Czechoslovakia. Throughout the communist decades, they were subject to economic, cultural, and educational policies that severely restricted their ability to reproduce their culture and improve their socioeconomic status. The relationship between the Czechs and the Slovaks was also tense from the beginning of cohabitation. Initial notions of a unified Czechoslovak identity were soon replaced by efforts to loosen Prague's control over the Slovak part of the land in a federative structure that better represented national interests.

Compared to Czechoslovakia, the postwar Romanian communist government adopted more minority-friendly policies. Because the ethnic Hungarian party was instrumental in the communist takeover in Romania, Hungarian minority leaders gained Moscow's support in achieving full citizenship rights, participation in the government, and the right to maintain cultural and educational institutions. The same Soviet government that in Czechoslovakia gave its full support to President Beneš's policies to expel the German and Hungarian minorities, in Romania facilitated the establishment of regional autonomy for Hungarians in Transylvania in 1952. Although this autonomous region was short-lived, the first communist-dominated Romanian government was much better disposed toward minorities overall than was the Beneš government in Czechoslovakia.[21] As the influence of ethnic Hungarian leaders in the Communist Party weakened, however, the government launched a nationalizing strategy that severely weakened the political status and social structure of the Hungarian community in Transylvania. Beginning in the mid-1960s, the government of Nicolae Ceaușescu launched a ruthless strategy to consolidate a centralized unitary national state. Ethnic Germans were offered incentives to emigrate to West Germany, and Hungarians were subjected to administrative, economic, and educational policies aimed at their assimilation. Against such a backdrop, ethnic Hungarians unsurprisingly played a significant role in the collapse of the Ceaușescu regime in December 1989.[22]

Of the unitary communist states in the region, Poland and Hungary were the only two that did not have sizable national minority groups. The small ethnic communities that existed in these states presented no systematic challenge to majority cultural dominance. Within the framework of the Moscow-led communist camp, the Hungarian government also indicated little interest in influencing the conditions of ethnic Hungarians living in the neighboring states. Under such circumstances, the significance of the national principle appeared less prominent in either case than it did in the region's multinational states. Yet the absence of internal national minorities did not make nationalist motivations irrelevant in these countries. In Poland, national aspirations contributed to the emergence of Solidarity, the most powerful anticommunist movement in the region in the 1980s. In Hungary, interest in the national principle strengthened by the end of the 1980s, especially with regard to Hungarian minorities living in the neighboring states.

Democratization and Nationalist Competition

With the collapse of communism came the promise of change, and for majorities and minorities alike, change brought a chance to redefine old ideas of citizenship and self-government. At the beginning of the process, most societies in the region experienced a unifying spirit of euphoria over the collapse of repressive regimes.[23] Democratization offered unprecedented opportunities for these societies to articulate differences through competitive elections, political parties, and parliamentary debates. The European Union offered a model of political integration and a way of transcending the nationalist competitions of the past. Yet the most influential political actors throughout the region articulated their intentions to achieve both stronger national sovereignty and European integration.

The international institutions that most of the newly elected governments aspired to join—the North Atlantic Treaty Organization (NATO), the Council of Europe, the Organization for Security and Co-operation in Europe (OSCE), the European Union—insisted on peaceful negotiations about sovereignty issues. As various majority and minority groups in the region asserted claims to "national" self-government, Western international institutions reasserted the principle of individual rights, but they also began adopting an impressive number of documents calling for the protection of the rights of minority cultures. These documents signaled increased international awareness that many states incorporate multiple nation-building processes and that tensions arising from these situations must find lasting solutions acceptable to all parties involved.[24]

Despite the relative consistency of international expectations and the shared objective of Central and East Europeans to return to a "common European home," the conditions under which this goal could be harmonized with nationalist aspirations varied. Consequently, there were significant variations in the way nationalism manifested itself throughout the region. The differences revealed themselves in the goals that leaders and groups articulated and the strategies they designed to achieve those goals. An overwhelming nationalist goal in the region was to establish national entities by creating new states (e.g., in former Yugoslavia and Czechoslovakia) or to reestablish precommunist state borders (in the Baltic region). Another form of nationalism pursued national dominance in existing states, despite minority opposition to this strategy (Romania and Bulgaria). A third form aimed at strengthening a common sense of nationhood beyond state borders (Hungary). The pages that follow offer explanations for these differences in nationalist strategy, emphasizing the influence of preexisting state structure (federal or unitary); national composition (whether national strategies involved internal or external national minorities); and the choices of national elites (to what extent majority and minority elites were willing to negotiate their claims within the emerging democratic institutions, employing the prospects of NATO and European integration in the process).

FROM MULTINATIONAL FEDERATIONS TO NATIONAL STATES

The nationalist movements that pursued state formation emerged in the three multinational federations: Czechoslovakia, the Soviet Union, and Yugoslavia. Although each of the three dissolving federal states was ethnically diverse, only a limited number of groups defined themselves in national terms and claimed rights to national self-government. In each case, the titular groups of substate administrative units were most likely to claim such rights. These were the Serbs, Slovenians, Macedonians, Montenegrins, and Croatians in former Yugoslavia; the Czechs and Slovaks in former Czechoslovakia; and the Estonians, Latvians, and Lithuanians in the former Soviet Union. In each case, those engaged in state formation had to answer the following questions: What would be the physical boundaries of the successor states? What would "the nation" mean within those boundaries? Who belonged to the new political community and under what terms? And what should happen to those who did not belong? In all cases, the political elites who led the movements for national independence played a very important role in shaping the debates about these questions. In the great majority of cases, nationalist claims were negotiated peacefully, within the channels of democratic political competition. In other cases, however, democratic forms of parliamentary debate and party competition were unable to contain national conflicts, and these conflicts escalated into devastating wars.

DEMOCRATIZATION DERAILED: NATIONALISM IN THE BALKANS

In former Yugoslavia, the substate borders of the republics did not coincide with people's mental maps of "historic homelands." Consequently, national self-determination became a vehemently contested idea in the Balkans, as multiple national groups living in a mixed demographic pattern claimed the same territory as "their own," and each group turned to a different national myth and conflicting interpretation of past relations of dominance and subordination, sacrifice and victimization.

Serbs and Croats composed the majority of the state's population as well as the overwhelming majority in the three largest republics—Serbia (and its autonomous provinces, Kosovo and Vojvodina), Croatia, and Bosnia-Herzegovina. Approximately 24 percent of Serbs lived outside the Republic of Serbia, and 22 percent of Croats lived outside Croatia. Tensions between these two groups influenced interethnic relations throughout Yugoslavia. Montenegrins generally identified with Serbs, and Muslims lived intermixed with Serbs and Croats. Only Slovenia and Macedonia, with their very small Serbian and Croatian populations, were not drawn into Serbian-Croatian competition.[25] In such a context, successive unilateral declarations of independence by nationalist elites contributed to a cycle of conflict that marked the entire decade of the 1990s and caused devastation and horror not seen in Europe since World War II.

The unilateral declaration of independence triggered military intervention even in Slovenia, where no other groups had articulated competing national claims for the same territory. The fight for independent Slovenia, however, was relatively uneventful compared to the brutal wars that followed in other parts of the disintegrating state. The Yugoslav army, by late 1991, had evolved into primarily a Serbian army. In the absence of Serbian claims for Slovenia as a "national homeland," European mediation quickly convinced the Yugoslav army to withdraw and hand over sovereignty to the Slovenian state in October 1991.

In other Yugoslav republics, where majority and minority political elites advanced competing and mutually incompatible claims for the same "national homeland," these claims mobilized large-scale ethnic support that led to violent conflict. The Serb Democratic Party in the Krajina region of Croatia, for instance, immediately challenged the emerging Croatian movement for an independent state by demanding administrative and cultural autonomy for the Serb-majority region. Unable to achieve this goal immediately, the leaders of the four Serb-controlled areas declared the formation of the Serb Autonomous Region of Krajina in January 1991 and added in March the same year that this region would "dissociate" from an independent Croatia and remain within Yugoslavia.

This sequence of unilateral declarations of national sovereignty exacerbated an already existing distrust and hostility among these groups and helped trigger a devastating war in Croatia. The government of Croatia on one side and the Yugoslav state presidency, as well as local Serbian authorities, on the other employed armed forces to resolve the crisis. The war ended in 1995 with the help of US and European mediation, after brutal destruction in Croatian cities and villages, great suffering among the civilian population, and "ethnic cleansing" on both sides that resulted in the displacement of more than a half million refugees. Today, the Serbian minority represents only slightly more than 4 percent of Croatia's population.

Competition over national sovereignty became particularly vicious in Bosnia-Herzegovina, a republic in which three groups began their armed fight for an acceptable state design in April 1992. The Party of Democratic Action, representing the majority Muslim population, advocated an independent and unitary Bosnia-Herzegovina, with no internal territorial division along national lines. The Serb Democratic Party first rejected separation from Yugoslavia and fought for a separate state in the Serb-populated areas—in the hope of future reunification with other Serbian-inhabited territories of (former) Yugoslavia. The Croatian Democratic Union allied itself with the Muslim party against the Bosnian Serbs but also staged its own secessionist attempt in Herzegovina from 1993 to 1994—a conflict resolved only through strong international pressure, which led to the formation of a Muslim-Croat federation. The war over the fate of Bosnia-Herzegovina lasted from 1992 to 1995 and involved the engagement of the Serbian and Croatian militaries as well as NATO forces. Although all three groups committed atrocities, Serbian troops were responsible for more crimes than their counterparts, and the Muslim population suffered most grievously.[26]

The Dayton Peace Accords, reached through international mediation in 1995, created a loose confederation that holds the Muslim-Croat federation and the Serb republic in the common state of Bosnia and Herzegovina, dividing the Muslim-Croat federation into separate national cantons and allowing the Bosnian Croats to maintain a close link with the Croatian state. Although the Serb Democratic Party no longer dominates politics in the Republika Srpska of Bosnia-Herzegovina, the main political parties representing the Serb population have continued to articulate desires for an independent state.

The other territory over which some of the most violent nationalist conflict emerged outside Bosnia-Herzegovina was Kosovo, a region that features prominently in the Serbian

Photo 5.2.   Croatian refugees fleeing from Bosnian forces in June 1993 near Travnik, when the Herzegovinan Croats turned on the Bosnians, creating an internal disaster. The Serbs reportedly sat in the hills laughing. (Jim Bartlett)

national myth. Before 1990, Kosovo was part of the Serbian republic of Yugoslavia but had a majority ethnic Albanian population. In 1990, Kosovo lost its autonomy under the emerging rule of Slobodan Milošević. As a result, the Albanians in this province were systematically excluded from institutions of political and economic power, and their means of cultural reproduction (such as education in the Albanian language) were virtually eliminated from state-sponsored institutions. When the opportunity for democratization presented itself, Albanian members of the Kosovo Assembly articulated the Kosovar Albanians' right to national self-determination as early as 1990. In September 1991, they organized a referendum in which an overwhelming majority of Kosovars (99.8 percent) voted for independence. After significant efforts to achieve independence through peaceful civil disobedience and the gradual construction of a "parallel state" (e.g., parallel institutions of education and health care), the National Movement for the Liberation of Kosovo (KLA) became impatient with this strategy and began a series of violent attacks against Serbs (police officers and civilians) in Kosovo. Serbian authorities responded with a massive offensive in July 1998, forcing the KLA to withdraw into the hills. The Serbs then began a ruthless and systematic process of ethnic cleansing, which resulted in approximately seven hundred thousand ethnic Albanian civilians from Kosovo being expelled from their villages and forced to flee to Albania or Macedonia. Despite international intervention, including two months of massive NATO bombings against military and industrial targets also in Serbia, the Serbian government refused to agree to an independent Kosovo. When Serb forces finally agreed in a June 1999 peace agreement to withdraw from Kosovo, the agreement guaranteed the continued territorial integrity of Yugoslavia (Serbia-Montenegro), including the province of Kosovo, which has been under United Nations administration since 1999. However, following the collapse of negotiations over the final status of Kosovo between local and international actors and the publication of a UN report calling for the independence of the former Serbian province[27] (albeit under international supervision), the Kosovo Assembly adopted a unilateral proclamation of independence on February 17, 2008. Swiftly recognized by the United States and some (though not all) EU member states, Kosovo's independence remains challenged by Serbia. Tensions over the border have decreased after an EU-brokered deal in April 2013 recognized Serb majority areas of Kosovo as autonomous at the municipal level; yet Kosovo suffers from weak state capacity and remains under considerable international supervision.[28]

INDEPENDENCE AND EU INTEGRATION: THE BALTIC STATES

The Baltic states of Estonia, Latvia, and Lithuania were reestablished without significant border disputes within the territorial boundaries that these states had before their forcible annexation to the Soviet Union in 1940. Although Russians had dominated the institutions of power at both the federal and republic levels and ethnic Russians had settled in these republics in significant numbers, there were no significant disputes over national territorial borders between Russian nationalist politicians and the leaders of independence movements in the Baltics.

An important factor in the absence of territorial disputes was that, although Russians were the ethnic group closely associated with Soviet federal power structures, the ethnic Russian population in the Baltic republics overwhelmingly comprised relatively recent settlers whom the native population viewed as colonizers. As the formerly dominant ethnic group in the Soviet Union, the Russians remaining in the Baltic states stood to lose the most at independence. Yet ethnic Russians articulated no systematic challenge to nationalist aspirations in the Baltics. The new states, with their prospects for European integration, offered better socioeconomic conditions than neighboring Russia. Rather than demanding self-government, let alone secession and unification with Russia, ethnic Russian political organizations contested the exclusionary aspects of citizenship and language laws and lobbied European institutions to pressure these governments to adopt more minority-friendly policies. At least at the beginning of the 1990s, speaking the Russian language did not signify ethnic or national identity in these states in the same way that language was the primary marker of Latvian, Estonian, or Lithuanian identity. The Russian-speaking population included people of different ethnicities who had switched to Russian as the language of advancement to higher status. Consequently, no commonly shared national myth existed among Russian speakers in the Baltic states that could have become the grounds for national sovereignty claims.[29] The only sizable historical minority in the Baltic region was the Polish minority in Lithuania. Although of roughly the same size as the state's Russian minority (at the time each made up roughly 10 percent of the population), the Polish minority articulated a stronger challenge to majority nation building than Russians in any of the three states—including Estonia and Latvia, where Russians made up a much higher proportion of the population.

The policies of the Russian government in Moscow constituted another significant factor accounting for differences between nation-building processes in the Yugoslav and Baltic regions. With over one hundred thousand Red Army troops stationed in the Baltic republics when the Soviet Union collapsed, many had feared violent Russian opposition to independence. Nevertheless, the Russian government agreed to withdraw these troops relatively quickly. In contrast to the Serbian leadership's involvement in mobilizing Serbian minorities in the secessionist republics and providing them with military resources, the Russian government aimed instead to eliminate discriminatory citizenship and language legislation in these countries through indirect pressure on their governments and complaints brought to European institutions.

In pursuit of national states, Baltic governments adopted policies to establish national dominance over the institutions of the new state. After 1990, there was a strong sense among these populations that democratization should bring national justice. Even though they were formally titular ethnicities in their republics during Soviet occupation, the share and status of indigenous ethnic groups had decreased dramatically due to large-scale deportation campaigns against the native population, the emigration of great numbers of Balts to the West, and the massive influx of Russians (see table 5.1).

As a result of these changes, Russian became the predominant language in the public domain, especially in the urban centers. The relationship between Russian and the titular national languages during the Soviet era remained that of one-sided bilingualism despite

Table 5.1.   Ethnic Composition of the Baltic States

Ethnic Composition of Estonia (2008 Census)

Nationality	Percentage of Population
Estonian	68.7
Russian	25.6
Ukrainian	2.1
Belarusian	1.2
Finn	0.8
Other	1.6

Ethnic Composition of Latvia (2009 Census)

Nationality	Percentage of Population
Latvian	59.3
Russian	27.8
Belarusian	3.6
Ukrainian	2.5
Polish	2.4
Lithuanian	1.3
Other	3.1

Ethnic Composition of Lithuania (2009 Census)

Nationality	Percentage of Population
Lithuanian	84.0
Polish	6.1
Russian	4.9
Other or unspecified	3.9

Source: CIA, *The World Factbook 2013*, https://www.cia.gov/library/publications/the-world-factbook.

language legislation adopted in the final years of Soviet political reform that aimed at "emancipating" the Baltic languages. Non-Russians had to be fluent in Russian in order to function fully and advance socioeconomically, but Russian speakers were not learning the languages of the republics in which they resided.[30]

Decades of aggressive linguistic Russification, however, seemed only to reinforce the Balts' national aspirations, and the notion that Russian presence represented "illegal occupation" became a significant building block in strategies of state reconstruction. After achieving independence in 1991, each of the three governments adopted citizenship and language policies that established the dominance of the titular language in the state. The policies of nationalist state building were most aggressive in Latvia, where the ratio of the native population compared to the Russian-speaking population was the highest, and most moderate in Lithuania, where the ratio of the Russian minority was the lowest. In Lithuania, all residents who had lived in the republic before independence obtained citizenship simply by applying. In Estonia and Latvia, only citizens of the interwar Estonian and Latvian states before Soviet annexation in 1940 and their descendants had an automatic right to citizenship. Citizenship laws required other residents to pass a language-proficiency test in order to become citizens of the reestablished states, even though during the Soviet era hardly any Russian school taught Latvian. As a result, roughly a third of the population of Estonia and Latvia was excluded from citizenship.[31] Citizenship laws also disadvantaged ethnic Russians in the distribution of resources. The 1991 Latvian privatization law, for instance, excluded noncitizens. In Estonia, property restitution similarly discriminated against Russians.[32]

In general, the story of state and nation building in the Baltic region is about harmonizing national sovereignty with European integration. "Returning to Europe" and obtaining protection from future Russian reannexation by joining the European Union were inextricable parts of the pursuit of national sovereignty in this region.[33] Employing the powerful leverage that these motivations provided, European institutions—especially the OSCE's High Commissioner on National Minorities, the Council of Europe, and the European Union—applied strong pressure on the Baltic governments to adopt more inclusive citizenship laws and more pluralistic educational and language policies that complied with "European norms."[34] After 1998, the governments of Estonia and Latvia began adopting amendments to their citizenship laws that made the naturalization of "nonhistoric" minorities easier. International pressure has been less successful in influencing them to liberalize their language policies. Language legislation in both states also continues to reflect a nationalist state-building strategy, although in most cases restrictive language legislation was only moderately implemented.[35] Tensions over language use continue. In Latvia, a new bilingual curriculum introduced in 2002 and 2003 required that minority-language schools teach certain subjects exclusively in Latvian. In Estonia, a 2007 education reform introduced similar requirements. In both states, policies that mandate the exclusive use of the majority language in subjects considered significant for the reproduction of national cultures, such as history and music, have reinforced fears among Russian-speakers that majorities intend to erase Russian culture from these states.[36]

In successor states of the Soviet Union, the parallel processes of democratization and EU integration described in this section unfolded only in the Baltic states. A brief account of developments in Ukraine helps to highlight how internal divisions over EU membership and national identity can contribute to a major state crisis in a post-Soviet European successor state where political elites failed to establish credible democratic institutions. Although the appeal of democratization is strong in Ukrainian society, the idea of EU membership remains deeply divisive. Given Ukraine's geographic position between the EU and Russia, the ambivalence about European integration has implications beyond the "Euroskepticism" found in current EU member states. A significant segment of Ukraine's political elite and public favors the pursuit of EU membership, but a sizable portion of the state's Russian speakers, especially in the eastern region close to the Russian border, is more interested in maintaining close ties with Russia. The Russian government, meanwhile, strongly opposes the idea of Ukraine's incorporation into Western political and security institutions. The combination of these conditions reinforced skepticism also among EU leaders about the prospects for Ukraine's inclusion in the European integration project. Given the large size of the Ukrainian territory and population in comparison with the Baltic states and the magnitude of Ukraine's socioeconomic problems, the prospects for Ukraine's EU integration remain weak, especially after the 2008 financial crisis. Although Ukraine became part of the EU's "Eastern Partnership" initiative,[37] this framework provides European institutions with no leverage to influence policies affecting interethnic relations in a partner state or to shape bilateral relations between Ukraine and Russia.

Ukraine includes a large Russian-speaking population with ambivalent attitudes toward the Ukrainian national identity pursued through policies designed in the state center. Under such conditions, a significant crisis of trust in the government can lead to a major state crisis in which even the political borders of the state become contested.[38] The evolution of the 2013–2014 Ukrainian state crisis manifests this logic. Ukraine's political elites failed to establish credible democratic institutions for the state created after 1991. President Viktor Yanukovych's decision to violently repress antigovernment demonstrations, which began in Kiev in November 2013 in response to the government's refusal to sign an association agreement with the EU, led to a major state crisis. The escalation of this crisis—involving the aggressive intrusion of the Russian state through a military annexation of the Crimean Peninsula, followed by secessionist mobilization in eastern Ukraine, all in the name of protecting Ukraine's Russian-speaking population—highlights not only the failure of democratization in Ukraine but also the continued salience of ethnicity in the politics of sovereignty and legitimacy in the region.

THE "VELVET DIVORCE" AND ITS AFTERMATH: THE CZECH AND SLOVAK STATES

In contrast with the violent conflicts over national sovereignty in former Yugoslavia and the powerful support for independence in the Baltic republics, the independent Czech Republic and Slovakia were created after the peaceful dissolution of Czechoslovakia in 1992. Some accounts of the separation emphasized cultural differences between Czechs and Slovaks and assigned a significant weight to Slovak aspirations for a national state.[39] Yet separation was not primarily the outcome of ethnic division between Slovaks and Czechs. Rather than the result of large-scale popular mobilization for independence, as in the Baltic states, the creation of independent Czech and Slovak states was an outcome negotiated among the political leaders of the two parts of the federation with only limited public support.[40] At the same time, each of these states was established democratically, by elected governing bodies, and in the absence of significant popular opposition.[41]

As with the separation of the Baltic states, a key reason for the absence of violent conflict over the dissolution of Czechoslovakia was that no disputes emerged between the Czechs and Slovaks over state borders, as the two groups did not initiate mutually exclusive "national homeland" claims to the same territory. Before the first establishment of Czechoslovakia in 1918, Slovaks had lived within the Hungarian kingdom for ten centuries, and the old territorial border remained a substate boundary in Czechoslovakia. After decades of coexistence with the prospect of mobility within a common state—first in interwar Czechoslovakia and then in communist Czechoslovakia—no sizable Czech national minority developed in Slovak territory or Slovak historic minority in the Czech Lands that would articulate a substate national challenge to either of the new states. Another important reason why the Czech and Slovak divorce lacked significant controversy was that the Hungarian minority in the Slovak part of the state, a historic minority with competing homeland claims in the southern region of Slovakia, did not challenge the Slovaks' right to independence.

For reasons described earlier in this chapter, at the time of independence the Czech Republic was one of the least ethnically diverse states in the region (see table 5.2). Czech political leaders therefore faced few challenges to pursuing a single, dominant culture in the new state. Of all the ethnicities in the state, the Roma continue to constitute the largest and most distinct cultural group, with a share of the population estimated at between 2 and 3 percent. Official policies and popular attitudes toward this minority after the creation of the new state indicated that the national majority had little desire to accommodate Roma culture. Citizenship laws limited the rights of Roma to become naturalized in the new state. On the level of local government, anti-Roma efforts included attempts to segregate swimming pools, construct walls separating Roma and Czech inhabitants, and provide subsidies for Roma willing to emigrate. The relatively small size and fragmentation of the Roma population, however, prevented these incidents from becoming a matter of broader debate about Czech national exclusivism.[42]

National aspirations found a more complex social context in newly independent Slovakia.[43] Before 1993, the primary question of Slovak national sovereignty had been whether an independent Slovak state was necessary to fulfill national aspirations. After the creation of Slovakia, the key question became how a Slovak "nation-state" could materialize on a

Table 5.2.   Ethnic Composition of the Czech Republic, 2011 Census

Nationality	Percentage of Population
Czech	64.3
Moravian	5.0
Slovak	1.4
Other or unspecified	29.3

Source: Czech Statistical Office (Český statistický úřad), "1-16 Obyvatelstvo podle národnosti podle výsledků sčítání lidu v letech 1921–2011 [Population by Ethnicity by 1921–2011 Censuses]," Czech Demographic Handbook 2013, http://www.czso.cz/csu/2013edicniplan.nsf/engt/8E001797ED/$File/4032130116.pdf.

territory that incorporated a relatively large, geographically concentrated, and politically well-organized historic Hungarian community (see table 5.3). During the first period of independence, from 1992 to 1998, the Slovak political parties in power, under the leadership of Prime Minister Vladimír Mečiar, opted for traditional nationalist policies.[44] In an attempt to suppress minority claims for substate institutional autonomy, these policies were aimed at establishing Slovak majority control over all institutions of government and cultural reproduction. Restrictive language legislation adopted in 1995 was designed to strengthen the status of the Slovak literary standard against dialects and to exclude minority languages from the spheres considered most important for the reproduction of national cultures: local government, territory markings, the media, and the educational system. Hungarian minority parties forcefully challenged these policies and pressed for a pluralist Slovak state. Employing the methods of party competition and parliamentary debate, Hungarian minority political elites asked that Slovakia's historic Hungarian minority be recognized as a state-constituting entity. To guarantee the reproduction of Hungarian minority culture in Slovakia, they demanded substate forms of autonomy, at various times emphasizing either the cultural, educational, or territorial aspects of self-government. Despite internal debates among Hungarian parties about the best institutional forms, they agreed on the importance of language rights and claimed the right to use the Hungarian language in the southern region of Slovakia in all public spheres and the educational system.

Majority-minority debates over these questions marked the first decade of democratization in Slovakia. The Mečiar government's policies of increasing centralized control over society also created sharp divisions within the Slovak majority. Based on their agreement about the necessity of moving Slovakia away from a recentralizing authoritarian regime, the Slovak and Hungarian parties in opposition eventually formed a strategic electoral alliance that defeated the Mečiar government in the 1998 parliamentary elections. This Slovak-Hungarian electoral alliance was able to form a governing coalition that changed the course of Slovak nationalist policies in the following years. Even though debates about minority self-government and language equality continued and often reflected vehement disagreements, the prospect of European integration provided a significant incentive to both majority and minority moderate parties to negotiate peacefully. They managed to design policies that, while preserving the predominance of the majority language throughout the country, gradually included the minority language in ways

Table 5.3. Ethnic Composition of Slovakia, 2011 Census

Nationality	Percentage of Population
Slovak	80.7
Hungarian	8.5
Roma	2.0
Czech	0.6
Ruthenian	0.6
Ukrainian	0.1
Other or unspecified	0.5

Source: Statistical Office of the Slovak Republic, "Table 10 Population by Nationality—2011, 2001, 1991," *2011 Population and Housing Census,* http://portal.statistics.sk/files/table-10.pdf.

Photo 5.3. With the expansion of the European Union, West European tourists have come in large numbers to places like this Hungarian village in Transylvania. Many buy "ethnic gifts" at new shops like this one. (Dana Stryk)

that satisfied the main aspirations of minority parties articulated from the beginning of the 1990s. The return of national exclusivist parties to the government after 2006 raised questions about the future of minority accommodation in the country. The controversy over June 2009 amendments to the Slovak language law restricting minority language use in official business reveals the limits of international pressure in the post-EU accession period, when the conditionality of prospective EU membership can no longer constrain majority policy makers. Still, the prospect of a more minority-friendly approach to nation building in the future remains open. The coalition government formed after the 2010 parliamentary elections included a new Hungarian-Slovak party that placed particular emphasis on interethnic reconciliation, and the government formed after the 2012 parliamentary elections did not include a Hungarian minority party. These changes in government had no significant impact on the position of Hungarians in Slovakia.

Consolidating National States: Nation-State or Pluralism?

The unitary states of Bulgaria, Hungary, Poland, and Romania continued their existence within unchanged state borders after the communist collapse. The absence of state collapse and new state creation, however, did not make nationalist ideology irrelevant in these countries. Wherever majority national elites chose to define the postcommunist state as the unitary "nation-state" of the majority national group, and the government engaged in aggressive policies to create majority dominance over sizable ethnic and national minority groups, nationalism became a deeply divisive political strategy.

FROM NATIONALIST COMMUNISM TO DEMOCRATIC NATIONALISM: ROMANIA

As in other multiethnic societies in the region, the legacies of past relations of dominance and subordination between ethnic groups continued to influence majority and minority perspectives in Romania about what "national sovereignty" should mean. With the end of World War II, the contested borders of the state were redrawn again, largely along the same lines created after World War I, and Romania fell under the influence of the Soviet Union.[45] Despite the ruthlessness of anti-Hungarian policies enacted during the dictatorship of Nicolae Ceaușescu, members of the Hungarian minority maintained a strong sense of national identity. Only days after the bloody December 1989 revolution that toppled perhaps the most repressive communist dictatorship in the region, ethnic Hungarians formed a political party that commanded the overwhelming majority of the votes of their population of 1.6 million in every subsequent election, and they became a significant force in the Romanian parliament.

Rather than discarding the nationalist policies of the Ceaușescu period, however, the government of Ion Iliescu, after 1990, designed a new constitution that defined the state as a "nation-state" based on the unity of an ethnically determined Romanian nation. The regime based its power on alliances with ultranationalist Romanian parties of the left and right and instituted minority policies that in some ways were more restrictive than their counterparts during the Ceaușescu dictatorship. The new constitution affirmed Romanian as the only official language in Romania. Laws adopted on public administration and public education also severely restricted the use of minority languages and became sources of intense controversy between the Romanian government and the Hungarian minority party. Like its counterpart in Slovakia, the Hungarian minority party demanded the right to Hungarian-language cultural and educational institutions and to use that

Table 5.4. Ethnic Composition of Romania, 2002 Census

Nationality	Percentage of Population
Romanian	89.5
Hungarian	6.6
Roma	2.5
German	0.3
Ukrainian	0.3
Russian	0.2
Turkish	0.2
Other	0.4

Source: CIA, World Factbook 2013, https://www.cia.gov/library/publications/the-world-factbook.

language in local and regional government. The Hungarians pressed for these demands through bargaining and negotiations with majority parties willing to compromise on national issues. Although all Romanian parties rejected Hungarian claims to substate autonomy, moderate Romanian parties were willing to form an electoral alliance with the Hungarian party, and—much in keeping with events in Slovakia—this strategic alliance defeated the Iliescu government in 1996, formed a coalition government, and began to change Romanian nation-building policies. Even though the Iliescu government returned to power in the 2000 elections, the prospect of membership in NATO and the European Union had become significant enough for the regime to expand the rights of language use in the spheres most important for minority cultural reproduction.[46] Consecutive Romanian governments have included the Hungarian minority party in their coalitions and continued to support minority-friendly language policies. The demand for substate territorial autonomy in a Hungarian-majority region is highly divisive, however, and the marginalization of Roma minorities remains a significant issue.

Nation Building across State Borders

Besides cohabitating with a national majority in the same state, most ethnic and national minorities in this region also have neighboring "kin-states"—that is, states in which their ethnic kin compose a titular majority.[47] A growing interest emerged among the governments in such kin-states to adopt legislation that would grant preferential treatment to ethnic kin living in other states. The constitutions of several states, such as Albania, Croatia, Hungary, and Macedonia, contain commitments to care for the well-being of kin living abroad. Several governments, such as in Bulgaria, Hungary, Poland, Romania, Russia, Serbia, Slovenia, and Slovakia, adopted legislation to provide benefits to ethnic kin living abroad. Although these constitutional clauses and benefit laws differ in their specific content, ranging from cultural and economic benefits to dual-citizenship rights, their common characteristic is that they support the preservation of national identity and aim to contribute to the fostering of relationships between a kin-state and those outside its borders who define themselves in some sense as conationals.[48]

HUNGARY AND VIRTUAL NATIONALISM

The Hungarian state's nation-building strategy after 1990 is the clearest example of the trans-sovereign type of nationalism in the region. This type of nationalism does not pursue a traditional nation-state through territorial changes or the repatriation of ethnic kin within its borders. Instead, it aims to maintain a sense of common cultural "nationhood" across existing state borders.[49] Close to 3 million ethnic Hungarians live in Hungary's neighboring states. In an integrated Europe, they compose one of the largest historical minority groups. After the collapse of communist regimes, Hungarian political elites were aware that revisionism was an unacceptable proposition if they wanted to join an integrated Europe. Instead of pressing for border changes, they created a network of institutions that link Hungarians living in the neighboring countries to Hungary while encouraging them to remain "in their homeland" and in effect withstand assimilation where they reside. To complement these cross-border institutions, the Hungarian government expressed support both for EU membership for Hungary and its neighbors and for Hungarian minority demands for local and institutional autonomy in their home states. According to the logic of these policies, if Hungary and all of its neighbors became EU members, and the European Union provided a supranational, decentralized structure for strong regional institutions, then Hungarians could live as though no political borders separated them.

Although the "virtualization of borders" appeared attractive to many Hungarians, the idea found little appeal among the majority political parties in neighboring countries. Seven states neighboring Hungary include ethnic Hungarian populations, and five of these states were newly established after the collapse of communist federations. As discussed earlier in this chapter, the majority national elites in both newly created and consolidating national states were highly reluctant to weaken their sovereignty and accommodate multiple nation-building processes in their territories. Thus, Hungarian efforts unilaterally to "virtualize" borders in the region triggered tensions between Hungary and its neighbors.

The adoption in June 2001 of the Law Concerning Hungarians Living in Neighboring Countries (commonly known as the Hungarian Status Law)—which defined all ethnic Hungarians in the region as part of the same cultural nation and on this basis offered a number of educational, cultural, and even economic benefits to those living in neighboring states—triggered significant attention from policy makers in the region, European institution officials, and scholars of nationalism.[50] The competitive dynamics of nation building in the region and its potentially large-scale regional impact made the Hungarian strategy particularly controversial. The governments of Romania and Slovakia, the two states with the largest Hungarian populations, expressed concern that the legislation weakened their exclusive sovereignty over ethnic Hungarian citizens and discriminated against majority nationals in neighboring countries. Although these neighboring governments themselves had adopted similar policies toward their own ethnic kin abroad, controversy over the Hungarian Status Law brought Hungary's relations with these neighbors to a dangerously low point. The fact that all of these governments were keenly interested in EU membership eventually helped them compromise. Hungary signed a bilateral agreement with Romania and altered the language of the law in response to European pressure in 2003. Yet the controversy over the Hungarian Status Law foreshadowed the challenges of reconciling European integration with the continuing power of divergent and competing national aspirations. The divisiveness of cross-border nationalism became particularly visible after 2010, when the newly elected Hungarian government began adopting legislation that made it easier for ethnic Hungarians living in neighboring countries to become Hungarian citizens and gain nonresident voting rights. These acts triggered strong resentment in Slovakia and also deepened political divisions in Hungary. The strong showing of the vehemently xenophobic Movement for a Better Hungary (Jobbik) in the 2009 European Parliament elections, together with this party's increasing success among the Hungarian electorate—in obtaining parliamentary seats in the 2010 elections and gaining 20 percent of the votes in the 2014 parliamentary elections—reveals the salience of exclusivist nationalism despite the earlier successes of democratic consolidation. The new Hungarian constitution adopted in 2011 has also been harshly criticized for provisions that can indirectly sanction discrimination against Hungary's large Roma minority.

Nationalism and the Expansion of Democracy

The continuing appeal of the national principle in Central and East European societies that have successfully acceded to the European Union challenges old assumptions about ethnicity, nationalism, and democratization. In these instances, democratization did not lead to the broad acceptance of liberal-individualist understandings of citizenship; nor did nationalism result in horror perpetuated in the name of ethnic kin throughout the region. Given the dramatic collapse of states and regimes in a region where state and nation building has always involved ethnic competition, the relatively low occurrence of violent conflict associated with these changes in the 1990s was remarkable.

The force and popular appeal of nationalist demands revealed that nationalism constitutes a significant element of continuity in this region. At the same time, the end of the Cold War and the promise of European integration altered the conditions under which nationalist interests could be articulated. Despite the commonality of these external influences, however, the specific goals that nationalist leaders and groups articulated, as well as the means by which they pursued those goals, varied across the region. Most of the former titular groups of multinational federations sought national independence. Where substate boundaries within the disintegrating multinational federation had coincided with the territories that titular groups defined as their historic homelands and secession encountered no significant challenge from other groups, nationalist state building unfolded without significant violence. In these cases, the prospects for integration into Western institutions helped reinforce initial interests in democratization. Examples of such nonviolent (or relatively nonviolent) state formation include the reestablishment of the Baltic states of Estonia, Latvia, and Lithuania; the secession of Slovenia and Macedonia; and the creation of independent Czech and Slovak states.

Where the state-building aspirations of a group encountered forceful challenge by another group claiming the same territory as a historic homeland within a dissolving federal state and the dominant political elites opted for unilateralism over sustained negotiation across ethnic lines, nationalist mobilization led to devastating wars. This was the situation in the former Yugoslav republics of Croatia, Bosnia-Herzegovina, and Kosovo. Competing national elites in these cases opted for national sovereignty or its violent denial even at the most horrific costs, and future prospects for European integration did not figure significantly in their calculations—despite the fact that, before the communist collapse, Yugoslavia had been better connected to international institutions than Soviet bloc countries. European integration became an important part of nationalist strategy only in Slovenia, where belonging to Europe constituted a strong element of national identity, and with no significant national minority, the issue of national sovereignty was most easily resolved.

Lithuania provides an important lesson about the significance of the choices that majority and minority political elites make in nationalist competition. In the same period that Croatian and Serbian majority and minority elites were fighting a devastating war in the southeastern part of the continent, the leaders of the Lithuanian national majority and the Polish minority opted for a consensual resolution of the tension over mutually claimed homelands. Eager to satisfy European expectations, they engaged in a bilateral and peaceful negotiation over the issues of autonomy and minority rights.

Governments in Bulgaria, Romania, and all of the multiethnic successor states of dissolving federations had to determine whether the democratic state could pursue the traditional nationalist aim of the political-cultural congruence of the nation or accommodate minority cultures in a more pluralist state. Excepting Croatia, Serbia, and Bosnia-Herzegovina, in all of these states majority and minority political parties remained committed to democratic means of negotiating their competing notions of sovereignty.

Complicating matters even further, however, many governments in the region juggle the dual roles of home state (in relation to their titular nation and national minorities living on their territory) and kin-state (in relation to ethnic kin populations living outside their territory). Such cases have prompted officials in European institutions to begin designing a common set of norms to assure minority protection and permit kin-states to build relations with external minorities while continuing to uphold the principle of state sovereignty.[51] In an enlarged European Union, harmonizing the principles of state sovereignty and individualism with the practice of multiple nation building within and across state borders will remain a continuing challenge.

Study Questions

1. State borders have changed many times in Central and Eastern Europe following the awakening of national movements in the second half of the nineteenth century. What were the most significant border changes, and in what ways have they exacerbated the competitive logic of nationalism and the problem of noncongruence between state and national boundaries?

2. Explain the "Janus-faced" character of nationalism and the way it has influenced post-communist democratic development in Central and East European countries. In what ways can we say that nation-building policies in this region have been both forward-looking and at the same time turned to the past?

3. Bearing in mind the significance of preexisting institutions, national composition, and the choices made by political elites, what seems to set apart the violent ethnic politics of the former Yugoslavia from the largely peaceful evolution of majority-minority conflicts in the rest of Central and Eastern Europe?

4. Most ethnic minorities in Central and Eastern Europe have kin-states in the region, and most governments have enacted legislation to extend various kinds of benefits to ethnic kin living abroad. Discuss the reasons why kin-state nationalism is controversial in this region and how it affects the evolution of democratic government and European integration.

5. The enlargement of the European Union to include democratized postcommunist states is commonly viewed as a source of success in democratic consolidation and interethnic peacemaking in significant parts of Central and Eastern Europe. At the same

time, the reassertion of Russian regional power under Vladimir Putin's government is viewed as a factor that weakens the prospects for democratic consolidation and can even endanger state stability in the successor states of the Soviet Union. What is the role of these processes of regional influence in explaining the successes and failures of nation building and minority inclusion throughout the postcommunist region?

Suggested Readings

Barany, Zoltan, and Robert G. Moser, eds. *Ethnic Politics after Communism*. Ithaca, NY: Cornell University Press, 2005.

Beissinger, Mark. "How Nationalisms Spread: Eastern Europe Adrift the Tides and Cycles of Nationalist Contention." *Social Research* 63, no. 1 (spring 1996): 97–146.

Brubaker, Rogers. *Nationalism Reframed: Nationhood and the National Question in the New Europe*. Cambridge: Cambridge University Press, 1996.

Bunce, Valerie. "Peaceful versus Violent State Dismemberment." *Politics and Society* 27, no. 2 (1999): 217–37.

Csergo, Zsuzsa. *Talk of the Nation: Language and Conflict in Romania and Slovakia*. Ithaca, NY: Cornell University Press, 2007.

Csergo, Zsuzsa, and James M. Goldgeier. "Nationalist Strategies and European Integration." *Perspectives on Politics* 2, no. 1 (2004): 21–37.

Gagnon, V. P., Jr. *The Myth of Ethnic War: Serbia and Croatia in the 1990s*. Ithaca, NY: Cornell University Press, 2004.

Gellner, Ernest. *Nations and Nationalism*. Ithaca, NY: Cornell University Press, 1983.

Hale, Henry. "Explaining Ethnicity." *Comparative Political Studies* 37, no. 4 (May 2004): 458–85.

Hroch, Miroslav. "From National Movement to the Fully-Formed Nation: The Nation-Building Process in Europe." *New Left Review* 198 (1993): 3–20.

Hutchinson, John, and Anthony D. Smith, eds. *Nationalism*. Oxford: Oxford University Press, 1994.

Karklins, Rasma. *Ethnopolitics and Transition to Democracy*. Washington, DC: Woodrow Wilson Center Press and Johns Hopkins University Press, 1994.

Kelley, Judith. *Ethnic Politics in Europe: The Power of Norms and Incentives*. Princeton, NJ: Princeton University Press, 2004.

King, Charles. *Extreme Politics: Nationalism, Violence, and the End of Eastern Europe*. Oxford: Oxford University Press, 2010.

King, Charles, and Neil Melvin, eds. *Nations Abroad: Diaspora Politics and International Relations in the Former Soviet Union*. Boulder, CO: Westview Press, 1998.

Kymlicka, Will, and Magda Opalski. *Can Liberal Pluralism Be Exported? Western Political Theory and Ethnic Relations in Eastern Europe*. Oxford: Oxford University Press, 2001.

Laitin, David. "The Cultural Identities of a European State." *Politics and Society* 25, no. 3 (September 1997): 277–302.

———. *Identity in Formation: The Russian-Speaking Populations in the Near Abroad*. Ithaca, NY: Cornell University Press, 1998.

Livezeanu, Irina. *Cultural Politics in Greater Romania: Regionalism, Nation Building, and Ethnic Struggle, 1918–1930*. Ithaca, NY: Cornell University Press, 1995.

Roeder, Philip. "The Triumph of Nation-States: Lessons from the Collapse of the Soviet Union, Yugoslavia, and Czechoslovakia." In *After the Collapse of Communism*, edited by Michael McFaul and Kathryn Stoner-Weiss, 21–57. Cambridge: Cambridge University Press, 2004.

Snyder, Jack. *From Voting to Violence: Democratization and Nationalist Conflict*. New York: W. W. Norton & Company, 2000.

Snyder, Timothy. *Bloodlands: Europe between Hitler and Stalin*. New York: Basic Books, 2010.

Subotic, Jelena. *Hijacked Justice: Dealing with the Past in the Balkans*. Ithaca, NY: Cornell University Press, 2009.

Tesser, Lynn. 2013. *Ethnic Cleansing and the European Union: An Interdisciplinary Approach to Security, Memory and Ethnography*. Basingstoke, UK: Palgrave Macmillan, 2013.

Tismaneanu, Vladimir. *Fantasies of Salvation: Democracy, Nationalism, and Myth in Post-communist Europe*. Princeton, NJ: Princeton University Press, 1998.

Verdery, Katherine. *National Ideology under Socialism: Identity and Cultural Politics in Ceauşescu's Romania*. Berkeley: University of California Press, 1991.

Wimmer, Andreas. *Ethnic Boundary Making: Institutions, Power, Networks*. New York: Oxford University Press, 2013.

Notes

1. Ernst Gellner, *Nations and Nationalism* (Ithaca, NY: Cornell University Press, 1983), 1.

2. For a comprehensive discussion of the literature about nationalism and modernization, see Anthony D. Smith, *Nationalism and Modernism: A Critical Survey of Recent Theories of Nations and Nationalism* (London: Routledge, 1998).

3. Robert Kaplan, *Balkan Ghosts: A Journey through History* (New York: Vintage Books, 1993); Mischa Glenny, *The Balkans 1804–1999* (New York: Viking, 2000).

4. Jack Snyder, *From Voting to Violence: Democratization and Nationalist Conflict* (New York: W. W. Norton & Co., 2000).

5. Smith, *Nationalism and Modernism*; Rogers Brubaker, *Nationalism Reframed: Nationhood and the National Question in the New Europe* (Cambridge: Cambridge University Press, 1996).

6. Henry Hale, "Explaining Ethnicity," *Comparative Political Studies* 37, no. 4 (May 2004): 458–85.

7. Tom Nairn, "The Modern Janus," in *The Break-Up of Britain: Crisis and Neo-nationalism*, ed. Tom Nairn (London: New Left Books, 1977).

8. Anthony D. Smith, *The Ethnic Origins of Nations* (Oxford, UK: Blackwell, 1986); Michael Billig, *Banal Nationalism* (London: SAGE Publications, 1995).

9. See also Mark Beissinger, "How Nationalisms Spread: Eastern Europe Adrift the Tides and Cycles of Nationalist Contention," *Social Research* 63, no. 1 (spring 1996): 135.

10. For a historical account, see Hugh L. Agnew, *The Czechs and the Lands of the Bohemian Crown* (Stanford, CA: Hoover Institution Press, 2004). About nationalism and competition, see Anthony W. Marx, *Faith in Nation: Exclusionary Origins of Nationalism* (Oxford: Oxford University Press, 2003). About resentment as an important motivation for nationalism, see Liah Greenfeld, *Nationalism: Five Roads to Modernity* (Cambridge: Cambridge University Press, 1992).

11. Stephen Krasner, ed., *Problematic Sovereignty: Contested Rules and Political Possibilities* (New York: Columbia University Press, 2001), 1–23.

12. J. Samuel Barkin and Bruce Cronin, "The State and the Nation: Changing Norms and the Rules of Sovereignty in International Relations," *International Organizations* 48 (winter 1994): 107–30.

13. Quoted in Arnold Suppan, "Yugoslavism versus Serbian, Croatian, and Slovene Nationalism," in *Yugoslavia and Its Historians: Understanding the Balkan Wars of the 1990s*, ed. Norman M. Naimark and Holly Case (Stanford, CA: Stanford University Press, 2003), 126.

14. Irina Livezeanu, *Cultural Politics in Greater Romania: Regionalism, Nation Building, and Ethnic Struggle, 1918–1930* (Ithaca, NY: Cornell University Press, 1995).

15. See Timothy Snyder, *Bloodlands: Europe between Hitler and Stalin* (New York: Basic Books, 2010).

16. For accounts of the significance of these processes of ethnic "unmixing" for the postcommunist political and social development of the region, see Rogers Brubaker, *Nationalism Reframed: Nationhood and the National Question in the New Europe* (Cambridge: Cambridge University Press, 1996); Lynn Tesser, *Ethnic Cleansing and the European Union: An Interdisciplinary Approach to Security, Memory and Ethnography* (Basingstoke, UK: Palgrave Macmillan, 2013).

17. The Czechoslovak and Yugoslav states pursued different policies of ethnicity. "Czechoslovakism" was officially abandoned after World War II, while the government of Yugoslavia remained interested in "Yugoslav" identity construction for decades after the war.

18. See Valerie Bunce, *Subversive Institutions: The Design and the Destruction of Socialism and the State* (Cambridge: Cambridge University Press, 1999).

19. About national ideology in Romania, see Katherine Verdery, *National Ideology under Socialism: Identity and Cultural Politics in Ceaușescu's Romania* (Berkeley and Los Angeles: University of California Press, 1991). For the national question in Czechoslovakia, see Sharon Wolchik, *Czechoslovakia in Transition: Politics, Economics, and Society* (London: Pinter, 1991).

20. Vojtech Mastny, "The Beneš Thesis: A Design for the Liquidation of National Minorities, Introduction," in *The Hungarians: A Divided Nation*, ed. Stephen Borsody, 231–43 (New Haven, CT: Yale Center for International and Area Studies, 1988).

21. Bennett Kovrig, "Peacemaking after World War II," in *The Hungarians: A Divided Nation*, ed. Stephen Borsody (New Haven, CT: Yale Center for International and Area Studies, 1988), 69–88.

22. Peter Siani-Davies, *The Romanian Revolution of December 1989* (Ithaca, NY: Cornell University Press, 2007).

23. Vladimir Tismaneanu, *Fantasies of Salvation: Democracy, Nationalism, and Myth in Postcommunist Europe* (Princeton, NJ: Princeton University Press, 1998).

24. These documents include the Commission on Security and Cooperation in Europe's (CSCE) Copenhagen Document (1990), known also as the European Constitution on Human Rights, which included a chapter on the protection of national minorities; the Council of Europe's (CE) European Charter on Regional and Minority Languages (1992); the United Nations Declaration on the Rights of Persons Belonging to National and Ethnic, Religious and Linguistic Minorities (1992); the CE's Framework Convention for the Protection of National Minorities (1995), which is commonly considered a major achievement as the first legally binding international tool for minority protection; and the Organization for Security and Co-operation in Europe's (OSCE) Oslo Recommendations regarding the Linguistic Rights of National Minorities (1998).

25. Aleksa Djilas, "Fear Thy Neighbor: The Breakup of Yugoslavia," in *Nationalism and Nationalities in the New Europe*, ed. Charles Kupchan et al. (Ithaca, NY: Cornell University Press, 1995), 88.

26. Djilas, "Fear Thy Neighbor," 102.

27. United Nations, *The Comprehensive Proposal for Kosovo Status Settlement* (New York: United Nations Office of the Special Envoy for Kosovo, March 26, 2007).

28. For different scholarly perspectives on the international consequences of Kosovo's unilateral declaration of independence, see the special issue titled "Self-Determination after Kosovo," published in *Europe-Asia Studies* 65, no. 5 (July 2013).

29. Zsuzsa Csergo and James M. Goldgeier, "Kin-State Activism in Hungary, Romania, and Russia: The Politics of Ethnic Demography," in *Divided Nations and European Integration*, ed. Tristan James Mabry, John McGarry, Margaret Moore, and Brendan O'Leary (Philadelphia: University of Pennsylvania Press, 2013): 89–126. On Soviet language policy, see Rasma Karklins,

Ethnopolitics and Transition to Democracy (Washington, DC: Woodrow Wilson Center Press and Johns Hopkins University Press, 1994), 151–52.

30. On Soviet language policy, see Karklins, *Ethnopolitics and Transition to Democracy*.

31. Graham Smith et al., *Nation-Building in the Post-Soviet Borderlands: The Politics of National Identities* (Cambridge: Cambridge University Press, 1998), 94.

32. Julie Bernier, "Nationalism in Transition: Nationalizing Impulses and International Counterweights in Latvia and Estonia," in *Minority Nationalism and the Changing International Order*, ed. Michael Keating and John McGarry (Oxford: Oxford University Press, 2001), 346.

33. Rawi Abdelal, *National Purpose in the World Economy* (Ithaca, NY: Cornell University Press, 2001).

34. Judith Kelley, *Ethnic Politics in Europe: The Power of Norms and Incentives* (Princeton, NJ: Princeton University Press, 2004). For a more skeptical view of the power of this leverage, see Bernd Rechel, ed., *Minority Rights in Central and Eastern Europe* (London: Routledge, 2009).

35. Rasma Karklins, "Ethnic Integration and School Policies in Latvia," *Nationalities Papers* 26, no. 2 (1998): 284.

36. Ojarrs Kalnins, "Latvia: The Language of Coexistence," *Transitions Online,* September 1, 2004, http://www.to.cz/TOL/home; Gerli Nimmerfeldt, "Integration of Second Generation Russians in Estonia: Country Report on TIES Survey in Estonia," Studies of Transition States and Societies 1, no. 1 (2009): 25–35; Tatjana Bulajeva and Gabrielle Hogan-Brun, "Language and Education Orientations in Lithuania: A Cross-Baltic Perspective Post-EU Accession," in *Multilingualism in Post-Soviet Countries*, ed. Aneta Pavlenko (Toronto: Multilingual Matters, 2008), 122–48.

37. The Eastern Partnership was established in 2008 as a venue for improving the EU's relations with neighboring states.

38. Maria Popova and Oxana Shevel, "What Doesn't Kill Ukraine," *Foreign Policy*, March 12, 2014.

39. See Gordon Wightman, "Czechoslovakia," in *New Political Parties of Eastern Europe and the Soviet Union*, ed. Bogdan Szajkowski (Detroit, MI: Longman, 1991), 67; Jiri Musil, "Czech and Slovak Society," in *The End of Czechoslovakia*, ed. Jiri Musil (Budapest: Central European University Press, 1995), 92.

40. Sharon Wolchik, "The Politics of Transition and the Break-Up of Czechoslovakia," in *The End of Czechoslovakia*, ed. Jiri Musil (Budapest: Central European University Press, 1995), 240–41; Abby Innes, "Breakup of Czechoslovakia: The Impact of Party Development on the Separation of the State," *East European Politics and Societies* 11, no. 3 (fall 1997): 393.

41. About negotiated transitions, see Juan J. Linz and Alfred Stepan, *Problems of Democratic Transition and Consolidation: Southern Europe, South America, and Post-communist Europe* (Baltimore: Johns Hopkins University Press, 1996), 316.

42. Zsuzsa Csergo and Kevin Deegan-Krause, "Liberalism and Cultural Claims in Central and Eastern Europe," *Nations and Nationalism* 17, no. 1 (January 2011): 85–107.

43. Kevin Deegan-Krause, *Elected Affinities: Democracy and Party Competition in Slovakia and the Czech Republic* (Stanford, CA: Stanford University Press, 2006).

44. The primary force behind national exclusivist policies was the Slovak National Party, which exerted pressure on the main governing party, Movement for a Democratic Slovakia. See Tim Haughton, "Vladimír Mečiar and His Role in the 1994–1998 Slovak Coalition Government," *Europe-Asia Studies* 54, no. 8 (2002): 1319–38.

45. For the history of the interwar period, see Joseph Rothschild, *East Central Europe between the Two World Wars* (Seattle: University of Washington Press, 1974).

46. Zsuzsa Csergo, *Talk of the Nation: Language and Conflict in Romania and Slovakia* (Ithaca, NY: Cornell University Press, 2007).

47. Brubaker, *Nationalism Reframed*.

48. Iván Halász, "Models of Kin-Minorities Protection in Eastern and Central Europe" (paper presented at the international conference titled "The Status Law Syndrome: A Post-communist Nation Building, Citizenship, and/or Minority Protection," Budapest, Hungary, October 2004).

49. Zsuzsa Csergo and James M. Goldgeier, "Nationalist Strategies and European Integration," *Perspectives on Politics* 2 (March 2004): 26.

50. Zoltán Kántor et al., eds., *The Hungarian Status Law: Nation Building and/or Minority Protection* (Sapporo, Japan: Slavic Research Center, 2004); Myra Waterbury, *Between State and Nation: Diaspora Politics and Kin-State Nationalism in Hungary* (Basingstoke, UK: Palgrave Macmillan, 2010).

51. See "Report on the Preferential Treatment of National Minorities by Their Kin-State" (adopted by the Venice Committee at its 48th plenary meeting, Venice, October 19–20, 2001), http://assembly.coe.int/ASP/Doc/XrefViewHTML.asp?FileID=10094&Language=EN (accessed August 25, 2014).

CHAPTER 6

Women's Participation in Postcommunist Politics

Marilyn Rueschemeyer

The end of communism in Central and Eastern Europe created new conditions for citizens to participate in politics. Women as well as men gained the opportunity to vote in meaningful elections, run for political office, form independent groups, and pressure political leaders to take action on issues of interest to them. But they also lost many provisions insuring that they were able to have families and engage in the work world as well as in social and political organizations. This chapter addresses the continuities and changes in women's interest and participation in political life, the share of women among elected political representatives, the pursuit of women's issues by elected women, and women leaders' relation to various constituencies, especially women's organizations.

Articulating women's interests in radically new economic, political, and social situations and making new goals attractive to women in very different life situations has inevitably been a slow process, one complicated by parallel and competing attempts to articulate class interests as well as the interests of religious and ethnic or national groups. Different definitions of women's needs and interests have frequently been connected to different actors' political goals. Some political actors emphasized cultural expectations for traditional roles for women. Others, often frustrated by the political and economic course of the transitions, tried to put forth an agenda that would include the interests of women seeking to continue to work and engage in other activities outside their homes. Finally, a renewed emphasis on national, religious, and ethnic themes entered the formation of competing political interests. This affected the ability of women to introduce other items to the political agenda.

The chapter begins with some reflections on the communist period, particularly on the importance of women's participation in the labor force in preparing them to take part in political life after the end of the communist regime. It then turns to some of the implications of the transition years for women's participation, the consequences of different electoral arrangements and parties' political positions for women's representation in elected bodies, and other factors that promote women's success in politics.[1] The benefits for and expectations of women in Central and Eastern Europe during the communist period broke the earlier tradition of women staying in the home by not only allowing but also requiring full participation of women in the workforce. In turn, they have influenced the women's position in the workplace and in politics since the 1989–1990 period.

To bring women into the workforce, these countries all offered, for both ideological and pragmatic reasons, comprehensive if austere social welfare provisions, including child care. While these policies did not lead to full equality, either in the family or in leading positions in the state or the economy, they did have an influence on creating more gender equality in education, positions in the labor force, and overall status in society, even if they did not eradicate gender differences in men's and women's professional training, income, and responsibility. There were, of course, differences in the impact of national traditions on gender roles and the government's commitments to and policies in all these areas among the countries of the region (for example, see table 6.1 for the percentage of women in higher education). There were also times when communist regimes sought to counter the drops in the birthrate that came with women being in the workforce and shortages in apartments, consumer goods, and even (in some cases) food. They did this by creating incentives in the form of payments for children and extended maternity leaves as well as propaganda and campaigns to encourage women to have children.

A quota system for women's political representation played itself out in different ways in different countries; the proportion of women deputies, for instance, ranged from a fifth to a third in national legislatures during the communist period. In reality, this representation was largely symbolic as these elective bodies had little power. Women were barely represented in the apparatus of the party and state, where real power lay. There were, in the communist period, no women party or state leaders. Most women's leadership in political organizations focused on groups representing what were seen as

Table 6.1. Percentage of Female Students in Tertiary Education

	1980	1990	2000	2008
Albania	48	48	60	—
Bosnia-Herzegovina[a]	36	55	—	—
Bulgaria	56	51	56	55
Croatia[b]	49	47	53	54
Czech Republic	43	44	49	55
Estonia[c]	52	51	60	62
Hungary	50	50	55	58
Latvia	57	55	62	64
Lithuania	55	57	60	60
Macedonia	48	52	56	56
Poland	56	56	58	57
Romania	43	48	54	56
Russian Federation	—	—	—	57
Serbia-Montenegro	52	52	55	45[d]
Slovakia	38	44	50	60
Slovenia	54	56	56	58
Ukraine	—	—	—	54

Sources: UNSESE Statistical Division, World Education Report. For 2008: UNESCO, Institute for Statistics, Global Education Report 2010.
[a] Data for 1996 instead of 2000.
[b] Data for 1996 instead of 2000; including International Standard Classification of Education (ISCED) levels 5 and 6.
[c] Including postsecondary technical education.
[d] Not including Montenegro in 2008.

"women's interests," although women comprised a significant portion of professionals, from engineers to doctors.

A large majority of women had important experiences and positions outside their households. As a result, "women learned not to derive their status from their husbands, but from their own educational and professional positions."[2] The communist model, whereby most women, even those with young children, worked outside the home, also taught women how to combine their work and family lives, a process facilitated by adaptations in employment practices and work legislation that benefitted employed mothers.[3] Even so, combining work and home was difficult for many women, particularly because the gender division of labor within the home did not change significantly. All this meant women had, even with limited political autonomy, considerable participatory experience in communist societies—in the workplace, in unions, and especially in work collectives and neighborhoods.[4]

Many policies and benefits identified as "women's policies" in the West were standard in Central and East European countries under communism.[5] Women had abortion rights (except in Romania under Nicolae Ceaușescu), maternity and child-care leave, guaranteed employment, and access to education. There has been some continuity in these areas of social policy in the postcommunist period, even though a number of these policies have been challenged and many benefits have been reduced or eliminated. Their legitimacy, though, has been recognized, at least among significant segments of the population, and they remain in the public arena of political discussion.

Developments after 1989–1990

After the end of communism, the experience and education women had gained in the communist period made them "ready" to be politically engaged and effective. At the same time, many changes made such participation more difficult. Social policies intended to achieve universal employment and increase gender equality disappeared or were dramatically decreased. The decrease in social welfare and state-funded child care, as well as the insecurity of employment for men and women, limited women's entry into the workforce.

Many women became full-time parents, making it even more difficult for them to search for work. Some employers discriminated against women with children because it meant they had other time commitments. In addition, the changes in health care and education meant that young mothers at home had to deal with a new health-care system and a new education system. For some young couples, finding affordable housing became difficult.[6] All of this meant that many women were not in a position to be active in politics.

A number of women did play a significant role in the transitions from communism through their activities in citizen movements, newly formed nongovernmental organizations, and political parties, some of which had a strong focus on the position of women. In the election to the Volkskammer of the then separate East Germany in March 1990, for example, more than 20 percent of the newly elected representatives were women.[7] Women also served as spokespersons for the umbrella political organizations formed to negotiate the end of communism and participated in large numbers in the mass demonstrations that toppled the communist regimes in Poland, the German Democratic Republic (GDR), Czechoslovakia, and

Romania. Yet, overall, women's political participation in leadership positions in post communist Central and Eastern Europe is still far lower than that of men, even though women and men generally vote in equal numbers. Women are underrepresented among elected representatives in all of the countries in the region, and women's issues are often sidelined.

While women have risen to top leadership roles in a few instances, their rise is unique enough to be newsworthy because they are women, not because they advocate for women's interests. In all but one case, women who have become prime ministers or presidents in Central and Eastern Europe have come to power as "iron ladies" with experience in finance or as interim prime ministers. Those who came to power as financial experts included Hanna Suchocka (prime minister of Poland, 1992–1993) and Dalia Grybauskaite (president of Lithuania, 2010–present). Vaira Vike-Freiberga served two terms as president of Latvia from 1999 to 2007. Yulia Tymoshenko partnered with Viktor Yushchenko during the Orange Revolution in Ukraine, went on to be prime minister twice during his term as president, and lost to their Orange Revolution rival Viktor Yanukovych in the 2010 presidential election.[8] She had been a mining entrepreneur and minister of energy under Leonid Kuchma before she broke with the regime and took a lead in the "Ukraine without

Photo 6.1.   Yulia Tymoshenko, Ukrainian prime minister under President Yushchenko, major player in the Orange Revolution, and unsuccessful presidential candidate in 2010. (This photo was taken through joint efforts of the UNIAN news agency [http://www.unian.net] and the International Renaissance Foundation/George Soros Foundation in Ukraine [http://www.irf.kiev.ua].)

Kuchma" opposition. Two women served as interim prime ministers: Kazimiera Danute Prunskiene (Lithuania, 1990–1991) and Renata Indzhova (Bulgaria, 1994–1995). Iveta Radičová, who became prime minister of Slovakia after the 2010 elections, is the main exception to this pattern. Active as a top party leader, Radičová is a sociologist who was active in Slovakia's nongovernmental organization, think tank, and academic worlds prior to becoming a party leader. She has also done research on gender and social issues. After entering politics, Radičová became the first woman candidate in the second round of elections for the presidency, although she lost to the incumbent in 2009.

While the proportions of women in the last communist and current parliaments do not yield a clear numerical contrast (see table 6.2), they do indicate a growing role for women because women now share in the greater power of the parliaments. The figures in this table also reflect an increase in women's representation in the last decade, as in most countries women's representation among legislators dropped dramatically in the first postcommunist elections. Women's concerns and issues have frequently been defined by (male) politicians as secondary to "more important needs." A fundamental problem has been that, given the shift to a market economy and political pluralism, many of these societies are now too poor to sustain the old communist-era social supports of virtually free health and educational services, child care, and other benefits that were key to women's participation in the labor force. The expectation that a new political economy would eventually produce enough to enable all citizens to live well has clearly not played out for many women any more than it has for the poor. Initially, the new governments had to adjust policy to fit the considerable economic constraints of the economic transitions, which in turn created conditions of real scarcity for many. Even as these economies have recovered and many are now prospering, however, the policy choices made have downplayed women's need to play significant professional and political roles. More often, the policy choices reflect not only pressures to respond to economic issues but, to a considerable extent, existing power relations in the area of gender.[9]

Table 6.2. Proportion of Seats Held by Women in National Parliaments

	Last Communist Elections	*Recent Elections for Lower/ Single Houses*
Czech Republic	29.4	20 (2013)
Estonia	32.8	21 (2012)
Hungary	8.3	9 (2010)
Latvia	32.8	23 (2011)
Lithuania	32.8	25 (2012)
Poland	20.1	24 (2011)
Romania	34.4	13 (2012)
Russia	32.8	14 (2011)
Slovakia	29.4	19 (2012)
Slovenia	17.7	32 (2011)
Ukraine	32.8	9 (2012)

Sources: For the last communist elections, see Steve Saxonberg, "Women in Eastern European Parliaments," *Journal of Democracy* 11, no. 2 (April 2000): 154–58. For the later elections, see World Bank, World Development Indicators, http://data.worldbank.org/indicator/SG.GEN.PARL.ZS (based on data from the Inter-Parliamentary Union [http://www.ipu.org/wmn-e/classif.htm]).

Unequal power relations characterize political life at all levels of society.[10] Group interests tend to be articulated from the experience of men who insist that "women's" issues—such as child and health care and decreased employment opportunities—wait until other critical issues are resolved.[11] And without social welfare benefits, women had fewer opportunities to be heard. They learned that they were not as valued in politics. Indeed, right-wing parties explicitly advocated the traditional roles of homemaker and mother for women rather than endorsing policies in support of women's and family interests. All this meant that few women had either the incentive or the voice to be heard in political debates.

Photo 6.2.   Elderly woman begging for change on the street. The economic transition hit older women particularly hard. (Peter Turnley/Corbis)

The decrease in social welfare and child care, as well as discrimination against women with children, meant that young mothers at home with small children often became responsible for new obligations, such as dealing with new health-care and education systems. As mentioned above, for some young couples, finding affordable housing became difficult. As a result of reductions in subsidized child-care centers in some areas, many women became full-time parents, making searching for work, much less becoming involved in political life, even more difficult.

With the shift to market economies, open unemployment increased sharply in most countries. Even in some of the more successful transitions, large numbers of men and women in Central and Eastern Europe are still unemployed, and some suffer from severe poverty. The 2008–2009 financial crisis hit Central and East European countries unevenly, and the long-term effects were not easily predictable. Unemployment in 2012 was somewhat reduced in the Czech Republic, Romania, and Slovakia. Poland had a considerable reduction in the percentage of unemployed men and women. The percentage of unemployed in several other Central and East European countries increased in 2012 (see table 6.3), and in 2013 the percentage of unemployed in Poland rose to 13.6 percent. In some countries, the percentage of unemployed women is now lower than that of men, and more women than men work part-time.[12]

There have been significant changes in women's work even in countries with relatively low unemployment, such as the Czech Republic.[13] But unemployment clearly aggravates other problems and inhibits social and political participation. Even with comparatively generous benefits for the unemployed, as found in Germany, those without work in eastern Germany often withdraw from friends and former colleagues. As a result certain groups of unemployed women find themselves more isolated.

Due to past experience as well as economic need, many women in Central and Eastern Europe have attempted to remain in the workforce, even with increased obligations.[14] Labor-force participation rates have remained high in the region. However, although engagement in the workforce gives women skills and interests that might lead to greater political involvement and makes them less isolated, employment also takes time away from participation in other activities.

Table 6.3. Unemployment Rates in Central and Eastern Europe

	Total			Men			Women		
	2000	2005	2012	2000	2005	2012	2000	2005	2012
Bulgaria	16.4	10.1	12.3	16.7	10.3	13.5	16.2	9.8	10.8
Czech Republic	8.7	7.9	7.0	7.3	6.5	6.0	10.3	9.8	8.2
Estonia	13.6	7.9	10.2	14.5	8.8	11.0	12.7	7.1	9.5
Hungary	6.4	7.2	10.9	7.0	7.0	11.2	5.6	7.4	10.8
Latvia	13.7	8.9	14.9	14.4	9.1	16.0	12.9	8.7	13.9
Lithuania	16.4	8.3	13.2	18.6	8.2	16.1	14.1	8.3	11.1
Poland	16.1	17.8	10.1	14.4	16.6	9.4	18.2	19.2	10.9
Romania	7.3	7.2	7.0	8.0	7.8	7.6	6.5	6.4	6.4
Slovakia	18.8	16.3	14.0	18.9	15.5	13.5	18.6	17.2	14.5
Slovenia	6.7	6.5	8.8	6.5	6.1	8.4	7.0	7.1	9.4

Sources: Eurostat, "Unemployment by Gender"; Eurostat "Unemployment Rates in the Regions of the European Union."

Women's political participation has also been shaped by developments in organized politics. Unions, women's organizations, and the parties themselves have attempted to educate potential voters on the issues and rising players. Not all of the new organizations have advocated for women's interests in working and having social supports for their families. Some, on the right and connected to the Catholic and Orthodox churches, have pushed for women to return to their traditional roles in the home rather than remaining in the workforce. But even this negative advocacy has increased many women's sense that politics makes a difference in their lives. As a result, women's support has gone to organizations that support their interests. In the Czech Republic, for instance, more women than men voted for conservative rather than for leftist parties in 1996, but women have subsequently moved to the left more than men, regardless of social class and age.[15]

The reemergence of nationalism and the politicization of ethnic identification in some of the postcommunist countries have also had a profound effect on the political salience of women's position in society, women's participation in public life, and women's concerns in public and political debate. Nationalism and strong ethnic identification have often been associated with more traditional conceptions of gender relations, challenging women's rights to an active life outside the household by putting the primary emphasis on their support for the family, as mothers, educators, and upholders of national or ethnic traditions. Efforts to restrict abortion and encourage larger families have been, in some places, related to the desire to make an ethnic or religious group more powerful. Furthermore, it is both common and expected for right-wing interests to attack any continuation of the state and social welfare policies of communism, with its commitment to promoting women's equality and social participation.[16]

Not all political parties either deal with issues that directly affect women or have consistent policies on social and labor policies, but two groups of parties have taken specific positions on women's issues even though they do not necessarily receive the votes of a majority of women. The Christian Democratic, church-affiliated, and nationalist parties tend to support a return to a strong family and women's traditional roles. The reformed communist, socialist, and social democratic parties generally emphasize gender equality, at least with respect to employment practices and social welfare policies. The liberal parties, though their policies vary even more than those of parties to the right and to the left, tend both to support women's right to abortion and to be open to women's rights issues, but they do not generally push for women's rights in the labor market or incorporate a women's agenda into their programs. Their lack of support for active measures in this respect reflects an important issue that separates liberals from reformed communists and social democrats.

Both the economic policy constraints and the new ideological landscape of these political systems meant that getting women elected did not necessarily mean women's issues were advanced. Especially at the beginning of the transition period, many women who engaged in politics did not have an agenda focused on the needs of women. If they did worry about developments that seemed to reduce work opportunities for women or the decline in more general social support that threatened women's lives, they hesitated in many cases to bring up these issues or press for a fair resolution in these moments of national change. Many women leaders were also uncertain of how to relate to the new independent women's organizations developing in their countries. Indeed, women have not been very successful in rising to positions of leadership when they have pushed for clearly female causes.[17]

There are frequently differences in what women's groups support, how women in parliament present their particular issues, and their very definitions of what women should do. Variations exist between those women who move in an international feminist environment and those who do not.[18] Those connected with Western feminist groups tend to focus on women's role in the economy and their liberation from household tasks as a part of Westernizing their societies. Those supporting nationalism tend to focus on women's roles as mothers and keepers of the home and national traditions. Women's groups also vary in their understanding of the role and responsibility of the state. Different conceptions of women's interests, and more broadly of gender relations, have had an impact on the actions of elected representatives. These conceptions also determine the organizational and advocacy goals for organizations that advocate for "women's concerns." There are independent women's organizations engaged in policy making and lobbying. Others concentrate on addressing the immediate needs of women through direct help, local projects of all sorts, and, in some cases, organizing centers for women. Often, differences in perspective and focus have prevented women's groups from supporting each other. Differences between women's groups in eastern and western Germany, for example, have hindered common actions. One vivid example of these differences occurred during a meeting of women affiliated with or interested in a German political party. The guest speaker was from the west; the meeting was held in the former GDR. Next to the meeting room were the children of those eastern German women who attended the discussion. After the western German speaker denounced the family as an institution, the eastern German women took over the meeting and ignored her. Some of these same discussions continue to be salient today in Central and Eastern Europe.

Electoral Arrangements and Political Parties

The chances for women to advance in political life depend, to an important extent, on structural conditions in the political system. Although the share of women among elected representatives does not correlate with the amount or kind of policy affecting women that is introduced and passed, it is clearly an important influence on the position of women and their issues in the political arena.

After the end of communism, there was considerable opposition to quotas for women in representative bodies. Quotas were attacked as undemocratically influencing the election process, being responsible for the participation of unqualified women under communism, and going against more traditional roles for women and men. Some of those who held these views also felt men were meant to do the work of politics. Proponents of quotas were frequently attacked as communist or as supporting a return to the old system.

Attitudes toward quotas have been somewhat different in Germany and seem to be changing in the same direction in other postcommunist countries as well. Quota systems for women in the Green Party and the Social Democratic Party, as well as in the Party of Democratic Socialism (PDS, the reformed Communist Party) and later the Left Party (an alliance of the PDS and a small segment of the Social Democratic Party), led to new opportunities for women. In the 2002, 2005, 2009, and the 2013 elections, about a third of the representatives elected to the German parliament were women. Women in the Czech Republic were more likely to support quotas in the late 1990s than in the immediate postcommunist period.[19] The Czech Social Democratic Party, the leading party in the Czech Republic in the early 2000s, initiated quotas for women occupying party offices.[20] Women in the Czech Republic were more likely to support quotas in the late 1990s than in the immediate postcommunist period. Other political parties in Poland have also initiated quotas.[21] The Polish Parliamentary Group of Women proposed a 30 percent quota but did not gain enough support to pass the measure in parliament.[22] In the Polish parliamentary elections of 2001, the Democratic Left Alliance and the Labor Union, as well as the Freedom Union, accepted a quota of at least 30 percent for women on their lists of candidates.[23] These quotas were also in effect in the 2005 elections. After extensive debate, the Hungarian Socialist Party endorsed a quota system that reserved for women and people under thirty-five one-fifth of seats in the party's elected bodies.[24] These are very important developments, reflecting a major change in political life in these countries since the beginning of the transition period.

Proportional representation systems are generally associated with increases in women's representation, while only modest gains are made in majoritarian systems.[25] When parties expect to win several seats, they are more likely to try to balance their tickets by gender, provided that women are effectively organized within the party. The more seats they expect to win, the more they are willing to include women as more than mere tokens. Although in 2005 in Poland neither the right-wing League of Polish Families nor the Self-Defense Party supported women's engagement in politics and work, both included a significant number of women on their candidate lists, though virtually none of these women had been politically active before. This meant that, in the 2005–2007 parliament, after unexpected vote gains, the right-wing parties had more women as deputies than the centrist parties, which had a greater political base from which to choose candidates. Although the parties' platforms did not change, women in these parties gained leadership experience. The rapid demise of these parties, though, meant that the women had no chance to use it.

Proportional representation systems also foster a contagion effect, as parties adopt policies initiated by other political parties. When a party that is dominant in an individual district in a single-member district system is challenged to nominate more women, it may be able to ignore the pressure because it is unwilling to lose the seat of an incumbent. In a proportional representation system, the loss of a few votes may lead to a loss for the party.[26] Closed lists, which give parties more control over the choice of candidates, are more helpful for women's participation than open lists.[27] Thus, although preferential voting systems in which voters choose individual candidates give voters the opportunity to promote women, they also give them the opportunity to do the opposite. A highly centralized party gives leaders the control to create openings for women if they desire to do so, and if they do not, a central party organization can be held responsible for the low number of women candidates. Preferential voting, on the other hand, leaves parties free of responsibility for insuring gender balance.[28] If the forces interested in women's representation are not effectively organized, however, the electoral system will probably have only limited effect.[29] It is thus only under certain conditions that proportional representation results in increased participation by women.

The way political parties deal with women's issues also has an impact on the number of women elected to parliament. In several countries, such as the Czech Republic and Hungary, as well as the eastern parts of Germany, left-leaning parties tend to have greater female representation than right-leaning parties. This pattern is in line with the broad characterizations of the parties' policy orientations on women's issues discussed earlier. Thus, it came as no surprise that after the 1998 elections in Hungary, when a more conservative coalition replaced the socialist-liberal government, the number of women in parliament dropped. In Ukraine, left-wing parties whose revival started in 1994 worked at promoting women candidates. At the same time, women's profile increased in other parties as well.[30] Yulia Tymoshenko played a major role in the Orange Revolution in Ukraine and served as prime minister under President Yushchenko. Although the percentage of women in the parliaments elected in 2005 and 2009 remained the same in Poland, the dominance of right-wing parties in 2005 (two with close ties to the Catholic Church) led to increasingly conservative policies related to women. Although these parties included a high percentage of women, rather than equal treatment, these women supported pro-family policies and pushed women to have and take of care of more children.

Other Factors Affecting Women's Roles in Politics

The education and professional training of women are crucial for their acceptance in political life, especially at the national level. In Czechoslovakia during the communist period, for example, women both in the government and among party elites were disproportionately drawn from working-class or peasant backgrounds and had less tenure and higher turnover than their male counterparts. There were no female heads of state or prime ministers in the communist period. Since the end of communism, although the number of women in public office has decreased, the qualifications of those women who have attained high political office have greatly improved.[31] Women leaders thus bring far more to the table when they exercise political power in postcommunist parliaments and have a greater impact on policy than they had under communism.

The educational and occupational patterns resulting from policies adopted during the communist era gave women skills and tools useful in political life. Women's higher qualifications are particularly important when they are political candidates. In several of the countries of Central and Eastern Europe, women attended university in numbers equal to or greater than men. The experience professional women gained in their work groups, as well as through activity in unions, is also important, even with all the limitations involved.[32]

Women's experience in professional and other nongovernmental associations also helps create the skills needed for wider political involvement. Not only do these activities increase women's experience, but the organizations can become a power base for those who are interested in becoming political candidates. They also give women visibility with the public.[33]

Photo 6.3.   Iveta Radičová, prime minister of Slovakia from 2010–2012, who also served as minister of labor in 2005 and 2006. She is a sociologist by training.

Local political experience may also be the beginning of a political career. In Hungary, as in many other countries, women's political engagement seems to be most prevalent at local levels,[34] and women's organizations tend to concentrate on local politics, where women are thought to be more at ease. Many of these early women's organizations tended to concentrate on social issues and assisting women in difficulty.[35] Many women also work in the professional administration of local governments.[36] Approximately equal numbers of all female deputies in the Czech parliament interviewed in the mid-1990s held an appointed or elected office at the local level prior to being elected to parliament.[37] Many women deputies in Romania in the late 1990s had done extensive work in their party organizations; a number also had experience in local politics and government.[38]

Even when involvement in local politics does not lead women to run for higher office, higher levels of women's participation have an impact on policy. Social spending by local governments in Hungary, for example, shows "significantly higher standards" where women represent the majority in decision-making bodies. As Julia Szalai, a Hungarian sociologist, writes,

> Their presence safeguards a sufficient level of expenditures on the moderniza-
> tion of local childcare facilities, day centers, and homes for the elderly. Simi-
> larly, welfare assistance reaches more of the needy and gives them more efficient

support in those communities in which women determine the orientation of local politics. These socially "sensitive" political bodies are also usually more open to civil initiatives, thus inviting an even larger circle of women into the shaping of community life.[39]

International organizations have played an important role in opening up possibilities for women. European women's sections of trade unions offered lectures and workshops at the invitation of women's groups in Hungary and elsewhere, for example, where working conditions, low pay, and problems after the end of maternity leave were discussed.[40] European and American groups and foundations, as well as governments, have provided funds for numerous women's nongovernmental organizations and sponsored programs.[41] On more substantive issues, international expectations were important for the 1997 bill passed in the Hungarian parliament that criminalized rape within marriage.[42]

The European Union has also had an important impact on the issues that Central and East European members of parliaments address. The Council of Ministers and the European Parliament recently reached agreement on a commission proposal for tight regulations that would combat sexual harassment at work as well as introduce additional changes to the laws on equality between men and women, for example.[43] After the June 1999 European parliamentary elections, women represented 30 percent of the total deputies in the European Parliament, a substantial increase from 1979, when women's representation was only 17 percent. In interviews with members of the European Parliament, it emerged that despite national and cultural differences, there were clearly certain women's rights issues, such as child care, sexual harassment, and employment, that the women parliamentarians thought they could affect positively. They also believed that the high percentage of women in the parliament made it easier to put those issues on the agenda.[44] As part of the accession process, candidate countries also have had to adopt "gender-equality machinery," including committees to monitor discrimination against women and anti-discriminatory legislation.

Women also participate in politics as members of women's groups as well as women's caucuses in unions and parties and in professional organizations. Challenges to social policies that benefit women and reproductive rights in particular can galvanize large numbers of women. The organization of women against attempts to criminalize abortion can be seen in a number of countries in the region. Poland is the best-known case because of the intense conflict with the Catholic Church; both women and men organized in protest against new abortion regulations. A large number of women's groups have also emerged in Hungary, where there was an effort to address the possible curtailment of reproductive rights, an increase in the retirement age, and decreased support for child care. Although successful with the first two issues, women's groups were not able to unify their forces sufficiently to prevent reductions in maternity and family benefits.

The possibilities for women leaders to work against the tight control of party decisions vary across countries. In Poland, a women's group formed in parliament that cut across party lines and included a majority of women delegates, but the creation and coordination of such a group was difficult when the right wing was dominant, so it did little. In most legislatures, tight party discipline and party control over the recruitment process limit women's cooperation across party lines. In some cases, women parliamentarians see no need to organize themselves as women within parliament.[45] In June 2009 in Poland, the Congress of Women, attended by women activists of different organizations, media people, and a few academics, concluded that the main goal of the congress was to introduce parity on electoral lists and began to collect the number of signatures required in preparation for the discussion in parliament.[46]

Women's success in politics also depends on their ability to frame their concerns and policy ideas in ways that are consistent with the dominant values and experiences of their constituencies. Understanding and taking into account the cultural, social, and political outlook of the people whom they seek to represent is of critical importance, even if—and perhaps especially if—women deputies are introducing innovative ideas or feminist ideologies.

Conclusion

Although there have been recent increases in women's political representation in some countries, women continue to play a secondary role in political life beyond voting in Central and Eastern Europe. Yet, despite the weak participation of women in the national political scene in nearly all postcommunist countries, women in much of the region retain an interest in politics equal to that of men. The obstacles women encounter in the postcommunist world, not their limited interest, explain their low participation. Most women attempt to remain active in the workplace outside the home, thus continuing their education, the use of their professional and vocational skills, and their contact and experience with the outside world. To the extent that they are active in professional associations, unions, and other voluntary organizations, they remain aware of and gain practice in activities that are important preparation for future political engagement. Social policies encouraging such engagement and political mechanisms that insure women's representation are crucial determinants of levels of women's political activism.

Participation in political life on the local level is typically part of the background of women who become active nationally. Women's activity at the local level in government, in women's associations, and in other nongovernmental organizations contributes not only to vital experience for women but also to the creation of viable social policies. In most of the countries discussed, women's groups have been important: first, by helping individuals in marginal social groups who are otherwise without sufficient supports and, second, by articulating the needs of these groups to the public and to governmental representatives, thus increasing the sensitivity of representatives to important social concerns. Links with international organizations have been helpful in this respect; links with supportive political parties may be even more important. Even with the frustrations that women active politically on the national level continue to experience, it is clear that in the years since the end of communism in Europe, women in several of the countries discussed in this chapter have gained more experience, have filled more important positions, and are more confident their ability to have an impact in the longer run.

Study Questions

1. Which features of the preceding communist systems were positive and which were negative for the later political participation of women?

2. What factors were most important for the declining involvement of women in post-communist politics?
3. Are electoral systems relevant for women's access to political office?
4. Did influences from other countries shape women's participation in postcommunist politics?
5. Are the politics advocated by women politicians shaped by their gender? Discuss other relevant factors.

Suggested Readings

Fodor, Eva. *Working Difference: Women's Working Lives in Hungary and Austria, 1945–1995.* Durham, NC: Duke University Press, 2003.

Gal, Susan, and Gail Kligman. *Reproducing Gender.* Princeton, NJ: Princeton University Press, 2000.

Hankivsky, Olena, and Anastasiya Salnykova, eds., *Gender Politics and Society in Ukraine.* Toronto: University of Toronto Press, 2012.

Kolinsky, Eva, and Hildegard Maria Nickel, eds. *Reinventing Gender: Women in Eastern Germany since Unification.* London: Frank Cass, 2003.

Matland, Richard E., and Kathleen A. Montgomery, eds. *Women's Access to Political Power in Postcommunist Europe.* Oxford: Oxford University Press, 2003.

Rueschemeyer, Marilyn, ed. *Women in the Politics of Postcommunist Eastern Europe.* London: M. E. Sharpe, 1998.

Rueschemeyer, Marilyn, and Sharon Wolchik, eds. *Women in Power in Post-communist Parliaments.* Washington, DC: Woodrow Wilson Center Press; Bloomington and Indianapolis: Indiana University Press, 2009.

Websites

Interparliamentary Union, "Women in National Parliaments": http://www.ipu.org/wmn-e/classif.htm

Parliamentary Assembly, "The Situation of Women in the Countries of Post-communist Transitions": Draft of a Committee Report for the Parliamentary Assembly of the Council of Europe, 2004. Instructive about the first ten years of transition. http://assembly.coe.int/ASP/Doc/XrefViewHTML.asp?FileID=10366&Language=EN

"Women in Government": http://en.wikipedia.org/wiki/Women_in_government (a general overview on Wikipedia)

Notes

1. An earlier version of this chapter was published as "Les nouvelles democraties eu-ropeennes de l'Europe de l'est," in *Femmes et parlements: Un regard international,* ed. Manon Tremblay (Montréal: Éditions du remue-ménage, 2004). Parts of the background material used appeared in Marilyn Rueschemeyer, "Frauen und Politik in Osteuropa: 10 jahre nach dem Zu-sammenbruch des Sozialismus," *Berliner Journal fur Soziologie* 11, no. 1 (2001): 7–18. It has been substantially revised and updated for this volume.

2. Marie Čermaková, "Women in Czech Society: Continuity or Change," in *Women, Work and Society*, ed. Marie Čermaková (Prague: Academy of Sciences of the Czech Republic, 1995), 19–32.

3. Hana Havelková, "Political Representation of Women and Political Culture in the Czech Republic" (paper presented at the Conference on Women's Political Representation in Eastern Europe, Bergen, Norway, 1999).

4. Marilyn Rueschemeyer, "The Work Collective: Response and Adaptation in the Structure of Work in the German Democratic Republic," *Dialectical Anthropology* 7 (1982): 155–63; Marilyn Rueschemeyer, "Integrating Work and Personal Life: An Analysis of Three Professional Work Collectives in the GDR," *GDR Monitor* (1983): 27–47. For a recent collection on direct research in communist Eastern Europe, see Marilyn Rueschemeyer, ed., "Research in Communist Countries," special issue of *Problems of Post-communism* 60, no. 4 (July–August 2013).

5. Jiřina Šiklová, "Inhibition Factors of Feminism in the Czech Republic after the 1989 Revolution," in *Women, Work and Society*, ed. Marie Čermaková (Prague: Academy of Sciences of the Czech Republic, 1995), 33–43.

6. During the early transition years in some of the countries, there was continuity in a number of the supports people had taken for granted. In the Czech Republic, for example, rent control kept housing expenses low, but young people looking for new housing often found the costs unaffordable. "The impact of the shift to market rates was compounded by . . . a dramatic decrease in new housing . . . but those who had housing did not face immediate evictions or immediate dislocations." See Marilyn Rueschemeyer and Sharon Wolchik, "The Return of Left-Oriented Parties in Eastern Germany and the Czech Republic and Their Social Policies," in *Left Parties and Social Policy in Postcommunist Europe*, ed. Linda Cook, Mitchell Orenstein, and Marilyn Rueschemeyer (Boulder, CO: Westview Press, 1999), 132.

7. Gunnar Winkler, ed., *Sozialreport 1990* (Stuttgart: Aktuell, 1990).

8. Marian J. Rubchak, "Discourse of Continuity and Change: The Legislative Path to Equality" (54–74) and Anastasiya Salnykova, "Electoral Reforms and Women's Representation in Ukraine" (75–97), *Gender Politics and Society in Ukraine* (Toronto: University of Toronto Press, 2012). At present (winter 2013–2014), Yanukovych has been ousted by the Euromaidan demonstrations, and in response Russia's president Vladimir Putin has annexed the Crimea.

9. Marilyn Rueschemeyer, ed., *Women in the Politics of Postcommunist Eastern Europe* (London: M. E. Sharpe, 1998).

10. During the early transition years in some of the countries, there was continuity in a number of the supports people had taken for granted. In the Czech Republic, for example, rent control kept housing expenses low, but young people looking for new housing often found the costs unaffordable. The impact of the shift to market rates was compounded by . . . a dramatic decrease in new housing . . . but those who had housing did not face immediate evictions or immediate dislocations," See Marilyn Rueschemeyer and Sharon Wolchik, The Return of Left-Oriented Parties in Eastern Germany and the Czech Republic and Their Social Policies,," in *Left Parties and Social Policy in Postcommunist Europe*, ed. Linda Cook, Mitchell Orenstein, and Marilyn Rueschemeyer (Boulder, CO: Westview Press, 1999), 132.

11. Ann Graham and Joanna Regulska, "Expanding Political Space for Women in Poland? An Analysis of Three Communities," *Communist and Post-communist Studies* 30, no. 1 (1997): 65–82.

12. For the latter, see the United Nations Economic Commission for Europe Gender Statistics Data Base: Statistics on Women and Men in the ECE Region, Regional Symposium on Mainstreaming Gender into Economic Policies, 2004, http://www.unece.org/fileadmin/DAM/Gender/documents/Symposium%20paper.pdf (accessed September 2, 2014).

13. Čermaková, "Women in Czech Society," 10; Marilyn Rueschemeyer, "Social Democrats after the End of Communist Rule: Eastern Germany and the Czech Republic," *Sociological Analysis* 1, no. 3 (1998): 41–59.

14. Hildegard Maria Nickel, "With a Head Start on Equality from the GDR into the Trap of Modernization in the Federal Republic: German Women Ten Years after the 'Wende'" (paper presented at the Center for European Studies, Harvard University, 1999).

15. Rueschemeyer and Wolchik, "The Return of Left-Oriented Parties."

16. Branka Andjelkovic, "Reflections on Nationalism and Its Impact on Women in Serbia," in *Women in the Politics of Postcommunist Eastern Europe*, ed. Marilyn Rueschemeyer (London: M. E. Sharpe, 1998), 235–48; Jill Irvine, "Public Opinion and the Political Position of Women in Croatia," in *Women in the Politics of Postcommunist Eastern Europe*, ed. Marilyn Rueschemeyer (London: M. E. Sharpe, 1998), 215–34.

17. Sarah Birch, "Women and Political Representation in Contemporary Ukraine" (paper presented at Conference on Women's Political Representation in Eastern Europe, Bergen, Norway, 1999).

18. Olga Lipowskaja, "Sisters or Stepsisters: How Close Is Sisterhood?" *Women's Studies International Forum* 17 (1994): 273–76.

19. Sharon Wolchik, "Men and Women as Leaders in the Czech and Slovak Republics" (paper presented for the Conference on Women's Political Representation in Eastern Europe, Bergen, Norway, 1999), 5.

20. Rueschemeyer, "Social Democrats," 49.

21. Joanna Regulska, personal communication, 1999.

22. Renata Siemienska, "Consequences of Economic and Political Changes for Women in Poland," in *Women and Democracy: Latin America and Eastern Europe*, ed. Jane S. Jaquette and Sharon L. Wolchik (Baltimore: Johns Hopkins University Press, 1998), 125–62.

23. Renata Siemienska, who has written about the quotas, has also noted a number of other legislative initiatives of the Parliamentary Group of Women, such as a proposal to modify the method of calculating taxes to protect single parents (usually single mothers), involvement in amending the Family and Guardian's Code, and the liberalization of the abortion law (personal communication, 2002).

24. Katalin Fabian, "Making an Appearance: Women in Contemporary Hungarian Politics" (paper presented at the annual meeting of the American Association for the Advancement of Slavic Studies, St. Louis, Missouri, 1999), 7.

25. Richard Matland, "Legislative Recruitment: A General Model and Discussion of Issues of Special Relevance to Women" (paper presented at the Conference on Women's Political Representation in Eastern Europe, Bergen, Norway, 1999).

26. Richard Matland and Donley Studlar, "The Contagion of Women Candidates in Single-Member and Multi-Member Districts," *Journal of Politics* 58, no. 3 (1996): 707–33.

27. Matland, "Legislative Recruitment," 13.

28. Miki Caul, "Women's Representation in Parliament: The Role of Political Parties" (paper presented for the annual meeting of the American Political Science Association, Washington, DC, 1997); Pippa Norris and Joni Lovenduski, *Political Recruitment: Gender, Race and Class in the British Parliament* (Cambridge: Cambridge University Press, 1995).

29. Matland, "Legislative Recruitment," 15.

30. Birch, "Women and Political Representation," 15.

31. Sharon Wolchik, "Women and the Politics of Transition in the Czech and Slovak Republics," in *Women in the Politics of Postcommunist Eastern Europe*, ed. Marilyn Rueschemeyer (London: M. E. Sharpe, 1998), 116–41.

32. Marilyn Rueschemeyer, *Professional Work and Marriage: An East-West Comparison* (Oxford, UK: St. Antony's Oxford/Macmillan, 1981), 138–64.

33. Matland, "Legislative Recruitment," 14.

34. Fabian, "Making an Appearance," 5.

35. Fabian, "Making an Appearance," 14.

36. Julia Szalai, "Women and Democratization: Some Notes on Recent Change in Hungary," in *Women and Democracy*, ed. Jane Jaquette and Sharon Wolchik (Baltimore: John Hopkins University Press, 1998).

37. Wolchik, "Men and Women as Leaders," 8.

38. Mary Ellen Fischer, "The Changing Status of Women in Romanian Politics," in *Women in the Politics of Postcommunist Eastern Europe*, ed. Marilyn Rueschemeyer (London: M. E. Sharpe, 1998), 168–95.

39. Szalai, "Women and Democratization," 200.

40. Fabian, "Making an Appearance," 18.

41. Fischer, "The Changing Status of Women," 186.

42. Urszula Nowakowska, "Violence against Women: International Standards, Polish Reality," *Journal of Communist Studies and Transition Politics* 15, no. 1 (1999): 41–63.

43. "Equal Opportunities: Parliament and Council Agree on Tough New Equality Rules," *European Social Policy* 128 (April 2002): 31–32.

44. Jane Freedman, "Women in the European Parliament," *Parliamentary Affairs* 55, no. 1 (January 2002): 179–88.

45. Fischer, "The Changing Status of Women," 187.

46. Professor Renata Siemienska, personal communication.

CHAPTER 7

Transitional Justice in Central and Eastern Europe

Peter Rožič and Brian Grodsky

The past still haunts Central and East European politics. Among the many postcommunist challenges, the issues of transitional justice have been particularly persistent. By means of transitional justice, successor states to authoritarian regimes have sought to overcome the legacy of repression and injustice. Individuals and whole societies have called for justice, truth, redress, and reconciliation to rectify past wrongs and their shadows. The communist world was not merely one of neighbors reporting on each other and controls on whether individuals could travel and where they lived or could go to school. It was also, depending on the time and place, a world of torture, murder, and imprisonment. As in other postauthoritarian countries, the aim of postcommunist transitional justice has been to acknowledge the coercive past, bring the perpetrators to justice, compensate the victims, revise historical narratives, work toward political transformation, prevent abuses from reoccurring, and move on.

This ambitious "justice" agenda was not as "transitional" as many had hoped, and many more have questioned the degree of its success. For some, the specter of communism has far from vanished. For instance, right and center-right politicians still denounce the supposedly insufficient accounting for past rights abuses. They assert that communism remains a threat, making dealing with the past a deciding factor in politics. Others blame the failed postcommunist privatization efforts for violent unrest, such as in Bosnia-Herzegovina in 2014. Still others link the tragic 2014 protests in Ukraine to President Viktor Yanukovych's communist past and his ties to Moscow. Twenty-five years after the collapse of communism and two decades after the postcommunist upheavals in Yugoslavia, making sense of the politics of Central and East Europe requires an understanding of how the past has and has not been dealt with in each country.

Postcommunist transitional justice was born in a charged political context. Legacies of corruption, authoritarian rule, planned economies, and communist ideologies have been difficult to overcome. Those picking up the pieces of communism were placed under an enormous burden. At the time of regime change, the political system was broken. The economy was imploding. Social structures were in disarray. Expectations were high. People who had demanded change now awaited the fruits of their victory. The benefits of regime change were to be delivered by former members of the opposition, who usually had little to no experience running a state. The new leaders risked losing power if they could not deliver. In addition to implementing extremely challenging political and economic reforms, the new regimes were supposed to carry out a variety of types of transitional justice.

There has been no universal model for transitional justice in Central and Eastern Europe. Countries have used judicial and symbolic measures of transitional justice, spanning from legal processes to reparation, truth processes, and institutional reform, to administrative adjudication. Immediately after regime change, states sought to decrease the influence of the former Communist Party by confiscating its property, penalizing the use of communist propaganda, introducing lustration laws, and opening communist files to the public. Other state responses to the legacy of repression have focused on retribution, including criminal trials. Victim-centered and reparatory perspectives have included truth commissions, property-restitution programs, compensation for imprisonment and career losses, public apologies, and the construction of memorials and museums. In some countries, a combination of these methods has been used. Other countries have implemented only a limited number of approaches. Still others have merely (if at all) discussed them.

Transitional Justice: A Trigger and Consequence

One of the most prevalent hypotheses explaining the differences in transitional justice has been the "politics of the present."[1] The decision to launch prosecutions and truth commissions or to conduct administrative purges, compensate victims, and build monuments has been seen as a function of the balance of power and political advantages among different groups. New leaders on the right, such as Hungary's prime minister Viktor Orbán and Poland's Law and Justice Party, led by the Kaczynski brothers, have frequently focused on the past. They have labeled former communist politicians who remain popular as evildoers. Such memory politics has been less about the communist past than about the future of political hegemony. On the other hand, most of the dissidents who fought the old communist system tended to "draw a thick line" between the past and present rather than focus on the past, especially in the early days, when the communist elite and security forces continued to play significant roles in governance.[2] Yet, the unsettled past accounts kept coming back up. Furthermore, former communists hoped initially that the old system would be remembered for its social services. Then, when that failed, they tried to implement a limited and regulated opening of the records on secret police agents and old Communist Party officials. Whatever was done, the past has remained a powerful part of contemporary politics in virtually every country.

What has been used from the tool kit of retributive, reparatory, or restorative justice depended on other factors as well: the timing of human rights violations, the nature of the abuses, the level of infiltration in the ranks of the anticommunist opposition, the political and economic power of former communist actors in the new system, security issues, and public demand. Moreover, a genuine concern for reconciliation and democratization led numerous political, religious, and social activists, as well as artists and scholars, to go beyond the simple political use of transitional justice. Some public figures made efforts to avoid attacks on the past and focus on building democracy: the first noncommunist prime minister of Poland, Tadeusz Mazowiecki; Czech writer, dissident, and politician Václav

Havel; assassinated prime minister of Serbia Zoran Đinđić; and Slovenian novelist Drago Jančar. These figures have encouraged many to embrace the quest for administrative and retributive adjudication, as well as for inclusion, forgiveness, and restorative justice.

How transitional justice was done has been not only a consequence of but also a trigger for ongoing contemporary sociopolitical developments. Tools of transitional justice have had different impacts. Some have led to amendments to constitutions and reforms of the judiciary and police. Others have fostered collective national identities. Still others have deepened social divisions and sharpened political battles. For example, postcommunist lustration, the regional form of limiting the influence of former elites, has contributed to a decrease in postcommunist corruption, but it has also fueled inflammatory politics. Property-restitution programs have recompensed many victims but have also created tense social dilemmas, such as whom to displace, what kind of property to return, to whom, and by whom. Finally, memories differ too. Transitional justice has influenced the way societies and individuals remember the past. Its focus on the negative has also at times conflicted with people's good memories of communism.

Repressive Past and Memory

However the communist period has been used in the postcommunist era, people's memories are complicated. There was, in every country, a repressive system with political murders and torture, denunciations, and long imprisonments for "political crimes." But the communist regimes also provided a sense of economic safety and equality. The level of repression decreased, in most places, after the death of Joseph Stalin in 1956. In some cases after 1956, outright repression gradually mutated into subtler forms of state control. But the memories of past extremes, like the 1968 repression of the Prague Spring, attacks on demonstrators in Poland, and the ongoing brutal rule in Albania, Bulgaria, and Romania, instilled in people a fear of speaking out. Even Yugoslavia, the least repressive among the communist regimes, silenced memories of long-standing ethnic conflicts until it fell apart and the tensions exploded.

Most of the controls exercised between 1956 and 1989 in the Soviet bloc involved spying on individuals. The secret police employed various surveillance techniques, most frequently through extensive informant networks, identifying and monitoring those who acted against the regime. Speaking out could result in anything from workplace dismissals and bans on foreign travel to the destruction of property, death threats, and abduction of the regime's most feared opponents. Mere criticism of the regime in some places could lead to property confiscation, long jail terms, and even denial of access to university education for dissidents' children.

The scope of (secret) police activity varied from one country to another and over time. Some have claimed that spying was correlated with a regime's legitimacy. Yet, while people's perceptions of rulers were often linked to the economic situation, the spying on citizens went on even in relatively well-to-do Czechoslovakia and Yugoslavia. Moreover, in Czechoslovakia, where interwar democracy had been strong, the communist police were as repressive as they were in Bulgaria, Romania, and Albania, which had no history of democracy.

When regimes responded to mass demands for change, popular memories were often reinforced by the use of harsh repression reminiscent of the Stalinist period. For instance, the police, the military, the militia, and even the Soviet Army were sporadically used to brutally repress those demanding change, most dramatically in Hungary in 1956, Czechoslovakia in 1968, and Poland (although without direct Soviet involvement) in response to its periodic upheavals. The efficient interplay between the secret police and the Communist Party, which orchestrated everything from national politics to apartment administration, reminded all of their vulnerable position in society.

Some memories were also good. Communist states did not rely solely on sticks. Leaders balanced political repression with economic carrots to increase their legitimacy. Most of the citizens tacitly gave up certain rights in exchange for the promise of economic security. Most people benefited from a sprawling state-controlled social safety net. There was virtually no unemployment. Social services, such as health care and education, even if substandard, were free. Official subsidy programs were often accompanied by informal networks of corruption, which originated in either economic growth and loans or empty store shelves and a scarcity of goods. In other words, the communist system was far from static. The massive demands for change in Hungary (1956), Czechoslovakia (1968), and Croats in Yugoslavia (1971) and repeatedly in Poland challenged a variety of Communist Party policies, including the economic ones, rather than simply the system of one-party rule. Ruling elites had no illusions of omnipotence and in some cases even promised concessions that would reduce political tension. A combination of not only repression but also popular cooptation through the provision of specific rewards for reporting to the secret police or simply being compliant helped to maintain the communist system for more than three decades after Stalin's brutal reign. With the communist politics of carrots and sticks, most citizens could usually, by keeping a low political profile, avoid harsh repression. Such submission kept despotic leaders in power, entangled citizens in a web of tacit assent, and censored various societal institutions, from media to culture, to keep the system far from transparent.

Public acceptance of the communist system was ultimately questioned more explicitly. While many saw institutions and the economy rotting in the face of corruption and mismanagement, by the 1980s, regimes' need for Western support or to buy off dissent allowed people to express their discontent. Communism was no longer capable of delivering the services promised in state-controlled newspapers, schoolbooks, and party declarations. True economic reform appeared to be impossible without political reform. The Soviet leader Mikhail Gorbachev pledged a major troop cutback in Europe. Dissent gained momentum, and people risked opposing the system.[3]

Buckling under the weight of economic and international pressures, the loss of institutional support, and an increasingly vocal citizenry, communist elites had not only to adapt, as in the past, but to drastically change their ways. For some states, the changes were negotiated. The communists initiated talks with the opposition that within months paved the way for democratic elections. For other states, where regimes held out for longer, such as in Albania and Romania, popular and sometimes violent protests without opposition leadership forced elites from power in an expedited and more spectacular end. In the Baltic states and Ukraine, the change occurred not only due to massive demonstrations but principally as a result of the collapse of the Soviet Union and the identification of communism with Russia. And in southeastern Europe, where onetime communists attempted to ride the coming wave by brandishing their own nationalist credentials, countries exploded in a stretch of violence that would postpone democracy for another decade. Although the Yugoslav leaders had squashed nationalism in the name of communism, they later helped generate the memories of national oppression, turning people on each other. In short, the memories of the communist past varied across Central and Eastern Europe after communism's end. And the nature of the end accordingly affected states' different patterns of historical justice.

Transition and Justice

The different mechanisms of transitional justice in Central and Eastern Europe are both inseparable from current-day politics and rooted in the region's repressive past. The type of transition and other aspects of the past create constraints on justice. In some of the states that were historically more repressive, new elites pursued administrative purges most aggressively. In Albania, hundreds of thousands of state employees were sacked by left and right governments in the early 1990s. Romania, however, was a highly repressive country, its transition most revolutionary, but it put justice off for a long time as its opposition had been decimated and the new political elite was unable to assemble pro-purge coalitions. The cases of Poland and Hungary show that aggressive types of justice were delayed or watered down as the new elites became aware that some dissidents would be hurt and the Catholic Church had been infiltrated. Moreover, their systems changed faster and through negotiated roundtable agreements with the communists.

A new regime's transitional justice policies provided new leaders political power through the ballot box and could be "politically productive."[4] As a result, new elites walked a delicate line. On the one hand, it was in the interest of political elites with seemingly untainted biographies to pursue justice. Their rationale may have been normative, such as furthering the rule of law, or pragmatic, such as proving their true anticommunist *bona fides* and eliminating political opponents. On the other hand, political and civil groups were constrained by the public's tolerance of policies that might be seen as a costly distraction from providing citizens with various goods and services. Leaders tasked with running the country, as well as ordinary citizens and victims of communism, pursued their preferred justice policies when these posed minimal political or economic risk. Yet they eschewed justice (or suffered from trying to impose it) when it was seen as overly costly.

In the transition period, many factors determined the path toward justice. One was the relative power of new political leaders vis-à-vis actors from the old regimes. In Czechoslovakia, the regime collapsed rapidly and left former communists particularly vulnerable. The new regime introduced perhaps the farthest-reaching policies of lustration, by which the new elite aimed at removing or limiting the influence of people who worked for or cooperated with the communist-era secret police. Unlike in Poland and Hungary, which after the roundtable compromises excluded political or criminal responsibility of communists for the past actions, in Czechoslovakia there was no roundtable negotiation to impede decommunization and lustration bills. Also, the former opposition was small, and the new reformers needed not only to protect democracy but also to demonstrate their skill in running the Czechoslovak state. Elsewhere, mechanisms such as lustration occurred several years after the transition. In negotiated cases such as Poland, lustration was delayed initially because communists still controlled top positions. These actors were often complicit in prior abuses and presumably opposed justice. And even the Czechs, who were among the first to introduce lustration, slowed its implementation as crucial members of the lustration commission proved to be former informants. In the Balkans, reckoning with former secret agents came late, if at all. There, the communists stayed in power under different hats, and many people felt that there was an agent in every family, so they did not want to open the files. In former Yugoslavia, both after Josip Broz Tito's death and after the wars of the 1990s, the degree of public support for administrative and political adjudication against former communists was lower than elsewhere. This could explain why the new elites shied away from measures that could inflame public opinion and increase instability.

Retributive Process: Criminal Prosecution

In any postrepressive state, criminal prosecutions can help further the rule of law, increase the legitimacy of state institutions, lessen the likelihood of vigilante justice, and demonstrate that those who violate others' rights will bear personal responsibility for their actions. The countries of Central and Eastern Europe all pursued criminal accountability to some degree, but the political context is crucial to understanding the means and targets they chose.

In Romania and Bulgaria, long considered to have experienced the slowest of Central and Eastern Europe's transitions away from communism, a handful of trials were held initially. In Romania, they focused on the perpetrators of the violence that occurred at the time of the 1989 transition. Justice was largely symbolic. The trials involved Nicolae Ceauşescu, who was summarily convicted and executed on December 25, 1989, and a small group of his high-profile associates, who were convicted but released within just a few years. In Bulgaria, criminal prosecutions, legalized by a 1990 law extending the statute of limitations, largely focused on just a few individuals and economic crimes, such as corruption, rather than on core human rights violations. Similarly, in Albania, the 1991 government issued a report attacking the former communists for economic rather than political crimes and then successfully prosecuted Albania's last communist leader and fellow Politburo members largely for their misuse of state funds. Only later, in the face of an impending electoral defeat, did noncommunists pursue a Law on Genocide and Crimes against Humanity Committed in Albania during Communist Rule. This led to the prosecutions of twenty-four former high-level officials—some of whom were already in jail for their convictions for economic crimes. The number of prosecutions—and especially convictions—elsewhere has been low. In Latvia, since a 1992 law suspended any statute of limitations for crimes against humanity, genocide, or peace, only eight former NKVD agents have been charged with genocide.

The Czechs have been the most aggressive in launching criminal trials, although most did not end in guilty verdicts. Czech legislation extended the statute of limitations to allow for prosecution of crimes committed between 1948 and 1989 and paved the way for the establishment in 1995 of the Office for the Documentation and Investigation of the Crimes of Communism. By August 2001, the office had investigated more than 3,000 cases and prepared 160 for prosecution. However, only eight alleged rights abusers from the communist era have been found guilty, and a majority of these never faced jail time.[5]

The case of Poland also highlights the difficulties of using the justice system. The Polish Institute of National Remembrance (IPN) was only established in 1998 over the postcommunist president's veto. One of its tasks was to prosecute cases from the communist era. As of 2013, the IPN had initiated just over three hundred prosecutions. Many were of officials from the pre-1956 Stalinist period, who were either elderly or so infirm that the prosecutions were suspended. These prosecutions were also hampered by a lack of evidence: there were no real reports on crimes, and the witnesses or their memories were gone. Moreover, after 2003, when the center-right lost elections, officials of the IPN raised the bar for evidence in crimes dealing with the communist era. Nonetheless, some critical cases were raised. While Wojciech Jaruzelski, the minister of defense during the 1970 Gdańsk killings, and others were eventually judged too old and sick to finish their trials, abundant documentation has since been made available.[6] Moreover, to break up the power of communist-era judges and prosecutors, the parliament in 1998 allowed these judges and prosecutors to face disciplinary courts. However, in practice, they were dismissed on the basis not of criminal charges but of corrupt pension privileges.

Photo 7.1.   General Wojciech Jaruzelski, president of Poland in 1989 and 1990 and former head of the Polish military, was tried for attacks on demonstrators in Gdańsk during the 1970 demonstrations. The trial ran for nearly a decade and then was dropped in 2013 due to his age and illness. (Adam Chelstoski/FORUM)

Another common barrier encountered in criminal prosecutions has been a legal one. In some places this was a simple question of weak institutions, as in Albania, where, after postcommunists won back power in 1997, politicized courts began overturning genocide convictions won by earlier prosecutors. In others, it was a more profound assessment of retroactive justice. While the Czech Constitutional Court upheld its country's extension of the statute of limitations, for example, Hungary's Constitutional Court struck down a similar 1991 law as a case of selective justice that promoted inequality in the new system. "A state under the rule of law cannot be created by undermining the rule of law," the court wrote in an opinion it would repeat with respect to a similar law passed in 1993.[7]

Due to the lack of political will and public support, countries such as Slovenia have had no criminal prosecutions related to the past. In Slovenia, several tens of thousands (some estimates exceed one hundred thousand) of prisoners of war and civilians were murdered in the immediate postwar period by the Titoist regime. Yet not a single person has been found guilty of these crimes. The situation was different in other former Yugoslav republics after the wars in the 1990s because of heavy international pressure. The International Criminal Tribunal for Yugoslavia (ICTY), created by the UN Security Council in 1993, effectively put the senior political and military leaders responsible for war and other crimes on trial. The ICTY made history by indicting a sitting head of state, Slobodan Milošević; however, the tribunal was only intended to prosecute a small number of offenders, and justice for the vast majority of the crimes committed in the wars has yet to be achieved.

Administrative Justice, Part I: Lustration and Decommunization

Lustration has been the most widely pursued justice policy to deal with the past in Central and Eastern Europe. This form of administrative justice systematically limits the political participation of former authoritarian actors. Lustration was, at least initially, designed to cleanse the society of its past evils, lessen corruption, and rebuild confidence in the democratic regime. A perceived need to free the country from corruption, distracting scandals, and the risk of blackmail was a common argument favoring lustration. During parliamentary debates in Romania, some of the themes were moralistic, but the majority were economic—for example, pushing ex-security agents from politically influential economic structures or allowing state leaders to focus their attention on delivery of political goods and prepare for European Union (EU) entry. Although lustration has often been a mechanism for a new set of political purges against anyone representing an oppositional force in the political or nongovernmental sphere, it also resulted in removing the former communist officials most prone to corruption.[8]

Czechoslovakia, in 1991, was the first to pursue lustration. While Václav Havel and other members of the former opposition opposed the policy, the new government started to exclude members of parliament and the government for their cooperation with, for example, the secret police, border service groups, and others. The government also disqualified from public positions anyone who had worked for certain repressive communist-era institutions.

Several other countries followed the Czech example. But the penalties for collaboration, as evidenced through secret police files, have varied from public shaming (in the case of parliamentarians) to employment bans in a broad range of positions, from elected posts and judgeships to management and state bureaucracy positions in state-owned enterprises, state-run media, or academia.[9] Although some lustration processes, including those in Albania and Bulgaria, have also included decommunization (i.e., by which communists were banned from certain positions regardless of their cooperation with the secret police), most in the region have focused on secret police collaborators.

No state, apart from East Germany, initially went as far as the Czechs, and in many countries, lustration was off the table in the early transition period. New elites often saw in lustration a potential political liability, especially since many secret police files were inaccurate, had been tampered with, or might hold embarrassing information about some members of the former opposition, as was the case in Hungary and Poland. In Albania, where one-quarter of the population is estimated to have collaborated with the secret police, highly aggressive justice efforts have been tempered by the fact that even many at the leadership level of anticommunist groupings have solid communist affiliations in their past. Fears that secret police archives could be used to blackmail the new generation of political and economic elites helped convince leaders from the Baltics to Romania to approach lustration with caution. Parliaments in Croatia and Slovenia attempted lustration, but it never passed, or if it did, as in Serbia in 2003, it was not implemented.

Lustration has been the most politically advantageous policy for new political elites eager to gain an edge over their opponents. When launching lustration, they exercised close control over it. For example, while Hungary did eventually pursue lustration in 1996, it helped to divert attention from the country's difficult situation and embarrass political rivals from the postcommunist camp. In Albania, lustration was conducted by a body overwhelmingly dominated by members chosen by the Democratic Party, which created the lustration law, written so its members were largely shielded. In Czechoslovakia, leaders of new parties have continued to use lustration to differentiate themselves from others. A similar process of differentiation took place in Poland, where right-wing elites worked to ensure that attitudes toward the communist past would be fundamental to political identity.

The Polish case highlights the irony of politicized justice. Except for a negligible lustrative provision of 1990, no lustration bill was passed when onetime oppositionists held power from 1989 to 1993. (The 1992 attempt ended in dismissal of the government when a minister presented a list of purported collaborators who were members of the parliament.) Curiously, the law was adopted once postcommunists had taken control of parliament and the presidency. The fall of postcommunist Józef Oleksy's government, under wild accusations that Oleksy had collaborated with the KGB, created a public fiasco. In order to save the left's reputation and limit "wild lustration" accusations, postcommunist president Aleksander Kwasniewski in 1997 signed a bill mandating that individuals serving in certain public offices provide a written declaration indicating whether they had collaborated with the secret services. Unlike under other lustration policies, collaboration itself did not entail punishment; only those filing false declarations would be banned from serving in certain public offices for a period of ten years. Voters did not seem to care; candidates who signed that they had been agents were elected anyway. Nevertheless, based on this law, in 2010 alone the Institute of National Remembrance analyzed over 150,000 lustration declarations and sent information to electoral committees about the status of 34,545 candidates.[10]

Over time, several political leaders throughout Central and Eastern Europe have made their careers by attacking the former system. Lithuania passed its first lustration law in 1999, banning former KGB officers from certain jobs and promising to publicize their names. Latvians also returned to lustration, passing separate laws in 1999 and 2000 banning those who had worked with or for the intelligence or state security services from becoming civil servants or judges. Among late attempts to lustrate was the Polish right's 2006 legislation, giving the Institute of National Remembrance the power to aggressively conduct lustration investigations and bar people in positions from local councilor up to president, including board members of majority state-owned companies, all academics and members of the legal community, journalists of public and private media, and others. That same year, Romanian anticommunist politicians, whose 1990 decommunization and lustration attempts were blocked by then postcommunist president Ion Iliescu, tried again to start lustration. The law promised to ban, from certain public offices for ten years, former leaders of the Communist Party, as well as high-up activists in institutions such as communist youth groups and those who were seen to have done their bidding (such as journalists, university professors, and legal professionals). Neither of these late lustration laws held up for long before being found unconstitutional by the Constitutional Court. The Polish court, for example, stopped implementation on the grounds that the law subjected individuals to self-incrimination, introduced retroactive justice, and overextended state power into the private sphere. Other countries, such as Lithuania, have moderated their lustration programs in the face of criticism from international institutions such as the Council of Europe, the European Court of Human Rights, and the International Labor Organization.

Lustration has been tempered by concerns that primary evidence of collaboration is normally drawn from official secret service records, many of which were at least partially destroyed or tampered with by the outgoing regime. The files were often falsified or had been rifled through, giving inordinate power to the secret police to disgrace people. In other cases, such as in the former Yugoslav republics, records were sold off to, or otherwise acquired by, private individuals, who could manipulate the information. Even where records were intact, they often proved deceptive or incorrect. In several high-profile incidents, innocent people were caught in the lustration web. Former Czech dissident Jan Kavan, for instance, was purged from parliament based on accusations of collaboration, only to clear his name after five years and eventually become the country's foreign minister.

While not all late lustration laws failed, they highlighted numerous dilemmas. In 2009, Macedonian politicians forbade onetime secret collaborators and informants, as well as anyone who utilized their information, from holding public office. Those seeking office were required to sign a statement of noncollaboration. Those who refused to sign were publicly called out. Rather than political purification, the result was political instability. Mimicking a process seen in neighboring Albania a few years earlier, newspapers were littered with political scandal. Accusers and those accused of collaborating publicly confronted each other as would-be defendants and others opposed to the process claimed much of the information released was false. The law was widely criticized for going after those with a relatively limited role in the repressive apparatus while leaving major perpetrators, as well as their victims, untouched.[11]

Administrative Justice, Part II: Opening of the Archives

There have been attempts all over Central and Eastern Europe to release the secret files. Declassification of files has been branded as an important form of historical accounting. These were methods of transitional justice because access to the documents compiled by the secret political police was available not only to journalist or academics but also to victims and, in some cases, ordinary citizens. The method represents a way for the public to become more informed and for victims to reach a degree of closure. Institutions created for declassification have attempted to reach this goal through their publications, searches for the graves of victims, and educational projects. Yet, there has been variation across the region in terms of who has access to the information and what information is revealed. In most cases, such access has been limited and available only decades after the fall of communism.

The Czech Institute for the Study of Totalitarian Regimes (USTR) was launched in 2008, aiming at the study and documentation of Nazi and communist crimes to "preserve the memory of the huge number of victims and to allow the public maximum possible access to the secret activity" of past regimes. The lengthy parliamentary deliberations of 2006 and 2007 were fueled by periodic leakage of secret police files and expedited by the creation of similar institutions in Hungary, Poland, and Slovakia. The USTR has made about 280 million pages available to the public through different research centers and the Internet. Opening of the files has also been controversial, divisive, and unsettling. It has resulted in public scandals and the resignation of many valuable experts from the institute.[12]

Some of the most restrictive approaches to declassification have occurred in Bulgaria, which at first claimed its files were all destroyed, and Romania, which under a postcommunist president initially promised to keep files closed for an extended period in order to avoid what some called witch hunts. After winning power in the mid-2000s, the Romanian center-right ordered the opening of 1 million security files. In Bulgaria, except minor legislative measures dealing with establishing archives for such materials in 1997 and 2001, no laws were adopted to provide for access and disclosure until 2006. The law on archives established a special commission to give people deemed to have been affected by the activity of the former secret service (KDS) full access to their files and conduct investigations. Many have seen this commission as the first successful Bulgarian transitional justice institution. It has verified the past of almost one hundred thousand people and identified forty-six hundred of them as former KDS collaborators.[13] Romania's declassification highlighted the political nature of justice.

Others countries pursued a middle ground, promising to open files but restrict access to those who had privileges, such as victims. In Poland, scholars, journalists, and court officials were initially promised access to files that extended from the start of communism to the end of Stalinism (1944–1956). However, two cabinets collapsed in the early 1990s because of the scandals caused by the information contained in the post-Stalinist secret police archives. To control access to the archives, former communists, who were in power themselves but faced an election, proposed the creation of a special archive, which was amended and accepted by a subsequent parliament. Although Poland's 1997 lustration law left file access highly restricted to the public, when the center-right won the elections later that year, it made the opening of the files a priority, hoping that many individuals would press charges against their abusers in an embarrassing show for the postcommunists. Poland has since published the contents of over five thousand public officers' files.[14]

Overall, there has been a low degree of interest in archival access. This may be due to the elite nature of justice, as well as to generational change coupled with the inaccessibility of the files in the immediate postcommunist period. In Serbia-Montenegro, then a country of more than 10 million, only 2,000 applied to see their files between 2001 and 2003. Numbers have also been low in Romania, where the National Council for the Study of the Securitate Archives, established in 2000, provided citizens the opportunity to access their own secret files. In Poland, between 1998 and 2004, the authorities received only 25,000 requests for files, a relatively paltry number considering that 10 million out of a total 40 million citizens were members of the Solidarity opposition in the early 1980s. In Slovenia, due to a low public demand, the calls for opening the files have fallen short. There, only 3,000 secret police files remain, due to the massive disappearance of documents in late 1980s, and although the abbreviated records of approximately 1 million files were leaked onto the Internet in 2003—among which 100,000 were listed as secret police files, as opposed to criminal files—relatively few Slovenians sought access to their own (abbreviated) files.

Truth Processes: Commissions

Truth commissions have largely been an overlooked solution to the human rights abuses of the communist era. Truth commissions seem to be most useful when victims and victimizers can be clearly delineated. But under communist regimes, many belonged to the party, and many offered information to security services, making it difficult to assign blame individually. The diffused guilt has not only inhibited the creation of truth commissions but also made those that did emerge more interested in (academic or historic) truth than in reconciliation. Postcommunist truth commissions do not represent restorative justice, in which all those with a direct stake in the conflict have a say in conflict resolution.

Although truth commissions are increasingly popular on other continents, only a few Central and East European countries have employed them: Estonia, Latvia, Lithuania, and Romania. Only in late 1998 were the Baltic commissions set up, partly due to the celebrated South African Truth and Reconciliation Commission, which by then had concluded its activity and helped truth commissions gain international acceptance. Once established, these truth commissions released final reports in a short period. Reports included the results of their investigations and the evidence collected to document the human rights abuses perpetrated during communism. Moreover, these formal, top-down efforts to establish the truth have been politicized—in some cases, by reframing the communist period to erase any positive associations that remained. In the Baltics, for instance, respective presidents established historical commissions to probe two now fused periods of occupation: the first under Nazi Germany and the second under the Soviet Union.[15]

Other countries have attempted to seek truth through specific commissions. In Poland, a 1991 law expanded and renamed the long-standing Chief Commission for the Investigation of Hitlerite Atrocities (established in 1945), which became the Chief Commission for the Prosecution of Crimes against the Polish Nation. One primary purpose of the commission before and after 1991 was educational—to investigate and publicize the crimes—while another was to recommend particular cases for prosecution by state prosecutors. Yugoslav truth commissions were set in Bosnia-Herzegovina, Croatia, and Serbia. These attempts were meant to address the human rights violations of the Yugoslav wars of the 1990s. They did not deal with communist crimes *per se*; nor did they produce significant results. For example, several working groups in Bosnia-Herzegovina produced draft legislation to establish working truth commissions, but ongoing disagreements among different ethnic groups on a viable makeup of the country prevented the truth-recovery attempts from being adopted and implemented. In Slovenia, soon after regime change, the parliament established a special commission for the investigation of postwar mass murders and dubious trials orchestrated by the communist regime. However, more than a decade has passed since the commission concluded its work, and the reports have yet to be made public. The failure of truth and investigation commissions in former Yugoslavia can be attributed to a relatively low level of secret police injustice and low public demand.

Reparatory Justice, Part I: Memorialization

Monuments, museums, and memorial sites of the communist era have mushroomed in recent years. With the purpose of honoring victims, helping societies reconcile, and establishing a record of history, postcommunist memorialization efforts have attempted to promote personal and social recovery after regime change. Memorialization also talks about the unspoken. It helps fill in the blanks, recognizing historical events that were ignored or everyone knew about but the state said did not happen. For example, in Ukraine, which has lacked other transitional justice mechanisms, about 300 monuments commemorate the victims of the great famine, the Holodomor, denied by the Soviets for decades. More than 150 memorial sites honor the victims of the 1956 Hungarian Revolution, which was hardly talked about during the communist era in Hungary.

However, the differing perceptions of communism often ignited conflicts over memorialization.[16] Multiple museums of (Soviet) "occupation" exist in Estonia, Georgia, Latvia, Lithuania, Moldova, and Ukraine. In Kyiv, the museum started as an exposition of "communist inquisition" in 2001 and received its current name (Museum of Soviet Occupation) in 2007 under the initiative of President Viktor Yushchenko. Moreover, although in the 2004 election year, President Leonid Kuchma ordered the construction of a national museum monument to Holodomor victims, Yushchenko made the commemoration of all communist-era victims a personal priority in his one term as president. He funded the construction of hundreds of monuments and museums, education programs, and media campaigns.

Central and East Europeans have tended to merge memorialization of two extraordinarily bloody periods of Nazism and communism. Examples are the creation of the Museum of the Occupation of Latvia 1940–1991 in 1993 and of Lithuania's Genocide Victims Museum in 1992. A similar case is the Warsaw Uprising Museum, which includes sections dedicated to Nazi- and Soviet-occupied Poland (there is no communist Poland permanent exhibition). Founded in 1983, the Uprising Museum was opened only in 2004, two years after Lech Kaczynski—an anticommunist who often used history to advance his agenda—was elected mayor of Warsaw. In Hungary, the head of the similar right-of-center FiDeSz party, Viktor Orbán, opened the House of Terror in Budapest, just ahead of the 2002 parliamentary elections. This museum quickly became a political pawn. While the museum professes to be a tribute to the struggle against fascism and communism, it has been criticized for treating the former with "white gloves" and the latter with "brass knuckles." This prompted an early fight with postcommunists, who publicly made known their displeasure with the museum and promised to investigate its financing on taking power in 2002. They subsequently slashed the museum's budget and withheld portions of the remaining funding.

Reparatory Justice, Part II: Rehabilitation, Property Restitution, Apologies

Central and East European reparatory justice has embraced, albeit sporadically, victim-oriented methods as well. These have included compensation for losses (such as harm or lost opportunities), restitution of confiscated property, and rehabilitation of victims. These approaches provided not only material benefits but also symbolic reparations, like commemoration and judicial rehabilitation. In Poland, for example, numerous political prisoners, particularly victims of Stalinism, were rehabilitated through specific parliamentary acts passed by an overwhelming majority of votes. In Latvia, the rehabilitation of victims of the communist regime started under Gorbachev in the late 1980s.

Political overtones often reach into forms of reparatory justice. In Latvia, politicians bundled victims from the Soviet era along with those from the Nazi period. In Poland, initial demands for national legislation were prompted by a need to ensure standardized justice and lessen the burden on courts when they were bombarded with applications from former prisoners from the Stalinist period (and families of deceased prisoners). They demanded that their names and records be cleared of political convictions and that they be given compensation. But during parliamentary debates, members of the formal opposition camp split, with some demanding quick compensation for those who faced repression at some point up to 1989, regardless of the qualitative difference in post-1956 rights abuses.

The Croatian case, in which rehabilitation was led by a former communist and then nationalist, Franjo Tuđman, is a stark reminder that rehabilitation and compensation are subject to political manipulation. In early 1992, Tudman's parliament passed two separate declarations providing for symbolic, though not legal, rehabilitation of two historic figures whose suffering was representative of that of thousands of Croats living in communist Yugoslavia. The declaration to rehabilitate Cardinal Alojzij Stepinac included a condemnation of the political trials against the clergy and faithful and was interpreted by many as an effort to gain support from the church, a powerful social institution. The declaration dedicated to Andrija Hebrang, who advocated for Croatian self-rule as a major figure in the early Yugoslav Communist Party, demonstrated how those who had been active in the Communist Party at some point, like Tudman, could cast the former system as a fundamentally benevolent one gone astray during implementation.

Property restitution has served as another important form of compensation in the region, where the Communist Party allowed for the confiscation of private property en masse during the first years of communist rule. Yet important questions surrounded restitution programs: What kind of property should be returned? Who should design the restitution programs? To whom should properties be returned? What will happen to those living there? To what extent does restitution legitimize the new political regime? The property taken included land, industries, artwork, jewels, places of worship, and schools. The property seized from private people had been retained by the state and communal agencies, such as agricultural collectives, or even transferred to other parties, such as in the 1948 transfer of Greek Catholic churches in Romania to the majority Orthodox Church.

Reparatory justice has been unevenly implemented in the region.[17] The Slovenian 1991 law on denationalization was fitfully implemented in the first half of the 1990s but stalled by 1995 and was frozen until 2000. However, the process gained speed during the country's EU accession process. In Bulgaria, the parliament dominated by the anticommunists adopted a restitution law in 1992. Most of the properties were returned, partly because of significant public support for the program.

In many countries where property restitution would have meant a way to create a capitalist class or a substantial redistribution of already private (and citizen-held) property to former property owners, as in Hungary, political leaders chose instead to issue to those demanding compensation vouchers that could be exchanged for state enterprises or land undergoing privatization. But a glimpse beyond the mechanics highlights the political aspects of this debate in several countries. Often, property restitution became a way for political leaders to bolster their competitive advantage. In the Baltics, even political leaders not known for their nationalist tendencies could profit from a restitution program that primarily benefitted the titular nationality (e.g., Estonians in Estonia, Lithuanians in Lithuania) at the expense of ethnic minorities, particularly Russians. Where property restitution was a no-win situation, it was halting. Such was the case in Poland, where postwar population transfers and territorial changes made restitution a fundamentally international issue, and political elites used the opportunity to warn that restitution could not be expected to include former German residents (of whom there were millions). Although many people have been compensated, no comprehensive restitution program was implemented in Poland.

Official sanctioning of the previous period and apologies, a far less costly version of justice, have tended to proceed at a tedious pace. Virtually all postcommunist states at least initiated declarations that the former period was illegal, though these were sometimes dropped because of legal confusion or perhaps, as some scholars have argued, out of respect for agreements made during the transition. Sometimes, after many years, condemnations came off as politically and socially irrelevant. Poland's first apology for the crimes of communism actually came from postcommunists themselves (anticommunist Tadeusz Mazowiecki deliberately avoided the topic) after their 1993 electoral victory. Members of the onetime anticommunist opposition issued a formal condemnation only in 1998 in a Senate resolution that few even among political elites had heard of. Prior to this, in the chaos of political and economic transformation, political elites shied away from condemning the system. The same might be true in other cases, including in Macedonia, where a condemnation took more than a decade, and Romania, where the process took more than a decade and a half from the fall of communism. These condemnations mattered little in comparison to people's material demands.

Conclusion

Transitional justice strives to help people feel they understand what happened in their systems or their societies as well as to ensure that it will not happen again. In the most general terms, transitional justice aims at facilitating reconciliation, promoting democracy, and ensuring accountability to serve peace. However, from the Baltic to the Black Seas, conflicts driven by painful shared history continue to complicate relations between and within societies more than two decades after the collapse of communism. Has transitional justice in Central and Eastern Europe therefore been a failure?

The evolution of the reckoning with past wrongs and their shadows makes most sense if understood in the context of both a messy transition from communism and the complexity of the communist era itself. On the one hand, postcommunist justice has often turned into a form of identity politics, or even victimology, used by new leaders for political advantage. Central and East European societies have dealt rarely, if at all, with their communist pasts through transitional justice in a comprehensive manner. While most of the countries used some tools of transitional justice, various measures implemented have highlighted the politicization of justice.

On the other hand, postcommunist justice depended on the nature of crimes and abuses. If South African and Latin American transitional justice was about crimes and violence against individuals and groups, leading to the identification of perpetrators, the crimes of communism were much more bureaucratic and involved people spying on one another. Since the communist violence against individuals most often happened long ago, it was remembered but less acute than in other world regions. For that reason, for instance, postcommunist memorialization represents a challenge because so many remember the good parts of communism and find some of the worst stories unbelievable. For the same reason, truth processes and prosecutions were more successful in Latin America and South Africa, as well as in former Yugoslavia. But for the rest of Central and Eastern Europe, the story may be too complex to deal with through truth commissions or trials. Instead, in postcommunist Europe the main issue has been dealing with communist-era agents and secret police, whose past activity led citizens to lose faith in the judgment of themselves and others, which in turn made postcommunist justice all more destructive politically.

Even in the Czech Republic, which has arguably accomplished the most in its transitional justice processes, just less than one-quarter of surveyed Czechs believe, after twenty years, that lustration in their country was successful. Perhaps more ominously, approximately half of respondents felt that social divisions from the past remained alive; just one in six said they were gone. In other countries, a large number of people still look at the communist period positively and are inclined to think a strong leader is what they need. Many, including political elites, have been deeply disaffected by the sociopolitical outcomes over the two decades since regime change. It is thus not surprising that transitional justice is looked on with cynicism or as political opportunism. However, the fact that transitional justice in Central and Eastern Europe has often turned into a complicated political game cannot distract us from the fact that the communist system was, at its worst, enormously repressive, lacking transparency and leaving a legacy of suspicion.

Transitional justice cannot, on its own, solve the legacy of repression. Most studies find that transitional justice has only a moderately beneficial impact on transitional societies. Perhaps we must expect less from transitional justice as an "off-the-shelf" approach. One of reasons is that, despite their common communist pasts, the countries of Central and Eastern Europe differ in culture and the causes for human rights abuses. Each country requires mechanisms matching best its particular context. Another reason is that the efficacy of transitional justice is difficult to quantify, and its broad aim suggests a tremendous complexity. Transitional justice is a multifaceted process, vulnerable to politicization, and therefore a very long-term project.

Study Questions

1. How have the societies of Central and Eastern Europe dealt with their pasts?
2. Why have different states pursued or not pursued the various forms of transitional justice?
3. How did transitional justice impact politics, and vice versa?
4. What explains the different patterns of postcommunist transitional justice?

Suggested Readings

Huyse, Luc. "Justice after Transition: On the Choices Successor Elites Make in Dealing with the Past." *Law and Social Inquiry* 20 (January 1995): 51–78.

Mayer-Rieckh, Alexander, and Pablo De Greiff, eds. *Justice as Prevention: Vetting Public Employees in Transitional Societies.* New York: Social Science Research Council, 2007.

Moran, John P. 1994. "The Communist Torturers of Eastern Europe: Prosecute and Punish or Forgive and Forget?" *Communist and Post-communist Studies* 27 (March 1994): 95–109.

Nalepa, Monika. *Skeletons in the Closet: Transitional Justice in Post-communist Europe.* New York: Cambridge University Press, 2010.

Nedelsky, Nadya. "Divergent Responses to a Common Past: Transitional Justice in the Czech Republic and Slovakia." *Theory and Society* 33 (February 2004): 65–115.

Pop-Eleches, Grigore, and Joshua A. Tucker. 2011. "Communism's Shadow: Postcommunist Legacies, Values, and Behavior." *Comparative Politics* 43 (July 2011): 379–408.

Stan, Lavinia. "The Vanishing Truth: Politics and Memory in Post-communist Europe." *East European Quarterly* 40 (December 2006): 303–408.

———. *Transitional Justice in Eastern Europe and the Former Soviet Union: Reckoning with the Communist Past.* London: Routledge, 2009.

———. "Truth Commissions in Post-communism: The Overlooked Solution?" *Open Political Science Journal* 2 (2009): 1–13.

Stan, Lavinia, and Nadya Nedelsky, eds. *Cambridge Encyclopedia of Transitional Justice.* New York: Cambridge University Press, 2013.

Welsh, Helga A. "Dealing with the Communist Past: Central and East European Experiences after 1990." *Europe-Asia Studies* 48 (May 1996): 413–28.

Williams, Kieran, Brigid Fowler, and Aleks Szczerbiak. "Explaining Lustration in Central Europe: A 'Post-communist Politics' Approach." *Democratization* 12 (February 2005): 22–43.

Notes

1. See, e.g., Kieran Williams, Brigid Fowler, and Aleks Szczerbiak, "Explaining Lustration in Central Europe: A 'Post-communist Politics' Approach," *Democratization* 12, no. 1 (2005): 22–43.

2. Among the first to use the "thick line" analogy was Tadeusz Mazowiecki, Poland's first noncommunist prime minister. In his opening statement to parliament, Mazowiecki declared, "We draw a thick line [*gruba linia*] between ourselves and the past," and stated that competence and loyalty toward the new government should be the only criteria for evaluating public officials. While he later insisted on the importance of the second part of the sentence, namely, that his government should only be held responsible for what it itself would do, the phrase "thick line" became proverbial to stand for a "Spanish" approach to the difficult past: let bygones be bygones. See Timothy Garton Ash, "Truth after Dictatorship," *New York Review of Books* (February 19, 1998): 35–40; Adam Michnik and Václav Havel, "Justice or Revenge?" *Journal of Democracy* 4, no. 1 (1993): 20–27.

3. Opposition movements were complex bodies. They existed mostly as informal organizations of a few members who met, wrote letters, or published underground papers. They fought in the name of varying and overlapping principles ranging from Western-style democracy and capitalism to nationalism. Despite this variety, oppositionists were united in their mainly apolitical hope of escaping a certain economic ruin connected with the political status quo. A certain economic welfare was necessary for dissent to grow. The opposition was weaker in states where the economy was the worst, such as in Ukraine, Romania, Bulgaria, and Albania. While their weakness there may be correlated with the level of repression, opposition grew faster where minimal economic standards were met. This is untrue for Yugoslavia, however, as it experienced not only a better overall economic standard but also less repression, providing weaker incentives for strong and univocal opposition.

4. Katherine Verdery, "Postsocialist Cleansing in Eastern Europe," in *Socialism Vanquished, Socialism Challenged: Eastern Europe and China, 1989–2009*, ed. Nina Bandelj and Dorothy J. Solinger (New York: Oxford University Press, 2012), 72.

5. Roman David, "Twenty Years of Transitional Justice in the Czech Lands," *Europe-Asia Studies* 64, no. 4 (2012): 761–84.

6. The 2008–2011 Institute of National Remembrance case against Jaruzelski and others found several defendants too old and sick as their average age was eighty-two and as the doctor's note advised they sit in court only three to four hours a day. See Monika Nalepa, "Poland," in *Encyclopedia of Transitional Justice*, ed. Lavinia Stan and Nadya Nedelsky (New York: Cambridge University Press, 2013): 2:389.

7. A subsequent attempt in Hungary to use international legal doctrine to frame only the 1956 crimes as "crimes against humanity" and "genocide" was better received by the court, which issued a series of recommendations for delineating what would fall into the former category (mass homicide). When parliament failed to adequately address these recommendations and the Supreme Court was forced to deal with appeals from prosecutions based on this law, the Constitutional Court again stepped in and declared the law unconstitutional based on procedural errors.

8. Yuliy A. Nisnevich and Peter Rožič, "Lustration as an Instrument of Counteracting Corruption," *Polis: Journal of Political Studies* 24, no. 1 (2014): 109–30.

9. For example, the 1994 Hungarian lustration law's targets included those who received reports from the political department of the secret police on a par with working as an informer or undercover officer, as well as music production and entertainment programs. The Bulgarian "Panev law" of 1992 targeted the activity of teaching (in effect, the former instructors of) Marxism-Leninism. The Albanian 1993 law #7666 targeted the exercise of the profession of advocacy, including professor at the faculty of law. Other lustrations targeted the rights of citizens to run for legislative office. While such laws usually target the national level, some aim at the candidates for the European Parliament. At the governmental level, lustration laws also target the employment of high government officials and bureaucrats, judges, and Supreme Court justices. For instance, the 1991 Czech law targets all nonelected politicians and civil servants and verifies their past involvement as secret police officers or informers, Communist Party officials, members of the People's Militia, or members of 1968 verification committees. For the most comprehensive analysis of lustration laws and practices, see Peter Rožič, *Lustration and Democracy: The Politics of Transitional Justice in the Post-communist World* (Washington, DC: Georgetown University, 2012), esp. 207–10.

10. Monika Nalepa, "Poland," in *Encyclopedia of Transitional Justice*, ed. Lavinia Stan and Nadya Nedelsky (New York: Cambridge University Press, 2013): 2:386–87, data based on Nalepa's correspondence with the Institute of National Remembrance (IPN). See also Lavinia Stan, "Poland," in *Transitional Justice in Eastern Europe and the Former Soviet Union: Reckoning with the Communist Past*, ed. Lavinia Stan (New York: Routledge, 2009).

11. Marko Krtolica, "The Process of Lustration in Republic of Macedonia: Facing the Past or Facing Political Opponents," *Iustinianus Primus Law Review* 4, no. 2 (2013): 1–13.

12. Roman David, *Lustration and Transitional Justice: Personnel Systems in the Czech Republic, Hungary, and Poland* (Philadelphia: University of Pennsylvania Press, 2011).

13. Momchil Metodiev, "Bulgaria," in *Transitional Justice in Eastern Europe and the Former Soviet Union: Reckoning with the Communist Past*, ed. Lavinia Stan (New York: Routledge, 2009).

14. Monika Nalepa and Emilia Klepacka, "Institute of National Remembrance—Commission for the Prosecution of Crimes against the Polish Nation," in *Encyclopedia of Transitional Justice*, ed. Lavinia Stan and Nadya Nedelsky (New York: Cambridge University Press, 2013), 3:200–205.

15. For a study on truth commissions in the Baltics and Poland, see Lavinia Stan, "Truth Commissions in Post-communism: The Overlooked Solution?," *Open Political Science Journal* 2 (2009): 1–13.

16. Uilleam Blacker, Alexander Etkind, and Julie Fedor, eds., *Memory and Theory in Eastern Europe* (New York: Palgrave Macmillan, 2013).

17. Hilary Appel, *A New Capitalist Order: Privatization and Ideology in Russia and Eastern Europe* (Pittsburgh: University of Pittsburgh Press, 2004).

CHAPTER 8

EU Accession and After

Ronald H. Linden with Shane Killian

After the extraordinary changes of 1989, virtually all of the newly democratizing states of Central and Eastern Europe made overtures to join the three major organizations of what was generally referred to as "Europe": the Council of Europe, the North Atlantic Treaty Organization (NATO), and the European Union (EU) (see table 8.1). They wanted to do so for a number of reasons. Some were practical: to allow the people of the region to partake of the prosperity and security that the EU and NATO, respectively, had afforded the West European states since the end of World War II. Some were psychological and symbolic: to heal the division of Europe and return to where they would have been had the Cold War not cut them off, and to be included among the world's democracies. This chapter offers some background on the region's international environment before 1989 and then focuses on the process undertaken by the Central and East European states to join the EU. A discussion of how the states have fared since joining and since the onset of the European economic crisis follows, with some questions raised for political science and for discussion posed at the end. As the chapter by Joshua Spero in this volume deals with NATO accession, this chapter does not discuss those issues.[1]

Eastern and Western Europe before 1989

After World War II the two parts of Europe moved in different directions, economically and politically. After being prevented by Joseph Stalin from participating in the US-funded Marshall Plan to rebuild Europe, Central and Eastern Europe was absorbed into the Soviet-dominated economic and political system and its organizations. All of the Central and East European states (except Yugoslavia) became members of the Council for Mutual Economic Assistance (CMEA), founded in 1949, and the Warsaw Pact, the Soviet-dominated military alliance, established in 1955. Most importantly, they were bound by bilateral economic, political, and military ties to the Soviet Union. Trade was sharply curtailed with the West and reoriented toward the Soviet Union (see table 8.2). Five-year plans approved by the respective communist parties ruled the region's economies, and private economic activity was reduced to insignificance or eliminated altogether.

Table 8.1.   Membership in European Organizations

Country	Date of Joining or Status with Organization		
	Council of Europe	European Union	NATO
Albania	7/13/1995	Potential candidate	4/1/2009
Bosnia-Herzegovina	4/24/2002	Potential candidate	MAP[d]
Bulgaria	7/5/1992	1/1/2007	3/29/2004
Croatia	11/6/1996	7/1/2013	4/1/2009
Czech Republic	6/30/1993	5/1/2004	3/16/1999
Hungary	11/6/1990	5/1/2004	3/16/1999
Kosovo	n/a	Potential candidate	KFOR[e]
Macedonia	11/9/1995	Candidate	MAP[d]
Montenegro	5/11/2007	Candidate	MAP[d]
Poland	11/26/1991	5/1/2004	3/16/1999
Romania	10/7/1993	1/1/2007	3/29/2004
Serbia	6/3/2006[a]	Candidate	Partnership for Peace
Slovakia	6/30/1993	5/1/2004[b]	3/29/2004
Slovenia	5/14/1993	5/1/2004[b]	3/29/2004
Ukraine	11/9/1995	Association agreement[c]	NATO–Ukraine Commission

Sources: Council of Europe (http://hub.coe.int); European Union (http://europa.eu); "EU-Ukraine Association Agreement," European Union External Action, http://eeas.europa.eu/images/top_stories/140912_eu-ukraine-associatin-agreement-quick_guide.pdf; NATO (http://www.nato.int).
[a] Continued membership of state of Serbia and Montenegro, dating from April 3, 2003.
[b] Eurozone member.
[c] A "new generation" agreement providing for political association and economic integration, including a free trade area, but not membership; signed March 21, 2014, and June 27, 2014.
[d] Membership Action Plan; consultation process with NATO aimed at membership but which does not guarantee membership.
[e] Kosovo Force; NATO-led security force in place since 1999.

Table 8.2.   Reorientation of Trade: Share of Central and Eastern Europe's Trade with Western Europe by Year

Country	Imports				Exports			
	1928	1989	1995	2002	1928	1989	1995	2002
Bulgaria	61.6	13.7	38.4	51.3	64.5	7.8	38.6	55.6
CZ/SL	54.8	15.4	45.4	62.0	43.9	16.5	45.7	64.2
Hungary	32.4	30.9	61.5	57.5	25.0	24.2	62.8	73.5
Poland	54.5	27.7	64.7	67.5	55.9	30.5	70.1	67.3
Romania	50.2	7.8	50.9	63.9	53.9	17.5	54.5	68.0

Sources: For 1928 and 1989, Susan M. Collins and Dani Rodrik, *Eastern Europe and the Soviet Union in the World Economy* (Washington, DC: Institute for International Economics, 1991), 39, 40. For 1995 and 2002, European Bank for Reconstruction and Development, *Transition Report 2003* (London: EBRD, 2003), 86. Data for 1928 and 1989 reflect trade with European countries that became or were members of the European Community; data for 1995 and 2002 reflect trade with members of the European Union. For 1995 and 2002 the average for the Czech Republic and Slovakia was used.

As a result, while Western Europe regained economic vitality, established convertible currencies, and began to participate actively in global trade and investment, Central and Eastern Europe did not. The states of the region did recover from the war and did make progress in providing basic goods and services for most of their populations, especially in comparison to the low level of economic development that had characterized most of the region (except for the Czech Lands) before the war. But the region was cut off from the stimulant of international trade competition, was not open to Western investment, and was in fact obliged to render economic support to the USSR, providing an estimated $20 billion worth of technology, machinery, skills, and manufactured goods in the first fifteen years after the war.[2]

The region remained a marginal global economic actor for the entire period of the Cold War. All of the Central and East European states together provided only 4.5 percent of the world's exports—equal to about one-third of the amount West Germany alone provided. The typical Central and East European state received from the USSR nearly 40 percent of its imports and sent to the USSR more than one-third of its exports.[3] None of the region's currencies were convertible, even in transactions among themselves. On the other hand, the region was shielded from sharp jumps in the price of internationally traded commodities like oil because these were provided to the region at the CMEA "friendship price" (a periodically adjusted fraction of the global price). Thus, the region's socialist economies avoided sharp recession and had little price inflation, but by the late 1970s and 1980s, they also began to show little or no growth.[4] The states of the region also received a substantial trade subsidy from the Soviet Union because they were able to purchase energy and other resources at lower than world prices in exchange for "soft" goods (i.e., those not salable in the West).[5] When Mikhail Gorbachev became the leader of the Soviet Union in 1985, he moved to change this "international division of labor" to adjust to economic realities. The revolutions of 1989 intervened, and the Central and East European states found themselves thrown onto the harsh playing field of the global economy without the experience or economic mechanisms to compete.

The Courtship of the EU: Toward the "Big Bang"

What is today an organization of twenty-eight countries with more than 500 million people began in the aftermath of World War II as a limited attempt to link key parts of the economies of former enemies France and Germany. In 1951, the European Coal and Steel Community (ECSC) was founded by those two countries, plus Italy, Belgium, the Netherlands, and Luxembourg. In the landmark Treaty of Rome of 1957 the European Economic Community was created to complement the ECSC and a new European Atomic Agency. These three were combined in 1965 into the European Community (EC). The members created a parliament and modified other parts of the organization, but over the next two decades, the organization grew slowly in terms of both number of members (adding the United Kingdom, Ireland, and Denmark in 1973; Greece in 1981; Spain and Portugal in 1986) and areas of policy responsibility. By the time the Berlin Wall fell in 1989, the EC still had only twelve members, but it had committed itself (through the Single European Act of 1986) to creating the mechanisms for a single European economy. The Treaty on European Union, referred to as the Maastricht Treaty after the Dutch town in which it was signed in 1992, renamed the organization the European Union and began to move the members toward more unified economic functioning as well as stronger common political institutions. Austria, Finland, and Sweden joined in 1995, bringing the number of members to fifteen. In 2002 the common European currency, the euro, was introduced in eleven of the member states.

After the overthrow of communism, the Central and East European states moved to try to join the EU as soon as possible. Hungary and Poland formally applied in 1994; Romania, Slovakia, and Bulgaria in 1995; and the Czech Republic and Slovenia in 1996. By that time, all had held at least one set of open elections deemed proper by international observers; had created conditions for the exercise of citizens' rights of expression, assembly, and participation; and were seeing the birth—in some cases explosion—of political parties and interest groups. The states of the region also rejected the idea of recreating the Soviet-era economic or political alliances in any new form in favor of joining the most successful and attractive international organization in history, the EU. That organization had never had to consider such a potentially large simultaneous expansion before. Moreover, in previous enlargements, the candidates for membership were not only functioning democracies but had established capitalist and Western-oriented economic systems. In Central and Eastern Europe, by contrast, the countries seeking membership were only just starting the process of creating such systems; were much more numerous; and, most importantly, were significantly poorer than even the poorest EU member. Among potential candidates, for example, the gross domestic product (GDP) per capita of Poland (the largest) was just over two-thirds that of Greece, the poorest EU member, and only 40 percent of the average of all EU members (see table 8.3).

It is not surprising, then, that the EU moved somewhat slowly to establish and implement standard procedures for bringing the Central and East European states into the organization. Along with financial assistance to help these states reform their economies (see below), the EU signed a series of association agreements, called the Europe Agreements, to govern trade with the Central and East European states. At the 1992 European Council at Lisbon, the organization for the first time pledged to help the Central and East European states not just to reform their economies but ultimately to become members of the organization. At the Copenhagen Council in 1993, the EU set forth the basic criteria that the new members would have to meet to be admitted. These criteria included stability of institutions guaranteeing democracy, the rule of law, human rights, and respect for and protection of minorities; the existence of a functioning market economy as well as the capacity to cope with competitive pressure and market forces within the union; and the ability to take on the obligations of membership, including adherence to the aims of political, economic, and monetary union.[6]

To fulfill these criteria, applicants were obliged to accept and pass into legislation the codes, practices, and laws in place in the European Union, referred to as the *acquis communautaire*. Starting in 1998, all of the applicant countries were evaluated annually to assess their progress toward establishing democratic practices, including the rule of law, the exercise of political rights by the population, and the protection of minority rights. Economic assessments judged the countries' movement toward establishing a market

**Table 8.3. Gross Domestic Product per
Capita of New and Old EU Members**

GDP in PPS per Inhabitant, 2001 (EU-15 = 100)

Luxembourg	190
Ireland	118
Netherlands	115
Denmark	115
Austria	111
Belgium	109
Finland	104
Italy	103
France	103
Germany	103
Sweden	102
United Kingdom	101
Spain	84
Cyprus	74
Slovenia	70
Portugal	69
Greece	65
Czech Republic	59
Hungary	53
Slovakia	48
Poland	41
Estonia	40
Lithuania	39
Latvia	33
Bulgaria	25
Romania	24
Turkey	23

Source: Eurostat, *Towards an Enlarged European Union*
(Brussels: European Commission, n.d.).
Note: In this chart gross domestic product per capita
is calculated on the basis of purchasing power standard (PPS), which takes into account differences in
prices across countries.

economy, including privatization, fiscal and monetary control, and openness to foreign investment. Each applicant's ability to undertake the "obligations of membership" was assessed by measuring the adoption of measures laid out in the *acquis*, covering, for example, agriculture, transportation, environmental policy, and justice and home affairs (e.g., the countries' legal systems, including courts, police, rights of accused, and use of the death penalty).[7] In all, there were thirty-one chapters of standards by which these countries were judged, and only when all chapters had been "closed," or judged satisfactory by the European Commission, were invitations for membership issued. That happened for eight Central and East European states in 2002, leading to their simultaneous admission in May 2004.[8] For Romania and Bulgaria, however, there were thirty-five chapters, and these two countries were subject to "enhanced monitoring" by the Commission. They were permitted to join as of January 1, 2007, but under an unprecedented "Cooperation and Verification Mechanism" that obliges them to report on their progress in judicial reform, the fight against corruption, and, in Bulgaria's case, the fight against organized crime.[9] In 2005 Croatia began formal negotiations and in July 2013 became the twenty-eighth member of the European Union.

The Costs of Joining

For most of the Central and East European states, making the transition to democratic practices with regard to individual freedoms, elections, political institutions, and parties was challenging. Although the countries' populations desired such institutions and practices after four decades of Communist Party rule, not all of the states moved equally quickly. In some cases communist-era practices—and people—remained powerful, as, for example, in Slovakia and Romania. It took electoral defeats in these cases to improve the EU's opinion and these countries' chances for joining the organization.

For the Central and East European governments, adapting their countries' political and legal processes to European norms involved making adjustments in a variety of policy arenas. Elimination of the death penalty and laws against homosexuality, for example, was required. Improvements in the legal system, including the formation of independent judges and constitutional courts, were needed in most cases. One of the most common areas of pressure lay in the EU's criticism of the countries' treatment of their Roma mi-

Photo 8.1.   EU Enlargement Day in May 2004. The flags of Cyprus, the Czech Republic, Estonia, Hungary, Latvia, Lithuania, Malta, Poland, the Slovak Republic, and Slovenia are raised at an EU building, marking their accession to the union. (European Community, 2007.)

Photo 8.2. Berlaymont building with "Welcome Bulgaria Romania to the European Union." After several delays due to slow conformance with European standards, particularly in the area of anticorruption reforms, Bulgaria and Romania joined the EU on January 1, 2007. (European Community, 2007.)

norities. Numbering over 4 million and scattered throughout the region,[10] Roma minorities suffered both legal and economic discrimination, exclusion from employment and political power, and, in some cases, actual physical harassment.[11] Even leading candidates for membership such as the Czech Republic were subject to criticism by the EU for restrictive citizenship laws and hostile actions toward Roma.[12]

The EU's involvement in minority issues in the region produced some skepticism even as it provided an opportunity for domestic minority groups and nongovernmental organizations to utilize EU influence on their behalf to secure better treatment from their governments. For example, the EU insisted that the candidate states implement full recognition and guarantees of minority rights that in some cases did not apply in member states.[13]

Setting up appropriate Western-style parliamentary and electoral institutions and getting them running in forms that the EU would approve was relatively simple compared to the process of wrenching the economies into line with EU expectations. These states were not as economically developed, had not traded in a competitive world market, and did not have the resources to make the economic transition without substantial pain. For example, in Central and Eastern Europe on average more than 13 percent of the workforce was employed in agriculture; the figure in Western Europe was just over 4 percent. The Central and East European economies were less productive, used more energy and human resources to produce the same number of goods as the West, and for the most part produced goods that were not competitive on the world market. To make matters worse, the goods these states could potentially sell globally were precisely those that the EU specialized in—farm products, steel, textiles—and the EU was at first not eager to open its markets. Within a few years, however, tariff and quota restrictions on Central and East European exports to Western Europe were removed. Still, given the uncompetitive nature of these economies, it took several years before any could achieve significant positive trade balances.

With the sharp shift in trade after 1989 (see table 8.2) and governments getting out of the business of running the economy, production in most of the Central and East European states declined dramatically. It took until the end of the decade for most of Central and Eastern Europe to reach the economic levels of 1989 and even longer for Romania and Bulgaria.[14] Unemployment, which had not officially existed under socialism, soared, reaching more than 12 percent of the workforce on average throughout the region. Part of the adjustment to EU economic policies involved improving the environment for competition, eliminating government support of industries, ending price controls, and allowing bankruptcies. The EU also exerted pressure to allow foreign investment on a nondiscriminatory basis, meaning that experienced, successful West European companies would be free to buy up valuable assets in these states, now available at bargain basement prices. After 1989 the region attracted more than $170 billion in foreign direct investment (through the year 2004), with the bulk going to the three Central European states, Poland, Hungary, and the Czech Republic.

While proceeding slowly on formal admission, the EU did move to provide the region with substantial economic aid. Through the PHARE program,[15] the organization provided more than $11 billion to Central and Eastern Europe, the Baltic states, and Bosnia between 1989 and 1999. Most of these funds went to infrastructure, education, training, and assistance in privatizing the economies. In 1999 the organization added the Special Action Program for Agriculture and Rural Development (SAPARD) and Instrument for Structural Policies for Pre-accession (ISPA) programs, which support rural and agricultural development and environmental and transportation projects, respectively. Together these programs provided more than $20 billion from 2000 to 2006 for new members in what was termed "pre-accession aid" even after they became members.

Perhaps the major challenge to the accession process involved agriculture. Since its formation, the EU has supported farmers by controlling imports, supporting prices, and providing direct payments through the Common Agricultural Policy (CAP).[16] CAP payments constitute the single largest item in the EU budget. With 7 million new farmers (and 40 percent more agricultural land) added by Central and East European accession to the 6 million already in the EU, the organization realized that it could not afford to extend to the new members the generous agricultural subsidies it had been providing to farmers in the EU-15 states. Moreover, in global trade negotiations the EU has pledged to reduce the level of its subsidies. Hence, as part of these states' accession, direct payments to Central and Eastern Europe's farmers were at first a fraction of those paid to farmers in Western Europe and were increased gradually.[17]

The Politics of Membership

When the European Union was founded, the driving idea was to link continental Europe's major economic powers, France and Germany, so inextricably as to make future wars between them impossible. As other functions became part of common responsibility, such as control of nuclear energy, control of agricultural production, and external trade ties, the organization not only grew in complexity but added members. Great Britain's membership had been vetoed by France in 1963 and was delayed for ten years, but adding democratic Portugal, Spain, and Greece in the 1980s and the relatively rich, capitalist Austria, Sweden, and Finland in 1995 was not controversial. However, adding eight or ten economically weak states that had operated as one-party dictatorships and state-run economies for four decades was not popular. Public opinion surveys among the members of the EU consistently showed a lack of enthusiasm for enlargement in most EU member states. Despite public ambivalence, movement toward membership proceeded, reinforcing the idea among some that the organization operates with a "democratic deficit"—that is, that decisions are made by distant elites who are not responsible to anyone and reflect bureaucratic imperatives in Brussels more than the desires of their constituents.[18]

In Central and Eastern Europe, though, accession to the EU was generally very popular. Public opinion polls in the 1990s showed that majorities of the populations in the region strongly supported joining the EU. In general, Central and East European populations trusted the EU and saw joining as the right thing to do for their country.[19] Support was not equally high throughout the region, however, as the costs of adjustment and the uneven distribution of such costs among the population became evident. In a 2002 survey, for example, roughly one-third of Estonians and Latvians thought that membership would be "a good thing," while more than two-thirds of Hungarians and Bulgarians thought so.[20] In most cases, as countries moved closer to joining the EU, public support for doing so fell off somewhat before rebounding.[21] Referenda on joining were held in each of the Central and East European countries due to join in 2004 and produced positive—though in some cases close—votes.[22] In the Croatian referendum in 2012, two-thirds of those voting supported accession, but the turnout (43 percent of eligible voters) was the lowest of any new member state.[23] By 2011, among the new member states, public views of the benefits of EU membership were similar to those held in countries with longer membership, but there was somewhat more uncertainty as to whether EU membership was a "good thing" than in the older member states.[24]

Apart from accommodating legal, political, and economic systems to the demands of the *acquis*, for several of the new members some issues provided a possible challenge to the depth of their commitment to join. Many worried that their inexperienced and weaker economies, especially in the agricultural sector, would not be able to compete with rich, subsidized EU enterprises. There was concern that West Europeans would buy up their countries' low-priced assets and land, leaving local people unemployed and without property. For their part, some politicians in the EU feared that economic dislocation and the attraction of the more prosperous West would produce a vast labor migration once borders were erased and full EU citizenship, including the right to live anywhere, was extended eastward. In the end, several countries were granted transition periods during which they could retain control over agricultural land purchase. But the "free movement of persons" was also limited for the new members, with restrictions remaining in place for not less than two and possibly up to seven years.[25]

Border issues continue to be complicated for some new members. All the new members were obliged to move toward adopting the provisions of the Schengen Treaty (1985) operating among most EU states. This treaty allows for free movement of citizens within the EU but mandates strict enforcement and guarding of the EU's external borders. With that border now pushed eastward, Poles and Hungarians living in Ukraine, for example, find visiting their ethnic kin in new EU member states more difficult and expensive. Citizens of non-EU states like Ukraine, Russia, and Moldova have to obtain visas to visit places they used to travel to more easily before. This requirement not only presents difficulties in human relations but also depresses the substantial transborder economic activity that had grown up, for example, between Poland and countries to the east. When some countries, such as Hungary, attempted to pass laws giving their ethnic kin in neighboring non-EU countries special rights and privileges, the EU criticized them and obliged them to water down or abandon such acts.[26]

Most of the new members also face serious issues in terms of compliance with environmental regulations. This chapter of the *acquis* includes extensive regulations affecting power generation (especially nuclear power), water, air cleanliness, and the burning of fossil fuels. Accommodating EU standards has been enormously expensive for these states and in some cases has obliged them to close down some power plants altogether. To ensure their entry, for example, Lithuania and Bulgaria agreed to close their nuclear reactors, which had the effect of increasing their dependence on Russian sources of energy.

Croatia, the EU's newest member, faced the most comprehensive and exacting scrutiny by the Commission due in part to criticisms of the poor performance of Romania and Bulgaria, which joined in 2007. As with those states, the issue of action against corruption slowed negotiations, which lasted six years. Unlike any other Central and East European applicant, Croatia arrested its own former prime minister, Ivo Sanader, in 2010, a move that seemed to convince EU officials of Zagreb's commitment to fighting corruption. But legacy issues from the state's time as part of Yugoslavia remained. One involved delineating the border with Slovenia, which was eventually submitted to arbitration. More difficult politically was Croatia's obligation—as part of its adherence to the Copenhagen criteria—to arrest and extradite those alleged to have committed war crimes during the wars with Serbia or in Bosnia. As the Croatian government acted on these demands and former military leaders were arrested and extradited, progress toward membership resumed.[27] (See chapter 17 on the successors to Yugoslavia.)

For all of the Central and East European states, the period after 1989 and before 2004 represented a wrenching shift in both real and symbolic terms. These states had been part of the Soviet Union's external empire for the four decades after World War II, and over the years Moscow had used political and economic ties and Soviet-dominated regional organizations to maintain control. When challenges emerged, as happened in Hungary in 1956 and Czechoslovakia in 1968, the USSR had been willing to use force to keep the countries subordinate. Only in 1989 did the USSR, under Mikhail Gorbachev, refrain from intervening to prevent far-reaching democratic change and the return of full sovereignty to the states of this region. The irony is that having finally achieved full control over their own affairs, the leaders of the newly democratic Central and East European states, with their populations' agreement, moved relatively quickly to surrender key parts of that sovereignty to a different power center, the EU. All were willing to remake virtually all of their institutions and practices to conform to standards set by Brussels. Finally, fifteen years after the revolutions that toppled dictatorships in Central and Eastern

Europe, and only after the EU was satisfied that national laws and institutions accorded with its norms, the east and west of Europe were formally reunited.

The EU and the Region since Membership

The enlargement of the EU to the east proved to be the high-water mark of an extraordinary period of enhancement and expansion. In 2005 a proposed European Constitution was defeated in referenda in Holland and France. A new, less ambitious Reform Treaty (referred to as the Lisbon Treaty) was drafted and finally ratified in 2009. The new treaty reflects Europe's emergence as an international actor, providing for the new political posts of President of the European Council and High Representative for Foreign Affairs and Security Policy. It also reflects a desire to improve decision making and reduce the democratic deficit by strengthening the ability of the European Parliament to affect decisions.[28]

The new treaty and the process of its approval were also part of the EU's efforts to adapt to its new size and to the concerns of some new members. Voting mechanisms in the European Council and the number of representatives in the European Parliament were adjusted, but the organization failed to reduce the size of the European Commission. Thus, all twenty-eight members will still nominate one commissioner.[29] More pointedly, the objections of national politicians like Czech president Václav Klaus had to be accommodated before he would sign and confirm Czech ratification of the treaty. Klaus, a well-known "Euroskeptic," refused to sign until the Czech Republic was assured that it would not be subject to compensation claims by descendants of Germans expelled from the country after World War II.[30] So, even though the new Central and East European members have shown little inclination to act as a "bloc" within the EU,[31] their presence has had an impact on the EU's future.

In terms of changes in the region itself, the aims of EU enlargement were multiple: establish security in a region known for conflict, bind the countries together and to Western Europe economically and politically, and help guide the creation of democratic institutions and societies. On virtually all of these counts, EU enlargement has succeeded, though some troubling developments worry observers.

For the first time in modern history, the possibility of military conflict in the heart of Europe is virtually nonexistent. Most of the Central and East European states have joined those in Western Europe as full members of both the EU and NATO. Others in the Balkans, including all the parts of what was once Yugoslavia, aspire to join these organizations. Across the membership area, international warfare of the type seen in the last century seems as unlikely as war between France and Germany. The significance of the organization's success on this dimension was thrown into sharp relief by the occurrence of military action just outside the EU domain in Georgia in 2008 and Ukraine in 2014. Economically, the region's trade and investment are overwhelmingly tied to fellow members (see below), and by 2013 the eighteen-member Eurozone included newer members Slovakia, Slovenia, Estonia, and Latvia.

In addition, the EU's aim of promoting democratic institutions and practices in the region has been broadly successful. Every one of the former dictatorships of Central and Eastern Europe is now judged as "free" by Freedom House, using an annual assessment of democratic processes.[32] Table 8.4 compares Freedom House rankings in more detail from the end of the 1990s—roughly the start of the EU accession process—through 2013 for new members and those still outside the organization. The effect of EU involvement on democracy support has been clear. The average democracy score for "New EU members" is 2.57 (a score of 1 being the best); the average for former Soviet states is 6.00.[33]

But it may not be permanent. In Hungary in 2010, the conservative Alliance of Young Democrats (FiDeSz), in coalition with the Christian Democratic People's Party, won a two-thirds majority in parliament. Since then the government of Viktor Orbán has adopted many measures, including a new constitution, that strengthen the hand of the ruling party, weaken electoral opposition, and erode the independence of the media, judiciary, and central bank. These measures have drawn criticism from the European Commission and European Parliament[34] and call into question the ability of the EU to exercise its "soft power" once states become members.[35]

The picture is also not as clear in the realm of democratic attitudes, as the demands of economic competition, combined with the slowness and unwieldy processes of democracy, have weakened public support for democratic governance. Surveys show a growing dissatisfaction with the way democracy operates in the region and a stubborn lack of trust in political parties and democratic institutions, such as presidents and parliaments.[36] Moreover, a disturbing rise in the fortunes of populist parties, both nationalist and those with a vague ideology that capitalizes on public dissatisfaction, has occurred in much of the region.[37] Still, compared to developments in the non-EU Balkans or further east (see table 8.4), and especially compared to where Central and Eastern Europe was twenty years ago, the region and all of Europe have benefited greatly from interactions with and joining European organizations.

The Eurozone Economic Crisis and the Region

In addition to expanding and changing its political structures, the European Union began in the early 1990s to create a single currency area—one in which members gave up their deutschmarks and francs, as well as their national control of monetary (currency) policies, in order to make cross-border transactions (payments, investments, lending) easier and cheaper. Although fiscal (budget) policies were still controlled by the states, they faced new limitations, in particular on total debt and annual deficit levels. According to the Treaty on European Union (1992), members of the Eurozone were not supposed to run deficits of more than 3 percent of GDP or have an overall public debt of more than 60 percent of GDP.[38] Since national currencies were to be abolished, no competitive devaluations could take place. In 1998, the European Central Bank was created; in 1999, eleven states, including Germany, France, and Italy, officially adopted the single currency (joined by Greece in 2001), and in 2002 national currencies were eliminated and the euro became a reality.

When the Central and East European states joined the European Union in 2004 and 2007, they were obliged to commit to eventually joining the Eurozone. So far Slovenia, Slovakia, Estonia, and Latvia (along with Cyprus and Malta) have done so (with Lithuania due to join in 2015).

Table 8.4. Democracy Scores for Central and Eastern Europe, the Balkans, and the States of the Former Soviet Union

	1999–2000	2001	2002	2003	2004	2005	2006	2007	2008	2009	2013
New EU Members											
Bulgaria	3.58	3.42	3.33	3.38	3.25	3.18	2.93	2.89	2.86	3.04	3.18
Croatia	4.46	3.54	3.54	3.79	3.83	3.75	3.71	3.75	3.64	3.71	3.61
Czech Republic	2.08	2.25	2.46	2.33	2.33	2.29	2.25	2.25	2.14	2.18	2.14
Estonia	2.25	2.13	2.00	2.00	1.92	1.96	1.96	1.96	1.93	1.93	1.96
Hungary	1.88	2.13	2.13	1.96	1.96	1.96	2.00	2.14	2.14	2.29	2.89
Latvia	2.29	2.21	2.25	2.25	2.17	2.14	2.07	2.07	2.07	2.18	2.07
Lithuania	2.29	2.21	2.21	2.13	2.13	2.21	2.21	2.29	2.25	2.29	2.32
Poland	1.58	1.58	1.63	1.75	1.75	2.00	2.14	2.36	2.39	2.25	2.18
Romania	3.54	3.67	3.71	3.63	3.58	3.39	3.39	3.29	3.36	3.36	3.50
Slovakia	2.71	2.50	2.17	2.08	2.08	2.00	1.96	2.14	2.29	2.46	2.57
Slovenia	1.88	1.88	1.83	1.79	1.75	1.68	1.75	1.82	1.86	1.93	1.89
Average	**2.41**	**2.40**	**2.37**	**2.33**	**2.29**	**2.28**	**2.27**	**2.32**	**2.33**	**2.39**	**2.57**
Median	**2.27**	**2.21**	**2.19**	**2.10**	**2.10**	**2.07**	**2.11**	**2.20**	**2.20**	**2.27**	**2.32**
The Balkans											
Albania	4.75	4.42	4.25	4.17	4.13	4.04	3.79	3.82	3.82	3.82	4.25
Bosnia	5.42	5.17	4.83	4.54	4.29	4.18	4.07	4.04	4.11	4.18	4.39
Macedonia	3.83	4.04	4.46	4.29	4.00	3.89	3.82	3.82	3.86	3.86	3.93
Yugoslavia	5.67	5.04	4.00	3.88	n/a	n/a	n/a	n/a	n/a	n/a	n/a
Serbia	n/a	n/a	n/a	n/a	3.83	3.75	3.71	3.68	3.79	3.79	3.64
Montenegro	n/a	n/a	n/a	n/a	3.83	3.79	3.89	3.93	3.79	3.79	3.82
Kosovo	n/a	n/a	n/a	n/a	5.50	5.32	5.36	5.36	5.21	5.11	5.25
Average	**4.83**	**4.44**	**4.22**	**4.13**	**4.20**	**4.10**	**4.05**	**4.05**	**4.03**	**4.04**	**4.21**
Median	**4.75**	**4.42**	**4.25**	**4.17**	**4.00**	**3.89**	**3.82**	**3.82**	**3.82**	**3.82**	**4.09**

(continued)

Table 8.4. *(Continued)*

	1999–2000	2001	2002	2003	2004	2005	2006	2007	2008	2009	2013
Non-Baltic Former Soviet States											
Armenia	4.79	4.83	4.83	4.92	5.00	5.18	5.14	5.21	5.21	5.39	5.36
Azerbaijan	5.58	5.63	5.54	5.46	5.63	5.86	5.93	6.00	6.00	6.25	6.64
Belarus	6.25	6.38	6.38	6.46	6.54	6.64	6.71	6.68	6.71	6.57	6.72
Georgia	4.17	4.33	4.58	4.83	4.83	4.96	4.86	4.68	4.79	4.93	4.75
Kazakhstan	5.50	5.71	5.96	6.17	6.25	6.29	6.39	6.39	6.39	6.32	6.57
Kyrgyzstan	5.08	5.29	5.46	5.67	5.67	5.64	5.68	5.68	5.93	6.04	5.96
Moldova	4.25	4.29	4.50	4.71	4.88	5.07	4.96	4.96	5.00	5.07	4.82
Russia	4.58	4.88	5.00	4.96	5.25	5.61	5.75	5.86	5.96	6.11	6.21
Tajikistan	5.75	5.58	5.63	5.63	5.71	5.79	5.93	5.96	6.07	6.14	6.25
Turkmenistan	6.75	6.83	6.83	6.83	6.88	6.93	6.96	6.96	6.93	6.93	6.93
Ukraine	4.63	4.71	4.92	4.71	4.88	4.50	4.21	4.25	4.25	4.39	4.86
Uzbekistan	6.38	6.42	6.46	6.46	6.46	6.43	6.82	6.82	6.86	6.89	6.93
Average	**5.31**	**5.41**	**5.51**	**5.57**	**5.66**	**5.74**	**5.78**	**5.79**	**5.84**	**5.92**	**6.00**
Median	**5.29**	**5.44**	**5.50**	**5.54**	**5.65**	**5.72**	**5.84**	**5.91**	**5.98**	**6.13**	**6.23**

Source: Freedom House, "Nations in Transit 2013," http://www.freedomhouse.org/report/nations-transit/nations-transit-2013# U2SP-1SJN3Ns.

Note: The Democracy Score ranges from 1, the highest level, to 7, the lowest level, and is an average of ratings for Electoral Process (EP); Civil Society (CS); Independent Media (IM); National Democratic Governance (NGO\1); Local Democratic Governance (LGO\1); Judicial Framework and Independence (JFI); and Corruption (CO).

At first, the promised benefits of the single currency were evident (and reflected in the growing strength of the euro). Cross-border transactions became easier; investments and lending flowed from the richer economies of Europe to governments and private actors (such as banks) in Eurozone countries without regard to risk. With easy borrowing terms, public and private debt stimulated growth for a while but was ultimately unsustainable. A series of "bubbles" (e.g., in housing) gave way to deep recessions. The causes were varied,[39] but without the ability to change their own fiscal policies—for instance, by running a deficit to allow greater government spending—or to devalue their currencies to make exports cheaper, one Eurozone country after another went into economic and then political crisis.

The negative results of poor domestic decisions were exacerbated by an international economic crisis beginning in 2008 that produced a dramatic slowing of growth in the United States and Europe. Thus, both investment funds and the market for exports for the affected countries shrank. A vicious circle then took hold, with businesses cutting back, unemployment increasing, and more borrowing needed to cover debt and government programs for people affected by the downturn. But now the lending rates were much less attractive and in some cases prohibitive.

The affected actors—chiefly Greece, Ireland, Spain, and Portugal—turned to Europe's "paymasters," Germany, the Netherlands, and Finland, to bail them out. But these countries, where the balance sheet was healthier, were not willing to simply write checks to continue what they saw as fiscally profligate policies. They pressured recipients of aid to implement austerity programs and contain spiraling deficits, while also seeking to implement these new aid measures through the EU and Eurozone. This led to a series of new European institutions. The European Financial Stability Mechanism (EFSM), which used the EU budget as collateral, and the European Financial Stability Facility (EFSF), which was financed directly by member states, were both implemented in 2010 as sources of aid to afflicted Eurozone countries. Both were succeeded by the European Stability Mechanism (ESM) in 2012, which has access to €500 billion in lending capacity. A "European Fiscal Compact" was also signed in 2012 and entered into force in 2013. The new compact forces states to implement new fiscal requirements in national law and creates automatic "correction mechanisms" that are triggered during periods of high deficit and debt. If states fail to implement these new requirements, the European Court of Justice can intervene, fining states up to 0.1 percent of GDP.[40]

Additionally, the European Central Bank (ECB) played a central role in responding to the crisis through a variety of policy avenues. The ECB helped to keep the financial system afloat during the crisis by providing long-term, low-interest loans to banks. In effect, these loans expanded the available money supply and, along with ECB purchases of Eurozone members' debt (called "outright monetary transactions"), helped keep interest rates at a level that allowed borrowing at reasonable rates. The combined effect of these actions did work to make the annual budget situation in Italy, Portugal, and Spain somewhat more manageable, and modest, though uneven, growth returned to the Eurozone in 2014. At the same time, EU institutions, especially those affecting Eurozone countries, have become stronger and reflect a tendency toward more intrusion by EU actors into domestic economic policy making.

The global economic crisis that hit Europe rippled across Central and Eastern Europe as well. This is not surprising, as the economies in Central and Eastern Europe have become more intertwined with those of their fellow EU and Eurozone members. By 2012 EU partners took nearly two-thirds of all exports from Central and Eastern Europe. Such exports are crucial to the economies of the region, accounting, for example, for 40 percent of GDP in the Czech Republic and 30 percent in Hungary, the Slovak Republic, and Slovenia from 2007 to 2009.[41] Thus, slowdowns in the Eurozone directly affect the region. Deep recessions have occurred in Hungary, Croatia, Bulgaria, Slovenia, and the Slovak Republic, as well as in the Baltic states. Only Poland has shown sustained growth.

In many new member countries, economic crisis led to political change. Governments in Croatia, the Czech Republic, and Eurozone members Slovenia and Slovakia succumbed to early collapse. In some Central and East European countries (as in the West) anti-EU sentiment strengthened the electoral showing of nationalist parties,[42] and across the region, public opinion has shown fading faith in the European Union (see figure 8.1). In Hungary, policies at odds with EU preferences twice led to suspensions of EU development funds.[43] At one point Prime Minister Viktor Orbán compared the EU's action to Soviet-style interference.[44] Such posturing did not hurt his political fortunes, as FiDeSz retained a two-thirds majority in the 2014 parliamentary elections, and the far-right Jobbik party—with a similar message—made modest gains.

In whatever way Europe and the European Union deal with the institutional and political challenges of managing a single market and a single currency during a time of

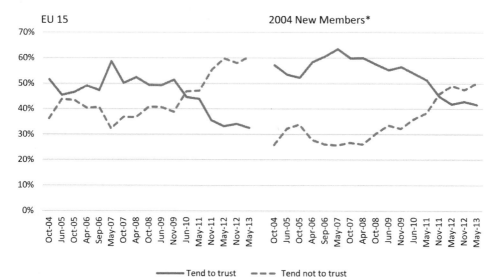

Figure 8.1.   Trust in the EU as an Institution

*2004 New Members include Estonia, Latvia, Lithuania, Poland, Czech Republic, Slovakia, Slovenia, and Hungary. Does not include Malta or Cyprus, or post-2004 accession states Bulgaria, Romania, and Croatia.

Original question: "For each of the following institutions, please tell me if you tend to trust it or tend not to trust it?"

Source: Constructed from Eurobarometer data at http://ec.europa.eu/public_opinion/cf/index.cfm ?lang=en.

epidemic crisis, the states of Central and Eastern Europe are directly affected. Whether they join the Eurozone immediately or hold off, their entrance into the European economic zone inextricably links their economies—and thus their politics—together.

The Future of EU Involvement: The Western Balkans and Ukraine

After the breakup of Yugoslavia, the EU has been working to admit as full members the states that emerged. Slovenia joined the organization in the first wave of enlargement, and Croatia did so in 2013. In 2003 the EU committed itself to continuing enlargement to include all of the states in what is referred to as "the Western Balkans."[45] Macedonia, Montenegro, and Serbia (along with Iceland and Turkey) are termed "candidate members" and are formally pursuing membership negotiations, while Albania, Bosnia-Herzegovina, and Kosovo are labeled "potential candidates." As with the earlier accessions, for some Balkan states there are special obstacles to membership. In Bosnia-Herzegovina, constitutional reform that would strengthen the country's ability to act as a unified entity is stalled despite vigorous EU involvement. (See chapter 17 on the post-Yugoslav states.) Macedonian progress toward membership is blocked by Greek objections to the country's name.[46]

Kosovo, which declared independence from Serbia in 2008, is not recognized by five EU members, and negotiations had failed to achieve Serbian acceptance of Kosovo's status. But in 2013 EU High Representative Catherine Ashton succeeded in brokering a power-sharing agreement that affects the northern part of the new country where most members of the Serb minority live.[47] This movement toward normalization of relations was a product of both sides' desire to enhance their prospects for EU membership and an important positive result of the EU's Western Balkans policy.[48]

Ukraine has always presented a special case for Brussels. It is the largest country in Central and Eastern Europe but has a bifurcated history and ethnic composition (see chapter 18 on Ukraine). The European Union and especially some members like Poland have been eager to exert influence on the country to push it toward democratization and a more open, better-run economy. The EU has not, however, offered a path to membership to Ukraine or any of the other former Soviet countries that are the focus of the EU's "Eastern Partnership" program unveiled in 2008.[49]

During the contested presidential elections at the end of 2004 (the Orange Revolution), the EU did not accept the election of Viktor Yanukovych and pushed strongly for new, fair elections. These made Viktor Yushchenko president. Ukraine was granted the status of "functioning market economy" and was considered a "priority partner country." EU-Ukrainian relations have been governed by a Partnership and Cooperation Agreement dating from 1998, and the EU has been the country's largest trading partner and the largest donor of technical assistance. Long negotiations eventually produced an association agreement, even though Viktor Yanukovych did succeed in becoming president in 2010. This agreement, the first of its kind for Partnership countries, was to provide for a stronger form of "political association" with the EU, including domestic reforms, and deeper economic ties, including the establishment of a free trade area.

Those very ties, however, alarmed Russia, which saw this as further Western incursion into a region in which it claims "privileged interests."[50] During 2013, a combination of political pressure and economic incentives (such as a lower price for natural gas) persuaded President Yanukovych to suspend plans to sign the association agreement. As a result of this action and accumulated frustrations with corrupt and ineffective government, huge demonstrations erupted in central Kyiv (labeled the "Euromaidan") that culminated in Yanukovych's fleeing the country to Russia in February 2014. (See chapter 18 on Ukraine for details.)

When a new interim government was formed, Russia continued to warn it against signing the agreement with the EU. At the same time, Moscow took advantage of upheaval in the country and secessionist sentiment in the Crimean Peninsula to forcibly wrest that territory from Ukraine. The EU, along with the United States, condemned the political machinations that accompanied this action, such as a referendum in which 96 percent of voters approved joining Russia, and applied targeted sanctions against Russian and pro-Russian Ukrainian elites. International condemnation notwithstanding, Crimea was annexed to Russia on March 21, 2014. The same day, the Ukrainian government signed the political provisions of the association agreement. The EU began immediately to implement free trade measures between the EU and Ukraine as part of a package of economic and political support measures designed to bolster Ukraine's economy and sovereignty.[51]

New presidential elections were held in May, even while a full-scale rebellion erupted in the eastern part of the country, led by forces opposed to the Kyiv government and supported by Russia. In June 2014 new president Petro Peroshenko signed the full association agreement with the EU, including its provisions for a Deep and Comprehensive Free Trade Area (DCFTA) and in September they were ratified.[52]

The EU and United States have applied an ever-widening package of sanctions against actors and sectors in the Russian economy because of their "illegal annexation of territory and deliberate destabilisation of a neighbouring sovereign country."[53] But the EU's leverage with Russia, as its largest export partner and leading investor, is blunted by its own dependence on Russian energy, especially natural gas. Some 30 percent of the gas Europe uses comes from Russia, and dependencies are highest among the new Central and East European members.[54] In addition to hurting its own consumers and weak economy, punitive action would also hurt Ukraine itself, the transit country for most of the Russian gas headed to Europe. In an attempt to assuage Russian concerns and reinforce a negotiated ceasefire in eastern Ukraine, the EU postponed implementation of the DCFTA until December 2015

The broader question for the new, larger EU is whether it will continue to have influence beyond its borders, as it did during the exhilarating time of the "big bang" enlargement and the ensuing decade. Expansion to Central and Eastern Europe was generally not violently opposed either externally or within the states. The wars fought in the Balkans were not about joining or not joining the EU—in fact, in the aftermath of that violence, all of the combatant states there are on a path to becoming members. But now the states and peoples in the non-EU post-Soviet world (Ukraine, Moldova, Armenia, Azerbaijan, and Georgia) have been put on notice by Moscow that movement toward integration with the Western organizations, even if short of membership, will not go unchallenged.[55]

Implications for Political Science

A central problem in the study of world politics has always been the question of why states act in certain ways. Do they do so out of considerations of pure power (the realist point of view), because of the nature of their governments (the liberal point of view), because of changes in their identity (the constructivist point of view), or because of the role of international institutions (the liberal institutionalist point of view)?[56] If a state's behavior seems to conform to the dictates of other more powerful states, is this because it has no choice, because it truly associates itself with the behavioral norms of its neighbors, or because it sees gains in acting that way? The case of the Central and East European states' accepting and implementing the norms of the EU provides a real-world experiment for such theories, though, like all such experiments, only an approximate one.[57] In the real world, states cannot be put in laboratories with some variables held constant and others allowed to vary. But for the years since the revolutions, the states of Central and Eastern Europe and their paths represent an observable group of outcomes that can be studied comparatively. These states, with different cultures and histories and different experiences of conflict, all became democratic and were freed from the dominant power that had ruled their region. They all had strong economic and political incentives to join the EU. Their leaders and populations all claimed to want to adhere to democratic norms, and in most cases they moved to do so. But why and how did they do so? Equally importantly, why do their outcomes seem so different from those of most of the countries that emerged directly from the USSR—for example, Ukraine? Looking for that answer takes us into the realm of international relations, to complement the focus on comparative political studies.

The questions raised for political scientists and policy makers are many. First, why were the Central and East European states so willing to dance to the EU's tune? Second, will they continue to do so now that membership is no longer an issue? Third, on the international stage, has the once dominant "soft power" influence of the EU been defeated by the "hard power" capabilities of traditional states like Russia?[58] This would mean, among other things, that the enlargement of the EU and the expansion of democracy have reached a high-water mark not because of domestic political dynamics but because of powerful global opposition.

Analysts of institutional behavior say that, generally speaking, actors accommodate their behavior either because of "the logic of consequences" (i.e., they do it because they fear a loss or anticipate a gain) or because of the "logic of appropriateness" (i.e., they do it because it is the right thing to do).[59] Such an approach underlies questions in both comparative politics and the study of international actions. In the case of Central and East European compliance, we have seen acceptance and emulation of EU norms across a range of domestic political and economic practices. Has this occurred as a product of rational calculation of costs and benefits? If so, we might expect the new Central and East European members to slide back on democratic practice, for example, once they are members. If they do, what can the EU do to ensure compliance? Alternatively, have the changes occurred because there has been a genuine acceptance of the norms of behavior that apply in democracies and market economies? In that case, the issue of enforcement will be much less important. In Central and Eastern Europe, we have seen, in general, a persistence of democratic and economic reforms, even in the face of significant challenges in recent years. But in some cases, most notably Hungary, critics have charged that democratic practices have been seriously weakened, and the EU, itself one of those critics, has been unable to reverse that trend.[60] Viewed at the global level, the contest between norms and power so often the subject of study in world politics is again on display in and around Ukraine. In the nearby "neighborhood" of both the EU and Central and Eastern Europe, the clash of soft and hard power has turned violent, with implications for people, systems, states, and international organizations that are part of or near the region.

Study Questions

1. What seems to explain the different paths to democracy and an open economy seen in Central and Eastern Europe? Is it determined by the past or culture or by contemporary political dynamics?
2. How do you explain the willingness of the Central and East European states to comply with comprehensive demands of the EU for membership so soon after regaining independence of action after the collapse of the Soviet alliance system?
3. Is there a link between economic success and democratization? Is democracy more successful in those Central and East European countries that are doing better economically, like Poland?
4. To what extent was the EU a beneficiary of movement toward democracy that would have occurred anyway in Central and Eastern Europe?
5. Is the new position of Central and Eastern Europe a historical repeat of its past as a group of marginal actors who have little choice but to accept the consequences of decisions taken elsewhere?

Suggested Readings

Berend, Ivan T. *From the Soviet Bloc to the European Union: The Economic and Social Transformation of Central and Eastern Europe since 1973*. New York: Cambridge University Press, 2009.

Grabbe, Heather. *The EU's Transformative Power: Europeanization through Conditionality in Central and Eastern Europe*. New York: Palgrave Macmillan, 2006.

Haughton, Tim, ed. *Party Politics in Central and Eastern Europe: Does EU Membership Matter?* New York: Routledge, 2011.

Jacoby, Wade. *The Enlargement of the European Union and NATO: Ordering from the Menu in Central Europe*. Cambridge: Cambridge University Press, 2004.

Linden, Ronald H., ed. *Norms and Nannies: The Impact of International Organizations on the Central and East European States*. Lanham, MD: Rowman & Littlefield, 2002.

Linden, Ronald H. ed. "The Meaning of 1989 and After." Special issue of *Problems of Post-Communism* 56, no. 5 (September–October 2009).

Poole, Peter A. *Europe Unites: The EU's Eastern Enlargement*. Westport, CT: Praeger, 2003.

Pravda, Alex, ed. *The End of the Outer Empire*. London: Royal Institute, 1992.

Schimmelfennig, Frank, and Ulrich Sedelmeier. *The Europeanization of Central and Eastern Europe*. Ithaca, NY: Cornell University Press, 2005.

Schwarzer, Daniela, "Crisis and Reform in the Euro Area." *Current History* 112, no. 752 (March 2013): 83–87.

Vachudova, Milada. *Europe Undivided: Democracy, Leverage, and Integration after Communism*. Oxford: Oxford University Press, 2005.

Websites

European Bank for Reconstruction and Development: http://www.ebrd.com/pages/homepage.shtml

European Union: http://europa.eu/index_en.htm

European Union, "Enlargement": http://europa.eu/pol/enlarg/index_en.htm

Freedom House, "Nations in Transit 2013: Authoritarian Aggression and the Pressures of Austerity": http://www.freedomhouse.org/report/nations-transit/nations-transit-2013

M. E. Sharpe, *Problems of Postcommunism*: http://www.mesharpe.com/mall/results1.asp ?ACR=PPC

Transitions Online: http://www.tol.org

Notes

I would like to thank Kristen Flanagan and Isabel Ranner for their research assistance on this chapter.

1. For a discussion of the enlargement of the Council of Europe, see Peter Leuprecht, "Innovations in the European System of Human Rights Protection: Is Enlargement Compatible with Reinforcement?" *Transnational Law and Contemporary Problems* 8 (1998): 313–36.

2. Paul Marer, "Has Eastern Europe Become a Liability to the Soviet Union? (III) The Economic Aspect," in *The International Politics of Eastern Europe*, ed. Charles Gati (New York: Praeger Publishers, 1976), 65.

3. James L. Ellis, "Eastern Europe: Changing Trade Patterns and Perspectives," in *East European Economies: Slow Growth in the 1980s*, US Congress, Joint Economic Committee, 99th Cong., 2nd sess., March 28, 1986, 17, 24. Figures are for 1980.

4. Thad P. Alton, "East European GNP's Domestic Final Uses of Gross Product, Rates of Growth, and International Comparisons," in *Pressures for Reform in the East European Economies*, US Congress, Joint Economic Committee, 101st Cong., 1st sess., October 20, 1989, 81.

5. Michael Marrese and Jan Vanous, *Soviet Subsidization of Trade with Eastern Europe* (Berkeley, CA: Institute of International Studies, 1983).

6. These criteria can be seen on the website of the EU at "Accession Criteria (Copenhagen Criteria)," European Union, http://europa.eu/legislation_summaries/glossary/accession_criteria_copenhague_en.htm.

7. These annual reports can be accessed at "New Member States Archives," European Union, Enlargement Archives, http://ec.europa.eu/enlargement/archives/enlargement_process/past_enlargements/eu10/index_en.htm.

8. In case a Central or East European state failed to fulfill its commitments in certain areas (internal market, justice and home affairs) after accession, "safeguard clauses" were included in the Accession Treaty, allowing for "appropriate measures" to be taken by the European Commission to ensure full compliance. The full text of the Accession Treaty can be seen at "EU 10-BG-RO," European Union, Enlargement Archives, http://ec.europa.eu/enlargement/archives/enlargement_process/future_prospects/negotiations/eu10_bulgaria_romania/index_en.htm.

9. For background on this process and the reports, see "Mechanism for Cooperation and Verification for Bulgaria and Romania," European Commission, http://ec.europa.eu/cvm/progress_reports_en.htm.

10. Estimates and censuses vary widely on the number of Roma. The best comparative assessment can be found in Zoltan Barany, *The East European Gypsies* (New York: Cambridge University Press, 2001), 157–64.

11. Dena Ringold, *Roma and the Transition in Central and Eastern Europe: Trends and Challenges* (Washington, DC: World Bank, 2000).

12. See, e.g., the 1999 European Commission Annual Report on the Czech Republic, which can be accessed at "New Member States_Archives," European Union, Enlargement Archives, http://ec.europa.eu/enlargement/archives/enlargement_process/past_enlargements/eu10/index_en.htm. See also Lynn M. Tesser, "The Geopolitics of Tolerance: Minority Rights under EU Expansion in East-Central Europe," *East European Politics and Societies* 17, no. 3 (summer 2003): 483–532.

13. Michael Johns, "Do as I Say, Not as I Do: The European Union, Eastern Europe and Minority Rights," *East European Politics and Societies* 17, no. 4 (fall 2003): 682–99.

14. Economic data can be found in the annual *Transition Reports* published by the European Bank for Reconstruction and Development in London.

15. The term "PHARE" was derived from the French title for the assistance program originally designed for Hungary and Poland and later expanded to all of the Central and East European countries.

16. For background on the CAP, see "The Common Agricultural Policy (CAP) and Agriculture in Europe—Frequently Asked Questions," European Union, http://europa.eu/rapid/press-release_MEMO-13-631_en.htm.

17. "Enlargement and Agriculture: An Integration Strategy for the EU's New Member States," European Union, http://europa.eu/rapid/pressReleasesAction.do?reference=IP/02/176&format=HTML&aged=1&language=EN&guiLanguage=en.

18. See Peter Mair, "Popular Democracy and EU Enlargement," *East European Politics and Societies* 17, no. 1 (winter 2003): 58–63.

19. Public opinion polls on enlargement can be found at "Public Opinion and the Enlargement," European Commission, http://ec.europa.eu/public_opinion/topics/enlargement_en.htm.

20. European Commission, *Candidate Countries Eurobarometer 2002* (Brussels: European Commission, 2002), http://ec.europa.eu/public_opinion/archives/cceb/2002/cceb_2002_highlights_en.pdf.

21. European Commission, *Eurobarometer 2003.2: Public Opinion in the Candidate Countries* (Brussels: European Commission, 2003), http://ec.europa.eu/public_opinion/archives/cceb/2003/2003.2_highlights.pdf.

22. Referenda results for states joining in 2004 can be seen on the website of the Danish EU Information Centre at "Which EU Referenda Have Taken Place in EU Member States?" Folketingets EU-Oplysning, http://www.eu-oplysningen.dk/euo_en/spsv/all/21.

23. Andrea Covic, "Referendum Briefing No 18 Croatia's EU Accession Referendum, 22 January 2012," European Parties Elections and Referendums Network, http://www.sussex.ac.uk/sei/documents/epern-ref-no18.pdf.

24. Eurobarometer data available at "Eurobarometer Interactive Search System," European Commission, http://ec.europa.eu/public_opinion/cf/index.cfm?lang=en.

25. "Report on Results of the Negotiations on the Accession of Cyprus, Malta, Hungary, Poland, the Slovak Republic, Latvia, Estonia, Lithuania, the Czech Republic and Slovenia to the European Union," European Commission, http://ec.europa.eu/enlargement/archives/pdf/enlargement_process/future_prospects/negotiations/eu10_bulgaria_romania/negotiations_report_to_ep_en.pdf.

26. Margit B. Williams, "'And the Walls Came Tumbling Down' . . . or Did They? European Union Accession, and New and Old Borders in Central and Eastern Europe," *Canadian-American Slavic Studies* 39, no. 4 (2005): 421–48. In 2010 the Hungarian parliament passed a law removing residency requirements for those who want to become citizens. "Stephen Deets: Hungary's New Citizenship Law," *Nationalities Blog*, June 15, 2010, http://nationalities.wordpress.com/2010/06/15/hungarys-new-citizenship-law. The new Hungarian constitution also gave Hungarians living abroad the right to vote in national elections, but this was found by the Venice Commission of the Council of Europe and the Organization for Security and Co-operation in

Europe (OSCE) to be in accordance with international standards. See "Joint Opinion on the Act on the Elections of Members of Parliament of Hungary," OSCE, June 18, 2012, http://www.osce .org/odihr/91534?download=true.

27. For background and a timeline of Croatia's accession, see "Croatia," European Commission, Enlargement, http://ec.europa.eu/enlargement/countries/detailed-country-information/ croatia.

28. For the text and a summary of the Lisbon Treaty, see "Treaty of Lisbon," Council of the European Union, http://www.consilium.europa.eu/documents/treaty-of-lisbon?lang=en. For discussion of the background and changes, see "The 'Treaty of Lisbon,'" EurActiv.com, http://www .euractiv.com/future-eu/treaty-lisbon/article-163412.

29. The website of the European Commission is http://ec.europa.eu/index_en.htm. Nomination to the Commission does not automatically ensure approval. In 2010, the Bulgarian nominee to be commissioner of humanitarian aid was obliged to withdraw because of criticism in the European Parliament. Stephen Castle, "Bulgarian Drops Candidacy for European Commission," *New York Times*, January 19, 2010.

30. Jan Cienski, "Czech President Signs Lisbon Treaty," FT.com, November 3, 2009; "Klaus Links EU Treaty Signature to WWII Claims," EurActiv.com, October 12, 2009.

31. David Armitage Jr., "Europe's Return: The Impact of the EU's Newest Members," Report No. 27, Center for European Policy Analysis, November 2009.

32. See "Country Ratings and Status by Region," Freedom House, Freedom in the World, http://www.freedomhouse.org/report-types/freedom-world#.U2Us0yjN3Ns.

33. See Nations in Transit 2013 assessments at "Tables," Freedom House, http://www .freedomhouse.org/sites/default/files/NIT2013_Tables_FINAL.pdf.

34. "EU Threatens Hungary with Legal Action over Constitution," EurActiv.com, April 15, 2013. For a text of the European Parliament's critical resolution, see http://www.europarl.europa .eu/sides/getDoc.do?type=REPORT&reference=A7-2013-0229&language=EN.

35. Alexandra Sarlo and Maia Otarashvili, "Can the EU Rescue Democracy in Hungary?" *Eurasia Review*, August 1, 2013.

36. Richard Rose, *Understanding Post-communist Transformation* (London: Routledge, 2009).

37. Grigorij Mesežnikov, Olga Gyárfášová, and Daniel Smilov, eds., *Populist Politics and Liberal Democracy in Central and Eastern Europe* (Bratislava: Institute for Public Affairs, 2008); Ronald H. Linden, "The New Populism in Central and Southeast Europe," special issue of *Problems of Post-Communism* 55, no. 3 (May–June 2008).

38. "Who Can Join and When?" European Commission, http://ec.europa.eu/economy_ finance/euro/adoption/who_can_join/index_en.htm.

39. "A Very Short History of the Crisis: The Causes," *Economist*, November 12, 2011, http:// www.economist.com/node/21536871.

40. For the text of the "Fiscal Compact," see "Treaty on Stability, Coordination and Governance in the Economic and Monetary Union," European Council, http://www.european-council .europa.eu/media/579087/treaty.pdf.

41. Jan Cienski, "Exports Buoy Fragile Recovery in Central and Eastern Europe," *Financial Times*, August 26, 2013, 4; Mark Allen, "The Impact of the Global Economic Crisis on Central and Eastern Europe," IMF, http://www.imf.org/external/region/bal/rr/2011/022511.pdf, 18.

42. Marcin Goettig and Christian Lowe, "Special Report: From Hungary, Far-Right Party Spreads Ideology, Tactics," Reuters, April 9, 2014.

43. "No Evidence of Fraud in Hungary Funding Freeze: EU Official," Reuters, August 14, 3013; Zoltan Simon and Edith Balazs, "Hungary Wins Reprieve from Planned EU Aid Halt after Budget Cuts," Bloomberg.com, June 22, 2012.

44. Simon Taylor, "Orbán Accuses EU of Colonialism," EuropeanVoice.com, March 16, 2012.

45. See the "Presidency Conclusions" of the Thessaloniki European Council, Council of the European Union, June 19 and 20, 2003, http://www.consilium.europa.eu/uedocs/cms_data/docs/pressdata/en/ec/76279.pdf.

46. For background on this dispute, see Sinisa Jakov Marusic, "Macedonia-Greece Name Dispute: What's in a Name?" *Balkan Insight*, June 30, 2011, http://www.balkaninsight.com/en/article/background-what-s-in-a-name.

47. Dan Bilefsky, "Serbia and Kosovo Reach Agreement on Power-Sharing," *New York Times*, April 19, 2013.

48. Stefan Lehne, "Serbia-Kosovo Deal Should Boost the EU's Western Balkans Policy," *Carnegie Europe*, April 23, 2012.

49. See "Eastern Partnership Roadmap 2012–13: The Multilateral Dimension," European Commission, SWD(2012) 108 final, May 15, 2012; "Joint Declaration of the Prague Eastern Partnership Summit, Prague, 7 May 2009" 8435/09 (Presse 78), Brussels, May 7, 2009.

50. Andrew Kramer, "Russia Claims Its Sphere of Influence in the World," *New York Times*, August 31, 2008.

51. For a text of the agreement, see "EU-Ukraine Association Agreement—the Complete Texts," European External Action Service, http://eeas.europa.eu/ukraine/assoagreement/assoagreement-2013_en.htm; *EU-Ukraine Relations* (Brussels: European External Action Service, April 29, 2014), 5, http://eeas.europa.eu/statements/docs/2014/140429_04_en.pdf.

52. "Countries and Regions: Ukraine," European Commission, http://ec.europa.eu/trade/policy/countries-and-regions/countries/ukraine.

53. European Commission, "Statement by President Barroso and President Van Rompuy in the Name of the European Union on the Agreed Additional Restrictive Measures against Russia European Commission—STATEMENT/14/244 29/07/2014," European Union, http://europa.eu/rapid/press-release_STATEMENT-14-244_en.htm. For more on the sanctions, see Julian Borger, Paul Lewis, and Rowena Mason, "EU and US Impose Sweeping Economic Sanctions on Russia," *Guardian*, July 29, 2014.

54. Guy Chazan and Ed Crooks, "Europe's Dangerous Addiction to Russian Gas Needs Radical Cure," Ft.com, April 3, 2014.

55. Nevertheless, at the same time Ukraine signed its DCFTA, Moldova and Georgia did also.

56. See James E. Dougherty and Robert L. Pfaltzgraff Jr., *Contending Theories of International Relations* (New York: Addison Wesley Longman, 2001), for a review of international relations theories.

57. Among those who see the postcommunist region as providing a "natural experiment," see Judith Kelley, "International Actors on the Domestic Scene: Membership Conditionality and Socialization by International Institutions," *International Organization* 58 (summer 2004): 425–57.

58. Joseph S. Nye Jr., "Hard Power, Soft Power and the 'War on Terrorism,'" in *American Power in the Twenty-First Century*, ed. David Held and Mathias Koenig-Archibugi (Cambridge, UK: Polity Press, 2004), 114–33.

59. James G. March and John P. Olsen, *Rediscovering Institutions: The Organizational Basis of Politics* (New York: Free Press, 1989).

60. Ulrich Sedelmeier, "Anchoring Democracy from Above? The European Union and Democratic Backsliding in Hungary and Romania after Accession," *Journal of Common Market Studies* 52, no. 1 (2014): 105–21.

CHAPTER 9

Security Issues

NATO AND BEYOND

Joshua Spero

One of the first foreign policy decisions of the new postcommunist states was to dissolve their forty-year-old military alliance, the Warsaw Pact. After the fall of the Berlin Wall, the Warsaw Pact's dissolution marked the institutional end of the Cold War and Europe's division into two competing blocs, one dominated by the Soviet Union and the other by the United States. In the process, the North Atlantic Treaty Organization (NATO) no longer needed to protect the West from a potential communist attack. Instead, NATO membership became a key incentive to help former communist states transition to democracy and eventual European integration.

How European democratization and integration continue certainly depends on developments between Russia and NATO nations, particularly for those independent nations in between East and West, and formerly part of the USSR, but not yet integrated into European institutions. Given the 2014 Russia-Ukraine geopolitical conflict, the potential for a greater regional crisis and the armed separatist insurgency in eastern Ukraine challenges NATO's twenty-first-century role. This conflict could reinvigorate the alliance and more prominently return NATO to the 1949 treaty's Article V collective defense commitment. However, the bottom line for NATO always delineates its collective action focus, where alliance cohesion stems from collective contributions politically, economically, and militarily.[1] Thus, NATO's long-term European crisis-management commitment and its partnership with the East may continue to provide a peaceful linchpin that bridges the European divide.

Even with the 2014 Russia-Ukraine crisis, NATO's post–Cold War focus remains intact, having shifted from protecting Europe's Cold War division toward bringing Eastern and Western Europe together, managing conflicts within Europe, and grappling with international terrorist networks, especially in the aftermath of September 11, 2001. To achieve such challenging goals, Central and East European states became NATO members as they transformed their military forces and NATO leaders deemed the states "democratic." During this period of rapid change, NATO forces deployed outside NATO member-state territories as peacekeepers, peace enforcers, and then as fighters in Bosnia, Kosovo, Macedonia, Afghanistan, Iraq, and Libya.

The Warsaw Pact and Its Legacy

The inclusion of former Warsaw Pact members in NATO did not mean simply shifting players on a chessboard. The Warsaw Pact was formally established in 1955 as a response to the establishment of NATO and attempted to enforce existing Central and East European subordination to Moscow as satellite nations. From weapons production to a politicized military leadership, the pact linked the militaries of the Soviet Union and its satellites together under Soviet control. Yugoslavia remained the only state in this region to avoid Warsaw Pact membership. After the invasion of Czechoslovakia in 1968, Albania withdrew from the Warsaw Pact, and Romania, which did not participate in the invasion, pursued its own independent foreign policies while still remaining a pact member.

Map 9.1. Warsaw Pact and NATO States, 1989

Although high-level officers from Central and Eastern Europe remained part of the Warsaw Pact's hierarchy, Soviet officers and commanders controlled planning and military action. One way the Soviets controlled the Warsaw Pact was by enforcing a policy of equipment interoperability. They insisted that all Warsaw Pact forces share the same equipment that fit Soviet anti-NATO specifications. From airplanes to guns, interdependence was further enforced by not allowing any single country to produce all weapons and by giving states specific tasks under the direction of the Warsaw Pact and the Council for Mutual Economic Assistance (CMEA). This intertwining of military control structures, therefore, prevented members from acting independently.

For the Soviet Union and Warsaw Pact, political control over all aspects of the military remained as important as military prowess and professionalism. The only military maneuvers the pact actually conducted were in 1968 to counter the liberalization in Czechoslovakia known as the Prague Spring. Later, although the Warsaw Pact did not intervene, the threat of maneuvers pressured Poland during the 1980–1981 unrest to impose martial law. For the conscripts and professional military, political and military training went hand in hand. Required military service for men out of school or during their college careers focused on indoctrination, though such indoctrination rarely succeeded. Even military oaths referred to defending the bloc and the Soviet Union rather than individual homelands.

The USSR also ensured the military reliability of the Warsaw Pact via the joint command and Warsaw Pact maneuvers. Pact forces upheld the mission of protecting the Soviet bloc. In the event of NATO action, each military was assigned a specific task. Ostensibly designated for offensive planning against the West, the pact lasted almost forty years until 1991. After the pact's collapse in 1991, crack troops from Soviet forces remained stationed along the Iron Curtain border between the East and West.[2]

After 1989, however, the pact itself immediately became a vestigial organization as newly democratizing Central and East European leaderships turned westward for economic and political guidance. The Soviet army's intervention in Latvia and Lithuania, then still part of the Soviet Union, in early 1991 to stop popular demands for independence made the Warsaw Pact's existence, even as a historical marker, unacceptable to Central and East European leaders. Soon after the intervention, the foreign ministers of Poland, Czechoslovakia, and Hungary demanded dissolution of pact military structures. In June 1991, the pact's foreign and defense ministers met to end its military functions. Nine months later, the USSR dissolved.[3]

Central and East European leaders whose countries had once been Warsaw Pact members now contended with dismantling the pact's Soviet-dominated political-military structures. For these countries to become members or partners of NATO, the once "ideological enemies" had to become trusted allies. A complete restructuring and reconstruction required several steps. First, each country needed to develop different, individual military chains of command separate from Russia's military. Second, each Central and East European country had to make a complete shift to Western weapons and equipment. Third, the logic for large militaries dependent on draftees needed to be rethought. The withdrawal of Soviet troops from the German Democratic Republic (East Germany), Poland, Czechoslovakia, and Hungary and their return to the USSR, a country whose economy at this point could not meet its population's demands, also had to be negotiated.

To join NATO, Central and East European states began restructuring their militaries and redefining civil-military relations, doing away with old pact weaponry, and investing in new equipment to fit NATO specifications. Professional high-ranking military officers from pact forces needed to become partners—at least "partners for peace"—with their old enemies. For these states, even with support and aid from the West, the cost of retooling militaries and committing to NATO membership was extremely high, given the costs of transition from communism and transition of the senior officers, many of whom were educated in Soviet military academies. But this first opportunity to become "official" parts of the West seemed worth the price, especially given some prominent political democratization debates across Central and East Europe in the early 1990s over how quickly to change communist security structures and integrate westward rather than try to remain neutral.

From New to Old: NATO and Europe

When NATO was established in 1949, its members (Belgium, Canada, Denmark, France, Great Britain, Iceland, Italy, Luxembourg, Netherlands, Norway, Portugal, and the United States) agreed that the Soviet Union and its Eastern bloc posed the main threat to Western security. NATO members committed to defend each other if any non-NATO nation attacked a NATO member. This guarantee was focused mainly against a Soviet bloc invasion of the West. The security umbrella NATO provided in the early 1950s extended to vital sea lanes from Greenland to Iceland and Britain. When NATO did expand, it strengthened its defense in 1952 during the Korean War by having Greece and Turkey become members to contain the Soviet Union on NATO's southeastern border. In 1955, the Federal Republic of Germany joined, putting NATO on the Iron Curtain's border dividing Germany and Europe as a whole, and in 1982, Spain was integrated into NATO. The membership of these two countries increased NATO's strategic depth and promoted democratization in those countries. In 1978, NATO reaffirmed its members' equal commitments by agreeing that 3 percent of each member's budget would be devoted to NATO.

The process of inclusion and developing NATO strategy avoided the strict Warsaw Pact hierarchical approach. Although a US general always headed NATO, the United States, which was the largest NATO donor, had limited influence in the organization because the many European-based US forces were separate from NATO. Joint maneuvers were "joint" rather than dominated by one leader over other countries. No attempt to meld these armies and the foreign policies of NATO states was allowed in the absence of an active threat. There was also no political training for forces involved in NATO missions.

Although many Cold War crises erupted in Europe and tensions between Greece and Turkey flared regularly, no attacks against NATO members occurred from outside NATO. Its troops did remain on high alert during the Berlin and Cuban crises, but they were never fully activated. Nonetheless, the presence of Soviet troops in Berlin, close to NATO's eastern borders, during the 1961 Berlin crisis and the Soviet-led Warsaw Pact invasion of Czechoslovakia in 1968 necessitated continual NATO vigilance against potential Soviet threats. Even after Western policy began to shift toward détente with the USSR, the United States and Western Europe continued to modernize their nuclear arsenals to defend Europe, if necessary. Ultimately, NATO held together even as the revolutions of 1989 changed European security rapidly.[4]

NATO's Redefinition

The collapse of communism first in Central and Eastern Europe and then the USSR exacerbated NATO's internal disagreements over the nature and purpose of the alliance given the lack of any clear "Soviet" threat. NATO's focus shifted rapidly during the initial postcommunist period from potential Soviet threats to NATO's enlargement, bringing the former Central and East European "enemy states" into NATO. However, the eruption of violence in Yugoslavia—the first post–World War II large-scale violence within Europe—quickly complicated the postcommunist transition and dual enlargement processes, just as NATO began redefining critical threats. Yugoslavia's disintegration in 1991, during a decade of armed conflicts as that country broke apart, proved difficult for NATO because members, such as Germany, France, and the United Kingdom, maintained different commitments toward and concerns about the emerging independent post-Yugoslav nations. Subsequent NATO intervention at several key junctures in the post-Yugoslav wars challenged NATO's unity.

NATO's effort to deal with the new European reality began right after the Warsaw Pact collapsed, with the November 1991 New Strategic Concept. This strategic approach focused on a new European security policy with former pact countries before any of them fully transformed. NATO's transformation continued at the 1994 Brussels Summit, where the groundwork for NATO's post–Cold War role was set out by establishing combined joint task forces to support Europe's security and defense identity. Such an initiative was intended to strengthen European states' ability to work more effectively together and take more initiative. This allied shift, though, led to ongoing debate over NATO's role that lasted through the 1999 Washington Summit celebrating NATO's fiftieth anniversary and integrating its three newest members—the Czech Republic, Hungary, and Poland.

NATO Expansion: Integrating the East

At the same time that NATO searched for a new mission and better balance between Europe and America, Central and East European leaders pressed to join NATO to affirm their Westernization and guard against Russian instability. NATO opted for a policy of inclusion to fulfill its long-term goal of a Europe "whole and free" but hesitated to enlarge immediately. In reality though, the process had begun, before the Warsaw Pact collapsed, at a NATO summit in London in July 1990, when NATO invited the Soviet Union and Warsaw Pact members "to establish regular diplomatic liaison with NATO."[5] Once the pact disbanded, NATO launched the North Atlantic Cooperation Council to include former communist countries, without moving toward formal enlargement.[6] After the USSR disintegrated, NATO included some former Soviet republics in the North Atlantic Cooperation Council.

Photo 9.1. NATO flag-raising ceremony marks the accession of the Czech Republic, Hungary, and Poland to the alliance. They were the first postcommunist countries to join NATO. In March 2004, Bulgaria, Estonia, Latvia, Lithuania, Romania, Slovakia, and Slovenia also joined, followed by Croatia and Albania in 2009. (NATO Photos, 1999.)

The North Atlantic Cooperation Council promoted dialogue on common security concerns with Central and Eastern Europe and post-Soviet states. The dialogue bridged the former East-West divide and started practical cooperation. It also helped Central and East European politicians understand how defense rooted in democracy-based politics and national security encompassing civil emergency planning signified more than just military priorities. The 1994 Brussels Summit moved NATO leaders closer to enlargement by establishing the Partnership for Peace (PfP), which included those countries deemed "able and willing to contribute to European security."[7] PfP eventually involved all Central and East European and post-Soviet states (except post-Yugoslav states at war during the 1990s) that desired to join and fulfilled the criteria for democratic and military reform. At the same time, membership was extended to Finland, Sweden, Austria, and Switzerland, established democracies that had maintained neutrality during the Cold War. Although the more democratic countries of Central and Eastern Europe saw PfP's establishment as more of "a policy for postponement," PfP addressed some of their key security concerns and established norms for partners wanting to contribute to common European security.[8] The Central and East European states that initially participated in PfP became the core group of new states in the expanded European security process. Participation in extended political and military coordination for search and rescue, humanitarian assistance, and peacekeeping operations not only set the stage for NATO membership for some PfP partner nations but also established crucial ties for NATO operations beyond member territories.

The PfP process provided the foundation for membership invitations issued to Poland, Hungary, and the Czech Republic at the July 1997 Madrid Summit since NATO deemed these country transitions successful at "produc[ing] political, economic, social and military security." During this summit, NATO also restructured PfP to allow members' actual involvement in NATO military operations. When NATO extended membership invitations, it underscored that "no European democratic country . . . would be excluded from consideration" in future enlargements.[9]

These initial invitees joined NATO on its fiftieth anniversary, on March 12, 1999. As they joined, NATO launched its Membership Action Plan (MAP) to prepare nine more states for possible membership invitations (Albania, Bulgaria, Estonia, Latvia, Lithuania, Romania, Slovakia, Slovenia, and Macedonia). MAP initiation depended not just on military readiness but also on continuing democratization and market expansion. In order to become acceptable members of NATO, MAP nations were required to become "producers" of security through equitable treatment of ethnic minorities, good neighbor relations with surrounding countries, and democratic oversight of the military.[10]

By the 2002 Prague Summit, many countries involved in the MAP process were deemed to have successfully fulfilled the action plan. As a result, NATO issued invitations to a large number of MAP countries, overcoming Russian opposition to having NATO integrate former Soviet republics. After Lithuania, Latvia, and Estonia were invited to join, NATO's eastern borders with Russia were extended. NATO also expanded into southeastern Europe with the addition of Bulgaria, Romania, and Slovenia; Slovakia was also included in this round of expansion. When these seven new members, comprising both former Soviet and former Yugoslav states, joined NATO in 2004, they demonstrated the impact of NATO on democratization and military cooperation. At successive NATO summits in Bucharest (2008) and on NATO's sixtieth anniversary in Strasbourg/Kehl (2009), Albania and Croatia joined the alliance, and Montenegro joined Macedonia as a MAP country. After the 2003 Rose Revolution in Georgia and the 2004 Orange Revolution in Ukraine, both of those countries expressed their desire to become MAP countries as NATO membership shifted to southeastern Europe and Eurasia. Given the sensitivity of inviting countries bordering Russia and former Soviet republics outside the Baltic nations, particularly in the aftermath of the Russo-Georgian War in summer 2008, NATO hesitated to issue MAP invitations to Georgia and Ukraine. Yet NATO attempted to maintain its long-term commitment to keep an "open door" policy for PfP and Euro-Atlantic partners to join NATO, including Russia.[11]

The Costs of Membership

Membership in NATO originally provided the fastest road for Central and East European countries to join the West and shed their communist past. For former communist and postcommunist leaders, membership signified that their countries had freed themselves from Soviet dominance and reinforced their mantle of Western democracy. Poland's president, Aleksander Kwasniewski, personified the ability of former communist leaders and states to transform into democracy-based NATO contributors. Despite being a former communist, on becoming president of Poland, Kwasniewski actively led

Photo 9.2. NATO summit in 1994, where the Partnership for Peace program was established. Currently, thirty-five countries are members of the program. (NATO Photos, 1994.)

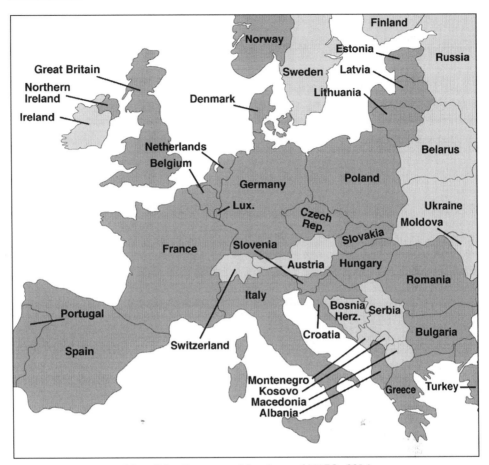

Map 9.2.   European Members of NATO, 2014

Poland's efforts to attain NATO membership. When Poland was accepted into NATO, he championed this step as proof that Poland had become a successful postcommunist democracy. NATO membership became most popular in Poland, among the original entrants, because of the country's long-held fear of Russian threats. Membership was less significant for Hungarians and Czechs because of their greater sense of geographical security and their much smaller armies. But NATO's membership and security guarantee under Article V served as proof of change, hope for protection, and promise of investment and foreign aid.

All of these benefits came with real costs. Although former pact members often invested far more in the military during the communist period, NATO membership remained expensive. Transitioning from their old force structures, purchasing Western equipment, and making force commitments, as well as contributing financially, cut deeply into the budgets of these former pact states. The costs of NATO membership also had a significant impact on these country budgets as they tried to become members of the European Union (EU). Membership did become a requirement for transitioning "into the West." Although it was a guarantee of security and not officially linked to EU membership, it emerged as a prerequisite for joining the European Union. As a result, economic conditions in new NATO countries initially worsened. Indeed, soon after the first entrants joined NATO, their economies declined precipitously, although only in part as a result of the costs of membership. Given these costs, the need to stay within the fiscal budget deficit limits imposed by the EU on these same new NATO members only posed more economic challenges.

The issue of "guns versus butter," then, signified real trade-offs: funding social programs in areas such as unemployment, education, and health care, making necessary infrastructure investments in roads and train lines to fulfill EU demands, or funding modernization to meet NATO demands. These choices occurred in a context in which the economies, even in their worst periods, were in far better shape than during communism, until the 2007–2008 global economic crisis. The monies paid for the military could double, as they did in the early years in Poland, Hungary, and Czech Republic, and the percentage of the budget going to the military remained relatively stable. Now, given the potential political backlash against the economic failure to "fund" the expected lifestyle improvements for large portions of the population, state expenditures on defense became politically difficult to justify. Some of these Central and East European NATO members may increase their military expenditures domestically and their budgetary contributions to NATO as a result of Russia's annexation of Crimea from Ukraine in the spring of 2014. Ironically, these newer NATO members may end up contributing more to NATO militarily than some of the older NATO nations, particularly in the aftermath of the pivotal developments in the Russia-Ukraine conflict, starting in early 2014.

Support for operations in Afghanistan, Iraq, and Libya also became politically charged and created economic problems. On the one hand, the prospect of having forces in Afghanistan and Iraq seemed to bring with it the promise of involvement in postwar reconstruction and alignment with the prestigious United States. On the other hand, it meant that new NATO members, which were also in most cases either new EU members or EU aspirants, might be seen as "Trojan horses" for US policy interests within NATO and also possibly within the EU. Contributing militarily to NATO- or to US-led operations in Afghanistan and/or Iraq arguably strengthened new members' and aspirants' integration into Europe institutionally in the first decade of NATO enlargement. European integration and the Eurozone crisis also pressured already fragile aspirant and new member economies as the global recession's impact endangered national budgets. These political and economic challenges reduced NATO's effort in Libya, where air operations were limited as the Europeans, with France and Britain in the lead, remained dependent on US military logistics and resupplies to reinforce those on the ground. Therefore, wary publics in aspirant and new member countries are skeptical of further NATO and EU enlargement.[12]

NATO's New Roles: Deploying outside Europe and Reconsidering Collective Defense

In the early and mid-1990s, even as NATO debated its role and integrated new members into the alliance, NATO forces deployed with old and new members in ways never before attempted. In 1996, as part of the 1995 Dayton Peace Accords that ended the Bosnian War, NATO and PfP nations contributed to the Implementation Force (IFOR) set up to enforce the fragile peace agreement. When IFOR's mission officially ended in December 1996, they continued to serve as members of the successful Stabilization Force, reinforcing Bosnia's rebuilding effort with the Organization for Security and Co-operation in Europe. This on-the-ground involvement, which was replayed in the Kosovo Force (KFOR) deployments to maintain the peace after NATO's bombing, also ended the Serb–Kosovar Albanian conflict and ethnic cleansing of Albanians that occurred in 1998 and 1999. Indeed, the seventy-eight-day NATO bombing campaign over Serbia and Kosovo drew NATO offensively into war, saving hundreds of thousands of Kosovar Albanians but reaching a new juncture in the defensive alliance's history, as nearly one thousand Serbs were killed.[13]

NATO's involvement in former Yugoslavia's wars severely tested the alliance's cohesion. Since the Kosovo bombing campaign failed to gain a UN mandate, real difficulties erupted in 1999 when NATO needed consensus on military intervention in Serbia and Kosovo. Although the postbombing KFOR operation did receive a UN mandate, justification for new military actions using old provisions complicated NATO's post–Cold

Photo 9.3.   The members of the Stabilization Force (SFOR) Multinational Honor Guard stand on the tarmac at Tuzla Air Base, Bosnia-Herzegovina. SFOR remained in Bosnia and Herzegovina from January 1996 to December 2005, when the EU's European Military Force (EUFOR) took over. (US Department of Defense, 1997.)

War missions because different allies had different ties and commitments to Serbia. More complications emerged from the interests of some new NATO members and PfP partners that opposed military action in Kosovo, in contrast to their positions concerning the Bosnian settlement. For the United States, NATO's involvement in Bosnia and then Kosovo occurred primarily because the United States wanted to enforce peace and counter large-scale Serb aggression militarily without entering into a politically untenable commitment of US ground forces. For most European NATO members, the worst post–World War II European violence raised the need to stem huge refugee inflows across Europe from former Yugoslavia, which created serious socioeconomic burdens.[14]

NATO's political decision to make the Balkans part of NATO's "area of responsibility" led, in addition to actions in Bosnia and Kosovo, to NATO force deployments in Macedonia, where they successfully prevented conflict. These deployments occurred before any of the Balkan states, including the newly independent post-Yugoslav nations, became NATO members. The hope was that the 2004 accession of Slovenia, Romania, and Bulgaria would increase Balkan stability by demonstrating to the other states in the region that NATO membership remained possible. These newly admitted states soon started advocating and formulating policy inside NATO to include the rest of the Balkans (Croatia, Albania, and Macedonia, as well as Bosnia-Herzegovina, Serbia, and Montenegro). In the aftermath of September 11, 2001, prior integration of PfP members into NATO and advanced NATO ties to PfP partners also meant that the United States could use Balkan as well as Central Asian military bases to support operations in Afghanistan. Consequently, new NATO member Poland particularly and other PfP nations, with NATO allies, contributed ground force contingents to Afghanistan and later Iraq, while comparable multinational units also continued to be stationed in Kosovo and Bosnia.

Since 9/11, NATO has struggled to reshape its defense capabilities to deal with the new risks of global terrorism. Due to these new globalized terrorist threats, NATO has included states in the Caucasus and Central Asia as participants, though they are not NATO members or potential members. It also has prompted more cooperation among NATO members against globalized terrorist networks, increasing the amount of shared intelligence and shared preparation for expanded nuclear, chemical, biological, or radiological threats. The risks, for NATO members, of undertaking collective defense increased dramatically after 9/11. Immediately after the attacks, NATO members invoked the Article V clause for the first time, ironically to support and protect the United States, although the United States only supported the implementation of the NATO collective defense enactment weeks later, NATO ambassadors unanimously voted on September 12, 2001, to invoke Article V. Once the United States finally sought NATO nation support in the aftermath of 9/11, NATO planes and ships began to protect the continental United States. Then, in 2002, when the United States needed reinforcement in Afghanistan, some NATO members and PfP partners joined US forces there. In 2003, the United States requested that NATO take the lead on one of the Afghanistan operations. In the NATO-led International Security Assistance Force (ISAF) in Afghanistan, Poland and the Czech Republic, among other NATO allies, led PfP member troops from Romania, Bulgaria, Ukraine, and Slovakia in combat. After the 2003 US-British-led invasion of Iraq, these NATO and PfP partner nations also contributed forces, as they did for counterinsurgency missions to rebuild Afghanistan. Poland commanded one of the three multinational sectors in Iraq alongside the United States and Britain.[15]

In the long run, the September 11 attacks triggered significant splits within NATO, reflecting differing threat perceptions and approaches to coalition building in NATO-led operations. Even though NATO membership involves a commitment to a broader set of responsibilities and wider geographical areas of engagement, most recently clarified in the New Strategic Concept in 2010, disputes arose among old and new NATO members over the Iraq War. Of the original NATO states, only Great Britain, Spain, Italy, and the Netherlands provided military forces. The newer NATO states, particularly Poland and Romania, committed themselves in the early part of the war and sent either forces or specialized noncombat support units, despite strong popular opposition.[16] Not only did strains exist among NATO members over the war in Iraq from 2003 to 2011, but most NATO states remain unwilling to increase their defense budgets despite the widening gap in military capabilities and investment between the United States, its longtime allies, and new members. NATO's ISAF mission in Afghanistan, which moved the alliance's focus away from European territorial defense, also lacked consensus as members differed on the importance of missions performed outside Europe.[17] Intra-allied consensus faces continued challenges as most NATO nations' forces withdraw from Afghanistan for the post-2014 transfer of security to Afghanistan, a decision taken at NATO's May 2012 Chicago Summit. Yet, a great likelihood exists that some allied forces will remain in Afghanistan for training, advising, and assistance missions after 2014, given the reality of continued instability in Afghanistan. This does take into consideration alliance objectives in the wake of the Russia-Ukraine crisis in 2014.[18]

Such intra-alliance tensions over force deployments beyond Europe also led to tensions within the alliance and with Russia over NATO's more recent strategic focus on the Black Sea, the Caucasus, and Central Asia, as well as over future NATO membership for Ukraine and Georgia. In an attempt to dilute and weaken NATO, Russia has tried to influence NATO debates about membership for Ukraine and Georgia. To a certain extent, Russian leaders see their Central and East European counterparts as working to bring countries that border Russia and that Russia regards as within its sphere of interest westward into NATO. However, Russian leaders also believe that many NATO allies remain hesitant to vote in new members, as many states do not want to irritate Russia, whose cooperation is needed for missions outside Europe and on whom many of the states in Western Europe depend largely for their energy needs.[19] Consequently, between 2008 and 2009, it was mainly the United States and the Central and East European states that supported potential NATO membership paths for Ukraine and Georgia. Although NATO allies voiced significant concern over Russian military tensions with Ukraine— particularly concerning the transit of Russian energy supplies to Europe via Ukraine, the Russo-Georgian War, and Russia's territorial annexation of Crimea—NATO found itself facing larger security dilemmas outside Europe where NATO either needed Russia's cooperation or NATO nations refused to confront Russia militarily. Thus, disagreements among members concerning how best to deal with the threat of periodic cutoffs of Russian oil and natural gas supplies for Western Europe via Central and East European pipelines and NATO nation military deployment commitments abroad, let alone within Europe, continually hampered NATO consensus on further enlargement.[20]

Russian endeavors to counter NATO actions were most effective in debating within the NATO-Russian Council, at least before the Russia-Ukraine crisis. Though alliance decisions occur at the North Atlantic Council, the highest NATO body, which excludes non-NATO PfP partners such as Russia, Russian concerns raised in the NATO-Russia Council affect the decisions arrived at by NATO members.[21] Before the Russo-Georgian War worsened NATO-Russia ties, Russia threatened NATO on future NATO MAP invitations for Ukraine and Georgia. Russian speeches at NATO headquarters and consistently after the NATO April 2008 summit threatened military intervention in Ukraine and Georgia if MAP invitations emerged. These threats caused major reactions in European capitals. Such Russian threats also set the stage for more antagonistic politico-military maneuvering to disrupt the NATO consensus, particularly in the aftermath of the Russo-Georgian War in August 2008.[22]

The geopolitical impact of the Russo-Georgian War on NATO-Russian relations became clearer both in NATO's suspension of NATO-Russia Council sessions for several months and in NATO's taking some decisions that favored Russian military strategy. NATO's sixtieth-anniversary summit in April 2009 demonstrated how the Russian military incursions in Georgia had slowed inroads toward greater alliance made by recent members and aspirant partners. The alliance distanced itself from enlargement with Ukraine and Georgia and retreated on missile defense in Poland and the Czech Republic. Divisiveness among allies grew over Russian military threats on NATO's eastern periphery, especially the postwar breakaway Georgian regions in Abkhazia and South Ossetia. The reduced commitment to enlargement and slowed MAP progress for Ukraine and Georgia evident in NATO declarations underscored allied divergence.[23] Indeed, the US missile defense system initiative in Poland and the Czech Republic before the April 2009 NATO summit initially gained alliance support. However, by the summit's end, NATO developments veered away from a US–Central European–NATO effort and, in fact, began to focus on a US-NATO-Russian one.[24] The April 2009 summit's declaration appeared to affirm Russian military objectives.[25] Russian arguments against missile defense influenced such important West European leaders as Germany to diverge from its Central and East European and US counterparts.[26] Dissension in NATO also emerged as NATO nations downplayed Iranian threats to Europe, while Russia rejected proposed US antiballistic missile defenses based on Russian territory. By the fall of 2009, the deal to trade US missile defense systems in Poland and the Czech Republic for suspension of sales of Russian S-300 surface-to-air missile systems to Iran emerged in US-Russian negotiations.[27]

By NATO's May 2012 Chicago Summit, NATO enlargement remained on the back burner, while NATO theater ballistic missile defense appeared to take priority. Such missile defense concentrated on Turkey and threats from the Syrian civil war rather than from Iran. At the same time, NATO allies and partners began to cooperate on some missile defense via the NATO-Russia Missile Data Fusion Center and joint Planning Operations Center. But the Russia-Ukraine crisis, particularly after Russia's annexation of Crimea in March 2014, ruptured NATO-Russia ties, suspending the NATO-Russia Council again. Only time will tell how enlargement, missile defense, and official NATO-Russia ties influence NATO's outreach to Central and southeastern Europe and the Caucasus and whether Russian military pressure will continue to spur divisiveness within the alliance.[28]

Given significant alliance tensions with Russia, along with declining NATO nation resource contributions to the alliance's trilateral approach of collective defense, crisis management, and cooperative security, NATO nations need not only to come to terms with Russia's renewed threats on NATO nation borders and to decide whether to enlarge to include more post-Soviet nations but also to confront the rapidly increasing threats, among others, of regional civil wars, massive refugee flows, and expanding international terrorist networks from North Africa and the Middle East. The uprisings across North Africa and the Arab nations between 2011 and 2013 resulted in NATO's air mobilization from spring through summer 2011 in Libya. Remarkably, the UN Security Council gave unanimous approval to have NATO help Libyans seek refuge within Libya as the country disintegrated. In Operation Unified Protector, NATO protected civilians from mass slaughter primarily with sortie and air-strike missions, a regional role that the Arab League supported. Yet, even as the initial UN mandate for NATO action in Libya received Russian support, primarily because NATO's leading nations pledged not to use the alliance offensively, Russia's approval evaporated when NATO decided to strike Libyan military forces as a means of protecting Libyan civilians. Hence, continued tensions within NATO and with Russia over Libya compounded intra-alliance tensions preceding the Russia-Ukraine crisis, while concerns persist about future out-of-area missions. Even more tellingly, although the United States pushed France and Britain to take the lead in Operation Unified Protector, without US logistical and operational military reinforcement for the sortie and strike missions, NATO's Libyan operation might have collapsed. Clearly, some of the lessons emerging from Unified Protector pointed toward long-lasting failures in full alliance interoperability and long-term European NATO member defense cuts. After the UN-mandated and NATO-led operation in Libya, such negative NATO military trends may prevent future NATO missions. Since large-scale upheaval hampers Libya and, regionally, Morocco, Algeria, Tunisia, Egypt, Mali, Niger, Sudan, and Somalia, in combination with upheavals projected from Syria, Jordan, Israel, Yemen, Iraq, Iran, Afghanistan, and Pakistan, security dilemmas across North Africa, the Middle East, and Southwest Asia portend more threats to NATO's members and partners in Europe and Eurasia, particularly from a reconstituted al-Qaeda's terrorist network offshoots.[29]

NATO Tomorrow

The fate of the new NATO and its impact on its new members remain challenging. Most European leaders remain focused on their Eurozone economic dilemmas, cannot secure increases to their defense budgets, and therefore fail to contribute more militarily to NATO and remain dependent on the US military for out-of-Europe NATO military operations. These military burden-sharing problems compound the European realization within NATO that the United States already has started refocusing militarily away from Europe and emphasizing the geostrategic priority of Asia and the Persian Gulf region. None of the newly democratizing states can refuse membership or risk being turned down, even as NATO allies continually reduce their NATO military contributions and consequently threaten to hollow out NATO and increase intra-alliance dysfunction.

NATO's integration of new members and partners shifting from authoritarianism toward democracy and capitalism needs to continue to reinforce an all-Europe defense force. Yet European forces remain limited primarily to territorial defense rather than the more significant out-of-NATO-area expeditionary capabilities needed. As a result, Europeans face the reality that, unless they contribute more militarily to NATO and become more militarily independent of the United States (as the EU's pull of resources away from NATO rises), Russia and other states will likely keep confronting vulnerable nations, knowing that the US projects lower European-based military force commitments. Although new threats and conflicts within Europe appeared to be declining, strategic concerns beyond Europe (e.g., in Afghanistan, Libya, and even Mali) underscore keen challenges for how many NATO allies can muster the resources and interoperability to contribute operationally.[30] After all, the growing conflicts in North and Central Africa, the Middle East, and Southwest Asia endanger NATO allies and partners significantly.

Taking these out-of-area concerns into account, NATO's revitalization may still result from its traditional fears of Eastern threats, primarily from Russia's growing military redeployments in and along the non-NATO Ukrainian border and three NATO nation Baltic borders. As NATO redefines Europe eastward, the Central and East European nations no longer delineate the border of West and East but act as bridges to the East from the heart of Europe. They need NATO's backing as long as threats exist from an increasingly authoritarian Russia and some of its unreformed allies along NATO's eastern periphery, and also on Afghanistan's borders that are vital to the NATO-led ISAF mission winding down there.[31]

Consequently, membership in NATO, as well as in the EU, for all its costs, remains necessary to becoming part of a democratized Europe in the twenty-first century. Even if Central and East European states continue to face challenges in consolidating durable political democracies in the coming decade, they appear unlikely to revert to communism. Instead, they will become even more significant players as NATO pushes the boundaries of Europe eastward and they move from new entrants to become players in European security and stability. Ultimately, 2014 may become pivotal to NATO's reemergence as the security institution of Europe. NATO's revival may well solidify because of Poland's key frontline border with Ukraine and its keen ties with Ukraine's post–Cold War leaders, and Germany's unique leadership linkages with Russia since the Cold War's collapse buttress the Poland-Germany partnership with Europe and the United States. For great powers and international institutions trying to defuse the Russia-Ukraine crisis, this Poland-Germany bridge building maintains West-East consultation and economic linkages to Ukraine and Russia. The Poland-Germany heartland bridge, having emerged with postcommunist Poland in 1989 and unified Germany to play the key Central and East European role[32] for twenty-first century European integration, will greatly influence together, more than separately, the next EU and NATO moves for Ukraine and Russia.[33]

At the same time, the alliance constantly faces new threats. The real challenge becomes managing or successfully overcoming the geostrategic maneuvering between and among Russia, the new members of the alliance in Central and Eastern Europe, and older European members, in the face of the United States' declining role in

Europe and its turn to East Asia and the Persian Gulf region.[34] From NATO's creation, the USSR and now Russia have long wanted to dilute NATO politically and militarily, if not cause its collapse.[35] Yet, NATO's survival may well depend on how well it manages intra-alliance differences over its operations in Afghanistan and its weakening due to declining alliance resources. Ironically, while a NATO failure in Southwest Asia imperils alliance unity and possibly the alliance's future, it could also destabilize the region, cast greater uncertainty throughout Eurasia, impact harshly on the gains made by Central and Eastern Europe, and end up harming Russian as well as European and US national security.

Study Questions

1. Is NATO the effective security institution for Europe in the twenty-first century?
2. How has NATO's mission changed since the end of the Cold War?
3. Should NATO have deployed forces from its contributing member and partner nations beyond the borders of its member states, starting in the mid-1990s for the first time?
4. What might be the most useful institutional relationship NATO could have with the European Union?
5. How might NATO consider its options if the United States decides to have its NATO allies take much more responsibility in the years ahead?

Suggested Readings

Asmus, Ronald. *Opening NATO's Door: How the Alliance Remade Itself for a New Era*. New York: Columbia University Press, 2002.

Goldgeier, James. *Not Whether but When: The U.S. Decision to Enlarge NATO*. Washington, DC: Brookings Institution, 1999.

Kaplan, Lawrence S. *NATO Divided, NATO United: The Evolution of an Alliance*. New York: Praeger, 2004.

Kay, Sean. *NATO and the Future of European Security*. Lanham, MD: Rowman & Littlefield, 2003.

Michta, Andrew A. *The Limits of Alliance: The United States, NATO and the EU in North and Central Europe*. Lanham, MD: Rowman & Littlefield, 2006.

Papacosma, Victor S., Sean Kay, and Mark R. Rubin, eds. *NATO after Fifty Years*. Wilmington, DE: Scholarly Resources, 2001.

Simon, Jeffrey, ed. *NATO Enlargement: Opinions and Options*. Washington, DC: National Defense University Press, 1996.

Sloan, Stanley R. *NATO, the European Union and the Atlantic Community*. 2nd ed. Lanham, MD: Rowman & Littlefield, 2005.

Spero, Joshua B. *Bridging the European Divide: Middle Power Politics and Regional Security Dilemmas*. Lanham, MD: Rowman & Littlefield, 2004.

Yost, David. *NATO Transformed: The Alliance's New Roles in International Security*. Washington, DC: United States Institute of Peace, 1999.

Websites

NATO on Twitter: https://twitter.com/NATO
NATO on YouTube: https://www.youtube.com/NATO
North Atlantic Treaty Organization (NATO): http://www.nato.int

Notes

The previous version of this chapter in the second edition of this volume was coauthored by Jeffrey Simon and Joshua Spero, based on Simon's chapter from the first edition.

1. Joshua B. Spero, "Considering NATO's Long-Term Revitalization," *E-International Relations*, July 30, 2014, http://www.e-ir.info/2014/07/30/considering-natos-long-term-revitalization (accessed August 14, 2014).

2. Zbigniew Brzezinski, *The Grand Failure: The Birth and Death of Communism in the Twentieth Century* (New York: Collier, 1989).

3. Andrew Michta, *East Central Europe after the Warsaw Pact: Security Dilemmas in the 1990s* (New York: Greenwood, 1992).

4. Jeffrey Simon, ed., *European Security Policy after the Revolutions of 1989* (Washington, DC: National Defense University Press, 1991).

5. Heads of State and Government, "London Declaration on a Transformed North Atlantic Alliance," meeting of the North Atlantic Council in London, July 6, 1990, paragraph 7.

6. Heads of State and Government, "Rome Declaration of Peace and Cooperation," meeting of the North Atlantic Council in Rome, Press Release S-1(91)86, November 8, 1991, paragraph 11.

7. "Declaration of the Heads of State and Government Participating in the Meeting of the North Atlantic Council in Brussels," Press Communiqué M-1(94)3, January 11, 1994, paragraph 13.

8. These occurred in the form of individual partnership programs (IPPs), which involved broad cooperation in the planning and review process, peace support operations, moves to ensure transparency, and the development of democratic oversight of the military.

9. Heads of State and Government, "Madrid Declaration on Euro-Atlantic Security and Cooperation," meeting of the North Atlantic Council in Madrid, July 8, 1997, paragraph 8.

10. North Atlantic Treaty Organization (NATO), "Study on NATO Enlargement," in *NATO Handbook*, October 8, 2002, http://www.nato.int/docu/handbook/2001/hb030101.htm (accessed January 11, 2010); "Membership Action Plan (MAP)," *Topics*, April 2, 2009, http://www.nato.int/issues/map/index.html (accessed January 11, 2010).

11. Sean Kay, *Global Security in the Twenty-First Century: The Quest for Power and the Search for Peace*, 2nd ed. (Lanham, MD: Roman & Littlefield, 2011); Andrew A. Michta, "NATO Enlargement Post-1989: Successful Adaptation or Decline?" *Contemporary European History* 18, no. 3 (2009): 363–76.

12. Joshua B. Spero, "Great Power Security Dilemmas for Pivotal Middle Power Bridging," *Contemporary Security Policy* 30, no. 1 (April 2009): 147–71; Sean Kay, "Indecision on Syria and Europe May Undermine America's Asia Pivot," Commentary and Analysis, *War on the Rocks*, July 8, 2013, http://warontherocks.com/2013/07/indecision-on-syria-and-europe-may-undermine-americas-asia-pivot (accessed August 20, 2013).

13. Ivo H. Daalder and Michael E. O'Hanlon, *Winning Ugly: NATO's War to Save Kosovo* (Washington, DC: Brookings Institution, 2000).

14. Steven L. Burg and Paul S. Shoup, *The War in Bosnia-Herzegovina: Ethnic Conflict and International Intervention* (Armonk, NY: M. E. Sharpe, 1999); Sabrina P. Ramet, *Thinking about Yugoslavia: Scholarly Debates about the Yugoslav Breakup and the Wars in Bosnia and Kosovo* (Cambridge: Cambridge University Press, 2005).

15. *East Europe's New Role in the Middle East*, Special Report, Woodrow Wilson International Center for Scholars, January 2004.

16. Joshua B. Spero, "Beyond Old and New Europe," *Current History* 103, no. 671 (March 2004): 135–38.

17. Zbigniew Brzezinski, "An Agenda for NATO," *Foreign Affairs* 88, no. 5 (September–October 2009): 2–20; Karl-Heinz Kamp, "Toward a New Strategy for NATO," *Survival* 51, no. 4 (August–September 2009): 21–27.

18. "Chicago Summit Declaration on Afghanistan," issued by the heads of state and government of Afghanistan and nations contributing to the NATO-led International Security Assistance Force (ISAF), NATO, May 21, 2012, http://www.nato.int/cps/en/SID-1BBDB541-FD5ACE96/natolive/official_texts_87595.htm (accessed August 20, 2013).

19. Adrian Karatnycky and Alexander J. Motyl, "The Key to Kiev," *Foreign Affairs* 88, no. 3 (May–June 2009): 106–20; Charles King, "The Five-Day War," *Foreign Affairs* 87, no. 6 (November–December 2008): 2–11.

20. Svante E. Cornell et al., *Regional Security in the South Caucasus: The Role of NATO* (Washington, DC: Johns Hopkins University, 2004); Paul Gallis, *NATO and Energy Security* (Washington, DC: Congressional Research Service, 2006).

21. "Chairman's Statement in Meeting of the NATO-Russia Council in Defence Minister's Session in Brussels," NATO-Russia Council, June 13, 2008, http://www.nato-russia-council.info/htm/EN/documents13jun08.shtml (accessed August 22, 2009).

22. Oksana Antonenko, "A War with No Winners," *Survival* 50, no. 5 (October–November 2008): 23–36.

23. NATO Final Communiqué, "Meeting of the North Atlantic Council at the Level of Foreign Ministers Held at NATO Headquarters, Brussels," NATO, December 3, 2008, http://www.nato.int/docu/pr/2008/p08-153e.html (accessed August 19, 2009).

24. "NATO Chief Expects Joint Missile Defense with Russia by 2020," *RIA Novosti*, December 17, 2009, http://en.rian.ru/world/20091217/157273894.html (accessed December 28, 2009).

25. NATO, "Strasbourg/Kehl NATO Summit Declaration: Issued by the Heads of State and Government Participating in the Meeting of the North Atlantic Council in Strasbourg/Kehl," section 54, April 4, 2009, http://www.nato.int/cps/en/natolive/news_52837.htm (accessed August 22, 2009).

26. Eugene Rumer and Angela Stent, "Russia and the West," *Survival* 51, no. 2 (April–May 2009): 91–104.

27. "U.S., Russia Trade European Missile Defense System for S-300 SAMs," *RBC Daily*, September 24, 2009, available at *RIA Novosti*, http://en.rian.ru/papers/20090924/156242202.html (accessed December 28, 2009); Oliver Thränert, "NATO, Missile Defence and Extended Deterrence," *Survival* 51, no. 6 (December 2009–January 2010): 63–76.

28. "2012 Chicago Summit Declaration," issued by the heads of state and government participating in the meeting of the North Atlantic Council in Chicago, NATO, May 20, 2012, http://www.nato.int/cps/en/SID-1BBDB541-FD5ACE96/natolive/official_texts_87593.htm (accessed August 20, 2013).

29. Rebecca C. Moore, *NATO's New Mission: Projecting Stability in a Post–Cold War World* (New York: Praeger, 2007); V. P. Malik and Jorg Schultz, eds., *Emerging NATO: Challenges for Asia and Europe* (New Delhi: Lancer Publishers, 2008); James W. Peterson, *NATO and Terrorism:*

Organizational Expansion and Mission Transformation (New York: Continuum, 2011); Stephanie C. Hoffmann, *European Security in NATO's Shadow* (Cambridge: Cambridge University Press, 2012).

30. Joshua B. Spero, "European Union Security Challenges," in International Affairs Forum, July 2011, http://ia-forum.org/Content/ViewInternalDocument.cfm?ContentID=7863 (accessed August 20, 2013).

31. Sean Kay, "NATO Revived? Not So Fast," *War on the Rocks*, March 6, 2014, http://waronthe rocks.com/2014/03/nato-revived-not-so-fast (accessed April 12, 2014).

32. Spero, "Great Power Security Dilemmas for Pivotal Middle Power Bridging."

33. Joshua B. Spero, "An East-West Bridge for Ukraine," *Duck of Minerva*, April 4, 2014, http://www.whiteoliphaunt.com/duckofminerva/2014/04/an-east-west-bridge-for-ukraine.html (accessed April 12, 2014).

34. Sean Kay, "Is NATO an Alliance for the 21st Century?" in *NATO's Current and Future Challenges*, ed. S. Victor Papacosma. Occasional Papers 6 (Kent, OH: Kent State University, 2008); Sean Kay, "The Russia Crisis Proves the Case for the Asia Pivot," *War on the Rocks*, March 27, 2014, http://warontherocks.com/2014/03/the-russia-crisis-proves-the-case-for-the-asia-pivot (accessed April 12, 2014).

35. Andrew A. Michta, "Central Europe and NATO: Still Married, but in Need of Counseling," *Center for European Policy Analysis*, Report No. 29, December 2009.

Part III

CASE STUDIES

Map 10.0. Poland

CHAPTER 10

Poland

THE POLITICS OF "GOD'S PLAYGROUND"

Jane Leftwich Curry

Poland was the first and one of the most successful transitions from a centralized communist state to a liberal, more Western-style democracy. During the European economic crisis, Poland's economy maintained one of the highest growth rates in the European Union (EU). Its political system stabilized. It has been both an active member of the EU and a strong advocate for liberalization of its eastern neighbors as well as for their inclusion in European initiatives. Its prime minister, Donald Tusk, was the first East European elected head of the Council of Europe in 2014. His successor, Ewa Karpacz, signaled a shift to more social welfare programs aimed at the middle and lower classes.

But getting there was not easy. Its early and fast start on democratization and economic reform, as well as reformers' fear of opposition from the Soviet Union or even from the police and military in Poland, created complications that impact Polish politics even today. Since Poland was the first state to begin a transformation out of communism, its new leaders went only as far as they thought the Soviet Union and the rest of the bloc would tolerate. But within months, communism had collapsed everywhere except the Soviet Union, which was clearly too weak to hold back change. So the other former Soviet bloc states went much further much faster. As a result, the Polish political system was a "work in progress" for years, changing its constitution and laws in response to what did and did not work. In the process, Poland went from an uneasy coalition of former communist leaders, Solidarity activists, and experts in 1989, to a system in which the right and then the former communists battled for power, and finally, by the end of its first two decades of democracy, to a stable system with two dominant parties close to the center and a number of smaller parties.

Capitalism worked on a macroeconomic level from the start but brought with it dramatic losses for much of the country. A "shock therapy" economic program was implemented in 1990 to stabilize the currency and allow prices to adjust to the marketplace so that a rapid shift to capitalism would be possible and Western aid would be approved. This process was the swiftest and most dramatic economic change in the region. But these reforms caused a dramatic drop in living standards for many. As a result, Poles were, for a long period, some of the least satisfied people in the former communist world, and Polish politics was often more about blaming and punishing the "bad guys" for economic problems than about building party loyalty or popular trust in the new democratic institutions and leadership.

When the European economic recession started in 2008, the Polish economy had been well enough reconstructed that it was not affected by problems elsewhere in Europe and was the only economy in Europe to grow throughout the recession. Now, though, as the recession tapers off elsewhere in Europe, an increase in the national debt, unemployment, and continued inequality may weaken some of Poland's macroeconomic success.

Poland came into the transition with a far more liberal political system than existed elsewhere. The three worker revolts before 1989 each ultimately resulted in concessions. Support for the Catholic Church was always strong enough to force rulers to concede to many of its demands and even seek its support. Solidarity, the trade union that emerged out of the 1980 Gdańsk workers strikes, had, at its height in 1981, over 10 million members, easily the majority of Poland's workforce. Even after it was declared illegal and its leaders and activists were interned, it remained a force with which the regime ultimately had to negotiate. And the shortages and hardships of "real socialism" in Poland created friendship and professional groups that helped people survive and counter the controls in the communist system. These groups, as well as the high level of social resistance, also allowed alternative elites to establish themselves, provided the personal ties between groups that helped in the transition, and gave people organizing experience that facilitated Poland's negotiated transition.

The weaknesses of the old communist system that made it liberal also complicated the transition. Poland was, by 1989, over $40 billion in debt to the West[1] and still enmeshed in the Soviet bloc economic system. This meant that its options for economic reform were limited by its need to satisfy its Western debtors. Its opposition had been the strongest in the communist world well before Solidarity's 1980–1981 advent, but it also had ideological divisions, and many suspected that others were reporting on them to the secret police. From the 1970s on, most Poles had real knowledge of and very high expectations for democracy and capitalism because they had been guest workers in the West, had ties to family members there, and had an elite that tried to buy them off with its openness to the West. The image of democracy and capitalism they took away from this was of prosperity not inequality. In Poland, they learned to work around or oppose the system. They did not learn, however, how to function as citizens in a normal democratic system. In the end, the communist-era reforms left them with high hopes for democracy, little practice with working within a democracy, and an economy of foreign debt, inflation, and failed factories.

The political ramifications of the communist past and the way the initial postcommunist leadership reformed the system and dealt with the past haunted Polish politics for almost two decades, even though Polish communism had been "communism light," with freedom for small businesses, peasants, and the Catholic Church and much more tolerance for dissent. The first prime minister in postcommunist Poland, Tadeusz Mazowiecki, having entered into a unity government with the communists who handed over power, tried to "draw a thick line" to avoid divisions over the abuses of the past as Poland struggled to deal with the many challenges of starting a new system. Doing this, though, left an opening for claims and counterclaims about what had happened and who had been responsible that reached its height in 2006 when the hard-liners of the right-wing

Law and Justice Party (PiS) led by President Lech Kaczynski and his twin brother, Prime Minister Jaroslaw Kaczynski, labeled anyone who disagreed with them a communist. In addition, the Mazowiecki government's choice of "shock therapy" to reform the economy by freeing the currency and prices while holding wages stable benefited the economy in the long run but, in the short run, impoverished many and turned them against the very reformers who had brought democracy to Poland. This further complicated political debates over options and popular faith in the new system. Substantive policy discussions often took a back seat to battles over what had happened and who was responsible.

Precommunist History

Situated in the "heart of Europe" between Germany and Russia, Poland has a long history of struggle against outside conquerors. By 1795, the Polish-Lithuanian Commonwealth had been split between the Russian, German, and Austrian empires. From then on, Poles fought at home and abroad for Polish independence. It took World War I and Woodrow Wilson's commitment to "national self-determination" for Poland to get its independence back. Within the boundaries set by the post–World War I peace accord, Poland stretched from western cities, like Poznań, that had long been part of Germany into the eastern areas with large Polish populations along with Ukrainians (Lwów/Lviv) and Lithuanians (Vilnius/Wilno).

In the interwar period, this made Poland a multiethnic state: one-third of its population was not ethnically Polish. This new state was burdened by having to establish national structures, deal with a diverse population of peoples with long histories of conflict, and build an economy and infrastructure out of parts of three empires, focused on Moscow, Berlin, and Vienna, as opposed to Warsaw. Democracy and capitalism enjoyed brief success in the initial years of independence, only to be virtually washed out by the Great Depression. From their history, Poles learned to maintain their culture and national identity under foreign occupation. The Catholic Church became closely identified with Polish national identity. Ultimately, all these lessons served Poles well in their resistance to the German occupation of World War II and remained with them for the more than forty years of communist rule.

Poland was devastated during World War II. In September 1939, it was first divided between the Soviets and Germans. Then, in 1941, the Germans turned on the Soviets and took over the rest of Poland. They used it as a base from which to annihilate Jews and Poles. Large numbers of Poles fought in a nationalist underground force against the Russians and Germans, while a far smaller group, identifying with communism, fought the Germans and the nationalist underground. Ultimately, one-third of Poland's population perished (including almost all of its Jewish population); its capital, Warsaw, was razed to the ground; and much of its industrial base and many of its other cities were destroyed. At the end of the war, the Soviet army took control despite Poles' attempts to prevent a Soviet takeover. In the process, the factories and infrastructure that survived were taken back to the Soviet Union to rebuild its own infrastructure. To add to the complications of rebuilding, in postwar agreements the boundaries of Poland were moved far to the west into what had been Germany, and most of Poland's eastern territories were annexed by the Soviet Union. With this shift came a massive population transfer: most Germans in what became western Poland were forced out or went willingly to Germany. Many Poles and Ukrainians moved or were forced west to settle in the areas the Germans had vacated.

Communist Experience

Soviet troops brought a communist regime in as a "baggage-train government" when they marched across Poland and pushed the Germans out in 1945. That new leadership was an uneasy alliance between Polish communist officials who had spent the war in the Soviet Union and communists who had fought in the small pro-communist underground. These new rulers had to rebuild most of the country and, at the same time, impose unwelcome communist rule. The Communist Party took control of the government, established state ownership of Poland's economy, and tried to control and limit the Catholic Church. With this came Stalinist terror, eased only by the communist leadership's reluctance to repeat Stalin's prewar destruction of the Polish Communist Party leadership by purging and killing those leaders who had spent the war years in Poland (as was done elsewhere in Central and Eastern Europe). The top leaders were also restrained by the refusal of the Catholic Church and the predominately Catholic population to submit totally to the new regime. At the same time, there were those who gained from the ongoing reconstruction and industrialization when large numbers of new industries were built and young peasants moved to cities to work in factories. In the process a whole new working class was established and educated.

With the deaths of Joseph Stalin in 1953 and of Poland's Stalinist leader, Bolesław Bierut, in March 1956, fear and control decreased. In the summer of 1956, Polish workers demonstrated in the Western city of Poznań, demanding "bread and freedom" and calling out, "The press lies." Polish troops fired on the demonstrators, killing almost a hundred. Open intellectual protests spread throughout Poland in the fall. Many Polish United Workers' Party (PUWP) members demanded reforms in the party itself. The party leadership tried to end this "Polish October" by bringing back Władysław Gomułka, a party leader jailed in the Stalinist period for his independence. When returned to power, he started "a Polish road to socialism," allowing private farming, small private enterprises, more freedoms for the Catholic Church, and greater freedom for public discussion. From then on, Poland remained on its own "freer" road.

These events were the first in a series of revolts against communism's failings, including student and intellectual demonstrations in 1968 and workers' riots in 1970, 1976, and 1980 triggered by price increases and economic failures. After each of the workers' demonstrations, the communist authorities made concessions to maintain their hold and buy support, only to fail to meet their promises. With each uprising, though, the opposition grew and became more organized until, after the 1976 workers' demonstrations, the Workers' Defense Committee (KOR) was formed to aid arrested workers and their families. It then produced underground publications to let people know about their rights and about human rights violations in Poland and to encourage independent thinking. By the late 1970s and early 1980s, this opposition had flowered into a massive underground press empire, a number of human rights organizations, and a whole alternate cultural milieu, including a "Flying University" offering courses taught by instructors not permitted in the communist curriculum.[2] It was from this opposition, in combination with the shipyard workers who had demonstrated and lost in 1970, that Solidarity emerged and the men and women who would take Poland into its transition gained influence.[3]

When Edward Gierek took over as head of the party after the December 1970 Gdańsk shipyard strikes, he promised Poles their lives would improve. To jump-start the economy and provide for a higher living standard, Poland borrowed from the West to build new factories with Western equipment and began importing Western consumer goods. These loans were to pay for themselves with earnings from the export of products to the West. However, the plan did not work: much of the money was wasted, Polish goods did not sell, and Poland had to borrow more and more just to pay the interest on its debts. By the beginning of the 1980s, the shelves of Polish stores were bare, and Poland was in the midst of a debt crisis with $8.1 billion—far more than its ready cash and assets would cover—of its over $20 billion debt to the West due in 1980.

The government was so desperate to placate Western creditors without touching off demonstrations that it imposed price increases on food staples (under Western pressure), region by region, with instructions to local leaders to negotiate pay increases if there were strikes or demonstrations. By August, rolling price increases on food and consumer goods had been imposed across the country.

The plan was that price increases would be imposed last in the seacoast towns where the 1970 riots had brought down the Gomułka regime. In response to the price increases, workers in the Gdańsk shipyards went on strike and simply refused to negotiate pay increases. Under the leadership of dissident worker Lech Wałęsa, workers occupied the shipyards in Gdansk and other Baltic towns, demanding not just the economic and social welfare benefits communism had promised but also the right to have an independent trade union, the right to strike, and more media freedom so that they would know what was really going on. Intellectuals joined them. Workers from other places in Poland sent messages of support, and some joined in support strikes. The Polish government conceded to the workers' demands by signing the Gdańsk Agreement. Solidarity became a national movement for economic and political change in Poland.

Poles were further emboldened to stand up to their leaders by the election of Karol Wojtyla, the former archbishop of Kraków, as pope in 1978 and his triumphant return to Poland in June 1979 as a conquering hero whose trip was organized and run by volunteers rather than the government, even as he was feted by communist leaders and the population alike. The rise of Solidarity was dramatic. By the end of its first year, more than one-third of the population had joined the movement. A farmers' Solidarity and a students' union had formed and forced the government to recognize them. Workplaces organized. Many party members joined Solidarity and sought to bring its openness into the Polish United Workers' Party. Independent press and discussions appeared everywhere. Solidarity elections and a national congress were held. Popular demands on the government increased. Poland's economy simply could not work well enough to feed its population, much less provide the gains the Gdańsk Agreements promised. As the economic situation worsened, strikes and demonstrations became the order of the day. What food supplies were available were rationed, or individuals had to use their connections to get meat and other necessities. The government could only make more and more political concessions, even as the Soviet Union and other Soviet bloc states pressed for a crackdown. For Polish leaders and their allies, the potential for chaos and threat of contagion were all too real. Party leader and head of the Polish military Wojciech Jaruzelski and those around him were convinced, by the end of 1981, that the Soviet Union would invade if popular actions and government concessions went any further.

On December 13, 1981, martial law was declared, and the freedoms Solidarity had enjoyed for fifteen months ended with a Polish military "takeover." Solidarity and other independent groups were declared illegal and shut down. Thousands of Solidarity and intellectual activists, as well as some top PUWP leaders accused of corruption and mismanagement during the Gierek era, were interned. Polish soldiers and police were on the streets when people woke up. Military officers supervised factories, schools, media, and government offices for months. Media freedom and free discussion ended. Individual parishes and Catholic organizations provided havens for discussion and distributed food and clothing to the struggling population. Most Poles were too shocked to act. The United States and some other Western countries imposed sanctions on Poland. Martial law under Jaruzelski, as head of the Polish military and Communist Party, continued formally for a year and a half.

Until the mid-1980s, the economic situation remained severely troubled. The sanctions imposed by the United States and some other Western countries remained in place. Some activists continued to be interned, and Solidarity and the other independent organizations were illegal, but an active underground movement functioned, and dissident publications and activities proliferated. At the same time, the difficulties of daily life amid constant shortages meant that most individuals focused on feeding and supplying their families rather than engaging in open political protest.

Transition from Communism

By the late eighties, Poland's economy had failed to rebound and provide what Poles thought they had been promised. The communists' efforts to win support or even draw in respected activists and intellectuals largely failed. Much of Poland's population was alienated from both Solidarity and the communist government. Random strikes with no specific goals worried both Solidarity leaders and the communists. To deal with this alienation, communist leaders reached out to the opposition as they tried to get the economy moving by decreasing controls on prices and forcing factories to be self-supporting. When none of these maneuvers worked, the government, with the support of the Catholic Church, sought Solidarity leaders' agreement to begin discussions on systemic change. Church leaders helped bring the two sides together and agreed to facilitate Roundtable talks between them.

No one thought communism would end. For the rulers, the Roundtables were a way to hold on to power by getting Solidarity to share responsibility for Poland's problems and move toward a new, more open system of government over the next four years. For Solidarity's self-appointed representatives, the most important goal of the Roundtables was to force the relegalization of Solidarity as a trade union (something the government conceded on the first day of the public Roundtables). The population hoped that the

Roundtable agreements would protect the economic guarantees of a social welfare state and that the freedoms of the Solidarity era would be returned. The Catholic Church wanted the Roundtables to stabilize Poland and ensure its interests and position.

After five months of private discussions and nine weeks of public discussions, the two sides agreed to defer decisions on economic reforms and move ahead with political reforms and parliamentary elections designed to give the PUWP and its former allies a majority of seats in a parliament that included Solidarity and other nonparty people as "junior partners." In the process, they created a system that broke taboos but did not initially violate the Soviet Union's old limits.

The Polish political system was redesigned to have a second legislative chamber (the Senate) and a president elected by the two houses together. To ensure the dominance of the communists and the two subsidiary parties that had run with it in the communist era, in this transitional election, 65 percent of the seats in the traditional parliament (Sejm) were designated for candidates who had been in one of these parties, and 35 percent of the seats were designated for candidates who had not belonged to a party in the communist era. The candidates of Solidarity and other opposition groups could run for the latter. Finally, forty seats were reserved for the so-called National List of the regime's notables and reformers. The new Senate, as a trade-off, was elected without any constraints. A majoritarian election system, in which those who did not get a majority in the first round had to run against the next-closest candidate in a second election, was used for both "party" and nonparty seats in the Sejm and new Senate as well as for the National List.

The results of the elections on June 4, 1989, defied all expectations. Candidates Solidarity identified as theirs (signaled by posters showing the candidate with Lech Wałęsa) won every nonparty seat in the Sejm and all but one in the Senate. Only a few of the Communist Party candidates, on the other hand, got the requisite majority to win in the first round. Most of the "party" seats had to be decided in the second round. All but the two men whose names were at the bottom of the National List lost in the first round, and few ran again in the second.[4] The presidency (elected by the Sejm and Senate) went, as had been tacitly promised, to Jaruzelski, the man who had both called for the hated martial law and championed the Roundtable talks. His victory was the result of a political compromise Solidarity leaders engineered to placate Communist Party and military hard-liners in Poland and hard-line leaders elsewhere in the Soviet bloc.

The 65 percent majority established for the Communist Party and its old allies did not hold. The smaller parties, long Trojan horses to draw peasants and small entrepreneurs into the system, broke with the PUWP and joined Solidarity. That reversed the percentages for the "establishment" and the "opposition" in the Sejm: people elected as PUWP members now held 35 percent of the seats, and 65 percent of the seats were held by Solidarity and its new allies from the old system.

The Soviet leaders accepted the results. But no one knew what would happen next. Solidarity deputies' platform had been against communism, but they had no actual plans for instituting real change in Poland. Communist deputies, on the other hand, were not prepared to be in the minority. They had expected to share power with nonparty members. They too had no plan for what would happen next. And their tries at forming a coalition government with Solidarity and their old allies failed.

A new, noncommunist government was formed in September 1989. Tadeusz Mazowiecki (longtime Catholic editor, dissident, and advisor to Solidarity leader Lech Wałęsa) was named prime minister on Wałęsa's recommendation. He formed a unity government of dissident intellectuals, experts in economics, specialists from the parties formerly aligned with the Communist Party, and three communist ministers to manage the most important ministries for Soviet interests: the Ministry of Interior (police and spy services), the Ministry of Defense, and the Ministry of Foreign Trade. Western-educated economist Leszek Balcerowicz was named minister of finance and deputy prime minister to manage economic reform.

The new government confronted the task of "unmaking communist control" and agreeing on concrete policies for the transition. What had been the Solidarity monolith against the communists dissolved into many factions. Faced with minority party membership after forty years of party rule, Communist Party deputies wanted as little to do with the rejected system as possible. By January 1990, the Communist Party, PUWP, had dissolved itself and passed its resources on to the new Social Democratic Party of the Polish Republic (SLDRP).

Solidarity and Communist deputies all worked to cut-and-paste the communist constitution to fit the election results and the Roundtable Accords. They excised from the constitution provisions like the "leading role of the party" and the promise of fealty to the Soviet Union. All national symbols dropped their communist elements. Then, under pressure from the United States and Western Europe, the Sejm passed bills instituting "shock therapy" economic reform (the Balcerowicz Plan) to make rapid privatization, foreign aid, and investment possible. This program—coupled with the inflation that began after the last communist government freed most food prices so they skyrocketed with the reforms (while salaries remained stable)—triggered a drop in the purchasing power of the zloty by 40 percent at the end of the plan's first month (January 1990) and brought a rapid end to popular euphoria over communism's end and Poland's "return to Europe."

For most Poles, their economic losses and gains were far more important public policy issues than Poland's foreign policy, dealing with the communist past, or imposing Catholic values by adding religion to the school curriculum and prohibiting abortion. Public opinion shows that, although Poles believed in democracy, their faith in the way the political system was run, its politicians, and its economic and political policies took a sharp dip after 1990 and declined over the years, only to begin to stabilize and even improve after 2007, when the economy stabilized and centrist parties dominated. Popular participation in elections has most often been under 60 percent—even during the euphoria of the first partially free elections and then communism's collapse. Respect for and involvement in the Catholic Church, once the symbol of the nation, has dropped steadily. There is also evidence of some popular nostalgia for the communist days and a decrease in faith in elected institutions and the Catholic Church.[5]

Political Institutions

For most of its postcommunist history, governance and political battles in Poland were more about which institution (president, prime minister and Council of Ministers, Sejm,

Photo 10.1.   Solidarity poster that covered the streets of Poland the morning of the June 1989 elections, based on a Gary Cooper poster for the film *High Noon*.

Senate, or courts) could do what. Initially, the "Small Constitution" of 1992 codified the additions and deletions made in 1990 to take communism out of the constitution and defined the powers of the major institutions. This did not, however, provide a framework to set out, coordinate, and balance what institutions could and could not do. So, in the first years, elected officials established the rights and responsibilities of their offices either, if they were legislators, by passing more legislation or, if they were the president or prime minister, by simply claiming the right to act and setting precedents. Only in 1997 was a full constitution passed.

Poland's constitutional system began as a strong semi-presidential one in which the president had the right to veto legislation or refer it to the constitutional court for review, disband parliament and call new elections, declare a state of emergency, play a role in selecting the prime minister and cabinet, appoint some top judges and officials to some supervisory councils, and represent the country in international politics and military affairs. Wojciech Jaruzelski, as Poland's first president and a remnant of the defeated regime, used virtually none of these powers unless asked to do so by the Solidarity government. After Lech Wałęsa, the former leader of Solidarity, became president, he took control by ignoring limits on his powers. In response, the 1992 and 1997 constitutions reined in the powers of the presidency and increased the powers of the prime minister and cabinet.

Under the 1997 constitution, the president has the right to step in and name a prime minister only if the Sejm is too divided to agree. The prime minister and his cabinet can be removed only by a vote of no confidence by the parliament. The prime minister is responsible for selecting his cabinet and presenting his choices to the Sejm for approval. The government also has the explicit responsibility to lead the policy-making process in domestic and foreign affairs, carry out the laws passed by the parliament, put forth regulations as authorized by the Sejm, and manage the state budget. Finally, the president and prime minister must cosign all laws.

The powers of legislation are concentrated in the Sejm. It also has the right to appoint officials to various public boards and to specific seats on the court. The Senate, on the other hand, is primarily a body to review and revise Sejm legislation and serve as a moderator in conflicts.

So, although the presidency formally retains most of its powers, each is now counterbalanced by the power of the legislature or the prime minister. Until 2005, even in the one period when the president and the government were from the same party—the Democratic Left Alliance (SLD)—these rules held. In 2005, the Law and Justice Party dominated the parliament, and its leader, Lech Kaczynski, was elected president. There were conflicts between the president and prime minister. These ended when Kaczynski appointed, as prime minister, his identical twin brother, Jaroslaw, who then lost the post after the 2007 early elections. Subsequently, Lech Kaczynski used his veto to block legislation by the Civic Platform (PO) majority and ignored constitutional limits by intervening in policy decisions in both domestic and foreign policy.

As is clear, the powers of the presidency, the prime minister, and the parliament have often stemmed from the politics and personalities of the moment rather than from constitutional provisions. Poland's first four presidents cut very different profiles. The first three claimed to represent not a political party but the Polish people as a whole. What they tried to do depended on their own interests and sense of power. Jaruzelski avoided conflict with the new Solidarity government and served as a figurehead. Lech Wałęsa rode in as the leader of the Solidarity movement and attempted an "imperial presidency." Although much of what he claimed he could do never happened, his threats alarmed many. Two years into his rule, he faced a very divided parliament. There were deadlocks with the government, public opposition to and disgust with his style of leadership, and even claims among former supporters that he had been a secret agent. All of these weakened not only his popular support but also his ability to lead. After he disbanded the parliament, following a vote of no confidence in the government in 1993, and an early

Photo 10.2.   Lech Wałęsa (president of Poland from 1991 to 1995), Tadeusz Mazowiecki (prime minister from 1989 to 1991), and Aleksander Kwasniewski (president from 1995 to 2005). (*Rzeczpospolita*)

parliamentary election, he found himself trapped in a continuous conflict with the SLD's majority and its prime minister and cabinet. In the end, no matter what Wałęsa did, he was checkmated by the parliamentary majority.

Aleksander Kwasniewski, who was elected president in 1995 and again in 2000, differed greatly from his predecessors. Given the public attacks on his party (SLD) and on him for having communist connections, he focused on disproving stereotypes about communists. He was a "by-the-book" president, taking no more power than was constitutionally mandated. At the same time, he was able to work effectively behind the scenes. In his first term, he had an SLD and Peasant Party parliamentary majority, so legislation was passed and conflicts avoided. As a result, in 1997, a full constitution was passed with support from all sides. After the 1997 parliamentary election, he worked with the right-wing coalition by focusing on avoiding direct conflict and presenting himself as a professional. He became the representative of Poland to the world, with a special emphasis on the West and leading Poland into the North Atlantic Treaty Organization (NATO). In the process, he returned prestige and the faith of the public to the presidency.

In 2000, Kwasniewski was so strong that other parties fielded candidates with little hope of winning. His slogan, "Poland: A Home for All," emphasized his apolitical leadership. One year later, the SLD returned as the dominant party balanced against a fragmented right wing. By default, Poland moved back to a semi-presidential state, with the president appointing economist Marek Belka as prime minister and taking leadership in areas like foreign policy that were the constitutional purview of the presidency.

In 2005, Lech Kaczynski of the Law and Justice Party was elected president, and parliamentary elections resulted in his party being the largest in the Sejm, so it could form a government with two very different but small radical parties (Samoobrona, or Self-Defense, and the League of Polish Families). He and his twin brother, Jaroslaw, in the role of prime minister, appointed allies to ministerial posts. There was no credible means to rein in his actions or his party and its fractious coalition. Changes in the electoral laws for local governments and leaders' commitment to "cleansing" the system of "agents" from the communist period enabled the Kaczynski brothers to expand their powers by claiming individuals who disagreed with them had been communists or agents. They then changed the lustration process, making all the old secret police files public and allowing the removal of individuals from public office based on the contents of their files. This

Photo 10.3. The late president Lech Kaczynski congratulating his twin brother, Jaroslaw Kaczynski, on his swearing in as prime minister in 2006. He left office in November 2007. (*Rzeczpospolita*)

made opposition to the government risky. At the same time, the Law and Justice Party and its allies engaged in continual internal battles over charges and countercharges.

Early parliamentary elections, held on October 24, 2007, showed popular disaffection with attacks regarding the past. A movement spearheaded by young people to get out the vote brought the more policy-focused Civic Platform to power. When the Civic Platform won parliamentary elections in 2007, that party's centrist leader, Donald Tusk, became prime minister. He worked to modernize the bureaucracy so that the government was more responsive. He and his coalition reversed what the rightest coalition had done by moving back to closer relations with Germany. Tusk's positive and professional style of leadership, as well as Poland's economic health during the recession, made him a popular leader. In the process, though, he faced constant attacks and vetoes of legislation by Kaczynski.

Lech Kaczynski essentially wielded right-wing power through his presidential veto powers and public attacks on his enemies as "communists." When Lech Kaczynski began his campaign for a second term as president in 2010, public opinion polls showed that he was not popular enough to win. He escalated the rhetoric in his battle for power with Tusk. In foreign policy, he battled with the prime minister were over who could speak for Poland. After Prime Minister Tusk's participation in the official Russian-Polish commemoration of the slaughter of Polish officers by Soviet soldiers at the start of World War II, Kaczynski, as president, led his own delegation of political leaders and survivors to the site in Russia. The plane carrying them crashed in Smolensk, killing all aboard and beginning a political battle between Polish authorities and his twin brother, the head of

Photo 10.4.   Donald Tusk, head of the Civic Platform, with supporters when they won the parliamentary election in 2011 and had a majority in parliament. (Adam Lach)

the Law and Justice Party, over whether the accident was the result of was pilot error, bad landing conditions, or a Russian attack.

Despite the tragedy and the battles over what happened and how to memorialize Lech Kaczynski, his brother, Jaroslaw, Law and Justice's candidate for president in the special election in 2010, lost to the Civic Platform's candidate, Bronislaw Komorowski, whose campaign focused on the promise of civility and compromise in governance rather than conflict. With Komorowski's election to the presidency in 2010, the Civic Platform has controlled both parliament and the presidency. The circle was, in some sense, closed since Komorowski had maintained close ties to the leaders of the postcommunist government of Tadeusz Mazowiecki. Although there have been tax increases and demonstrations over the low incomes of professionals in health care and education as well as mini-scandals, the Civic Platform remained popular and cohesive under Donald Tusk. It will, though, face Law and Justice again in the presidential and parliamentary elections in 2015, with its top leader, Tusk, serving not as prime minister but as head of the Council of Europe.

Parties and Elections

After 1989, holding elections became politicians' way of solving political conflicts and battles over institutional powers. In the process, rather than clear policy divisions, elections came to reflect the individual battles of increasingly radicalized political leaders. As a result, until the mid-2000s, elections actually increased fragmentation, parties came and went, and the public was often disenchanted with its elected officials.

In the first decade after the fall of communism, parties on the right fought with each other and attacked other parties as "communist." The clearest divide, among voters and parties, was between those who saw the communist system in a positive light and those who identified with the Catholic Church. This divide was more significant than economic interests in determining how people voted.[6] By 2007, though, the parties (and their leaders) on the far right and those connected with communists had destroyed themselves, leaving two major parties, the moderate Civic Platform and the populist Law and Justice, to do battle.

In the first year after the end of communism, a rush to elections began in the summer of 1990. Local government elections were held before the duties and new powers of the various levels of local government had been established. Almost at the same time, a campaign by Lech Wałęsa and his followers got underway to force Jaruzelski's resignation and the passage of a law for direct popular election of the president. Jaruzelski conceded to this pressure and resigned.

Lech Wałęsa won the first popular presidential election, defeating then Prime Minister Tadeusz Mazowiecki and, more narrowly, defeating Stanislaw Tyminski, an émigré with no clear platform or qualifications who promised instant wealth for everyone. This election, in the fall of 1990, caused more fragmentation of Solidarity.

Voting for someone new who promised dramatic improvement in living conditions and, on the right, condemned all opponents became the pattern in Poland's first decade and a half of democratic elections. Two other long-term features of party affiliation in Poland also began at this point. One was the regional difference in party support between the prosperous west, with its big cities, which supported pro-reform candidates, and the impoverished east and other areas where factories had gone bankrupt and small-scale agriculture had failed, which supported the right with its promises of social welfare and condemnations of those who had made the changes initially. The other feature that emerged was the focus of right-wing parties and voters on accounting for the communist past as a way of explaining and dealing with current economic problems.

Initially, a plethora of tiny parties emerged, making coalitions difficult if not impossible after the initial free elections. In the early parliamentary elections of 1991, one hundred parties ran candidates, and twenty-nine parties were elected in the Sejm's proportional representation elections. The Senate was also fragmented after its elections. In addition to two warring Solidarity-based parties and the Solidarity trade union, there were various small right-wing parties that condemned both the former communists and Solidarity deputies for the losses "caused by" the Balcerowicz Plan, in a campaign marked by nationalist and religious rhetoric. Only the former communists, the Social Democratic Party of the Polish Republic, remained unified.

So divided was this parliament that, within two years, it was unable to make policy and turned in on itself. In the process, the largest of the many parties in the Sejm pushed through two laws that impacted party politics. First, to cut down on the fragmentation of the Sejm, political parties were required to win 5 percent of the national vote and coalitions 7 percent to hold seats in the Sejm. Second, the Sejm legalized a system allowing parties represented in parliament to receive national government funding for their campaigns if they had won at least 3 percent in the election. The amount of this funding was proportional to the number of seats a party won in the Sejm or Senate.

In 1993, this electoral law resulted in the SLD, with only 20.41 percent of the votes, and its former allies, the renamed Polish Peasant Party, with 15.4 percent of the vote, winning 60.5 percent of Sejm seats. The nine right-wing parties that ran could not form a coalition, and none reached the 5 percent of the vote required to hold seats in parliament, so they got no seats even though, together, they polled 34.45 percent of the vote.

Polish parties, with the exception of parties from the old communist system, have had neither the incentive nor the resources to do ground-level organization and build an infrastructure. After the era of Communist Party rule, the very word "party" and the notion of being a party member had negative connotations, so most of the groups that ran for elections eschewed the word "party" and did not build structures or enroll members. Candidates, even from the most established parties, have had to invest their own money in campaigns; only if they win seats in parliament are they reimbursed. The expenses of being in parliament are paid through their party directly from the parliament's budget. This financing is complicated by defections from parliamentary parties while the parliament is in session.

This funding has not resulted in political parties with permanent structures. Only the former communists (SLD) invested in the infrastructures typical of European parties. It started ahead because it had inherited some of the PUWP's buildings, equipment, and membership lists, as well as old members who had long organized for the party. These cadres of old party workers were willing to work for the SLD, even though it voiced a pro-capitalist ideology, because the other parties attacked or shunned anyone who had been in the Communist Party. Then, after the 2001 elections, when the collapse of the right-wing coalition handed victory to the SLD, the party destroyed itself by trying to expand its leadership, bringing in new people, and allowing them to profit from their positions in the party.

The other political groups in Poland initially did not have the resources or desire to invest in increasingly expensive infrastructure and offices. In the early years of Poland's democracy, some right-wing parties received support and facilities from the Catholic Church in exchange for advocating for its interests. But in the years between elections, even the more successful parties remained essentially "couch parties," focused on individual leaders and existing only during political campaigns. Most still have no real formal membership; leaders and parliamentary deputies only hold together because they get funding, beyond their salaries, from their party in parliament, not as individuals. Even the dominant party since 2007, Civic Platform, has not built a strong party organization. It has basically functioned as a Western catchall party focused on its strong and popular leadership.

Parties' ideologies have been unstable and confusing at best. The dramatic defeat of the Communist Party in 1989 resulted in the dissolution of the Polish Communist Party (PUWP). Its legacy party, the Democratic Left Alliance (SLD), cast off its Marxist ideology and voted for the Balcerowicz Plan, then shifted to advocating for "trickle-down economics," holding that the poor would gain from excess profits in a capitalist economy. This position was amplified by the victory of SLD leader Aleksander Kwasniewski in the presidential race in 1995 and again in 2000. He essentially ran as a modern, pro-capitalist, European leader who was above the political fray. The SLD, once it won the 2001 parliamentary election, became known for corruption at its lower levels and, as a result, lost its popular support. And Kwasniewski's attempt to save the left by linking those from the old Solidarity who stood for workers' rights and social democracy—who had never gotten an electoral foothold—and the SLD together in a group called Left and Democrats in the 2007 elections failed. Little remains of the left except for small groups of young politicians who began in the SLD who advocate for what are marginal issues in Poland.

The initial political center (Freedom Union) could not disassociate itself from the losses people had suffered due to the Balcerowicz Plan. As a result, its candidates were defeated in the 1990 presidential election and the 1991 parliamentary elections and returned to government as an element of the Civic Platform. This center stands against Polish nationalism and for establishing a liberal market economy, democratization, and a return to Europe. Although some of its leaders were lay Catholic opposition leaders during the communist era, this center has not supported giving the Catholic Church real power in politics.

In 2001, the center reemerged with 12.7 percent of the vote as the Civic Platform and came in second to the Democratic Left Alliance with its 41.0 percent. In 2007 and 2011 the Civic Platform won the parliamentary as well as the presidential elections in 2010. It maintains a pro-European and pro–free market position and supports a strong Polish presence in the European Union. Equally important is its reputation for rational and reasoned political action rather than politics marked by strong rhetoric, charges, and countercharges, seen as a negative characteristic of the right.

The right wing has focused and focuses on Poles' bitterness over their losses in the initial move to capitalism. It has advocated for social welfare and protecting workers even as it has railed against communist-era repression, the profits communists made by using their positions to buy up valuable properties during the transition, and communists' supposed connections to Russia and the old secret police. Most right-wing parties, including the League of Polish Families, Solidarity Electoral Action, and Law and Justice, also, implicitly or explicitly, support Catholic religious values and Church authority as the core of public policy. In identifying themselves as Polish nationalists, they have opposed Poland's deep involvement with both the West and the governments of the former Soviet states. As such, they did not fully support joining the European Union and wanted to insure that Poland had a strong position even vis-à-vis Germany in spite of Germany's greater population.

The most powerful and long-standing of these parties, Law and Justice, led with calls against corruption by government officials and "the elite" and with promises to end inequality and to punish communists and their agents and to exclude them from power. Since their defeat in 2007 in early parliamentary elections after their 2005 coalition with the centrist PO fell apart, they have continued to focus on this mix of attacks and demonstrations of Polish nationalism.

None of these parties on the right or their small successors today ever claimed to have had a clear, viable plan to solve the problems they identified. With the exception of those closely tied to the church, they have run "against" elements of the status quo—ranging from women's rights to "Europeanization"—rather than for any specific policy. Although many campaigned promising social benefits, most are parties of outspoken politicians rather than ideologically based organizations. As a result their coalitions have fallen apart every time they have taken the lead in parliament.

The other stable party in the political constellation has been the Polish Peasant Party. It has never failed to hold seats in the Sejm and Senate even as it has lost support since 1993. It has been in coalitions with both sides. Initially, it focused on the interests of the agricultural sector; more recently, it has positioned itself as a moderate party supporting both economic development and a preservation of social supports. In the 2005 election it did lose some of its peasant supporters to the radical Self-Defense Party; in 2007, however, it regained voter support as a party not involved in the ideological fights and also as the one major party that did not support the war in Iraq.

In the long run, these fluid and irresolvable noneconomic divisions have meant that the battles in Polish politics have been more over issues of the past and religion than over how best to deal with the economy and the needs of people for state support services. As a result, without alternative policies on soluble problems, political rhetoric has often focused on charges and countercharges. In the end, the rationality and professionalism of the SDP under Aleksander Kwasniewski and the Civic Union's image allowed them to win sequential elections.

Civil Society

Unlike the rest of the postcommunist world, Poland began with well-established alternative institutions from the communist period, including the Catholic Church, the intellectual opposition, and Solidarity. Intellectual opposition groups had clear leaders known to the public, produced elaborate and regular sets of publications, ran an alternative educational system, and provided legal and financial support for individuals working in the opposition or workers punished for participation in demonstrations. Professional associations also acted more independently than their equivalents elsewhere in the Soviet bloc as they pressed for privileges and power for their groups. At the same time, in the communist period, Poles were part of elaborate friendship networks that often crossed lines between the regime and the opposition. These facilitated the negotiations that made the transition possible.

Tragically, these institutions rapidly lost out in the transition. The informal networks were no longer necessary. Professional groups did not work in a system where there was competition for jobs within professions. And while established opposition groups and Solidarity retained their symbolism, they lost popular support when they had to be for something (particularly economic reform) rather than simply against communism. Their authority was also tarnished by allegations and some revelations that some prominent figures had been, at some time, agents of the secret police.

Solidarity, the trade union formed as a result of shipyard workers' requirement for ending their strike in 1980, was a powerful, if decentralized, organization until martial law was imposed to end its activities in December 1981. Initially, strikes and other work actions (or the threat of them) brought concessions from the government. Solidarity also spun off unions of students and peasants. After it was declared illegal and a broad swath of its leadership was interned, it remained a powerful force as a symbol and rallying point for broad popular opposition. When the government sought a partner for negotiations in 1988 and 1989, it turned to Solidarity's former leaders, who generally sent their intellectual advisors as negotiators to the Roundtables. Solidarity, under the guise of the Citizens' Electoral Committees, then organized a massive campaign for the 1989 elections, signifying the candidates it supported in every district by papering the streets on election day with posters showing them with Solidarity leader Lech Wałęsa.

After the formation of a Solidarity-based government and the passage of the Balcerowicz Plan, Solidarity lost public support. Its old unity against communism's failures fragmented rapidly when policy had to be made. First, there were splits between the intellectuals who had advised Solidarity and those who had come to leadership from the working class over who should lead and what policy should be. Its dual role as trade union fighting for workers' rights and reformist political party dissuaded supporters.

More recently, organizations identifying themselves as Solidarity have appeared but have not had the draw or power that Solidarity did in 1980 and 1981 and then in 1989 and 1990. Solidarity has not been able to focus on the interests of workers in private businesses and industries (now the vast majority of Polish workers).[7] As inflation ate away at their salaries, public-sector employees, such as teachers and medical personnel, marched under the Solidarity banner against changes in benefits, but they were never able to gather enough demonstrators to gain real traction.

The Catholic Church was once such a popular force that the communists allowed it to function as a religious institution and symbol of the limits of communist rule. In the communist period, going to church became not just a religious obligation but also a political act for many. Catholic intellectuals and students groups, the Catholic University of Lublin, and a number of theological schools also helped link the church to the secular dissident movement. In the 1980s, its role was magnified by the election of Karol Wojtyla, the former archbishop of Kraków, as the first non-Italian pope in four hundred years. The pope's first trip to Poland served as proof that people could organize without the state. This was critical in the mobilization of Solidarity a year later. The church served as a symbol for Solidarity and a haven that provided donated food and clothing for the needy during martial law

From the first semi-free elections on, local churches and the national hierarchy inserted themselves directly into politics, supporting individual candidates and parties. The Catholic Church and the parties they supported pushed through and won required religious education in all schools and, eventually, strict limits on abortion. In the process, the church went from Poland's most respected institution to one of its least respected. Although Poland remains one of the most Catholic countries in Europe (88 percent identify as Catholic, although only 58 percent claim to be practicing[8]), the number of births out of wedlock and the number of abortions continue to increase. So, while Polish politicians were and are wary of going against the Church's wishes, much of the public sees the church as having too much influence in politics and so ignores its directives.[9] At the same time, Catholic institutions have fragmented. The right-wing, privately owned Radio Maryja, with its xenophobia, racism, and anti-Semitism, became so powerful and popular that the Church hierarchy had no way to moderate it or stop it.

As the economic transition reduced the free time and resources of most people, other civil society institutions failed to fill the void left by the reduced influence of intellectual and professional groups, the Catholic Church, and Solidarity. Initially, Western foundations created or funded civil society organizations in Poland. Most of these lasted only as long as the funding from the outside did. Other organizations appeared. Some were charities for needy groups, but most focused on providing special benefits and privileges for their members or substituting for poor state services. They have not been significant political actors or avenues for popular participation in politics.

The Economic Transformation

The economy was the Achilles' heel of Poland's leaders in the communist period and during the transition. But, in the years that have followed, Poland's economy has become one of the stronger in the postcommunist world. In fact, Poland had the highest growth rate of any EU country during the European recession that began in 2008.

In 1989, the economic reformers inherited an economy distorted by the communists' attempts to avert disaster with piecemeal reforms and their efforts to placate the population by importing Western goods and allowing some privatization. So, reformers faced a population with higher expectations than elsewhere and a crushing debt to the West.

Western countries also had more power over Poland's economic decisions than they did in the rest of the communist world because Poland was so heavily indebted to the West. After all, Poland's attempt to jump-start its economy in the early 1970s by borrowing from the West had failed, pinning it under more than $43 billion of debt by 1989 (making it, then, the third most internationally indebted country in the world). This meant that Poles' decisions about how they transformed their economy were very much dependent on the approval of their Western creditors because they needed debt write-offs as well as aid.

Postcommunist economic reform began with "shock therapy," or the Balcerowicz Plan to curb high inflation and open the Polish market to competition with the outside. This reform involved ending all price controls January 1, 1990, a month after the bill was passed. This made the Polish zloty convertible to Western currencies, eliminating trade barriers and government subsidies for state enterprises so that they would be self-supporting, restricting wage increases, reducing the money supply, and increasing interest rates. Its results were disastrous for most individuals. By the end of January 1990, individual purchasing power had dropped 43.2 percent. Registered unemployment went from 0.3 percent in December 1989 to 6.5 percent a year later, jumping to 11.4 percent in December 1991 and 16.4 percent in 1993.[10] Declines in all the major economic indicators for the next two years were equally dramatic. Gross domestic product (GDP) dropped over 18 percent. In the first month of 1990 alone, industrial production dropped 30 percent, and the purchasing power of wages and salaries went down more than one-third. Peasant incomes fell by about half. Polish agricultural goods lost out to better-packaged and heavily subsidized Western goods that were often cheaper than their now unsubsidized Polish equivalents. Old state cooperatives and private enterprises that had survived the communist era collapsed because they could not compete with mass-produced Western goods or pay soaring costs for rent, materials, and salaries. At the same time, a small group of wealthy "owners and consultants" emerged. Poles reacted by voting government after government out. By 1993, the economy had begun an upswing that lasted through the mid-1990s, when it slowed perceptibly. Growth hovered around 5 percent per year in the mid-1990s.

Even as the economy grew, however, there were problems. The growth was happening only in specific areas where new technology brought productivity increases and job losses. The export sector lagged behind, leaving Poland with a serious deficit. Inflation remained high. For a large percentage of Poles, the new buildings and foreign investments in the major cities were coupled with bankruptcies in the smaller cities and rural regions. These triggered significant regional unemployment outside the major cities in what was known as "second Poland" and a slide into poverty for a majority of the population, even as a small but ever increasing number of people gained from the changes. This socioeconomic division remains today.

The solution for the government was to push privatization. New small firms, largely based on imports and street trade, blossomed. They often began by working around the existing rules, selling on the street and paying little or no tax. Many state stores were simply privatized by their employees. As a result, the share of employment and the national income in the private sector grew from less than one-third to more than half of the Polish economy by 1993, even though larger and weaker state firms continued on, virtually untouched by privatization.

The next step proved extremely complex and contentious. Solidarity leaders advocated moving toward employee ownership and maintaining cooperative enterprises. Leszek Balcerowicz, as deputy prime minister and minister of finance, and his supporters wanted simply to privatize state industries as quickly and completely as possible by establishing a stock market and letting weak industries go bankrupt. Only after eleven draft laws were rejected did this Margaret Thatcher–style privatization become law.

In the end, Poland's privatization was piecemeal, done largely through foreign investment and mass privatization, where salable firms were consolidated into national investment funds. In this process, only 512 of the 8,453 state firms were included, most of them small. As a result, initially only about 2 percent of the total workforce was involved. Much of the money earmarked to prepare firms for privatization went to managers rather than to upgrading and reorganizing the firms. Every adult Pole got a share certificate for 180 zlotys (about $40) to invest in these funds. For most Poles, this minimal "mass privatization" was far from enticing. Rather than enlivening the market, the process caused the worth of the firms and the certificates to fall to less than half their original value.[11]

Most foreign direct investment involved government and private firms buying up state firms and Western businesses moving in to renovate them or open new businesses. The bulk of new investments were in construction and the opening of huge supermarkets and discount stores. In the end, the Polish economy, 75 percent of which was in private hands by 2000, was a "subsidiary economy" of foreign firms. At the turn of the century, after these initial investments, foreign investment decreased dramatically: between 2000 and 2002, the total direct foreign investment dropped from $9.341 billion to $4.131 billion.[12]

There were serious political complications in both mass privatization and foreign direct investment. For most Poles, privatization seemed to hurt rather than help. Newly privatized firms were often sold or transformed to make money for their managements. Wages and work conditions in many foreign firms have been below Polish standards. Many Poles felt Poland was being sold off, at bargain prices, to the West. Almost 75 percent of banking services are controlled by Western capital, and large parts of other key institutions, such as the media, some postal services, and telephone services, are owned by outside interests. The public's disgust at not getting the benefits it expected from capitalism was magnified by accusations and revelations of corruption involved in selling off, with huge tax and price breaks, Polish industries and resources to Western firms and, in early 2000, Russian interests.

The growth in Poland's GDP during the European recession was in large part a result of the funding benefits the European Union gave to prepare Poland's economy and infrastructure for accession; the comparatively small amount of its GDP that comprised foreign trade (and the fact that most of that trade was in agricultural products rather than modern, large-scale manufacturing); the slowness of its banking sector to modernize and lower its standards for loans or loans in foreign currency; and the fact that it had not joined the Eurozone. This meant that the Polish economy had funding for investment projects and was not as affected by the economic problems of other states when the recession hit. Its agricultural sector, after opposing joining the EU, found itself actually benefiting from Poland's membership. Not only did the EU provide substantial agricultural aid as Poland was joining, but Poland's small, traditional farms found a valuable niche as producers of organic foods.

As Poland moves ahead, the one troubling economic factor is the level of its national debt (more than 50 percent of its GDP since 2009), even though it is far lower than in many economies in Europe. Efforts to reduce the debt by cutting state costs and benefits have not been well received. And the pressure of unemployment on the economy has grown as the loss of jobs elsewhere in Europe has forced Poles who had left to work abroad to return, heightening unemployment, particularly among youth.

Social Conditions

For all of Poland's macroeconomic successes, those gains have not been matched by the growth of salaries and employment rates for most of the population. The unemployed population has grown, and the worth of most workers' earnings has dropped because of high inflation rates. To keep the state sector solvent, many (mostly larger) firms that could not easily be sold off were closed down or sold off at low prices. Because so much of Poland's industry had been concentrated in single-industry towns and regions, outside the major cities, there were areas of mass unemployment in what came to be known as "second Poland." That still remains a problem alleviated only by the out-migration of workers to other areas where there are jobs.

Indeed, Poland now has one of the highest levels of inequality in the European Union: 17 percent of the population lived below the government-established social minimum (enough income to cover not only food and housing but also clothes, limited cultural events, and education) in 2005, and 26 percent of children lived in poverty.[13] By 2013, unemployment hovered around 10.3 percent, down from 19.1 percent in 2004, with approximately 27.3 percent registered unemployment among youth, down from 39 percent in 2004. Much of this is long-term unemployment. These decreases occurred, in large part, because the elderly population is decreasing; as of 2010, nearly 5 million people were on early retirement, unemployment, or social welfare. The cohort of young people entering the labor market was much smaller than it had been previously because, as of 2010, nearly 2 million were working abroad and others were attending universities. But by 2013, many young people going into the labor market, after working abroad or finishing their educations, found there were no jobs for them.

The impact of these inequities and demographic changes has been aggravated by the economic reforms' negative effect on the very aspects of social welfare that were "givens" in the communist era—free education and health care and guaranteed pensions. Reforming the welfare system has never been high on the government's agenda. That, coupled with EU pressures for a low budget deficit, made either reforming or supporting social services difficult at best. So, doctors and teachers experienced a steady decline in their salaries, financial support for hospitals, schools, and other social welfare institutions dried up, and the wealthier segment of the population now uses private hospitals, clinics, and schools. Many professionals shifted to the new private sector in education and health care, took on multiple jobs, or left the country.

These trends were also aggravated by the heightened demand on and costs to the state for health care and education as well as unemployment assistance and pensions. The economic reforms increased the cost of basic necessities dramatically, even as privatization and the commitment to an exchangeable currency and meeting EU requirements decreased the money the state could spend on such services.

The results of these social demands and the inability of the state to meet them have resulted in a number of changes in society. Unemployment and family support funds are most often so limited that no one can live above the biological minimum level on only unemployment benefits or the family subsidies regions give out. Most of the unemployed have drifted away into the gray economy of illegal trade and crime. Particularly in the rural areas and small towns, poverty has become a steady state. After 2000, youth unemployment and the promise of work for those with the right training increased the demand for some form of higher education. This in turn resulted in the proliferation of private schools not only at the lower levels but also in higher education. A decade later, universities, even the more prestigious ones, are unable to fill their departments, and many of their graduates are left to survive on part-time jobs.

State support in these areas has been limited at best. After 1989, Jacek Kuron, a longtime member of the opposition and the first noncommunist minister of social welfare, fought for decent unemployment benefits and even set up his own soup kitchens as a model for private action to deal with problems for which there was no government money. Only after the 1997 election was there an attempt to create coherent public programs to reorganize the health-care and pension systems and their funding. But by 2005, neither the right-wing Solidarity Electoral Action government nor its social democratic successor had been able to implement effective reforms in these areas. Hospitals closed down for months at a time because of a lack of funds. In one case, the Constitutional Court declared a health-care reform law unconstitutional, leaving the health-care system to function with no legal structure for more than a year until a new law was passed in 2004. The crisis in the public sector has decreased slightly with the passage of some health-care and education legislation, but it is far from over. Salaries for public-sector employees remain a major political issue, as does the extent to which cutbacks can be made in government programs to reduce Poland's debt.

Transitional Justice

Poland's negotiated revolution and the unwillingness of many of its leading dissidents, once they became leaders, to punish the men and women of the former regime, its secret police, and network of agents led to "drawing a thick line" between the past and present. This action deferred dealing with what had happened under communist rule until 1996, when the first lustration law was passed. In the void this delay caused, politicians on the right made accusations and claimed to have proof in what came to be called "wild lustration." This forced politicians on the left to move to establish a legal process for dealing with the past, complicated as it was by the fact that the secret police files had remained in the hands of the police, vulnerable to being destroyed or tampered with, until 2007. The Institute of National Memory was opened after a more developed and broader law was passed.

Transitional justice in Poland has officially focused on three processes: trying leaders accused of ordering attacks on major demonstrations, lustrating politicians listed as agents in the past, and setting up programs for recognizing and getting information out on long-ignored moments in Polish history. Ironically, public opinion surveys show that these processes have not been of great interest to the population; they have, however, been significant in political battles.

Until 2007, individual politicians were "lustrated" (barred from public office for having served as agents of the secret police) only if they lied in the declaration required of each candidate and some state officials by claiming not to have been such an agent. These declarations were posted in election district polling stations but did not deter voters from supporting strong candidates even if they had lied about their pasts. If top government officials were found to have lied on their forms, they were given the choice of either vacating their positions or going through a trial in a special, closed court. In 2006, the Law and Justice Party pushed through legislation expanding the requirement for lustration to the legal, media, and education professions, as well as to other state offices, and opening up the police files of those who had been spied on not just to the victims but to journalists and scholars as well. That legislation, though, was largely eviscerated by the courts as against European rights standards. Even with the opening of files and lustration, however, charges of having been an agent of the secret police or the Soviet Union, as well as references to the past, remain regular parts of political discourse. To the extent that they had credibility, these attacks not only muddied political battles but also the public image of the Church and the opposition movement, both prime targets for secret police pressure. And although most of the victims and perpetrators are now dead or elderly and there is little political support for the politics of attacks, the secret police and their agents remain a popular topic in Polish film, and "who did what" is of interest to younger generations as well.

Pressure from the right also resulted in trials of Wojciech Jaruzelski and others around him for the killing of workers in 1970 (although Jaruzelski did not sign the order and was not in the area when the attacks happened) and for the imposition of martial law. The trial for the 1970 killings dragged on for years. In 2007, based on documents in the files taken over by the Institute of National Memory, a trial of Jaruzelski and his close associates over the declaration of martial law in 1980 began. Both trials drew little public interest and were ended because the defendants were too old and ill. Ultimately, they had no effect on public opinion: a significant part of the population saw martial law as "the lesser evil."

The institute has also taken an active role in historical discussions of the communist period, publishing books, sponsoring meetings, and even producing games designed to remind people and teach youth about the problems of life in communist systems. At the same time, new museums and monuments are being opened on issues ignored in the communist era: the Warsaw Uprising at the end of the war, the history of Jews in Poland, and repression under the communists.

Foreign Policy

Poland's foreign policy has tried to bridge three worlds: the United States, Western Europe, and the former Soviet bloc. Given the strength of the Polish lobby and the size of the Polish economy and unpaid debt, US interests were early and powerful players, as were West European interests.

For all the initial government's interest in returning to Europe, it was impossible to turn away from the Soviet Union totally. The Soviet responses were key to how the Poles designed the limits of their transition. The Soviet Union and former Soviet states that border Poland (Ukraine, Belarus, and Russia) have been an established market for Polish goods. Russia was also the major source of energy resources for Poland.

Former Soviet peoples' desire to go to the West or have their systems follow Poland's model proved to be a blessing. On the one hand, Poles first worried that there would be a mass exodus from these poorer states to the West, flooding Poland with refugees. Instead, they got a plethora of skilled laborers from Ukraine and other former Soviet states ready to work at low wages in Poland to cover their expenses in their home countries. On the other hand, foreign policy leaders came to value the idea of Poland as a bridge between East and West. In playing this out, Poland has been far more engaged than other countries in Central and Eastern Europe in working with countries to the east and advocating for their democratization. Aleksander Kwasniewski, as a former communist and president of Poland, was used by the Ukrainian government and the Our Ukraine candidates to lead top-level negotiations that ended the Orange Revolution. And then, once Russian engagement in Ukraine began in 2014, Polish politicians were leaders in NATO and the EU, pushing for strong stands against the repression and Russian actions.

This balancing act was complicated as it was coupled with incentives, largely for those on the left, to legitimize themselves by being welcomed by US leaders, NATO, and the European Union. For all of Poland's former politicians, especially the former communists, one key way to legitimize themselves and the economic reforms they advocated was to stress Western ties and the fact that reforms were required for Poland to rejoin Europe as a part of the transatlantic alliance.

It fell to the right wing to emphasize Polish nationalism and the risks and costs of alignment. Those on the right were inclined to picture Poland as being sold off to Western (and former Soviet) interests. Hence, the Euroskeptic candidates in European Parliament elections were, most often, from right-wing parties in Poland.

The balancing act required was not easy; nor was responding to the demands of membership in the EU and NATO or to US demands. Although Poland was the central geographic corridor for NATO and the European Union's expansion eastward, it lagged in making the necessary reforms. It also did not always side with the Europeans in economic and political matters. In fact, Poland was long called by some "America's Trojan horse." When faced with a choice between American and European producers, it leaned toward US products. At the same time, for Poles, the United States' refusal to lift its visa requirement, as it has for the other Central European countries, has been a serious issue, especially now that Poles have money and there is no longer any real incentive to work illegally in the United States.

NATO membership was an important symbol of Poland's turn to the West. It was, for Poles, a guarantee that they were safe from their eastern neighbors, even though there was no commitment, until Russia's intervention in Ukraine, to protect Poland in the event of an attack. The costs of joining and retooling its military were partially cushioned by Western aid it had received earlier and aid targeted to smooth its movement into NATO. After Britain, Poland was one of the first European states to join the "coalition of the willing in Iraq," with a sizable contingent of troops that governments on both the right and left maintained, and one of the last to withdraw. In response to Russian actions in Ukraine, NATO agreed to station rapid response forces in Poland.

Poland's membership in the European Union was guaranteed by its geographic position. Even if it lagged in its preparations, it could not be ignored and could not have its membership delayed. Many in Poland and the West feared the results of Poland's inclusion in the European Union, even as they cheered this visible end to the division of Europe. Many thought Poles would leave en masse to work in Western Europe. To calm fear of what came to be known as "the Polish plumber," provisions were enacted allowing many countries not to give Central and East Europeans, particularly Poles, work permits for long-term stays in most of Western Europe. But until the recession, the emigration of Poles to Great Britain and Ireland proved a boon for those economies.

In its east, Poland built (with West European money) one of the most heavily guarded borders in the world to keep emigrants from getting into "Europe" through Poland. And yet, Poland's neighbors from Ukraine and Belarus could enter with only a visa—given out for free at embassies and consulates. So, Poles have been able to maintain their temporary-worker labor force and to provide a haven in times of political repression in Belarus and Ukraine. This new border had unexpected side effects: it cut off or reduced the barter trade that had been "big business" for eastern Poland, where factories were so poorly developed and produced such low-quality goods that they could only trade with the even poorer countries to the east.

European Union subsidies and special provisions eased the major concerns about the domestic impact of entry into the EU, which also triggered fear that Germans would retake their prewar property in western Poland. The European Union responded to the latter concern by ruling that, for the first seven years after Poland joined the EU in 2004, foreigners could not purchase Polish land.

Poles' limited enthusiasm for joining the European Union was clear in the initial vote for EU membership in May 2003, when 77 percent of those who went to the polls voted yes for membership—less than in any other Central and East European state except the Czech Republic and Slovakia—after an active government campaign in favor. In the elections for the European Parliament in June 2004 (less than two months after May 1, 2004, when Poland officially joined the EU), only 20.4 percent voted, and of those, 55 percent supported candidates from parties that were, at best, skeptical of the EU. In the 2009 EU elections, participation had risen slightly to 24.5 percent, and the Euroskeptic vote had decreased, with 44 percent of the Polish vote (and half the seats) going to Civic Platform candidates.

As a result, Polish policy toward the European Union has been split. On the one hand, the social democratic government treated membership in NATO and the EU as its great achievement. The Law and Justice government that began in 2005 was Euroskeptic, painting itself as the defender of Polish interests and the traditional Catholic faith in the EU. With a majority of Poland's deputies hailing from the Euroskeptic right, Poland did not always go along with standard EU procedures. So Poland was a leader in the demand that the EU constitution define Europe as a Christian society. Poland has also worked to increase its power in the EU, going so far in 2007 as to nearly block an agreement on vote counting provisions for the new EU constitution. A last minute compromise delaying the new voting system until 2012 ultimately placated the Poles.

The victory of the Civic Platform in 2007 resulted in a dramatic turn toward closer ties with Western Europe and the United States, despite the objections of President Kaczynski. Prime Minister Donald Tusk rapidly developed close ties with Angela Merkel of Germany and other West European leaders. His work with these leaders facilitated his election to the Council of Europe, giving him even greater influence in European policy toward Russia.

As it has moved westward in its foreign policy, Poland has also maintained strong ties to Russia and the former Soviet states. In the process, Polish governments have tried to ensure continued access to Russian energy resources and markets. The Polish economy has also benefited from the cheap laborers that have come west to Poland to work. Poland's delay in dealing with the past complicated policy debates with accusations about who did what in the past. Then, as the European recession began and politics grew more troubled elsewhere, Poland's was the only economy that had a constant growth rate; it returned to being a model for politics in the region and became a leader in Europe itself. Polish foreign policy has, explicitly and implicitly, advocated for democratization in the countries to its east. When Russia under Vladimir Putin became more authoritarian and popular upheavals took place in Georgia and Ukraine in 2003 and 2004, Poland's ability to maintain itself as a bridge between East and West declined. Indeed, particularly since Aleksander Kwasniewski helped broker the transition in Ukraine in 2004, Russian-Polish relations, along with Polish-Belarusian relations, have grown colder, with Russia circumventing Poland in building an oil pipeline from Russia to Germany. But the conflict never went so far as to threaten Polish supplies of Russian energy.

In 2013, beginning with the Euromaidan, Poles were engaged. Then, when the agreement fell apart and Russia entered Crimea, Polish foreign minister Radoslaw Sikorski took the lead in pressing NATO, the G7, and the European Union to take a strong stance against Russian aggression. In Poland, Poles watched the events closely and collected clothes and money to help the Ukrainians. And Poland moved to provide financial support for Ukraine until International Monetary Fund and other monetary aid could be agreed on and delivered to Ukraine.

Conclusion

The grand irony of the Polish transition is that Poland had veered the furthest from Soviet-style communism (with the exception of Slovenia) before the transition began, had the best-developed civil society, and was the first state to begin the transition. Of the former communist states that are new entrants to the EU, Poland is the largest country with the biggest economy. Yet its initial transition, while clearly oriented toward democracy and capitalism, was one of the most troubled, with the public quite willing to vote out regime after regime; serious economic problems, even when it had the fastest-growing economy in the region; and real popular disaffection. In the end, the weakness of Poland's communist regime and the success of the former communists in returning to power as pro-democracy politicians not only opened the door for a negotiated transition but also made the construction of a new polity difficult. At the same time, these "rebranded" politicians took the lead in tying Poland to the West.

Poland entered the EU haunted by old problems. For many individuals, the pains of the economic transition and the gap between their expectations and reality delegitimized the new system. Its failure to provide for youth employment decreased young people's excitement about building a "new Poland." The original reformers and the communists who turned democrats lost credibility, leaving Poland's political system bereft of parties that participated in the change or are supported because of their work on economic reform and Poland's new position as a part of NATO and the EU. At the same time, Poland's delay in dealing with the past and the secret police files on agents, who came to symbolize the evils of communism, made the past a political football to shut down opposition and explain away economic failures.

But with the recession in Europe, Poland's problems with reform worked to its advantage. Poland had been less successful, after the transition, in getting foreign investment, opening up lending, and borrowing to modernize its economy. That meant it had not taken the steps that backfired for other countries. Politically, the back-and-forth of Polish politics destroyed both the ideological left and right. It reduced people's expectations of politics and politicians. And it left Poland with only a center of less ideological parties and a population with few expectations of their government.

As this plays out, there is a clear move by most of the public toward rational and civil rather than extremist political parties. The policies of Civic Platform candidates may not all be popular, but their style of governance is. The geographic divide remains, with the eastern territories being far more impoverished; however, people there are far less politically active. In the end, Poland's parties have moved to the center, and the radical rhetoric and leadership battles have largely given way to more rational policy debates. And because of both its geographic position and its commitment to bridging divides, Poland is a major player in Europe itself.

Study Questions

1. Why was Poland's communism less repressive and more inclined to liberalization of the economy and some aspects of society than that of other states? How did this impact the nature of the transition?
2. Why was Poland's transition a fully negotiated one, and how did this impact the nature of the initial government and the making of its critical decisions? Why did its politics evolve, over nearly twenty-five years, into a centrist two-party system?
3. How was Poland's economic transition begun? What was the political effect?
4. What are the structures of government and their powers in postcommunist Poland? How were they established formally and informally?
5. What are the key political parties and civic society organizations in Poland, and why have they proved weak?
6. How did Poland's initial economic transition happen? How has it worked for people in Poland?

Suggested Readings

Curry, Jane L., and Luba Fajfer. *Poland's Permanent Revolution*. Washington, DC: American University Press, 1995.
Davies, Norman. *The Heart of Europe: The Past in Poland's Present*. Oxford: Oxford University Press, 2001.
Garton Ash, Timothy. *The Polish Revolution: Solidarity*. New Haven, CT: Yale University Press, 2002.
Kowalik, Tadeusz. *From Solidarity to Sellout*. Translated by Eliza Lewandowska. New York: Monthly Review Press, 2012.

Websites

Center for Public Opinion Research: http://www.cbos.pl/EN/home_en/cbos_en.php
Gazeta.pl: http://www.gazeta.pl (general news website with limited English translation)
Government Central Statistical Office: http://stat.gov.pl/en/
Polish Ministry of Foreign Affairs: http://www.msz.gov.pl/en/ministry_of_foreign_affairs
Warsaw Voice: http://www.warsawvoice.pl (weekly English-language publication)

Notes

God's Playground is a two-volume history of Poland by Norman Davies (New York: Columbia University Press, 1982). In the title of this definitive history of Poland, Davies makes the point that Poland has been the country most conquered and fought over in Europe and has undergone successive experiments and disasters.

1. David S. Mason, "Poland," in *Developments in East European Politics*, ed. Stephen White, Judy Blatt, and Paul G. Lewis (Durham, NC: Duke University Press, 1993), 45.
2. Padraic Kenney, *Carnival of Revolution* (Princeton, NJ: Princeton University Press, 2002).
3. Jane Curry and Luba Fajfer, *Poland's Permanent Revolution* (Washington, DC: American University Press, 1995).
4. Those two probably won only because, for the National List, voters could use a single *x* to mark out all the candidates on the two-column National List ballot. The names at the bottom of the two columns often fell below the *x* and so were not counted as being crossed out.
5. These results come largely from the research of the Center for Research on Public Opinion (CBOS), which publishes its results online in English monthly at http://www.cbos.pl/EN/home_en/cbos_en.php.
6. Miroslawa Grabowska, *Podzial postkomunistyczny: Spoleczne podstawy polityki w Polsce po 1989 roku* (Warsaw: Wydawnictwo naukowe SCHOLAR, 2004).
7. Agnieszka Cybulska et al., "Demokracja w praktyce," in *Nowa rzeczywistosc*, ed. Krzysztof Zagorski and Michal Strzeszewski (Warsaw: Dialog, 2000), 80–84.
8. CBOS, "Religinosc: 2013" (yearly report).
9. Beata Roguska and Bogna Wciorka, "Religijnosc i stosunek do kosciola," in *Nowa rzeczywistosc*, ed. Krzysztof Zagorski and Michal Strzeszewski (Warsaw: Dialog, 2000).
10. World Economy Research Institute, *Transforming the Polish Economy* (Warsaw: World Economic Research Institute, 1993), 6.
11. Barbara Blaszczyk and Richard Woodward, *Privatization and Company Restructuring in Poland*. Report No. 18 (Warsaw: CASE, 1999).
12. *Rocznik statystyczny 2004* (Warsaw: GUS, 2005), 597.
13. Daniele Checchi, Vito Peragine, and Laura Serlenga, "Fair and Unfair Income Inequalities in Europe," DP No. 5025, IZA, June 2010, http://ftp.iza.org/dp5025.pdf.

Map 11.0.   The Czech and Slovak Republics

CHAPTER 11

The Czech and Slovak Republics

TWO PATHS TO THE SAME DESTINATION

Sharon L. Wolchik

In November 1989, mass demonstrations in Prague, Bratislava, and other cities caused the hard-line communist system in Czechoslovakia to fall. Preceded by nearly twenty years of stagnation, the Velvet Revolution, as these events came to be called, ushered in a broad process of change designed to reinstitute democracy, re-create a market economy, and reclaim the nation's rightful place on the European stage. It soon became evident, however, that the impact of the transition in the Czech Lands and Slovakia, as well as the perspectives and ambitions of political leaders in the two areas, differed significantly.

After the peaceful breakup of the common state and the creation of two independent states in January 1993, the transition process diverged considerably. Progress in the Czech Republic was recognized by that country's admission to the North Atlantic Treaty Organization (NATO) in the first round of NATO expansion in March 1999. In Slovakia, on the other hand, the antidemocratic actions of the government of Vladimír Mečiar and lack of progress in privatization cast doubt on Slovakia's fitness to join the Western club of nations and resulted in the country's exclusion from the first round of NATO expansion. The victory of the opposition in Slovakia in the 1998 parliamentary elections put the country back on track, a fact recognized in Slovakia's inclusion in the second round of NATO expansion in 2004 and its accession, along with the Czech Republic, Poland, Hungary, Latvia, Lithuania, Estonia, and Slovenia, to the European Union (EU) in the same year.

Leaders in both countries continue to face numerous challenges in consolidating democratic governance. Thus, political attitudes and values still reflect an amalgam of precommunist, communist, and postcommunist influences at the mass and elite levels, civil society remains weak, and the political party systems are still fluid. In both, coalition governments have proved fragile and corruption, particularly at the elite level, is an ongoing political issue. There are also significant problems in both countries in terms of incorporating minorities and dealing with the inequalities of opportunity and outcome created by the shift to the market. However, both remain among the most successful cases of transition in the region.

Precommunist History

Many of the differences between the Czech and Slovak republics date to the precommunist era. Prior to the creation of an independent Czechoslovak state in 1918, both regions were part of the Austro-Hungarian Empire. In contrast to several other ethnic groups in the region, neither Slovaks nor Czechs, after the Battle of White Mountain in 1620, had a native nobility. However, the Czech Lands were ruled by Austria, whereas Slovakia formed part of the Hungarian kingdom for nearly a thousand years. As a result, the Czechs had greater opportunities to develop a mass-based national movement and participate in politics in Bohemia and Vienna. The Czech Lands also became the center of the empire's industry.

In Slovakia, on the other hand, efforts to Magyarize, or Hungarianize, the population prevented the formation of a broad-based national movement. These efforts, which were particularly strong after 1878, also kept Slovaks from receiving secondary or higher education in their own language. In contrast to the Czech Lands, which were among the most developed parts of the empire, Slovakia remained predominantly agrarian. Tax codes designed to preserve the political power of the landowning aristocracy in Hungary stifled industrial development, although numerous mining and other centers, largely inhabited by Germans, did develop.

A final difference between the two regions was evident in the sphere of religion. Both peoples were predominantly Roman Catholic, but the population in the Czech Lands was far more secular than that in Slovakia, where levels of religious observance were much higher. There were also important differences in the relationship between Catholicism and national identity, as well as in the role of Protestantism in the two areas. Although the Czech national movement that developed in the nineteenth century included Catholic figures and symbols, such as Saint Wenceslas, Protestant figures, such as Jan Hus, the fifteenth-century precursor of Martin Luther who called on the church to reform and was burned as a heretic in 1415, were equally if not more important, and Catholicism played a relatively small role in the development of Czech national identity. A small Protestant minority in Slovakia also played an important role in efforts to create a national revival. However, Catholic figures and, in the interwar period, Catholic priests and the church were much more closely linked to the emerging sense of Slovak identity. Slovaks were also much more likely to attend church and turn to church ceremonies to mark major life passages such as birth, marriage, and death.[1]

These differences came to the fore very soon after the formation of the Czechoslovak republic in 1918. The result of efforts by leaders in exile such as Tomáš Masaryk and Milan Štefánik, as well as the need to fill the void created by the fall of the Austro-Hungarian Empire at the end of World War I, the new state, which came to include Ruthenia in 1919, brought together regions at very different levels of development, populated by peoples with very different experiences.

The impact of these differences was evident throughout the interwar period. The government in Prague was committed to industrializing Slovakia and closing the gap in development levels between the two parts of the country. However, very little progress was made in this respect before the Great Depression plunged Czechoslovakia, as much of the rest of the world, into economic decline. Levels of unemployment skyrocketed, and emigration increased.[2]

Other policies of the government also fed Slovak dissatisfaction. Faced with the need to staff bureaucratic positions vacated by Germans, the government turned to the generally better-educated Czechs. Czech administrators, as well as Czech businessmen and specialists who came to Slovakia as part of the development effort, frequently provoked resentment. The expansion of opportunities for education in the Slovak language during the interwar period led to a significant increase in the numbers of Slovaks with secondary and higher education, but there were relatively few Slovaks with these qualifications at the beginning of the period.[3] The unitary nature of the state, which was a centralized government based in Prague, also provoked dissatisfaction among many Slovaks, who came to feel that they had merely traded rule from Budapest for rule from Prague.

As a result of these factors, support for nationalist groups grew in Slovakia. Founded by Father Andrej Hlinka, the Slovak People's Party (after 1925, Hlinka's Slovak People's Party; after 1938, Hlinka's Slovak People's Party–Party of Slovak National Unity) gained an increasing share of the vote in Slovakia. As Adolf Hitler gained power in Germany, many leaders and members of the party adopted the trappings of Nazism and looked to Hitler to support their goal of an independent Slovak state.

The German minority in the Czech Lands also became increasingly dissatisfied with the state. Konrad Heinlein's Sudeten German Party received the overwhelming share of the vote of the Germans in the Sudetenland, and the dissatisfaction of this group provided the pretext for Hitler's demand at the September 1938 Munich Conference that Czechoslovakia cede the Sudetenland to the Third Reich. Faced with the unwillingness of his British, French, and Russian allies to come to Czechoslovakia's aid, President Eduard Beneš acceded to Hitler's demands. Beneš also agreed to autonomy for Slovakia in October 1938. These steps only temporarily spared his country, however, as the Germans invaded on March 15, 1939, and established the Protectorate of Bohemia and Moravia under German control. Slovak leaders, threatened with invasion as well if they did not comply with Hitler's demands that they declare independence, declared Slovakia an independent state on March 14, 1939.

Czechoslovakia was the only state in the region to retain democratic government until it was ended by outside forces. The interwar democratic system, which is often idealized, was certainly more successful than those in neighboring states in dealing with many of the pressing issues of the day. Progressive labor and occupational safety legislation and an extensive social welfare system succeeded in incorporating the growing working class and deflecting dissent. Elite political culture, heavily influenced by President Masaryk, also played an important role in supporting democracy, although the country in fact had a dual political culture as evident in the large size of the legal Communist Party.[4] The dominant role of the *pětka*, the five-party coalition that ruled the country for much of this period and often set policy in discussions among party leaders outside parliament, resulted in a form of democracy dominated by disciplined political parties and their leaders. The interwar leadership was less successful in dealing with ethnic issues than with social problems, a weakness that eventually contributed to the end of the interwar state.

Inhabitants of the Czech Lands and Slovakia had rather different experiences during World War II. Both areas experienced lower levels of human and property loss than states such as Poland and Yugoslavia, which had large, active resistance groups and were scenes of heavy fighting. Occupied by the Germans, the Czech Lands were considered a source of manufactured goods and labor for the war effort. Beneš formed an exile government in Britain, but aside from sporadic acts against German rule, there was little armed resistance. Although they had little real autonomy, many Slovaks saw the Slovak state led by Jozef Tiso as the realization of Slovak aspirations for independence. As Hitler's ally, Slovakia was also spared heavy destruction. In August 1944, Slovak anti-Nazi opposition leaders staged what has come to be known as the Slovak National Uprising against the Germans in central Slovakia. This action came to be seen after the war as a symbol of Slovak resistance and a counter to the policies of the Slovak state.

Most Jews in both the Czech Lands and Slovakia perished in the Holocaust. Roughly ninety thousand Jews lived in the Czech Lands before the outbreak of World War II. In 1942 alone, fifty-five thousand of them were sent to Theresienstadt; many of these were later deported to Auschwitz and other death camps. An estimated eighty thousand Czech Jews, or 90 percent of the community, perished in the course of the war. In Slovakia, only fifteen thousand of the estimated ninety thousand Jews survived.[5]

With the exception of the area of western Bohemia around Plzeň, which was liberated by US troops, Czechoslovakia was liberated by the Red Army. Afterward, the country was reestablished according to its interwar boundaries with the exception of Subcarpathian Ruthenia, which became part of the newly expanded Ukrainian Soviet Socialist Republic. From 1945 until February 1948, the country experienced a modified form of pluralism. The Communist Party enjoyed certain advantages, including control of the ministries of information, the interior, and agriculture, but other political parties existed and were free to participate in political life. In the 1946 elections, which were generally considered free and fair, although the political spectrum was truncated because several parties were banned for collaborating with the Nazis, the Communist Party emerged as the most popular party with 38.6 percent of the vote. Declining support on the eve of the 1948 elections, coupled with changes in Joseph Stalin's plans for the region in light of the beginning of the Cold War, led the party to instigate a government crisis in February 1948 over control of the police. The democratic members of the government resigned, and after President Beneš accepted their resignations, a government clearly dominated by the Communist Party took power.

The Communist Experience

After the February coup, the Czechoslovak communist leadership began implementing the Soviet model in earnest. The few political parties allowed to continue to exist were subordinated to the Communist Party, which became the only effective party. The new government also stepped up the nationalization of industry, which had begun under the previous government, and aggressively collectivized agriculture. A central planning board was established to set binding five-year plans based on reorienting the country's economy to focus on heavy industry to the neglect of light industry, the consumer and service sectors, and agriculture. Efforts were also made to industrialize Slovakia, which was much less developed economically than the Czech Lands at the outset of the communist period.

As in other states in the region, the leadership also implemented measures designed to change the social structure by improving the status of previously disadvantaged groups, such as workers and farmers, and remove the privileges of the previous elites. The associational life of the country was simplified. Most voluntary organizations were outlawed and replaced by large, unitary mass organizations under the control of the party. The independent media were disbanded, and a system of strict control of information and censorship was established. The party also asserted its control in the areas of education, culture, and leisure. Political criteria became important for admission to higher education, and the content of education was politicized. The elites also made efforts to use culture and leisure to propagate values and behaviors consistent with Marxism-Leninism.

Since the changes involved in implementing the Soviet model affected almost every area of life and were not chosen by the population but rather imposed from the top down, it is not surprising that the leadership came to rely increasingly on coercion. The purge trials in Czechoslovakia were among the harshest in the region, and numerous high party officials, including the secretary-general of the party, Rudolf Slánský, as well as Vladimír Clementis and several other Slovak party leaders, were executed after highly publicized show trials.[6]

Czechoslovakia remained a model Soviet satellite throughout the 1950s and early 1960s. An uprising in Plzeň after Stalin's death in 1953 was quickly put down. The regime survived de-Stalinization, which led to the Revolution of 1956 in Hungary, and popular protests and strikes in Poland in 1956, with only modest changes in personnel and lip service to the need to rout the cult of personality and restore socialist legality. By 1961, however, the previously dynamic economy in Czechoslovakia also began to show the effects of Stalinism. After the economy registered a negative growth rate in that year, party leaders commissioned a team of loyal party economists at the Academy of Science to propose economic reforms. This step, which was followed by the formation of other commissions to examine ways to reform other areas of life, initiated a large-scale process of renewal and rethinking at the elite level. Coupled with growing demands for intellectual freedom on the part of creative intellectuals, particularly writers, it resulted in the elaboration of a new model of socialism that its creators deemed more appropriate to a Western, developed society. The mid-1960s also saw the growth of Slovak dissatisfaction with Slovakia's position in the common state with the Czechs, as well as greater activism on the part of youth and several of the mass organizations.[7]

In late 1967, the reform process spread to the Communist Party, and in January 1968 Alexander Dubček replaced Antonín Novotný as head of the statewide party. Despite the persistence in the leadership of a hard-line faction, under Dubček and his supporters, the reform developed an explicitly political aspect. With the end of censorship in March 1968, the movement for change also spread to groups outside the party and its loyal intellectuals. More radical in its demands than those of the reformists within and associated with the party, this mass current kept pressure on Dubček and his colleagues in the party leadership to continue their efforts to create "socialism with a human face," as the model they were elaborating came to be called.

The reformist communist leadership that supported Dubček wanted to pursue reforms within the system. Best expressed in the Action Program adopted by the party in April, these demands did not include an end to the Communist Party's monopoly of power or any effort to renounce membership in the Warsaw Pact or separate Czechoslovakia from the Soviet Union and other socialist countries.[8] However, conservative leaders in East Germany and Poland, as well as the Soviet leadership, became increasingly fearful that the reformist spirit would spread to their countries.

Dubček and his supporters were caught between the need to maintain the slowly growing trust of the population and the need to satisfy their allies that socialism was not under threat. The growth of groups outside the party, including the Club of Engaged Nonparty People (KAN) and Club 231 (a club of former political prisoners), as well as the increasingly radical demands being voiced by some intellectuals,[9] led reformist leaders to consider the use of force to rein in the reform process, even as they attempted to reassure their colleagues in other socialist states.[10] After several meetings with the Soviet leadership in the summer of 1968 failed to produce the desired results, Soviet and other Warsaw Treaty Organization forces invaded Czechoslovakia on August 21, 1968.

After returning to Prague from Moscow, where they had been forcibly taken during the invasion, Dubček and his supporters attempted to preserve the reform course. It became increasingly difficult to do so, particularly with Soviet forces now stationed in the country once again, and in April 1969, when Gustáv Husák, also a Slovak leader, replaced Dubček at the head of the party, it was clear that the reform era was over. Husák presided over the effort to restore orthodoxy in a process known at the time as "normalization." An attempt to reverse the reforms in all areas of life, "normalization" involved the reassertion of a clear monopoly of political power by the Communist Party, the restoration of censorship, and the end of economic reform. It was accompanied by a massive personnel purge that removed most of the most talented figures in areas as diverse as culture, education, the economy, and politics from their public and professional positions. The loss of these reformists, estimated to have included from two hundred thousand to five hundred thousand people, and the restoration of party control over the mass organizations and media led to an almost twenty-year period of stagnation. During this time, Czechoslovakia once again became a model satellite. All discussion of reform became taboo, and only small numbers of intellectuals, soon labeled dissidents by the regime, engaged in independent activity.

During this period, the regime relied on a combination of material incentives and coercion to gain the population's compliance. The standard of living improved, and many families acquired summer or weekend cottages. Coercion was used primarily against dissident intellectuals who refused to accept the status quo or were active in the small number of independent groups that developed to protest the regime's disregard for human rights and to support independent activity. Charter 77, formed in response to the regime's signing of the Helsinki Accords and the prosecution of a group of young rock musicians, the Plastic People of the Universe, in 1977, was the most important of these. Founded by Václav Havel and other intellectuals centered mainly in Prague and other large cities in Bohemia and Moravia, Charter 77 was named for the document to which these intellectuals were signatories, which circulated in *samizdat* (unauthorized material reproduced and circulated clandestinely). In the last years of communist rule in particular, the group came to serve as the center of a growing community of independent activists, and many people who remained in good standing with the official world came to rely on its analyses for alternate information about problems that the regime either did not want to discuss or handled in a clearly biased way.[11] In 1989 and the years immediately following the end of communist rule, Charter 77 exerted an influence disproportionate to its numbers, as its leaders founded Civic Forum, and many of its members moved into prominent positions in public life in the early postcommunist period. In Slovakia, where few intellectuals signed the charter, dissent based on religious grounds was the most prominent form of opposition. Unauthorized pilgrimages to religious shrines drew upward of five hundred thousand people in the late 1980s, and lay Catholic activists organized a candlelight demonstration in Bratislava in December 1988 demanding religious freedom. Some Slovak intellectuals also participated in what came to be called "islands of creative deviation"—that is, groups of people who still held their positions in the official world and used approved organizations as venues for conducting unauthorized, noncomformist activities.

On November 17, 1989, the process that came to be known as the Velvet Revolution was set in motion by police brutality during a peaceful demonstration called to commemorate the death of a student during the period of Nazi occupation. Encouraged by the fall of the Berlin Wall and changes in Hungary and Poland earlier that year, hundreds of thousands of citizens participated in mass demonstrations against the regime. As it became clear that the demonstrators were not going to give up and that the Soviet Union would not intervene to preserve communism in Czechoslovakia, leaders of the Communist Party began negotiations with Civic Forum in Prague and Public against Violence in Bratislava—umbrella groups formed by Charter 77 and other dissidents in Prague and members of the opposition in Bratislava to coordinate the mass demonstrations.

Photo 11.1. Citizens of Prague, Czechoslovakia, turn out by the thousands in November 1989 to protest the communist regime led by Miloš Jakeš. Just one month later, the regime had toppled, paving the way for the election of Václav Havel as president in December of that year and for democratic elections in June 1990. (David Turnley/Corbis)

Within twenty-one days, the rigid, seemingly all-powerful, repressive communist system in Czechoslovakia fell. Many of the most conservative, compromised party members were removed from the federal legislature, and new elections were scheduled for June 1990. The election of former dissident playwright Václav Havel as president of Czechoslovakia on December 31, 1989, by a parliament still dominated by Communist Party members marked the victory of the so called Velvet Revolution.

The Transition and the Velvet Divorce

After the end of communism, Czech and Slovak leaders faced many of the same tasks as leaders in other postcommunist states. The top-priority goals were aptly summarized in the election slogans of almost all parties that ran candidates in the June 1990 parliamentary elections: democracy, the market, and a return to Europe. In the political realm, the country's new leaders had to come to terms with the communist past and establish new institutions or reorient the work of existing institutions so that they could function democratically. Other tasks included the recruitment of new leaders to replace the discredited old elite; the repluralization of the political landscape, both in terms of political parties and associational life; and the need to combat the legacy of communism on political values and attitudes and to create a new political culture suitable to a democratic polity.

In the economic realm, the new elites had to enact the legislative basis for the recreation of private ownership and private enterprise; find a way to privatize state assets, which in Czechoslovakia accounted for over 90 percent of all economic activity at the end of communist rule; encourage the development of new private enterprises; restore economic assets to their rightful owners or their heirs; deal with rising unemployment, poverty, and inequality in a previously very egalitarian society; and address the environmental consequences of the communist pattern of industrialization. With the breakup of the Soviet Union and the Council for Mutual Economic Assistance (CMEA), they also were required to reorient the country's trade, which had remained heavily centered in the socialist bloc, to the West.

In the area of foreign policy, the new leaders soon reasserted the country's status as a sovereign nation by negotiating the withdrawal of Soviet troops from its territory and began the process of reclaiming their rightful place on the European stage. In the early years after 1989, this process involved discussion about the abolition of NATO as well as the Warsaw Treaty Organization, which was dissolved in 1991. After the breakup of the Soviet Union in 1991, however, Czech and Slovak leaders began a campaign to join existing European and transatlantic institutions. The EU and NATO were the main targets of these efforts.

The new leadership of the country, as well as its citizens, also had to cope with the social and psychological aspects of the far-reaching changes the transition entailed. In the social realm, these included changes in the social structure, as well as the emergence into the open and exacerbation of old social problems, such as juvenile delinquency, alcoholism, drug abuse, crime, and domestic abuse, as well as the creation of new issues, such as human trafficking and organized crime. The widespread dislocations, as well as in many cases the positive effects of the transition, including the vastly expanded choices available to citizens, also had psychological effects on many members of the population.

Very soon after the end of communism, it became evident that the transition, and particularly the shift to the market, would be more difficult in many ways in Slovakia. Because Slovakia had industrialized largely during the communist era, it had more of the "monuments of socialist industry," or very large, inefficient factories that could not compete in market conditions. Slovakia had also become the center of the country's sizable arms industry. The shift to the market, with its emphasis on profit and the ability to compete on the world market, therefore, created much greater economic disruption in Slovakia, where levels of unemployment were significantly higher than in the Czech Lands. In 1993, for example, when 3 percent of the population was unemployed in the Czech Republic, close to 15 percent was unemployed in Slovakia.

The nature of the Czechoslovak federation was another irritant to many Slovaks. Although the adoption of a federal system was one of the few changes discussed during the reform period of 1968 that actually was implemented in 1969, the provisions that granted Slovakia a great deal of autonomy in managing its own economic as well as cultural and educational affairs were soon rescinded as the country was "normalized." After 1971, the federation functioned largely as a unitary state. Growing Slovak dissatisfaction with Slovakia's position in the common state was reflected in public opinion polls conducted in the early 1990s that showed that some 80 percent of Slovaks were dissatisfied with the federation.[12] Although most Czechs and Slovaks continued to say that they did not want the state to break up, Czech and Slovak leaders were unable to agree on an acceptable division of power between the republic and federal governments. After the June 1992 parliamentary elections led to the victory of the center-right under Václav Klaus in the Czech Lands and the center-left led by Vladimír Mečiar in Slovakia, the two leaders oversaw the process of dissolving the federation. This step formally occurred on January 1, 1993, when the Czechoslovak Federative Republic, as it was called, was replaced by the Czech Republic and the Slovak Republic.

Initially, political and economic developments diverged markedly in the two independent states. Initial expectations that the transition would be smoother in the Czech Republic were borne out by that country's inclusion in the first round of expansion of both NATO and the EU. Vladimír Mečiar's dominance of political life in Slovakia, on the other hand, and the antidemocratic actions of his government stalled economic reform and resulted in Slovakia's exclusion from the first round of NATO expansion. The victory of Citizens' Campaign 98 (OK'98) in the 1998 parliamentary elections brought a broad coalition of parties favoring reform to office. The government of Prime Minister Mikuláš Dzurinda quickly restarted economic reforms, included representatives of the 460,000-strong Hungarian minority in the government, rescinded anti-Hungarian measures adopted by the Mečiar government, and restored the rule of law and respect for human rights and political liberties. These steps put Slovakia back on track, and the country was admitted to NATO in the second round of expansion and included in the EU's first round of expansion to the postcommunist world in 2004.

As the pages to follow illustrate, both the Czech Republic and Slovakia have largely achieved the major goals, articulated soon after the end of communism, of restoring democracy and the market and returning to Europe. However, in both, important problems persist in consolidating democracy and dealing with the economic aftermath of communism.

Photo 11.2.   Václav Havel, Václav Klaus, and Vladimír Mečiar hold a press conference about the future of the country. A month later, the Velvet Divorce was announced, separating the once unified country into the Czech and Slovak republics. (Czech News Agency)

Political Institutions

The legislature elected for a two-year term in Czechoslovakia in June 1990 was to have been a constitutive assembly: its main task was to revise the country's constitution and reform its legal system to be compatible with democratic government and the creation of a market economy. Although the country's new leaders made a great deal of progress in the latter area, their inability to agree on a division of power between the federal and republican governments contributed to the breakup of the state.

The two new states that replaced the federation in January 1993 were both unitary. Their constitutions, adopted in both countries on January 1, 1993, identify them as parliamentary democracies and include provisions guaranteeing their citizens broad political and civil liberties.

In both states, the government is formed based on the results of parliamentary elections and is responsible to the legislature. The Czech Republic has a bicameral legislature. The lower house consists of two hundred members elected for four-year terms on the basis of proportional representation. The upper house, the Senate, created in 1996, consists of eighty-one members elected according to the majority principle for six-year terms. One-third of senators are elected every two years. Slovakia has a unicameral legislature. Its 150 members are elected to four-year terms according to proportional representation.

In addition to governments headed by prime ministers responsible to parliament, both countries also have presidents who serve as head of state. The president is directly elected in Slovakia and, since 2013, in the Czech Republic. Previously, the Czech president was elected by parliament. Officially, the duties of the president are largely ceremonial in both countries. However, in both cases, the office has sometimes been used to counteract or counterbalance actions by the government in ways that go beyond its formal powers. These activities were most evident in Slovakia during the Mečiar period, when President Michal Kováč, formerly a close colleague of Prime Minister Mečiar, came to be seen as an opponent of Mečiar's more authoritarian actions. Václav Havel, who was both the first postcommunist president of the federation and the first president of the independent Czech Republic, exercised influence that far exceeded the powers of his office due to his enormous moral authority and reputation around the world.[13]

The next Czech president, Václav Klaus, a known Euroskeptic, held up Czech ratification of the Lisbon Treaty in October 2009 by refusing to sign without certain EU guarantees. He finally signed on November 3 after the Constitutional Court rejected a challenge from the Civic Democrats, making the Czech Republic the last country to approve the treaty. His successor, Milos Zeman, the first popularly elected president in the Czech Republic, has attempted since his election in 2013 to expand the powers of the office beyond its ceremonial duties.

Political Parties and Movements

After the end of communism, one-party rule by the Communist Party was replaced by a plethora of political parties. The most important of these initially were the broad umbrella groups formed in November 1989 to direct the mass demonstrations and negotiate with the government: Civic Forum in the Czech Lands and Public against Violence in Slovakia. Almost immediately, however, other political parties began to form. These included successors to parties that had been active in the interwar period and were banned under communism, new parties with links to parties in the rest of Europe, nationalist or regional parties and movements, and single-issue groups and parties focused on new issues. Several small parties that had been allowed to exist under communism, albeit under the control of the Communist Party, began to act independently. Reformed and unreformed versions of the Communist Party also participated in politics in both regions.[14]

Although they won the June 1990 elections resoundingly, Civic Forum and Public against Violence soon splintered into smaller groups. In the Czech Lands, then finance minister Václav Klaus broke away from Civic Forum in April 1991 to form the Civic Democratic Party. Those who remained in Civic Forum founded the Civic Democratic Movement and the Civic Democratic Alliance, which succeeded in electing candidates to the Federal Assembly in the 1992 elections but were not viable political entities after that. In Slovakia, Vladimír Mečiar, initially part of Public against Violence, broke away in April 1991 to found the Movement for a Democratic Slovakia, which became the most popular party or movement in that republic. Public against Violence was replaced by a variety of other parties on the center-right.

As table 11.1 illustrates, the number of political parties and movements that have fielded candidates has in fact increased in both the Czech Republic and Slovakia since 1990. However, many of these were unable to obtain enough votes to pass the threshold of 3 or 5 percent of the vote required to seat deputies in parliament. Thus, four parties gained enough votes to seat deputies in the federal legislature in the Czech Lands and five in Slovakia in 1990; in 1992 six parties crossed the threshold in the Czech Lands and

Table 11.1.   Ratio of the Number of Parties Seating Deputies to the Number of Parties Fielding Candidates by Election

Czechoslovakia Federal Assembly (Chamber of Nations and Chamber of People)			
	Czech National Council	Czech Lands	Slovakia	Slovak National Council
1990	4/13	4/15 + 4/16	5/17 + 5/17	7/16
1992	8/19	6/20 + 6/21	6/22 + 5/22	5/23

	Czech Republic Chamber of Deputies		Slovakia National Council
1996	6/15	1994	7/17
1998	5/12	1998	6/17
2002	4/28	2002	7/25
2006	5/25	2006	6/21
2010	8/26	2010	6/18
2013	7/23	2012	6/26

five in Slovakia. Six parties were represented in the Czech Chamber of Deputies in 1996, five in 1998, and four in 2002. In Slovakia, seven parties seated deputies in parliament in 1994, six in 1998, and seven in 2002. After the 2006 elections, there were once again six parties in the parliament in Slovakia and five in the Czech Chamber of Deputies. In the 2010 elections, eight parties seated deputies in the Czech Chamber of Deputies and six in the Slovak National Council. In the early elections in Slovakia in 2012, six parties seated deputies in the Slovak National Council; in the Czech Republic's early elections in October 2013, seven parties seated deputies in the Chamber of Deputies, including one newly formed party.

Although a relatively small and stable number of parties have seated deputies in the legislatures since 1990, the figures in table 11.1 mask an important aspect of politics in the period since 1989. As table 11.2 illustrates, parties continue to appear and disappear with great frequency. Thus, seventeen of the twenty-five parties that competed in the 2002 elections in Slovakia were new or newly formed combinations of previous political groups, as were two of the seven parties that seated deputies. In the Czech Republic, twenty-one of the twenty-five parties that fielded candidates in the 2002 parliamentary elections were either new or reincarnations of previous parties. In the 2006 Czech parliamentary elections, the pattern remained the same, as thirteen of the twenty-six parties that fielded candidates were new. In Slovakia, however, only eight of the twenty-one parties that fielded candidates in 2006 were new. In 2010, there were thirteen new Czech parties out of twenty-five fielding candidates and nine new Slovak parties in a field of eighteen. Fifteen of the twenty-six parties that competed in the Slovak elections of 2012 were newly formed, as were ten of the twenty-six parties that contested the early Czech elections in 2013.

Analysts of politics in both countries have disagreed about how to characterize the political party system that followed the breakup of the initial umbrella organizations. By the mid-1990s, some analysts argued that the proliferation of political parties that followed the demise of these groups was coming to an end and that a simplified party

Table 11.2.   Number of Parties Fielding Candidates and Number of New Parties in the Czech Republic and Slovakia since Independence

	Czech Republic			Slovakia	
	New Parties	Total Parties		New Parties	Total Parties
2013	10	23	2012	15	26
2010	13	26	2010	9	18
2006	13	25	2006	8	21
2002	21	28	2002	17	25
1998	5	12	1998	13	17
1996	8	15	1994	12	17

system was emerging. Others argued that, although party labels continued to change, the electorate was sorting itself into two coherent, identifiable large blocs that corresponded in a general way to the left-right division seen in many other European polities.[15] As subsequent elections have demonstrated, events since that time have not supported either view. Instead, voter support for most parties, with few exceptions, has continued to be fluid, as voters have generally tended to "throw the rascals out" at each election. As table 11.2 illustrates, both the number of parties and the parties themselves have also tended to change from one election to another. The reelection of a center-right government in Slovakia in the 2002 elections and a center-left government in the Czech Republic in the same year, although both with changes in the composition of the coalition, was unusual not only in those countries but in the postcommunist region as a whole.

In the 2006 parliamentary elections, voters in both countries reverted to the more common pattern of defeating the incumbent government. In Slovakia, the Smer (Direction) movement led by Robert Fico won the largest number of votes, soundly defeating the center-right government of Mikuláš Dzurinda. Fico eventually formed a coalition government with deputies from Vladimír Mečiar's center-left Movement for a Democratic Slovakia and the extreme right-wing Slovak National Party. In the Czech Republic, the center-right Civic Democrats emerged as the strongest party in the June elections, but the minority government they led, which was formed only several months after the election, was a fragile coalition with the Christian Democrats and the Greens that survived four no-confidence votes between 2006 and 2009 but was toppled by a vote of no confidence in March 2009, when the Czech Republic held the presidency of the EU. An interim government led by Jan Fischer, former head of the State Statistical Office, governed the country until early elections in May 2010. Both of the largest parties, the Czech Social Democratic Party (CSSD) and the Civic Democratic Party (ODS), lost votes in the 2010 elections, although the socialists received more votes than any other party (22.08 percent).[16] In the 2013 elections, held after a scandal involving corruption and misuse of government resources led to the resignation of the prime minister and the appointment of a caretaker government, ODS, the dominant party in the three-party coalition formed after the 2010 elections and a constant in the Czech political party scene since its founding in 1991, barely received enough votes to seat deputies in parliament.

Although Robert Fico's Smer won by far the largest share of the vote (29.14 percent) in the 2010 parliamentary elections in Slovakia, he was unable to form a coalition due to the failure of Mečiar's party to cross the 5 percent threshold necessary to seat deputies and the unwillingness of all parties except the Slovak National Party, which won 11.73 percent of the vote, to form a coalition with him.[17] A center-right coalition consisting of the Slovak Democratic Christian Union–Democratic Party (SDKU-DS), Christian Democratic Movement (KDH), and two new parties, Most-Híd, which broke off from the Hungarian Coalition Party prior to the elections, and the Freedom and Solidarity Party (SaS), a center-right party focused on the need for tax reform, thus formed the new government with Iveta Radičová, a sociologist and longtime civic activist before she joined the SDKU-DS, as prime minister. In the early 2012 elections held after the Radičová government fell in 2011, Smer gained 44.42 percent of the vote, which translated into 83 of the 150 seats in parliament, enabling the party to form a government without forming a coalition. Support for the Slovak Democratic Christian Union–Democratic Party fell dramatically to 6.10 percent of the vote, in large part due to the so-called Gorilla corruption scandal, in which former prime minister Dzurinda and other top center-right leaders were caught on tape discussing bribes.

In the 2014 presidential elections in Slovakia, Andrej Kiska (see photo 11.3), a wealthy businessman and philanthropist with no previous political experience, won an upset victory over Robert Fico, the current prime minister, with 59.4 percent of the vote in the first round. Fico's election, had it occurred, would have meant that both the majority in parliament and president were from the same party, an outcome Slovak voters evidently wanted to avoid. Kiska, who is thought to be a moderate politically, has no affiliation with a political party.

Photo 11.3.   Andrej Kiska was elected in 2014 as Slovakia's fourth president. (Corbis)

Most political parties in the Czech Republic and Slovakia are weak organizationally, with small memberships and poorly staffed local organizations. The unreformed Communist Party in the Czech Republic and the Christian democratic parties in both countries have larger memberships than most other parties, but their memberships are also relatively small. Levels of party identification, which in more established democracies helps simplify political choices, links citizens to the political system, and moderates conflict, have also remained low. Many citizens do not believe that parties play an essential role in a democratic state, and many continue to hold parties and party leaders in low regard.

In part, these trends reflect the legacy of the communist period. In reaction to the need to be a member of the Communist Party or its youth organization if one wanted to study at university or hold many professional jobs, many people have refused to join any party. Low levels of party membership may also reflect, however, the trend in much of the rest of Europe for parties to change from being membership organizations that influence many aspects of their members' lives to electoral parties more along the lines of US political parties. The lack of willingness to become a member of a party or take part in party-sponsored activities, as well as negative attitudes toward parties, may also reflect citizens' experiences in the postcommunist era. The tendency of parties to come and go, the similarities in the platforms of many parties, and the frequent change in the party affiliation of political figures all make it difficult and costly in terms of time and attention for citizens to affiliate with particular parties. These trends also reinforce citizens' views of parties as vehicles to advance the personal fortunes of their leaders rather than as mechanisms to aggregate interests and pursue broader policy objectives.

Photo 11.4. Former Czech prime minister Mirek Topolánek and former and current Slovak prime minister Robert Fico. (Official website of the government of the Slovak Republic, http://www.government.gov.sk)

Civil Society

In contrast to the situation in Poland and Hungary, where strong civil societies independent of the government had begun to form prior to the end of communism, there were very few independent groups in Czechoslovakia prior to 1989. Due to heavy repression and the very real threat of imprisonment, removal from jobs, and other forms of retaliation, the number of independent organizations remained very small even after Mikhail Gorbachev's reforms in the Soviet Union began to have some impact in Czechoslovakia. Experts estimated that there were approximately fifteen hundred independent groups in Hungary in the late 1980s.[18] In Czechoslovakia, there were approximately thirty at that time.[19]

Following the end of communism, Czechoslovakia experienced the same resurgence of associations and voluntary organizations that occurred elsewhere in the postcommunist world. As with political parties, some of these groups had ties to groups that had been active in the interwar or immediate post–World War II periods. Some were attached to the newly emerging parties or were branches of international organizations. Still others were new groups designed to further the interests of their members, provide charitable services, or unite citizens with similar hobbies.

Most of these new nongovernmental organizations (NGOs) were funded in the early years after the end of communism by outside sources, and many remained heads without bodies, that is, groups of intellectuals in the major cities with few links to ordinary citizens or members. Domestic philanthropy has increased over time, as has the number of NGOs that no longer rely on foreign funders. Similarly, citizens are more likely to participate in the work of NGOs than in that of partisan political organizations, and the number of citizens who indicate that they participate in the work of such organizations has increased in both the Czech Republic and Slovakia.[20]

The NGO sector was particularly well organized in Slovakia during the mid-1990s when Vladimír Mečiar dominated partisan politics. A coordinating committee known as the Gremium included representatives of the main sectors of the NGO community and sponsored an annual conference to discuss issues of importance to the sector. The Gremium and activists who had participated in NGO campaigns formed the core of those who organized the OK'98 campaign of civic actions that increased voter turnout sufficiently to oust Mečiar as prime minister in 1998. The impact of this campaign, the first full elaboration of the electoral model of ousting semi-authoritarian leaders in the postcommunist world, was not limited to Slovak politics but served as an inspiration and model for NGO activists in other postcommunist countries.[21]

Once the Dzurinda government was formed, NGO activists articulated their desire to continue to serve as watchdogs of the government and succeeded in passing a freedom-of-information law. With the end of government harassment of NGO activists and the return of respect for democratic procedures, the unity of the sector has diminished. During the 2002 election campaign, individual NGOs sponsored election-related actions. However, there was no repetition of the large-scale NGO campaign to get out the vote that occurred in 1998. Although some NGOs continue to lobby political leaders and monitor their actions, most NGOs have returned to focusing on their particular areas of activity.[22] Others have redirected their activities toward providing assistance to NGOs seeking to promote democracy in other countries.

Political Values and Attitudes

As in many other postcommunist countries, the political attitudes and values of citizens in the Czech Republic and Slovakia continue to reflect a variety of influences. Some of these stem from the precommunist political culture, which contained both democratic and nondemocratic elements in both countries. Others derive from the communist era, and still others have developed in response to the politics and economic policies of the transition since 1989.

The political attitudes of citizens of the Czech Republic and Slovakia differ somewhat from those of citizens in non-postcommunist members of the EU. These differences are most evident in perceptions of and levels of trust in government institutions and in citizens' perceptions of their own political roles. Thus, although citizens' levels of interest in politics in the Czech Republic and Slovakia, as well as in Hungary and Poland, do not differ greatly from those in older EU member states, citizens of postcommunist states have lower levels of trust in government institutions. They also have lower levels of political efficacy, or the sense that they can make a difference at either the local or national level if their interests are threatened.[23]

Surveys conducted in 1994 and 2004 in the Czech Republic and Slovakia found that most citizens in both countries supported democracy. They also held views of democracy that included protection of individual rights and other political liberties; they also believed that democracy should bring with it a high level of well-being. In the early 1990s, citizens in the Czech Lands were more likely than those in Slovakia to agree with the notion that citizens should be responsible for ensuring their own well-being; they also accepted the idea that a certain level of unemployment was an inevitable element of the shift to the market. As unemployment rates grew in the Czech Republic, however, differences between the two countries in this regard decreased. Popular resistance to the institution of fees for higher education and medical services, as well as to other measures that have decreased the government's responsibility for services and welfare, are further indications of the extent to which citizens internalized the belief common during the communist period that the state owes citizens a great deal of material security.[24]

Early studies of tolerance in the two areas found that levels of anti-Semitism were lower in the Czech Republic than in Slovakia, Poland, and Hungary.[25] However, studies done at that time and more recently have repeatedly documented very high levels of prejudice against the Roma in the Czech Republic as well as in Slovakia.[26]

The Economic Transition

Shortly after the end of communism, Czechoslovakia's new elites began debating the best way to return to a market economy. Early discussions of a more gradual, or third, way to transform the economy soon gave way, under the direction of then federal finance minister Václav Klaus, to the decision to move rapidly and decisively to the market. This decision—accompanied by the end of or decreases in government subsides, a rapid increase in prices, and efforts to privatize the economy, which was almost entirely in state hands—led to a steep drop in production and an increase in unemployment, economic hardship, and poverty. The negative effects of the shift to the market were especially evident in Slovakia.

The country's new leaders used a variety of methods to privatize economic assets. These included auctions, sales to foreign investors, and, most distinctively, the use of vouchers or coupons. Under the latter system, citizens were able to buy vouchers or coupons very inexpensively, which they could then exchange for shares in privatizing companies. This system, which became a sort of parlor game at the time, was designed to compensate for the lack of domestic capital at the end of communism as well as to give most citizens a personal stake in the continuation of market reforms. However, because it was not accompanied by changes in the banking sector or even, until several years later, the adoption of a bankruptcy law, it did little to restructure the economy. As in other postcommunist countries, privatization was also accompanied by massive fraud and corruption.[27]

Political elites also adopted laws to regulate restitution, the return of property that had been seized by the state to its rightful owners or their heirs, and stimulate the development of new private enterprises. The country's trade was also rapidly reoriented to the West, particularly after the collapse of CMEA and the Soviet Union.

Eventually, the shift to the market created more favorable economic conditions in both the Czech Republic and Slovakia. However, in the period soon after the end of communism, policies designed to achieve this goal created greater hardship in Slovakia. They also affected different groups of the population very differently. Thus, the economic transition created both winners and losers. The former were those who had the education, contacts, and ability to benefit from the new opportunities to increase their skills and qualifications, travel abroad for study or work, practice their occupations free of ideological interference, take the risk of working for a private or international corporation, or found a private business. These were primarily the young, urban, and well educated. For those lacking such skills and opportunities (those who were older, rural, and less educated, as well as families with several or many children and the Roma), the shift to the market and other economic changes brought primarily hardships.

As chapter 3 in this volume on economics indicates, both the Czech and Slovak economies have attracted sizable amounts of foreign investment. In the Slovak case, outside investors began to seriously consider investing in Slovakia after the victory of the liberal opposition in the 1998 elections. Both countries now play an important role in producing many products for the European market, including, most notably, automobiles. After nearly a decade of high growth rates, both countries suffered from the 2008–2009 global economic crisis. Gross domestic product contracted in 2009 by 4.1 percent in the Czech Republic and 4.7 percent in Slovakia, after 2.5 percent growth in the Czech Republic and 6.2 percent growth in Slovakia in 2008.[28] Both economies began to recover in 2010 but grew at slower rates than in the 1990s.

As planned, Slovakia adopted the euro on January 1, 2009. Despite fears about the impact of this move on more vulnerable parts of the population, most analysts believe that it helped Slovakia weather the global crisis.

Social Consequences

In addition to bringing poverty and unemployment to some groups, the shift to the market and the broader transition also had a number of social consequences. First among these was growing inequality. Although inequalities in terms of lifestyles, values, and access to higher education existed under communism[29] and the communist leadership clearly had many material privileges, Czech and Slovak societies were generally very egalitarian, and those who had greater wealth were fairly circumspect about it. With the return to the market, inequalities increased dramatically. Wage differentials, which had been among the lowest in the communist world, widened significantly, and with expanded availability of consumer durables and goods, it suddenly became clear to many families that they were not living as well as their neighbors.

Czech and Slovak societies have once again become more complex, as the return of the market led to the emergence of new occupations and groups, particularly in the rapidly expanding service and financial sectors. Restitution and the growth of the private sector also led to the reemergence of certain previously banned social categories, such as capitalists and entrepreneurs. There were also important shifts in the status and prestige, as well as the incomes, of different occupations and groups. At the same time that these changes opened up many new opportunities for some citizens, the situation of members of other groups, such as agricultural workers, unskilled and skilled manual workers, and some members of the party's former apparatus, worsened.

The opening of the borders and decline of tight political and police control also led to the intensification of all forms of social pathology, such as alcoholism, drug use, and abuse within the family, and to the emergence of new issues, such as trafficking in persons, smuggling, and HIV/AIDS. Many of these problems were intensified by the economic transition, as economic hardship took its toll on families.

The end of communism also allowed certain issues, such as ethnic tensions and issues related to sexuality, to emerge into the open and get onto the political agenda. Hungarian activists in Slovakia formed their own political parties and began to make demands for greater respect for minority culture and more attention to minority rights. The positive start to forging new relationships evident in the inclusion of a Hungarian party in the first postcommunist coalition government in Slovakia was interrupted temporarily by Mečiar's government, which enacted a number of laws that, among other things, restricted the right of the Hungarian minority to use its language in official dealings, removed dual-language street signs, and required Hungarian women to add the Slavic suffix *ová* to their last names.

With the victory of the democratically oriented opposition in 1998, the by-now-single Hungarian party was once again included in governing coalitions, and the most offensive legislation of the Mečiar era was reversed. Hungarian leaders continued to press for greater recognition of minority rights but played a constructive role within the coalition government on many issues. The inclusion of the nationalist, anti-Hungarian Slovak National Party in Prime Minister Robert Fico's coalition after the 2006 elections halted the progress made in this regard. There were several isolated incidents of violence by Slovaks against ethnic Hungarians who were speaking Hungarian. The inflammatory rhetoric used by some political leaders at this time heightened tensions within Slovakia and also contributed to worsening relations between Slovakia and Hungary. Ethnic relations and Slovak-Hungarian relations took a turn for the worse in 2009 when a language law was enacted that restricted the use of Hungarian and other non-Slovak languages in official contacts in Slovakia. The government's effort to replace Hungarian geographic names with Slovak names in Hungarian-language textbooks, which Hungarian-language schools refused to use,[30] further angered ethnic Hungarians in Slovakia. The center-right government formed after the 2010 elections, which once again included representatives of a Hungarian party, worked to improve Slovak-Hungarian relations within the country and Slovakia's relations with Hungary. The formation of a political party explicitly designed to cross the ethnic divide, Most-Híd (a party whose name consists of the Slovak and Hungarian words for "bridge") reflects the effort of some Hungarian and Slovak leaders to foster good relations among the two groups.

The status of the Roma community has also become an important issue. Subject to various measures to foster assimilation during the communist era, the Roma continue to face widespread prejudice and discrimination in both the Czech Republic and Slovakia. Education levels among the Roma are very low, and the practice of sending Roma children to special schools for the mentally handicapped remains widespread. Unemployment rates approach 85 percent in many Roma communities. The living conditions of many Roma, who reside in "settlements" on the outskirts of towns and cities, are very poor, as many Roma communities lack running water, electricity, and other public services. Violence against the Roma has also been an ongoing problem in the last twenty-five years. Unlike the Hungarian minority, the Roma have not developed effective political organizations to raise their claims in the political arena. Both the Czech and Slovak governments have adopted programs, in part at the prodding of the European Union, to improve the status of the Roma, but serious problems, including overwhelmingly negative public attitudes toward the group, remain in both countries.[31]

Gender issues have also emerged as political issues since 1989. In part because women's equality was an official goal during the communist era, and in part because the uneven pattern of change in women's roles created great stress for women and their families,[32] many Czechs and Slovaks rejected the idea of women's equality after the end of communism. This backlash was reflected in the view that women should emphasize their maternal rather than economic roles, as well as in the reluctance on the part of women to be actively involved in politics. Although most women continued to be employed, women were more likely than men to lose their jobs in the Czech Republic as a result of the transition. In both countries they also faced increased competition from men for jobs in areas such as tourism, law, and financial services, which became more attractive under market conditions, and like men, they encountered new pressure to work productively. Given the continued traditional division of labor within the home, the task of dealing with the results of declining social services and the need to stretch family budgets to cover necessities also fell most heavily on women during the early part of the transition.

Women's political representation also declined in the early postcommunist period. Many women appeared to share the view of male leaders, including some former dissidents, who argued that politics was too dirty for women or that women had more important tasks than arguing about political issues. This pattern began to change in the late 1990s, as levels of women's representation increased in both the Czech Republic and Slovakia. However, as chapter 6 on women's issues indicates, women are still underrepresented among the political elite, and it is still difficult for women leaders to raise issues of particular concern for women.[33] As a result of the 2010 elections, Iveta Radičová, a former NGO activist and sociologist who has done research on gender issues, became Slovakia's first woman prime minister. She also became the first woman candidate for president to advance to the second round, although she lost to the incumbent. Despite Radičová's position as head of the government, the number of women in the Slovak parliament decreased from 18 to 15.3 percent after the 2010 elections. In the Czech Republic, 22 percent of members of the lower house of parliament were women after the 2010 elections. Women's representation remained at approximately the same level in Slovakia (16 percent) after the 2012 elections and decreased slightly to 19.5 percent in the Czech lower house after the 2013 early elections.[34]

By the mid-1990s, the backlash against even considering or discussing issues related to women's status began to decrease. Social scientists and women's advocates succeeded in getting certain issues related to women's situation onto the political agenda. Women's groups, particularly the small number of such groups that identify themselves as feminist, have also succeeded in establishing links with a few political leaders and have provided background materials as well as position papers on issues such as same-sex partnerships and legislation prohibiting sexual harassment in the workplace. Public discussion of women's issues in the media also increased. The EU accession process accelerated these trends in both countries, as political leaders were forced to adopt certain laws and establish government institutions to address issues related to women's status as part of that process.

Foreign Policy

As noted earlier in this chapter, foreign policy concerns were a major element of the transition in both the Czech Republic and Slovakia. A first step of the new government was to negotiate the withdrawal of Soviet troops from Czechoslovakia. The country's new leaders also sought to reclaim Czechoslovakia's place on the world stage as an independent country once again. Helped by the international stature of then president Václav Havel, Czech and Slovak leaders played an active role in upgrading the status of the Organization for Security and Co-operation (OSCE) in Europe. They also were key players in establishing the Visegrad group of Czechoslovakia, Hungary, and Poland, which sought to coordinate the three countries' efforts to join NATO and the EU and continues to coordinate the initiatives of the Czech Republic, Slovakia, Poland, and Hungary in these organizations now that these countries are members.

After the breakup of the federation, the foreign policies of the newly created Czech and Slovak republics diverged for several years. The Czech Republic maintained its status as a candidate for inclusion in the first round of NATO expansion, a goal it achieved in 1999, and began negotiations for EU accession. Although the Slovak leadership never renounced the goals of joining NATO and the EU, under Mečiar Slovakia fell out of the group of countries included in the first round of NATO expansion and was in danger of being excluded from EU expansion as well. The Mečiar government also sought to increase Slovakia's ties with Russia. After the victory of the opposition in the 1998 elections, Slovakia's foreign policy once again emphasized EU accession and NATO membership. Slovakia was included in the second round of NATO expansion in 2004 and became a member of the EU, along with the Czech Republic and eight other countries, that year.

In 2009, the Czech Republic became the second postcommunist country to hold the presidency of the EU. The country's ability to pursue its three announced priorities—economy, energy, and Europe in the world—was hampered by the fall of the government in March. Although the interim government received praise in some quarters, the Czech presidency received mixed reviews. The fact that President Klaus was the last holdout in signing the Lisbon Treaty further tarnished the country's reputation in the EU.

As members of NATO and the EU, both Slovakia and the Czech Republic at times have faced competing pressures from their European and US allies. These became evident almost immediately after the Czech Republic joined NATO in 1999 in the context of the NATO bombing campaign in Serbia and Kosovo in reaction to Slobodan Milošević's expulsion of most of the Albanian population from Kosovo. The governments of both countries supported this effort, but this step was unpopular with citizens of both.

US actions in Afghanistan and particularly the war in Iraq posed even more starkly the dilemma these countries face in trying to maintain good relations with other EU members and the United States. Both countries sent specialized units to Afghanistan and Iraq. However, as in most of Central and Eastern Europe, citizens in both countries opposed these deployments. Most Czech citizens welcomed the decision in 2009 by the Barack Obama administration to scrap the George W. Bush administration's plans to place a radar station in the Czech Republic as part of a missile defense system as there was widespread popular opposition to the plan, despite the Czech government's approval.

The reaction of both governments to the crisis posed by events in Ukraine in 2013 and by Russia's occupation and annexation of Crimea, fomenting of separatist activities and arming of separatists in eastern Ukraine, and invasion of eastern Ukrainian in 2014 reflected their previous experiences with Russia and the obligations of their existing foreign policy commitments as members of the EU and NATO. The Czech government condemned the use of violence against protestors by the Victor Yanukovych regime and flew many of those wounded to hospitals in the Czech Republic for treatment and rehabilitation. Government spokespersons also condemned the illegal annexation of Crimea and supported EU sanctions, although President Milos Zeman took a more ambiguous position. In Slovakia—which, unlike the Czech Republic, which has coal, is more dependent on Russia for its energy supplies—Prime Minister Robert Fico has taken a more neutral stance on Crimea and Russian actions in eastern Ukraine. Arguing that they would hurt Slovakia's economy, he urged caution in applying sanctions.

Future Challenges

As the preceding pages have illustrated, both Slovakia and the Czech Republic are among the success stories in the postcommunist world. Although political and economic developments diverged in Slovakia under Mečiar, in the period since 1998, political leaders have successfully achieved many of the objectives set out after the fall of communism in 1989. Thus, both Slovakia and the Czech Republic are now among those countries classified as "free" by Freedom House and other international ranking bodies. Although important problems remain with the party system, as well as with elite and mass political culture, both are widely recognized as functioning liberal democracies.

Both countries' economies have also been among the success stories in the region. Economic growth rates were among the highest in Europe prior to the 2008 crisis in the world economy, and foreign direct investment continues to increase. Privatization was successfully accomplished, and the standard of living has long surpassed its 1989 level in both countries. Although both economies were hurt by the worldwide economic crisis of 2008 and 2009, both have since recovered. Securely anchored in European and transatlantic institutions, both Slovakia and the Czech Republic have also achieved recognition for their roles in supporting pro-democracy movements abroad, particularly in the postcommunist world.

As in other postcommunist, as well as many other developed, Western countries, numerous problems remain in all of these areas. In the political realm, these include the need to develop a stable system of political parties and to increase linkages between political leaders and citizens, as well as between political leaders and the NGO sector. They also include the need to foster tolerance as well as a political culture that supports democracy and includes a greater sense of citizens' responsibility to take action to resolve public problems and actively join with others to address common issues.

There is also room for improvement in dealing with corruption in the political and economic arenas in both countries. Both have experienced major political scandals in the recent past that have tainted political life and called into question the competence of political elites. In Slovakia, the Gorilla scandal continues to hamper the development of a strong center-right party. In the Czech Republic, the forced resignation of Prime Minister Petr Nečas after revelations that his chief of staff had improperly used state resources to spy on his estranged wife and about his own role in offering bribes to parliamentary deputies led to a caretaker government for several months and to the near elimination from political life of his party, the Civic Democratic Party, which had been a mainstay of the Czech party system since 1991.

In the economic arena, both governments continue to face regional disparities in growth and unemployment, as well as a host of problems arising from aging and declining populations. They also must address the problem of persistent poverty among certain groups, particularly the Roma, as well as other unresolved issues related to the marginal status of the Roma in both societies. Gender issues are another area requiring greater attention. As their economies continue to grow and the wage differentials compared to more developed EU members that have made both countries attractive to foreign investors change, Czech and Slovak leaders will also need to find other incentives to attract outside capital. They must also deal with the lingering impact of the 2008–2009 economic crisis on their economies.

In the area of foreign policy, leaders in both countries will continue to face the need to balance their relations with the rest of Europe and the United States. They must also find a way to play constructive roles as small countries within the EU as well as in regional groupings and to define their relations with countries to the east.

As this listing of areas indicates, political leaders and citizens face important challenges in both Slovakia and the Czech Republic. Some of these continue to reflect the legacy of communism and its impact on the transition. Others derive from the transition process itself and its unintended or, in some cases, seemingly inevitable consequences. Increasingly, however, the problems that dominate the political agenda in both Slovakia and the Czech Republic are those that confront leaders in other developed, Western societies.

Study Questions

1. How were developments in the precommunist and communist periods reflected in the postcommunist period in the Czech Lands and Slovakia?
2. What caused the Velvet Divorce, and what were its consequences?
3. What role did NGOs play in the ouster of Mečiar in Slovakia in 1998?
4. What trends are evident in the party systems in each country?
5. What major challenges face leaders and citizens in each country?

Suggested Readings

Bunce, Valerie J., and Sharon L. Wolchik. *Defeating Authoritarian Leaders in Postcommunist Countries*. New York: Cambridge University Press, 2011.

Fisher, Sharon. *Political Change in Post-communist Slovakia and Croatia: From Nationalist to Europeanist*. New York: Palgrave Macmillan, 2006.

Haughton, Tim, Teresa Novotna, and Kevin Deegan-Krause. "The 2010 Czech and Slovak Parliamentary Elections: Red Cards to the 'Winners.'" *West European Politics* 34 (2011): 394–402.

Innes, Abby. *Czechoslovakia: The Short Goodbye*. New Haven, CT: Yale University Press, 2001.

Krause, Kevin Deegan. "Slovakia's Second Transition." *Journal of Democracy* 14, no. 2 (April 2003): 65–79.

Leff, Carol Skalnik. *The Czech and Slovak Republics: Nation vs. State*. Boulder, CO: Westview Press, 1996.

Prečan, Vilém. *Prague-Washington-Prague: Reports from the United States Embassy in Czechoslovakia, November–December 1989*. Washington, DC: National Security Archive, 2004.

Skilling, H. Gordon. *Czechoslovakia's Interrupted Revolution*. Princeton, NJ: Princeton University Press, 1976.

Vachudova, Milada Anna. *Europe Undivided: Democracy, Leverage, and Integration after Communism*. Oxford: Oxford University Press, 2005.

Wolchik, Sharon L. *Czechoslovakia in Transition: Politics, Economics, and Society*. London: Pinter Publishers, 1991.

Websites

CZECH REPUBLIC

Prague Daily Monitor: http://praguemonitor.com
Prague Post: http://www.praguepost.com

SLOVAKIA

Slovak Spectator: http://spectator.sme.sk
Pozor Blog: http://pozorblog.com

Notes

1. Samuel Harrison Thomson, *Czechoslovakia in European History* (Princeton, NJ: Princeton University Press, 1953).

2. Zora Pryor, "Czechoslovak Economic Development in the Interwar Period," in *A History of the Czechoslovak Republic: 1918–1948*, ed. Victor S. Mamatey and Radomír Luza (Princeton, NJ: Princeton University Press, 1973).

3. Owen V. Johnson, *Slovakia, 1918–1938: Education and the Making of a Nation* (New York: Columbia University Press, 1985).

4. H. Gordon Skilling, "Stalinism and Czechoslovak Political Culture," in *Stalinism: Essays in Historical Interpretation*, ed. Robert C. Tucker (New York: W. W. Norton & Co., 1977).

5. Lucy S. Dawidowicz, *The War against the Jews: 1933–1945* (New York: Bantam Books, 1975).

6. See Arthur Koestler, *Darkness at Noon* (New York: Macmillan Press, 1941), for a fictionalized account of the purges.

7. Barbara Jancar, *Czechoslovakia and the Absolute Monopoly of Power: A Study of Political Power in a Communist System* (New York: Praeger Press, 1978); Golia Golan, *The Czechoslovak Reform Movement: Communism in Crisis, 1962–1968* (Cambridge: Cambridge University Press, 1971).

8. Robin Alison Remington, ed., *Winter in Prague: Documents on Czechoslovak Communism in Crisis* (Cambridge, MA: MIT Press, 1969).

9. Ludvík Vaculík, "2,000 Words to Workers, Farmers, Scientists, Artists and Everyone," in *Winter in Prague: Documents on Czechoslovak Communism in Crisis*, ed. Robin Alison Remington (Cambridge, MA: MIT Press, 1969).

10. Kieran Williams, *The Prague Spring and Its Aftermath: Czechoslovak Politics, 1968–1970* (Cambridge: Cambridge University Press, 1997); Jaromír Navrátil, ed., *The Prague Spring '68* (Budapest: Central European University Press, 1998).

11. Sharon L. Wolchik, "Czechoslovakia," in *The Columbia History of Eastern Europe in the Twentieth Century*, ed. Joseph Held (New York: Columbia University Press, 1992).

12. Sharon L. Wolchik, "Institutional Factors in the Break-Up of Czechoslovakia," in *Irreconcilable Differences: Explaining Czechoslovakia's Dissolution*, ed. Michael Kraus and Allison Stanger (New York: Rowman & Littlefield, 2000).

13. Sharon L. Wolchik, "The Czech Republic: Havel and the Evolution of the Presidency since 1989," in *Postcommunist Presidents*, ed. Ray Taras (Cambridge: Cambridge University Press, 1997).

14. Sharon L. Wolchik, "The Repluralization of Politics in Czechoslovakia," *Communist and Post-communist Studies* 26 (December 1993): 412–31.

15. Tomáš Kostelecký, *Political Parties after Communism: Development in East Central Europe* (Baltimore: Johns Hopkins University Press, 2002).

16. "Volby do Poslanecké sněmovny Parlamentu České republiky konané ve dnech 28.05.–29.05.2010," Volby.cz, http://www.volby.cz/pls/ps2010/ps2?xjazyk=CZ. A center-right coalition, led by Petr Nečas of the ODS and consisting of the ODS and two new parties, TOP 09 (Tradition, Responsibility, and Prosperity) led by Karel Schwarzenberg and VV (Public Affairs), a fiscally conservative party, took office in July 2010.

17. http://www.volbysr.sk/nrsr2010/sr/tab3.html.

18. Rudolf Tokes, "Hungary's New Political Elites: Adaptation and Change, 1989–1990," *Problems of Communism* 39 (November–December 1990): 44–65. http://www.unz.org/Pub/ProblemsCommunism.

19. George Schopflin, Rudolf Tokes, and Ivan Volgyes, "Leadership Change and Crisis in Hungary," *Problems of Communism* 37, no. 5 (September–October 1988): 23–46.

20. Tereza Vajdová, *An Assessment of Czech Civil Society in 2004: After Fifteen Years of Development* (Prague: Civicus, 2005).

21. See Pavol Demeš, "Non-governmental Organizations and Volunteerism," in *Global Report on Society, Slovakia 2002*, ed. Grigorij Mesežnikov, Miroslav Kollár, and Tom Nicholson (Bratislava: Institute for Public Affairs, 2002); Valerie J. Bunce and Sharon L. Wolchik, "Favorable Conditions and Electoral Revolutions," *Journal of Democracy* 17, no. 4 (October 2006): 5–18.

22. Jana Kadlecová and Katarina Vajdová, "Non-governmental Organizations and Volunteerism," in *Global Report on Society, Slovakia 2003*, ed. Grigorij Mesežnikov and Miroslav Kollár (Bratislava: Institute for Public Affairs, 2004), 605–23.

23. Zdenka Vajdová and Jana Stachová, "Politická kultura české populace v regionálním rozméru," *Czech Sociological Review* 41, no. 5 (2005): 881–903; Zora Bútorová, *Political Culture in Slovakia* (Bratislava: Institute for Public Affairs, 1999).

24. See Sharon Wolchik et al., results of "Citizens Political Attitudes and Values in the Czech Republic and Slovakia," in 1994 and 2004, as reported by STEM, Prague, Czech Republic, FOCUS, and the Institute for Public Affairs, Bratislava, Slovakia.

25. Sharon L. Wolchik, *Czechoslovakia in Transition: Politics, Economics, and Society* (London: Pinter Publishers, 1991).

26. Michal Vašečka, Martina Jurásková, and Tom Nicholson, eds., *Global Report on Roma in Slovakia* (Bratislava: Institute for Public Affairs, 2003).

27. Jiří Pehe, *Vytunelování demokracie* (Prague: Academia, 2002).

28. Economist Intelligence Unit, "Country Report: Czech Republic" (London: Economist Intelligence Unit, 2009), 19; Economist Intelligence Unit, "Country Report: Slovakia" (London: Economist Intelligence Unit, 2009), 18.

29. David Lane, *The End of Inequality? Stratification under State Socialism* (New York: Penguin Books, 1971).

30. Freedom House, "Slovakia," in *Nations in Transit 2009* (Washington, DC: Freedom House, 2009), 494, http://www.freedomhouse.org/report/nations-transit/2009/slovakia#.U9f80lYSAeI.

31. Vašečka, Jurásková, and Nicholson, *Global Report on Roma in Slovakia*; Freedom House, "Slovakia," 494.

32. Jane S. Jaquette and Sharon L. Wolchik, eds., *Women and Democracy: Latin America and Central and Eastern Europe* (Baltimore: Johns Hopkins University Press, 1998).

33. See also Marilyn Rueschemeyer and Sharon L. Wolchik, eds., *Women in Power in Post-communist Parliaments* (Bloomington: Indiana University Press, 2009), for the results of interviews with women deputies in six postcommunist parliaments.

34. "Women in National Parliaments," Inter-parliamentary Union, http://www.ipu.org/wmn-e/classif.htm.

Map 12.0.   Hungary

CHAPTER 12

Hungary

FROM POSTCOMMUNISM TO POPULIST NATIONALISM

Federigo Argentieri

Hungary's transition out of communism began over three decades before 1989 with the 1956 revolution. After the latter was suppressed, its programs remained on a virtual agenda and were gradually reintroduced in the late 1980s, opening the door for the demise of communism elsewhere in Central and Eastern Europe: it was, after all, Hungary that cut the barbed wire to bring down the Iron Curtain in the summer of 1989, starting a chain of events that forced the hand of the East German and Czechoslovak leaderships. In large part, the smoothness of its transition was a result of the distance Hungary had traveled in economic reforms and its limited political liberalization after the repression of the late 1950s, as well as the success of reform movements within the party and of intellectual dissent in the late 1980s. From the mid-1960s on, Hungarians had lived with "goulash communism" and its guarantees of satisfactory supplies of food and consumer goods in exchange for the appearance of support for the regime. Whereas other systems actively repressed dissidents and those who questioned the system, Hungary was renowned for the mantra "He who is not against us is with us." Not surprisingly then, Hungary's transition was the product of ongoing and overlapping discussions and a series of roundtables that involved reform communists and intellectual groups whose roots were framed by Hungarian historical debates. The democracy that resulted has been one of the most politically stable and—at least until 2008—economically prosperous of the postcommunist world.

Hungary was also the first country, in 1994, to vote former communists back into power with an absolute majority of parliamentary seats. In 2010, a new phase began, characterized by a stronger emphasis on nationalism and the central role of a charismatic leader, which, along with a catchall economic policy and some authoritarian features, constitute the classic ingredients of populism.[1]

In the late spring of 1989, a twenty-six-year-old bearded graduate in law spoke in extremely blunt terms to a large crowd in Budapest's Heroes' Square: the occasion was the solemn reburial of Imre Nagy and his associates, who had been executed thirty-one years earlier and dumped into mass graves. The speech demanded the immediate withdrawal of Soviet troops from Hungary, which frightened many an observer on grounds that such request was premature and could have backfired; the speaker was Viktor Orbán, who became the favorite politician of international public opinion supporting democratic change in the region.

A quarter century later, that same Viktor Orbán triumphed in the April 2014 parliamentary elections, securing for the second legislature in a row a supermajority (i.e., two-thirds) of 133 out of 199 available seats for his party, the Alliance of Young Democrats (FiDeSz), and its junior ally, the Christian Democratic People's Party (KDNP). True, the coalition's percentage of the vote was considerably smaller than in 2010, and the opposition forces increased their score, but it all happened in the context of a new electoral law that downsized seats from 386 to 199 and redesigned electoral districts in a way almost admittedly meant to help the incumbents retain a majority. Quite aptly, Princeton professor Kim Lane Scheppele, the most relentless Western critic of Orbán's policies, defined the 2014 elections as "legal but not fair"; the Organization for Security and Co-operation in Europe expressed a similar sentiment.[2]

In spring 2010, Hungary had celebrated the twentieth anniversary of the first democratic election after communism with a remarkable political turnaround. In April, the center-right party FiDeSz had won a stunning 68.14 percent of votes—that is, a two-thirds majority—leaving the rival Hungarian Socialist Party (MSzP), which had been in office since 2002 and between 1994 and 1998, with a meager 15.28 percent, less than one-fourth the FiDeSz score. The other four parties that had gained seats in 1990 disappeared from parliament and were replaced by the far-right Jobbik, with 12.18 percent of the vote, and the new Politics Can Be Different (LMP) environmental party, with 4.15 percent. The victorious party was thus empowered to amend the constitution and immediately started to pass legislation such as granting Magyar citizenship to Hungarians abroad—a move that raised suspicion and concern in neighboring Slovakia and Romania.[3] On June 29, 2010, former Olympic champion Pál Schmitt (individual sword, Munich 1972) was elected the fourth president of the Hungarian Republic since 1990, only to resign less than two years later over a plagiarism scandal. He was replaced by János Áder, a member of the European Parliament and former speaker of parliament.

In 2011, one year into its two-thirds majority, FiDeSz passed its own new Fundamental Law[4] (all other parliamentary groups voted against it). It subsequently amended it in ways that many commentators viewed as authoritarian,[5] capping it all with a new electoral system that allegedly goes in the same (i.e., authoritarian) direction.

Historical Background and Communist Experiences

Hungary's history has played a major role in its present. Its triumphs and defeats left a complicated legacy for both the communist rulers and the postcommunist system. Reunified as of 1713 inside the Austrian Empire, Hungarians had far greater cultural independence than the nations that were part of the Ottoman and Russian empires. The Age of Reforms triggered a revolution in 1848–1849 in Hungary for freedom and independence. That revolution failed, but changes in the geopolitical realities of Central Europe subsequently resulted in a dual Austro-Hungarian Empire in which Hungarians had separate administrations in every field but military and foreign affairs. As a result, by the end of the nineteenth century, Hungary's economy and culture had blossomed. In the cities, the workers prospered, even as the countryside remained backward and relations with most ethnic and religious minorities remained tense.

All this came to an end when the expansion of the Austro-Hungarian Empire into Bosnia-Herzegovina and its alliance with Germany brought the empire into World War I. As punishment for its defeat, large portions of what had been Hungarian land were occupied by Czechoslovakia and the Balkan states of Romania and Serbia with the endorsement of Western powers. Meanwhile, a democratic republic was proclaimed in Hungary, which was quickly replaced by the Bolshevik Republic of Councils in the spring and summer of 1919. Bolshevism in Hungary, although it often disregarded Vladimir Lenin's instructions and had a certain cultural liveliness, was still characterized by mostly brutal and chaotic policies, which left communism with a quite negative image. The Bolshevik experiment ended in a counterrevolutionary offensive by part of Hungary's new military, led by Admiral Miklós Horthy. By August 1919, he and his forces had suppressed the Red regime and appointed a new regency government under Horthy, who encouraged anti-Jewish pogroms on account of the infamous equivalence between Bolshevism and Jewishness. To compound the political battles, the Trianon peace treaty, signed in 1920, resulted in Hungary losing not only the areas inhabited by other ethnic groups but also much of its own historic territory: 120,000 square miles and half its population were taken. Over 3 million Hungarians were cut off from Hungary.

These losses, coupled with the toppled Red regime and the debacle of World War I, left Hungarians wary of and at odds with both the Soviets and the West. During the interwar years, students began their classes by chanting, "Nem, nem, soha!" (No, no, never!), meaning that they would never accept the injustice of the Trianon treaty. In domestic politics, a semi-authoritarian system emerged that outlawed the Communist Party and limited voting rights as well as Jews' access to universities,[6] the latter based on the false assumption that automatically linked Jews to communism. As pointed out in a classic essay by István Bibó (1911–1979), one of the most original political thinkers of the region (and a main inspiration for the young Viktor Orbán), this policy was part of a more general problem caused by the collapse of prewar Hungary, which took with it the gradually successful assimilation of most of the Jewish population into Magyar society and made the Jews suddenly appear responsible for all of the catastrophes that had befallen the nation.[7]

After the end of communism in Hungary, this stereotypical anti-Jewish prejudice would pop up anew—not only in the surge of parties of the far right, such as Miép and Jobbik, but also inside pro-government forces. Current prime minister Orbán's longtime friend and proud carrier of FiDeSz party card number five, Zsolt Bayer, for instance, uttered in an infamous article published in the daily *Magyar Hirlap* (January 4, 2011), his regret for "all the Jews not having been buried to their necks at Orgovány," the site of one of the most gruesome Horthy-sponsored pogroms carried out in the fall of 1919.[8]

The combination of the Great Depression and Hungarians' interest in reclaiming their territory drew Hungary into the orbit of Adolf Hitler's Germany. After the Munich Agreement and the 1938–1939 dismantling of Czechoslovakia, southern Slovakia and Ruthenia were returned to Hungary. Then, after the Molotov-Ribbentrop Pact, Hungary regained most of Transylvania. In return, Hungary had to not only increase its restrictions on Jews but also participate in the 1941 invasions of Yugoslavia and the Soviet

Union. At the end of World War II, as Hitler's position weakened with the German defeat at Stalingrad and the Allied landing in Italy, Admiral Horthy tried to switch sides. Hitler responded by occupying Hungary in March 1944 and replacing Horthy (who was arrested in October 1944) with Ferenc Szálasi, head of the Arrow Cross Party, the Hungarian equivalent of the Nazis. More than half a million Jews were deported and killed. At the same time, the Soviets invaded Hungarian territory, which they occupied by April 1945, after a merciless and destructive fight.

Hungary's communist experience proved an even more complicated legacy for its transition. During the forty-four years between the end of World War II and 1989, communist rule in Hungary swung from relative liberalism to extreme repression and back again. These shifts left memories of a democratic regime that was rapidly co-opted or paralyzed by the communists; a moment of hope for freedom and a return to the West in 1956, followed by a brutal Soviet invasion and years of repression; and then the placating of the opposition with goulash communism. Ultimately, communist rule disintegrated on its own when the economy began to fail in the 1980s. This history included liberal communists and repressive communists, as well as good memories of economic and social welfare and bad memories of tanks rolling into Budapest and shooting at demonstrators and innocent civilians.

The communist takeover of Hungary took almost three years. Winston Churchill and Joseph Stalin had agreed in October 1944 that Hungary would be evenly split between the Soviet sphere of influence and the West. Although Hungary was occupied by the Red Army, the first parliamentary elections in November 1945 were free and fair, although their follow-up was not. The centrist, Christian, anticommunist Independent Smallholders Party won an absolute majority of over 57 percent of the votes, yet was unable to form a government by itself because the Allied Control Commission, dominated by the Soviets, forced it to go into a coalition with three left-of-center parties: the social democrats, the communists, and the National Peasant Party. In February 1946, Smallholder Zoltán Tildy was elected president in what would prove to be democracy's last gasp.

Even as Hungary was establishing a democratic government, albeit in an awkward coalition of anticommunist centrists and left-wing parties, Mátyás Rákosi, head of the Hungarian Communist Party, was engaged in cutting democracy down through what he called "salami tactics" (using the secret police and other pressures to slice off pieces of the noncommunist parties until there was nothing left). The communists first pressured the Smallholders to expel their "right wing." Then, as soon as the Treaty of Paris was signed in 1947 and the Allied Control Commission was dissolved, the main leader of the Smallholders, Béla Kovács, was arrested for "espionage" by the Soviet troops, who had remained in Hungary in order to secure connections with their contingent in Austria. Finally, Prime Minister Ferenc Nagy, who had resisted every attempt to nationalize property, was forced into exile. The social democrats were then given the choice of merging with the communists or facing serious consequences. Some accepted the unification. Others refused and were, at the least, forced out of public life. Some, such as the particularly stubborn Anna Kéthly, were imprisoned. The Hungarian Workers' Party was born of this unification in June 1948, signaling clearly the communists' final victory.

Having successfully taken over the political institutions, the communists openly imposed control over all other sectors of society. The economy was transformed:

agriculture was forcibly collectivized, and the rest of the economy was nationalized. A massive industrialization drive shifted the economy from an agricultural to an industrial one. These policies were accompanied by an exodus from the countryside to the cities, and millions of young people suddenly got a chance at education. Religious institutions were attacked. Not only were citizens punished for supporting religion but the head of the Hungarian Catholic Church, Cardinal József Mindszenty, was arrested, tried, and sentenced to life imprisonment. Terror even hit the Communist Party's own elite. The show trial and execution of Minister of the Interior László Rajk for being a Titoist agent in 1949 came to symbolize the spiral of terror that lasted until Stalin's death in 1953.

After Stalin's death, the different factions in the Kremlin manipulated Hungarian politics. Control of the state and the party was split between Rákosi, as head of the party, and Imre Nagy, the first communist minister of agriculture, as prime minister. The Soviets pressed the Hungarian leadership to shift from attempts at establishing heavy industry to greater production of consumer goods. Nagy pushed reform further to include a relaxation of the terror and an end to the permanent hunt for "traitors" that had paralyzed Hungarian life since the communist takeover. But as the balance of power shifted from liberals to conservatives in the Kremlin, Nagy was forced out, and Rákosi returned to power.

In 1955 and 1956, to achieve an accord with Yugoslavia and follow through on the denunciations of Stalin and his cult of the personality, Nikita Khrushchev, the new Soviet leader, forced more change in Hungary. Rákosi, who had boasted of being "Stalin's best Hungarian disciple," was dismissed from office and went into exile in the Soviet Union. He was replaced as head of the Communist Party by the equally Stalinist Ernő Gerő. At the same time, the verdict against László Rajk was nullified, and his body was publicly reburied. This step, coupled with the example of liberalization in Poland during the Poznań events and the Polish October, as well as the constant shifts in leadership, convinced Hungarians that change was possible.

The Hungarian Revolution[9] would remain seared in the national memory even though it was an officially taboo subject until 1989. It began with student demonstrations on October 23, 1956. Within a few hours, Soviet tanks entered and fired on the demonstrators. Three days later, a new government was brought in, with János Kádár as head of the Communist Party and Imre Nagy as prime minister. By this time, though, virtually the entire population was engaged in the struggle for freedom and the effort to create a genuine pluralist democracy. Parties abolished in 1948 resurfaced and were brought into Nagy's executive. The Hungarian Workers' Party dissolved itself and formed a new Hungarian Socialist Workers' Party (HSWP), and grassroots national committees and workers' councils mushroomed. After briefly starting to withdraw their troops, the Soviets intervened a second time on November 4 to suppress the revolution, at which point the Hungarian government, buoyed by the increasingly loud demands of insurgents and the population throughout the country, denounced the Warsaw Pact even as Soviet troops killed thousands of demonstrators, jailed thousands more, and sent thousands into exile.

János Kádár went to the Soviet Union and agreed to lead a new government with the support of the occupying Soviet troops. When Nagy refused to resign as prime minister,

Photo 12.1.   This statue of Imre Nagy in Budapest was put up in 1996 for the centennial of his birth. In 1989, a state funeral and reburial of Nagy and the other 1956 leaders who had been given the death penalty and buried in unmarked graves in 1958 had set the stage for the transition away from communism.

he and other leaders loyal to the revolution were arrested and deported to Romania. In 1958, they were secretly tried in Hungary, sentenced to death, executed the next day, and buried in unmarked graves. Much as the Rajk reburial had opened the floodgates in 1956, the memorial service for and reburial of Nagy and others in June 1989 signaled the end of communist control and was followed by the dissolution of the HSWP.

The repression that accompanied the Soviet occupation and the reestablishment of a one-party system under Kádár's control lasted into the 1960s. In 1963, following negotiations with the United Nations, some surviving freedom fighters and leaders were released from prison, and Kádár turned away from repression. The New Economic Mechanism (NEM) was introduced in 1968 and brought a real improvement in the Hungarian standard of living and the availability of goods. It provided for "profit" to become a motive for state enterprises and for open wage differentiation. Although the central planning process persisted under the NEM, it no longer dictated the details of what was produced and how. Instead, it set priorities and left decisions about production and pay to factory managers. Once collectivization of the agricultural sector was quite ruthlessly completed in 1961, farms were allowed to direct their own production and engage in side businesses. Peasants, along with the urban population, also received cradle-to-grave social welfare benefits. In the process, the NEM recognized a range of unions and professional organizations as players in the policy process. Although Hungary remained a part of the Council for Mutual Economic Assistance (CMEA) and was tied to ruble-based exchange rates and Soviet bloc economic priorities, it opened up to Western investment and became the recipient of sizable loans, which were used almost exclusively to support improved living standards. In the 1970s that investment brought in some Hungarian refugees from 1956 as well as West Europeans who set up factories in Hungary and imported and exported goods. The result was a consumer economy vibrant and varied enough to make Hungary "the happiest barrack in the camp" until the 1980s, when the forward and backward moves in the NEM and the aging of the economy showed in the failings of the consumer sector.

Politically, communism in Hungary from the mid-1960s was consistently less repressive than elsewhere in the bloc. This difference was due in part to the fact that the population was both satisfied with what it had economically and wary of trying for political change after the experience of 1956. In part, it resulted from János Kádár's equally vivid memory of 1956 and his concern with preventing tensions inside the party and between the party and the populace. Dissident groups, far weaker than in Poland, existed without any real repression or mass popular support. After the mid-1960s, Hungary's borders were more open for its own citizens and for émigrés and tourists. Life, for Hungarians, was a trade-off: political silence for comparative economic prosperity.

By mid-1980s, however, the elaborate system of carrots and sticks that had held Hungarian communist rule in place was crumbling. The New Economic Mechanism, which had already suffered a political setback between 1972 and 1977, was now worn down. The annual growth in gross domestic product (GDP) decreased from 4.8 percent in the 1970s to 1.8 percent between 1980 and 1985 and continued on a rapid downward trajectory.[10] For workers, tensions over wages grew more acute because the instruments being used to manage the economy did not allow employers to raise wages to improve enterprise performance.[11] Thus, Hungarians' real incomes stagnated and began declining, causing savings to decrease.

At the same time, changes in the Kremlin reduced whatever fear remained of Soviet repression. The Soviet occupation troops meant little when Mikhail Gorbachev came to power and made it clear that reform in the Soviet Union would evolve in ways the Hungarians had not dared attempt and that the Soviet Union would no longer rein in its satellites. The rise of Poland's Solidarity movement in the early 1980s inspired Hungarian dissidents to publish journals that challenged historical taboos. Repression of dissidents was not an option: Hungary had signed the Helsinki Final Act in 1975. Perhaps more importantly, it was increasingly indebted to the International Monetary Fund (IMF) and other Western financial institutions. So its leaders could not risk the kinds of financial sanctions imposed on Poland after the imposition of martial law if it was going to try to keep its economic bargain with the Hungarian people. And dissent involved only a tiny section of the population.

In addition, Kádár himself had aged. Whereas Hungary had changed, he had not. When he did appear in public, his hands shook, and his speeches fell flat. The men who had risen up behind him in the party, Károly Grósz, György Lázár, and Miklós Németh, began to take the lead in the public eye and behind the scenes. Their postures, though, were increasingly critical of Hungary's status quo and divided over what should come next and how to deal publicly with the past and present. In 1988, Kádár was forced to retire.

The Transition

As the regime's system of carrots and sticks crumbled, intellectuals in and out of the party began to meet and push the old limits. In June 1985, a good part of Hungary's intellectual elite met at Monor to discuss the failings of the system since 1956. In these discussions, which happened with no interference from the party or police, the political divide that had characterized Hungarian thinking from the 1930s reemerged. The "people's nation-alists" looked on the peasantry and Christianity as the base of the Hungarian spirit and wanted to find a "third way" between capitalism and communism. The "urbanists" were secular and not nationalist. The people's nationalists pressed for Hungary to intervene to prevent the increasing repression of Hungarians abroad, particularly in Romania, where Nicolae Ceaușescu was engaged in a full-scale assault on Romania's sizable Hungarian minority. The urbanists, on the other hand, emerged as liberal democrats and defenders of human rights at home and sponsored radical pro-market economic reforms along with North Atlantic Treaty Organization (NATO) and European Union (EU) membership.

This initial meeting, the crumbling of the economy, and the visible decrease in Soviet power or interest in Central and Eastern Europe triggered the emergence of a plethora of different political groupings that have played a role not only in the transition but also in democratic Hungary. In 1987, the Hungarian Democratic Forum (MDF) formed as a political and cultural movement based on Christian democracy and the traditions of "people's nationalism." Its members were quite willing to tolerate and even compromise with the reformist wing of the HSWP. In 1988, a group of young lawyers founded the

Alliance of Young Democrats, or FiDeSz. It was far more outspoken than earlier movements and opposed both the reformist and nonreformist versions of the communist system. Months later, the Committee for an Act of Historical Justice (TIB) emerged, demanding the political, civic, and moral rehabilitation of the veterans of the 1956 revolution and pension benefits for its survivors. Then, a Network of Free Democratic Initiatives appeared and pushed for a reduced role of the state and the protection of individual rights; it later transformed into the Alliance of Free Democrats (SzDSz), the third of the key noncommunist parties in democratic Hungary.

These parties and two associations representing the intelligentsia met between March and June 1989 in what was known as the Opposition Roundtable (ORT). Their ultimate goal was to come to a consensus so that they could be monolithic in their negotiations with the regime before it had a chance to pass reform legislation and take control of the transition. They agreed to negotiate with the HSWP but only about holding free elections, not about what would follow. In the process, the ORT discussions spilled out and further challenged communist control.

As the opposition crystallized into groups and then political parties, the HSWP began to fall apart. After Kádár was forced to resign, Károly Grósz, a relative conservative, took over. But his was not the only faction in the HSWP. Younger reformers like Miklós Németh and Imre Pozsgay, in alliance with older ones such as Rezsö Nyers, struggled within the party. On the outside, the party's position vacillated. Grósz ordered the suppression of the demonstrations on the anniversary of Imre Nagy's execution in June 1988, which had been promoted by all the new organizations. Then, the younger and more liberal leaders began to reconsider the "1956 events," met with opposition leaders, and symbolically removed the Iron Curtain in May 1989 by cutting the barbed-wire fence between Austria and Hungary. As a compromise between the two groups, a "committee of experts" made up of scholars and politicians was established in 1989 to investigate the real causes of the 1956 events. Its report created a major political stir. The Kádárist notion that the 1956 events were a "counterrevolution" was rejected, and the events were designated a "legitimate national uprising."

Preparations began for the reburial of Nagy and the other leaders of the Hungarian Revolution. Kádárist-style rule was clearly in its last days. In the spring, the party divested itself of much of its power, even shifting the responsibility for dealing with the politically explosive reburial to the state. Old parties that had been a part of Hungary's moment of democracy and reemerged briefly in 1956 reappeared only to fade away once the transition had happened. Despite the objections of some in the HSWP and leaders in Bulgaria, Germany, Romania, and Czechoslovakia, the funeral of Imre Nagy was held as a public ceremony in Budapest's Heroes' Square. As more than 250,000 people observed in the square and millions more watched on television, the reform communists stood as honorary pallbearers. New political leaders from the new and old parties gave speeches. The leaders who had survived, including Nagy's press spokesman, Miklós Vásárhelyi, "spoke of justice, national unity, and the opportunity for 'a peaceful transition to a free and democratic society.'" As already mentioned, the then young FiDeSz leader, Viktor Orbán, explicitly demanded the withdrawal of Soviet troops.[12]

With the Communist Party shifting its powers to the state, the history of 1956 rewritten, and the reburial of Nagy complete, there was no stopping the transition. Negotiations between the ORT and the regime began on June 13, 1989 (simultaneously with the semi-free Polish elections). The HSWP agreed to focus only on establishing the rules for free elections and amendments to the communist constitution rather than to try to follow the Polish model of negotiating political, social, and economic issues as well. In exchange, the ORT parties had to agree to a triangular table, with the HSWP's voting power aided by the inclusion of the trade unions as minor players in the negotiations. On October 23, 1989, the Third Hungarian Republic was proclaimed. A week earlier, the communist HSWP had declared its transformation into the Western-style, social democratic Hungarian Socialist Party (HSP) and announced its intention to participate in the forthcoming elections.

The final battle of the transition was over whether to elect the president or the parliament first. For the ex-communists, the best scenario was to hold the presidential election first because their leader, Pozsgay, was still popular for dismantling the Communist Party and was the best-known politician. The Alliance of Free Democrats and FiDeSz refused to agree to this plan and instead organized a referendum on whether to first elect the president or the parliament (whose members would then elect the president). On this issue, the ORT groups split from the Hungarian Democratic Forum, urging abstention rather than changing the roundtable agreement to elect the president and then the parliament. In that referendum, the option of holding the parliamentary elections first won with 50.07 percent. The monolithic opposition started to divide.

Political Institutions

The Roundtable Accords, as they were modified after the referendum, and the old parliament's vote for the president to be directly elected provided for a parliamentary system. After its election in March 1990, the initial center-right parliament revised the transitional constitution so that only a simple majority was needed to pass most laws and the president was elected by the parliament every five years by a two-thirds majority. The single-house parliament was to be elected every four years with a mixed electoral system and also to select the prime minister. The prime minister was responsible for selecting and guiding the ministers. The president had ceremonial powers and some ability to intervene when there were problems within the system. None of these powers were decisive, however.

Árpád Göncz, elected president by the parliament, created a model for the Hungarian presidency that generated criticism but also secured his reelection in 1995. His model entitled the president, who represents the country, to work behind the scenes to reach consensus among the various political groups. Through this process, Göncz and his successors have tried to avoid identifying with one side or the other. At the same time, Göncz used the ability to approve the removal of such officials as the heads of radio and television to push the parties away from partisanship in these areas. His successor, Ferenc Mádl (elected in 2000) followed this model. László Sólyom, who was president from 2005 to 2010, on the other hand, was often criticized for an alleged bias toward FiDeSz.

Dominant coalitions shifted from election to election. Until 2010, all of the cabinets were products of coalitions of centrist parties, and none was controlled by a single party. József Antall, Péter Boross, and Viktor Orbán served as conservative prime ministers. There have been four socialist-sponsored prime ministers since 1990—Gyula Horn, Péter Medgyessy, Ferenc Gyurcsány, and Gordon Bajnai. None of the prime ministers carried out real policy shifts until Orbán's 2010 triumph. A former left-leaning liberal, yet consistently anticommunist, Orbán had astutely moved to the right in 1993 and 1994 on realizing that the death of Antall, founding member of the MDF, had created a huge vacuum on that side of the political spectrum. In his first mandate as leader of a supermajority, he imposed a style of government that left little or no room for collegiality.

The stability of Hungary's political system was clear early on when József Antall, the first postcommunist prime minister, died in office in late 1993. He was immediately replaced by another Hungarian Democratic Forum leader, Péter Boross, who served six months until that parliament's term ended. After the socialist's loss in the 2004 elections to the European Parliament, the Hungarian Socialist Party shifted its leadership to respond to the public's disaffection. This allowed Ferenc Gyurcsány to become the first prime minister to serve two successive terms until he also resigned in spring 2009, to be replaced by Bajnai.

Although the ministers have changed with every election, the upper ranks of the state bureaucracy have remained quite stable. Because no effective legislation purged the state of workers from the communist era, they were allowed to remain in their positions if they declared allegiance to the new system. Where changes have occurred, they have been the result of the government's efforts to make Hungary's overall bureaucracy smaller and more professional. In the 2010–2014 legislature, the supermajority FiDeSz government made an effort to ensure political loyalty from all sectors of the state apparatus, thereby attracting severe criticism and frequent accusations of authoritarianism. The Orbán government's reply argues that most formerly communist bureaucrats had remained glued to their posts and were inclined to be disloyal toward the new government, thereby requiring serious streamlining in the country's interest.

Elections and Political Parties

Elections for the first freely elected parliament since 1945 were scheduled for March 25, 1990, with a runoff on April 8. The electoral system provided for a parliament of 386 seats, of which 176 were to be elected in single-member districts with a French-type, double-ballot, majoritarian system, and 152 were to be selected from party lists for each region using a proportional system. The remaining seats (a minimum of 58) would be distributed to national party lists to compensate for "extra votes" that were over and above what a candidate needed to get elected or had been cast for losing candidates in the single-member districts. The goal of this redistribution was to keep the parliament truly representative of the overall national vote. At the same time, any party that received less than 4 percent of the vote nationally was disqualified from seating deputies in the parliament. Although the system has been responsive to changes in Hungarian public opinion, until 2010 it was also extremely stable, with governing coalitions shifting regularly from right to left but both sides remaining close to the center and ready to step over ideological divides.

The unquestionable winner of the first election was the MDF, whose president, József Antall, was inaugurated as prime minister in May 1990. Six parties received enough votes to make it into that parliament. Three (MDF, SzDSz, and FiDeSz) were brand-new. They won 277 seats in this first election and would remain the centerpieces of Hungarian politics into the twenty-first century. One (the HSP) could be called both new and old, as it was made up mostly of the reform wing of the old HSWP. The remaining two (the Independent Smallholders Party and the People's Christian Democrats) had existed before the communist period. Together, these two got a total of sixty-five seats. Among these parties, there was a clear consensus about the direction Hungary should take: toward Europe, democracy, and capitalism. The differences had more to do with the details of Hungary's move forward and assessments of the past. These divisions reflected the old Hungarian separation of people's nationalists and urbanists. As Bill Lomax has observed,

> Hungarian parties are, almost without exception, elite groups of intellectuals, often long-standing personal friends more like political clubs than representative institutions. Many of Antall's government ministers went to the same school with him. Most of the Free Democrats were together in the democratic opposition. Several of [FiDeSz]'s leaders studied law together. . . . The political identities and cleavages they do represent are based neither on social interests, nor political programmes, nor structured belief systems. In fact, to the extent that such cleavages do exist in Hungarian politics, they are found to cut across the parties almost equally—each party has its liberals, its nationalists, its conservatives, its social-democrats, its populists, its radicals.[13]

Initially, the leaders of all the parties (except FiDeSz) were intellectuals from academia and the arts. The leaders and members of FiDeSz, or the Young Democrats, were different. They and their constituents were young people. Most of the party leaders had studied law together in the 1980s. As a result, until 1993, they were less bound by ideology and more West European in their thinking and presentation.

In 1994, the Hungarian Socialist Party was the first successor to an old ruling Communist Party of Central and Eastern Europe to be reelected and returned to power with an absolute majority of seats. Yet, in the first of a series of unlikely coalitions, the HSP joined with the Alliance of Free Democrats. Their gains were a reaction to people's initial disappointment with what the transition had brought and also to the weakness in the Hungarian Democratic Forum brought to a head by József Antall's death and the splintering effect of the Hungarian Truth and Life Party led by István Csurka. Like the Polish social democrats, leaders of the HSP talked not of returning to the old communist system but of modernization, economic and political reform, and joining Europe. The Alliance of Free Democrats actually lost votes in 1994, but the Hungarian Democratic Forum lost far more, and the Alliance of Free Democrats was—despite its history of opposition to communism—the largest and most viable partner for the HSP.

In 1998, there was a shift in all the major players' positions and strengths. The Hungarian Democratic Forum had essentially collapsed by 1998. Most of the precommunist parties could no longer get enough votes to seat deputies in parliament. In the aftermath of Antall's death and the partnership of the Alliance of Free Democrats and HSP (confirmed by their signing of the Democratic Charter in 1991), FiDeSz moved to the right. Its leaders were able, despite the simultaneous success of the extreme rightist Truth and Life Party, to present themselves as the legitimate successors of the declining MDF. The party leader, Viktor Orbán, when he became prime minister, openly claimed Antall's legacy. Their coalition was made up of the Smallholders and the remnants of the MDF. To further their popularity, they also added "Hungarian Civic Party" to their name (it later became "Hungarian Civic Alliance").

Toward the end of the legislature, Orbán signaled his intentions to profoundly revise recent Hungarian history as told in the communist and postcommunist versions. In late February 2002, he inaugurated a statue to Béla Kovács on the fifty-fifth anniversary of his arrest and deportation, as well as Budapest's Terror House Museum, a controversial yet interesting institution intended to equate the Hungarian versions of Nazism and communism and the crimes committed by their proponents. While nobody took issue with the first decision, the second was seriously questioned for its portrayal of historical accuracy.[14]

A few weeks later, the balance shifted back to the coalition of the socialists and the Alliance of Free Democrats after a close race with the Young Democrats and the Democratic Forum Alliance. The two parties were able to govern with a razor-thin majority. However, when the coalition lost in its first elections to the European Parliament and right-wing and Euroskeptic candidates took a number of districts, Péter Medgyessy (who had been a member of the HSWP, a banker in France, and a leader in the private sector in Hungary) resigned. He was replaced by Ferenc Gyurcsány, who had gone on from the Communist Youth Organization to become one of the wealthiest businessmen in Hungary. Under his leadership, the Socialist–Free Democratic Alliance was the first coalition to win two successive elections. This made Gyurcsany the first Hungarian prime minister to serve more than one term, as he led the party to a much clearer victory in 2006.

Until the riots that followed the revelation that Gyurcsány had lied about the status of the Hungarian economy just before the fiftieth anniversary celebrations of the 1956 Hungarian Revolution, political parties and groups in Hungary were quite restrained and remained very centrist. The closeness of the parties ideologically, their ability to form coalitions, and the low turnout rate in Hungarian elections at all levels since the transition began are all reasons for and demonstrations of Hungarian voters' lack of engagement with particular parties and political battles. In fact, many local government elections have had to be held a second time because less than 50 percent of the population voted in the regular election round. This disengagement changed, at least momentarily, after the Gyurcsány revelation. Budapest and other major cities were rocked by riots by angry and disillusioned voters, which in the long run led to Gyurcsány's resignation in 2009 and the

Photo 12.2. Riots in Budapest in 2006 after a recording of Prime Minister Ferenc Gyurcsány admitting to party members that he had lied to the country about the economy was leaked to the public. (MTI Foto, Olah Tibor)

installation of a caretaker government until the next elections. Gyurcsány's resignation, however, did not prevent a crushing defeat for the socialists in 2010.

Economic Transition

Economic weakness has been the Achilles' heel of Hungarian politics. In the last decade of communism, borrowing money from abroad was the regime's only way to sustain the living standards of its population and keep itself in power. Even with that infusion of foreign loan money, the transition in Hungary was stirred by the stagnation of the economy and its double-digit inflation. The new leaders of Hungary inherited far less debt and a far better economy than their Polish counterparts, but they still faced high popular expectations, a debt of over $20 billion from the Kádár regime's borrowing, and the disaster wrought by the collapse of the CMEA market.

Hungary avoided the Polish "shock therapy" model. Instead, it began by creating a "social market economy" that moved toward private ownership in industries producing consumer goods and providing services. Although legislation promised to begin bankruptcy actions against failing enterprises, very few large-scale industries were closed. Instead, foreign investment and ownership were used as tools to get the economy going.

Hungary's transition was complicated by its high debt to the West, the collapse of the Soviet market, and the end of cheap Soviet oil and natural gas supplies. Between 1989 and 1992, Hungary's GDP had collapsed by 18 percent, "a decline comparable only to the worst of the Great Depression of the 1930s."[15] Western banks and governments wrote off much of Hungary's debt when they wrote off the Polish debt as part of a package to help both the Hungarian and Polish economies correct themselves. The IMF, European Community, and World Bank also provided large loans.

Only in March 1995 was the Bokros Plan for serious economic reform implemented. This reform program encouraged privatization with monetary incentives and openness to foreign investment. At the same time, state enterprises were allowed to survive, and new private enterprises were established alongside them. The goal was for these private enterprises to edge out the state enterprises. A similar policy governed the reforms in agriculture and social services. The costs of health care and education ballooned as the state continued to provide funds, while the wealthy opted out and provided for themselves by creating private health and educational institutions. By 2005, 80 percent of the Hungarian economy was in private hands. Foreign ownership went from about 4 percent in 1990 to 52.1 percent in 1997.

The reforms all seemed to work in the first decade. The population was satisfied. By 1997, the economy had begun to grow by 4 to 5 percent annually. However, the gains came with real hidden costs; many hard economic moves were avoided, and the economy depended instead on its Kádár-era base and foreign investment. Keeping costly social welfare programs and encouraging foreign investment by allowing profits to go abroad meant that the apparent upward course was far from secure. Government accounting only hid the problem. In 2006, as Gyurcsány's leaked admission to party elites indicated, Hungary's deficit stood at 10 percent. The rhetoric of the ensuing demonstrations and the opposition politicians who led them showed that they had no alternative economic proposal. Rather than deal with the social consequences of how Hungary could best deal with its budget deficit and rationalize its economy, political rhetoric focused on accusations that individuals were communist or anti-Semitic. The promised tax reduction was not to be; taxes actually had to go up to pay for increases in government spending and inflation and to placate foreign investors. The plan for Hungary to adopt the euro in 2010 (which required a deficit below 3 percent) was also called into question as pure wishful thinking and turned out to be utterly unrealistic. But the anger dissipated when it was clear there were no alternatives to the course Hungary was on.

On winning the elections in 2010, Orbán set the country on a path characterized by strong anti–foreign capital rhetoric (and deeds) and various measures declared to be aimed at enhancing domestic resources as opposed to leaving a peripheral Hungary at the mercy of the global market. According to the pronouncements of FiDeSz, only in this context can the necessary budget cuts be implemented and economic growth encouraged. By late 2013, the results were encouraging on both accounts, which was one of the key factors leading to the 2014 FiDeSz victory.[16]

Social Consequences

The social consequences in Hungary were no different from those in other countries when they began to transform their economic and political systems. Despite the problems in the

Hungarian economy in 1989, Hungarians started the transition with higher expectations because they were accustomed to living better than most in the bloc. As Prime Minister Antall detailed in his presentation of the government program after the 1990 elections, the country faced declining health and falling living standards. He stated that Hungarians' life expectancy was the lowest in Europe, that for the past decade the number of deaths had exceeded the number of births, and that because of the polluted environment and the need to work long hours, the health and life expectancy of middle-aged Hungarians were the worst among civilized nations.[17]

The limited economic reforms Hungary undertook at the start of the 1990s left 1 million of Hungary's population of 10.6 million living below subsistence level and 2 million living at the officially defined social minimum. Those hardest hit were pensioners, families with more than two children, and those who found themselves unemployed. Homelessness also appeared because factories closed workers' hostels, citizens were unable to pay the increases in their rent, and people came to Budapest in search of jobs. Roma and illegal aliens—largely ethnic Romanians or Hungarians who had "escaped" the more disastrous Romanian economy—added to the numbers of homeless.[18]

In the decade and a half that followed, Hungary's living standards continued to fall. Hungarians, accustomed to rising consumption, have proved less willing than Poles to tolerate a considerable drop in living standards. Also, public opinion has focused on whether consumer goods markets function reasonably well, whether most goods are readily available, and whether there is a "visible" economic crisis.[19] Hence, consumption rose more slowly than incomes, and with real income actually falling, consumption has declined sharply. Increases in consumer prices were exacerbated by subsidy reductions and price liberalization.

While some had prospered during the 1980s, those lacking the skills needed to access the wealth from the "second economy" and those reliant on state incomes did relatively badly.[20] Job opportunities for unskilled or uneducated people diminished throughout this time as a result of a continuing decrease in the number of vacant jobs and the shift in labor demand toward skilled workers.[21]

Hungary became steadily more polarized, and Hungary's ethnic groups, particularly the Roma and illegal aliens, suffered from the economic reforms. While in 1971 Roma males and females had been regularly employed and earned incomes, from the late 1980s onward, they were systematically pushed out of the labor market.[22] By 1993, this trend resulted in shockingly high unemployment figures for the Roma. Less than half of the Roma unemployment rate could be accounted for by factors like Romas' lower educational levels and disadvantageous distribution of labor power. The rest was due to discrimination by employers. Thus, the Roma are generally described as major losers in the economic transition. Although they make up only 5 percent of the total population, approximately 25 percent of the 2 million poor in Hungary are Roma. Moreover, the Roma in Hungary are discriminated against not only by employers but also by state or state-controlled institutions like public education, the national health service, the police, and the courts.[23] In addition, between 2008 and 2009, six apparently random but clearly racially motivated assassinations of Roma people illustrated

Photo 12.3.   Viktor Orbán speaking at the opening of a new industry in 2013. (László Balogh/Reuters/Corbis)

the unresolved situation in which they live and reawakened fearsome ghosts of the country's past. The above-mentioned FiDeSz number five cardholder, Zsolt Bayer, in yet another deplorable outburst in the daily *Magyar Hirlap* (January 5, 2013) exactly two years after his anti-Semitic article, commented on a felony allegedly committed by Roma, calling them "animals deserving to be punished" and stirring up another domestic and international scandal. Although some government and FiDeSz officials distanced themselves from him and he subsequently retracted his statement, at least in part, the government left the impression of taking an ambiguous stand on anti-Roma prejudice and violence.

In its struggle to keep up economic growth and deal with its budget deficit, Hungary has essentially ignored the need to reform its social services. According to the Organisation for Economic Co-operation and Development country survey for 2005, Hungary needed to take strong measures to prevent "failure in the welfare regime change."[24] The problem is that unpopular political decisions must be made to streamline the public health system, limit disability pensions to the really disabled, make labor mobility more effective, and deal with problems in most other state welfare sectors. No political group wants to deal with these issues directly. Conservatives and liberal-socialists are separated more by rhetoric than by concrete differences in economic and social policy.

Neither the left nor the right has championed the needs of Hungary's poor. Instead, they have talked about "trickle-down economics." In the early years of the transition, the government gave in when faced with demonstrations by those who had suffered from the economic reforms. The most famous of these demonstrations were the so-called Taxi Wars in 1990, when taxi drivers and others blocked the streets of Budapest and roads around the country in response to the government's sudden decision to raise the price of gasoline by 66 percent overnight and announcement that the price of other energy products would increase in order to deal with shortages caused by decreases in sales by the Soviet Union. In the end, the government backed down.

Until the 2006 demonstrations, other responses to social problems were far smaller and more subdued. Groups have, when they could, taken matters into their own hands. Some self-help and advocacy groups have been organized, and many, like the homeless, have broken the law to provide for themselves.

Foreign Policy

Hungary was a leader in the move toward Europe. It was the first member of the Soviet bloc to become a member of the Council of Europe. On June 4, 1990, the new and free Hungarian parliament marked the seventieth anniversary of the Trianon peace treaty by adopting a resolution that reiterated the acceptance of its existing borders.

Following the dissolution of Yugoslavia, the CMEA, the Warsaw Treaty Organization, and the Soviet Union itself (all of which happened between June 25 and December 25, 1991), Hungary attempted to conduct bilateral negotiations with its old and new neighbors and to march resolutely toward membership in NATO and the EU. Its attempts to deal with its eastern neighbors were far more politically problematic. The state treaty with Ukraine, signed in 1991, caused major repercussions in domestic politics. A faction within the MDF, led by the playwright István Csurka, openly rejected the agreement on borders and walked out of that party, eventually forming a new group called the Hungarian Truth and Life Party.[25] As the 2013–2014 "Revolution of Dignity" unfolded in Hungary's main eastern neighbor, Orbán took an ambivalent stance on the nature of events, focusing more on the never-threatened status of the Magyar minority rather than on the evident similarity with the 1956 events, thereby "freeing the Hungarian Left of their most important political burden."[26]

After the 1991 agreement with Ukraine, further treaties were signed with Croatia and Slovenia (1992), Slovakia (1995), and Romania (1996). These treaties settled Hungarian affairs to the east and left Hungary open to move toward the EU.

The process of gaining EU membership began with the signing of an association agreement with the EU in 1994, followed by the transformation of the former Soviet base of Taszár in southwestern Hungary into a NATO logistical base in 1996 and receipt of full NATO membership in March 1999, on the eve of the Kosovo War. As relations between the United States and parts of the EU deteriorated in 2003 because of the invasion of Iraq, Hungary cautiously supported the George W. Bush administration, while making the point that good relations with all EU members were a priority. In May 2004 full EU membership was achieved.

Conclusion

The remarkable unity displayed by the Hungarians in 1956 and 1989 did not last for the transition. Yet, although the two traditional political factions (i.e., people's nationalists and secular liberals) have railed at each other rhetorically, the Hungarian parties have never seemed far apart in their actual policy goals, at least until recently. The economy still suffers from the huge burden of trying to move from goulash communism (which in the long run proved a major liability) to goulash capitalism, but the upheavals in 2006 over revelations of the economy's true problems were more about being misled than about the financial restraints that had to be imposed. For Hungary, joining the European Union has been a decided benefit. Clearly, there is no interest in turning back or slowing Hungary's move forward. And yet, the Orbán government's legislation—while taking full advantage of the benefits of membership—has repeatedly challenged various EU institutions, particularly regarding civil liberties, resulting in numerous warnings and admonishments but no substantial consequences. The truth of the matter is that, as long as the European People's Party—the EU's grouping of conservative and Christian democratic parties of which FiDeSz is a member—and its most relevant leader, German chancellor Angela Merkel, refuse to oppose Orbán and his choices, things are unlikely to change. Despite his renunciation of "liberal" democracy in a speech in Romania in 2014,[27] Orbán will most probably stay in power until the opposition proves capable of rallying a majority of Hungarians behind it.

Study Questions

1. Why are the Jewish and Roma questions so relevant in Hungarian politics?
2. What are the main reasons for Orbán's continued support by a majority of Hungarians?
3. To what extent can Hungary be called a parliamentary democracy and a state based on the rule of law?
4. Is Orbán proving more successful in economic policy than his socialist predecessors?
5. How should the Hungarian center-left opposition act in order to increase its future chances of electoral victory?

Suggested Readings

Barany, Zoltan. *The East European Gypsies: Regime Change, Marginality and Ethnopolitics.* Cambridge: Cambridge University Press, 2002.

Braun, Aurel, and Zoltan Barany, eds. *Dilemmas of Transition: The Hungarian Experience.* Lanham, MD: Rowman & Littlefield, 1998.

De Nevers, Renée. *Comrades No More: The Seeds of Change in Eastern Europe,* Cambridge, MA: MIT Press, 2003.

Fábián, Katalin. *Contemporary Women's Movements in Hungary: Globalization, Democracy, and Gender Equality*. Washington, DC: Woodrow Wilson Center Press; Baltimore: Johns Hopkins University Press, 2009.

Gati, Charles. *Failed Illusions*. Stanford, CA: Stanford University Press, 2006.

Guy, Will, ed. *From Victimhood to Citizenship: The Path of Roma Integration*. Budapest: Kossuth, 2013.

Gyuricza, Péter. *The Media War II—Evolution of the Media in Hungary 2010–2013*. North Charleston, SC: CreateSpace, 2014.

——. *The Media War in Hungary I—Media and Power in Hungary from 1989–2009*. 2nd ed. North Charleston, SC: CreateSpace, 2014.

Janos, Andrew C. *East Central Europe in the Modern World*. Stanford, CA: Stanford University Press, 2000.

Király, Béla K., and Bozóki András, eds. *Lawful Revolution in Hungary, 1989–1994*. Boulder, CO, and New York: Social Science Monographs and Columbia University Press, 1995.

Körösényi, András. *Government and Politics in Hungary*. Budapest: Central European University, 2000.

Körösényi, András, Tóth Csaba, and Török Gábor. *The Hungarian Political System*. Budapest: Hungarian Center for Democracy Studies Foundation, 2009.

Kun, J. C. *Hungarian Foreign Policy: The Experience of a New Democracy*. Washington Papers 160. Westport, CT: Praeger, 1993.

Lendvai, Paul. *Hungary: Between Democracy and Authoritarianism*. London: Hurst & Co., 2012.

Lomax, Bill. "The Strange Death of Civil Society in Post-communist Hungary." *Journal of Communist Studies and Transition Politics* 13 (1997): 41–63.

Morlang, Diana. "Hungary: Socialists Building Capitalism." In *The Left Transformed in Post-communist Societies*, edited by Jane Curry and Joan Urban, 61–98. Lanham, MD: Rowman & Littlefield, 2003.

Pittaway, Mark. *The Workers' State: Industrial Labor and the Making of Socialist Hungary, 1944–1958*. Pittsburgh: University of Pittsburgh Press, 2012.

Sárközy, Tamás. *Magyarország kormányzása 1978–2012* [*The Governing of Hungary, 1978–2012*]. Budapest: Park, 2012.

Schmidt, Mária, and Tóth Gy. László. *Transition with Contradictions: The Case of Hungary, 1990–1998*. Budapest: Kairosz 1999.

Tokes, Rudolf. *Hungary's Negotiated Revolution: Economic Reform, Social Change, and Political Succession*. Cambridge: Cambridge University Press, 1996.

Volgyes, Ivan, and Nancy Volgyes. *The Liberated Female: Life, Work and Sex in Socialist Hungary*. Boulder, CO: Westview Press, 1977.

Websites

Politics.hu: http://www.politics.hu
Hungarian Spectrum: http://hungarianspectrum.wordpress.com
National Széchényi Library, 1956 Institute and Oral History Archive: http://www.rev.hu

Notes

1. Ghiţa Ionescu and Ernst Gellner, eds., *Populism: Its Meaning and National Characteristics* (London: Weidenfeld & Nicholson, 1970); Yves Mény and Yves Surel, *Democracies and the Populist Challenge* (New York: Palgrave 2002).

2. See, respectively, Paul Krugman, "Legal but Not Fair (Hungary)," New York Times, April 13, 2014, http://krugman.blogs.nytimes.com/2014/04/13/legal-but-not-fair-hungary; International Election Observation Mission, Hungary—Parliamentary Elections, April 6, 2014, "Statement of Preliminary Findings and Conclusions," Organization for Security and Co-operation in Europe, http://www.osce.org/odihr/elections/117205?download=true. For a questioning of Scheppele's objectivity, see the message of former British academic, now member of the European Parliament for FiDeSz, George Schöpflin, at Princeton University Program in Law and Public Affairs, http://lapa.princeton.edu/hosteddocs/hungary/schopflin -scheppele_letter.pdf.

3. See Eva S. Balogh, "Fidesz Gathering in Front of Parliament," Hungarian Spectrum, May 2010, http://hungarianspectrum.wordpress.com/2010/05.

4. See the text in English at "The Fundamental Law of Hungary (25 April 2011)," Website of the Hungarian Government, http://www.kormany.hu/download/e/02/00000/The New Funda mental Law of Hungary.pdf, and the main drafter's viewpoint at Max Harden, "The New Hungarian Constitution," John Cabot University, http://www.johncabot.edu/about_jcu/guarini-institute/ past-events/New-Hungarian-Constitution.aspx.

5. For a complete description and honest discussion of the amendments, see "Hungary: Constitutional Amendments Adopted," Library of Congress, http://www.loc.gov/lawweb/servlet/ lloc_news?disp3_l205403520_text.

6. Andrew Janos, The Politics of Backwardness in Hungary: 1825–1945 (Princeton, NJ: Princeton University Press, 1982), 176–82.

7. I. Bibó, Democracy, Revolution, Self-Determination (Highland Lakes, NY: Atlantic Research and Publication, 1991), 155–322. See also Paul Lendvai's observations in Hungary: Between Democracy and Authoritarianism (London: Hurst & Co.), 2012, 53–65.

8. See a rough translation of the article in Eva S. Balogh, "Zsolt Bayer Vents against Hungarian Jews and the Foreign Press," Hungarian Spectrum, https://hungarianspectrum.wordpress. com/2011/01/05/zsolt_bayer_vents_against_hungarian_jews_and_the_foreign_press. Neither Orbán nor any other FiDeSz official ever said anything to the effect of distancing him- or herself from, let alone against, Bayer—apparently (and interestingly) of Jewish origin himself—on this occasion or when he dismissed Imre Kertész, the 2002 Nobel laureate in literature, as a "non-Hungarian author," a definition that Kertész subsequently endorsed on moving to Berlin. Even more interestingly, in late June 2013, the Constitutional Court, renamed Curia, despite its reputation as a government tool, ruled that the accusations of anti-Semitism made by the liberal Klubrádió (see http://www.klubradio.hu/index.php?id=215) against Bayer, following which the latter had filed a libel suit, were legitimate.

In the summer of 2014, two contradictory nominations happened. In July, a man called Péter Szentmihályi Szabó, a notorious anti-Semite with no diplomatic record, was appointed to be Hungary's ambassador to Italy. Following loud protest in both countries and internationally (and some embarrassment inside of FiDeSz), he decided to withdraw from the scene. On August 20, 2014, the recently restored Order of Saint Stephen, the highest Hungarian state decoration, was bestowed on Kertész, who shared the honor with Ernő Rubik, inventor of the famous cube. It is difficult to not see here a deliberate "stick-and-carrot" approach by the Orbán government, which is trying to appease Jobbik, the center-left opposition, and international public opinion. See Hungary around the Clock, "Fidesz Members Worried by Italy Ambassador Nomination," Politics.hu, July 25, 2014, http://www.politics.hu/20140725/fidesz-members-worried-by-italy-ambassador-nomination; MTI, "Contested Appointee Declines Ambassador to Italy Role," Politics.hu, July 25, 2014, http://www.politics.hu/20140725/contested-appointee-declines-ambassador-to-italy-role; MTI, "Jobbik Protests Planned State Award to Kertesz," Politics.hu, August 25, 2014, http:// www.politics.hu/20140815/jobbik-protests-planned-state-award-to-kertesz; MTI, "Kertész, Rubik Presented High State Award," Politics.hu, August 20, 2014, http://www.politics.hu/20140820/ kertesz-rubik-presented-high-state-award.

9. For a database of the Hungarian Revolution and all the actors involved, see "The 1956 Revolution," National Széchényi Library, 1956 Institute and Oral History Archive, http://www .rev.hu/history_of_56/naviga/index.htm.

10. Paul Hare and Tamas Revisz, "Hungary's Transition to the Market: The Case against a 'Big Bang,'" *Economic Policy: A European Forum* 14 (April 1992): 236.

11. Hare and Revisz, "Hungary's Transition to the Market," 241.

12. Rudolf Tokes, *Hungary's Negotiated Revolution* (Cambridge: Cambridge University Press, 1996), 330.

13. Bill Lomax, "From Death to Resurrection: The Metamorphosis of Power in Eastern Europe," *Critique* 25 (1993): 68.

14. Béla Kovács (1908–1959) had been, in 1930, one of the founders of the Independent Smallholders Party, a political force characterized by a strong pro–land reform and antidictatorial stand. He led it to the November 1945 electoral triumph (57 percent of the votes), only to be arrested and deported to a forced-labor camp in the USSR, where he remained until after the Twentieth Congress of the Communist Party of the Soviet Union in 1956. During the revolution later that year, he briefly resumed his position and stated that "the land and the factories shouldn't be turned back to their old owners," a position unpopular with FiDeSz, eager to emphasize solely his anticommunist relevance.

As for the Terror House Museum, established in the infamous building on Andrássy Avenue that played an important role under both the Nazi and Stalinist regimes, several observers pointed to the fact that only one hall is devoted to Nazism and the Arrow Cross, and many more treat the communist regime in all its variants, which is acceptable in terms of years in power but not victims. However, Socialist-led executives from 2002 to 2010 did not alter the structure of the museum, which has since become one of the cultural attractions of Budapest.

15. Eva Ehrlich and Gabor Revesz, "Coming In from the Cold: Hungary's Economy in the 20th Century," *Hungarian Quarterly* 41, no. 157 (spring 2000): 18.

16. "Economic Survey of Hungary 2014," OECD, http://www.oecd.org/economy/economic -survey-hungary.htm.

17. Karoly Okolicsanyi, "Prime Minister Presents New Government's Program," *Report on Eastern Europe* (June 18, 1990): 21.

18. Edith Oltay, "Poverty on the Rise," *Report on Eastern Europe* (January 25, 1991): 13–14.

19. Hare and Revisz, "Hungary's Transition to the Market," 230.

20. Hare and Revisz, "Hungary's Transition to the Market," 229.

21. Csaba Halmos, "Political and Economic Reform and Labour Policy in Hungary," *International Labour Review* 129, no. 1 (1990): 47.

22. Project on Ethnic Relations, *Roma in Hungary: Government Policies, Minority Expectations, and the International Community* (Princeton, NJ: Project on Ethnic Relations, 2000), 16.

23. Project on Ethnic Relations, *Roma in Hungary*, 8.

24. *A jóléti rendszerváltás csődje—Gyurcsány-kormány első* éve [*The Failure of Welfare Regime Change—Gyurcsány's Government's First Year*] (Budapest: Századvég, 2005). This is the third volume of a yearbook on the activity of the executive, sponsored by FiDeSz.

25. Over the 2000–2010 decade, Csurka's party was gradually replaced by another one called Jobbik, which actually is more outspoken in its extreme rightist approaches and the related racist features, including a more explicit reference to Hungary's past fascist-type ideas and rulers; after winning three seats at the 2009 European elections, Jobbik gained forty-seven parliamentary seats at the April 2010 vote and became the third-largest party of the country, just below the socialist MSzP. Such a position was maintained in 2014, placing Jobbik again long after FiDeSz and just below the fragmented galaxy of center-left parties and electoral alliances.

26. "Hungary's Reaction to Ukraine Crisis Illustrates Tensions within Fidesz's Foreign Policy Discourse," Politics.hu, March 21, 2014, http://www.politics.hu/20140321/hungarys-reaction-to-ukraine-crisis-illustrates-tensions-within-fideszs-foreign-policy-discourse.

27. Kester Eddy, "EU Urged to Monitor Hungary as Orban Hits at 'liberal Democracy,'" *Financial Times*, July 30, 2014, http://www.ft.com/intl/cms/s/0/0574f7f2-17f3-11e4-b842-00144 feabdc0.html#axzz3IEtu9evR.

Map 13.0. The Baltic States

CHAPTER 13

The Baltic Countries

CHANGES AND CHALLENGES IN THE NEW EUROPE

Daina S. Eglitis

Together, the Baltic countries of Latvia, Lithuania, and Estonia have a population of about 7 million. Located on the Baltic Sea to the west of the Russian Federation and east of Scandinavia, the three countries survived a tumultuous twentieth century, at the dawn of which Latvia and Estonia were provinces of the Russian Empire, and Lithuania was divided between Germany and Russia. The Baltic countries also experienced the turmoil of revolution in Russia, beginning in 1905 and continuing through the end of the empire and the beginning of Bolshevik rule.

Following World War I, the Baltic countries were among the progeny of an era that brought into being a host of small states, and all three became independent. Independence was, however, short-lived, and the nonaggression pact between Adolf Hitler's Germany and Joseph Stalin's Soviet Union sealed their political fate as victims of more powerful neighbors. By the end of World War II, during which the Baltic countries lost a substantial proportion of their populations to war, deportation, political murder, and the flight of refugees, all three were occupied republics of the USSR.

Nearly half a century later, the ascent of Mikhail Gorbachev created unprecedented opportunities for open discussion and dissent. The Baltics were among the first republics to take advantage of new freedoms and to demand change. The collapse of the Eastern bloc and, subsequently, the USSR opened the door to the reestablishment of independence in Latvia, Lithuania, and Estonia, with its accompanying challenges, choices, and changes.

Early-Twentieth-Century History

The Baltic countries had just two decades of experience with independence when they regained autonomous statehood in 1991. In all three cases, independence was declared for the first time in 1918, though formal recognition by the international community came later. The Soviet Union recognized the independence of the former provinces in separate peace treaties concluded between February and August 1920. Between 1921 and 1922, the international community extended its acceptance of the new states and welcomed them into the League of Nations.

The first period of independence was a time of dramatic transformations. Emerging from World War I (1914–1918), the Baltics had to overcome the burdens of decimated populations and devastated economies. For example, Latvia's population plummeted from 2.5 million in the prewar period to just 1.58 million in 1920. Estonia and Lithuania also lost substantial proportions of their populations to fighting and refugee flight. Agriculture, a key economic sector, was deeply damaged by the war, and farmlands lay virtually fallow. The nascent industrial sector, which had taken root in the Latvian and Estonian territories, was in ruins, as most heavy equipment had been moved to the Russian interior during the war. The economic foundations for the new states were tenuous.

The Baltics undertook massive land reforms focused on the transfer of land from private estates concentrated largely in the hands of Baltic Germans to the landless peasantry, who had tilled the soil for generations but never owned the land. One goal of reform was to create a rural economy based on small family farms. There was also an interest in transferring more rural land to indigenous populations: in Latvia, most private land was in the hands of non-Latvians. Fear in the government of Bolshevik sympathies among the rural peasantry compounded the perceived urgency of reform. Land reform was relatively successful in meeting its goals. In Latvia, by 1925 over 70 percent of rural dwellers, many of them Latvians, were landowners. Though the states regulated some sectors of their economies, the trajectories in all three pointed toward the creation of capitalist economies rooted in private ownership, agriculture, and entrepreneurship.

Political pioneers in the Baltics laid the foundations for democratic states, putting in place the constitutional and institutional building blocks of parliamentary democracies with universal suffrage (they were among the first European states to guarantee voting rights for women), equality before the law, and guarantees for minority rights. The parliamentary systems were characterized by weak executive powers (Estonia, in fact, had no head of state separate from the legislative branch) and, following the constitutional model of Weimar Germany, proportional representation in the legislature based on party lists. One intention of the parliamentary system was to guard against authoritarianism. Paradoxically, the fragmented legislatures that emerged from this system contributed to the later rise of authoritarian governments.

The Baltic governments suffered instability, in part because parliaments were populated by a multitude of small parties characterized by a spectrum of narrow interests. Governments were short-lived, and political alliances were ever shifting. By 1926, Lithuania was under an authoritarian presidential regime, led by Antanas Smetona. In Estonia and Latvia, democratic parliamentary systems lasted longer but were also plagued by political problems rendered more acute by a worldwide economic depression. In Estonia, between 1919 and 1933, the average duration of governments was eight months, and in early 1934, Konstantin Päts rose to rule by presidential decree. Later that year, Latvia's parliament was dismissed and its political parties dissolved by President Karlis Ulmanis.[1]

While the regimes of Smetona, Päts, and Ulmanis severely limited political opposition, they succeeded in establishing stability that benefited the economy, including private business and agriculture, which had responded poorly to the unpredictability of unstable governments. Cultural life and education for titular populations flourished. However, the nationalist sentiment embraced by the regimes adversely affected opportunities for minority populations to fully realize their aspirations. In Latvia, the slogan "Latvia for Latvians" was manifested in policies that marginalized the interests of minority populations in areas like business ownership and education.

Although the Baltics sought to remain neutral in the face of growing tensions in Europe, the world around them was erupting in violence. Germany had embarked on the decimation of its Jewish population, and the Third Reich cast a menacing shadow over its neighbors as well. Stalin's regime in the Soviet Union had already engineered a devastating famine in the republic of Ukraine and conducted murderous purges of enemies real and perceived throughout the USSR. The partnering of these powers against the Baltics sealed their fate: the Molotov-Ribbentrop Pact, signed by Germany and the Soviet Union in August 1939, contained a "secret protocol" (the existence of which the Soviets denied until the glasnost era) that divided the Baltic countries (as well as Poland, Romania, and Finland) into spheres of influence: Latvia and Estonia were ceded to the USSR, Lithuania to Germany (though later Lithuania would be claimed by the Soviets). Notably, even today, Russia, the USSR's legatee, denies that an occupation took place, arguing that the Baltics voluntarily joined the USSR in 1940.

History of the Communist Period

Between September and October 1939, Estonia, Latvia, and Lithuania were forced to accept the terms of mutual-assistance treaties with the USSR. The treaties permitted the stationing of Soviet troops on the Baltic countries' territories, and tanks rolled across the their borders with no resistance: this capitulation in the face of the Soviet threat remains an object of historical debate, as many have wondered if resistance could have prevented a half-century-long occupation.

In July 1940, new governments, "elected" from a slate of regime-approved candidates in compulsory voting, requested admission to the USSR. This electoral farce took place against a bloody backdrop: the violence that had been limited during the initial occupation exploded in what Balts call the "year of terror," which began with arrests in the summer of 1940 and reached its pinnacle on the night of June 14, 1941, with the mass deportations to Siberia of, it is estimated, more than twelve thousand Estonians, fifteen thousand Latvians, and thirty-four thousand Lithuanians, as well as members of minority populations like the Poles of Lithuania.[2]

Between 1941 and 1944, German occupation interrupted the Soviet occupation of the region. World War II was catastrophic for the Baltic states not only because of the human and economic toll that the war took on all of Europe but because it divided their populations. Thousands of Balts evacuated with the Red Army after Germany's attack on the USSR and were eventually mobilized to fight for the Soviets. Thousands of others fought on the opposite side, either volunteering for the German army in order to keep the Red Army from returning or being drafted for service. Fighting for the great powers of the era, Balts faced one another on the battlefield.[3] Even members of the same family could be found on opposite sides of the bloody war.

The occupation years (1940–1990) cannot be uniformly characterized. The Stalin era represented a stranglehold of social control and fear. The collectivization of agriculture gained momentum in the late 1940s and was nearly completed by 1952. The process in the Baltics was slow, in part because there was rural resistance to collectivization. Resistance was broken by a new round of deportations in 1949, in which about one hundred thousand rural dwellers, including women and children, were deported from the Baltic republics.[4]

Violent repression and public fear declined with Stalin's death in 1953. Although the persecution of individual dissidents continued under his successor, Nikita Khrushchev, most of the population, if willing to abide by Soviet norms and laws, could live in relative normalcy. Cultural and social life was still controlled, though less stringently restricted than before.

In terms of economic life, the Baltics were considered among the "prosperous" Soviet republics and known for a generally higher standard of living. This made them a magnet for migration from other republics, further shifting the demographics and driving the titular population, particularly in Latvia and Estonia, closer to minority status.[5] One consequence of this development was linguistic: whereas most Balts spoke fluent Russian, few Russians learned the republics' languages. The 1970 census in the Latvian Soviet Socialist Republic, for instance, showed that over half of Latvians (and a higher proportion in younger generations) spoke Russian, but fewer than a fifth of ethnic Russians could speak Latvian.[6]

In 1964, Leonid Brezhnev came to power. His regime continued to exercise stringent social control, and in the 1970s he initiated a concentrated campaign against nationalism: as in Khrushchev's time, the goal was to create *Homo sovieticus*, the Soviet man, exorcised of his bourgeois inclinations toward ethnic allegiances. Episodes of dissent were few and far between, though they arose periodically in the Baltics. The public self-immolation in 1972 of Romas Kalanta, a Lithuanian student, sparked demonstrations in Kaunas. Most opposition, however, remained small and contained, though apparently there was enough concern about simmering discontent that Khrushchev's short-lived successor, Yuri Andropov, a former KGB chief, cracked down on dissent, real and perceived.

Discontent in the Baltics was centered in the indigenous populations, whose older members retained the living memory of independence. These populations also feared demographic marginalization. All three countries, but particularly Latvia and Estonia, had below-replacement fertility rates and aging populations. Latvia and Estonia also had large Russian-speaking populations, whose numbers had risen again in a wave of immigration in the 1970s. Soviet population data showed Latvians approaching the 50 percent mark in their republic, a proportional downward slide that showed few signs of abating. The fear of ethnic extinction would become an important issue in the mobilization of civil society in the Gorbachev era.

In the Baltic countries, mobilization of independent civil society and, ultimately, the path to independence proceeded along similar lines. Prior to 1987, independent mass demonstrations were forbidden in the USSR, and a culture of fear wrought by decades of repression made such collective action unlikely. Whereas individual and small group dissident activities dotted the Soviet historical map, most citizens were docile, unwilling or unable to openly oppose the regime. Gorbachev's ascent to power in the Soviet Union and his adoption of a policy of glasnost, with the accompanying possibilities for freer expression, opened the door to Baltic social movements that evolved from small demonstrations of discontent to massive manifestations of open opposition to the state and regime, the economic, environmental, and ethnic policies of the USSR, and the refusal of the Soviet government to recognize the illegal occupation of the three countries in 1940.

Early opposition focused on the preservation of folk culture and the environment, issues that were less politically sensitive than secession from the USSR or Soviet distortions of history. At the same time, the elevation of issues of nature and culture was profoundly symbolic. In Latvia, early civic activism centered on a hydroelectric station (HES) proposed for the Daugava, a river central in Latvian history, folktales, and poems: it has been called Latvia's "river of destiny." Opponents of the HES argued that its construction would damage the river and flood surrounding arable lands. The response to an article on the topic published in a progressive weekly newspaper, *Literature and Art*, in 1986 was tremendous: thousands of Latvians wrote to the newspaper to voice their criticism of the project. In early 1987, construction of the HES was halted by the USSR Council of Ministers. The voices of civil society, long suppressed, had achieved a significant victory, setting the stage for the coming years of opposition.[7]

In neighboring Lithuania, as in the other Baltic countries, indigenous elites played an important role in the early construction of independent civil society. In Lithuania, an important part of the active elite included scientists. Widespread discussion and, eventually, opposition focused on the Ignalina Atomic Energy Station (AES), built in the 1970s just eighty miles from Vilnius, the capital city of the republic. Some scientists and other activists questioned the environmental and safety standards of the AES. The disaster at Chernobyl in Ukraine in 1986 rendered these questions even more critical, though widespread public activism around Ignalina did not begin until 1988. Leaders of the initially small opposition appealed to the public with science and symbols: the Lithuanian nation was rooted in the earth, and Ignalina posed a threat to both nature and nation. While the nascent opposition could not speak out overtly against the Soviet government in 1988, environmental issues provided a platform for civil society to gain a foothold.[8]

Civil Society and the Transition from Communism

By 1989, the opposition was openly asking questions about historic distortions, demographic issues, and autonomy for the republics. There was quiet but persistent discussion of secession from the USSR. Symbolic restoration of independent nationhood was already under way, as the interwar flags flew over demonstrations and Balts began publicly celebrating pre-Soviet national holidays. Demonstrations grew to the tens and then hundreds of thousands. The largest demonstration, the Baltic Way, took place on August 23, 1989, the fiftieth anniversary of the Molotov-Ribbentrop Pact. On this day, nearly 1 million Balts joined hands across the three countries, forming a human chain stretching from Vilnius in the south, through Riga, to Tallinn in the north. At the same time, opposition was becoming institutionalized, and changes in some political structures of the USSR and the republics offered new opportunities for challenging the Soviet system from within.

Competitive elections began in the Baltic countries before those countries regained independence in 1991. In early 1990, the Soviet government permitted partially open elections, and opposition groups in the Baltics fielded candidates for the Supreme Soviets of their respective republics. In Lithuania, which had the distinction of hosting the first multiparty elections in the history of the USSR, pro-independence candidates carried the election. In Latvia and Estonia, which held their elections later, the results were mixed but tilted toward pro-independence candidates. Ethnic Latvians and Estonians overwhelmingly favored these candidates, but a notable proportion of Russian-speaking residents also selected pro-independence candidates.[9]

The legislative activities in the three republics were important, but the speed at which changes were taking place meant that legislative change, especially within existing Soviet-era political structures, would trail the initiatives of civil society. The opposition, already demanding independence, was further radicalized by events in Lithuania and Latvia in January 1991. In that month, conservative Soviet forces sought to take over the Vilnius television tower, which was defended by thousands of Lithuanians. In the violence that followed, Soviet forces killed fifteen protesters and injured hundreds: the graphic images of Lithuanians crushed beneath the treads of a Soviet tank received global coverage and signaled a new turn in the political climate, as Gorbachev sought to distance himself from both the Vilnius killings and the deaths of five civilians that occurred when Soviet special forces attacked buildings belonging to the Ministry of the Interior in Latvia.

In a widespread rejection of the evolutionary change offered by Gorbachev or the regressive course embraced by conservative elements, the Baltic countries voted in February and March 1991 in referenda on independence. In February, fully 90 percent of participants in Lithuania (who were required to be eighteen years of age or older and permanent residents, a category that essentially excluded only Soviet military forces stationed in the republic) voted for independence. In March, 78 and 74 percent of inhabitants of Estonia and Latvia, respectively, voted in the affirmative.

The hard-line coup attempt that took place in Moscow in August 1991 did not substantially change the Baltic course, which pointed toward independence. The failed coup effectively destroyed the remaining legitimacy of the Soviet Communist Party, and the Soviet Union itself was rendered little more than a shell of a country. These developments brought independence more rapidly than most people had expected: on September 6, 1991, the USSR recognized the Baltic countries as independent entities, and less than two weeks later they were admitted to the United Nations.

Institutional Structures and Electoral Systems in the Baltics

Latvia, Lithuania, and Estonia built their early postcommunist political institutions based on the assumption that independence was being "restored" rather than "established" in 1991. Consequently, constitutions, electoral systems, judicial structures, and other key political institutions were initially renewed rather than constructed from scratch. Although the tension between those who wished to follow a more conservative and nationalistic path of restoration (rhetorically constructed in Latvia as the "renewal of the First Republic of Latvia") and those who wished to construct a historically grounded but modern and "European" state (articulated as the creation of the "Second Republic

Photo 13.1. Independence demonstrations that began in Lithuania in 1989. These culminated with the Baltic Way, a human chain of 2 million Baltic inhabitants, that went through all three Baltic states on August 23, 1989. (Peter Turnley/Corbis)

Photo 13.2. Vytautas Landsbergis voting in Lithuania's first free elections since World War II. From 1990 to 1992, he held constitutional authority as both the leader of the state and the speaker of parliament. In 1993, he founded a new political party, the Homeland Union, which won the 1996 parliamentary elections, allowing him to serve as speaker of the Lithuanian parliament from 1996 to 2000. (Giedrus Pocius/Sygma/Corbis)

of Latvia") would grow as time passed, all three states were initially inclined to ground themselves in the foundation of the independent past.[10]

Restoration of independence included the renewal of prewar constitutions, which underscored the legal continuity of institutions. In Estonia, the new constitution of 1992 was based on the constitution of 1938. In Latvia, the 1922 constitution was restored in 1993. In Lithuania, the 1938 constitution was temporarily accepted, but the leadership of the country opted ultimately to write a new constitution, as the prewar document, despite its symbolic importance, was declared authoritarian and not well suited to the country.[11]

There is also some continuity with the electoral systems of the past in the Baltics. In the postcommunist period, Latvia's one-hundred-member Saeima (parliament) has been elected through a system of proportional representation with a 5 percent threshold. In the interwar period, this electoral system brought a multitude of small parties into the Saeima. Political fragmentation in the legislature was a justification for President Ulmanis's 1933 assumption of authoritarian leadership in a coup. Indeed, the 1995 election in Latvia produced a parliament with nine parties, none of which earned more than 16 percent of the vote. By 2011, however, the number of parties both competing and winning had fallen: just five of seven competitors earned seats.

In Lithuania, the Seimas (parliament) is elected through a mix of proportional representation and direct constituency voting. The voting is split across two nonconsecutive days: for instance, in 2012, election days were on October 14 and 28. The first 70 of the 141 available seats were elected through open-list proportional representation on the first date; the remaining 71 were filled in two-round voting in single-member districts. Estonia's Riigikogu is also a unicameral body; its 101 seats are filled using a complex proportional representation system (the d'Hondt method).

Lithuanian and Estonian legislatures have also been characterized by the presence of a multitude of parties, though the number is shrinking. Lithuania's most recent elections (2008 and 2012) produced bodies with, respectively, eleven and eight parties (and some independent legislators). Estonia's first elections of the new millennium (2003 and 2007) saw the seating of six parties each; in 2011, however, just four parties were seated. These elections have established left- and right-oriented poles in mainstream political life; center-right parties have been most influential in the Baltics, though Lithuanian voters recently made the Lithuanian Social Democratic Party the largest in the Seimas, signaling a turn to the left (and a rejection of the austere policies embraced by the outgoing center-right coalition).

Another historical continuity between the interwar and new states is the relatively short life span of governments. In the interwar parliamentary period, short-lived governments characterized the three countries. The new states have inherited this dubious legacy: in Latvia, between 1990 (when the Latvian legislature declared its independence from Soviet control) and 2013, there were twelve different prime ministers (several of whom served more than once) and more than sixteen different coalition governments, several of them weak minority coalitions. The large number of parties and coalitions competing for legislative seats and the low threshold required for winning places create optimal conditions for shifting allegiances and alliances, though recent governments have been among the most enduring in the postcommunist period.

Political Leadership

All three Baltic countries have a titular head of state with limited powers. The president is elected by the parliament by secret ballot for a term of five years in Estonia and four in Latvia. In Lithuania, the president is elected by popular vote. The prime minister has greater power over policy, though the presidency has also been a vehicle for the exercise of significant leadership.

Notably, Estonia had no presidency during most of the first independence period: from 1918 to 1938, the parliament governed alone. Revisions to the 1938 constitution, however, brought the office into being, and Estonia's postcommunist presidents have exercised significant public influence. Estonia's president, Toomas Hendrik Ilves, has been in power since his election by the Riigikogu in 2006. He is serving his second term as Estonia's third postcommunist president.

The Latvian president has the power to dissolve the legislature and to convene and preside over extraordinary sessions of the cabinet, though a good deal of the president's power rests on his or her ability to set a public agenda with a visible presence in the media and society, as Latvia's second postcommunist president, Vaira Vike-Freiberga, did during her tenure (1999–2007). Her strong support of Latvia's entrance into the European Union (EU) and the North Atlantic Treaty Organization (NATO) helped solidify societal support for membership.

More recently, Vike-Freiberga's successor, President Valdis Zatlers, used his presidential powers to dissolve the parliament. In May 2011, just days before the Saeima was scheduled to vote for a president, Zatlers responded with this dramatic action to the legislative body's failure to permit the search of a legislator's home on suspicion of corruption. Although Zatlers was not subsequently reelected to a second term by the Saeima, in a required referendum on the action a large majority of voters supported his dissolution of the body. He has remained engaged in politics, creating a new political party, the Zatlers Reform Party, which won seats in the 2011 election.

Postcommunist Political Culture, Parties, and Elections

Political parties in the Baltic countries are still at an early stage of development. While parties put forth candidates for election, candidates also run on lists associated with political organizations that are not formally political parties. Even most of the parties themselves are not political parties as that institution is understood in the West: they are not mass organizations with broad memberships, and very few residents are official members of any party. Some "parties" are financed by private businesses. In Latvia, due to the lack of party-subsidy legislation, which offers state subsidies to parties winning a minimum percentage of votes, some parties have been the financial "projects" of local oligarchs rather than representative political organizations. Among other problems, the low and shifting support of individual parties translates into an unstable political party system. As Daunis Auers and Andres Kasekamp note, "A remarkable feature of the Latvian political party system is that, until 2006, all national elections were won by a party which had not existed at the time of the previous national elections. Though the Estonian political party system can be characterized as more consolidated, it was only in 2007 that an Estonian prime minster and his party were re-elected."[12] In Estonia, the March 2011 national election was the first in which no new parties participated. While parties are likely to evolve in the direction of a West European model, most continue to be ephemeral entities, reflecting short-term political and financial interests and charismatic personalities as much as clear political ideologies.

Lack of confidence in or identification with parties may be linked to declines in electoral participation. Voter participation in elections has declined markedly since the early years of independence. More than 91 percent of eligible voters cast ballots in Latvia's first postcommunist elections in 1993. In the next elections in 1995, just over 72 percent of citizens opted to participate; in subsequent elections (1998 and 2002), the proportion of participants held steady at about 71 percent, then dropped below 63 percent in 2006. It has since continued to fall, reaching just over 59 percent in the 2011 elections. Lithuanian participation has been still lower: in 2012, just under 53 percent of voters participated in the first phase of national elections (which filled 70 of 141 seats in the legislature), and fewer than 36 percent took part in the second phase (which filled the remaining 71 seats).

Like its Baltic neighbors, Estonia has experienced low rates of voting after the initial activism of the early 1990s: while nearly 70 percent voted in parliamentary elections in

Photo 13.3. Former Estonian president Lennart Meri. He served as Estonia's second president from 1992 to 2001. An active leader of the independence movement in Estonia, he was also a writer and film director. (Erik Peinar)

1995, only about 58 percent of eligible voters opted to participate in 1999 and 2003. In 2007, however, Estonia instituted an innovative Internet-based voting option and remains the only country in the world with full online e-voting available. In the 2011 elections, about 15 percent of Estonian citizens voted in advance via the Internet. This may account for a rise in participation: nearly 62 percent of eligible voters cast ballots.

Photo 13.4.   Former federal president of Germany Horst Kohler (L), former president of Latvia Vaira Vike-Freiberga, and president of Italy Giorgio Napolitano during their joint press conference at the Fourth Informal Debates of European Presidents on the Future of Europe, in Riga. (Toms Kalnins/epa/Corbis)

Estonia is also one of the few countries in the world that permits legal residents (including noncitizens) to vote in local elections.

While many residents have chosen not to vote, others have not been eligible to participate. In Estonia and Latvia, automatic citizenship was granted first to citizens of the interwar republics and their descendants. These laws had the effect of creating a substantial population of stateless persons (mostly ethnic Russians) who were citizens of neither the renewed countries nor the defunct USSR. While both Latvia and Estonia offered legal residency, neither was eager to introduce a large number of Soviet-era migrants into the pool of potential voters. In Lithuania, citizenship was granted more broadly, as that country had a far lower proportion of non-Lithuanians living in the territory than did Latvia or Estonia. The body of citizenry in Estonia and Latvia has grown as well, however. Whereas in 1992, just 68 percent of residents in Estonia held citizenship, in 2012, the figure was fully 84 percent; most of this change was driven by high levels of naturalization in the 1990s, though some is also the result of noncitizen emigration. In Latvia, in 2000, just over three-quarters of residents were citizens; by 2010, nearly 84 percent held citizenship, and noncitizens constituted only 14 percent of residents (2 percent are foreign nationals). Some legal residents eligible for citizenship have opted not to pursue it, while others remain ineligible due to, for example, their lack of language knowledge or failure to meet residency requirements.

Economic Transition

The Baltic countries have undergone substantial economic changes in the transformation from command to free market economies. From a comparative perspective, the Baltics fared better in the first decade and a half than other former Soviet republics, though perhaps not as well as Central and East European states such as Hungary and the Czech Republic. Growth rates in the Baltics largely met or exceeded expectations, with the exception of a crisis in 1998, when the crash of the Russian ruble damaged neighboring economies. One hallmark of the Baltics' transformation was the speed with which they privatized formerly state-owned industries. In Latvia and Estonia, privatization at the ten-year mark of independence was almost complete, with most formerly state-owned small and medium-size enterprises fully privatized.

Another key dimension of the construction of an economic and social order rooted in private property was the restitution to prewar owners of the urban and rural properties taken from them when Soviet occupiers nationalized property and drove many members of the "ownership class" out of their countries. This move was symbolically significant because it "righted" a Soviet wrong: in the early postcommunist period, nearly any action seen as undoing what the communists had done was likely to find a sympathetic constituency. Restitution was also intended to restore the grid of private property that existed in the interwar period and reestablish an ownership society, the basis of the new capitalism.

The advent of free markets and the spread of ownership, investment, and entrepreneurship fueled powerful growth in the Baltics.[13] In the early years of the new millennium, the economies of all three states were characterized by dynamic development and a rapid rise in gross domestic product (GDP), which translated into rising wages, consumption, and living standards for the new middle class. Perhaps ominously, these welcome developments were accompanied by a steep rise in housing prices, widespread use of credit, and inflation. Latvia's real GDP growth of 10 percent in 2007, for instance, was matched by an inflation rate of 10 percent.

Baltic economic expansion came to an abrupt and dramatic halt in late 2008, as key economic indicators turned downward and the Baltics, like much of the globe, slid into recession. Lithuania experienced strong GDP growth in the new millennium: this economic indicator rose from 3.3 percent in 2000 to a stunning 9.8 percent in 2007. It turned down in 2008, falling to 2.8 percent before crashing in 2009 and dropping to −18.1 percent. Latvia followed a similar trajectory, reaching a real GDP growth rate of 12.2 percent in 2006 before tumbling to −18 percent in 2009. Estonia's fall from the heights was smaller but still deep: its real GDP growth fell to −13.7 percent in 2009.[14]

Arguably, the severity of human distress in the crisis period was exacerbated by the condition of deep stratification already in place when the economies were flourishing. Even in this period of prosperity, the rising tide failed to lift all boats: macroeconomic policies did little to alleviate economic distress at the bottom of the ladder. In Latvia, for instance, the measured "poverty risk" grew from 16 percent in 1996 to 23 percent in 2006, though it declined to 21 percent in 2007. Notably, this measure is relative rather than absolute: according to Eurostat, which compiles social and economic indicators on European states, the indicator "is defined as the share of persons with an equivalized disposable income below the risk-of-poverty threshold, which is set at 60 per cent of the national median equivalized disposable income (after social transfers)." As such, it reflects the position of the lowest earners relative to the median. As the median rose in the years of prosperity, absolute poverty may not have risen, but the gap between the worst off and the middle and upper classes grew.[15]

The greatest risk of poverty across the postcommunist period has been in rural regions and small towns, while the risk has been smaller in most large cities, where employment options are more varied. At the same time, rural dwellers, particularly those who work the land, have benefited in times of crisis from their ability to ensure their own food supply.

The depths of the economic crisis in the Baltics, however, have been matched by the dramatic climb back to economic growth. In Latvia, the fall in GDP approached 20 percent in 2009, but the rebound brought Latvia the fastest-growing economy in Europe in 2013. Estonia too has roared back: the Estonian economy is experiencing robust growth of 2.9 percent, and about 15 percent of GDP is rooted in a highly entrepreneurial and creative high-technology sector. Lithuania has come back more slowly but also registered growth of nearly 3 percent in 2012. Economic recovery in the Baltics has largely been built on austerity measures pushed through by national governments and advocated by the European Union and International Monetary Fund. These measures temporarily pushed up unemployment and shrank wages in the large public sector. Interestingly, whereas the governments that imposed austerity in Latvia and Estonia were returned to office in the most recent elections, Lithuanians in late 2012 elected an antiausterity center-left government.

In January 2014, Latvia became the second of the three Baltic countries to join the Eurozone. The Maastricht Treaty, which set the rules of the Eurozone, has a host of requirements for aspirants, including the demand that countries achieve a budget deficit equivalent to about 3 percent of GDP and maintain low inflation. Estonia was the first to meet the requirements and became a Eurozone member in 2011. Latvia joined in January 2014, and Lithuania has set a goal of joining no later than 2015. While the governments of all three countries have not wavered in their goal of Eurozone membership, public attitudes toward the new currency have ranged from ambivalence to anger. In late 2013, only about a third of Latvians were in favor of joining the Eurozone. One reason behind the negative reactions is a fear of currency instability caused by the deep economic crises of Eurozone members like Greece and Spain. Another reason is rooted in Latvia's history of currency conversion: the shift from the ruble to the Latvian lats in the wake of independence effectively wiped out the savings of thousands of residents when the value of the ruble collapsed.

While official data are helpful in understanding the economies of the Baltics, it is notable that all three have substantial "gray economies" (in the terminology of the World Bank), comprising both illegal economic activities (such as the sex, narcotics, and arms trades) and legal ones (such as the sale of used clothing or furniture) that are not reported to governments and thus are not subject to taxation and regulation. A recent study by the SEB bank and Riga's Stockholm School of Economics estimates that in each of the Baltic countries, about a fifth of the economy is "in the shadows."[16] By contrast, the European Union average is 15 percent.

Social Transition

Communism embraced an ideology of equality. Capitalism, by contrast, embraces an ideology of competition. In the period of Soviet communism, all citizens were theoretically equal: women and men, Russians and non-Russians, professionals and laborers. In reality, the situation was more complex.

Although well represented in the workforce, women tended to occupy positions with less prestige and authority. They also carried the double burden of paid work and primary, if not sole, responsibility for domestic work. Some observers suggested that women bore a "triple burden," the third being that they were usually the ones to wait in long shop lines for groceries or other goods.

In addition, despite ostensible ethnic equality, some Soviet citizens, to paraphrase George Orwell's *Animal Farm*, were "more equal than others." Russian was the lingua franca of the USSR, and all nationalities were expected to learn the language. Russians were often given priority in acquiring housing while others waited many years for an apartment.

In the capitalist and democratic context of postcommunism, there have been both changes and continuities in the forms of inequality experienced in the Baltics. In terms of gender, women are legally equal to men and have comparable opportunities to gain educational training. In fact, women are more likely than men to be highly educated, and they make up the majority of students in most institutions of higher education. At the same time, women still suffer a gender wage gap and are less likely to occupy positions of power and authority, particularly in business and politics (although Latvia was home to Central and Eastern Europe's first female president, Vaira Vike-Freiberga).[17]

Although women are well represented in the paid labor force, the postcommunist period has also seen a push from some conservative political organizations for women to return to home and hearth in order to ensure the creation of new Latvians, Estonians, and Lithuanians. In the demographic and social context of the Baltics, issues of family formation are widely deemed to be of public importance: none of the countries has replacement rate fertility (defined as a total fertility rate of 2.1), and all have lost population through declining birth rates as well as emigration. All three states have pro-natalist policies and programs of social support for parenting.

The sands of ethnic equality have also shifted in the Baltics. Whereas in the Soviet period, Russians were the "most equal" of all legally equal nationalities, in the postcommunist Baltics, legal equality is extended to all, but the titular nationalities have asserted dominance in areas like language-law and educational policies.

Although the Baltic countries have not experienced serious political violence and day-to-day relations between ethnic groups are peaceful, recent years have seen manifestations of tensions over these issues. A constitutional referendum to make Russian an official second language in Latvia was held in February 2012. The referendum was the result of a petition drive, organized largely by ethnic Russians, which successfully gathered enough signatures to prompt the vote. Notably, the referendum saw voter turnout much higher than that of recent parliamentary elections: fully 70 percent of eligible voters opted to participate. The effort to make Russian an official second language failed, with only 25 percent of voters supporting the constitutional change. While some observers feared a backlash after the failure, most negative reactions were limited to the Russian-language press.

On the one hand, interethnic relations have been and will continue to be influenced by state policies and actions: laws about language, education, and equal access to opportunities will contribute to the integration or alienation of Russian speakers in the Baltics. On the other hand, social and economic factors not controlled by the state influence the issue of Russian speakers' acquiring titular languages and ethnic relations. In Latvia, the rate of ethnic intermarriage is high: many families are mixed, and children learn both languages and bridge both cultures. As well, the practical imperative of profit making in capitalism has induced young people and other would-be entrepreneurs to learn multiple languages in order to serve customers more effectively. In sum, while ethnic tensions are present in the Baltics, macro- and microlevel forces help maintain equilibrium and reduce potential for the ethnic conflict that has devastated areas like former Yugoslavia.

Civil Society

Public opinion polling suggests that trust in political institutions, particularly parliament and political parties, among the masses has been low in the past decade and a half. Little of this discontent, however, has been reflected in public activism: after the end of several years of civil society activism in the opposition period, some observers lamented the "death of civil society."

All, however, has not been quiet. In Latvia, anger at government corruption was manifested in 2007 in large public protest actions not seen since the late years of anti-Soviet protest. In November 2007, an estimated eight to ten thousand people gathered in central Riga to protest rampant graft, an action that contributed to the resignation that month of the sitting prime minister. Public anger was sharpened by the economic crisis in the region, and another large anti-government demonstration in January 2009 ended with violence. While ten thousand protesters gathered in Riga's city center to speak against economic mismanagement and to demand early elections, riots involving several hundred demonstrators followed the peaceful action.

Most protest actions across the Baltics, however, have been relatively small and nonviolent. In Latvia in early 2013, demonstrators picketed the parliament building to protest Latvia's effort to join the Eurozone. Estonians have also turned out to make their voices heard over economic issues: in the spring of 2013, thousands of school teachers crowded into Tallinn's Freedom Square to draw attention to poor salaries.

Most activity in Baltic civil society takes place in the sphere of nongovernmental organizations (NGOs), which are plentiful across the region and embrace issues ranging from environmental protection to worker rights to Internet freedoms. NGOs focused on women's issues date back to the early 1990s, though only recently have some prominent

NGOs expanded their issue range to include support for victims of domestic violence, an issue long subject to public silence.

Contemporary civil society in the Baltics also includes some new groups of actors, including sexual minorities, whose social marginality dates back to the Soviet era. In the summer of 2004, the first gay-pride march took place in Estonia, followed a year later by a similar event in Latvia. Lithuanian activists held the first gay-pride march in 2012. The marches have taken place annually, though they have generated some resistance from both police, who have suggested that they cannot guarantee the safety of the marchers, and conservatives, who have aggressively opposed the them: in Vilnius in 2012, for instance, the "March for Equality" encountered hundreds of protesters, who rejected the message of equality for sexual minorities. While the Baltic countries largely mirror their Scandinavian neighbors in liberal attitudes toward practices such as nonmarital cohabitation and child-bearing, these societies are conservative in their attitudes toward sexual minorities.

Foreign Policy

After a half century as citizens of the Soviet Union, many in the Baltics embraced the slogan "Back to Europe." Having regained independent statehood in 1991, the Baltic countries sought seats in the United Nations, and all three became members in September of that year, an important symbolic step that signaled international acceptance of the states. The accession of the three Baltic countries to the European Union in May 2004 represents another important symbolic and substantive step. In terms of symbolism, the EU's expansion signals the first time since the historical Hanseatic League that nearly the entire Baltic Sea region is part of a single economic and political bloc. In terms of modernity, it brings a geographic part of Europe back into economic and political Europe.[18]

In March 2004, another major foreign policy goal was realized: the Baltic countries became members of the North Atlantic Treaty Organization. NATO membership represents an important symbolic link to Europe and, critically for the Balts, confers a right to and obligation to provide mutual defense. Even before formally joining NATO, the Baltics deployed small contingents of soldiers and specialists to Western missions, joining the "coalition of the willing" for service in Iraq in 2003. Baltic troops also served with the NATO mission in Afghanistan.

Whereas the Baltics have cultivated close relations with many of their western neighbors, relations with Russia have been tense. Despite cooperation in some areas of mutual interest, including trade relations, there have been ample sources of dispute, ranging from Russian displeasure over citizenship and language laws in Latvia and Estonia to tensions over the extension of NATO to Russia's western doorstep and even disputes over history.

It is notable that dominant Baltic and Russian (previously Soviet) historical narratives about World War II differ markedly. In brief, whereas the former highlight Soviet occupation and oppression, the latter embrace the story of a heroic Red Army liberating Europe (including the Baltics) from the deadly grip of Nazism.[19] In early 2007, the Estonian government decided to relocate the Bronze Soldier, a monument to the "Soviet liberators" erected during the communist period, from central Tallinn to a more remote location. While Estonian nationalists supported the decision, seeing the soldier as an affront to the suffering of Estonians under the Soviet regime, the removal of the monument sparked two nights of rioting and looting, mostly by young Russians, in the capital. At least eleven hundred persons were detained in the worst collective violence of the independence period. Russia also took a public stand against the Estonian state's decision to remove the soldier, calling the act, among other things, "blasphemous." Estonians, in return, accused the Russian media of stoking unrest with allegations that the monument had been destroyed (it was moved but not damaged).

Shortly after the dispute over the Bronze Soldier, Estonia experienced a massive cyberattack, which effectively disabled the entire Internet structure of the country, paralyzing financial, government, media, and even personal transactions (mobile phone networks were temporarily frozen as well). As a state that has taken pride in establishing one of the world's first e-governments, where much of the business of the state is conducted electronically, the attack was deeply damaging. NATO responded by sending cyberterrorism experts to Estonia to study the attack and assist in recovery.

Estonia and a host of Western observers accused Russia of being behind the attacks based on both timing and technical evidence. Notably, in 2013, Lithuania also experienced a distributed denial-of-service (DDOS) cyberattack, which, though not as serious as that experienced by Estonia, slowed Internet traffic considerably and rendered some Lithuania-based pages temporarily unavailable to the outside world. This DDOS followed an article published by the Lithuanian DELFI news portal that alleged Russian vote buying at the popular continental music festival Eurovision. As in the Estonian case, definitive proof of the source of the attack has been elusive.

Clearly, Baltic security can no longer be understood only in terms of borders, troops, and Western alliances. At the same time, Russian military activities continue to cause fear in the Baltics. A recent military exercise between Russia and Belarus, designated Zapad 2013 (zapad is the Russian word for "west"), was watched in the Baltics with trepidation: the September joint-service exercise, which involved over twelve thousand troops, took place in the Kaliningrad Oblast, an exclave located just to the east of Lithuania. The USSR's earlier use of exercises as a cover for real military operations may have been one source of concern, as was the assertion, expressed by Lithuania's Ministry of National Defense, that exercises were likely offensive, not just defensive.[20]

Tensions with Russia have also spilled into other international relationships. In July 2011, officials in Austria arrested Mikhail Golovatov, a former commander of the elite Soviet Alpha Troops implicated in the January 1991 attacks on the Vilnius television tower, which ended in the death of fourteen civilians. Less than a year earlier, Lithuanian officials had issued a European arrest warrant for Golovatov, accusing him of war crimes and crimes against humanity. However, Golovatov was released just a day later, ostensibly on technical grounds related to the extradition paperwork. Although an Austrian official acknowledged Lithuania's "old wounds," many Lithuanians saw the action as dismissive of their pursuit of historical justice. Lithuania responded with a recall of its ambassador in Vienna and a boycott of Austrian goods. In this instance, the violent events of January 1991 in Vilnius took on international dimensions, pitting Lithuania (and the other Baltic countries, which supported it) against both a Russian state that rejected responsibility for Soviet-era crimes and a European Union country that elevated bureaucratic rationality over what Lithuanians perceived as recognition of their historical victimhood.

Significant Political Developments

Although accession to the European Union has brought important political and economic support to the Baltics, it has also brought consequences, including substantial labor migration out of the three countries. While Baltic emigration began before accession, new opportunities to work and live legally in some European states have spurred a significant migration wave. The government does not keep systematic data, but it is estimated that between 5 and 8 percent of Latvia's working-age population has engaged in productive labor outside the country[21] and that the economic crisis has increased the likelihood that both Latvians and Russians will emigrate. According to the country's most recent census, conducted in 2010, in the decade following 2000, Latvia's population declined from about 2.3 million to just over 1.9 million.

During postcommunist period and including natural decrease (a death rate that exceeds the birthrate) and migration, Lithuania's population has fallen nearly 17 percent. The flow of labor migration has been particularly pronounced during the economic crisis: in 2010, an estimated 85 percent of emigrants from Lithuania cited this as the reason for their departure. While opportunities to work abroad offer an important way for Balts to build connections and human capital, long-term or permanent loss of working-age adults has the potential to impede economic growth and to exacerbate the woes of countries with falling birthrates and aging populations.

While the Baltics have experienced net population loss in the decades after communism's end, a recent controversy in Latvia revolves around migration into the country. In 2010, the Latvian Saeima accepted an amendment to the immigration law allowing foreigners who make a minimum investment in real estate or a new or existing company in the country to obtain a five-year residency permit. Beyond legal residence for the investor and his or her family, approved applicants also gain access to visa-free, open travel across the twenty-five countries of the Schengen zone (though not permission to work in other countries). In 2012, there were about twenty-four hundred applications, and since its inception, the law has been a vehicle for residency for an estimated forty-seven hundred people (as of February 2013), including investors from Russia and China. While advocates praise the law for kick-starting a real estate market devastated by the economic crisis, critics, including nationalist political parties and their supporters, have been critical of a law that may be pushing real estate prices out of the reach of many indigenous residents and that, from their perspective, is opening the door to greater foreign influence, particularly through Russian immigration.

What Makes the Case Interesting?

The evolution of postcommunist states and societies has followed some similar patterns across the region. The Baltics are not alone in their effort to chart a path toward democratic and capitalist development; nor are they unique in encountering both internal and external obstacles on that road. The Baltic countries have frequently led the region in both dramatic economic growth and devastating economic crises, which have created some of the most stratified societies in the European Union. At the same time, Baltic entrepreneurship, particularly Estonian innovation in the high-technology sector, has been robust and remains a promising foundation for the development of an economically secure middle class.

Unlike their neighbors in Central Europe, the Baltics carry legacies of the Soviet occupation, including large Russian-speaking populations, which have had a profound effect on citizenship policies, debates over education and language, electoral politics, and, most recently, foreign and security policy. In the wake of the 2014 crisis, in which Russia occupied Ukraine's Crimean region on the pretext of "protecting the Russian-speaking population," there has been serious trepidation in the Baltic countries, particularly Latvia and Estonia, about Russia's potential imperialist intentions. This was exacerbated when Russia's ambassador to Latvia, in the midst of the crisis, opted to offer Russian passports and even pensions to ethnic Russians in that country. As of this writing, there appears to be sentiment among NATO leaders in favor of upping both the reality and the appearance of military security in the Baltics with a stronger NATO presence.

Conclusion

The outlook for the Baltic countries of Latvia, Lithuania, and Estonia cannot be uniformly or easily characterized. On the one hand, the Baltics have achieved many of the important goals they set in the early postcommunist period. The basic mechanisms of democracy and free markets have been put in place, membership in those European organizations that ideally bring them closer to security (NATO) and prosperity (EU) has been achieved, and the countries are recognized as postcommunist success stories without the violence and upheavals that have cast a shadow over transition in some other states in the region.

On the other hand, the Baltic countries face both internal and external challenges. Even in the years of prosperity that preceded the recent economic crisis, all three countries experienced a dramatic rise in social stratification, as a segment of the population expanded its human capital, wealth, and power, while other groups were left powerless and poor. The global and local economic crisis brought acute threats to stability and prosperity in these countries, but recovery has also been robust and sustained in recent years. Other challenges to maintaining stable and prosperous states and societies lie in addressing substantial socioeconomic stratification, corruption, public health threats, demographic declines, and aging populations.

Externally, the Baltics continue to seek their footing in the global economy, which presents particular challenges to small states with educated and mobile populations. Relations with Russia, as that country attempts to assert its influence over smaller neighbors, are likely to remain tense. Baltic attention to maintaining stable ethnic relations internally may help to mitigate tension, though it is unlikely to solve the larger problems of the fragile relationship. Responsive, democratic governments and institutions, combined with the active voices of civil society, are the best hope to address societal problems and to foster the positive future progress of three small countries that have experienced dramatic changes and challenges.

Study Questions

1. The Baltic states are commonly presented as a single entity in published works on the region. Based on your reading of the chapter, is this tendency justified? Do the commonalties outweigh the differences in history and contemporary experiences? How readily can "the Baltic states" be characterized as a single unit?
2. How has civil society changed from the late 1980s and early 1990s to today? What key issues drove early activism, and what issues underpin social activism today?
3. A half century of occupation denied residents of the Baltic countries the opportunity to freely choose candidates in democratic elections. In the postcommunist period, high participation in elections early on has been followed by comparatively low rates of voter participation. What factors cited in the chapter might account for the decline in voting?
4. Based on the discussion of security issues in the chapter and your knowledge of contemporary news events, how would you assess the level of military or other security threats to the Baltic countries from neighboring Russia?
5. Compared to other countries about which you have read, what advantages do the Baltic countries appear to have in terms of successful political, economic, and social development? What disadvantages can you identify?

Suggested Readings

Buttar, Prit. *Between Giants: The Battle for the Baltics in World War II*. New York: Osprey Publishing, 2013.

Eksteins, Modris. *Walking since Daybreak: A Story of Eastern Europe, World War II, and the Heart of Our Century*. New York: Houghton Mifflin, 1999.

Lieven, Anatol. *The Baltic Revolution: Estonia, Latvia, Lithuania and the Path to Independence*. New Haven, CT: Yale University Press, 1993.

Lumans, Valdis. *Latvia in World War II*. New York: Fordham University Press, 2006.

Misiunas, Romuald, and Rein Taagepera. *The Baltic States: Years of Dependence, 1940–1990*. Berkeley: University of California Press, 1993.

Purs, Aldis. *Baltic Facades: Estonia, Latvia, and Lithuania since 1945*. London: Reaktion Books, 2012.

Smith, David J., ed. *The Baltic States and Their Region: New Europe or Old?* New York: Rodopi, 2005.

Websites

Baltic Times: http://www.baltictimes.com (a long-standing English-language newspaper that offers both up-to-the-minute news and analytical and investigative reporting)

Baltic Course: http://www.baltic-course.com (English-language media platform offering news on the Baltics, focusing primarily on business and economics)

Latvian Institute: http://www.latvia.eu (English-language website based in Latvia providing contemporary information on social, cultural, and political life in Latvia and links to further sources)

Notes

1. David Kirby, *The Baltic World, 1772–1993: Europe's Northern Periphery in an Age of Change* (New York: Longman, 1995), 317–28.

2. Walter C. Clemens Jr., *Baltic Independence and Russian Empire* (New York: St. Martin's Press, 1991), 53.

3. Prit Buttar, *Between Giants: The Battle for the Baltics in World War II* (Oxford, UK: Osprey Publishing, 2013).

4. Kevin O'Connor, *The History of the Baltic States* (Westport, CT: Greenwood Press, 2003), 126.

5. Alan Palmer, *The Baltic: A New History of the Region and Its People* (New York: Overlook Press, 2005), 380–81.

6. For broad examination of interethnic relations with a focus on the Baltic republics, see Rasma Karklins, *Ethnic Relations in the U.S.S.R.: The Perspective from Below* (New York: Routledge, 1988). On the glasnost-era discourse about Russian knowledge of the Baltic languages, see Clemens, *Baltic Independence and Russian Empire*, 78–82.

7. Daina S. Eglitis, *Imagining the Nation: History, Modernity, and Revolution in Latvia* (University Park: Pennsylvania State University Press, 2002), 34–36.

8. For an interesting discussion of the impact of environmental activism in opposition movements, see Jane I. Dawson, *Eco-nationalism: Anti-nuclear Activism in Russia, Lithuania, and Ukraine* (Durham, NC: Duke University Press, 1996).

9. For a comprehensive discussion of the opposition and early postcommunist periods, see Anatol Lieven, *The Baltic Revolution: Estonia, Latvia, Lithuania and the Path to Independence* (New Haven, CT: Yale University Press, 1993).

10. The tension between political currents favoring the past as a model for transformation and those favoring Western Europe as a model is discussed in Eglitis, *Imagining the Nation*.

11. Thomas Lane, *Lithuania: Stepping Westward* (New York: Routledge, 2002), 132.

12. Daunis Auers and Andres Kasekamp, "Explaining the Electoral Failure of Extreme-Right Parties in Estonia and Latvia," *Journal of Contemporary European Studies* 17, no. 2 (August 2009): 251.

13. For a discussion of the "radical" neoliberal economics embraced by the Baltics, see Dorothy Bohle and Bela Greskovits, "Neoliberalism, Embedded Neoliberalism, and Neocorporatism: Towards Transnational Capitalism in Central-Eastern Europe," *West European Politics* 30 (2007): 443–66.

14. Updated economic data and forecasts for the region are available at the European Bank for Reconstruction and Development website: http://www.ebrd.com.

15. Daina S. Eglitis and Tana Lace, "Stratification and the Poverty of Progress in Post-communist Latvian Capitalism," *Acta Sociologica* 52, no. 4 (December 2009): 329–49.

16. "Shadow Economy Share at 20% of GDP," Estonian Public Broadcasting, http://news.err .ee/economy/5bb4ecee-efe6-43d1-86ad-23132641dcba (accessed October 2013).

17. Akvile Motiejunaite, *Female Employment, Gender Roles, and Attitudes: The Baltic Countries in a Broader Context* (Stockholm: Stockholm University, 2008).

18. For a review of Baltic foreign policies, see David J. Galbreath, Ainius Lasas, and Jeremy W. Lamoreaux, *Continuity and Change in the Baltic Sea Region: Comparing Foreign Policies* (New York: Rodopi, 2008).

19. For a broad-ranging examination of issues of collective memory and history in the region, including the dispute over the Bronze Soldier in Estonia, see "Contested and Shared Places of Memory, History and Politics in North Eastern Europe," special issue of *Journal of Baltic Studies* 39, no. 4 (December 2008).

20. Boris Egorov, "Polish and Baltic Leaders Concerned about Upcoming Russian War Games," Atlantic Council, July 22, 2013, http://www.atlanticcouncil.org/blogs/natosource/polish -and-baltic-leaders-concerned-about-upcoming-russian-war-games (accessed October 2013).

21. Ivars Indans et al., "Latvija un briva darbaspeka kustiba: Irijas piemers" ["Latvia and the Free Migration of Labor: The Irish Case"], in *Strategiskas analizes komisijas zinojumi 2006* (Riga: Zinatne, 2007).

Map 14.0.   Bulgaria

CHAPTER 14

Bulgaria

PROGRESS AND DEVELOPMENT

Janusz Bugajski

In the last twenty-four years, Bulgaria successfully conducted two historic transformations: from a centrally controlled communist system to a pluralistic market-oriented democracy and from the closest ally of the Soviet Union in the former Warsaw Pact to a full member of the North Atlantic Treaty Organization (NATO). This dual transformation was neither consistent nor predictable. For much of the early and mid-1990s, the postcommunist Bulgarian socialists ruled. They resisted full-blown capitalism and a close alliance with the West largely in an effort to preserve their political and economic positions and maintain their traditional ties with Moscow. Sofia's turn toward Western institutions and economic models accelerated after 1998, when a reformist coalition government was elected. Bulgaria became a member of NATO in 2004 and of the European Union (EU) in 2007.

Precommunist Bulgaria

Bulgaria emerged as an independent state from the Ottoman Empire in several stages. In 1878, following the Russo-Turkish War, the Treaty of San Stefano created a large Bulgarian state stretching from the Danube to the Aegean and including most of present-day Macedonia. The Treaty of Berlin in July 1878 reduced this territory at the insistence of the great powers because of fears of Russian dominance throughout the Balkans. Bulgaria subsequently included the region between the Danube and the Balkan Mountains. The area between the Balkan Mountains in the north and the Rhodope Mountains in the south formed the autonomous Ottoman province of Eastern Rumelia. These border readjustments and Bulgaria's reversion to a semiautonomous Ottoman principality under a German ruler created widespread resentments. However, in 1879, Sofia adopted the progressive Turnovo Constitution that guaranteed individual rights, and in the following two decades, a number of political parties were established, including the National Liberal Party and the Bulgarian Agrarian Union.

The country proclaimed its full independence from Turkey in 1908 after several popular revolts, including the Ilinden uprising in August 1903, centered in the Macedonian and Thracian regions. Bulgaria's territorial claims contributed to fueling two Balkan wars in 1912 and 1913. In the first, the new Balkan states combined their forces to drive the Ottoman armies out of the region. In the second, Bulgaria was unsuccessful in its military campaign against Serbia and Greece and once again lost territories in Macedonia and Thrace to its two neighbors. The result left a lasting sense of injustice in Sofia with regard to Bulgaria's rightful frontiers. Sofia retained only a small slice of Pirin Macedonia and a sector of the Thracian coastline. During World War I, Bulgaria allied itself with Germany and Austria, but with the defeat of the Central Powers, it was forced to accept a harsh peace treaty at Neuilly in November 1919 and lost all access to the Aegean Sea.

For most of the interwar period, Bulgaria witnessed political turmoil and economic crisis, particularly after the overthrow of the Agrarian government led by Aleksandur Stamboliyski in 1923. Following a military coup d'état supported by political rivals and nationalist Macedonian activists, Stamboliyski and other Agrarian leaders were murdered. After a decade of political instability and conflict, another coup in May 1934 led by military officers resulted in the formation of a personalistic regime under King Boris III. During World War II, Sofia imposed a royal dictatorship and capitalized on the German occupation of Yugoslavia and Greece to forge an alliance with Berlin to regain parts of Macedonia and Thrace. Sofia also repossessed the region of southern Dobruja from Romania. King Boris died in August 1943. For the rest of the war, the country was ruled by a regency, as Boris's successor, Simeon, was only six years old. Bulgaria's territorial advances, including access to the Aegean coastline, were again reversed at the close of World War II, as Sofia found itself once more on the losing side.

Communist Experience

Communist forces, with Soviet military and political assistance, seized power in Bulgaria in September 1944 during the closing stages of World War II. At the end of 1947, they eliminated all organized political and social opposition. They then held falsified elections to legitimize their assumption of absolute power. Former Moscow-directed Communist International (Comintern) agent Georgi Dimitrov returned to Bulgaria from exile and assumed leadership of the Communist Party and the state. A new Stalinist "Dimitrov" constitution was passed in December 1947 that replicated the Soviet prototype. The communist regime, under Soviet supervision, began to place tight restrictions on cultural and political life, conducted a full-scale drive toward state control over the economy, and pursued agricultural collectivization among the peasantry.

Dimitrov died in July 1949 and was replaced by Vulko Chervenkov, another hardline Stalinist. Chervenkov in turn was replaced by Todor Zhivkov in April 1956 during the slow process of de-Stalinization. However, Zhivkov and his Communist Party maintained tight control over the country for the next thirty-four years until the collapse of the centralized system. Zhivkov's absolute loyalty to Moscow and his ability to thwart any organized domestic opposition to Leninist rule earned him the complete support of the Soviet leadership. There is even evidence that the Bulgarian regime sought to join the USSR as the sixteenth republic. Bulgaria was thus considered to be Moscow's closest and most loyal ally in the entire Soviet bloc.

Transition from Communism

Following a wave of public protests and increasing political pressures against the communist regime, on November 10, 1989, the Bulgarian Communist Party (BCP) Central Committee announced the resignation of Todor Zhivkov as secretary-general and his replacement by foreign minister Petar Mladenov. The new leader promised sweeping political and economic changes to transform Bulgaria into a "modern democratic state." The BCP organized pro-Mladenov rallies, depicting itself as the initiator of progressive reforms, scapegoating the Zhivkov leadership for all of the country's maladies, and trying to deny the reformist initiative to the emerging, but still embryonic, democratic opposition movement.

As head of the Bulgarian Communist Party, Mladenov held meetings with dissident activists in mid-November 1989 and pledged to implement substantive democratic reforms and legalize all types of independent groups and activities. The BCP's subordinate bodies, including the Komsomol youth association, were allowed to be more critical in an attempt to deflate some of the opposition's demands. Reshuffles were conducted in the BCP's governing Politburo and Central Committee, and Mladenov declared himself in favor of free general elections. Following massive public protests in Sofia, the regime dropped the BCP's "guiding force" role from the constitution and promised to curtail the repressive role of the security services. These steps paved the way for the creation of a multiparty system. While the BCP endeavored to maintain its political initiative, dozens of new political groups were forming during this time.

Some reform communists demanded the resignation of the entire BCP Central Committee as divisions deepened with the emergence of the Alternative Socialist Association as a faction within the party. In early December 1989, a preparatory meeting was held between BCP officials and representatives of some independent groups. Mladenov promised that the authorities would hold a constructive dialogue with all groups "supporting socialism." In order to incorporate leading opposition elements in some workable coalition and to prevent destructive splits within the party, the BCP initiated roundtable discussions with officially sponsored organizations and some of the newly formed opposition groups in January 1990.[1]

The regime continued to be treated with mistrust by most of the opposition, which refused to enter the Government of National Consensus proposed by the communists. At its Extraordinary Congress, held in early February 1990, the BCP selected Alexander Lilov as its new secretary-general and replaced the Central Committee with a smaller Supreme Party Council and the ruling Politburo with a new presidency. BCP leaders also initiated steps to separate the party from the state (which they had fully controlled), and the party itself was renamed the Bulgarian Socialist Party (BSP) to distance it from its totalitarian past.

The National Assembly (parliament), controlled by the BSP, elected Andrey Lukanov as the new prime minister. Lukanov attempted to form a more broadly based coalition government, but the initiative was rejected by the Union of Democratic Forces (UDF), which had grown into the chief democratic opposition alliance. The new cabinet became an all-communist body as the BSP's former communist era coalition partner, the Agrarian People's Union, refused to join the Lukanov government and purged itself of compromised older leaders. In addition, reformist BSP intellectuals established an Alternative Socialist Party and cast serious doubts on the BSP's ability to democratize. Meanwhile, the UDF organized public demonstrations to protest the slow progress in the roundtable negotiations and the limitations on the democratic transition.

By mid-March 1990, the BSP and UDF had reached an agreement on the transition to a democratic system and the scheduling of competitive national elections. The BSP won the parliamentary elections held on June 10 and 17, 1990, with 47.15 percent of the vote, giving the party 211 of the 400 parliamentary seats. The UDF obtained a disappointing 36.20 percent (144 seats). The Agrarian People's Union took 8 percent (16 seats), and the Turkish party, Movement for Rights and Freedoms (MRF), garnered 6 percent of the vote (23 seats). The UDF accused the regime of ballot rigging and maintaining a monopoly over the media. The opposition had insufficient time to organize an effective election campaign and scored particularly poorly in rural areas where the communist-socialist apparatus remained largely intact.

In April 1990, parliament formally created the office of the president but limited its authority to security matters and ceremonial functions by giving the president no veto power over parliamentary legislation. On July 6, 1990, Mladenov resigned as acting president, and the BSP threw its support behind Zheliu Zhelev as the country's new head of state. When the UDF refused to form a coalition to ensure a two-thirds parliamentary majority, the Lukanov government was stalemated. The BSP-led Lukanov government resigned at the end of November 1990 and was replaced a month later by a coalition headed by Prime Minister Dimitur Popov that included the BSP, the UDF, the Agrarians, and independents.

Political Institutions

The unicameral National Assembly also became a constitutional assembly that drafted Bulgaria's new democratic constitution. The document defined Bulgaria as a parliamentary democracy and a unitary state and prohibited any form of territorial autonomy or the creation of political parties founded on an "ethnic, racial, or religious" basis. Parliament was given legislative supremacy; the president had the right to veto legislation passed by the National Assembly. This constitution was eventually adopted in July 1991 despite opposition from some UDF factions. The National Assembly is elected every four years by a popular ballot, and the majority party or a coalition that consists of a parliamentary majority forms the new government. The president of Bulgaria is elected in a general election every five years. According to the constitution, his or her role is more ceremonial and symbolic than substantive in terms of decision making. Any amendments to the constitution require a three-fourths majority in parliament. However, a completely new constitution would need to be adopted by a newly elected Grand National Assembly. Bulgaria's local government consists of twenty-eight provinces named after the provincial capitals, with the national capital itself forming a separate province. The provinces are further subdivided into a total of 264 municipalities, which are the main units of local government.

Parties and Elections

Prior to the October 1991 elections, the UDF split because its largest coalition partners, the Social Democratic Party and the Agrarian National Union "Nikola Petkov," were refused a more prominent voice on the UDF Council or a greater number of candidates on the UDF electoral list. In addition, it was divided between advocates of a moderate line toward the BSP (the "light blues") and a majority demanding far-reaching decommunization and a settling of scores with the repressive communist leadership (the "dark blues"). The light blues withdrew from the union and formed the UDF-Liberals. The dark blues became known as the UDF-Movement and inherited the coalition's organizational network and media outlets.

In the October 1991 elections, the UDF-Movement narrowly won a plurality of votes despite declining support for the BSP. The UDF received 34.36 percent of the vote (110 of 240 parliamentary seats). The BSP gained 33.14 percent, claiming 106 seats. The only other party to clear the 4 percent threshold and gain parliamentary seats was the Turkish-based Movement for Rights and Freedoms. Not surprisingly, the parliament became highly polarized, and the UDF had to form a coalition government with the MRF, headed by Prime Minister Filip Dimitrov, who was installed in office in November 1991.

A top priority of the UDF-MRF administration was decommunization in all public institutions and the elimination of subversive activities by secret service officers who were trying to obstruct market reform. This task proved difficult because of the entrenched interests that pervaded most state bodies and enterprises. The National Assembly passed a law to confiscate communist property. The prosecution of former communist officials was intensified. About fifty prominent figures were indicted, including Todor Zhivkov. Former members of the defunct communist structures depicted the decommunization campaign as a witch hunt that undermined economic progress and failed to do anything for ordinary citizens. The UDF leadership asserted that, without the ouster of communist officials and the elimination of special interests, which were undermining the Bulgarian economy, the market reform program would not succeed.

The Dimitrov government gave qualified support for Zheliu Zhelev in the first direct presidential ballot in January 1992. Zhelev was a sociologist who had been expelled from the Communist Party in the late 1980s for organizing a group to support political reform. The president was pressured to accept as his running mate prominent Bulgarian writer Blaga Dimitrova from the UDF-Movement in return for the party's endorsement. Zhelev received only 45 percent of the votes in the first round of balloting and 53 percent in the second round against the BSP candidate Velko Vulkanov. There was incessant hostility between the UDF administration and President Zhelev, who represented a more moderate policy line toward the socialists. Both the government and parliament criticized Zhelev for appointing ex-communists, and both institutions tried to further undercut the president's powers.

By the summer of 1992, the Dimitrov government faced internal splits over such issues as the return of the monarchy, the leadership of the Bulgarian Orthodox Church, and the pace of economic reform. The MRF was particularly disturbed: the decline in the economy seriously affected the Turkish rural population since the land reforms implemented favored former Bulgarian owners, and the state was slow to redistribute property to minorities from the state land fund. MRF leader Ahmed Dogan called for a change of policy, but when this failed in October 1992, the MRF parliamentary delegation joined with the BSP in a vote of no confidence in the UDF government. This motion was supported by Zhelev, who accused Dimitrov of undermining the presidency and alienating the population.

Prime Minister Dimitrov resigned on October 28, 1992. His cabinet was replaced by an "expert" government headed by the socialist Lyuben Berov that survived until September 2, 1994. It came under mounting criticism for rampant corruption and ties to clandestine business interests. As a result, it was replaced by a caretaker administration under Reneta Indzhova on October 17, 1994, that was to hold power until early general elections were held.

The BSP returned to power in the elections of December 18, 1994, winning 43.5 percent of the popular vote and 125 parliamentary seats. This time, only five parties were able to cross the 4 percent threshold to gain parliamentary representation, compared to the seven parties that entered parliament after the June 1990 elections. BSP leader Zhan Videnov, known as a hard-liner and antireformer, became the new prime minister.[2] Two allied parties, the Bulgarian Agrarian People's Union "Alexander Stamboliyski" and the Political Club Ecoglasnost, which were on the same list as the BSP in the elections, joined the government coalition. The popular swing toward the BSP was confirmed during local elections in October 1994, when socialist candidates received 41 percent of the votes and the UDF only 25 percent.

The UDF had suffered substantial losses in these elections, gaining only sixty-nine parliamentary seats. The party's defeat was blamed largely on the preelection economic downturn and on internal squabbling that made a coherent and determined policy line impossible. Following their defeat, the UDF leadership resigned en masse. In early 1995, Ivan Kostov, a liberal reformer and former professor at Sofia Technical University, was elected to replace Filip Dimitrov as UDF leader. He moved to better coordinate the UDF, undercut the independence of its constituent parties and factions, and improve relations with the MRF and other opposition formations.

During its term in office, the socialist administration under Videnov's leadership, which took power after the December 1994 elections, was accused of maintaining secret connections with business conglomerates siphoning off state funds for the benefit of the old communist apparatus. Failure to follow through on reform measures also led to a rapid downturn of the economy that seriously affected living standards. Policy differences between reformists and conservatives became insurmountable, and the opposition frequently called for votes of no confidence in the administration.

The slow progress of the BSP during 1995 and 1996 in implementing reforms, as well as its mishandling of the economy, led to a host of financial, social, and economic problems. These reached crisis proportions by the mid-1990s. Meanwhile, the UDF gradually began to regain its popular support by promoting a pro-reform and pro-Western agenda. The UDF had several splits, but it remained the most credible center-right force in Bulgarian politics throughout the 1990s. It operated as a broad anticommunist movement from its inception, with support drawn mostly from among the young, educated, entrepreneurial, and urban populations.

The year 1996 proved to be a watershed in Bulgaria. The country experienced serious economic difficulties caused by the absence of systematic market reforms, widespread corruption, and even outright theft by government officials. Pressures increased for an early parliamentary ballot that could dislodge the former communists from power. However, the BSP and its coalition partners maintained a secure parliamentary majority despite growing pressures from the major opposition bloc, the UDF. The political scene remained polarized between these two formations. Their ideological differences were evident in all major issues affecting Bulgarian society. The socialists were determined to maintain the economic status quo and stalled the mass privatization program, leading to an even more serious economic decline. Moreover, the government was opposed to NATO membership and strengthened its relations with Russia, despite criticisms from the opposition.

Rifts were also evident within the Socialist Party between the harder-line members linked to Prime Minister Zhan Videnov and reformist elements critical of government policy. These divisions widened after the assassination of former prime minister Andrey Lukanov at the beginning of October 1996. Lukanov had become an outspoken critic of official resistance to reform. Allegedly, he also possessed information on corruption at the highest levels of government that he reportedly planned to make public.[3] Observers contended that Lukanov himself was deeply involved in corruption, and his killing resembled a gangland assassination.

The presidential elections further undermined the socialist administration. UDF candidate Petar Stoyanov gained an overwhelming percentage of votes (44 percent) over the socialist Ivan Marazov (27 percent) in the first round of voting on October 27, 1996. Stoyanov was elected president in the second-round runoff on November 3, 1996, with 59.7 percent of the vote to Marazov's 40.3 percent.[4] Although the post of president was primarily ceremonial, the result emboldened the opposition to push for a no-confidence vote in the socialist government.

During 1996, Bulgaria faced a major financial crisis. Its hard-currency reserves plummeted, and there were growing doubts that Sofia could meet its critical foreign debt payments. The government continued to prop up obsolete and uncompetitive state-owned industries. Moreover, the former communist apparatus still controlled and exploited much of the economy through shady "economic groups," where corruption was believed to be rampant. An ambitious mass-privatization program remained stalled in parliament because of powerful vested interests. As the financial crisis deepened and the currency collapsed, prices soared dramatically. Bread shortages were reported in various parts of the country, and analysts warned of severe food and fuel shortages during the winter months. Bulgaria was in the midst of a banking crisis and entered a period of hyperinflation, which surpassed 2,000 percent on an annual basis in March 1997.[5]

Large sectors of the public were angry about the rapid decline in their living standards and the reports of widespread corruption among government officials. Following several months of protests and public demonstrations, the increasingly isolated socialist government of Prime Minister Videnov resigned in December 1996. The newly inaugurated President Stoyanov called for early parliamentary elections in April 1997 and appointed the mayor of Sofia, the popular and charismatic reformer Stefan Sofianski, as caretaker prime minister.

The Union of Democratic Forces (UDF) participated in the presidential elections in October and November 1996 and in the April 1997 parliamentary elections as part of a broader coalition, the United Democratic Forces (UDF). Its chief allies in the coalition included the Democratic Party and the Agrarian People's Union, which formed the People's Union alliance. The Agrarian People's Union, originally a founder of the UDF in 1989 under the name Agrarian People's Union "Nikola Petkov," was one of about twenty groups claiming to be the successors of the precommunist Agrarians. Most of them were right-of-center formations.

The United Democratic Forces won the April 1997 election overwhelmingly with 52 percent of the vote, gaining 137 of 240 parliamentary seats; the BSP only got 22 percent of the vote and 58 seats. Ivan Kostov, the UDF leader, was appointed prime minister. The composition of his cabinet reflected Bulgaria's commitment to intensive economic and political reforms and included pro-Western liberal reformers. The new administration benefited from broad public support even though the impact of the planned economic reforms was painful for workers in state industries.

The key priorities of the UDF-led coalition government were stabilizing the economy, combating crime and corruption, and pursuing Euro-Atlantic integration. The UDF-dominated legislature passed a number of important measures to root out the corruption that had become endemic among state officials and industrial managers. A new law passed in September 1997 prohibited members of the former communist apparatus from obtaining high positions in the civil service for a period of five years. Parliament also approved the opening up of secret police files to determine which top officials had collaborated with the communist-era security services and engaged in repressive acts. This move indicated that the authorities favored openness and transparency in government operations. Investigations into large-scale corruption were also initiated since some former socialist officials were believed to have embezzled millions of dollars from state funds.

The authorities were determined to pursue a radical economic reform program to avert a major financial crisis. In consultation with the International Monetary Fund (IMF), Sofia launched a far-reaching "stabilization program" that lifted most price controls, pegged the national currency to the German mark, and established a currency board to control government spending. As a result, the inflation rate decreased dramatically. Parliament also approved a new budget that cut state spending and reduced the subsidies on unprofitable industries. An extensive privatization program was launched that had an impact on the majority of state-owned enterprises. The possibility for social unrest remained since living standards declined sharply as a result of the government's austerity measures and budgetary discipline.

The new government was also determined to pursue Bulgaria's integration into various Euro-Atlantic institutions. President Stoyanov declared that Bulgaria was seeking membership in NATO and was willing to undertake the necessary reforms of its military structure. The previous socialist administration had been ambiguous about alliance membership and preferred a policy of neutrality and close relations with Russia. The new pro-NATO policy dismayed Bulgaria's traditional ally Russia. As a result, relations between Sofia and Moscow grew tense. Bulgaria's interior minister also accused Moscow of racketeering because of its manipulation of gas prices and control over Bulgarian energy supplies.

The parliamentary majority held by the UDF ensured that the reform program was not seriously challenged by the socialist opposition. Stoyanov remained very popular despite the painful austerity program imposed by the UDF authorities. However, the local elections in October 1999 were a setback for the UDF, which only narrowly defeated the socialists in a majority of Bulgarian municipalities. Growing public frustration with layoffs and state spending cuts resulted in a decreased voter turnout of some 50 percent. However, the UDF retained control of the two major cities, Sofia and Plovdiv. Despite the progress achieved by the UDF in securing macroeconomic stability and fulfilling the criteria for international loans, the living standards of the majority of citizens actually stagnated or fell after the elections, especially among pensioners, rural workers, and blue-collar employees, angering the population.

The Bulgarian political scene changed dramatically in April 2001 with the return of the exiled King Simeon II. The ex-monarch, deposed by the communists after World War II, formed his own political group, styled as the National Movement Simeon II (NMS). This center-right organization drew support away from both the UDF and the opposition socialists. In the parliamentary elections held on June 17, 2001, the NMS scored a landslide victory, gaining 42.73 percent of the vote and 120 seats in the 240-seat legislature. The UDF finished a distant second with 18.17 percent and 51 seats. Two other parties passed the electoral threshold: the Socialist Party captured 17.14 percent of the vote and 48 seats; the Turkish minority-based MRF garnered 7.45 percent and 21 seats.

Simeon II thus became the first monarch to return to power in postcommunist Central and Eastern Europe, although he made no attempt to re-create the monarchy. His party captured the protest vote of impoverished elements of the Bulgarian population, and his selection of young Western-educated professionals as parliamentarians and ministers increased public support for him and his party. The king himself did not run in the elections and, at first, did not even put himself forward as prime minister. He also denied that there were any plans to restore the monarchy and pointed out that the country had far more pressing issues to contend with, such as unemployment, poverty, and corruption.

Critics charged that the NMS message was too populist and insufficiently specific on economic policies. NMS leaders countered that they would continue with the reform program launched by the UDF while paying more attention to combating corruption, attracting foreign investment, reforming the judicial system, and creating new employment opportunities. Moreover, Simeon underscored his government's commitment to the European Union and NATO integration.

The NMS triumph jettisoned what had essentially become a two-party system. However, the victors indicated they were intent on creating a coalition government to achieve broader political consensus and ensure effective government during a difficult reform process. The Bulgarian public seemed to reject the continued polarization of public life by voting for this movement that pledged to unify the nation. The MRF was the first party to offer its cooperation, indicating a valuable opportunity for involving the sizable Turkish population in the governing process. In mid-July 2001, Simeon agreed to assume the post of prime minister and proceeded to form a new cabinet.

The NMS electoral base proved diverse. The party's ministers were a mixture of young bankers with Western experience, older Bulgarian lawyers, and representatives of local business groups. However, the NMS government's failure to meet unrealistic popular expectations led to a progressive drop in support for the government and its programs, as well as increasing divisions within the NMS itself. By late 2003, 11 members of parliament (MPs) had defected from the NMS's initial parliamentary contingent of 120; 10 of them formed the National Ideal of Unity faction to the left of the NMS. The New Time group of 22 MPs on the NMS's right also became largely independent. NMS candidates performed poorly in local elections in October 2003, especially as the movement lacked any significant local structures. Although it declared its intention to transform itself into a political party, the NMS lacked cohesion and was principally based on the personality of its leader.

Following its defeat in the 2001 elections, the UDF disintegrated. In fact, by 2004 the center-right splintered into several rival formations, most with weak organizational structures but with charismatic leaders. Some activists were concerned that this development would exclude them from parliament or enable the socialists to form a workable governing coalition. Mayor of Sofia and former caretaker prime minister Stefan Sofianski broke away from the UDF in late 2001 after failing to persuade his colleagues to form a coalition with the NMS. He founded a separate party, the Union of Free Democrats. Although the party was small, Sofianski benefited from high ratings on a national level. Ivan Kostov resigned as the UDF's leader and created the Democrats for a Strong Bulgaria (DSB) in May 2004, pulling some supporters away from the UDF. Other center-right groupings included the Bulgarian Agrarian People's Union, the St. George's Day Movement (Gergyovden), and the New Time.[6]

The appointment of Nadezhda Mihailova, the former foreign minister, as UDF caretaker leader in March 2002 provoked intense criticism and did not improve the UDF's popularity ratings. The UDF's performance in the local elections in October 2003 was disappointing for the party. Mihailova came under increasing attack from Kostov and other UDF leaders at that time. UDF's public support had dropped even further by the 2005 elections.

In 2005, the Bulgarian electorate followed its pattern of always voting out the ruling coalition. This time it was motivated by disappointment that the NMS had not managed to transform the economy enough to benefit the older and less educated part of the population or achieve its promises to control both corruption and organized crime. Beyond this, the "kingmaker" MRF gained from the emergence of a far-right, anticommunist, xenophobic party, Ataka, which ultimately got 8.75 percent of the vote. Its attacks stimulated MRF voters to go to the polls, allowing the MRF to do far better than had been expected.

This time, both the UDF and the NMS lost to the Coalition for Bulgaria, which centered on the Bulgarian Socialist Party, the successor to the Bulgarian Communist Party. Its victory was marginal; with only 34.17 percent of the vote for the BSP and 14.17 percent for the MRF, the two could not form a majority coalition. The Bulgarian Socialist Party, therefore, had to reach out to the NMS (22.8 percent) to join forces for a three-party center-left coalition. This process was facilitated by the BSP's campaign commitment to continuing the economic reforms and maintaining a centrist posture to keep Bulgaria turned toward the West. The resulting government was peopled by men and women in their thirties and forties, with Sergey Stanishev, the thirty-nine-year-old BSP leader, as prime minister. The three deputy prime ministers represented the three coalition partners. Financial issues were given to a former member of the UDF. The

Photo 14.1. Ultranationalist party Union Attack members demonstrate against a loudspeaker at a mosque in Sofia. In Bulgaria's 2005 parliamentary elections, Union Attack received nearly 9 percent of the vote. (Nadya Kotseva/Sofia Photo Agency)

minister of European affairs, charged with moving Bulgaria toward its 2007 entry into the European Union, continued on from the NMS movement.

Despite all these political splits, by the early 2000s, Bulgaria had developed a relatively stable democratic system with a functioning market economy. The country had held several free and democratic elections, and the political transition between governing parties had been smooth and trouble free. The policies of all the major political forces had been pro-reform and pro-NATO, and even the postcommunist Socialist Party developed a Western and pro-NATO orientation after losing power in 1997.

Most of the BSP social base consisted of pensioners, peasants, some of the technical intelligentsia, and Bulgarians in ethnically mixed areas who veered toward nationalism. The party itself incorporated a spectrum of political trends, from Marxist dogmatists to social democrats. The more market-oriented social democrats began to prevail in the late 1990s after the party's credibility was undermined by the 1996–1997 economic collapse. Georgi Parvanov, elected BSP leader in 1996, pursued a policy of economic reform, social democracy, and pro-Westernism, including support for NATO membership. His position was buttressed by his victory in the presidential ballot in 2001. Perceived as a young reformist at the time, Sergey Stanishev was elected to be his successor as Socialist Party leader in December 2001.

During 2003 and 2004, the BSP increased its popularity largely in reaction to falling public support for the incumbent NMS-led government as a result of hard-hitting reforms. This fact was demonstrated in its performance in the 2003 municipal elections.

Photo 14.2.   Georgi Parvanov was elected president in 2001. In 1996, he was elected head of the Bulgarian Socialist Party, where he pursued a policy of economic reform, social democracy, and a pro-Western foreign policy, including support for NATO membership. (Website of the president of the Republic of Bulgaria, http://www .president.bg)

However, the party also has experienced internal divisions. It has endeavored to consolidate its popularity by broadening its appeal among younger citizens. Most of the BSP's political partners are small, center-left formations with limited public support, including the Bulgarian Social Democratic Party and the United Labor Bloc. A relatively successful center-left formation in the late 1990s called Euroleft formed as a breakaway group from the BSP. It entered parliament in 1997 but failed to gain seats in 2001 and subsequently disappeared from the political scene.

Bulgaria has come a long way in its transformation process, as demonstrated by its accession into NATO and the EU in 2007. However, economic development, structural reform, judicial effectiveness, and public trust continue to be undermined by official corruption and organized cross-border criminality.[7] Political corruption deepened in 2008 and 2009 involving cases bordering on state capture, flagrant instances of conflict of interest, and the use of public resources for personal benefit. Although corruption among business decreased by 50 percent after Bulgaria's EU accession, procurement of public funds, and particularly EU funding for a number of development projects, became the new target for corruption schemes. As a result, the European Commission withdrew millions of euros allocated to agriculture and administrative modernization in Bulgaria. The impunity of high-level corruption and organized crime earned Bulgaria the label of "the most corrupt EU country."[8]

Bulgarian parliamentary elections on July 5, 2009, revolved around tackling official corruption and controlling the economic recession. Because of widespread dissatisfaction with the ruling socialists and public outrage with misappropriation of EU funds, the elections were comfortably won by the center-right Citizens for the European Development of Bulgaria (GERB), which received 39.7 percent of the vote. The BSP slipped to 17.7 percent; the Turkish MRF gained 14.4 percent, the ultranationalist Ataka, 9.4 percent, the center-right Blue Coalition (led by the UDF), 6.8 percent, and the rightist Order, Lawfulness, and Justice (RZS), 4.1 percent. GERB gained 116 out of 240 parliamentary seats, followed by BSP (40), MRF (38), Ataka (21), the Blue Coalition (15), and RZS (10). Boyko Borisov, a former chief secretary of the Interior Ministry and former mayor of Sofia, became prime minister on July 27, 2009.

The GERB government undertook measures to combat corruption and organized crime and restore confidence in Bulgaria's ability to manage EU funds. Shortly after taking office, Borisov's government adopted a fifty-seven-point plan to implement the EU's recommendations to reform law enforcement and the judiciary. The EU unblocked €156 million in pre-accession agriculture funds due to the new government's initial efforts to implement EU recommendations. Specialized police operations against organized criminal groups eliminated the most notorious ones, and a number of high-profile criminal bosses were imprisoned. However, little improvement was observed in reform of the judicial system. Media freedom also declined with the few remaining independent news outlets subjected to political pressure. Concentrated media ownership by interrelated oligarchic structures raised EU criticism.[9]

In the midst of Europe's financial crisis, the Borisov government managed to maintain financial stability and largely preserve the country's fiscal reserves. Austerity measures helped keep the budget deficit low—it was 0.8 percent of gross domestic product (GDP) in 2012.

The government revised three major Russian energy projects signed by the previous socialist-led coalition: the Burgas-Alexandropulos oil pipeline with a 51 percent Russian share, the second nuclear power plant at Belene with Russian-built reactors, and the South Stream natural gas pipeline with 50 percent Russian ownership. The government scraped the first two projects, backing only South Stream. The GERB-controlled parliament adopted an indefinite moratorium on shale gas exploration and extraction under pressure from green groups and lobbyists for Russian energy interests in Bulgaria.[10]

Increased electricity prices provoked massive public protests in January and February 2013, forcing the government to resign on February 20. On March 13, President Rosen Plevneliev appointed a caretaker government headed by career diplomat Marin Raykov. Parliamentary elections took place on May 12, 2013, with only four political parties passing the threshold. GERB won the elections with 30.54 percent of the vote, gaining 97 of the 240 seats in parliament, but it was unable to form a government without a coalition partner. The elections produced a hung parliament, with BSP and its junior partner, MRF, together gaining exactly half the seats in the National Assembly. BSP received 26.61 percent of the vote and 84 parliamentary seats; MRF took 11.31 percent and 36 seats; Ataka received 7.30 percent and 23 seats. Ataka declared it would not enter into coalition with GERB and refrained from formally entering into a coalition with BSP and

MRF. However, the ultranationalists eventually sided with the socialist-led coalition and helped it form a government. For the first time, none of the traditional center-right parties instrumental in Bulgaria's democratic transition made it to parliament, including the Union of Democratic Forces and Democrats for a Strong Bulgaria.

On May 29, the Socialist Party, in coalition with the ethnic Turkish MRF, formed a government supported by Ataka. Two weeks later, parliament provoked public outrage with the appointment of controversial media mogul Delyan Peevski, an MP from the Turkish party, as chairman of the State Agency for National Security. Peevski's name has been linked to corruption and shady business interests.[11] A wave of public protests continued even after the appointment was revoked, with thousands of demonstrators demanding the government's resignation. Daily demonstrations took place in Sofia during the summer and fall of 2013 as Bulgaria entered a period of political turmoil with a government that had little credibility. An October 2013 opinion poll showed that only 23 percent of citizens trusted the government, and 76 percent wanted early elections.[12] President Plevneliev expressed support for the protestors and called for early elections. But the government survived, and as the crisis in Ukraine began in late 2013, security concerns preoccupied the politicians and the public, along with preparations for the May 2014 elections for the European Parliament. The MRF nominated Delyan Peevski as its leading candidate for the European Parliament, sparking new controversies.[13]

Civil Society

A host of independent groups appeared in the early 1990s, ranging from environmental movements to consumer organizations and public policy institutes.[14] A new nongovernmental organization (NGO) law adopted in 2000 introduced the concept of public benefit organizations. This legislation created special financial and tax incentives for NGOs because they were seen as complementary to the state in dealing with important social issues. Parliament also formed the Civil Society Committee, a special standing committee to promote the development of civil society. It provides NGOs with an opportunity to publicly present their issues. However, because of the diversity of civil society, not all of its members' important issues are presented at this forum. To increase its legitimacy, the Civil Society Committee has created its own consultative body, the Public Council, with NGO representatives from different fields of expertise and diverse geographic regions to more effectively promote its agenda in parliament.

In some areas, the NGO-government partnership has developed fruitfully, especially in terms of providing social services at the local level. Often, municipalities contract with NGOs to be independent providers of social services. NGOs are allowed to perform a few health activities in the areas of mental health and health education.

Economic Transition

By the end of the 1990s, Bulgaria had made steady progress in stabilizing its economy under the center-right government elected in 1997. The administration remained focused on privatizing major state-owned enterprises and proved successful in stabilizing the banking sector and reforming social security, health care, and the pension system. Major economic reforms were implemented largely under the auspices of the IMF. These included price liberalization, reduction of tariffs, a balanced state budget, liquidation of unprofitable companies, privatization, removal of state subsidies, a simple taxation system without preferential treatment for any social sector, and the deregulation of the energy and telecommunications sectors.

The Bulgarian economy was stabilized at the macroeconomic level under the UDF government in the late 1990s when it introduced an effective currency board system to control state spending. When the NMS government came to power in 2001, it maintained the commitment to privatization, economic growth, and attracting foreign investment. The country registered a steady growth in GDP in the early 2000s, reaching a nearly 5 percent growth rate in 2002, 4.2 percent in 2003, 5.8 percent in 2004, and 4.3 percent in 2005. Agriculture has been steadily declining in Bulgaria in terms of overall economic growth, from just under 17 percent of GDP in 1999 to under 12 percent in 2003 and 9.3 percent in 2005. The service sector contributed some 58 percent of GDP and industry about 29 percent. Fruits, livestock, tobacco, vegetables, and wine continue to be among Bulgaria's chief exports, while imports mainly include machinery, equipment, technology, mineral fuels, and processed goods. Bulgaria's national debt continued to climb and stood at $13.7 billion in 2003 and €14.5 billion ($17.5 billion) at the close of 2005, an indication that the economy continued to be at least partially reliant on borrowing from overseas sources. Nevertheless, the government was able to meet its debt-repayment requirements on schedule.

During the 1990s, Bulgaria diversified its trade and became less reliant on the former Soviet bloc. Trade with the European Union increased steadily, especially with Italy, Germany, and Greece. Bulgaria's exports to the ten new EU member states increased by 10.5 percent in the first quarter of 2004, while imports from these countries grew 29.4 percent. In its trade with the Commonwealth of Independent States (CIS), Bulgaria's exports dropped slightly; imports from the CIS increased 15 percent. Bulgarian exports overall increased to Russia and all neighboring countries except Turkey. As Bulgaria wanted to join the European Union, it increasingly geared its economy toward compatibility with the European market and sought investments from Western countries.

The rate of foreign direct investment (FDI) steadily increased during the term of the center-right governments after 1997 as Western business felt more confident in Bulgaria's institutional, fiscal, and social stability. Anticorruption measures were implemented, although Western businesses and the European Union pressured Sofia to pursue more comprehensive judicial and administrative reform to increase investor confidence. According to data from the Bulgarian National Bank (BNB), between 2000 and 2003 Bulgaria attracted around $3 billion in direct business investment from abroad, which was about half of the total investment attracted for the previous eleven years. In 2003 alone, foreign investment was estimated to be $1.32 billion, or 7 percent of the country's GDP. FDI inflows in 2005 reached $3 billion and continued to climb until the global economic downturn in 2008.

Most of the measures adopted by the NMS government after it came to power in 2001 were aimed at supporting specific business sectors. These measures involved the introduction of tax preferences and concessions in public procurement and increased subsidies for agriculture, tobacco growing, and certain state-owned enterprises. At the same time, in order to maintain fiscal discipline, public spending in 2002 was reduced to 39 percent of GDP, compared to 40 percent in 1998 and 44 percent in 2000. The percentage rose after 2007 as Bulgaria began to make its first contributions to the EU budget.[15]

The government's involvement in the economy remains significant. By May 2003, about 53.6 percent of state-owned assets were privatized. The public sector constituted 24 percent of GDP. Since then, the privatization process has accelerated, and a number of large enterprises, including the Bulgarian Telecommunications Company; the tobacco-industrial complex, Bulgartabac; seven electric-power distribution companies; and thirty-six hydroelectric power plants have been earmarked for sale. The privatization program was implemented in three ways: capital market offerings, centralized public auctions, and cash privatization. Among the bigger enterprises offered for sale were the Pleven oil and gas prospecting company; the Energoremont companies for power facility repairs in Ruse, Bobov Dol, Varna, and Sofia; and the Maritsa 3 thermal power plant in Dimitrovgrad.

The restitution of land and other assets to property owners or their relatives dispossessed by communist nationalization and collectivization proved complicated. Many of the private holdings acquired by farmers after 1990 were small and required owners to band together in some form of cooperative in order to afford mechanized equipment or irrigation. Compensation notes and vouchers were issued in the restitution process to owners who could not recover their actual property for a variety of reasons.

Although the Bulgarian economy continued to grow until 2008, income distribution remained a serious problem. Several parts of the population have not felt any improvement in their living standards. The most deprived groups are those who live in rural communities, ethnic minorities, and unemployed citizens. Large sectors of the population continue to experience low standards of living, long-term unemployment, and low salaries, while the extent of foreign investment has been limited compared to that in other postcommunist states such as Poland or Hungary.[16] The unemployment rate remained high throughout the transition. It stood at 16.3 percent of the total workforce by the end of the 1990s and climbed to 17.6 percent in 2002 before falling to 10 percent in 2005 and rising again during the economic recession in 2008 and 2009. The reasons are common for most postcommunist states: the closure of old loss-making enterprises, the unstable business environment in a fragile market economy, and the slow development of new businesses, which are mostly small or medium sized. In 2009, the booming construction market in Bulgaria collapsed, seriously impacting unemployment rates. The labor market is also relatively rigid; bureaucratic restraints make hiring and firing very costly. In addition, privatization, enterprise restructuring, and military downsizing have left many people jobless.

Faced with the challenge of high unemployment statistics, the government implemented various reforms aimed at removing some of the bureaucratic restraints, encouraging labor market flexibility, and funding a variety of retraining programs for job seekers. These reforms proved relatively successful, and the unemployment rate slowly decreased after early 2004 and stood at around 10 percent by the second quarter of 2005.

After the government reforms, the job market improved with steady 5 to 6 percent economic growth between 2003 and 2008 and increased foreign investment in this period. Urban unemployment is drastically lower than in rural areas. In Sofia, the rate in May 2004 stood at 3.44 percent, followed by Burgas and Varna, with 3.75 and 4.86 percent, respectively. In comparison, smaller towns like Turgovishte and Montana suffered from 27.29 and 22.87 percent unemployment, respectively. In 2012, the difference between employment rates in rural and urban regions stood at 12.8 percent, according to Eurostat. EU regional development funds and various government and private initiatives are intended to remedy the situation.

According to a report by the National Statistical Institute (NSI) released in June 2004, the total average personal income in April 2004 reached 157 leva ($96.86) per month, while the average income per household per month totaled 406.47 leva ($250.60). Average personal income increased steadily during the 2000s and kept pace with the inflation rate until the global recession began to impact the Bulgarian economy at the end of the decade. In 2013, the average salary in Bulgaria was estimated at 789 leva ($548).

The International Monetary Fund registered an 11.7 percent fall in Bulgaria's GDP in 2009, bringing it to −5.5 percent. GDP growth returned to barely positive levels in 2010 (0.4 percent) and remained insignificant in 2011 (1.7 percent) and 2012 (0.8 percent). However, economists and EU governments applauded the fiscal restraint shown by the government of Prime Minister Borisov, elected on a promise to combat corruption, a problem that led the EU to freeze $1.56 billion in aid to Bulgaria in 2008. Under his administration Bulgaria's economy avoided emergency financing and the double-digit economic contractions seen in Latvia, Lithuania, and Estonia. Nonetheless, the unemployment rate reached 10.2 percent in 2010 as the government was planning to streamline the state bureaucracy and cut back on official spending. According to the NSI, unemployment in 2011 was 11.3 percent and in 2012, it was 12.3 percent. In the second quarter of 2013, the jobless rate went up to 12.9 percent, or 437,300 people.[17] According to the IMF, unemployment will remain high in 2014, registering 12.5 percent at the end of the year. The IMF expects a further increase of 2.5 percent in 2015, reaching 15 percent, the highest levels since 2002, when unemployment reached 18 percent.[18] The socialist-led coalition introduced a program of social assistance for vulnerable groups such as young mothers and first graders, which caused concerns that Bulgaria's fiscal reserve will be depleted.

Social Impact

In an attempt to bridge the poverty gap, the government undertook a series of initiatives and social welfare programs. It increased the subsidies for agriculture, tobacco growing, and state-owned enterprises. The ratio of subsidies as a portion of GDP increased from 2.1 percent in 1998 to 2.4 percent in 2002; social and welfare spending increased from 11 percent of GDP in 1998 to 14.6 percent in 2002.[19] However, simultaneously under IMF requirements, Bulgaria needed to balance the state budget. Doing so was difficult without increasing the tax burden on besieged small and medium enterprises, which make up the majority of the economy. Instead of increasing such taxes, the authorities have tried to broaden the tax base and make tax collection more effective. Although the government faced difficulties in meeting the IMF's budgetary targets in some years, in 2003 it registered a budgetary surplus, which remained in place until 2009, when a budgetary deficit of −0.9

percent was registered. The budgetary deficit was –3.9 percent in 2010, dropped slightly to –2.1 percent in 2011, and decreased further to –1.9 in 2012.

An ongoing problem for Bulgaria, as for several other Central and East European countries, is a steady decline in the population, especially as many of the most economically productive, skilled, and educated younger generation have emigrated to find more lucrative employment in Western Europe and the United States. Officials estimate that approximately 50,000 citizens have emigrated annually since 1995; according to official data, some 850,000 people have left Bulgaria since the early 1990s. Out of a population of 8.7 million in the early 1990s, the total declined to 7.28 million by 2012, when the annual growth rate stood at –0.8 percent. Birthrates have fluctuated but generally remained low. There were 9 births per thousand people in 2000, only 8.4 births per thousand by 2003, and 9.2 births per thousand in 2012. After a peak of 81,000 births in 2009, the number of new births fell to 62,000 in 2012, the lowest since the end of World War II. The demographic crisis continued to deepen due to immigration and the high death rate, which remained at 14.32 per 1,000 in 2012.

About 85 percent of Bulgaria's population of approximately 7.2 million is Slavic Bulgarian. The country's three largest minorities are the Turks, at about 9 percent of the population, the Roma, estimated at around 4 percent, and the Pomaks, or Slavic Muslims, who make up less than 1 percent of the population. Under the communist regime, during the 1980s, there was a policy of forced assimilation directed primarily at the ethnic Turkish minority, which led to a mass exodus to neighboring Turkey. Since the collapse of communism, Bulgaria has not suffered through any significant ethnic conflicts. After Todor Zhivkov's ouster, Bulgarian officials made strenuous efforts to improve the country's minority policies and to repair the damage suffered by ethnic Turks during the repressive government campaigns of the 1980s. During Zhivkov's assimilation campaign, for instance, Turks had to "Bulgarize" by adopting Slavic names—typically, a Slavic suffix was added to a Muslim name, or an entirely new name could be chosen from a list of acceptable Bulgarian names—and giving up many of their national customs. Over three hundred thousand Turks fled the country fearing even more severe repression. Their properties were confiscated by the state or sold at low prices to Bulgarians. About half this number of Turks returned to Bulgaria after the democratic changes, but many faced problems in reclaiming their houses and other possessions.

During the summer of 1989, at the height of the Turkish exodus from Bulgaria to Turkey, the bulk of the Pomak (Slavic Muslim) population opposed efforts at forcible integration, and some sought to emigrate. The Pomaks, ethnic Bulgarians who had converted to Islam during the Ottoman occupation, numbered about seventy thousand people. The authorities proved reluctant to allow them to leave the country and denied passports to people residing in predominantly Pomak regions. These policies resulted in several substantial Pomak protests. Pomak regions suffered steep economic decline with the closure of local industries. Observers feared that economic problems would intensify political tensions. Bulgarian officials warned that unemployment and economic deprivations in regions with ethnically and religiously mixed groups were alarmingly high, and minorities complained about increasing discrimination in employment. After 1989, many Pomaks adopted a Turkish identity or demanded Turkish-language education, viewing it as advantageous to associate with a stronger and more influential minority.

The ethnic repression of its communist regime was one of the first parts of its past that Bulgaria jettisoned. In December 1989, the BSP (then still named the Bulgarian Communist Party) renounced forcible assimilation, allowing Muslims the freedom to choose their own names, practice Islam, observe traditional customs, and speak their native language. In January 1990, the National Assembly recommended the adoption of a special statute for minority rights. With Sofia's policy reversal, thousands of ethnic Turks returned to Bulgaria and faced new problems of adjustment. Most had lost their jobs and sold their houses for less than their true value. On their return, they demanded appropriate reparations. Ahmed Dogan, the political leader of Bulgaria's Turks, demanded a legal resolution that would restore property to victims of the exodus. Turkish deputies in parliament eventually introduced a law that was adopted in July 1992. It stipulated that all Turks were to be given back their property by April 1993 for the low price at which it had been sold. Those who proved unable to buy back their former homes would be given low-interest loans toward the purchase of alternative housing.[20]

In March 1990, the country's major political forces agreed to pass a Bulgarian Citizens' Names Law that allowed all victims of forcible assimilation to return to their old names. New birth certificates were issued, and the process of changing names was simplified from a judicial process to a straightforward administrative measure. The process was complicated and costly only for those Muslims who did not act before December 31, 1990.[21]

The issue of minority rights, particularly language use, education, and access to the mass media, generated some controversy. According to the 1991 constitution, Bulgarian was to be the sole official language. Under the Zhivkov regime, ethnic Turks were forbidden to use their mother tongue officially. The legacy of language discrimination persisted in a variety of forms. For example, parliament was reluctant to implement Turkish-language programs in secondary schools for fear of ultranationalist reactions.[22] In January 1991, a consultative council, including the Bulgarian prime minister, decided that the teaching of Turkish as part of the secondary school curriculum was constitutional. The Bulgarian parliament promised to implement a state-controlled Turkish program in all public schools with a significant minority enrollment. Bulgaria's nationalist opposition claimed that these programs were unconstitutional, so parliament issued assurances that they would not jeopardize the "unity of the Bulgarian nation."[23]

The Bulgarian constitution adopted in 1991 prohibits the creation of political parties based on "ethnic, racial, or religious lines" and organizations that "seek the violent usurpation of power."[24] Although intended to protect the Bulgarian state, these stipulations were frequently cited in efforts by nationalists to undermine the rights of minorities. Nationalist organizations capitalized on Bulgarian fears of alleged Turkish subversion and applied pressure on government organs to outlaw ethnic-based associations on the grounds that they were politically motivated and therefore "antistate."

Even with the regime's repudiation of the old communist-era ways, the Turks have had a hard time advocating for themselves. The main Turkish organization, the Movement for Rights and Freedoms, was singled out for attention. In August 1991, the Sofia City Court decided that a political party formed by the MRF was unconstitutional because it was ethnically based. As a result, it could not participate in any elections. The MRF, in turn, claimed that it was not an entirely ethnic party and harbored no separatist ambitions. In September 1991, the Supreme Court barred the Rights and Freedoms Party (the political wing of the MRF) from participation in general elections on the grounds that it propounded an exclusivist ethnic and religious platform.[25] Nonetheless, the MRF itself and various Turkish cultural and social organizations were not prohibited from functioning, and the MRF legally competed in the second general elections in October 1991. It gained twenty-four parliamentary seats, with 7.55 percent of the popular vote, making it the third strongest party in Bulgaria and a coalition partner for the UDF.

The MRF also became a coalition partner in the government of the National Movement Simeon II in April 2001. The party represents Bulgaria's 746,000 ethnic Turks, although formally there is a constitutional ban on ethnic-based parties. The MRF is a moderate formation. It resisted the demands of separatists within the Turkish community and concentrates on cultural and religious rights and the defense of Turkish economic interests. Smaller, more radical groups have not captured public support. In the NMS government, the MRF had two ministers and several deputy ministers. Its influence has expanded as it has asserted itself on several fiscal and privatization issues by supporting low taxation and transparency in selling state property. In recent years, the MRF also opened itself to non-Turks to increase its membership and voter base. The party has good relations with the socialists and is now the pivotal party in their coalition with the NMS. It holds the three ministries that most directly affect the agricultural sector.

In some respects, Macedonian groups have been more persecuted than either Turks or Pomaks. The Bulgarian government, together with most Bulgarian political parties, has refused to accept Macedonians as a legitimate minority. Instead they have defined them as Slavic Bulgarians with the same language and history as the rest of the country. They persist in this policy even though the Council of Europe and some human rights groups continue to criticize Sofia for its alleged political discrimination against the Macedonian minority.[26] For instance, according to Bulgarian leaders, a Macedonian minority did not exist in the Pirin region in western Bulgaria despite the activities of local radicals who wanted some form of regional autonomy or even unification with the independent state of Macedonia. An openly Macedonian organization styled as Ilinden was established in the Pirin area and applied for official registration only to be turned down in July 1990 by a district court.

Protests by Ilinden supporters were suppressed, and Bulgaria's Supreme Court ruled that Ilinden violated the unity of the Bulgarian nation. Ilinden's statutes promoted the recognition of a sovereign Macedonian minority, a fact that evidently served as evidence that the organization intended to achieve "a united Macedonian state." Ilinden was ordered to disband but persisted in a covert fashion, claiming that the decisions of the Bulgarian courts were in violation of international law.[27] In November 1998, the local court in Blagoevgrad reversed its earlier decision and allowed the registration of a Macedonian organization, OMO "Ilinden"–Pirin, with its headquarters in Blagoevgrad.[28]

Nationalist pro-Macedonian groupings were active in Bulgaria in the 1990s and called for closer social, economic, and political links with Macedonia that they hoped would culminate in eventual reabsorption of this former Yugoslav republic by Bulgaria. At the same time, some autonomist Macedonian organizations became active in western Bulgaria, amid suspicions that they were funded by Belgrade and by some militant groups in the Republic of Macedonia to sow discord within Bulgaria and press for the separation of the Pirin region from the Bulgarian state.

Although Bulgaria addressed its most pervasive ethnic problems during the 1990s and early 2000s, the treatment and position of the large Roma minority remains a problem. Bulgarian officials claim the country's policies have been guided by the Human Rights Charter and the Bulgarian constitution. Clearly, they were in part a response to the tragic treatment of the Turkish population at the end of the communist era. Just as clearly, the outside pressures and aid by international human rights organizations and the European institutions Bulgaria wished to join have influenced the Bulgarian government to develop more coherent legislation that balances concerns over national security and state integrity with full respect for minority rights and ethnic aspirations.

The social and economic position of the large Roma minority and the persistent prejudice and discrimination against it remain major problems. The Roma themselves are split on what they want and need. Unlike the Turks in Bulgaria, whose leaders perceived the gravest threat as coming from forcible assimilation, Romani spokesmen have been particularly opposed to the segregation and marginalization of the Roma population. Many representatives of the Roma have opposed separate schooling for Roma children because it results in inferior education, insufficient exposure to the Bulgarian language, and stymied career advancement. On the other side, some Roma leaders are pressing for a revival of Romani culture, education, and ethnic identity, fearing gradual assimilation by either the Bulgarian or Turkish communities. In addition, the law on political parties, which prohibited the registration of organizations established according to ethnic or religious criteria, worked to the detriment of Romani self-organization. After all, even though the Roma clearly do not represent a threat to Bulgaria's "territorial integrity" and the "unity of the nation" or "incite national, ethnic, and religious hostilities," they are barred from forming electoral associations.[29] But their ethnic traditions and migrant lifestyles make it impossible for them to fit into other parties, which, at best, do not advocate for Romani interests.

A few populist and nationalist groupings have been formed to advocate for "Bulgarian" national interests. A newly established party, Ataka, managed to win twenty-one seats in the June 2005 parliamentary elections and tried to mobilize anti-Roma sentiments in Bulgarian society. The party gained twenty-three seats during the 2013 parliamentary elections. Its program has been opposed by the majority of parliamentary deputies, but as the "kingmaker" in the government coalition, it had a significant impact on official policy. The socialist-led coalition government would likely collapse if Ataka withdrew its support.

Most other nationalist groups are not significant political players. These have included the Nationwide Committee for the Defense of National Interests and various parties working together as the Internal Macedonian Revolutionary Organization (IMRO). IMRO has campaigned for Bulgarian "national interests" on issues such as the rights of Bulgarian minorities abroad. It has attracted some support in a few regions and posts in local government. IMRO and Gergyovden stood together for parliament in 2001, narrowly missing the 4 percent threshold.

Foreign Policy

After the end of World War II, Bulgaria became part of the Soviet bloc. Its security revolved around membership in the Warsaw Pact, dominated by the Soviet Union, which ensured communist rule in each of the Central and East European countries. Bulgaria was largely isolated from the West and even from its Balkan neighbors, such as the Yugoslavs. Its economy was tied to the Moscow-centered Council for Mutual Economic Assistance. Since the collapse of the Soviet bloc, Bulgaria has made substantial progress in developing relations with all of its Balkan neighbors. It has also succeeded in joining NATO and became a member of the EU in 2007.

Bulgaria was one of the few countries to recognize Macedonia immediately after the republic declared its independence from Yugoslavia in early 1992. At the same time, the Bulgarian authorities were not willing to recognize the existence of a separate Macedonian nation and refused to recognize the Macedonian ethnic minority within Bulgaria. Sofia and Skopje ended a period of political deadlock concerning Bulgaria's recognition of a separate Macedonian language with the signing of a joint declaration and a number of accords on February 22, 1999. Bulgarian prime minister Ivan Kostov and his Macedonian counterpart, Ljubčo Georgievski, signed an agreement to settle the language dispute and to open the way to normalize relations. The joint declaration, signed in both Bulgarian and Macedonian, stipulated that the two countries would not undertake, incite, or support unfriendly activities against each other, including making territorial claims or applying pressure to ensure minority rights. Seven other bilateral agreements were signed at the same time to promote cooperation, trade, and investment.

Bulgaria has played a leading role in a number of regional cooperation formats, including the multinational South-Eastern Europe Brigade (SEEBRIG), headquartered in the city of Plovdiv, which promoted military interoperability between participating states. Sofia has participated in the regional security initiative South-Eastern Europe Defense Ministerial (SEDM). Following the ouster of Serbian president Slobodan Milošević in October 2000, Bulgaria has also contributed to democratic developments in Serbia by assisting nongovernmental organizations and local authorities in Serbia.

The crisis in Yugoslavia posed one of the most difficult foreign policy problems for postcommunist Bulgaria. Bulgaria's relations with Yugoslavia deteriorated under the Milošević regime in the 1990s, and NATO's war with Serbia worsened these relations. Sofia was outspoken about the culpability of Milošević in Balkan instability and supported NATO in its efforts to restore security to Kosovo despite some opposition to this policy inside the country. Bulgaria suffered from a loss of trade as a result of the Yugoslav wars, primarily because of United Nations sanctions on Yugoslavia and the blockage of traffic along the Danube River. Sofia has continued to develop good relations with both Greece and Turkey by balancing its ties with the two Balkan rivals. The government has also been active in developing regional initiatives to enhance security and cooperation across Balkan borders.

In its relations with Russia, Bulgaria has had to deal with significant pressures from Moscow. Moscow considers the Black Sea states of Bulgaria and Romania strategically significant for several reasons. Traditionally, Russia sought to keep open the Bosporus Strait between the Black Sea and the Mediterranean for its navy and raw materials. This goal was accomplished in the late nineteenth century at the expense of the independence of all the states in the region, including Bulgaria and Serbia, which became Russian quasi-protectorates. Continuing influence over these countries is critical for several reasons. First, it projects Russian political and economic ambitions throughout southeastern Europe and keeps the Black Sea itself as a zone of Russian dominance. Second, Bulgaria and Romania can provide the infrastructure and energy linkage between Europe and the Caucasus and Caspian regions. And third, Bulgaria is viewed as a historic ally that can help restore Russia's outreach. Currently, Russian strategic ambitions primarily mean the unhindered flow of Russia's energy supplies westward, not necessarily through the Bosporus. Moscow intends to secure alternative routes across the Balkan Peninsula as a shield against potential blockages in Turkey. This goal places Bulgaria in a strategically important position.

In the early 1990s, politicians in Moscow hoped they could draw Bulgaria into a closer political orbit through membership in the CIS or in alliance with the pro-Russian quadrilateral inner core of the commonwealth (Russia, Belarus, Kazakhstan, Kyrgyzstan). These proposals by President Boris Yeltsin were viewed with dismay in Sofia, leading President Zheliu Zhelev to declare them an "insult to Bulgarian sovereignty and national dignity."[30] Moscow concluded a bilateral treaty with Bulgaria during Yeltsin's visit to Sofia in August 1992. Nevertheless, relations did not develop smoothly, and there was no agreement on the repayment of Russia's debt to Bulgaria, which stood at $38.5 million by the end of 2004. Russia vowed to repay the bulk of this debt in military equipment and other goods. Trade between the two countries declined, largely as a result of disputes over the price of Russian gas sold to Bulgaria. The disintegration of the Soviet bloc raised the question of how Sofia could protect its independence and promote economic development while maintaining balanced relations with Moscow.[31] Bulgaria elected a pro-NATO reformist government in April 1997, and its progress toward NATO entry generated political tensions with Moscow.

President Vladimir Putin's policy proved more focused and politically active than Yeltsin's. It relied on Russian businesses to sponsor public relations campaigns aimed at redirecting Bulgaria's national strategy toward Moscow. However, Russian leaders were perturbed once again when they "lost" Bulgaria in the parliamentary election victory of the King Simeon movement in June 2001. This result prevented the Bulgarian socialists from regaining power and potentially redirecting the country toward Moscow, as they had in the mid-1990s.

Despite Bulgaria's NATO entry, Putin repeatedly sought to revive the Russian-Bulgarian relationship. During a visit to Bulgaria in March 2003 to mark Bulgaria's liberation from the Ottoman Empire and the 125th anniversary of the Russo-Turkish War, Putin stressed that Russo-Bulgarian collaboration would "significantly contribute to the development of a prosperous and self-determining Europe."[32]

Under the socialist administration (2005–2009), relations between Sofia and Moscow improved, and Bulgaria agreed to several large-scale economic contracts with Russian energy companies. However, in the fall of 2009, Bulgaria's newly elected center-right government began to review several projects with Russia, including the South Stream natural gas pipeline, intended to transit Russian gas under the Black Sea to the Balkans, the construction of the Belene nuclear power plant, and participation in a trans-Balkan oil pipeline between the Bulgarian port of Burgas and the Greek port of Alexandroupolis. Borisov stated that the government would give priority to the EU-sponsored Nabucco pipeline project, due to bring Caspian gas to Europe via the Balkans and reduce dependence on Russia. Regarding Belene, Sofia sought a clearer and more transparent financing structure because of soaring costs and dwindling budget revenues. Eventually, the government scrapped the project for lack of economic feasibility and inability to attract a major Western investment. Sofia also quit the Burgas-Alexandroupolis oil pipeline in December 2011 but signed an investment agreement with Russia for the construction of South Stream.

Bulgaria considers itself a partner and ally of the United States. There is overall agreement on major decisions related to Bulgaria's contribution to NATO and the antiterrorist campaign. As a nonpermanent member of the UN Security Council during the 2002–2003 period, Bulgaria supported US positions more consistently than several of the United States' West European NATO allies. The center-right government of the National Movement Simeon II (2001–2005) backed Washington in the Iraq War despite verbal criticism by socialist president Georgi Parvanov and the socialist opposition in parliament. Although the socialists are supportive of NATO membership, some of their leaders have also maintained close links with Russian authorities, who seek to diminish the United States' global role.

To join NATO, Bulgaria had to transform its military and its weaponry to fit NATO standards and consolidate democratic civilian control over the armed forces. The government restated its commitment to downsizing and modernizing the armed forces in line with its Defense Plan 2004. The Bulgarian army became fully professional in January 2008, two years ahead of the government's schedule. According to the Development Program of the Bulgarian Armed Forces of 2010, Bulgaria is to have 27,000 standing troops by 2014, consisting of 14,310 troops in the land forces, 6,750 in the air force, 3,510 in the navy, and 2,420 in the joint command.[33]

There was comprehensive political and public support for Bulgaria's NATO membership, despite the country's financial constraints, with a firm commitment to allocate approximately 3 percent of GDP to defense spending over the coming years. The government calculated that the benefits of NATO membership, in terms of military modernization, downsizing, and international interoperability, outweighed the high costs of maintaining an obsolete military structure. There is a high level of protection of classified information in compliance with NATO standards, and the government has tightened controls over the export of possible dual-use weapons and technologies.

Bulgaria supported US and NATO military operations in both word and deed. It granted airspace for the NATO Allied Force operation in Serbia in March through June 1999. Bulgaria played an important role in avoiding a possible crisis in relations between NATO and Russia in June 1999 by denying Russian forces overflight rights during NATO's intervention in Kosovo. Sofia facilitated NATO's actions when Kosovo-bound forces were allowed through. Bulgaria also participated in two NATO-led peacekeeping operations: in Stabilization Force (SFOR) in Bosnia-Herzegovina and in Kosovo Force (KFOR).

In the US-led antiterrorist and anti-rogue-state campaign since September 11, 2001, Bulgaria has allowed air, land, and sea transit to coalition forces and the temporary deployment of US aircraft for refueling and cargo-lifting purposes in both the Afghanistan and Iraq operations. It has allocated military units to the International Security Assistance Force (ISAF) in Afghanistan and dispatched an anti–nuclear, biological, and chemical unit to Iraq. Bulgaria sent a total of 485 soldiers to Iraq between 2003 and 2008 and maintained a larger contingent in Afghanistan as part of ISAF, with the highest number of 681 in 2012. According to the ISAF website, as of April 2014, Bulgaria had a 387-member contingent in Afghanistan.

Moreover, Bulgaria has consistently supported the US position on the Iraqi question in the UN Security Council and dispatched a contingent of troops to the country after the American-led military invasion. Although several Bulgarian soldiers died in Iraq, Sofia remained steadfast in its involvement in the peace-enforcement coalition.

Bulgaria signed a defense cooperation agreement with the United States in 2006. It has welcomed the construction of small US bases on Bulgarian soil that could be valuable for America's strategic access to areas of potential crisis in the Middle East.

In April 2005, Bulgaria signed an accession treaty with the European Union; it became a full EU member on January 1, 2007. The government had successfully completed the implementation of all thirty-one chapters of the EU's voluminous *acquis communautaire*, which stipulated the reforms that needed to be enacted in various areas of the economy and administrative structure for Bulgaria to meet EU standards. Brussels also included a clause in the treaty that could have led to a delay in Bulgaria's entry if the remaining reforms in the judicial system and in combating corruption were not implemented.

EU membership itself closed an important chapter in Bulgaria's post–Cold War history, as it signaled that the country had successfully completed its transformation from a communist dictatorship to a capitalist democracy. However, following EU entry, some turbulence has been evident in Bulgaria's relations with several West European partners over its relations with Washington. Sofia and other Central and East European capitals seek to strengthen the transatlantic link within the EU. At the same time, they are subject to increasing pressures from Brussels and various West European capitals to coordinate their policies more closely with the EU's emerging security and foreign policy, even if the latter is sometimes at odds with Washington. For instance, tensions were evident during the George W. Bush administration when Sofia supported US policy in Iraq despite opposition from several large EU members.

Bulgaria found itself at odds with the EU over the prospective Russian-led South Stream natural gas pipeline. In December 2013, the EU Energy Commission pronounced illegal all contracts signed between six EU members and Gazprom regarding the construction of the pipeline. The contracts fell short of complying with the EU's Third Energy Package on competitiveness. As the EU Energy Commission took the lead in renegotiating the contracts with Moscow, the Bulgarian parliament decided to amend the Energy Act in order to try to bypass the provisions of the Third Energy Package. The EU warned Bulgaria that such actions would lead to a heavy infringement procedure against the country.[34]

The crisis in Ukraine in March 2014 over Russia's annexation of Crimea had a significant impact on Bulgarian society, which was torn between loyalty to the EU and to NATO on the one hand and a historic affinity for Russia reinforced by dependence on Russian energy sources. As the government endorsed the sanctions against Russia and took a strong stand supporting the territorial integrity of Ukraine, the nationalist Ataka party leadership called for a veto of the sanctions and recognition of the disputed March referendum in Crimea. Moreover, holding the balance of power in the Bulgarian parliament, Ataka threatened to topple the government if it supported further sanctions against Moscow. Party members transformed themselves from Bulgarian nationalists to

Photo 14.3. Kristalina Georgieva, currently UN Commissioner for International Cooperation, Humanitarian Aid, and Crisis Response. She has been the most popular politician in Bulgaria in recent years. (*Capital Weekly*, Bulgaria)

pro-Russian nationalists, sending over twenty representatives to help the ethnic Russians in Crimea. The public debate about events in Ukraine has raised questions concerning the extent to which Bulgaria remains a reliable EU and NATO member.[35]

Future Challenges

It will take many years for Bulgaria to achieve the economic level of its West European partners, but EU membership also means access to the union's structural funds, which will help to develop the country's economy. The government will seek to attract greater volumes of investment from Western Europe and to reverse the outflow of the most educated sectors of society. It will also plan to recover from the impact of the global recession.

The European Union itself is undergoing a major transformation as a more integrated international actor. Bulgaria will seek to have more influence in EU decision making, and it will need to achieve a beneficial balance in its relations with Washington and Brussels. Like other new democracies, Bulgaria wants the EU to become a united and effective organization. At the same time, it wants to maintain close relations with the United States and maintain a prominent role for the NATO alliance in international security. For this to happen, though, Bulgaria must develop its infrastructure and halt the illegal drug trade that traverses the country. It must also prepare its economy and legal structures to meet EU standards. Persistent problems with the rule of law, corruption, and media freedom, as well as Bulgaria's commitment to the Russian-led South Stream natural gas pipeline, undermine Bulgaria's position within the EU.

Bulgaria is particularly affected by the crisis in Ukraine as Russian military planes are crisscrossing the Black Sea, raising security alarms. The country may request a NATO military presence on its soil if provocations persist. Potential disruptions of Russian gas supplies may also have a devastating impact on Bulgaria, as the country has no alternative energy supplies and very limited gas storage capacity.

The main challenge for Bulgaria is the prolonged political crisis that the country entered with the resignation of Boyko Borisov's government in February 2012. The next government of an unstable Socialist-led coalition survived for only a year, giving way to an interim government, followed by yet another electoral cycle. The fractured political party system that undermines public trust, pervasive corruption, and the lack of an efficient judicial system will be the main reasons for economic stagnation and a high rate of immigration among young Bulgarians in the future.

Study Questions

1. Why did communism collapse in Bulgaria?
2. What are the key components in the construction of a democratic system in Bulgaria?
3. How did Bulgaria qualify for NATO and EU membership?
4. How important and extensive are ethnic minority rights in Bulgaria?
5. Why did the traditional center-right coalition lose its place in parliament in 2013?
6. What are the major characteristics of Bulgarian nationalism, and why is it rising?

Suggested Readings

Anguelov, Zlatko. *Communism and the Remorse of an Innocent Victimizer*. College Station: Texas A&M University Press, 2002.

Bell, John D., ed. *Bulgaria in Transition: Politics, Economics, Society, and Culture after Communism*. Boulder, CO: Westview Press, 1998.

———. *The Bulgarian Communist Party from Blagoev to Zhivkov*. Stanford, CA: Hoover Institution Press, 1986.

Crampton, R. J. *A Concise History of Bulgaria*. New York: Cambridge University Press, 2005.

Ganev, Venelin I. *Preying on the State: The Transformation of Bulgaria after 1989*. Ithaca, NY: Cornell University Press, 2007.

Groueff, Stephane. *Crown of Thorns: The Reign of King Boris III of Bulgaria, 1918–1943*. Lanham, MD: Madison Books, 1987.

Marushiakova, Elena, and Vesselin Popov. 1997. *Gypsies (Roma) in Bulgaria*. Frankfurt am Main: Peter Lang, 1993.

Neuburger, Mary. *The Orient Within: Muslim Minorities and the Negotiation of Nationhood in Modern Bulgaria*. Ithaca, NY: Cornell University Press, 2004.

Perry, Charles M., Dimitris Keridis, and Monica R. P. d'Assunção Carlos. *Bulgaria in Europe: Charting a Path toward Reform and Integration*. Dulles, VA: Potomac Books, 2006.

Websites

Bulgarian government portal: http://www.government.bg/fce/index.shtml?s=001&p=0023

Bulgarian National Statistical Institute: http://www.nsi.bg/Index_e.htm

Center for Liberal Strategies: http://www.cls-sofia.org

Embassy of the Republic of Bulgaria in the United States: http://www.bulgaria-embassy.org

European Commission in Bulgaria: http://ec.europa.eu/bulgaria/index_bg.htm

European Foreign Policy Council in Bulgaria: http://ecfr.eu/sofia

National Assembly: http://www.parliament.bg

MAJOR ENGLISH-LANGUAGE BULGARIAN MEDIA

Bulgarian News Agency: http://www.bta.bg/en/home/index

Sofia Echo: http://www.sofiaecho.com

Sofia News Agency: http://www.novinite.com

NEWS WEBSITES

Investor.bg: http://www.investor.bg

Mediapool.bg: http://www.mediapool.bg

MAJOR PRINT MEDIA

24 Hours Daily: http://www.24chasa.bg
Dnevnik Daily: http://www.dnevnik.bg
Kapital Weekly: http://www.capital.bg
Sega Daily: http://www.segabg.com
Standart Daily: http://www.standartnews.com
Trud Daily: http://www.trud.bg

Notes

1. For a valuable account of postcommunist Bulgaria, see John D. Bell, "Democratization and Political Participation in 'Postcommunist' Bulgaria," in *Politics, Power, and the Struggle for Democracy in South-East Europe*, ed. Karen Dawisha and Bruce Parrott, 353–402 (Cambridge: Cambridge University Press, 1997).

2. Stefan Krause, "Socialists at the Helm," *Transition* 1, no. 4 (March 1995): 33–36.

3. Ivo Georgiev, "Indecisive Socialist Party Stumbles into Crisis," *Transition* 2, no. 26 (December 1996): 26–28.

4. Stefan Krause, "United Opposition Triumphs in Presidential Elections," *Transition* 2, no. 26 (December 1996): 20–23.

5. Anne-Mary Gulde, "The Role of the Currency Board in Bulgaria's Stabilization," *Finance and Development Magazine*, IMF, December 1999, http://www.imf.org/external/pubs/ft/fandd/1999/09/gulde.htm.

6. For an overview of the center-right, see Dilyana Tsenova, "SDS to Have Golden Moment in 40th Parliament," *24 Chasa* (April 2004).

7. Center for the Study of Democracy, *Corruption, Contraband, and Organized Crime in Southeast Europe* (Sofia: Center for the Study of Democracy, 2003); *Corruption Assessment Report, 2003* (Sofia: Coalition 2000, 2004); *On the Eve of EU Accession: Anti-corruption Reforms in Bulgaria* (Sofia: Center for the Study of Democracy, 2006); *Anti-corruption Reforms in Bulgaria: Key Results and Risks* (Sofia: Center for the Study of Democracy, 2007).

8. Center for the Study of Democracy, *Crime without Punishment: Countering Corruption and Organized Crime in Bulgaria* (Sofia: Center for the Study of Democracy, 2009).

9. "Bulgarian Media Ownership Trends Worrying, German Ambassador Says," Sofia News Agency, October 2, 2013, http://www.novinite.com/articles/154145/Bulgarian+Media+Ownership+Trends+Worrying,+Says+German+Ambassador; "A Few Media Magnates Create 'a State within the State,'" *Dnevnik Daily*, October 2, 2013, http://www.dnevnik.bg/analizi/2013/10/02/2152421_niakolko_mediini_magnati_si_suzdavat_durjava_v_durjava.

10. For more information, see *Eurasia Daily Monitor* reporting on Bulgaria from 2011 to 2014 by Margarita Assenova at http://www.jamestown.org/programs/edm, or articles by the author on the Jamestown Foundation website at http://www.jamestown.org/articles-by-author/?no_cache=1&tx_cablanttnewsstaffrelation_pi1%5Bauthor%5D=651.

11. "Who Is the New Chairman of the NSC Delyan Peevski?," *Capital Daily*, June 14, 2013, http://www.capital.bg/politika_i_ikonomika/bulgaria/2013/06/14/2081416_koi_e_noviiat_predsedatel_na_dans_delian_peevski; Margarita Assenova, "Is Organized Crime Taking over the Bulgarian State?" *Jamestown Foundation Blog*, June 14, 2013, http://jamestownfoundation.blogspot.com/2013/06/is-organized-crime-taking-over.html.

12. "'Alpha Research': The Delitimization of the Institutions and a Sense of Instability in the Beginning of the Political Season," *Dnevnik Daily*, October 2, 2013, http://www.dnevnik.bg /analizi/2013/10/02/2152409_alfa_risurch_delegitimaciia_na_instituciite_i/?ref=substory.

13. "DPS: Delyan Peevski Is Most Suitable for MEP," Sofia News Agency, April 9, 2014, http://www.novinite.com/articles/159652/DPS%3A+Delyan+Peevski+Is+Most+Suitable+For+ MEP.

14. For more details, see Luben Panov, "NGOs and the State in Bulgaria: Towards Greater Cooperation," *Social Economy and Law Journal* (winter 2003–spring 2004): 42–43.

15. For useful economic statistics, see "Economic Structure: Annual Indicators," Economist Intelligence Unit, Country Report Subscription, October 1, 2006.

16. For more details, see Institute for Regional and International Studies, *Country Report: Bulgaria, State of Democracy, Roadmap for Reforms, 2001* (Sofia: Institute for Regional and International Studies, 2002).

17. "Unemployment in Bulgaria in Q2013 was 12.9 percent—NSI," *Sofia Globe*, October 1, 2013, http://sofiaglobe.com/2013/10/01/unemployment-in-bulgaria-in-q2-2013-was-12-9-nsi.

18. International Monetary Fund (IMF), *World Economic Outlook* (Washington, DC: IMF, April 2014), http://www.imf.org/external/pubs/ft/weo/2014/01/pdf/text.pdf.

19. Krassen Stanchev, "Bulgarian Economic Policy Is Not Rightist," A study by the Institute for Market Economics, *Capital Weekly*, July 19, 2003.

20. Stephen Ashley, "Migration from Bulgaria," Radio Free Europe/Radio Liberty (RFE/RL) Research Institute, *Report on Eastern Europe*, December 1, 1989; Stephen Ashley, "Ethnic Unrest during January," RFE/RL, *Report on Eastern Europe* 1, no. 6 (February 9, 1990); Kjell Engelbrekt, "The Movement for Rights and Freedoms," RFE/RL, *Report on Eastern Europe* 2, no. 22 (May 31, 1991).

21. For a discussion of cultural assimilation and the Name Change Law, see "Minority Problems Persist: Elections Set for June," in *News from Helsinki Watch*, "News from Bulgaria," March 1990. On the new law on names, see "Deep Tensions Continue in Turkish Provinces, despite Some Human Rights Improvements," in *News from Helsinki Watch*, "News from Bulgaria," August 1990.

22. Goran Ahren, "Helsinki Committee on Turkish Bulgarians: Continued Political Oppression," *Dagens Nyheter* (Stockholm), December 24, 1989, *JPRS-EER-90-009*, January 24, 1990.

23. Mitko Krumov, "New Deputies Yuriy Borisov and Vasil Kostov Replace Dobri Dzhurov and Georgi Velichkov Who Resigned," *Duma* (Sofia), January 10, 1991, *FBIS-EEU-91-013*, January 18, 1991. For a discussion of the major strikes in Kardzhali, see Bulgarian News Agency (BTA), February 26, 1991, *FBIS-EEU-91-038*, February 26, 1991.

24. Constitution of the Republic of Bulgaria, adopted July 12, 1991.

25. "Second Yilmaz Letter Is Unprecedented and Greatly Alarms Nationwide Committee of Defense of National Interests," *Duma* (Sofia), August 30, 1991, *FBIS-EEU-91-172*, September 5, 1991; Kjell Engelbrekt, "The Movement for Rights and Freedoms to Compete in Elections," RFE/RL, *Report on Eastern Europe* 2, no. 91 (October 4, 1991).

26. See the January 2004 report on Bulgaria on the website of the Council of Europe's Committee against Racism and Intolerance (http://hudoc.ecri.coe.int/XMLEcri/ENGLISH/ Cycle_03/03_CbC_eng/BGR-CbC-III-2004-2-ENG.pdf).

27. See Duncan M. Perry, "The Macedonian Question Revitalized," RFE/RL, *Report on Eastern Europe* 1, no. 24 (August 24, 1990); Evgeni Gavrilov, *Duma* (Sofia), November 14, 1990, *FBIS-EEU-90-223*, November 19, 1990; Bulgarian News Agency (BTA), September 23, 1991, *FBIS-EEU-91-185*, September 24, 1991.

28. *State Gazette* (Sofia), February 23, 1999, and March 14, 1999; Bulgarian News Agency (BTA), November 3, 1998.

29. See Helsinki Watch, *Destroying Ethnic Identity: The Gypsies of Bulgaria* (New York: Human Rights Watch, 1991).

30. President Zhelev quoted in Bulgarian News Agency (BTA), April 2, 1996. Bulgaria's Foreign Ministry called Yeltsin's "invitation" to Bulgaria "a cause for concern." Leaders of the opposition UDF claimed that Russia's ultimate aim was the restoration of the Soviet Union, in which Bulgaria would be a constituent element. In 1963, Bulgaria's Communist Party leader had offered to make Bulgaria the sixteenth republic of the USSR; the Kremlin seemed to believe that such offers were still valid. The incident mobilized the pro-NATO opposition against the Russian-oriented socialist government led by Prime Minister Zhan Videnov and backfired against Moscow's policy.

31. Ognyan Minchev, "Bulgaria and Russia," in *Bulgaria for NATO* (Sofia: Institute for Regional and International Studies, 2002). Even though Bulgarian-Russian friendship has a long pedigree, relations have also been marked by conflicts, as Russia's tsars demanded that the newly liberated Bulgarian state in the late nineteenth century demonstrate "total economic and political dependence on Russia" (ibid., 120).

32. "Putin Expresses Aspirations for Russia and Bulgaria Together in a Self-Determining Europe," Mediapool.bg, March 3, 2003. Mediapool is an influential electronic news portal in Bulgaria.

33. *White Paper on Defense and the Armed Forces of the Republic of Bulgaria*, Ministry of Defense of Bulgaria, October 2010, http://www.md.government.bg/en/doc/misc/20101130_WP_EN.pdf.

34. Margarita Assenova, "Bulgaria: The Cost of Resuscitating South Stream," *Eurasia Daily Monitor* 11, no. 65 (April 7, 2014), http://www.jamestown.org/single/?tx_ttnews%5Bswords %5D=8fd5893941d69d0be3f378576261ae3e&tx_ttnews%5Ball_the_words%5D=bulgaria%20 nabucco&tx_ttnews%5Bpointer%5D=2&tx_ttnews%5Btt_news%5D=42193&tx_ttnews%5Bba ckPid%5D=7&cHash=4501a453bdd9d08a5f33cb661caa8560#.U9gPuFYSAeI.

35. "Bulgarian Nationalists May Topple Government over Russia Sanctions," Reuters, April 1, 2014.

Map 15.0.   Romania

CHAPTER 15

Romania

OLD PROBLEMS AND NEW CHALLENGES

Daniel Brett

When compared to those of other states of the region, Romania's recent history appears problematic and troublesome. The Romanian communist regime was among the most repressive, atomizing, and atavistic in its totalitarianism, outside the USSR and Albania. Despite the country's revolution in 1989, unreconstructed members of the Communist Party with scant democratic commitment dominated the emerging government. Since 1989, Romania has suffered from economic, social, ethnic, and environmental issues as the state has failed to confront problems that emerged during communism and grew worse with the impact of transition. Moreover, a self-interested political and economic elite with a weak commitment to democratic politics has dismantled the resources of the state and distributed the rewards among themselves. And yet, despite the presence of a large Hungarian ethnic minority and the domination of Romanian political discourse by populist and nationalist rhetoric, Romania did not succumb to civil war like Yugoslavia. Despite attempts to roll back democratic institutions, Romania has not yet seen the full-scale undermining of democratic institutions comparable to Orbán's moves in Hungary. Romania has managed to join the European Union, and the process of tackling corruption has seen the very public jailing of former prime minister Adrian Năstase.

Given this juxtaposition of negative and positive aspects, where does Romania lie? What is the political, social, economic, and cultural landscape of the contemporary state? What problems does it face, and what are the causes of those problems? This chapter addresses these questions by examining the problems that arose during the emergence and development of the Romanian state, as well as those associated with communist rule and the transition from communism that still have consequences for contemporary Romania. It then examines domestic politics and the foreign policy of Romania since 1989.

Precommunist History

Unlike some of the other states of the region, we cannot speak of a "historic" Romanian state, despite the claims of nationalist authors. The Romanian state (the Old Kingdom) first came into being in 1859 with the unification of the Ottoman provinces of Moldavia and Wallachia and their claim of independence after the Russo-Turkish War of 1871. The Romanian space was influenced from the north by the Russian Empire, from the south by the Ottomans, and from the west by the Habsburg Monarchy. The territory of each region thus had very different political, social, and cultural experiences.

Only after 1918, at the end of World War I with the Paris Peace Conference, did Romanian "national unification" take place as additional territory was obtained: Transylvania, the Banat, and Bukovina from Austria-Hungary; Bessarabia from revolutionary Russia; and Southern Dobruja from Bulgaria. This newly obtained territory roughly doubled the size of the Romanian state, but each territory also brought its own system of governance, differed in degree of economic development, and introduced significant new minority populations. Trying to consolidate, harmonize, and improve these varied economic and governance systems, as well as to integrate or adjust to greatly enlarged minority populations, would prove very troublesome for the state during the interwar period.

In economic terms, Romania in 1918 was predominantly agricultural with few areas of urbanization and industrialization. In an attempt to modernize the country and lift citizens out of poverty, land reform was introduced. The hope of the reform was to grant the peasants sufficient land to produce a surplus of produce that could be sold to the cities or abroad. This money could then be invested in agricultural modernization, leading to a greater surplus and increased profits. However, land reform failed. There were simply too many peasants and not enough land. The plots were too small to produce a surplus, and without improvements in infrastructure, produce failed to reach a wider market. Despite state efforts, by 1930, 79 percent of the population was still rural. Efforts at industrialization also failed, although some progress occurred in the 1920s. When the Great Depression hit in 1929, the crisis proved too severe for the state to overcome. Extreme economic insecurity contributed to the rise of radical, extreme, and fascist politics, which came to dominate Romania in the 1930s.

Like the other newly created states, Romania faced the difficulty of integrating now sizable minority populations in both urban and rural areas into the state and nation. Before 1918, in estimates and census data, between 7 and 19 percent of the population were minorities.[1] After the territorial revisions following World War I, this number rose precipitously to 28.9 percent[2] with the annexations. A contradiction emerged. As Romania had based its claim to territory after World War I on the grounds of national self-determination, its claim to legitimacy on the basis of the cultural and numerical rights of the ethnic Romanian majority was called into question, as almost one-third of the population was denied the right to self-determination. The Bucharest political elite responded by advocating a highly centralized state, and Bucharest itself, rather than the more ethnically diverse but geographically better-situated city of Braşov, was chosen as the capital in part due to its "Romanian-ness."[3] At the time of unification, political autonomy had been promised, along with the right to education, representation, and justice in the minority languages. However, by 1924 this had been abandoned in favor of centralization, which alienated minorities and also Romanians from the rural regions who were isolated from what increased opportunities centralization offered. Political difficulties and frictions arose because the large minority groups, especially the Hungarian, German, and Jewish minorities (see table 15.1), not only were concentrated in urban centers in these territories but were more educated than the Romanians there and often comprised the political, economic, and professional elite. Centralization shifted toward increased ethnization after the Great Depression as the economy declined and jobs became scarcer. As the Romanian state sought to increase the presence of ethnic Romanians in all of these positions through better education of the ethnic Romanian population, competition for slots at the university, as well as for professional positions (in professions such as medicine and law), arose between the Romanians and the Hungarian, German, and Jewish minorities.

The impact of this effort to form a centralized unitary national state from a multinational one by limiting the participation of educated minorities in the economic life and governance of the new state, in the words of one expert, "destroyed the civil traditions" and "civil experience" they could have brought to governance.[4] The problem was especially acute for the Jewish minority. The efforts by the Romanian government, especially in the 1930s, to promote "Romanization," which employed nationalist, populist, and anti-Semitic rhetoric, later institutionalized anti-Semitism through discriminatory legislation. These actions not only deprived the state of expertise but, together with university student groups' rhetoric and actions, led to the rise of the Legion of the Archangel Michael, also called the Iron Guard, Romania's own native fascist movement.

It is unclear if better governance could have saved Romania in the interwar period from extremist and radical politics. Politics and politicians in the interwar period were a direct carryover from the politics and politicians of the pre-1918 period. Electoral politics in the Kingdom of Romania (the Regat) and Transylvania before 1918 had been marked by fraud, corruption, and chicanery, with incumbent power holders seeing the state as a resource to be captured and then deployed against their rivals. The narrow electoral franchise of the period before World War I facilitated the formation of cadre parties dominated by personal networks and patrimonial power.

Table 15.1.   Romanian Population by Self-Declared Ethnicity, 1930

Ethnicity	Total Number	Percentage of the Population
Romanian	12,981,324	71.9
Hungarian	1,425,507	7.9
German	745,421	4.1
Jewish	728,115	4.0
Ukrainian	582,115	3.2
Russian	409,150	2.3
Bulgarian	366,384	2.0
Roma	262,501	1.5
Turkish	176,913	1.0
Others	170,944	0.9
Gaguaz	105,750	0.6
Czech and Slovak	51,842	0.3
Serb, Croat, Slovene	51,062	0.3
Total	18,057,028	100

Source: Joseph Rothschild, *East Central Europe between the Two World Wars* (Seattle: Washington University Press, 1992), 284.

With the formation of Greater Romania in 1918, the nature of politics did not change. Despite the appearance of Western-style institutions, such as the constitution of 1923, that provided for elections, increased the franchise, allowing peasants (largely ethnic Romanians) and Jews to vote, and divided power between the king and a parliament, scholars generally agree that these institutions were more a facade than an actuality. Party politics, although superficially ideological, lacked strong ideological commitment from politicians. It was not uncommon for politicians to change parties four or five times during their careers, often driven by the promise of promotion and rewards rather than by ideology. Elites viewed the state as a source of personal wealth for the taking, and "amongst a ruling elite which looked upon rapacity as proof of dexterity and cunning, corruption of principles became widespread."[5] Nonetheless, despite nine different governments, the 1920s are still looked on today by many Romanians, as a period of stability. Under the guidance of the king and the National Peasants Party (PNŢ) and the National Liberal Party (PNL), politics, in this period, were more democratic than they had been before.

This situation changed in 1929 with the Great Depression. The 1930s were an extremely turbulent time in Romanian politics as extremist and radical parties dominated political life. In response to the economic crisis and the failure of mainstream politicians, a widespread shift toward authoritarian and extremist politics took place. The initial success of extremist movements in turn prompted formerly mainstream politicians and disenfranchised minorities alike to support their own extremist parties. The rejection of parliamentary politics led to the widespread use of violence. The anti-Semitic Iron Guard was a relatively small but extremely violent movement, which murdered a number of politicians and opponents, including two prime ministers.

In contrast to the rest of the Romanian political scene, the members and leaders of the Iron Guard were younger and driven to action. Given the inertia of mainstream politics, this approach appealed to many who had suffered economically after 1929. The Guard also established its own mythology and its embrace of Romanian Orthodoxy attracted significant support, drawing in many future senior church leaders. Mainstream politicians took three different approaches to dealing with the Guard: King Carol II saw it as a threat to his government and the country and repressed it; others mimicked it in trying to appeal for supporters; and still others, such as National Peasants Party leader Iuliu Maniu, tried to ally themselves with it against Carol, whom they considered the greater threat. This action caused tensions in PNŢ, given the discomfort of some with the Guard's antidemocratic tendencies.

In addition to domestic factors, external forces affected the direction of Romania's politics during the interwar period and through World War II. Although Romania sought to remain neutral, its geographic position between two large powers, Nazi Germany and the Soviet Union, physical separation from its ally France, the West's unwillingness to assure its security after the Munich Agreement of 1938, Britain's unwillingness to buy one of Romania's largest export products, wheat, and Nazi Germany's interest in another of Romania's exports, oil, slowly led Romania into an increasingly tight economic dependency on Nazi Germany. Though its leaders affirmed the policy of "equilibrium" between the two powers through June 1939, the country was driven to the side of Nazi Germany by major territorial losses in 1940, when Romania forfeited a third of its territory to its neighbors. Following an ultimatum from Russia, it lost Bessarabia and Northern Bukovina. As the result of the second Vienna Award in July, it lost northern Transylvania to Hungary, and, finally, it lost Southern Dobruja to Bulgaria.

At this point, Romania's King Carol II's personal dictatorship, which he had instituted in 1938, collapsed. He abdicated, taking with him as many possessions and as much gold as he could. Into this vacuum stepped the Iron Guard. From September 1940 to January 1941, the National Legionary State emerged, consisting of the Iron Guard and the head of the army, Ion Antonescu. This anti-Semitic regime allied itself with Nazi Germany.

Four months of bloodletting by the Guard followed, as political rivals, including another former prime minister, were murdered. In January the Guard simultaneously launched a bloody and violent anti-Semitic pogrom and a coup against Antonescu. In the end, Antonescu managed to suppress the rebellion and the Guard. He instituted a pro-German military dictatorship, ensuring that Romania would fight on the Axis side until 1944. As part of this alliance, Romania joined with Nazi Germany to invade the USSR. As a result, Romania regained Bessarabia.

Romania under Antonescu actively participated in the Holocaust, killing two-thirds of the country's prewar Jewish population. Between 280,000 and 380,000 Jews were murdered in Romania and Romanian controlled territories, as were another 135,000 from northern Transylvania (under Hungarian control between 1940 and 1945);[6] in addition, 11,000 Roma were killed.

On August 23, 1944, a coup d'état removed Antonescu from power, and a communist-dominated government took over. This new government ordered a change of sides, so Romania would finish the war in the Allied camp. Bessarabia and Nortern Bukovina were directly occupied by the Soviets in 1944 and 1945 and then incorporated into the USSR.

In conclusion, the interwar period was a very dynamic political period for the new Romanian state, which doubled in size after World War I. The newly annexed territories contributed to the size of the new state but also, due to the Romanian government's policies, created issues that it could not resolve successfully. Although the 1920s had been the "most democratic" moment in Romania's short history, attempts to create good democratic governance and a unitary national cultural and political state out of a multinational one failed. This failure, in combination with poor governance, economic problems, and external factors, contributed to a descent into political extremism and radicalism that, for the next sixteen years, from 1929 to 1945, resulted in a succession of dictatorships by the king, a fascist military regime allied with the Nazis, and communists in a takeover at the end of the war.

Romania under Communism

Many Romanians today view the communist period as a uniquely dark one in Romanian history, an alien system imposed from outside that subverted not only the state but society as well. However, as is clear from Romania's interwar history, the communists were not the first group to subvert state and society in Romania. As we will see, the country's particular history shaped its communist period in significant ways.

Ending the war on the Allied side meant Romania regained territory it had lost during the war, including northern Transylvania, which had been taken over by Hungary during the war. Other regions in its east were occupied by the Soviet army. These territorial gains and losses, though, did not ease the way for communist rule. In 1944, the Romanian Communist Party (RCP) was a small, outlawed group, split between members who had been imprisoned in Romania and those who had been exiled in the USSR. The democratic opposition had its own problems: an ageing leadership, party networks fractured during the wartime fighting, and the desertion of many alienated younger members to more radical movements than the democratic opposition. The weakness of the opposition, the unwillingness of the Western Allies to intervene to stop a communist takeover, the material support of the Red Army, and the ability of the communists to capture and subvert the security apparatus all enabled the communists to sweep aside their enemies and gain total and absolute power by the end of 1947. At the same time, the communists benefitted from some of their positive political moves between 1945 and 1947, including granting political autonomy to the Hungarians in Transylvania so they could present themselves as ethnically inclusive in contrast to the divisive ethnic politics of the interwar period.

In the years after World War II ended, communism was instituted in much the same way as it was instituted elsewhere in Central and Eastern Europe. In the process, though, communist control built on the repressive organs of the prewar period and planted the seeds for the excesses of Nicolae Ceacescu's rule in the 1970s and 1980s. Gheorghe Gheorghiu Dej rose to power by removing his rivals violently (having party leader Stefan Foris murdered),[7] and from 1948 he took control of the Communist Party, after which he consolidated his position further, purging his rivals, such as Foreign Minister Ana Pauker, and having his most dangerous rival, Lucrețiu Pătrășcanu, purged and then executed in 1954. Through these means Dej retained power until his death. During this time, like many other "little Stalins" in the bloc, he instituted the main tenets of "high Stalinism," which included the political persecution and jailing of his primary internal opponents, along with the concomitant show trials to solidify his control of the political apparatus. He used the secret police, the Securitate, to terrorize and bring to heel a rather anticommunist population. The communists did not introduce the secret police in Romania; nor were they the first to politicize it—this had already taken place during the interwar period. The communists under Dej did, however, massively extend the reach of the police apparatus, which had been used as a tool for removing political opponents and securing communist power, turning it not only on wider society but also against anyone Dej perceived as a threat to his leadership. This created a political atmosphere of paranoia and fear.

Dej also put into place two other main practices of a Stalinist political program: (1) removing the peasants from their land and herding into cooperatives, and (2) industrialization along Soviet lines (i.e., with a focus on heavy industry with binding targets set by the central planning authority). Given the extent to which Romania was still largely a country of peasants who privately owned small pieces of land, along with the degree to which the country was still not industrialized, the rapidity and severity with which these programs were enacted forced wrenching and frequently unwelcome changes in the lives of Romanian citizens. During collectivization, peasants who resisted were subject to retribution from the state in the form of imprisonment and loss of land.[8] The early phase of communism witnessed the creation of a political, economic, and bureaucratic framework that would dominate Romanian life for the remainder of the twentieth century.

In response to Nikita Khrushchev's 1956 condemnation of Stalinism and the subsequent thawing of politics and society, many hard-line "little Stalins" in Central and Eastern Europe were quickly ousted as the states attempted limited liberalization, using national independence from the USSR to legitimize themselves. De-Stalinization presented a challenge to Dej, who survived by subverting it while embracing the national-independence line. Rather than liberalizing, he maintained his hard-line Stalinist approach. Taking advantage of anti-Russian sentiment in Romania, he portrayed Khrushchev's call as Soviet imperialism and argued that by rejecting this, he was asserting Romania's independence.[9] This marked the birth of Romanian nationalist communism, which attracted the support of both the Orthodox Church and many intellectuals.

After Dej's death in 1964, Nicolae Ceaușescu came to power and ruled for the next twenty-five years. Until 1971, his rule was marked by a limited domestic thaw and a further break from the USSR, especially after 1968, when Romania became the only member of the Warsaw Pact not to participate in the invasion of Czechoslovakia. This decision won Ceaușescu support not only at home, where he further embraced Romanian nationalism, but also in the West. Charles de Gaulle, Richard Nixon, and other leaders praised Ceaușescu as "another Tito" willing to break with the USSR. This period also marked, however, the start of Ceaușescu's cult of personality, which dominated all aspects of Romanian life from that point onward and intensified after 1971, when Ceaușescu visited North Korea and China. Particularly impressed with Kim Il Sung's bombastic projects, Ceaușescu abandoned the thaw of the 1960s and sought to bring Romania into a self-proclaimed "golden age" led by the *Conducător*. The cult, which extended beyond Ceaușescu to include his wife, Elena, most commonly took the form of eulogistic praise in the media. In physical terms, Ceaușescu began rebuilding Bucharest and other cities to conform to his vision of a communist city. These and other grandiose projects consumed vast amounts of state resources but were often poorly designed and poorly constructed.

The 1980 crisis in Poland that led to the formation of Solidarity and brought down the government of Edward Gierek caused a major shift in Ceaușescu's domestic policy. Believing that the crisis had been caused by Poland's debts to foreign states, he decided to pay off all of Romania's foreign debts as quickly as possible—a goal he could only reach by imposing massive domestic austerity, resulting in rationing, food shortages, and power cuts as basic services crumbled.

Many have asked why no Romanian Solidarity emerged in the face of such conditions. The common explanation, the degree of Securitate repression, only represents one element. Additional factors include division and isolation among those who opposed the regime, along with the practical difficulties caused by the crisis that made organizing an opposition impossible. The hard-line defensive nationalism of the regime served two purposes: it provided a scapegoat by allowing any problems to be blamed on anti-Romanian forces, and it co-opted many intellectuals who elsewhere might have formed part of an opposition movement. Likewise, the Orthodox Church provided no home for opposition.

By the late 1980s some indications of open dissent finally emerged both from the Romanian people and the Romanian Communist Party. In 1987, when the economic situation of workers was dire, factory workers at the Red Flag Truck Factory in Braşov struck for the restoration of their recently cut wages. Unlike the thirty to forty thousand Jiu Valley miners who had conducted a sit-in strike for benefits in 1977 (and had obtained them from Ceauşescu, who negotiated with them personally), the Braşov workers started a procession from the factory to the town hall. Significantly, along the procession route, they were joined by citizens and the cries for better wages quickly became shouts of "Down with Ceauşescu." Less than twenty-four hours after it began, the Braşov strike was crushed, and arrests and imprisonment swiftly followed. By 1989, Communist Party officials also had begun to show their disquiet. In March 1989, six party veterans wrote an open letter expressing their concerns at what they then regarded as Ceauşescu's erratic behavior and excesses. Several courageous individual dissidents also spoke out.

In early 1989, however, nothing appeared likely to break the power of the communists in Romania. Foreign pressure from both the West and the USSR had no effect. Domestic pressure had proven equally ineffective. When the regime did collapse, its fall was rapid, bloody, and violent. Yet, when the dust settled and the new leadership appeared, many wondered if there had been any revolution at all.

THE END OF COMMUNISM AND POST-1989 POLITICS

For many of the other communist states in Europe, 1989 represented a moment of national liberation. For states like Romania, which had asserted national independence from the Soviets earlier, the revolutions instead took the form of bloody rebellions against local leadership.

The Romanian revolution remains one of the most controversial aspects of the state's history. It served to highlight the underdeveloped nature of civil society in the state and how "backward" Romania was compared to its neighbors. It did not have a base in the democratic opposition movements found in other states; nor did leaders spring from the trade union movement or the intelligentsia. Instead, a dead dictator and a former second-tier communist with weak democratic credentials emerged from the dust.

The Romanian revolution began with a series of protests against the removal of the Hungarian pastor Laszló Tökés in the western city of Timişoara. It is no accident that the revolution began there. The city's close proximity to the border with Hungary and Yugoslavia meant that the public had access to information from the media in those states; Bucharest and Braşov, by contrast, were isolated from foreign media. Despite the unrest in Timişoara, Ceauşescu chose to continue his December visit to Iran. In his absence a power vacuum emerged, leaving the regime unable to respond to the crisis. Internal divisions within the leadership appeared, and the protests spread. Once Ceauşescu returned, to show that he was still in control and also to announce increases in wages and pensions, he gave the infamous balcony speech, televised live across Romania. When an incident sparked panic in the crowd, Ceauşescu was shown looking bemused and confused by his inability to deal with the situation. Although control was regained in the crowd, this symbolic loss of the usual scripted control brought additional people onto the streets. Then, the authorities did lose control.

Ceaușescu's decision to use force to stop the demonstration failed as the security forces began to switch sides. His public flight by helicopter from Bucharest created a power vacuum. In the absence of authority, chaotic fighting broke out between protesters and loyalists. The actual events remain murky to this day. Many deaths were the result of mistaken identity as fears and rumors of a countercoup by Ceaușescu and his supporters led spontaneous groups of fighters to suspect each other as being Securitate and to fire on one another. The situation is complicated further by the extent to which Ceaușescu loyalists and Securitate were active with no clear sense of who was giving the orders.

Photo 15.1.   Bucharest's youth celebrate the flight of Nicolae Ceaușescu in December 1989. (Dan Dusleag)

Ceaușescu's capture, hastily convened show trial, and rapid execution did little to bring about peace or to establish a democratic Romania.

The Romanian revolution[10] had all the marks of a classic revolution from below: people on the streets, protests spreading across the country, a government unable to respond, the power of the dictator collapsing before everyone's eyes, and eventually the execution of the Ceaușescus. But what emerged was not revolutionary. In addition to historical factors, the way in which the cards were dealt in the early 1990s has profoundly affected how politics, the state, and society have functioned since then.

Out of the vacuum emerged the National Salvation Front (NSF) led by Ion Iliescu. It proclaimed itself a transitional government, barring members of the former interwar parties and other organizations that tried to enter the television station during the revolution. This allowed Iliescu, a senior communist before falling out with Ceaușescu, to quickly position himself as the leader of the revolution. Despite its sudden appearance, the NSF—made up of former senior communist officials—seemed well organized and prepared, rapidly taking over the offices of the Communist Party and declaring Iliescu president of the new party.

Iliescu[11] in 1990 had no commitment to democracy. He initially rejected liberal democracy in favor of what he described as "original democracy," in which democracy would be conducted through the NSF as a type of "one-party democracy," or a "form of political pluralism . . . [based on] maintaining and consolidating the national consensus."[12] The government was composed largely of former members of the party *nomenklatura*, most of whom had fallen out with Ceaușescu before 1989. To counteract the image of continuity, Iliescu appointed Petre Roman as prime minister. The Western-educated Roman represented a different, younger generation than the Moscow-educated Iliescu. While Roman showed some interest in reform, Iliescu showed none.

In its initial statements in December 1989, the NSF proclaimed itself the guardian of the revolution: it was committed to democratic principles and a multiparty system and promised to organize free and fair elections. No one, it stated, should be elected for more than one or two terms. As a guarantor of the principles of the revolution, to ensure fairness, it promised that it would not become a party and field candidates. Rather, it would step down after the first elections. Finally, the NSF declared that it represented a clear break with the communist regime. Although all of the primary leaders of NSF were former communists, many people knew that Iliescu had been banished to lower-level positions by Ceaușescu in the 1970s and had lost his Central Committee seat. Silviu Brucan, another NSF leader, while remaining in highly visible positions under Ceaușescu, had been against the brutal suppression of the Brașov workers' protest in 1987 and had signed the open "Letter of Six" in March 1989 protesting Ceaușescu's erratic leadership and policies. Several known dissidents, such as human rights activist Doina Cornea and poet Mircea Dinescu, also joined the NSF, although not in leadership positions. In short, it appeared initially that the leaders of the NSF were sincere. However, that belief would prove illusory.

The first full month that the NSF was in power, January 1990, was one of great fluidity. Though almost nonexistent under communism, civil society groups began to appear, especially among students and intellectuals. In the first week of January, political parties, especially the "historical" political parties—namely, the National Peasants Party, Social

Democratic Party, and National Liberal Party—began to reconstitute themselves. New parties and political organizations were also formed, including the Democratic Union of Hungarians in Romania. Despite the NSF's declaration that the "Communist Party was dead,"[13] an official order disbanding the hated Securitate, and Iliescu's reassurances in his New Year's address that the NSF sought to institute political pluralism, many remained skeptical.

On January 7, students took the lead in expressing their unease: three thousand students gathered in a Bucharest University lecture hall to mourn the loss of their fellow students in the December revolution and raise their uncertainty about the intentions of the NSF. Five days later, less than three full weeks after the NSF had appointed itself the "guardian" of the revolution, five thousand people protested against the Communist Party. Gathered outside the NSF headquarters, they shouted slogans like "Down with communism, kill the communists."[14] Such demonstrations, differing in size though usually numbering at least one thousand, continued to take place sporadically throughout the month of January. Although no single demonstration opposing the NSF was particularly large until the one on January 28, these protests reflected the public's fear that the revolution had been usurped by the communists in the guise of the NSF.

Indeed, the NSF had moved quickly to stabilize the revolutionary situation, establish a provisional government, and consolidate its own power. It rapidly took full control of the organizations and assets of the Romanian Communist Party. In mid-January, it officially confiscated all the large industrial enterprises (which had recently brought in more than $220 million in hard currency) and the agroindustrial "complexes," which included more than eighteen thousand state farmers, not to mention Ceauşescu's twenty-one palaces and forty-one residential villas. A short time later it also claimed control over all state-owned transportation. From the outset it had controlled the TV station and most major media. The Securitate, which was officially disbanded, was reconstituted with 60 percent of the same personnel a few months later. The NSF also captured and utilized the strong and deeply rooted clientelistic networks of the RCP.

The declaration on January 23 that the leaders of the NSF were going to run in the first elections as a political party and that there would be restrictions on demonstrations magnified the public's unease. *Romania Libre*, one of the more independent newspapers, ran a headline reading, "Illusions Lasted Only One Month." Three of the political parties called on the NSF to resign and appoint a technocratic caretaker government until the elections.[15] Together with civil society actors, they called for demonstrations. Although the initial demonstrations on January 23 and 24 were only about one thousand people strong, the demonstration on January 28 brought out between twenty and thirty thousand people in Bucharest, the largest gathering since the revolution. In sympathy, workers struck in three major cities: Sibiu, Braşov, and Timişoara. Nothing, though, changed.

Iliescu's self-interested approach to politics and lack of democratic commitment came to the fore in June 1990, when anti-Iliescu and anti-NSF demonstrations in Bucharest began to turn contentious. The security services that had inherited the role of the Securitate, with Iliescu's support, used violence against the pro-reform demonstrators. The NSF and security services mobilized some sixteen thousand civilians, specifically coal miners from the Jiu Valley in Transylvania, for what were called *Mineriada*—responses to demonstrations for which miners were transported to Bucharest and encouraged to attack anyone who expressed opposition to Iliescu and the NSF. The security services were later accused of infiltrating opposition rallies and distributing fake Legionary leaflets to discredit Iliescu's opponents and support Iliescu's charges of fascism.[16]

During these *Mineriadă* the headquarters of opposition parties were ransacked, and pro-democracy advocates were beaten and arrested.[17] The violence carried out by both miners and members of the security services shocked observers inside and outside Romania.[18] The hope that postrevolutionary politics would break with the past proved false. Miners returned again in 1991 to oust Petre Roman after he began to challenge Iliescu's dominance. The exact number of protesters killed during the four *Mineriadă* remains unknown but has been estimated at around two hundred.

Thus, the initial political environment after the end of communism was marked by a weak commitment to the rules of democracy when the self-appointed leaders were confronted with an overt challenge by the population. The willingness to use violence and provocateurs and the hostility toward critics at home and abroad reflected a continuation of Ceauşescu-era political culture. Neither the political elite nor their conduct changed in 1989; Romanian politics remained a politics of intolerance.[19]

Between January and the elections in May, the NSF also continued consolidating the assets of the RCP to assure its victory in the May. As early as the second week of January, opposition political parties correctly complained about their lack of media access, despite an election decree guaranteeing them free access to the media. In a country where the NSF controlled every major media outlet, the opposition had trouble getting its message heard. The opposition was also hampered by the timing of the elections: in January the NSF declared that the elections would be held in three months. In April, opposition parties absent for forty or more years and trying to reconstitute themselves, as well as new parties attempting to form, requested that the elections be postponed until September or October. The NSF refused, although it did move the elections to May. It also passed an election-financing law stating that each party would get a state subsidy and banning outside or foreign financing. Since the NSF had "inherited" all of the monetary assets of the RCP, limiting the funding sources for other parties put them at a severe disadvantage. It prevented émigré Romanian politicians, who had returned to the country, from using any of the money they had amassed during their exile and other parties from getting foreign sponsors.

The NSF also had the highly organized, fairly well-disciplined former Communist Party machine to utilize. In its election campaign, the NSF employed smear and scare tactics; it told the electorate that anyone else they elected would allow foreign capitalists to close factories, leading to mass unemployment, that the Hungarians would get Transylvania back, and that the "historic" parties wanted to return the country to the state of social inequality that existed in the interwar period. In short, NSF officials painted a picture that promised citizens instability, economic insecurity, and chaos if they did not elect NSF leaders to be their guarantors and protectors. Finally, the opposition parties themselves were disorganized and did not run strong campaigns. Given that their leaders had been silenced or forced out of the country in the communist period, the new parties had little to say. They largely counted on people having positive memories of them from the interwar years.

As a result of its resources and the weakness of the new parties, the NSF easily won the elections in May 1990. Iliescu took 85 percent of the presidential vote, and the NSF won two-thirds of the parliamentary seats.[20] Following the ouster of Petre Roman, violence as a means to consolidate power gave way to a more formal approach by Iliescu and his supporters. Iliescu again won the 1992 presidential elections despite a reduction in support, and his party garnered just over a third of the seats in parliament.

In short, during the period from December 22, 1989, through the first founding election, not only were former higher-ranking communists not displaced by the revolution, but they managed to capture and consolidate their hold on the resources of the state. Using these institutional advantages, as well as other extrajudicial measures, the men who came to power shaped the subsequent direction of Romanian politics.

The government formed in 1992, led by Prime Minister Nicolae Văcăroiu, continued the same course and focused on ensuring that the basic structures of power remained in the hands of the ex-communist elite: 96 percent of the members of the new government were former Communist Party members.[21] As Vladimir Tismaneanu has argued, rather than progressing toward a consolidated democracy, Romania between 1989 and 1996 was "very close to a populist regime, [a] corporatist, semi-fascist" system—one in which "corruption [was] the principal form of perpetuating the elite."[22]

Parties that considered themselves the "democratic opposition" to the NSF formed the Democratic Convention of Romania (CDR) in November 1991. The leading parties of the CDR declared themselves to be center-right and drew from the revived precommunist parties (the PNȚ and the PNL). The CDR grew in strength over the years and, by the 1996 elections, contained more than ten parties. Unified more by a desire to see Iliescu and the NSF removed from power than by any real ideology, this diverse political grouping coalesced under the slogan "We can only succeed together."[23]

The CDR developed into a formidable opposition force led by university administrator Emil Constantinescu, who proposed sweeping reforms through the "Contract with Romania,"[24] which emphasized the need for swift economic restructuring, including privatization, and called for the introduction of a serious anticorruption program. After the stagnation and corruption of the Iliescu years, the tide was turning. The CDR won the parliamentary and presidential elections of 1996. Constantinescu beat Iliescu decisively with 54.21 percent of the vote. The CDR garnered 30 percent of the vote in the lower house of parliament, while the NSF, renamed the Party of Social Democracy in Romania,[25] came in second with 22 percent. The CDR formed a multiparty coalition with other anti-Iliescu parties and formed a new government under Prime Minister Victor Ciorbea.

Neither the CDR nor Constantinescu managed to live up to the expectations of the Romanian people, who hoped that the 1996 elections would mark a decisive break with the past and that the delayed democratic transition would finally come. Once in office, the coalition faced the realities of governing a systemically corrupt bureaucracy and a structurally weak economy. Under these conditions, they found effective and popular government an elusive goal. The public's initial support for reforms also began to dwindle as the social costs of economic restructuring hit.

As it became clear that the CDR could not deliver on its promises, divisions began to appear, and the coalition fragmented. The Democratic Party (PD),[26] led by Petre Roman, withdrew from the government, forcing Ciorbea to resign. The PNL later withdrew as well, reducing the CDR to a shell organization. After the CDR's collapse, Constantinescu refused to run for a second term as president in 2000, warning that incumbent politicians, seeking only private gain, had imperiled the country and made real change nearly impossible.

With a crumbling government and an opposition that had retained control over significant political and economic resources, the electoral landscape changed dramatically in the 2000 elections. The Social Democratic Party (PSD) became the largest party in parliament, and Iliescu returned to the presidency. A number of parties strongly affiliated with the CDR were defeated in the parliamentary elections, never to return, or were reduced to a mere handful of representatives.

The performance of the extremist Greater Romania Party (PRM) caught the attention of many observers and the international community. The party's leader, Corneliu Vadim Tudor, had effectively been Ceauşescu's court poet during the communist period. A writer known for his bombastic paeans to the Romanian nation and to the dictator's genius during his rule, Vadim went on to endorse the miners' violence of the 1990s and served as editor of his party's newspaper, *România mare* (*Greater Romania*), a publication known for its anti-Semitic and anti-Hungarian articles. His ties with Ceauşescu and the fact that the party was extremist, anti-Semitic, and racist awoke fears of the returning ghost of interwar extremism and violence. The international press feared that in an ethnically diverse state such as Romania, such politics could result in the same ethnic violence seen in Yugoslavia a few years previously.

In fact, however, the execution and results of the 2000 elections were encouraging in a number of ways, and the strong showing of an extreme nationalist leader was hardly exceptional for a European state in the early 2000s. Moreover, the success of the PRM did not reflect a deeply xenophobic citizenry; it was a product of Vadim's vehement anti-corruption campaign and Romanians' disenchantment with the other major parties. The collapse of the CDR and the parties associated with it opened up a space into which the PRM could step. Ultimately Vadim's ability to catch the protest vote proved short-lived, and support for the PRM dwindled after 2000. Its vote declined in the 2004 elections and, by 2008, it failed to reach the 5 percent electoral threshold and ceased to have any political representation in parliament. In 2012 it received below 2 percent of the vote.[27]

Romania under Social Democratic leaders Ion Iliescu, president from 1990 to 1996 and 2000 to 2004, and Adrian Năstase, prime minster from 2000 to 2004, experienced both progress and stagnation. These two leaders represent the most negative elements in Romanian politics: authoritarianism, antagonism toward opposition, and rampant self-enriching corruption. They sought to create PSD hegemony for their own benefit. During their rule, there was also the start of constitutional tinkering, such as increasing presidential terms from four to five years. While Iliescu sought to protect his legacy, Năstase sought to create his. Nonetheless, during this period Romania made its delayed journey toward the European Union (EU) and North Atlantic Treaty Organization (NATO). It was also a period of relative economic stability, in contrast to the CDR years, because of the structural funds Romania received from the EU to improve infrastructure.

The country's desire to join the EU and NATO placed severe constraints on the actions of the Romanian political and economic elite. Increased international attention limited the ability of Iliescu and Năstase to undermine democracy, as EU criticism and threats of further delays to accession forced them to adhere to democratic norms.

However, corruption and a self-aggrandizing approach to public office have remained problematic aspects of politics in Romania.

The center-right remerged after 2000 in the form of the Truth and Justice Alliance (DA) of the Democratic Party (PD) and National Liberal Party (PNL). This alliance grew out of parliamentary cooperation instigated by former CDR justice minister and PNL parliamentarian Valeriu Stoica in 2002 and developed into an anti-PSD bloc for the 2004 election. It built on the charisma of presidential candidate Traian Băsescu, the popular former mayor of Bucharest, and voters' unease with PSD presidential candidate Adrian Năstase. Băsescu's willingness to use populist rhetoric and anticorruption discourses put him in stark contrast to Năstase, who had earned the nickname "Patru Casa Năstase" (Four Houses Năstase) because of the wealth he had accumulated through corruption. The antidemocratic tendencies of the PSD under Năstase rose to the fore during the campaign with threats against journalists and critics of the PSD.

Băsescu and the DA aligned themselves with the turn toward liberalism and redemocratization in the region that had begun with Georgia's Rose Revolution in 2003 and continued with Ukraine's Orange Revolution in 2004. The DA even adopted the same orange banners seen waving on the streets of Kyiv earlier that year.[28] Thus, as the CDR had done previously, the DA positioned itself as finally breaking with Romania's past.

Although Năstase won the first round of the presidential election, concerns about the direction Romania might take under him led to a surge in support for Băsescu in the second round of voting. While the PSD remained the largest single party in parliament, Băsescu's victory drew smaller parties to the DA, allowing for the formation of a coalition government led by Călin Popescu-Tăriceanu of the PNL as prime minister.

The new government seemed to mark a clear generational shift in Romanian politics with young ministers appointed to important portfolios such as foreign affairs and justice. Momentum also began to gather in favor of punishing those who had ties with the communist regime. In 2006, new legislation led to the opening of parliamentarians' communist-era secret service files for public scrutiny. Several leading figures from the PSD, PNL, and other parties were disgraced after their records showed collaboration with the Securitate. The question of the communist past became a central issue of Băsescu's presidency. Băsescu publicly denounced the communist system as "an illegitimate and criminal regime."[29] This stance, along with his success, earned him the long-standing animosity of the PSD. The threat of possible lustration legislation motivated politicians who would be subject to this legislation to seek to impeach Băsescu in 2007. This attempt failed when a national referendum yielded strong public support for the president.

The DA, like the CDR before it, proved a fragile coalition. Political egos and personal vanity, as well as material interests, undermined it. The coalition only held together for as long as it did for one reason: the prospect of EU membership. The EU cast a very critical eye at Romania, and the fear that internal political instability might delay accession forced politicians to work together. Călin Tăriceanu, as prime minister and head of the PNL, clashed with Băsescu, head of the Democratic Party and president, for preeminence, and in April 2007 the PNL announced its intention to withdraw from the alliance. Its leaders then formed a minority government with the Democratic Union of Hungarians in Romania (UDMR). Breaking the alliance led to the removal of the most reform-minded and anticorruption ministers from their positions and their replacement with PNL loyalists. It also allowed Băsescu to maintain his anticorruption stance as some PNL leaders were under scrutiny for corruption and Securitate links. The minority government survived until the parliamentary elections of November 2008. However, the breaking of the alliance was not well received by the public: the PNL ran a clear third behind the PDL (formed of the PD and a splinter group of the PNL in 2007)[30] and the PSD.

The 2008 elections took place under the new but highly complex mixed electoral system, which even party leaders admitted they had trouble understanding. The PSD won the largest percentage of the vote in the Chamber of Deputies (33 percent), but the PDL won the most seats (34 percent). This split between two parties that hated one another made the process of constructing a government difficult. But ultimately they agreed to forge a "coalition of convenience" under Emil Boc, leader of the PDL. The agreement meant the end of any reform or anticorruption measures, which suited the PSD, as a focus on these issues would have hurt it in the run-up to the 2009 elections.

The Boc government was unstable from the outset. In September 2009, once it no longer saw the partnership as useful, the PSD withdrew, hoping to weaken Băsescu's credibility prior to presidential elections in November and December 2009. It achieved its aim, as Băsescu's popular support slipped. In the first round of the elections, Băsescu won 32 percent of the vote to the PSD's Mircea Geoană's 31 percent. Băsescu managed to retain the presidency, however, with 50.3 percent support in the second round. Votes from the young and émigré Romanians in Western Europe, as they had in the 2007 impeachment vote, proved critical.

After losing the 2004 elections, the PSD removed Iliescu and Năstase as party leaders and replaced them with the younger Mircea Geoană. However, following the defeat of Geoană in the 2009 elections, the Iliescu-Năstase faction and the barons of the PSD returned. They chose a new, younger leader, Victor Ponta. Năstase's former PhD student, Ponta was widely viewed as a weak leader who would follow the orders of senior party officials. His past quickly became an issue, however, as it was revealed that he had plagiarized his PhD and been investigated in the suspicious 2002 death of a former colleague tasked with investigating Adrian Năstase.

Following defeat in 2008, the PNL replaced Tăriceanu with Crin Antonescu. Both the PNL and the PSD felt deep animosity toward Băsescu and the PDL. The PNL hated the PDL for replacing them as the primary anti-PSD party, while the PSD hated Băsescu for the anticorruption measures that had targeted Năstase and other leading PSD barons. The PNL and PSD began to work together to establish a political alliance in 2011 to oppose Băsescu. Just as the CDR and DA had been anti-Iliescu alliances, the Social Liberal Union (USL) is a purely anti-Băsescu alliance. The two parties have no common ideological ground, and each believes that it should be the leading party. Significantly, the PSD's declining support in each election means it can now only govern via a broad coalition.

Following the collapse of the Boc and then the short-lived Mihai Razvan Ungureanu governments in the spring of 2012, the USL took over. A division of offices had been agreed to, with Ponta to become prime minister and Antonescu to be the USL's future presidential candidate. Tensions within the USL as well as impending corruption cases drove the USL to seek to impeach Băsescu.

At a time of major economic crisis, many Romanians saw this effort as yet more self-indulgent politicking by the elite. Worryingly, the USL sought to amend the constitution, and when the Constitutional Court blocked this, the USL threatened to ignore the ruling. Coming so soon after events in Hungary, this threat stirred the international community. Both the United States and the EU condemned the moves and warned of political and economic consequences if such measures went ahead. In response, the USL retreated into defensive nationalist discourse reminiscent of the Ceauşescu years, attacking the EU and United States for interfering in Romanian affairs. Ultimately the referendum to impeach Băsescu failed due to low turnout; however, for several months, Romania underwent political paralysis, and the USL's commitment to democracy was questioned.

The USL won the parliamentary elections with an absolute majority, which would appear to indicate widespread support for them. However, turnout was only 47.11 percent.[31] Despite having resisted austerity measures when in opposition, the USL has retracted many of its promises since taking office.

In 2014 the USL alliance broke up when it became apparent that Victor Ponta intended to run for president in 2015. As a result the PNL exited the alliance, leaving Ponta governing with the UDMR. Another round of infighting has begun as Ponta has been named in a graft investigation, while Ponta and his supporters in the parliament have launched an attempt to have Băsescu investigated over a land purchase.

Institutional Politics

Institutionally, Romania is a mixed system. The president, the head of state, is directly elected via two rounds of elections for a term of five years (changed from four years in 2004). The president appoints the prime minister, the head of government; however, this depends on parliamentary support, and the government can and will fall in the event of a parliamentary vote of no confidence.

The parliament is bicameral, consisting of a 412-member Chamber of Deputies and a 176-member Senate. Parliamentary elections occur every four years. The Romanian parliamentary electoral system, which changed in 2008, is a complex mixed system of proportional representation and single-member districts.[32]

The Constitutional Court provides a further check and balance. It is empowered to strike down legislation that it deems unconstitutional. It consists of nine members serving nine-year terms that cannot be extended, with three members each appointed by the president, the Senate, and the Chamber of Deputies. Every three years, three members are subject to replacement.

The impetus for the constitutional design was both practical and cultural. The Romanian system echoes the French system, reflecting the close cultural ties that much of the elite had with France. More importantly, one legacy of Romanian history has been a desire to prevent the concentration of too much power in the hands of one individual or institution. As a result, a complex series of checks and balances exists within the written constitution, itself highly complex and often contradictory. There are three main areas of gridlock. First, the division of powers and roles between the president and prime minister is ambiguously stated within the constitution. In periods of cohabitation, when the president and prime minister are from different parties, this lack of clarity leads to conflict between the two. Second, the president and both the Senate and Chamber of Deputies have the ability to block and delay legislation. The uncoupling of presidential and parliamentary elections after 2004 has increased the likelihood of cohabitation and thus legislative gridlock or resort to the use of the emergency decree. Third, the president and parliament select Constitutional Court judges for nine-year terms; thus presidential and parliamentary power can endure through these court appointments even after given politicians' terms end. For instance, Iliescu's court appointees could veto legislation, such as transitional justice legislation, that went against his wishes even after Iliescu left office.

Political Parties

Party politics in postcommunist Romania have been marked by two constants—namely, the stability of political parties derived from the former Romanian Communist Party and the instability of opposition parties. The development of the party system has been influenced by two important themes: the absence of any strong ideological commitment and a weak commitment to democracy and the rules of democratic politics. The political elite's greatest commitment is to power and self-enrichment. Paradoxically, despite the sense of perpetual crisis and instability, until 2012, all Romanian parliaments completed their full terms, in part because membership in parliament effectively guarantees immunity from prosecution. All Romanian parties are "office-seeking" as opposed to vote- or policy-seeking parties. In other words, they seek to "maximize their control over political office benefits, that is, private goods bestowed on recipients of politically discretionary governmental or sub-governmental appointments." [33]

Postcommunist political parties arose from three distinct sources and fall into three distinct groupings: those that emerged out of the RCP, those that claimed to be the successors to precommunist parties, and genuinely new parties. The parties have been volatile, with frequent mergers and splits between factions as well as name changes. However, there has been remarkable continuity in personnel, and the divisions and coalitions have generally been driven by political opportunism rather than ideology.

All current parties strongly favor the free market while remaining socially conservative. The PSD has moved away from the statist view of the economy under Iliescu toward an embrace of privatization. This shift reflects less an ideological move than the growing domination of the economic elite among the party barons and the clientelistic nature of party politics.

Romanian political parties are largely top-down organizations; although they have extensive local organizations, party members have very little control over or say in policy. All parties depend on wealthy supporters for material aid and on local elites to bring supporters and votes to the table. Politics is largely based on patronage, clientelism, and networks rather than ideology or political commitment. Although in recent years leadership of political parties has begun to shift from those who were active during the communist years to a younger generation, many of these new leaders are the children of the old communist *nomenklatura*.

Until recently the PSD could count on sufficient electoral support to ensure a majority, and its opponents had to form large coalitions to stand any chance of taking power. Two such groupings include the Democratic Convention of Romania and the Truth and Justice Alliance. These large alliances of very different parties held together by their dislike of the PSD proved unstable once they had achieved their primary objective of denying the PSD power.

Electoral results show that reformist parties draw their support mainly from urban areas and the west of the country.[34] Their supporters tend to be younger than PSD supporters and often mobilize against the perceived embedded corruption of the PSD within the state.

The PSD draws its support from the countryside and the poorer regions of Romania, and its electorate tends to be elderly and more dependent on the state. However, in recent years residual support for the PSD has declined, forcing the party into an alliance with the National Liberal Party and the Social Liberal Union in order to win the 2012 parliamentary elections and assume the prime ministership.

It is no accident that since 1989 every Romanian president has embraced populist rhetoric and ethnonationalism. This approach, a continuation of Ceauşescu-era nationalist discourse, has proved successful in mobilizing supporters to vote at key elections, especially among working-class and rural voters. Politicians who have distanced themselves from such rhetoric have often failed.

All parties as well as the media in Romania make use of what Michael Shafir has described as "utilitarian" nationalism,[35] meaning that politicians play on certain anti-Semitic or nationalistic prejudices, even though they may not personally share these beliefs, for political ends. Thus, politicians will play the anti-Hungarian card or invoke nationalist discourses in response to criticism.

Minorities can be represented through one of two mechanisms. The first involves standing for election at the national level. Thus, multiple deputies and senators can be elected from a single minority party, but only if they cross the electoral threshold. The second mechanism, guaranteed minority representation, follows the constitutional provision that entitles all minorities to political representation. So as long as enough people claim to be part of an ethnic minority, that minority is entitled to a single representative, chosen via an election within the minority itself. Thus, minorities have to choose between guaranteed but limited representation and unguaranteed but potentially greater representation.[36]

The Hungarian minority is represented by the Democratic Union of Hungarians in Romania, which acts as a vehicle for ethnic representation. Like other political parties in Romania, it is an office-seeking party, willing to align with any political faction in order to secure office. It would be incorrect to view the Hungarian ethnic vote as homogeneous. Within the Hungarian community, divisions exist along social lines as well between moderates and radicals with regard to the position of ethnic Hungarians in Romania. These divisions result in a highly volatile internal political environment. However, members of the UDMR recognize that if the party were to factionalize and split, it would almost certainly fall below the electoral threshold. Successful distribution of the spoils of office is thus central to maintaining the cohesion of the UDMR as a political organization and helps to explain its willingness to act as a coalition partner with any governing party in Romania.

Civil Society: The Politics of Protest and the Environment[37]

The absence of a strong Romanian civil society is frequently attributed to the atomizing, atavistic effects of the communist regime, in particular the Ceaușescu years, which helped to turn Romanian society in on itself, destroy social networks, and turn individuals inward psychologically. The state of perpetual fear under Dej that continued under Ceaușescu, combined with the shortage economy of the 1970s and 1980s, which necessitated self-interest, are cited as the causes. The evidence for the impact on civil society is the absence of any democratic movement before 1989. Romania produced no Lech Wałęsa or Václav Havel; there was no Romanian Solidarity or Public against Violence; nor was there even an environmentalist movement equivalent to that in Bulgaria. However, this explanation ignores the fact that Romanian society even before 1944 was deeply polarized, with cleavages that stood in the way of developing social networks. The culture of mistrust among both individuals and social groups predates communism; it was exploited by the communists and continues to be exploited by those who fear the emergence of a genuinely autonomous civil society beyond the control of the political and economic elite.

It is thus impossible to talk about an autonomous civil society in Romania. Sectional interests primarily in the economic sphere are mobilized from the top down by opportunistic political and economic actors seeking to parlay discontent into political office. The protests of 2011 and 2012 organized by the USL were one such example. On the flipside, small-scale autonomous actions exist to advance the interests of either cultural or social groups and tend to be limited to one interest or in their social appeal. The groups are often from the political extremes and naturally hostile to one another. Intellectuals steadfastly refuse to establish points of contact with the working class and peasantry, and the peasants and workers mistrust the intellectuals. Socially liberal intellectuals consider the lower classes to be beyond help and to be naturally right-wing and reactionary.

The only political issue that has produced collective action has been the environmental issue, and this is a recent development. The Romanian environmental movement has started to play an important role in the country's emerging climate of protest. A consideration of these dynamics illustrates both the continued influence of the communist legacy and the ways that citizens are responding to the current social and political context. Romania's main environmental problems include water and air pollution and land degradation, stemming from both communist-era industrialization and more recent increased capitalist consumption.

ENVIRONMENTAL ACTIVISM AND PROTEST

Environmental activism did not emerge during communism due to strict control of environmental groups by Ceaușescu. Afterward, some activism emerged in response to specific problems, and some environmental political parties had early success. However, as short-term economic issues took center stage, the environment was again largely ignored. As mentioned above, environmental organizations proliferated along with funding during preparations for EU accession. However, as European funding was cut off after accession, many such groups disappeared or turned to corporate funding, which does not always lead to environmental benefits.[38]

One issue in particular, the planned creation of Europe's largest opencast gold mine at Rosia Montana in Transylvania, has led to the growth of grassroots environmental activism in Romania. The Save Rosia Montana campaign has fought since the late 1990s against Gabriel Resources, the Canadian company that wants to open the mine, which would displace the residents of sixteen villages, create a large cyanide lake, and destroy extensive Roman-era mining galleries.[39] The issue has become well known throughout Romania, occasionally making international headlines. Recently, support for the campaign has increased, especially in light of larger frustrations with the government and a renewed willingness to protest.

After peaceful demonstrations were crushed violently in the early 1990s, as seen in the above discussion of the *Mineriadă*, Romanians have been hesitant to protest. However, as the economic crisis and resulting austerity measures have resulted in slashed salaries and pensions, public unrest has grown, culminating in the 2012 protests, also described above. Many activists became discouraged in the months following the protests, as the government failed to change yet again. Then in 2013, the Rosia Montana issue came into the spotlight as the government tried to pass legislation that would allow the gold corporation to bypass multiple regulations and begin operations. In response, protesters again took to the streets. The campaign attracted support in large part because the issue incorporates many of the problems that concern the Romanian public.

This case illustrates the fact that, as in many other Central and East European countries at the end of communism, environmentalism has become an arena for more general criticism of and outrage toward the government. As such, protests have attracted people and groups with a wide variety of concerns, including not just the environment but also the effects of capitalism and governmental corruption, and diverse motivations, including nationalism and religion.[40] Thus, while environmentalism has become an umbrella for many interests, its continued ability to remain a coherent movement—and the effects this could have on Romanian politics and society—remain to be seen.

Economic Transition

Romania remains one of the poorest states in the region today, largely due to communist-era mismanagement. While Romania had severe economic problems in 1989, it also possessed a number of advantages over its neighbors. These were quickly squandered, however, by Iliescu.

In 1989 under communism, the Romanian economy was, as the joke goes, the world's most advanced nineteenth-century economy. Based on outmoded heavy industry and collective agriculture, strained by the austerity of the 1980s, and burdened with outdated technology and a lack of investment, it ground to a halt. The massive industrial complexes generated more pollution than products. The oil and coal industries on which Romania depended contracted, while agriculture suffered from poor production and management. All industries suffered due to crumbling infrastructure.

Despite its many economic problems, Romania did have one advantage over a number of its neighbors. Ceaușescu's obsession with the eradication of Romania's foreign debt meant that Romania began its economic transition without any. Of course, paying off of the debt caused many structural problems. Nonetheless, Romania also had large quantities of foreign reserves and was the only state in the region that was a member of the International Monetary Fund (IMF).

While Petre Roman made early attempts at liberalization, Iliescu and his supporters resisted making the hard decisions associated with shock therapy that could have jump-started the economy in the early 1990s. State-owned enterprises continued functioning, and little effort was made toward large-scale privatization as seen in other states of the region. Thus, the public sector still accounted for 55 percent of Romania's gross domestic product (GDP) in 1995. By comparison, 70 percent of wealth was privately generated in neighboring Hungary by 1996.[41]

Iliescu consistently argued that he felt a responsibility to Romanian citizens not to apply the shock therapy reforms that had been advocated in other parts of Central and Eastern Europe. However, two other factors were likely at play. First, Iliescu feared that large-scale unemployment would turn the population against the government and erode the ambiguous legitimacy with which he and his associates had begun the postcommunist period. Any reform measures were thus executed in a way that would maximize popular support for the NSF's initiatives, not necessarily because they would boost national economic output. Decollectivization and land reform, for example, illustrate this approach. Despite the popularity of these policies with those granted land at the time, they have ultimately resulted in a Romanian landscape dotted with a huge number of inefficient, unconsolidated microplots that continue to produce subsistence and small-trade crops.

The second element involved a lack of transparency in the many privatization deals that did take place, a problem that remains today. For many it appeared that privatization aimed to allow the NSF/PSD elite to convert their political power into economic wealth. Corruption was, and has remained, a major challenge to economic stability and a cause of inequality. Until recently, the EU and Romanian citizens agreed that systemic corruption was the number one economic concern, ahead of poverty and unemployment.[42] World Bank surveys suggest that one out of every two Romanians sees corruption as a "part of everyday life."[43] The abuse of public office for private gain is perceived to be most widespread among customs officials, the judiciary, parliamentarians, the police, and health officials—but no sector is thought to be free of its effects. Most perniciously, however, during the early period many of the "barons and boyars" who form a wealthy and powerful elite gained control over much of the economy and the media. Iliescu and the NSF/PSD had once again put their own self-interests ahead of the interests of Romania. The legacy of the 1990–1996 period thus entails not only an unreconstructed, uneconomic agricultural sector but also the concentration of wealth and power in the hands of a few with strong connections to the NSF and the security services.

Immediately after its election in November 1996, the center-right CDR began to introduce structural reforms under pressure from international financial institutions. The unreconstructed mining sector, which represented about a quarter of all losses in the economy since 1990, received special attention.[44] In December 1998, after the CDR announced plans to close nearly 150 mines, local miners again began to mobilize for a violent descent on Bucharest. Although halted by the police, the miners managed to force the government to scale back the closures. They repeated this process in other areas, and the government abandoned the reform to avoid protest.

From 2000 until 2008, the Romanian economy grew in absolute terms, and the government achieved a level of fiscal stability. Initial growth was slow, but it rapidly accelerated after 2006. As the likelihood of Romania's joining the EU increased, foreign direct investment rose, and domestic credit eased. From 2006 to 2008, Romania had one of Europe's fastest-growing economies with annual growth rates of around 8 percent and huge year-on-year increases in average real wages (up to 17 percent in 2007).[45] The World Bank attributed these trends to the country's increased integration into the world economy[46] via the EU and its willingness to exploit comparative advantages in the production of textiles, clothing, furniture, automobiles, mid-level technologies, and information services. In contrast, the Economist Intelligence Unit argued that the immediate impetus to growth was the rapid expansion of easy credit and a commensurate increase in domestic consumer demand and spending, which grew by 13 percent in 2007.[47] Although some outside observers were concerned about the structural soundness of the Romanian economy, domestic conspicuous consumption increased.

The global economic crisis of 2008 and 2009 hit Romania hard. As the country fell into the deepest recession of all of the states in the region, the economy shrank by 7 percent in 2009. This decline partially reflected the massive growth over the previous three years. However, fiscal mismanagement by Tăriceanu played a larger role.[48] The government ran loose fiscal and wage policies, allowing consumer demand to continue

Photo 15.2.   Poor technology and infrastructure are rendering Romania's coal-mining industry obsolete. (John Gledhill)

to expand with the backing of foreign capital inflows and easy credit. Credit-backed consumption of imported goods saw Romania's current-account deficit balloon to around 14 percent of the country's GDP in 2007 and 2008.[49] When the global crisis hit, foreign investment quickly dried up, and loans were called in. With a rapidly contracting economy and spiraling unemployment, both the state and private individuals struggled to service their debts. In March 2009 the government turned to the IMF, EU, and European Bank for Reconstruction and Development, which offered a loan of €19.5 billion on the condition that the government introduce a series of austerity measures and structural adjustment. Wages in the public sector were to be cut, some public employees were to be forced to take unpaid leave, and pension plans were to be reformed.

The imposition of these reforms caused a renewed awareness of social divisions. Inequality of wealth had grown rapidly during the mid-2000s, and anticorruption measures had been weakened after 2007. Yet the demands of the IMF hit those at the lowest levels of society—namely, pensioners and the many poorly paid public-sector employees—hardest. Meanwhile, the government did not tackle the structural issues of corruption; nor did the political elite offer a mea culpa for their economic mismanagement between 2000 and 2008. The situation came to a head over the proposed privatization of the country's SMURD ambulance service. The highly respected health minister Raed Arafat resigned in protest, and this incident sparked public anger and demonstrations. Despite cultivating an image as a man of the people, Băsescu turned a deaf ear to their concerns, attacking those who criticized austerity as "leftists."[50] This made the situation worse and brought more people onto the streets.

The recent upturn in the Romanian economy has been driven by strong harvests and high world food prices rather than economic reform instigated by the IMF. The country remains vulnerable should a harvest be poor or food prices collapse.

Inequality, Corruption, and Transitional Justice

Romania has the fourth worst income inequality in the EU. In 2012 the top 20 percent of the population in terms of equivalized disposable income[51] received 6.3 times as much income as the bottom 20 percent.[52] This inequality has been increasing since 2003. Inequality can be blamed, in part, on the unequal distribution of resources and concentration of wealth and power in the hands of the few. Corruption is a strong contributing factor, as many among the economic and political elite had strong connections to the communist regime and security apparatus, which they used to benefit themselves in the new system.

Romania has resisted engaging in transitional justice, which would present a serious challenge to the power of the postcommunist elite. Thus, parties with a reformist agenda tend to fuse anticorruption and reckoning with the past. The relationship between corruption and the wealth gap also gives the issue a strong populist resonance with the electorate. The PSD, on the other hand, considers moves toward reform to be less about resolving corruption than about its opponents trying to settle political scores and prevent it from taking office and power.

The transfer of power away from the PSD in 1996 and again in 2004 saw certain anticorruption programs introduced. However, the real impetus for reform has come from the EU, which has been harsh in its criticism. With the carrot of European integration dangling in front of Romania, real efforts were made to curtail corruption before Romania joined the EU in January 2007. In 2000 the National Section for Combating Corruption and Organized Crime under the direction of the general prosecutor's office was established; additional organizations were established in 2005. A 2003 law brought Romania further into line with EU norms by increasing freedom of information and clarifying the kinds of acts that constitute corruption.

The EU gave impetus to civil society to support the anticorruption fight, and the prospect of EU accession also seemed to boost grassroots anticorruption campaigns. Groups including the Coalition for a Clean Parliament rose to prominence and had some real success in bringing down corrupt politicians through public-awareness campaigns that focused on obvious disparities between public representatives' relatively low salaries and their often vast wealth. This coalition played a large role in turning power over to the Democratic Alliance in the 2004 elections. In what seemed like a break with the past, civil rights activist Monica Macovei was appointed justice minister under the new government and immediately made corruption her number one priority. Macovei's success made her a target, and when the governing coalition broke up after EU accession in April 2007, she was one of the first ministers to be removed by her opponents. As a result, the prosecution of high-level corruption cases has slowed. Romania is the bottom-ranked member of the EU in Transparency International's annual corruption index.[53] Furthermore, after accession, the threat of delayed membership ceased to have any leverage over Romania, and politicians have been emboldened to seek to water down or ignore anticorruption legislation.

Corruption is linked to the lack of transitional justice and the failure to remove former members of the *nomenklatura*. Since the revolution, all three presidents, nine of ten prime ministers, and most ministers and parliamentarians have been drawn from the former Communist Party. Lavinia Stan describes lustration[54] as the "revolution's still-born child."[55] The first calls for transitional justice appeared in the Timişoara declaration issued in March 1990, a citizens' response to the apparent capture of the revolution by the NSF.[56] This declaration demanded that Communist Party officials, state dignitaries, and members of the Securitate be banned from holding office until 2002 (twelve years, or three full electoral cycles). Unsurprisingly, the NSF attacked the declaration, which was ultimately ignored.

Constantinescu's rejection of lustration in 1996 angered many anti-communists.[57] Even parties supporting the concept of lustration were deeply divided on the issue. When two CDR deputies sought to introduce amendments to the electoral law to ban former communist officials from running in the 2000 and 2004 elections, the PSD attacked this effort as an attempt by opponents to stop Iliescu from running for a third term as president. In the absence of lustration, citizen groups took matters into their own hands. The Coalition for a Clean Parliament used publicly available information to denounce controversial candidates and encourage voters not to support them. As a result, many were not elected.

After years of being blocked in parliament, in May 2010 a lustration law was passed banning communist officials from holding public office for five years. In June 2010, however, after an appeal by the PSD, the Constitutional Court (which included many

PSD appointees who were liable to be lustrated) rejected the law as unconstitutional. Parliament made a further attempt to pass a watered-down lustration law in 2012. The Constitutional Court again rejected this, specifically objecting to the section of the law that applied to communist-era prosecutors.[58] Even President Băsescu, who had previously supported lustration and transitional justice, came to argue that it was too late for these measures to have any effect.[59]

The advances and failures of anticorruption efforts can be illustrated using two cases. The first involves Adrian Năstase, Romania's prime minister between 2000 and 2004. Năstase was accused of corruption, bribery, and embezzlement in three court cases. In the first indictment, in 2006, Năstase's status as former prime minister and his parliamentary immunity resulted in delays and obstruction in prosecuting his case. In 2011, the "Aunt Tamara" case, in which Năstase was accused of embezzling money and removing legal evidence, ended in his and his accomplices' acquittal. In 2012, however, Năstase was sentenced to two years in prison for embezzling €1.6 million of public money to fund his presidential campaign in 2004. As the police came to arrest him, Năstase claimed to have shot himself in the neck and was hospitalized. Despite the efforts of Victor Ponta and the PSD in this elaborate bid to stay out of jail, Năstase was taken to Jilava prison near Bucharest, then released early on medical grounds. Despite the short sentence, the jailing of Năstase shocked many Romanians who believed that, as a very well-connected member of the elite, he would get away with his misdeeds, just as he and others had done previously.[60]

The other side of the coin regarding the difficulty of prosecuting corruption charges is exemplified by the case of Dan Voiculescu. Voiculescu, a member of parliament who owns several television stations and newspapers, was unmasked in 2008 as a previous informer for the Securitate. He was accused of embezzling €60 million through influence peddling and money laundering during the privatization of the Institute for Food Research. Voiculescu's lawyers questioned the evidence brought against him, stalled for time, and continuously asked for reconsideration of the evidence, new expertise, invalidation of old evidence, and new witnesses. The case moved from one court to another following Voiculescu's game of hide-and-seek with the system, in which he resigned three times between 2007 and 2012, each time forcing the case to change courts. In the meantime, the statute of limitations on some of the charges expired.[61]

Foreign Policy

Romanian foreign policy since 1996 has been firmly oriented westward. Romania joined NATO in 2004, but its accession to the EU was delayed until 2007 because of concerns about the Romanian economy, corruption, and political reform. The EU has criticized Romania since 2007 for the slowness of reform, and during the political crisis of 2012, both the EU and the United States were openly critical of the actions of the USL and expressed concerns that democracy was being undermined.[62]

Romania took part in the Afghan and Iraq wars and has also provided airbases to the United States. Along with Poland, the country actively participated in the extraordinary rendition program carried out by the United States during these wars. This program involved transporting prisoners from Iraq, Afghanistan, and other states during the "War on Terror" to the US airbases in Romania or via Romania to other US military prisons where they were subject to torture.[63]

Romania, as noted earlier, is a member of NATO and the EU. Moldova, however, is not. Romanian politicians have been happy to float implicitly the idea of "unification" between Romania and Moldova as a way to mobilize nationalist support within Romania. However, recent events have shown the dangers of this discourse. Vladimir Putin's revanchism in Ukraine, Russian annexation of Crimea, and separatist and Russian actions in eastern Ukraine have brought the Transnistrian issue to the fore and called Moldovan sovereignty into doubt.

Photo 15.3.   The street sign reads, "Romania: That'll do." (Ion Barbu)

Transnistrian politicians on April 16, 2014, asked Moscow to allow them to join Russia.[64] This was not the first time they had made the request, and they referred to the 2006 referendum held on the issue. The next day Putin gave an ambiguous response that the issue was complicated but that the people should be allowed to decide their own fate.[65] The Moldovans expressed concern about this[66] as an example of mixed signals from the Putin regime, as only a month previously Russian foreign minister Sergei Lavrov had stated that Moscow respects Moldovan territorial integrity.[67] However, concern has been growing that, given Putin's apparent expansionist and revisionist foreign policy, Transnistria may be the next object of his attention. There is concern that this could open up the ethnic tensions between ethnic Moldovans and the ethnic Russians in Moldova as well as with the Gagauz minority currently seeking greater political representation and autonomy.

The Romanian political elite now face a problem. Having talked of support for largely Romanian-speaking Moldova and used the idea of Moldova as "the lost family," they are now attempting to temper expectations that, should any conflict in Moldova take place, Romania will intervene militarily on behalf of Moldova. As a result, as Russian engagement in eastern Ukraine has increased, Romanian politicians have been simultaneously encouraging and supporting the inclusion of Moldova in the European Union while arguing that the potential for their intervention in Moldova could only come within the framework of NATO.

Current Issues and Future Challenges

A look at Romania's past and present reveals many significant positive developments that have improved the situation of the Romanian population. At the same time, the country continues to face many challenges, some old and some new. Romanian society has experienced many of the same phenomena that have occurred across Europe; however, their problems are often more severe than elsewhere. Yet we should not be trapped in a view of Romania as a victim.

Romanian history has played a role in shaping the options available to current political actors, but this fact does not make Romania a prisoner of its history. Many of the social, political, and economic issues facing Romania are structural in character. However, Romanian actors individually and collectively have often chosen to put their short-term self-interests above those of society as a whole. This was the case particularly during the interwar period but has also been so from the post-1989 period up to the present. Those interested in understanding Romania must therefore continue to appreciate both structural factors and the role of individuals in shaping Romania's future.

Study Questions

1. Is the history of Romania really one dominated by ethnic tension and violence?
2. What are the primary sources of tension in Romanian society?
3. To what extent is Romanian politics one of continuity with the appearance of rupture and change?

4. Why did Romania not develop a coherent civil society before or after 1989?

5. Why do Romanian political institutions not function as they are intended?

Suggested Readings

Deletant, Dennis. *Ceauşescu and the Securitate: Coercion and Dissent in Romania, 1965–1989.* London: Hurst, 1995.

Gallagher, Tom. *Modern Romania: The End of Communism, the Failure of Democratic Reform, and the Theft of a Nation.* New York: New York University Press, 2008.

Hitchins, Keith. *Rumania: 1866–1947.* New York: Oxford University Press, 1994.

King, Charles. *The Moldovans: Romania, Russia and the Politics of Culture.* Stanford, CA: Hoover Institution Press, 2000.

Livezeanu, Irina. *Cultural Politics in Greater Romania: Regionalism, Nation Building, and Ethnic Struggle, 1918–1930.* Ithaca, NY: Cornell University Press, 1995.

Marin, Irina. *Contested Frontiers in the Balkans: Ottoman, Habsburg and Communist Rivalries in Eastern Europe,* London: I. B. Tauris, 2012.

Papadimitriou, Dimitris, and David Phinnemore. *Romania and the European Union: From Marginalisation to Membership.* New York: Routledge, 2008.

Siani-Davies, Peter. *The Romanian Revolution of December 1989.* Ithaca, NY: Cornell University Press, 2005.

Tismaneanu, Vladimir. *Stalinism for All Seasons: A Political History of Romanian Communism.* Berkeley: University of California Press, 2003.

Websites

NineO'clock.ro: http://www.nineoclock.ro (although somewhat basic, the best site for current news from Romania)

Romania-Insider.com: http://www.romania-insider.com (a similar site)

Notes

This chapter draws in part on that by Charles King and John Gledhill in a previous edition of this volume, as well as on work by Nancy L. Meyers.

1. HHStA, PA Rumaenien 1880, Karton 50, Judenfrage, *Memoire sur la revision de l'article 7 de la Constitution roumaine* (Paris, 1879), 12–13: according to the 1859 census, population of Romania: 4,582,602; of these, 218,304 were Jews.

2. Joseph Rothschild, *East Central Europe between the Two World Wars* (Seattle: University of Washington Press, 1992), 284.

3. See Joanne Roberts, "The City of Bucharest, 1918–1940," PhD diss., University of London, 2009.

4. Dennis Deletant, review of *Cultural Politics in Greater Romania: Regionalism, Nation Building and Ethnic Struggle, 1918–1930* by Irina Livezeanu in *Slavonic and East European Review* 74, no. 4 (1996): 765.

5. Dennis Deletant, "A Balancing Act—Romania 1914–1940," *History Today* 42 no. 6 (1992): 52.

6. *Final Report of the International Commission on the Holocaust in Romania* (Yad Vashem, Holocaust Martyrs' and Heroes' Remembrance Authority, November 11, 2004), 1–2.

7. See Dennis Deletant, *Communist Terror in Romania: Gheorghui-Dej and the Police State, 1948–1965* (London: Hurst & Co., 1999); Dennis Deletant, *Romania under Communist Rule* (Bucharest: Fundația academia civică, 1998).

8. See Deletant, *Communist Terror in Romania*; Deletant, *Romania under Communist Rule*.

9. Vladimir Tismaneanu, *Stalinism for All Seasons: A Political History of Romanian Communism* (Berkeley: University of California Press, 2003).

10. The most detailed treatment of the revolution itself is Peter Siani-Davies, *The Romanian Revolution of December 1989* (Ithaca, NY: Cornell University Press, 2005).

11. See Siani-Davies, *The Romanian Revolution*.

12. Quoted in Georgeta Pourchot, "Mass Media and Democracy in Romania: Lessons from the Past, Prospects for the Future," in *Romania in Transition*, ed. Lavinia Stan (Aldershot, UK: Dartmouth Publishing Co., 1997), 70.

13. Comment by Deputy Foreign Minister Corneliu Bogdan, on Sunday, December 31, 1989, to reporters as cited in "Romanians Move to Dissolve Party," *Chicago Tribune*, January 1, 1990, N1.

14. "Communist Party Is Outlawed, Romania's Chief Says," *Montreal Gazette*, January 13, 1990, A10.

15. Part of the communiqué read by party leader Corneliu Coposu on January 24, 1990, as cited in "1,000 Protestors Demand 'Communists in Disguise' Give Up Power in Romania," *Montreal Gazette*, January 25, 1990, A9.

16. See V. G. Baleanu, "The Enemy Within: The Romanian Intelligence Service in Transition," Federation of American Scientists, January 1995, http://www.fas.org/irp/world/romania/g43.html.

17. For a treatment of these events, known as the *Mineriadă*, see Vladimir Tismaneanu, "Homage to Golania," *New Republic*, July 30, 1990; Mihnea Berindei et al., *Roumanie, le livre blanc: La réalité d'un pouvoir néo-communiste* (Paris: Éditions la découverte, 1990); John Gledhill, "Three Days in Bucharest: Romania's Transitional Violence, 20 Years On," *Europe-Asia Studies* 63, no. 9: 1639–69.

18. Dennis Deletant, "The Security Services since 1989: Turning Over a New Leaf," in *Romania since 1989: Politics, Economics, and Society*, ed. Henry F. Carey (Lanham, MD: Lexington Books, 2004), 507.

19. The accusation of hooliganism and fascism remains a refrain of the government when faced with protests, and during the recent antigovernment protests, current prime minister Victor Ponta accused the protesters of being legionaries. See "Ponta cere intervenție 'fără complexe' la proteste violente și face comparații cu legionarii," Realitatea.net, October 18, 2013, http://www.realitatea.net/ponta-cere-interventie-fara-complexe-la-proteste-violente-si-face-comparatii-cu-legionarii_1295924.html.

20. On the first elections and the early postrevolutionary years, see Tismaneanu, *Stalinism for All Seasons*; Vladimir Tismaneanu, "The Quasi-Revolution and Its Discontents: Emerging Political Pluralism in Post-Ceaușescu Romania," *East European Politics and Societies* 7, no. 2 (spring 1993): 309–48.

21. Sorina Soare, "La construction du système partisan roumain entre sorties et entrées imprévues," *Studia politică* 4, no. 1 (2004): 92.

22. Vladimir Tismaneanu (in conversation with Mircea Mihaieș), *Balul mascat* (Iași, Romania: Polirom, 1996), 31, 140.

23. For an excellent overview of Romania's postcommunist period, see Tom Gallagher, *Theft of a Nation: Romania since Communism* (London: Hurst, 2005).

24. For an outline of the convention's program, see "Contractul cu România: Programul celor 200 de zile," in *"Nu putem reuşi decât impreună": O istorie analitică a Convenţiei Democratice, 1989–2000*, ed. Dan Pavel and Iulia Huiu (Iaşi, Romania: Polirom, 2003), 556–57.

25. The party now known as the PSD began as Frontul salvării naţionale (FSN); after the split with Petre Roman in 1992, it became Frontul democrat al salvării naţionale (FDSN). In 1993 it merged with some smaller parties and changed its name to Partidul democraţiei sociale in România (PDSR), and following another merger in 2001, it became Partidul social democrat (PSD). Throughout these changes, the party elite has remained constant and thus has an unbroken linage back to the FSN and the RCP.

26. Following the split of the NSF in 1992, when Iliescu ousted Petre Roman, disaffected members of the NSF led by Roman founded the Democratic Party as a rival movement.

27. It should be noted that a core electorate supports populist parties, all of which hit on common themes of anticorruption combined with authoritarian rhetoric; these are often personalized parties led by charismatic leaders. Between 2004 and 2012, the New Generation Party (PNG), led by Steaua Bucharest owner and former Securitate informer Gigi Becali, gained considerable media attention, if not many votes. More recently, in 2012, the Popular Party Dan Diaconescu (PPDD) gained almost 15 percent of the vote. Diaconescu, who owns the OTV and DDTV television stations, has been accused of racism, anti-Semitism, and corruption. In all three cases, the profile granted these politicians by the Romanian media has far exceeded their electoral power or appeal, reflecting the media's desire for scandal and sensationalism, which all three provide through their statements and actions.

28. The initials "DA," spelling "yes" in Romanian, echoed the "Tak" ("yes" in Ukrainian) banners seen during the Orange Revolution.

29. Traian Băsescu, "Un regim ilegitim şi criminal," *Revista 22*, December 19–25, 2006,.

30. PD was now named the Liberal Democratic Party (PDL). Following PNL's decision to leave the coalition, a faction split from PNL and joined PD. The party renamed itself to reflect this merger.

31. See "lista secţiilor de votare," Biroul electoral central, http://www.becparlamentare2012.ro/index.html.

32. See Daniel Brett, "Romania's Election Law: Everything You Always Wanted to Know . . . " Dr. Sean's Diary, March 16, 2008, http://drseansdiary.wordpress.com/2008/03/16/romanias-election-law-everything-you-always-wanted-to-know.

33. Wolfgang C. Müller and Kaare Strøm, "Political Parties and Hard Choices," in *Policy, Office, Votes: How Political Parties in Western Europe Make Hard Decisions*, ed. Wolfgang C. Müller and Kaare Strøm (Cambridge: Cambridge University Press, 1999), 1–22.

34. For information about election results, see "Romania: Parliamentary Elections: Electoral System," Norwegian Social Science Data Services, European Election Database, http://www.nsd.uib.no/european_election_database/country/romania/parliamentary_elections.html, and "Lista," Biroul Electoral Central, http://www.becparlamentare2008.ro/index.html.

35. Michael Shafir, "Memories, Memorials and Membership: Romanian Utilitarian Anti-Semitism and Marshal Antonescu," in *Romania since 1989: Politics, Economics, and Society*, ed. Henry F. Carey (Lanham, MD: Lexington Books, 2004), 71.

36. See Andreea Carstocea, "Ethno-business: The Unexpected Consequence of National Minority Policies in Romania," in *Informal Relations from Democratic Representation to Corruption*, ed. Zdenka Mansfeldova and Heiko Pleines. Case Studies from Central and Eastern Europe Changing Europe Series 8 (Stuttgart: Ibidem Publishers, 2011), 163–83.

37. See Amy Samuelson, *Youth and Environmentalism in Post-Socialist Romania and Moldova*, in *New Europe College Yearbook, 2011–2012* (Bucharest: Humanitas and New Europe College, 2014).

38. For a critique of corporate funding for environmentalism, see Thaddeus Guldbrandsen and Dorothy Holland, "Encounters with the Super-Citizen: Neoliberalism, Environmental Activism, and the American Heritage Rivers Initiative," *Anthropological Quarterly* 74, no. 3 (2001): 124–134.

39. Filip Alexandrescu, "Gold and Displacement in Eastern Europe: Risks and Uncertainty at Rosia Montana," *Revista romana de sociologie* 1–2 (2011): 78–107.

40. For more on the diversity of Romanian protesters and potential implications for a coherent movement, see Florin Poenaru, "Romanian Protests: From the Love of Democracy to the Hatred of Politics," Reviews and Critical Commentary, October 2, 2013, http://councilforeuropean studies.org/critcom/romanian-protests-from-the-love-of-democracy-to-the-hatred-of-politics.

41. Data taken from the Economist Intelligence Unit (EIU), *Country Profile: Romania, 1996– 97* (London: EIU, 1996), 14; EIU, *Country Profile: Hungary, 1996–97* (London: EIU, 1997), 11.

42. Southeast European Legal Development Initiative (SELDI), "Corruption Indexes: Regional Corruption Monitoring in Albania, Bosnia and Herzegovina, Bulgaria, Croatia, Macedonia, Romania, and Yugoslavia," *Bulgaria Online*, April 2002," http://www.online.bg/vr/SELDI01_e.htm.

43. World Bank, *Diagnostic Surveys of Corruption in Romania* (Washington, DC: World Bank, 2000), vi.

44. Vlad Fonta, "Valea Jiului: Un caz atipic în economia românească," *Sfera politicii* 67 (1998), http://www.dntb.ro/sfera/67/mineriade-4.html.

45. EIU, *Romania: Country Profile 2009* (London: EIU, 2009), 17, 20.

46. World Bank Country Memorandum, *Romania: Restructuring for EU Integration—the Policy Agenda* (Washington, DC: World Bank, June 2004), 6.

47. EIU, *Romania: Country Profile 2009*, 17.

48. EIU, *Romania: Country Report December 2009* (London: EIU), 6.

49. EIU, *Romania: Country Profile 2009,* 21.

50. "Traian Basescu catre Raed Arafat: Sa nu cream o psihoza ca acest guvern ticalos vrea sa distruga sistemul de ambulanta. Daca asta e mesajul, e mincinos si incorrect," HotNews.ro, January 9, 2012, http://www.hotnews.ro/stiri-esential-11149580-traian-basescu-catre-raed-arafat -nu-cream-psihoza-acest-guvern-ticalos-vrea-distruga-sistemul-ambulanta-daca-asta-mesajul-minci nos-incorect.htm.

51. Equivalization is a technique in economics in which members of a household receive different weightings. Total household income is then divided by the sum of the weightings to yield a representative income. The Organisation for Economic Co-operation and Development (OECD) works out the value by taking household income and dividing it by the square root of the household size. See "What Are Equivalence Scales?" OECD, http://www.oecd.org/els/soc/OECD-Note -EquivalenceScales.pdf.

52. Income quintile share ratio by sex and selected age group. See "S80/S20 Income Quintile Share Ratio by Sex and Selected Age Group (Source: SILC)," European Commission Eurostat, July 28, 2014, http://appsso.eurostat.ec.europa.eu/nui/show.do?wai=true&dataset=ilc_di11.

53. See information for Romania at "Corruption Perceptions Index 2012," Transparency International, http://www.transparency.org/cpi2012/results.

54. Lustration is used in the broadest sense of transitional justice as defined by Susanne Karstedt and consists of two procedures: "Criminal proceedings against members of the elite and authorities over the lower ranks of the state bureaucracy" and "mass screening procedures, which are conducted against collaborators, party members or employees (police, security agencies) mainly from the middle and lower ranks of the hierarchy." Karstedt, "Coming to Terms with the Past in Germany after 1945 and 1989: Public Judgements on Procedures and Justice," *Law and Policy* 20, no. 1 (1998): 16.

55. Lavinia Stan, "Lustration in Romania: The Revolution's Stillborn?" International Political Science Association, 2006, http://paperroom.ipsa.org/papers/paper_5041.pdf; for more detail, see

Lavinia Stan, "Romania," in *Transitional Justice in Eastern Europe and the Former Soviet Union: Reckoning with the Communist Past*, ed. Lavinia Stan (London: Routledge, 2008), 128–51.

56. Stan, "Lustration in Romania," 2–6.

57. Stan, "Romania," 134–135.

58. "Legea lustratiei este neconstitutionala, a decis CCR," Ziare.com, March 28, 2012, http://www.ziare.com/ccr/decizii/legea-lustratiei-este-neconstitutionala-a-decis-ccr-1158666.

59. "Basescu, despre legea lustratiei: Prea tarziu!" Ziare.com, October 2, 2013, http://www.ziare.com/basescu/presedinte/basescu-despre-legea-lustratiei-prea-tarziu-1260190.

60. Dan Bilefsky, "Former Romanian Premier Ordered Released from Prison," *New York Times*, March 18, 2013, http://www.nytimes.com/2013/03/19/world/europe/former-romanian-premier-adrian-nastase-to-be-released-from-prison.html.

61. Virgil Burlă and Antoaneta Etves, "Fuga de justiție. Dan Voiculescu versus DNA. Al 6-lea termen de la întoarcerea la Tribunal. Băsescu, chemat ca martor de Voiculescu în dosarul ICA,, April 30, 2013, http://www.evz.ro/detalii/stiri/fuga-de-justitie-dan-voiculescu-versus-dna-al-6-lea-termen-de-la-intoarcerea-la-tribunal-1035168.html.

62. Luiza Ilie and Sam Cage, "Romanian President Survives Impeachment Referendum," *Chicago Tribune*, July 29, 2012, http://articles.chicagotribune.com/2012-07-29/news/sns-rt-us-romania-politicsbre86s0i4-20120729_1_romanian-president-social-liberal-union-voter-turnout.

63. See the Rendition Project (http://www.therenditionproject.org.uk).

64. "Transdniestrian Authorities Ask Moscow for Recognition of Independence," NineO'clock.ro, April 16, 2014, http://www.nineoclock.ro/transdniestrian-authorities-ask-moscow-for-recognition-of-independence.

65. "Putin: 'The People of Transnistria Should Be Allowed to Decide Their Fate Themselves,'" APA.az, April 17, 2014, http://en.apa.az/xeber_putin_____the_people_of_transnistria_shoul_210000.html.

66. Radio Free Europe/Radio Liberty (RFE/RL), "Moldova Awaits Russian Reaction to Transdniester's Appeal," RFE/RL, April 18, 2014, http://www.rferl.org/content/moldova-awaits-russian-reaction/25354262.html.

67. RFE/RL, "Moldova's Breakaway Transdniester Urges Moscow to Recognize Independence," RFE/RL, April 16, 2014, http://www.rferl.org/content/moldovas-breakaway-transdniester-urge-moscow-to-recognize-independence/25351540.html.

Map 16.0. Albania

CHAPTER 16

Albania

THE CHALLENGES OF TRANSITION

Elez Biberaj

Since the demise of its communist regime in the early 1990s, Albania has undergone a profound political, economic, and social transformation. Once one of the most reclusive and oppressive communist societies, Albania has achieved an impressive level of democratic maturity in recent years, with a well-established political system and relatively stable democratic institutions, and has emerged as a key factor in promoting regional stability and democratic values in southeastern Europe. In April 2009, Albania joined the North Atlantic Treaty Organization (NATO), and in June 2014 it was granted EU candidate status.

Domestically, after a series of contested elections and postelection disputes that resulted in political gridlock and set the tiny southeast European country apart from its neighbors, Albania conducted free and fair parliamentary elections in June 2013, whose results were certified by domestic and international observers and accepted by the major players.[1] The opposition Socialist Party–led coalition won a landslide victory, ending eight years of rule by the center-right Democratic Party led by Sali Berisha. The elections were followed by a smooth transition of power and a new coalition government composed of the Socialist Party and the Socialist Movement for Integration (SMI). Controlling 84 out of the 140 seats in parliament, Prime Minister Edi Rama's government has the political capital to enact meaningful economic and political reforms.

But despite Albania's enormous progress, much about the quality of its democracy is tentative and fragile.[2] Albania finds itself at a critical crossroads and, more than any other country in southeastern Europe, suffers from weak governance, ineffective institutions, and a failure to fully embrace the rule of law. Albanian politics remain highly divisive and confrontational, adversely affecting Albanians' aspirations for national prosperity, democratic consolidation, and European integration. Freedom House rates Albania as partly free, while Transparency International ranks it as one of the most corrupt countries in Europe.

Albania also faces daunting social and economic challenges. It is one of the smallest and poorest countries in Europe with an estimated gross domestic product (GDP) per capita of $6,500. More than a quarter of the population lives below the national poverty line. Agriculture accounts for 23 percent of GDP and industry 19 percent. Albania is rich in mineral resources—chromium, copper, and nickel—but after 1990 mineral production collapsed because of civil unrest, lack of investment, outdated technology, and a sharp fall in prices on international markets. Albania also has one of the highest birthrates in Europe. Yet the country's population has been declining because of the high rate of emigration. In 2011, Albania's population was estimated at 2.8 million, the same as it was in 1989.[3] Since the early 1990s, about 1 million Albanians have fled their country in search of a better life abroad. Most of them settled in Greece, Italy, and the United States. Arguably, Albania has experienced a higher brain drain than any other country in southeastern Europe.

Political Background

Albania's overriding objective historically has been to preserve its independence and territorial integrity from its more powerful neighbors. Although one of the most ethnically homogeneous countries in the region, it has long lacked national cohesion. Its political development has been obstructed by regional, tribal, and religious differences. At several points in its troubled history and as recently as 1997, it came close to being classified as a "failed state." Albania had a short-lived experiment with a multiparty system in the 1920s. But virtually all of its history has been one of repressive governments that were not responsive to the needs of the population and displayed no sense of accountability or transparency.

Albanians, the descendants of the Illyrians, are considered the oldest inhabitants of the Balkans. Turks overran the country in 1478, following the death of Gjergj Kastriot Skenderbeu, the leader of a twenty-five-year resistance to the Ottomans. For the next five centuries, the country remained under Ottoman occupation. And in the seventeenth century, the majority of Albania's population converted to Islam.

Albania gained its independence in 1912 during the Balkan wars. When the international community recognized its independence in 1913, some 40 percent of the Albanian population and half of its territory, including Kosovo and Çameria, remained outside its borders. From then on, Albania has been unique because more Albanians lived outside its borders than inside, and it is bordered almost on all sides by Albanian-speaking populations. This mismatch between state and national/ethnic borders severely hindered the country's political and economic development and complicated its ties with its neighbors. After the country gained its independence in 1912, Albanian politics were dominated by forces and parties whose main objectives were focused on its sovereignty and independence and on regaining Kosovo. The internal organization of the Albanian polity was far less clear. Western political ideas were slow to penetrate, as few Albanians had been educated in the West. The country also lacked a well-developed middle class imbued with democratic ideals, and most of the emerging political, cultural, and military elites had been educated in Turkey rather than in the more democratic societies of Western Europe. The semifeudal Albanian society was characterized by widespread authoritarian tendencies.

In the early 1920s, Albania witnessed the emergence of several parties, the most important of which were the People's Party, led by Fan S. Noli, a Harvard-educated Orthodox clergyman, and the Progressive Party, led by Ahmet Zogu, a chieftain from central Albania. This experiment with a multiparty system was short-lived. The country's main forces could not agree on much. After a period of political instability, Ahmet Zogu took power by force in December 1924. After restoring order and eliminating his political enemies, Zogu in 1928 declared himself king. His exact title was "King of the Albanians," making it clear that Albania had not given up on liberating Kosovo. The king instituted significant social, political, and economic changes and laid the foundations of a modern state. His rule was interrupted in April 1939 when Italy invaded Albania. For the next six years, Albania remained under Italian and/or German rule.[4]

Communist Experience and Transition to Democracy

Albania's communist history was unique: the state was ruled by one of the most repressive, Stalinist leaders for a longer period than any other Central or East European country.[5] The main pillars of Enver Hoxha's regime were the military and the secret police, the Sigurimi. Through a continuous reign of terror and purges, the communist regime succeeded in eliminating all traces of open opposition to its rule. Purges eventually extended to the top echelons of the Communist Party, leading to the demise of even its most prominent leaders, including in 1981 Mehmet Shehu, who had been prime minister for three decades. Hoxha also skillfully exploited disagreements within the communist bloc to consolidate his power and ensure the survival of his regime. He first allied Albania with Yugoslavia. He then took advantage of Josip Broz Tito's break with Joseph Stalin to align himself with Moscow. When Soviet leader Nikita Khrushchev's de-Stalinization policy in the middle to late 1950s threatened his tenure in office, he switched alliances and sided with Mao Zedong's China, at the time the most dogmatic communist regime. And finally, when China moved toward a rapprochement with the United States, Tirana broke with Beijing and embarked on a policy of self-reliance. This move had very serious repercussions for the country's political and economic development. Private property was abolished, and the country was prohibited by law from seeking foreign assistance, including loans and credits.

As most other communist countries experimented with economic and political reforms, Albania became progressively more repressive and isolated. In the late 1960s, Hoxha launched his own version of the Chinese Cultural Revolution to extend the Communist Party's control over all aspects of life and to eliminate any center of potential power that could threaten its primacy. All religious institutions were closed down, and Albania became the world's first official atheist state. Many mosques and churches, some dating back centuries, were destroyed. Imams and priests were imprisoned or executed. The intelligentsia, long distrusted by Hoxha, came under severe attack. Prominent intellectuals were chastised for ideological deformations. Intellectuals also were ordered to live in the countryside for extended periods. The party launched a well-coordinated campaign for the emancipation of women. By the mid-1980s, women had made significant strides in securing equal social and political rights and held important posts in the party and the government. Whereas the trend in most other socialist countries was toward increased liberalization and a decrease in the party's tight grip on society, in Albania the opposite occurred. By the time Ramiz Alia became party leader following Hoxha's death in April 1985, Albania faced a serious economic crisis and a dispirited and apathetic population.

Alia had been among the youngest members of the postwar communist elite. He skillfully survived Hoxha's violent purges. From the very beginning of his reign in 1985, he came under pressure from both the conservative and the more liberal elements of the party. In an attempt to institute some changes in the country's highly centralized economic system, he loosened the party's grip on the cultural sector and took measures to end Albania's international isolation. At the same time, he was determined to preserve the party's leading role. This process of controlled reforms could not keep up with internal demands for changes, fueled by the end of the 1980s by a seriously deteriorating economic situation and the revolutions in other Central and East European countries.

Albania was the last communist domino to fall. In December 1990, a year after the downfall of Romania's regime, Alia's government was forced to sanction the creation of noncommunist political parties. The Communist Party won the first multiparty elections in March 1991. Alia was elected to a five-year term as president, and a new government was formed, led by Prime Minister Fatos Nano, a thirty-nine-year old economist. Nano's government, however, was short-lived. He was forced to resign in June 1991, paving the way for the creation of a broad coalition government dominated by noncommunists. Early elections were held in March 1992, and the opposition Democratic Party won an overwhelming victory, capturing 92 seats in the 140-seat parliament. Alia then resigned as president and was succeeded by the Democratic Party's leader, Sali Berisha.

Photo 16.1. Albanians topple a statue of Enver Hoxha as their belated revolution gathered momentum in 1991. (Reuters/Corbis)

Political Institutions

Immediately following the demise of the communist regime in 1990 and 1991, the newly created Democratic Party and other opposition forces pushed for a radical transformation of the country's political institutions, demanding a modern, democratic constitution. The communists, who held the necessary two-thirds majority in parliament, tried to preserve as much as possible of the old order. However, under strong pressure from the opposition and the international community, they were forced to compromise. The parliament rejected a draft-constitution submitted by Alia that retained many of the features of the 1976 constitution and granted substantial powers to the president. Instead, it approved the Law on the Main Constitutional Provisions. The constitutional law endorsed political pluralism and a multiparty system and guaranteed human rights. The document defined Albania as a parliamentary republic and limited the powers of the country's president.

Following the Democratic Party's landslide victory in the March 1992 elections, the Law on the Main Constitutional Provisions was completely revamped, and a new constitutional order was created with checks and balances, safeguards for fundamental rights and freedoms, and judicial review. Because the new president needed expanded powers to deal with the serious problems facing Albania, the parliament amended the April 1991 law, granting extensive powers to the presidency. Although Albania was defined as a parliamentary republic, the constitutional provisions granted the president broad authority, including the capacity to appoint the prime minister and, from his nominations, other members of the cabinet. The document also granted the president the power, after consultations with the prime minister and speaker of the parliament, to dissolve the legislature if it was unable to exercise its own functions. While the prime minister was granted a leading role in the government, the president was empowered, in special instances, to chair meetings of the Council of Ministers and to set the agenda. The parliament was vested with substantial powers, including electing the president, determining the basic orientation of the country's domestic and foreign policy, and approving the government's programs.

The 1991 Law on the Main Constitutional Provisions had not contained separate chapters on the judiciary and the protection of fundamental human rights. So, in April 1992, the parliament adopted a chapter on the organization of the judiciary and the Constitutional Court, which provided for judicial independence and created a bipartite system, composed of the regular court system headed by a Court of Cassation and a separate Constitutional Court. A year later, the parliament adopted the Charter on Fundamental Human Rights and Freedoms, which contained guarantees of the freedoms of speech, religion, conscience, press, assembly, and association, as well as assurances on the due process of law.

The unicameral People's Assembly consists of 140 deputies who serve a four-year term. The parliament is the highest institution. It elects the president, the prime minister, and members of cabinet. The most recent constitution was adopted by a national referendum in 1998 and was amended in 2008. The president is the head of state and serves a five-year term. Initially, the president was to be elected by a three-fifths vote. Amendments approved in 2008 stipulate that the president is selected by a simple majority of votes if, in the first three rounds of voting, a candidate cannot secure a three-fifths majority. Although the presidency is largely ceremonial, the constitution does make the president the commander in chief of the armed forces and chairman of the National Security Commission.

Albania's justice system is similar to that of other European countries and consists of a Constitutional Court, a Supreme Court, and appeals and district courts. The president appoints, with the consent of the parliament, the nine members of the Constitutional Court, which interprets the constitution, determines the constitutionality of laws, and resolves disputes between different branches of government and between national and local authorities. The Supreme Court, the country's highest court of appeal, is composed of eleven members appointed by the president with the consent of parliament. The judicial system is overseen by a fifteen-member High Council of Justice chaired by the president.

Although the constitutional provisions provided for a parliamentary republic, during Berisha's tenure as president (1992–1997), Albania developed a hybrid presidential-parliamentary system. Not unlike his counterparts in other transitional countries, such as Russia's Boris Yeltsin and Poland's Lech Wałęsa, the Albanian president amassed enormous powers, exercised broad decision-making powers, and eclipsed the prime minister and the cabinet.

The 1991 constitutional law was intended to be in force for a limited period until a new constitution was promulgated. However, strong disagreements between the ruling Democratic Party and the opposition Socialist Party, the successor to the Communist Party, on the institutional alternatives and the specific powers of each branch of government prevented the adoption of a new constitution. The democrats argued that Albania needed strong executive leadership. The socialists, on the other hand, advocated reducing the president's powers, essentially confining the head of state to a merely ceremonial role. In an attempt to break the constitutional deadlock, Berisha bypassed the parliament and submitted a draft constitution to a national referendum in November 1994. His efforts failed, as Albanian voters rejected the draft. He then resigned as president after the socialists won the June 1997 elections held in the wake of popular unrest sparked by the collapse of pyramid schemes. In 1998, the socialist-controlled parliament adopted a new constitution, which apportioned the largest share of political power to the prime minister and the cabinet.[6]

Berisha's successor, Rexhep Meidani, was a moderate figure who served during very challenging times as Albania was engulfed in widespread civil unrest, the Democratic Party's boycott of institutions, and the 1999 war in Kosovo. Because Meidani was so closely associated with the Socialist Party and faced with the hostility and unwillingness of Berisha to work with him, he was never able to play the role of a unifying figure. By the end of his tenure, he did not have sufficient support within his own Socialist Party to run for a second term. After his plans to become president failed, Socialist Party chairman Fatos Nano, in a rare example of cooperation between the ruling party and the opposition, agreed to a compromise candidate proposed by Berisha, Alfred Moisiu, who was elected president on June 24, 2002. A career military man and the son of famous World War II commander Spiro Moisiu, he had held senior positions in the communist regime but was supported by the Democratic Party from the very beginning. In the early 1990s, he served as deputy defense minister and subsequently headed the North Atlantic Association that promoted Albania's membership in NATO.

Critics questioned Moisiu's credentials, calling him a political novice unprepared for Albanian political combat. He lacked an independent political base and soon came under strong pressure from both Nano and Berisha. Following the Democratic Party's return to power in 2005, Moisiu clashed repeatedly with Prime Minister Berisha. He vetoed several laws approved by the parliament and, in October 2006, rejected the legislature's recommendation to dismiss Prosecutor General Theodhori Sollaku, whom the democrats accused of having failed to prosecute high-profile corruption cases and of having links with criminal groups. This step led to a dysfunctional relationship with Berisha, the speaker of the parliament Josefina Topalli, and other Democratic Party officials.[7]

As the end of Moisiu's tenure approached in July 2007, political life in Albania was dominated by a single issue: the election of his successor. The ruling Democratic Party and the opposition Socialist Party engaged in a prolonged and tense political struggle over the next presidential election. It had been widely believed that Berisha and Nano had reached an understanding in 2002 that, since the democrats had proposed Moisiu for president, the socialists would select his successor. Following his resignation as chairman of the Socialist Party when Berisha won in the 2005 election, Nano openly campaigned for president. Berisha sought to work with the opposition to find a consensus candidate but, in return, demanded that the socialists support the dismissal of Prosecutor General Sollaku. Edi Rama, Nano's successor as Socialist Party chairman, was interested neither in supporting Nano's candidacy for president nor in working with Berisha on finding a consensus candidate. Emboldened by his party's good showing in the local elections in February 2007, Rama wanted to block the election of the president—the democrats lacked the necessary eighty-four votes to elect their own candidate—and force the country to hold early parliamentary elections.

Having failed in his efforts to find a compromise with the socialists, Berisha named Bamir Topi as the Democratic Party's candidate for president. Topi, the number two man in the Democratic Party and leader of the party's parliamentary group, was a surprise choice because he was seen as too important for a ceremonial post. After three rounds of voting, when it appeared that parliament would not be able to elect the president and there would have to be new elections, Nano, disappointed that Rama did not support his bid to become president, convinced six of his supporters in parliament to vote for Topi. The fifty-year-old Topi had been elected to parliament in 1996 and served as minister of agriculture in 1996 and 1997. He developed a good reputation as a moderate and was able to represent the Democratic Party successfully in difficult negotiations with the socialists. Topi's election averted the potential crisis of early elections and was a major boost for the governing coalition.

In early 2008, parliament, on the basis of a consensus reached by the democrats and socialists, approved a package of reforms including important constitutional changes in the way the president was elected, the establishment of a system of proportional representation based on regions for electing members of parliament, and limiting the prosecutor general to a fixed five-year term of office instead of an unlimited one.[8] Berisha described the changes as "a historic victory for Albanian democracy," while Rama maintained that the electoral reform "closes a long chapter of grave distortions of the electors' will."[9]

While the two big parties hailed the constitutional changes, small parties were fiercely critical, arguing that the new rules would make it very difficult for them to win national

Photo 16.2.   President Bamir Topi meets with Edi Rama, chairman of the opposition Socialist Party, and Prime Minister Sali Berisha in Tirana. (Arben Celi/Reuters/Corbis)

representation. President Topi, who evidently had not been consulted by his own party, was also strongly critical of the new measures. He showed his displeasure by vetoing several laws passed by parliament. As a result, his relations with the democrats were severely strained. Given his limited constitutional powers and alienation of both the democrats and the socialists, Topi was not able to lead efforts to develop a broader political and social consensus by deepening legal and judicial reforms.

In June 2012, Bujar Nishani, a close Berisha ally, was elected president. The international community had exerted considerable pressure on both sides to elect a consensus candidate. However, Rama refused to propose a candidate or endorse the nomination of Xhezair Zaganjori, a respected member of the Constitutional Court. Nishani was elected with a simple majority in the fourth round of voting. A founding member of the Democratic Party, Nishani had held senior positions in Berisha's cabinet, first as minister of justice and then as minister of internal affairs. The socialists criticized Nishani's election, claiming that he was too closely associated with the democrats to play the role of a nonpartisan head of state. The president pledged to live up to his constitutional role as a unifying force above party politics and to be a voice of moral authority. Following the socialists' landslide victory in June 2013, Nishani has come under increased criticism, with senior government officials threatening to replace him.

Elections and Political Parties

Since the end of communism, Albania has held eight multiparty parliamentary elections: in March 1991, March 1992, May 1996, June 1997, May 2001, July 2005, June 2009, and June 2013. With the exception of the 1992 and 2013 elections, all have been problematic and contested by the losing party. While it has made significant progress and every election has represented a qualitative step forward, Albania's difficulty in holding elections in full accordance with international standards has adversely impact its democratic development and integration into the EU.

The electoral system was changed on numerous occasions. Before 2008, the electoral code combined single-member electoral districts with proportional representation. Under that system, one hundred members of parliament were elected by direct popular vote in districts, and the remaining forty seats were allocated based on the political parties' shares of national votes. The threshold was 2.5 percent. In 2008, the Democratic Party and the Socialist Party agreed to revise the electoral code, addressing several recommendations offered by the Office for Democratic Institutions and Human Rights of the Organization for Security and Co-operation in Europe (OSCE) and the Council of Europe's European Commission for Democracy through Law (Venice Commission) to alleviate abuses and shortcomings under the previous electoral law. The old system tended to favor the smaller parties. The new electoral law, approved by parliament in early 2009, provides for a regional proportional system with 140 members of parliament elected in twelve regional constituencies corresponding to the country's administrative regions. The law sets a 3 percent threshold for political parties and a 5 percent threshold for coalitions. The law favors big parties and grants special rights to the chairpersons of political parties, allowing them to run on their party's lists in each of the twelve electoral districts simultaneously.[10] The democrats and the socialists maintained that the new electoral system would ensure a more stable government by producing clear majorities and reducing the inflated presence of small political parties. However, smaller parties across the political spectrum fiercely objected to the new electoral code, arguing that the regional proportional system would favor the two largest parties.

Although there are more than thirty political parties across the political spectrum and most of them field candidates in national and local elections, Albanian politics has been dominated by the country's two major political forces—the center-right Democratic Party and the Socialist Party, the successor to the Albanian Communist Party.[11] These two have tended to view elections in terms of a zero-sum game, often disregarding democratic norms, manipulating electoral procedures, intimidating the judiciary and the media, and contesting unfavorable results. The two big parties have alternated power: the democrats governed from 1992 to 1997 and from 2005 to 2013 and the socialists from 1997 to 2005 and since 2013. They have largely governed in a partisan and nontransparent fashion. Despite occasional calls to work constructively with each other, the democrats and the socialists have generally failed to find much common ground. When in opposition, each party has done its best to make life as difficult as possible for the government.

The Albanian electorate continues to be polarized around strong Democratic Party and Socialist Party positions. The two dominant parties claim to reflect competing strains of public opinion and hold contrasting views of Albania's future. However, a close analysis of their platforms reveals that they have become largely indistinguishable. Indeed, in recent years, the ideological gap between them has narrowed. There are no deep philosophical differences, and their approach to most issues is pragmatic and nonideological.

The Democratic Party, led by Sali Berisha, came to power in 1992. From 1992 to 1996, Berisha's government was viewed as one of the most progressive in the region. During this period, Berisha had a virtual free ride from an admiring West. He moved swiftly to fill the political vacuum created during the turmoil following the sanctioning of political pluralism. The immediate priority of the new government was to arrest the nation's economic decline, restore law and order, begin the difficult task of institution building, and reintegrate the country into the international community after decades of isolation. Albania witnessed rapid and significant institutional and legislative transformations. Berisha was able to secure substantial foreign assistance—Albania became the largest recipient of Western aid on a per capita basis in Central and Eastern Europe. Outside aid helped Albania institute radical economic reforms and an ambitious mass-privatization program. By 1996, Albania had emerged from the ruins of a totally state-owned economy as a market economy, with the private sector accounting for more than 65 percent of GDP and about 70 percent of the national wealth.

The implementation of painful austerity measures also caused considerable social dislocation. The opposition sought to capitalize on the resulting discontent caused by austerity measures by condemning the reforms for bringing unacceptable suffering on the public, increasing economic inequality, concentrating wealth in a few hands, and creating a vast mass of poor people. By the mid-1990s, Berisha's almost universal popularity had eroded as he turned increasingly autocratic. He showed no qualms about jailing Socialist Party leader Fatos Nano on what many saw as dubious corruption charges, imposed restrictions on basic political actions, introduced a restrictive media law, and allowed corruption and pyramid schemes to flourish. The wind shifted markedly against him after the flawed elections in 1996. These elections were followed by a falling out between Berisha and the international community, including the United States, his key foreign backer. Berisha resorted to increasingly repressive measures against his opponents (particularly the socialists), restricting freedom of the press and becoming less and less tolerant of dissent within his own Democratic Party.

The political crisis was compounded by rising economic problems caused by the mushrooming of pyramid schemes. The collapse of those firms in 1997 sparked an armed revolt. State institutions folded, and the police and armed forces disintegrated. In March 1997, the government reached an accord with the opposition, agreeing to form a national unity government and hold early elections. Under a state of emergency, Albania held early elections in June 1997. The democrats suffered a humiliating defeat, and the socialists were swept back into power. Berisha resigned as president and was succeeded by the Socialist Party's general secretary, Rexhep Meidani. Nano, who had escaped from prison during the March unrest and was subsequently pardoned by Berisha, became prime minister. He formed a coalition government with several smaller parties, including the Social Democratic Party, the Democratic Alliance, and the Union for Human Rights Party.

During the next eight years (1997–2005), the Socialist Party held a monopoly on political power nationally and locally. Within a relatively short period, the socialist-led government rebuilt the country's police and armed forces and restored law and order in most parts of the country. Albania adopted a new constitution through a national referendum, enacted important legal reforms, and experienced significant economic growth. However, socialist rule was characterized by political instability, infighting within the Socialist Party, a lack of cooperation between the government and the opposition, and a dramatic rise in corruption and organized crime activities. The Socialist Party was also consumed with personal strife between Nano and Ilir Meta, the former head of the party's youth organization and a rising star in the Socialist Party. Nano was forced to resign as prime minister following the assassination of student leader and close Berisha associate Azem Hajdari in September 1998. His successor, Pandeli Majko, was in turn forced to resign under pressure from the Socialist Party chairman after only one year in office, paving the way in November 1999 for Meta to become prime minister.

Nano and Meta reached a temporary truce on the eve of the June 2001 parliamentary elections, the first elections after the tumultuous events of 1997. The Socialist Party won seventy-three seats, while its allies—the Social Democratic Party, the Union for Human Rights Party, the Agrarian Party, and the Democratic Alliance—secured thirteen seats. The democrats and their allies garnered forty-six seats. The elections were seriously flawed: five rounds of voting were required to complete the process. In October, the OSCE election observation mission issued its final report, expressing concern about the government's interference in the election process and noting serious irregularities, police intimidation, Socialist Party manipulation, and dubious decisions by the Central Electoral Commission. The report, however, was unusually restrained in its criticism and largely dismissive of opposition complaints.[12]

Meta was reconfirmed as prime minister. However, he was unable to show any political resolve to undertake pressing domestic reforms or improve relations with the opposition. He faced an immediate and open challenge from Nano, which destabilized the government, paralyzed the state administration, and eventually delegitimized the ruling coalition. Resorting to press leaks, political pressure, and petty harassment, Nano launched a devastating campaign against Meta driven by two main considerations. First, although he was the party leader and had organized and led the electoral campaign, Meta had largely excluded Nano and his closest allies from the spoils of victory. Second, Meta refused to endorse Nano's candidacy for president. Nano focused his campaign on corruption, raising questions about Meta's role in the privatization of large, strategic state assets and portraying his administration as geared toward powerful, entrenched interests. As prime minister, Meta had displayed authoritarian tendencies, amassed too much power, and become very arrogant, alienating significant groups within the party. Unable to resist Nano's onslaught, Meta resigned in January 2002. He was succeeded by Pandeli Majko, his predecessor, who had served as prime minister from 1998 to 1999.

The Democratic Party made great efforts to seek partisan advantages from the string of scandals that befell the socialists. In an attempt to improve his image, Berisha expressed readiness for a compromise with the socialists and willingness to work with the government. The democrats ended their disruptive street tactics, expanded their international contacts, and returned to parliament. Under pressure from the international community and faced with a serious challenge from Meta's faction and the opposition, Nano reached out to Berisha. The two agreed to recommend Alfred Moisiu as a consensus candidate for president. Following Moisiu's election as president, Majko resigned, paving the way for Nano to return to the post of prime minister. Meta was appointed deputy prime minister and foreign minister. But Nano's thaw with both Berisha and Meta was short-lived. Rancorous skirmishes followed partial elections in Elbasan, with the democrats accusing the socialists of rigging the voting. Disagreements over changes in the electoral code and property issues brought parliamentary proceedings to a standstill. Meta, on the other hand, found himself largely marginalized in Nano's government and resigned in 2003. After several years of acrimony, in September 2004 Meta and his closest associates broke away from the Socialist Party and formed the Socialist Movement for Integration. The split, amid rising disenchantment with socialist rule, was a very significant factor in the Socialist Party's defeat in the next parliamentary elections.

Democratic Party Rule (2005–2013)

The Democratic Party remained the most important opposition force because the post-1997 efforts of other parties and forces to supplant it as the only viable alternative to the Socialist Party have failed. The democrats had made great efforts to exploit opportunities created by the splits within the Socialist Party and the rising disenchantment with social-ist rule. In the 2003 local elections, the Democratic Party expanded its base of support, winning in socialist strongholds in the south. Berisha launched a charm offensive aimed at improving his image and relations with the international community. He took measures to open up his party and worked hard to form a broad coalition, similar to the one in 1992. In January 2005, Berisha announced the creation of the Policy Orientation Com-mittee, bringing together some forty prominent experts from civil society. This group played a major role in drafting the party's electoral platform. Berisha welcomed back into the party Gramoz Pashko, Genc Ruli, Arben Imami, and Preç Zogaj, former prominent officials who had been expelled from or left the Democratic Party as a result of policy and/or personality conflicts in the early and mid-1990s. The democrats focused their campaign on the Socialist Party's failings and pledged to improve the economy, gener-ate employment, fight corruption, and speed up Albania's membership in Euro-Atlantic institutions. Faced with the decrease in its popularity, the Socialist Party's message was vague and muddled. Nano presented a rosy picture of socialist achievements that bore little relationship to reality. Meta, for his part, attempted to position himself as the logical alternative to Nano and Berisha.

The Democratic Party won fifty-six seats. Other parties that made it into parliament were the Republican Party, with eleven seats; the New Democratic Party, four seats; the Agrarian and Environmentalist Party, four seats; the Christian Democratic Party, two seats; the Union for Human Rights Party, two seats; and the Liberal Democratic Union, one seat. In addition, one independent candidate won a seat. On the left, the Socialist Party won forty-two seats; the Social Democratic Party, seven seats; the Democratic Alliance, three seats; and the Party of Social Democracy, two seats. Meta's Socialist Movement for Integration secured only five seats. The election results showed that the government's ineptitude in dealing with the economic crisis, corruption, and organized crime had driven the discontented toward Berisha and Meta. The socialists were driven out of power. Nano resigned as chairman of the Socialist Party and was replaced by Edi Rama, the mayor of Tirana.

The election results represented an astonishing comeback not only for Berisha personally—in the wake of Albania's implosion on his watch in 1997, most observers had discounted him—but also for his Democratic Party after it had fallen from grace with Albanian voters. The democrats formed a coalition government with six other parties, and Berisha became prime minister. In addition to giving cabinet posts to their traditional ally (the Republican Party), the democrats broadened the governing coalition, giving cabinet posts to the Union for Human Rights Party and the Agrarian and Environmentalist Party, both of which had been part of the Socialist Party–led coalition between 1997 and 2005. The democrats and their allies held a comfortable majority of eighty-one seats but lacked the three-fifths majority necessary to elect the president.

Berisha's government laid out an aggressive agenda to combat the economic crisis, improve the business environment, fight corruption and organized crime, and speed up Albania's integration into NATO and the European Union. During the next four years, the government made significant progress in its efforts to create a stable political environment with functional democratic institutions. Albania experienced strong economic growth, averaging an annual real GDP growth of 7 percent. Poverty and unemployment were reduced, and pensions and wages in the public sector increased.

Perhaps the government's greatest achievement was Albania's membership in NATO. Berisha termed Albania's attainment of this strategic objective as the most important event since independence. However, membership in the European Union, Tirana's other major foreign policy objective, eluded Albania because of the poisonous relationship between the government and the opposition and the slow progress in implementing reforms aimed at strengthening the judicial system, enforcing property rights, fighting corruption, and respecting media freedom.[13]

The June 2009 election results showed that the Albanian electorate remained deeply and closely divided between the two major political parties. The democrats won 68 out of 140 seats, three more than their socialist opponents; Ilir Meta's SMI won 4 seats; two parties allied with the democrats and one allied with the socialists won 1 seat each. Though the Democratic Party emerged with most parliamentary seats, it fell short of the majority required to form the government. In an abrupt about-face, Berisha entered into a coalition agreement with the Socialist Movement for Integration, denying the socialists the chance to form the new government. Berisha's coalition with Meta came as a surprise. They were archenemies, and on the eve of the elections, Berisha had ruled out the possibility of entering into a coalition with either Meta or Rama.[14] Meta had been one of Berisha's fiercest critics, at one point calling him "the most dangerous enemy of the Albanian state."[15] Although the coalition caused some rumblings within both the Democratic Party and the SMI, the two leaders had no difficulty justifying it to their electorates. Given the narrow margin of his victory, Berisha had limited options, and without Meta's support, he could not form the new government. Meta, for his part, was bitter that Rama had bluntly rejected his repeated offers for a preelection coalition and had made every effort to marginalize the SMI. Had Rama accepted Meta's offer to join forces, they, rather than Berisha, would most likely have won the election. Meta maintained that he accepted Berisha's offer for a coalition in order to avert a dangerous political crisis and to help advance Albania's EU membership aspirations. Meta became deputy prime minister and foreign minister. His party received two other posts: the Ministry of Health and the powerful Ministry of Economy, Trade, and Energy. In addition, Meta's party got to name its own to 20 percent of all senior posts in the administration. Berisha's new coalition government pledged to continue the implementation of market reforms and to pursue an aggressive campaign against corruption and organized crime, as well as other reforms aimed at improving Albania's chances for EU integration.

Following the elections, relations between the government and the opposition were marked by constant tensions. Rama refused to accept the results, although international observers had deemed them sufficiently credible.[16] The socialists boycotted the parliament and resorted to threats, ultimatums, and disruptive actions in pursuit of their demands. They shunned government calls for cooperation and stymied efforts to pass important legislation. Rama heightened his antigovernment rhetoric and organized protests in several cities demanding that the ballot boxes be opened in several districts where the socialists had alleged irregularities. He vowed to oust Berisha through street protests if his party's demands were not met.[17] The democrats maintained an uncompromising attitude and refused to take any meaningful measures to reach out to the opposition.

The dispute over the elections led to a long political impasse, diverted attention from pressing economic and social challenges, stalled progress on key reforms, and tarnished Albania's image and democratic credentials. While there is a wide consensus on the importance and potential benefits of Albania's integration into the European Union, Albanian leaders permitted short-term political considerations to trump the country's EU integration. In December 2012, the European Commission refused, for the third year in a row, to grant Albania candidate status.

Whereas the Democratic Party's first term was marked by significant progress in all areas, its second term (2009–2013) was characterized by sluggish economic growth, prolonged political gridlock, and the inability to implement significant political and economic reforms, strengthen the rule of law, or effectively fight corruption and organized crime. Despite the government's anticorruption strategy, corruption continued to worsen, as reflected in reports by Transparency International. In 2011, Albania was ranked in 95th place, but two years later it dropped to 116th position out of 177 countries and territories.[18] Senior government officials and politicians were reputed to have used their positions to build huge private fortunes, but no senior official was prosecuted. Berisha's inability to significantly reduce corruption dimmed public confidence in his government.

Ilir Meta's trial on corruption charges—based on a video released by his former deputy, Dritan Prifti, which purported to show Meta discussing bribe taking—eroded the coalition's popularity. His case became a source of acute embarrassment and cast an unflattering light not only on Meta and his party but also on Berisha's government. The socialists made Meta the focus of their corruption criticism, and the violence that erupted in January 2011, in which four opposition supporters were killed in clashes with police forces, was sparked by popular anger at Meta. The socialists vehemently criticized Meta's acquittal in early 2012. There was a widespread perception that Meta had escaped prosecution because of the government's undue influence over the courts.

Following Meta's acquittal, Berisha struggled to keep the coalition intact. Jockeying, increased competition among coalition partners, and politicking in the run-up to the June 2013 elections significantly impacted the government's reform and legislative agendas. Meta undermined the coalition by adopting positions on major issues that were likely to improve his party's election prospects. Finally, in April 2013, Meta quit the coalition and signed an election alliance with the Socialist Party, virtually sealing the Democratic Party's election defeat.

The 2013 Elections: The Socialists Return to Power

The June 2013 parliamentary elections, which resulted in a landslide victory for the Socialist Party–led coalition and the defeat of the Democratic Party, marked a milestone in Albania's political development and ushered in a major political realignment. These were perhaps the most credible and peaceful elections since 1992 and improved Albania's democratic reputation and its EU membership prospects.

The elections were fiercely contested by the democrats and the socialists. However, the election campaign was conducted in a much calmer environment than in past elections. While there are dozens of political parties, the democrats and the socialists continue to dominate Albanian politics. Other, smaller parties have limited popular support, and most of them are led by politicians who split off from the Democratic or Socialist parties over disagreements with their top leaderships. Only two new forces contested the elections on their own: former president Bamir Topi's New Democratic Spirit and the Red and Black Alliance. Other parties joined the two major parties' coalitions. The Democratic Party–led Alliance for Employment, Well-Being, and Integration had some twenty-five parties in its coalition, including the Republican Party, the Movement for National Development, and the Party for Justice Integration and Unity. In addition to the SMI, the Socialist Party–led Alliance for a European Albania grouped together more than thirty-five parties, including the Social Democratic Party, the Union for Human Rights Party, and other parties spanning the country's political spectrum.

The democrats presented a report of accomplishments during their eight years of rule but no credible road map detailing the direction in which they intended to take the country. There is no question that between 2005 and 2013, Albania made progress on many fronts. But after eight years in power, the ruling party had experienced a significant erosion of popularity. Many blamed the government for the post-2009 election gridlock and slow progress toward EU integration. In addition, the ruling party faced growing economic hardships, its inability to address the corruption issue decisively, and increased social discontent. The socialists made very ambitious election pledges, focusing their campaign on accusations of poor governance, mismanagement, corruption, and the democratic stranglehold on institutional power. They advocated government-supported social programs, rapid economic development, job creation, and tax reform. Evidently recognizing that his confrontational approach had backfired and under increased pressure from party rank and file, Rama had changed his strategy following his loss of the mayoral elections in 2011. He focused on counteracting perceptions of him as a polarizing figure and improving his relations with the international community.

The socialist-led coalition won a landslide victory, gaining 83 out of 140 seats; the socialists won 66 seats, only one more than four years earlier; the democratic-led coalition received 57 seats. Meta's Movement for Socialist Integration emerged as the unexpected big winner of the election with sixteen seats, a fourfold increase from the 2009 elections. In September 2013, Rama became prime minister and formed the new government. Out of nineteen ministerships, Meta's party received five; most ministers had never held high position. Meta took the post of the speaker of parliament. The government has a clear mandate and the political capital to advance its political and economic agenda. Moreover, the defection of a deputy from the democratic-led coalition gave the socialists the three-fifths of votes in the parliament required to enact important legislation, including constitutional changes. Prime Minister Rama unveiled his government's program, promising a different governing model from that of Berisha. He articulated an ambitious agenda: accelerating EU integration, restoring law and order, fighting corruption, improving the efficiency of the public administration, strengthening the independence of the judiciary, reducing public debt, addressing economic problems, replacing the flat income tax of 10 percent with a progressive tax system, and creating three hundred thousand jobs within the next four years.[19] Expectations are very high, and Rama will have difficulty fulfilling his election promises because of budgetary constraints and declining revenues and growth. He must demonstrate his government's commitment to fight corruption and bolster Albanians' faith in the democratic system. Meta, widely considered an astute politician but one of the most corrupt in Albania, will likely provide tough competition for Rama.

The Democratic Party, which suffered a humiliating defeat and lost badly even in previously secure constituencies, was not in a position to contest the results of the elections, which were certified by international observers. Berisha, the unchallenged democratic leader for over two decades, accepted responsibility for the defeat and resigned as party chairman. He was succeeded by Lulzim Basha, the incumbent mayor of Tirana who previously had served as minister of transportation and public works, minister of foreign affairs, and minister of internal affairs. Basha, who has had very close links with Berisha, attempted to keep the party together and bring the various factions back into the fold. The Democratic Party, riddled with factional fighting and undergoing a major crisis following Berisha's resignation, will need time to rehabilitate itself with the Albanian electorate.

Economic and Social Transition

Albania has carried out fundamental reforms aimed at establishing a functioning market economy. These have resulted in solid growth rates, infrastructure improvements, significant reduction in poverty, and an overhaul of the financial sector. Between 1998 and 2008, Albania averaged an annual real GDP growth of 7 percent. Between 2002 and 2008, poverty declined by one-third, from 25.4 to 12.4 percent. Unemployment fell from 15.8 percent in 2002 to 12.7 percent in 2009. In the public sector, wages in real terms increased by 36.5 percent between 2005 and 2008. The government also made great efforts to improve the country's business climate, establishing a one-stop-shop registration system that reduced the time and money required to open a business, introducing a 10 percent flat tax rate on personal and corporate income, and implementing a series of measures to increase tax revenues. In 2009, the World Bank's *Doing Business* report ranked Albania 82nd out of 183 countries; in 2008, Albania was ranked 135th.[20]

Berisha's government launched a huge public infrastructure program, the most important project being the highway linking Albania's port city of Durrës with Kosovo; it was Albania's largest and most ambitious project since the fall of communism. The new road significantly increased cooperation with Kosovo. Berisha had come to power in 2005 with the promise to rule "by clean hands," insisting that rooting out corruption was "fundamental" to Albania's democratization. Throughout his first four years as prime minister, he maintained a strong anticorruption stance. There is no question that this campaign advanced Albania's aspirations for Euro-Atlantic integration. But despite undeniable gains, corruption remained pervasive. Transparency International ranked Albania 85th out of 180 countries in its 2008 Corruption Perceptions Index; a year later, Albania was ranked ten places lower; and in 2013, it listed Albania as the most corrupt country in Europe. The government came under domestic and international criticism for failing to respect the independence of the judiciary and interfering with investigations into a March 2008 blast at an army ammunition dump in Gerdec that killed twenty-six people.

Despite the significant economic and social transformations, Albania is still one of the poorest countries in Europe. According to the World Bank, one out of three Albanians is poor. Some five hundred thousand Albanians live in extreme poverty, subsisting on less than $1 per day. Albania has yet to move from consumption-based to investment- and export-led growth to encourage foreign direct investments. Close to 1 million Albanians have emigrated, with those between the ages of twenty and forty emigrating in the largest numbers. As a result, Albania has experienced a major brain drain. The remittances of emigrants, estimated at close to $1 billion annually, are an important factor in the country's stability, but such a high emigration flow also has significant political, social, demographic, and economic ramifications. Despite the boom and apparent prosperity of Albania's major cities—Tirana, Durrës, and Vlore—much of the rest of the country remains poor and overwhelmingly agrarian. The rural areas are characterized by economic stagnation and endemic poverty, with the population relying mostly on the informal economic sector and with poor access to education and health services. In central and south Albania, there has been significant progress and social change. The north has experienced less social and economic development. If these regional disparities are not addressed, growing resentment will likely provide a fertile breeding ground for political demagogues.[21]

Albania's main challenges over the midterm are the strengthening of state institutions (particularly the judiciary), developing infrastructure, fortifying the banking system, and taking further measures to encourage foreign investments. While the constitution guarantees the judiciary's independence, the justice system is seen as one of the most corrupt institutions in Albania, with its decisions subject to political pressure. Despite campaign pledges to ensure the judiciary's independence, both the socialists and the democrats have failed to implement meaningful reforms of the judicial system or to depoliticize the judiciary.

The global economic crisis impacted Albania, causing a decrease in exports, a significant decline in remittances from Albanians abroad, and lower foreign investments. Real GDP growth slowed to 1.6 percent in 2012, from 3 percent in 2011, and to 0.9 percent in 2013. Public debt soared, reaching 60 percent of GDP, and the budget deficit widened to 6 percent of GDP.

Civil Society and the Media

A vibrant civil society has already developed. Numerous nongovernmental organizations—women's organizations, human rights organizations, environmental groups, professional associations, and policy institutes—operate freely, engaging in a wide range of activities.

However, nongovernmental organizations have had limited success in influencing policy and enhancing government accountability, transparency, and openness. They have had increasing difficulties securing funding, so most are almost totally dependent on foreign donors. In addition, the failure of many nongovernmental organizations to preserve their independence from the government and political parties has seriously undermined their effectiveness.

During the more than twenty years since the demise of communism, the media in Albania have undergone dramatic changes. From a totally government-controlled media, Albania has seen the emergence of diverse and dynamic media outlets. There are more than twenty daily newspapers, some ninety television stations, and more than forty radio stations. However, the Albanian media has made slow progress in becoming a functioning fourth estate and ranks low among trusted institutions. Most media outlets are associated with the government or a particular political party or politician. While various Albanian governments have cast themselves as champions of press freedom, they have often resorted to various instruments of pressure on the media, including denying advertisements and putting pressure on owners and their businesses. Prominent businessmen, closely allied with the government or opposition political parties, have bought key newspapers and television stations that serve as major news sources for the population. Many journalists, vulnerable to political and economic pressures, engage in widespread self-censorship and lack professionalism and ethics. If truly free media are to take hold, local journalists must take a stronger position in defending their rights. Closely related to this is the need for local journalists to adhere to professional journalism standards. In most cases, there is no firewall between government officials and owners, on the one hand, and reporters, on the other, to ensure editorial integrity and independence.

Foreign Policy

Under the communist regime, Albania had pursued a maverick policy, with high costs for the country's development and international standing. After its break with China in the mid-1970s, Albania embarked on an isolationist policy, almost totally cutting itself off from the outside world and maintaining contacts with only a limited number of countries. With the collapse of the communist government, Albania moved rapidly to end its international isolation, restoring ties with the United States, joining the OSCE, the International Monetary Fund, and the World Bank, and reaching out to neighboring countries. Tirana forged a special relationship with the United States, which openly supported the Democratic Party in the 1992 elections; developed extensive ties with Italy and Greece; and embarked on a policy of integration into Euro-Atlantic institutions. Tirana pursued a constructive policy vis-à-vis ethnic Albanians in Kosovo and was among the first to recognize the independence of Macedonia. Ties with Italy and Greece improved, although periodic crises over Tirana's treatment of the ethnic Greek minority characterized its relationship with Athens.

The downfall of Berisha's government in 1997 had no significant impact on the country's foreign policy. Initially Nano displayed an ambivalent attitude toward the United States, his predecessor Berisha's strongest international benefactor, and showed a preference for Italy and Greece. Eventually, he became a strong proponent of Albania's strategic partnership with the United States. His successors, Majko and Meta, pursued similar policies. The war in Kosovo in 1999 provided an unprecedented opportunity for Albania to appear on the world stage. Albania hosted NATO troops and played a major role in the alliance's strategy of ending the ethnic cleansing of Albanians in Kosovo.

Albania has played a major role in advocating regional economic cooperation, forging close relations with former Yugoslav republics, particularly Macedonia, Montenegro, and Croatia. Tirana's contacts with Belgrade have remained limited. Its extensive ties with Kosovo raised concern in Belgrade with senior Serbian officials accusing Tirana of working for the creation of a "Greater Albania." Albanian-Russian relations have not experienced significant improvements because of Russia's support for Belgrade and strong opposition to Kosovo's independence.

Despite government changes in Tirana, the goal of integration into Euro-Atlantic institutions has remained constant and enjoys overwhelming popular support. While Albanian politics have been characterized by fragmentation and politicization, the prospect of integration has served as an important stimulus for political and economic reforms. Albania was the first former communist country to seek membership in NATO. With the outbreak of the conflict in former Yugoslavia in the early 1990s, Albania developed close relations with the alliance and in 1994 joined NATO's Partnership for Peace program. Albania played an important role in NATO's strategy of preventing the expansion of the Yugoslav conflict, placing its air and port facilities at the alliance's disposal. During the war in Kosovo in 1999, NATO troops were stationed in Albania. A staunch supporter of NATO's engagements, Tirana deployed troops in Afghanistan and Iraq as part of the American-led multinational forces in those countries. The United States was the driving force behind Albania's accession to NATO in 2009.

Albania, for its part, was very supportive of the US policy of fighting extreme nationalism and promoting regional stability and cooperation in southeastern Europe. Tirana also condemned Russia's annexation of Crimea in March 2014 and the Kremlin's efforts to provoke instability in eastern Ukraine. Senior Albanian officials expressed concern about Russia's growing assertiveness and urged a strong and coordinated Western response to what they called Russia's aggression against Ukraine.

Aspirations to join the EU have been closely related to Albania's NATO membership. In 2009 Albania submitted its membership application, but for three years in a row, the European Commission ruled that Albania had not made sufficient progress to be granted candidate status. The adoption of a series of key electoral, judicial, and public administration reforms in 2012 and 2013 stipulated by the EU as required to achieve candidate status, as well as the conduct of orderly elections in June 2013, significantly improved Albania's EU prospects. In its annual progress report in October 2013, the European Commission concluded that Albania had made significant progress and recommended it be granted candidate status on the understanding that it will continue to take action in the fight against organized crime and corruption.[22] In June 2014, the European Commission, acknowledging that Rama's government had demonstrated a commitment in the fight against organized crime and corruption, granted Albania EU candidacy status. Although Albania is expected to open accession talks in 2015, full membership is likely to take at least a decade.

The hallmark of Albania's foreign policy has been the development of a strategic partnership with the United States. The United States played a major role in assisting Albania in fostering its democratic institutions and furthering economic growth and was the

Photo 16.3.   Albanian prime minister Rama meets with Angela Merkel in Berlin. (Corbis)

driving force behind Albania's accession to NATO and Kosovo's independence. Albania, for its part, has been a staunch ally of the United States, supporting American actions in both Afghanistan and Iraq. Former president George W. Bush received a hero's welcome during a visit to Tirana in 2007.

The declaration of Kosovo's independence in February 2008 was perhaps one of the most momentous events in the Albanian nation's contemporary history and led to a massive expression of pan-Albanian sentiments throughout the Balkans. Kosovo's independence, along with Albania's membership in NATO and the increasing empowerment of Albanians in Macedonia and Montenegro, gives Albanians throughout the region a new sense of confidence and unprecedented security. Long known as the underdogs in the Balkans, the Albanians have never been in a more favorable geopolitical position. The relationship between Albanians in Albania and Albanians in the countries of former Yugoslavia has undergone significant transformations. Albanian communities have not only restored old ties but are fostering new types of community relations. These developments have led some observers to raise questions about Albanians' long-term plans and nationalist aspirations.

Undoubtedly, Kosovo's independence has revived the idea of the national unification of Albanians. However, with the exception of a few extremists, Albanians, in general, and their leaders, in particular, have maintained a healthy balance between realism and idealism on the unification issue. Albanians have pursued a pragmatic and rational approach and realize that the benefits of continuing with their current pro-Western agenda of Euro-Atlantic integration and intensified regional cooperation far outweigh the perceived benefits of pursuing political unification and change in current state borders. Unification seems to be overshadowed by other, more urgent challenges, such as the strengthening of governance and democratic institutions in Albania, the consolidation of Kosovo's statehood, and securing a greater share of power for Albanians in Macedonia and protection for Albanian minorities in southern Serbia and Montenegro.

National unification has not been a dominant theme in the Albanian public discourse. To the extent that the idea of unification is present, it is advocated by diverse individuals and groups that currently do not seem to enjoy much popular support and therefore are not likely to be in a position to mobilize masses in pursuit of the unification objective. Official Tirana has been eager to please the United States and the European Union and has not taken any independent stand on Kosovo. Instead, the leadership's goal has been engagement with neighbors, giving priority to the interests of the state of Albania over those of the wider Albanian "nation." Even in the case of Serbia, Tirana has repeatedly approached Belgrade with a readiness to expand ties and explore areas of common interest, without in any way contesting Serbia's objectionable policies and actions vis-à-vis Kosovo. Moreover, Albanian elites in Kosovo and Macedonia have different priorities and tend to take independent action. Tirana's leaders have little clout in Pristina. Albanians in Kosovo, in particular, see themselves as equal to their brethren in Albania. With the erosion of the Serbian threat after 1999, Kosovar elites and the population at large are less enthusiastic than in the past about reunification with Albania. Arguably, Kosovar leaders have a strong motivation and self-interest in the consolidation of a separate Kosovar state. They cannot expect to play the same prominent role in a "Greater Albania." Finally, the Kosovars rightly fear that any move toward reunification would lead to the partition of Kosovo.

The downfall of communism, Kosovo's independence, the rapid advances in information technology, and the erosion of government control over information have, however, transformed the relationship among Albanians in the region, restoring old ties and fostering new types of community relations. Officials in Albania, Kosovo, and western Macedonia do not speak with one political voice; nor do they have one national platform. Yet a remarkable consensus has emerged between decision makers and political actors in Tirana, Pristina, and Tetova. Albanians have publicly rejected unification while subtly coordinating policies and strengthening cooperation in all fields, particularly economic and cultural ties. Since Kosovo's independence, the Balkans have witnessed the emergence of an Albanian "space"—with open borders and a free trade zone but lacking a political center and joint state and government institutions.

The spectacular celebration of Albania's one-hundredth anniversary of independence in November 2012 throughout Albania, Kosovo, Macedonia, Montenegro, and southern Serbia was associated with a sudden and dramatic increase in nationalistic rhetoric. The centennial celebrations kicked off in Skopje, the capital of Macedonia. In a speech at the event, which was attended by senior Albanian leaders from Albania and Kosovo, Berisha said that while Albanians were committed to EU integration, their dream was national unification. The prime minister invoked the historical Albanian narrative and raised the specter of the unification of all Albanians into one state, adding, "From Skopje, I call on the Albanians to work, every minute, every hour, every day, every week, every month and every year for their union."[23]

This nationalist rhetoric triggered a harsh international response. Although the airing of nationalist views was evident across the political spectrum and in the media, criticism focused on Berisha. The prime minister was accused of using nationalism to channel popular discontent away from the failures of his government to deal with domestic problems.

He was forced to temper his nationalist rhetoric following international criticism that this rhetoric threatened US and EU security objectives of regional cooperation promotion. Although Rama, too, had taken an increasingly pan-Albanian position, organizing an exhibition of historical Albanian national flags and traveling to Kosovo, Macedonia, and southern Serbia on the eve of the centennial of Albania's independence, he was quick to denounce Berisha, accusing him of damaging Albania's relations with its strategic partners. While criticizing Berisha for advocating what he termed "primitive nationalism," the Socialist Party leader called for the deepening of cooperation between Albania and Kosovo, including a unified educational system, a customs union, and joint projects for the development of energy and tourism.[24] Once in power, Rama pressed for closer coordination of policies between Tirana and Pristina. In January 2014, the two governments held a joint cabinet meeting in Prizren and agreed on a series of measures aimed at increasing cooperation in all areas. Both sides were careful to assure neighboring countries that they had nothing to fear from closer Tirana-Pristina ties.[25]

Conclusion

The postcommunist period has proved that there are deep-seated obstacles to Albania's democratization that go well beyond the totalitarian nature of Enver Hoxha's regime and the lack of a democratic tradition. They span a host of historical, economic, and sociopolitical factors. These obstacles, combined with the general failure of postcommunist political elites to look beyond their own personal interests or the narrow interests of their parties, groups, and clans, account for the fact that Albania's transition has been very painful and the pace of democratization slow. But despite the myriad political, economic, and social difficulties, Albania has made enormous progress and has achieved an impressive level of democratic maturity and economic and social development. While it has made significant progress, Albania still needs difficult political, legal, and economic reforms that are imperative to complete its transition to a truly consolidated democracy. The main threats to Albanian democracy remain poor governance, weak democratic institutions, corruption, crime, and the long-standing rivalry between the two major parties that has served as a serious barrier to speedy, fundamental reform. Albania must make greater efforts to strengthen the rule of law, ensure the judiciary's independence, demonstrate a real commitment to fighting corruption, develop strong, enduring democratic institutions, and modernize the economy.

Albania's foreign policy will probably remain constant and will continue to be heavily driven by Tirana's long-standing priorities of strengthened strategic partnership with the United States, membership in the European Union, and improved regional cooperation through advocacy of greater political, economic, security, and cultural links. The United States and the European Union have considered Albania an important part of their vision for southeastern Europe: the spread of democracy, the establishment of a multiethnic society, protection of minority rights, and the promotion of peaceful conflict resolution. Washington and Brussels have pursued a common strategy and have devoted enormous resources aimed at advancing Albania's democratization. But while the international community can provide valuable assistance and support, in the final analysis it is up to Albania's leading political forces to create a climate of trust within the body politic, end the political polarization that has impeded the country's progress, and develop a broader political and social consensus in deepening political, legal, and judicial reforms. For Albania to achieve these objectives, the country's leaders will have to put aside their narrow interests and take responsibility for tackling the myriad uncertainties and daunting challenges that their country is likely to face in the near and mid term.

Study Questions

1. What was the nature of Albania's communist system, and how did it contrast with that of other communist states in Central and Eastern Europe?
2. What challenges has Albania faced in its transition from a Communist Party state to a multiparty system and market economy?
3. What role did Albania play during the conflict in former Yugoslavia in the mid-1990s?
4. When did Albania join NATO?
5. What are the main objectives of Albania's foreign policy?

Suggested Readings

Biberaj, Elez. *Albania in Transition: The Rocky Road to Democracy.* Boulder, CO: Westview Press, 1998.

Fischer, Bernd J. *Albania at War, 1939–1945.* West Lafayette, IN: Purdue University Press, 1999.

Gjonça, Arjan. *Communism, Health, and Lifestyle: The Paradox of Mortality Transition in Albania, 1950–1990.* Westport, CT: Greenwood Press, 2001.

Kola, Paulin. *The Myth of Greater Albania.* New York: New York University Press, 2003.

Schwandner-Sievers, Stephanie, and Bernd J. Fischer, eds. *Albanian Identities: Myth and History.* Bloomington: Indiana University Press, 2002.

Vickers, Miranda, and James Pettifer. *Albania: From Anarchy to a Balkan Identity.* New York: New York University Press, 1997.

Websites

Balkan Web: http://www.balkanweb.com/indexi.php
Freedom House: http://www.freedomhouse.org
National Democratic Institute, "Albania": http://www.ndi.org/albania
World Bank, "Albania": http://www.worldbank.org/en/country/albania
Zëri i Amerikës: http://www.zeriamerikes.com (Voice of America)

Notes

1. Organization for Security and Co-operation in Europe (OSCE), "Albania, Parliamentary Elections, 23 June 2013: Final Report," OSCE, October 10, 2013, http://www.osce.org/odihr/elections/106963.

2. For general information on Albania, see Freedom House, http://www.freedomhouse.org; "Albania," World Bank, http://www.worldbank.org/en/country/albania; "Albania," National Democratic Institute, http://www.ndi.org/albania; Balkan Web, http://www.balkanweb.com.

3. According to the census conducted in October 2011, Albania had a residential population of 2,831,741, a decline of about 8 percent compared to the 2001 census (3,069,275 residents). Some 83 percent (2,312,356) declared themselves Albanian, 0.87 percent (24,243) Greek, 0.3 percent (8,301) Roma, 0.3 percent (8,266) Aromanian, and 0.2 percent (5,512) Macedonian; 14 percent (390,938) of respondents refused to declare their nationality. In terms of religious affiliation, Muslims accounted for 56.70 percent (1,587,608) of the population, Bektashi 2.09 percent (58,628), Catholics 10.03 percent (280,921), Orthodox 6.75 percent (188,992). Some 386,024 respondents (13.79 percent) refused to declare their religious affiliation. See the Institute of Statistics, *Population and Housing Census in Albania,* Part 1 (Tirana: Institute of Statistics, 2012), 14, 71, http://www.instat.gov.al/media/177354/main_results__population_and_housing_census_2011.pdf.

4. Stavro Skendi, *The Albanian National Awakening, 1878–1912* (Princeton, NJ: Princeton University Press, 1967); Edwin E. Jacques, *The Albanians: An Ethnic History from Prehistoric Times to the Present* (Jefferson, NC: McFarland & Co., 1995); Miranda Vickers, *The Albanians: A Modern History* (London: I. B. Taurus, 1995); Bernd J. Fischer, *King Zog and the Struggle for Stability in Albania* (Boulder, CO: East European Monographs, distributed by Columbia University Press, 1984); Bernd J. Fischer, *Albania at War, 1939–1945* (West Lafayette, IN: Purdue University Press, 1999).

5. Nicholas C. Pano, *The People's Republic of Albania* (Baltimore: Johns Hopkins Press, 1968); Elez Biberaj, *Albania and China: A Study of an Unequal Alliance* (Boulder, CO: Westview Press, 1986); Elez Biberaj, *Albania: A Socialist Maverick* (Boulder, CO: Westview Press, 1990); William E. Griffith, *Albania and the Sino-Soviet Rift* (Cambridge, MA: MIT Press, 1963); Arshi Pipa, *Albanian Stalinism: Ideo-political Aspects* (Boulder, CO: East European Monographs, distributed by Columbia University Press, 1990); Peter R. Prifti, *Socialist Albania since 1944* (Cambridge, MA: MIT Press, 1978); Anton Logoreci, *The Albanians: Europe's Forgotten Survivors* (London: Victor Gollancz, 1977).

6. Elez Biberaj, *Albania in Transition: The Rocky Road to Democracy* (Boulder, CO: Westview Press, 1998); Miranda Vickers and James Pettifer, *Albania: From Anarchy to a Balkan Identity* (New York: New York University Press, 1997).

7. Alfred S. Moisiu, *Midis Nanos dhe Berishës* [*Between Nano and Berisha*], vol. 3 (Tirana: Toena, 2009).

8. *Gazeta shqiptare*, April 22, 2008, 2.

9. *Shekulli*, April 25, 2008, 4; ATA [Albanian Telegraphic Agency] in English, April 22, 2008.

10. *The Electoral Code of the Republic of Albania* (Tirana, 2009), http://www.refworld.org/pdfid/4c1f93e32.pdf. See also the European Commission for Democracy through Law (Venice Commission), "Joint Opinion on the Electoral Code of the Republic of Albania," Opinion No. 513/2009, Strasbourg/Warsaw, March 13, 2009. For a critical assessment of the electoral code, see Claude Moniquet, "Albania: The Adoption of a New Electoral Code Compromises Possibilities for Holding Free Elections," European Strategic Intelligence and Security Center, Background Note, December 17, 2008, http://www.esisc.org/publications/analyses/albanie-ladoption-du-nouveau-code-electoral.

11. Afrim Krasniqi, *Partitë politike në Shqipëri* [*Political Parties in Albania*] (Tirana: Eurorilindja, 2006).

12. See OSCE Office for Democratic Institutions and Human Rights, "Republic of Albania: Parliamentary Elections, 28 June 2009," Warsaw, October 11, 2001, http://www.osce.org/odihr/elections/albania/38598?download=true.

13. Commission of the European Communities, *Albania 2009 Progress Report* (Brussels: Commission of the European Communities, October 2009).

14. In a television interview three days before the elections, Berisha said a coalition with the Socialist Movement for Integration was "out of the question. I will never do this with the Socialist

Party or the Socialist Movement for Integration. Absolutely not! I can never enter into a coalition with either of these parties." See *Koha Jonë*, June 25, 2009, 2–3.

15. "Meta to Rama: 'Leave Berisha, Go Left,'" *Albania* (Tirana), April 26, 2008, 4. Meta made these comments on the eve of the parliament's approval of constitutional changes that introduced a new electoral system and stipulated that the president be elected by a simple majority.

16. OSCE Office for Democratic Institutions and Human Rights, "Republic of Albania: Parliamentary Elections, 28 June 2009," Final Report, Warsaw, September 14, 2009, 1, http://www.osce.org/odihr/elections/albania/38598?download=true.

17. "Ballot Boxes or We Will Overthrow Berisha before Election," *Gazeta shqiptare*, November 11, 2009, 7.

18. "Corruption Perceptions Index 2013," Transparency International, http://www.transparency.org/cpi2013/results. See also Marsida Nence, "Corruption, Albania's Biggest Challenge for Integration in E.U.," Portal on Central Eastern and Balkan Europe (PECOB), December 2013, http://www.pecob.eu/Corruption-Albania-biggest-challenge-integration-E-U.

19. "Government Program: Sectors Where 300,000 New Jobs Will Be Created," *Gazeta shqiptare*, September 11, 2013, 2–3; Alliance for a European Albania, *Programi i qeverisë, 2013–2017* (Tirana, 2013).

20. The European Bank for Reconstruction and Development (EBRD), *Strategy for Albania, 2009–2012* (London: EBRD, 2009), 15–16. See also International Bank for Reconstruction and Development, *Country Assistance Strategy Progress Report for Albania for the Period FY06–FY08*, Report No. 43346-AL (Washington, DC: World Bank, 2008).

21. See World Bank, *Albania: World Bank Group Partnership Program Snapshot* (Washington, DC: World Bank, October 2013).

22. European Commission, *Key Findings of the 2013 Progress Report on Albania* (Brussels), European Commission, October 16, 2013, http://europa.eu/rapid/press-release_MEMO-13-888_en.htm; European Commission, *Albania 2013 Progress Report* (Brussels: European Commission, October 2013), http://ec.europa.eu/enlargement/pdf/key_documents/2013/package/al_rapport_2013.pdf.

23. *Panorama*, November 26, 2012; *Gazeta shqiptare*, November 26, 2013. At a conference in Tirana on Kosovo's role in the creation of the Albanian state, Berisha said, "We should work hard to overcome thousands of divisions created in the Albanian lands over the past century. We should do everything to make the borders between us insignificant. We should not forget that when it comes to the status, the status of the Albanians can be nothing but that of one nation. Any other stance is absolutely illusionary. Today we have a platform to implement, the platform for our integration into the EU. It is through this platform that we will realize our major objectives of the process for our national unification. Again, we do not believe, we do not think that this platform is sufficient to materialize our ideal fully. Therefore, we need other, additional measures, which will help us to totally unify our standards, norms, and practices so that the Albanians feel themselves the same wherever they are living." Quoted in Fation Binjaku, "National Unification: Sacred Right," *Panorama*, November 20, 2012, 4.

24. Edit Rama, "Nationalist's Cries: Government's Offer," *Shekulli* (Tirana), December 29, 2012, 9.

25. See joint article by the two foreign ministers, Ditmir Bushati and Enver Hoxhaj, "Strategic Partnership: A Model of Regional Cooperation," *Shqip* (Tirana), January 14, 2014, 8.

Map 17.0.   Former Yugoslavia and Its Successors

CHAPTER 17

Former Yugoslavia and
Its Successors

Mark Baskin and Paula Pickering

It is impossible to compress the story of the Socialist Federal Republic of Yugoslavia (SFRY) and its successor states into a neat and simple story of transition. Its succession twists and turns through pathways of war, reconstruction, and reconstitution into national states—a process not yet completed. In this contentious tale, observers sharply differ on the sources of dissolution, the causes of war, and the current state and future prospects of the post-Yugoslav governments.[1]

The tragedies that occurred are all the more painful since it seemed, in 1990, that the SFRY was on the verge of joining the European Community. It had long ago done away with many of the overtly repressive trappings of Central and East European socialism. Since the 1950s, Yugoslav leaders had been experimenting with liberalizing economic and political reforms, and Yugoslavia had been broadly integrated into international economic, political, and cultural developments. Yugoslavia's socialist regime was more open, transparent, and accepting of non-Marxist ideologies than any in Central and Eastern Europe. And since the 1960s, its citizens had massively enjoyed the opportunities to travel, study, and work abroad.[2] Literature and culture forbidden in the east, from George Orwell's *1984* to punk rock and neoliberal economics, were long prominent on the Yugoslav market.

By 1989, Yugoslav efforts to find a "third way" between Western capitalism and Soviet socialism had clearly run into a dead end. A burgeoning civil society, a business-oriented prime minister, and the popular Slovenian cry, "Europa Zdaj!" (Europe Now!) appeared to move Yugoslavia toward an evolving Europe. But Yugoslavia's other republics and provinces did not share Slovenia's relatively smooth ascension to the European Union (EU), and most have remained outside the "European home."

This chapter explores the causes and consequences of the SFRY's demise. It suggests that the agenda for the dissolution of multinational Yugoslavia was set by a series of incomplete economic and political reforms that left Yugoslavia without the institutional resilience to overcome increasing interregional differences. The national revivals that swept unevenly across Yugoslavia in the 1980s enabled the rise of the uniquely talented leader Slobodan Milošević, who advanced Serbian interests in the name of preserving Yugoslavia. The wars of Yugoslav succession were the outcome of unequal bargaining in the absence of compelling central authority, the failure of ambitious republican leaders to find a basis for future common existence, and the initial disinterest of Europe and the United States. Yugoslavia's violent dissolution led to a delayed international intervention, settlements that have helped to define the newly independent states, the prominence of international agencies in domestic developments, and transitions that have lasted far longer than foreseen in the early 1990s.

Precommunist History

The heterogeneous cultural, social, and political precommunist traditions in the lands of former Yugoslavia stem from their location amid the divisions in Europe between the Eastern and Western Roman Empires; Eastern Orthodoxy, Western Catholicism, and Islam; the Ottoman Empire, the Republic of Venice, and the Hapsburg Monarchy; and the Warsaw Pact and the North Atlantic Treaty Organization (NATO).[3] Nineteenth-century national movements appeared on the heels of wars, invasions, migrations of peoples, shifting boundaries, and religious conversion.

Many national leaders who emerged in the 1990s focused on the historical antecedents to the post-Yugoslav national states. The medieval Croatian, Serbian, and Bosnian states were relatively brief preludes to their integration into larger, imperial state structures. An agreement with the Hungarian throne in 1102 led to a separate but unequal existence for Croatia within the Kingdom of Hungary until 1918, which put it under the Hapsburg Monarchy after 1526. The battle on a Kosovo field in 1389 between Serbian and Ottoman forces led to the ultimate end of medieval Serbia in 1459. By the time Serbian power again controlled this area in the early part of the twentieth century, Serbs were greatly outnumbered by Albanians in Kosovo. The Ottoman forces conquered independent Bosnia in 1463 and Herzegovina in 1483. The Slovenes lost their political independence in the eighth century and were incorporated into the Hapsburg Monarchy by the fourteenth century. Macedonia did not enjoy independence during the medieval era and fell under Byzantine, Bulgarian, Ottoman, and Serbian rule in the period before World War I. The departure of the Serbian state northward after 1389 enabled the development of a Montenegrin state, where the bishops of the Orthodox Church became rulers after 1516.

The legacies of imperial rule continue to be felt in these lands. The Ottomans imposed a centrally controlled regime of land tenure, tax collection, and native religious rights that gave extensive autonomy to religious communities. Large-scale conversions to Islam took place only among Bosnians and Albanians, but the forced conversion of young boys to Islam for the Ottoman officer corps remains a potent anti-Islamic symbol. The Ottomans twice advanced to the gates of Vienna and the Hapsburg court and administration: in 1529 and 1682. In response to the Ottoman threats, the Hapsburgs established a military border populated largely by Orthodox Serbs on the Croatian side of Bosnia-Herzegovina. The aspirations of the Hapsburg Monarchy in the eighteenth century to impose enlightened absolutism and bureaucratic uniformity did not succeed in providing a unifying link within the empire—especially as the Croatian lands did not constitute a single administrative entity in the pre-Yugoslav period. Similarly, Ottoman efforts at internal reform throughout the nineteenth century did not provide a basis for reviving the authority of the center in these far-flung parts of the empire. By the eve of World War I, the Austro-Hungarian Dual Monarchy was neither a vital nor an authoritative state, and in the First Balkan War in 1912, the Ottoman Empire had been pushed out of the Balkans by an alliance consisting of Bulgaria, Greece, Serbia, and Montenegro.

This imperial decline was attended by the spread of ideas of the Enlightenment, the romantic movement, and Napoleonic revolution of the early nineteenth century, which led, among the peoples of former Yugoslavia, to the emergence of modern national movements rooted in the language and culture of the common people. As discussed below, contending notions of the Yugoslav state combined with the uneven appearance of national movements in the nineteenth century. Serbia was the first state to emerge in a series of uprisings against the Ottomans that began in 1804 and culminated in formal independence at the Congress of Berlin in 1878. It gained experience in administration, in exercising influence in the region, and in its difficult relations with the government of the Hapsburg Dual Monarchy. The small state of Montenegro also gained international recognition in 1878 in Berlin as a separate government under Russian tutelage. Independence movements in different parts of Croatia and Slovenia were constrained by their relative weakness within the Hapsburg state and by a shifting set of goals rooted in some form of pan-south-Slav federalism, liberalism, integral nationalism, and an enhanced position within the Hapsburg Monarchy. At the Congress of Berlin, the Dual Monarchy took over the administration of Bosnia and, to great Serbian protest, formally annexed it in 1908. In the First Balkan War, the Ottomans lost both Kosovo to Serbia and Macedonia to a larger coalition. But the Second Balkan War in 1913 saw Serbia annex a great deal of Macedonia from Bulgaria. The end of World War I created conditions for the formation of a common state for Serbs, Croats, Slovenes, Bosnian Muslims, and Montenegrins that would also house significant numbers of Albanians, Hungarians, Turks, Italians, and others.

The decline of the Ottomans and the Hapsburgs set an agenda that did not favor the emergence of democratic institutions following World War I because of many unanswered questions in economic development, administration, cultural policy, and foreign policy. In his magisterial *The Yugoslav National Question*, Ivo Banac suggests, "The national question permeated every aspect of Yugoslavia's public life after 1918. It was reflected in the internal, external, social, economic, and even cultural affairs. It was solved by democrats and autocrats, kings and Communists. It was solved by day and unsolved by night. Some days were particularly bright for building, some nights particularly dark for destroying. One horn of the dilemma was that a single solution could not satisfy all sides. Was the other that a firm citadel could be maintained only by human sacrifice?"[4]

The Communist Experience

The felicitous title of Dennison Rusinow's superb *The Yugoslav Experiment* effectively captures socialist Yugoslavia's policy of permanent political improvisation.[5] The communist-led Partisans' seizure of power during World War II, with minimal assistance from the Soviet Union, began a search for a governing formula that would combine an efficient and equitable strategy of economic development with an approach to governance balanced between the leadership of a Leninist party and the broad inclusion of mass organizations. The communists' capacity to mobilize mass and external support during World War II provided the new regime, led by Josip Broz Tito, with the resilience, absent in other Central and East European socialist regimes, to resist the domination of its internal political and policy agendas by the Soviet Union. This toughness was essential for the experiments in governance that were conducted in an unusual international environment and that addressed economic decision making and organization and the evolution of national communities within the Yugoslav federation.

In the first element of the experiment, socialist Yugoslavia found itself in a unique international environment in which it was a member of neither the Warsaw Treaty Organization nor NATO, where it was viewed as a communist country by the West and as a capitalist country by the Soviet bloc. Joseph Stalin's expulsion of Yugoslavia from the Communist Information Bureau, or Cominform, in 1948 provided a context to search for a legitimizing formula that would leave Yugoslavia both independent and socialist.[6] Military spending increased from the necessity to maintain a Yugoslav National Army (JNA) that could deter attack. While the top officer corps was ethnically balanced, the middle and noncommissioned officer corps were dominated by Serbs and Montenegrins—a matter of great significance, as most Yugoslav military assets fell to the Serbs during the wars of succession in the 1990s.

By the early 1960s, the Yugoslav government under Tito had adopted an "open" foreign policy between the two Cold War blocs and the newly independent countries in the developing world in which it came to play a prominent role in the movement of nonaligned countries.[7] Tito's Yugoslavia actively pursued an independent political course within the United Nations. It simultaneously traded extensively with communist-bloc countries and developed relations with multilateral financial institutions, such as the International Monetary Fund. It opened up its borders so that by the early 1970s, over 1 million Yugoslav citizens lived and worked abroad. From the early 1950s, in other words, an increasingly diverse set of foreign relationships helped maintain Yugoslav independence and came to shape the character of internal policy choices.[8] However, by the fall of the Berlin Wall in 1989, Yugoslavia had ceased to represent a daring experiment that commanded Western and Soviet support.

The second element of the experiment lay in a strategy of economic development that was socialist but non-Soviet. Abandoning central planning early on, Yugoslav leaders adopted "self-management" decision making within firms as the regime's central economic symbol. From the early 1950s onward, Yugoslav leaders engaged in a series of partial economic reforms that fell short of creating a market economy similar to those in Europe or North America. These reforms included the decollectivization of agriculture; the decentralization of economic decision making; the establishment of workers' councils in firms; liberalization of foreign trade; banking reforms; the creation of a Fund for the Development of Underdeveloped Regions; efforts to simulate or create financial, commodity, and labor markets; efforts to remove the party from everyday decision making in the economy; the redesign of the economy in the mid-1970s into a "contractual economy"; and a policy of liberalizing "shock therapy" in 1990.[9]

The reforms did not work very well over the medium term, mainly because they neither fully embraced the implications of liberalizing reforms that would lead to significant privatization of economic assets nor ensured that the economy would remain "socialist." They did not provide stable economic growth based on a productive agriculture. Instead of narrowing intra-Yugoslav inequality, they were associated with increased economic inequality across and within republics. They appeared to increase Yugoslav dependence on the international economy and led to significantly increasing unemployment and the wholesale departure of labor to jobs in the West. They also continued political meddling in production. By 1990, Yugoslav debt to Western banks had grown to $20 billion. Unemployment reached 15.9 percent and in the least developed region, Kosovo, was 38.4 percent.[10] At one point in 1989, inflation had grown to 1,750 percent. In the best of political times, the Yugoslav government might have overcome these difficulties, but by 1991 it was the worst of times.

The final element of the experiment lay in political reforms embodied in large-scale efforts to define new constitutional orders in 1946, 1954, 1963, and 1974. Among other things, these constitutions attempted to devolve power away from the Communist Party of Yugoslavia to mass organizations that were more sensitive to diverse popular aspirations. Signs of this devolution included renaming the party the League of Communists of Yugoslavia (LCY) at its sixth congress in 1952, taking the party out of a command position in the mid-1960s by investing more authority in the regional organizations, and purging the hard-line secret police. The LCY leadership attempted to enhance the authority of nonparty governmental and administrative institutions but stopped short of divorcing the party from power. The purges of liberal party leaders throughout Yugoslavia in the early 1970s led to the re-Leninization of party organizations, which became incubators of the fractious nationalism they were meant to eliminate. This party-led regionalism provided the context for the end of the Yugoslav experiment in brotherhood and unity, the dissolution of the state, and war.

The idea of brotherhood and unity was central to the Yugoslav experiment. Yugoslavia, in reality, was a heterogeneous collection of Muslims, Eastern Orthodox, and Catholics; Serbs, Croats, Slovenes, Bosniacs,[11] Macedonians, and Montenegrins; and Albanians, Hungarians, Italians, Slovaks, Czechs, Turks, and others. These peoples had acquired their modern national consciousness within the Hapsburg Monarchy and the Ottoman Empire. Their modern national movements began at different times throughout the nineteenth century and enjoyed different degrees of success. The idea of creating some sort of state of South Slavs, or Yugoslavia, was also in the mix. But even the nineteenth century saw tensions between the idea of creating an overarching common identity and that of a Yugoslav identity that would merely bind together national groups sharing a common political space. This tension characterized political debates between centralizing "unitarists" and decentralizing "federalists" in both royalist and socialist Yugoslavia. And there was nothing inevitable about the creation of the Kingdom of Serbs, Croats, and Slovenes at the end of World War I, an entity that became known as Yugoslavia in 1929. Its Serbian royal dictatorship tried to push a common cultural Yugoslav identity that was in practice Serb-dominated. Serb-Croat political conflicts wracked the country right up until its dismemberment by the Nazis in 1941 into puppet regimes in Slovenia, Croatia, and Serbia and the annexation of Kosovo, Macedonia, and parts of Croatia by neighboring countries with their own claims to these regions. The communist-led Partisans won the civil war that took place during World War II in good measure because the symbol of Yugoslav "brotherhood and unity" was a supranational appeal to reason and survival.

To recognize and balance national interests, the SFRY was a federation of six republics: Serbia, Croatia, Montenegro, Slovenia, Macedonia, and Bosnia-Herzegovina. Bosnia-Herzegovina, the only republic without a titular nation, was a "community of Moslems, Croats, and Serbs."[12] There were two autonomous provinces within Serbia: Vojvodina, which was home to large numbers of Hungarians, and Kosovo, which had been predominantly Albanian since the end of World War II.[13] Croatia's population was 12 percent Serb in 1991. Many Serbs in Croatia lived in compact settlements in areas that comprised the Hapsburg military border from the sixteenth century, and others lived in large urban settlements. The Serbs were the SFRY's most dispersed nationality; more Serbs than any other ethnic group lived outside their nominal republic.

Successive constitutions defined a series of increasingly complex power-sharing arrangements between federal, republican, and regional governments that came to resemble consociational institutions theorized to build stable democracies in culturally plural societies.[14] By 1974, the pattern of representation in all federal-level decision-making bodies was carefully allotted to individuals from each republic (with attention paid to the intrarepublican nationality composition of such delegations) in order to ensure the formal picture of federal multinationalism. There was an intricate pattern of interrepublican decision making, wherein republican and provincial representatives in state and government institutions held a virtual veto over each stage of federal decision making.[15] All federal-level institutions were guided by the ethnic key. The presidency, parliamentary delegations, and cabinets included representatives of all republics and autonomous provinces. Under the 1974 constitution, the republics became the SFRY's most significant centers of power. But decentralization of politics left the LCY as "the one ring to bind them all," in Rusinow's phrase, despite the party's loss of political coherence.

Tito also tried to ensure that the country would remain unified by establishing a collective state presidency in 1971. Thus, each republic seat had a member to serve as part of the collective head of state. The president of the collective state presidency, who was Tito until his death, rotated among the republics and provinces each May, according to a predetermined arrangement.

With Tito's death in 1980, the fragility of this house of cards became increasingly apparent. As the winds of change began sweeping through socialist Europe, official Yugoslav politics remained committed to the methods of economic and political half reforms of the earlier socialist era. The bankruptcy of politics-as-usual could be seen in the suppression of demonstrations calling for republican status in Kosovo, in trumped-up show trials of Bosnian Muslims for ostensibly advocating an Islamic republic, and in a series of other public "political cases" meant to demonstrate the strength of the political center against disloyal enemies. But the absence of an authoritative political center was exposed in the failure of successive federal governments to identify an effective strategy of economic development and in the failure of republican oligarchs to agree on amendments to the 1974 constitution. The loss of a central vision was clearest in the failure of the Yugoslav presidency to act with any independent authority and the minor role relegated to federal prime minister Ante Marković in the political drama of succession. The torch had passed to republican leaders who were unable to reach agreement on a constructive course forward.

Most ominously, this political impasse led to the rise of Slobodan Milošević in Serbian politics in a 1987 coup against his close friend and political patron, Ivan Stambolić.

Milošević revolutionized Yugoslav politics as the first party leader to depart from a convoluted and ideological public language to simple and direct rhetoric comprehensible to the broad masses. He explicitly integrated Serbian national goals into an "antibureaucratic revolution" that was supposed to preserve socialist Yugoslavia but actually provided an Orwellian tinge to his accumulation of greater power. Aside from taking over the Serbian media, Milošević employed sophisticated techniques of mass mobilization to make credible threats against the socialist governments in Slovenia and Croatia after he had put his loyal minions in power in Kosovo, Vojvodina, and Montenegro, thereby giving him political control over four of the eight Yugoslav political units. This tactic made him the single most influential political force in late socialist Yugoslavia, but he had neither Tito's goal of inclusion nor his command of the levers of power. Still, he was the commanding force in Serbian politics until his electoral defeat in autumn 2000 and arrest by the International Criminal Tribunal for the former Yugoslavia (ICTY)—a decade after the first window of democratic transition closed.[16]

The silver lining to this political cloud might have been the opening up of civil society throughout Yugoslavia in the middle and late 1980s. This process involved publicly confronting previously suppressed conflicts and official excesses and beginning multiple processes of reconciliation. In theory, a new democratic politics would be inclusive and strive to integrate all citizens and groups into a series of nested political communities that began locally and grew outward to the federation. In practice, it opened a Pandora's box and sometimes resulted in such inflammatory programs as the Serbian Academy of Sciences' "Memorandum" of 1986, which gave a cogent critique of economic mismanagement alongside a nationalist program aimed at protecting Serbs throughout Yugoslavia. The increasing openness of Yugoslav society meant that former officials and political prisoners could gather at meetings of the Association for Yugoslav Democratic Initiative to search for common ground for the future. It meant the return of *gastarbeiteri,* or Yugoslav guest workers who had been working abroad, and the entry of political émigrés into a rapidly evolving political mainstream. It meant coming to terms with the transnational character of ethnopolitical communities in the 1980s and 1990s—whether in the selection of an American citizen, Milan Panić, as the Serbian prime minister in 1992, the prominent role played by overseas Croats in Croatian domestic politics in the 1990s, or the substantial support of Albanian émigré communities for political and military action in Kosovo.

Greater pluralism combined with mounting economic problems to deepen the antagonism between political and economic development strategies pursued in the more economically developed regions (Slovenia and Croatia) and those regions that were less economically developed.[17] Slovenian and Croatian elites favored a looser, asymmetrical federation together with liberal political and economic reforms. Serbian leaders countered with reforms calling for a recentralization of the state and political system together with a streamlined self-management system. Each plan suited the self-interest of the regionally rooted elites who proposed it. Forces for compromise—federal prime minister Ante Marković and leaders of the less developed and ethnically diverse republics of Bosnia and Macedonia—were easily drowned out. Already disgruntled over having to foot what they considered more than their fair share of the bill for central government and economic development in poorer regions of the country, leaders in Slovenia and Croatia in the late

1980s balked when asked to contribute to Serbia's strong-arm tactics over restive Kosovo. Fearing they would lose the battle with Belgrade over reform of Yugoslavia, the Slovenian party elite in 1989 saw the benefit of "giving in" to the increasing demands of republic youth and intellectuals for pluralism and sovereignty. The pursuit of liberal reform was more contentious in Croatia, where 12 percent of the population was Serb, and reformers only gained the upper hand at the end of 1989.

By 1989, the pressure for comprehensive change was great. The federal LCY ceased to exist in January 1990 when the Croat and Slovene delegations walked out of the Fourteenth Extraordinary Congress of the LCY after the Serbian bloc rejected all Slovene motions—for example, to confederalize the party, ban the use of torture, and provide clearer guarantees of the right of dissociation—without any meaningful discussion. Most former republican LCY organizations soon morphed into social democratic parties (SDPs).[18] This development did not auger a happy outcome for the intense interrepublican political bargaining about Yugoslavia's future architecture. For the first time since World War II, nationalist ideas were viewed as legitimate, and nationalist "enemies" of socialism became centrally important actors in Yugoslav politics. By 1991, few political or institutional constraints were commonly accepted throughout Yugoslavia. There was also a sense that the window of political opportunity would not remain open long. The Serbian government viewed itself as the protector of Serbs throughout former Yugoslavia, and Croatian president Franjo Tudjman would soon make the error of trying to extend the Croatian state into Bosnia.

State Formation and War

The Yugoslav government barely paused at the precipice of dissolution and war in 1990 and 1991. As described in more detail below, elections throughout the federation in 1990 selected republican leaderships accountable to ethnically based republican constituencies. These leaders failed to reach consensus on the shape of a democratic Yugoslav federation. Slovenian and Croatian leaders held well-orchestrated referenda on independence and began transforming their reserve forces into armies. European mediators failed to prevent a war at this "hour of Europe," and the US government was not sufficiently interested at this early moment to act.[19] While the underlying causes of the wars of Yugoslav succession remain in sharp dispute, most scholars have rejected simplistic explanations that conjure up centuries of ethnic enmity in favor of more complex explanations in which ambitious elites exacerbated ethnic tensions and dramatically increased the potential for violence. On the eve of war, the SFRY's economy was in decline and the legitimacy of its socialist institutions in disrepair to the increasing frustration of ordinary citizens. With no authoritative political center, the emergence of politicized ethnicity that awoke unresolved grievances from World War II allowed little room for compromise among elites. Against this background, the republican elections that took place throughout 1990 and negotiations that failed in the first half of 1991 propagated an "ethnic crisis" that led to war in mid-1991.[20] Five interconnected armed conflicts took place that still cast long shadows on developments in the successor states. It has been difficult to establish precise figures, but an estimate of people killed during the entire conflict is somewhat under 150,000;

over 4.5 million people were displaced at some point in the conflicts. By early 2013, the United Nations High Commissioner for Refugees estimated that some 300,000 refugees remained in exile, and more than 218,500 internally displaced persons were still seeking durable solutions by returning home.[21]

SLOVENIA

The Slovene government declared independence on June 25, 1991, following careful preparations for defense that effectively stymied an ill-prepared Yugoslav National Army offensive. By June 30, Serbian leaders ordered the JNA to prepare to abandon Slovenia. There were eight military and five civilian deaths among the Slovenes, and thirty-nine members of the JNA died. Slovenian independence was formally acknowledged on July 18.[22] Slovenia subsequently entered the EU in 2004 together with nine other countries, became the first new member to adopt the euro as its currency in 2007, and was invited to become a member of the Organisation for Economic Co-operation and Development in October 2010.[23]

CROATIA

The Croatian government declared independence on June 26, 1991. Following the initially artful invitation to the leader of the Serb Democratic Party to become a vice president in the Croatian government in spring 1990, the Tudjman government awkwardly began firing Serb administrators and police throughout Croatia in the name of achieving ethnic balance in official employment. Armed conflict began in 1990 with a series of skirmishes and the Serbs' consolidation of control in the illegally constituted Serb Autonomous Regions with the aid of JNA officers and arms by mid-March 1991. Croatian Serbs largely boycotted the Croatian referendum on independence. The war featured sieges of Croatia's Danubian city of Vukovar and the Adriatic city of Dubrovnik. Former US secretary of state and United Nations negotiator Cyrus Vance devised a plan that allowed 13,500 UN troops to deploy to oversee the reintegration of the one-third of the republic's territory controlled by Serbs into Croatia.[24] An estimated twenty thousand people died during the war. Despite European Community concerns over the Croatian government's treatment of its Serb minority, Germany recognized Croatia's independence in early 1992; the United States and other European governments soon followed.

International negotiators from the United Nations, the European Community, the United States, and Russia presided over three years of inconclusive negotiations between the Croatian government and rebel Serbs, who repeatedly refused to begin talks concerning the reintegration of Serb-held territory into Croatia in accordance with the Vance Plan. The Croatian government launched two offensives to regain control of most Serb-held territory in May and August 1995, after which approximately three hundred thousand Serbs fled Croatia.[25] As part of the larger process of ending the war in Bosnia-Herzegovina, the UN Transitional Administration in Eastern Slavonia (UNTAES) mediated the formal return of territory by early 1998. The Organization for Security and

Co-operation in Europe (OSCE) later remained to monitor aspects of policing, media, and the return of refugees. The Croatian government's reassertion of control over its entire territory by 1998 was a turning point that removed the issue of Serb occupation and enabled the emergence of more normal political bargaining and political reform that ultimately led to Croatia's membership in the EU, as discussed below.

BOSNIA-HERZEGOVINA

By autumn 1991, a delicately balanced coalition government among Muslim, Serb, and Croat parties broke down with disputes over Bosnia's relationship to rump Yugoslavia, the departure of the Serb Democratic Party delegation led by Radovan Karadžić, and the formation of multiple Serb Autonomous Regions with JNA support. Croatian president Tudjman had already discussed the partition of Bosnia-Herzegovina with Serbian president Slobodan Milošević by March 1991, in an initiative that would betray Croatia's image as a victim of aggression, strengthen the hand of radically nationalist Croats in Herzegovina, and establish the "territorial integrity of the Croat nation in its historic and natural borders" in a way that would expand the Tudjman government's influence in Bosnia.[26]

The Bosnian government's declaration of independence was recognized by several Western governments on April 6, 1992. Initial Serb campaigns in 1992 rapidly led to the capture of about 60 percent of Bosnia's territory, gains that remained basically intact until the fighting ended in autumn 1995. In an attempt to homogenize Bosnia's ethnically complex social geography in order to control territory, the Serb military engaged in ethnic cleansing[27] and created prison camps. The radical Croatian Defense Council (HVO) subsequently launched offensives in Herzegovina and central Bosnia. Radicalized by foreign Muslim volunteers, a Muslim brigade in central Bosnia also committed crimes, while both Serb and Croat forces destroyed Islamic cultural monuments.[28] The war in Bosnia generated 2.5 million refugees and internally displaced persons, well over half of the prewar population.

The international community proved ineffective at ending the war. The United Nations Security Council passed over one hundred normative acts that established an arms embargo that de facto favored the well-armed Bosnian Serb Army against the poorly equipped Army of the Republic of Bosnia-Herzegovina, created six poorly defended "safe areas" for civilians, and addressed daily crises in the provision of humanitarian assistance and protection of civilians. Concurrently, diplomatic negotiators from the European Community, United Nations, United States, and others drafted a series of peace plans but took few steps to compel the parties to reach agreement and did not intervene in support of the elected Bosnian government headed by Alija Izetbegović. The UN Security Council deployed twenty-six thousand lightly armed troops in the UN Protection Force scattered throughout Bosnia-Herzegovina during the fighting in support of humanitarian efforts. But these troops were not in a position to compel compliance with the UN mandate and were, in effect, at the mercy of the strongest party on the ground—the Bosnian Serb Army. International negotiators succeeded in compelling Croat forces in Herzegovina and the Bosnian government to cooperate against Serb forces by forming the

Federation of Bosnia and Herzegovina in early 1994. By mid-1995, Serb forces became increasingly assertive, culminating in their conquest of Srebrenica in the largest single post–World War II European massacre. Soon afterward, NATO air intervention and a Bosniac-Croat offensive ended the fighting and culminated in the US-led negotiations in Dayton, Ohio, in November 1995. The most respected, though still contentious, estimate holds that just over 97,100 people died in the conflict.[29]

The US-led negotiations in Dayton resulted in peace accords that created a Bosnia that largely recognized the "facts" created on the ground by the war. Dayton Bosnia consists of an unwieldy configuration of two entities: Republika Srpska (RS; 49 percent) and the Bosniac-Croat Federation (51 percent), each with its own police and army. The RS is relatively centralized, while the federation is composed of ten cantons with substantial autonomy. Two cantons are explicitly mixed, three are dominated by Croats, and five are dominated by Bosniacs. A large NATO military implementation force and complex civilian intervention began in early 1996, and its work is continued by a considerably smaller multinational force led by the European Union.[30] Under the authority of the fifty-five-member Peace Implementation Council (PIC), the High Representative for Bosnia and Herzegovina has overseen efforts to implement the Dayton Peace Accords by the United Nations, the European Union, the OSCE, the World Bank, and a host of nongovernmental organizations. The High Representative won extraordinary powers at a meeting of the Peace Implementation Committee in Bonn in December 1997, which has enabled him to override Bosnian institutions to pass legislation and remove domestic officials from office. Since 2006, the PIC has aspired to close the Office of the High Representative in an effort to stand Bosnian institutions on their own feet to "take responsibility for the peace process and the problems that the country faces," but the failure to settle all of the war's outstanding issues has not permitted this to take place.[31]

KOSOVO

Kosovo has long been an apple of discord between Serbs and Albanians. It served both as the center of the medieval Serbian state and as the birthplace of the modern Albanian national movement in the nineteenth century. In the period immediately after World War II, the Serbian-dominated secret police imposed a harsh anti-Albanian order in Kosovo; in the 1950s the situation was so bad that many Albanians declared themselves Turks and emigrated to Turkey. The pendulum swung in the other direction after the fall of secret police chief Aleksandar Ranković in 1966; by 1974, Kosovo had become almost an equal member of the federation, and Albanians were the largest ethnic group in the province. But beginning with demonstrations in 1981, the pendulum again began swinging back against Albanian interests. Between 1988 and 1990, the Serbian government took steps to limit Kosovo's autonomy. It forced the province's two top leaders to resign; forced the federal assembly to adopt amendments reducing the province's autonomy; suppressed the provincial assembly and the Executive Council; terminated Albanian-language instruction in the schools; caused well over one hundred thousand Kosovar Albanians to lose their jobs in the administrative, education, and health sectors; and changed street names in the capital, Pristina, to Serbian ones. These measures led to large-scale emigration from

Photo 17.1.   Signing of the Dayton Peace Accords. Leaders of six other nations look on as the presidents of Serbia, Croatia, and Bosnia sign the Peace Accords at the Elysée Palace. (Peter Turnley/Corbis)

Kosovo and were accompanied by official efforts to resettle Serbs (including refugees from Croatia) there.[32]

In response to these developments, a peaceful movement for autonomy and then for independence developed, headed by the Democratic League of Kosovo (LDK) under the leadership of Ibrahim Rugova. In parallel elections, the LDK won the broad support of Albanians in Kosovo. It established a parallel administration in education and health care that was widely used and supported by Albanians. However, Rugova did not succeed in winning a place at any international negotiating table beyond that of observer, partly because international negotiators viewed Milošević as essential to ending other conflicts. This failure created the conditions for a more militant phase of the national movement when the Kosovo Liberation Army (KLA) took the initiative in support of independence for Kosovo. Beginning with violent assaults against Serbian police stations in December 1997, the KLA began more sustained operations, which elicited increasingly harsh responses from Serbian forces. International diplomatic efforts to establish an OSCE Verification Mission in the autumn of 1998 did not succeed in deterring further violence. The failure of the Rambouillet negotiations in France in early 1999 led to a seventy-seven-day NATO air campaign against Serbia and Serb positions in Kosovo and to more intense ethnic cleansing of Albanians from Kosovo. The campaign ended with a Military-Technical Agreement between the International Security Force and the governments of the Federal Republic of Yugoslavia and Serbia on June 9 and with UN Security Council Resolution 1244 on June 10, which created an interim administration for Kosovo meant to provide a framework for a political settlement of the crisis.

From June 1999 through February 2008, the UN Mission in Kosovo cooperated with newly evolving domestic institutions and the NATO-led Kosovo Force to oversee the establishment of political and administrative institutions in Kosovo. From the initial establishment of the Joint Interim Administrative Structure in late 1999 through the passage of a constitutional framework in mid-2001, elections to local government in October 2000, and creation of the Assembly of Kosovo in November 2001, the United Nations oversaw efforts to establish security and judicial institutions, administration, and services and to regulate economic activity and trade. Beginning in November 2005, former president of Finland Martti Ahtisaari led negotiations among all relevant stakeholders that led to the Final Comprehensive Proposal for a Kosovo Status Settlement in March 2007 as a basis for negotiations among the political leaderships in Serbia and Kosovo.

The parties failed to reach an agreement over Kosovo's future status. At minimum, it was believed, some leaders of the Serbian government sought to partition Kosovo so that several northern municipalities, including industrially developed Mitrovica, would remain part of Serbia. Kosovar Albanian leaders have insisted that Kosovo retain its prewar administrative borders. Consequently, on February 17, 2008, the Kosovo Assembly declared Kosovo "an independent and sovereign state" that would "be a democratic, secular and multiethnic republic, guided by the principles of non-discrimination and equal protection under the law."[33] Following a period of "supervised independence" guided by the International Civilian Office that ended in September 2012, a substantial international presence remains in Kosovo, including the European rule of law mission called EULEX, the Kosovo Force, and a number of other multilateral aid missions and influential bilateral diplomatic missions. By late 2013, well over ninety governments have recognized Kosovo's independence, but this number excludes important powers such as Russia and China and European governments such as Spain, Slovakia, and Romania. This partially reflects the diplomatic efforts of the Serbian government, which formally objected to Kosovo's independence before the International Court of Justice.[34] The EU's success in facilitating a political dialogue between the governments of Serbia and Kosovo leveraged the desire of both governments for EU accession. In spring 2013, Serbian prime minister Ivica Dačić and Kosovo prime minister Hashim Thaqi concluded two years of meetings with an agreement and implementation plan to establish an association of Kosovo Serb municipalities, to integrate Serbian police and judicial structures into Kosovo, and to prepare for local elections.[35]

MACEDONIA

The enduring sources of the "Macedonian question," including Bulgarian, Greek, and Serbian claims to the region, have not figured into the ethnic conflict between Macedonians and Albanians in the period since 1990.[36] Albanians constitute 25 percent of the population of Macedonia and inhabit the area in the northwest bordering on Kosovo and Albania and in the capital, Skopje.[37] The government of Greece has consistently "objected to Macedonia's 'appropriation' of a name and symbols it deem[s] exclusively Hellenic since 1990," has obstructed Macedonian accession to European institutions, and has accepted its UN membership as the "Former Yugoslav Republic of Macedonia."[38] A "policy of half-hearted, half-reluctant ethnic cohabitation" in a series of multiethnic coalition governments since the early 1990s helped maintain a fragile peace but did not provide a basis for integrating the two groups into a common community.[39] Nor did the international presence of the UN Preventive Deployment Force, the European Community, or the OSCE in the mid-1990s lead to political integration. These delaying actions led to a series of skirmishes in 2001 in northwestern Macedonia between Albanian guerillas supported by Kosovar irregulars and Macedonian forces. After several months, international diplomats brokered the Ohrid Agreement, which provides for constitutional amendments and reforms to improve the status of Albanians while maintaining the unity of the Macedonian state. NATO briefly deployed in Macedonia in order to collect weapons, and an OSCE mission remains in place.

MONTENEGRO

The declaration of Montenegrin independence on June 3, 2006, was another significant act in the post-Yugoslav drama of succession. Through 1996, the Montenegrin government largely supported Yugoslav war aims, and Montenegrin soldiers actively participated in the siege of Dubrovnik and surrounding areas in October 1991. In 1992, Montenegro joined Serbia in a truncated Federal Republic of Yugoslavia, which on February 4, 2004, devolved into the State Union of Serbia and Montenegro; on May 21, 2006, Montenegro won full independence in a referendum, with a relatively narrow vote of 55.5 percent of voters supporting independence and 44.5 percent opposing. This was the culmination of a process of alienation between Serbia and Montenegro and an internal divide in Montenegro over relations with Serbia that began in 1991.[40] Elections in 1997 and 1998 put a reform wing of the former League of Communists led by Milo Djukanovic firmly in power. And with the adoption of the German mark as the parallel currency and abolishing of visas for foreigners in 1999, the Montenegrin government staked out its future claim to independence. The Montenegrin government's most dramatic departure from Serbian policy has been its recognition of Kosovo's independence in October 2008. In June 2012 the European Council of the EU endorsed the opening of accession negotiations with the Montenegrin government.

In sum, the Socialist Federal Republic of Yugoslavia violently dissolved into seven small countries following the first democratic elections in 1990, and the aftershocks of this dissolution have not yet fully ended. A mid-size country of 21 million citizens had been subdivided into seven countries with populations ranging from 625,000 to just over 7 million citizens. The failure of the international community to act in a timely fashion in the late 1980s and early 1990s contributed to the uncertainty that permitted stronger and more aggressive forces to gain strength and undermined efforts to move toward peace and the construction of normal political systems. The wars of Yugoslav succession have made the transition from socialism in the countries of former Yugoslavia significantly more complicated than transitions in other parts of Central and Eastern Europe. The influence of the wars becomes clearer when we survey domestic developments, including elite transformation, party politics, the development of civil society, attitudes toward politics, and economic development and policies in the successor states.

Political Transitions and Political Institutions

The chaotic political transition and the wars of Yugoslav succession have left a deep imprint on the patterns of elite transformation in the successor states. Old and new leaderships easily blended together. Former communists, such as Serbian president Milošević and Croatian president Tudjman became nationalist leaders in the new regimes, and former SFRY finance minister and president of the National Assembly Kiro Gligorov became the first president of Macedonia and pursued a moderate vision. Many former democratic dissidents also became nationalist leaders and ideologues. Some former nationalists became liberal, democratic human rights advocates. Returning political émigrés blended effectively with former communists in nationalist parties. Among the older generation, former communists were able to work easily with former nationalist "enemies." Younger, able, and politically nimble politicians and administrators rose quickly to prominence in all parties and states. A careful examination of elite transformation in Croatia, Serbia, Bosnia-Herzegovina, and Kosovo would certainly show how nationalist leaders employed the wars to deepen their hold on power and expand political machines that limited significant interparty electoral competition. The wars thus delayed political democratization and economic liberalization.

The international community also contributed to this delay. The command systems that were established during the wars facilitated alliances between external agencies and the warring parties at the expense of the citizens for whom the assistance was intended. For example, in Bosnia-Herzegovina, the warring parties took a cut of all humanitarian aid intended for civilians as part of their war effort.[41] After peace agreements, "peace-building" international agencies tacitly helped to buttress the authority of corrupt ethnic leaders and helped to legitimate efforts to resist democratization simply by dealing primarily with them. The peace accords in Kosovo and Bosnia-Herzegovina did not settle disputes about sovereignty or provide a road map to stable and democratic institutions. The failure to resolve open issues peacefully—for example, the status of Kosovo, the capture of indicted war criminals, the return of refugees and displaced persons, and the relationship between Republika Srpska and Serbia—ensured that recalcitrant leaders would find little reason to commit to the implementation of the peace accords. Finally, many important domestic functions were taken over by international officials from the United Nations, OSCE, Office of the High Representative, and EU. These often inexperienced officials generally spoke none of the languages and knew little about the region. As a result, their actions have often made the transition even more difficult.

By 2006, all former Yugoslav republics had adopted proportional representation (PR) electoral systems, and all but Bosnia and Kosovo in practice could be described as parliamentary democracies. However, most did not start the postcommunist period that way. Domestic and international forces helped alter the distribution of power between the president and the parliament, as well as the electoral systems of the former Yugoslav states. For example, as democratic groups gained strength in Croatia and Serbia, they weakened their countries' presidencies, by building up and increasing the independence of nonpresidential political institutions. In Croatia, they also jettisoned the single-member district system and adopted the more inclusive and representative PR system.

Institutional engineering was the most elaborate in those regions of former Yugoslavia that experienced significant international intervention. There, international diplomats compelled the adoption of sophisticated power-sharing arrangements that they hoped would ensure members of all ethnic groups a stake in the postconflict political systems. At the end of war in Bosnia, international institutional designers drafted a constitution as Annex IV in the Dayton Accords, which featured complex and rigid multilayered political institutions that enshrined ethnic power sharing in the collective presidency as well as in most other political and administrative institutions. Bosnia's weak national-level government and strong regional (entity and canton) governments have enabled ethnically exclusive parties to dominate public life. International engineers induced the adoption of PR systems in Macedonia and Kosovo, as well as the redrawing of electoral district lines in Macedonia, to improve the chances of candidates from minorities and small parties. In addition to drafting Bosnia's elaborate rules for representation of all major ethnicities, international officials compelled Kosovo to reserve parliamentary seats for minorities. The pull of the EU encouraged dedicated seats for minorities in Montenegro and Slovenia, though the latter reserves seats only for its indigenous minorities. Germany helped convince Croatia also to reserve seats for minorities. In addition, Croatia reserved seats for representatives chosen by the Croatian diaspora.[42] Electoral engineers also added gender quotas in Macedonia, Bosnia, and Kosovo to ensure the representation of women in political offices. Despite all the attention to crafting political institutions in Bosnia and Kosovo, these domestic institutions currently share power with unelected international officials who exercise executive authority.

Elections and Political Parties

The countries of former Yugoslavia have often been left out of the bulk of comparative literature on political competition in the postcommunist region. Yet these countries share characteristics of their Central and East European neighbors, including weak party systems, a rather amorphous ideological spectrum, party fragmentation, inconsistent commitment to programs, and problems with internal party democracy.[43] Former Yugoslav governments are riddled with personalistic parties with few deep roots in their communities, whose members lack strong relationships with constituents and rely primarily on strong patronage networks. Taken together with the frequent formation of new parties and disappearance of other parties, these characteristics have significantly undermined their capacity to aggregate interests effectively. Bosnia and Macedonia have been subjected to intensive international involvement in domestic politics and also feature entrenched ethnic party systems. Valerie Bunce suggests that the victory of a liberal, anticommunist opposition in the first multiparty election permits a decisive break with the authoritarian past and a launching of a liberal program. In contrast, the victory of an ethnically exclusive opposition can obviate democratization and lead to challenges to state boundaries.[44] Communist parties can also adopt nationalist agendas in order to maintain their hold on power.

By these criteria, only Slovenia experienced a relatively smooth democratic transition and process of state formation in its first post-Yugoslav election, the founding parliamentary election. The noncommunist coalition Democratic Opposition of Slovenia (DEMOS) won. The leader of the reformed Communist Party won the presidency.

This new government enacted pluralist and market reforms and declared Slovenia's independence from Yugoslavia. After the movement-based DEMOS disintegrated, the fragmented party system consolidated into four strong parties: the left-oriented Social Democrat Party, the moderate-left Liberal Democracy of Slovenia, the center-right Slovenian Democratic Party, and the Christian Democratic Party. Broad agreement among Slovenia's elite that their future was tied to European and Euro-Atlantic institutions helped the country achieve early membership in the EU and NATO. In addition, the absence of substantial minorities allowed Slovenia's significant illiberal forces to remain relatively harmless during its march into Europe.[45] The heavy impact of the 2008 global recession, 2011 Eurozone crisis, and domestic austerity policies generated conditions for a vote of no confidence in September 2011, the formation of two new political parties, and the holding of the first early elections in the postcommunist period in December 2011. These developments have exposed the weaknesses in Slovenian governance.[46]

By contrast, the first post-Yugoslav elections in Croatia and Serbia enabled nationalist forces to advance narrow ethnic agendas and undermine democratization with wars in Croatia and Bosnia-Herzegovina. Only at the end of these conflicts could opposition coalitions overcome their own bickering to win elections in second transitions and initiate reform programs that contributed to more normal political competition, albeit within the weak party systems described above.

In Serbia, Milošević weathered several waves of antiregime demonstrations in the 1990s and intraparty conflict and remade the League of Communists of Serbia into an authoritarian nationalist party with its own satellite, the United Yugoslav Left, headed by Milošević's wife, Mirjana Marković. In the founding election in 1990, his Socialist Party of Serbia (SPS) ensured that it would dominate the parliament. The SPS's program appealed to socialist conformists as well as to Serbs who had criticized Tito's "weakening of Serb interests" in Yugoslavia in the 1980s.[47] The party was strongest outside Belgrade and in the Serbian heartland. Milošević used existing structures to retain power, acquire wealth, distribute patronage to his family and allies among his criminalized support structure,[48] and manage "Serb" territories outside Serbia. War and a monopoly over politics, effective propaganda through government-directed media, and control of the security forces allowed Milošević to demobilize political opposition and eliminate political alternatives.[49]

With the end of the war over Kosovo, the SPS could no longer label oppositionists as traitors. Ordinary Serbs increasingly attributed their poverty to the SPS's poor governance. Milošević's supporters among the criminal class had become independent of his patronage. The leaders of the liberal opposition finally set aside personal antagonism to unite, and the youth organization Otpor (Resistance) effectively led civic mobilization. These forces overturned Milošević's plans to rig the 2000 presidential elections and helped secure the victory of Vojislav Koštunica, who was supported by an eighteen-party opposition coalition, the Democratic Opposition of Serbia (DOS). The DOS coalition convincingly won the December 2000 parliamentary elections, selecting the Democratic Party's (DS) Zoran Djindjić as prime minister. However, differences between Koštunica and Djindjić over a bargaining strategy with the West on reform led to the disintegration of the coalition. Not long thereafter, war profiteers assassinated Djindjić in response to his plans to reform the security sector and prospects for closer cooperation with the war crimes tribunal in The Hague.

Photo 17.2.   Funeral procession for Serbian prime minister Zoran Djindjić, who was assassinated by Serbian radicals in 2003. Djindjić had made many enemies for his pro-Western stance, reformist economic policies, and clampdown on organized crime. He also had Slobodan Milošević arrested and handed over to the International Criminal Tribunal for the Former Yugoslavia at The Hague. (Website of the Serbian Government, http://www.srbija.gov.rs)

In the 2003 and 2007 parliamentary elections, Vojislav Šešelj's extremist Serb Radical Party (SRS) received more votes than any other party, gaining popular support from dissatisfaction with incumbents, unpopular sacrifices connected to economic reform, and resentment of Western demands for closer Serbian cooperation with the ICTY and for the relinquishment of Kosovo. However, pressure from the West led Koštunica to form center-right coalitions after both elections that denied the SRS a formal role.[50] But SRS influence was felt in the National Assembly's quickly and nontransparently drafted constitution that was unanimously adopted in September 2006. Prime Minister Koštunica struggled to balance demands within his broad coalition: the government's liberal partners, G17 Plus, and President Boris Tadić of the DS pushed for the reforms needed to resume talks with the EU on a stabilization and association agreement (SAA), while their powerful and populist supporters remained resentful of EU pressure on Serbia. With the formation of a government and closer cooperation with the ICTY in capturing high-profile indictees, the EU resumed SAA talks with Belgrade in June 2007.

New elections were held within a year. In the first presidential elections since the dissolution of Serbia's state union with Montenegro, President Tadić narrowly won reelection in January 2008 over SRS candidate Tomislav Nikolić. In May 2008 parliamentary elections, the DS-led For a European Serbia group narrowly won the election and formed a coalition government with DS, G17 Plus, the leftist coalition led by the SPS—for the first time since 2000—and parties of national minorities: Hungarians, Bosniacs, and Albanians. Under its current leader, Ivica Dačić, the SPS has become a party with European aspirations that has been exploring membership in the Socialist International and whose cadres are among the most practical in Serbian public life.

In September 2008, because of differences with ICTY-indicted leader Vojislav Šešelj over EU membership, Tomislav Nikolić led a bloc of twenty members of parliament out of the SRS to form the considerably more moderate Serbian Progressive Party (SNS). The SNS quickly established its credibility in opposition to the government dominated by President Tadić by appealing to Serbs in small towns outside the capital and reaching out to Serbia's key international partners abroad. This strategy paid off in the elections held in spring 2012. Nikolić defeated President Tadić in the second round of voting, and the SNS's Let's Get Serbia Moving coalition defeated the DS's Choice for a Better Life coalition in parliamentary elections, then formed a coalition with Dačić's SPS, which placed third in the voting. However, as of late 2013, formerly important smaller parties, such as the Liberal Democratic Party, G17 Plus, and Democratic Party of Serbia are apparently in eclipse.

It was noteworthy that the leading candidates and parties in the 2012 presidential and parliamentary elections, for the first time in the postcommunist period, all pledged to support Serbia's integration into the EU.[51] Although the Serbian government has not committed to formal recognition of the independence of Kosovo, the European Commission concluded that Serbia had made progress in fulfilling the political criteria and conditions for an SAA, and the European Council granted Serbia candidate country status in March 2012. Aside from its progress in developing a market economy and parliamentary democracy, the report noted the Serbian government's cooperation with the ICTY and a number of agreements with the government of Kosovo as part of its process of dialogue.[52]

In Croatia, the nationalist movement was led by the Croatian Democratic Union (HDZ) under the leadership of former Partisan general and later political dissident Franjo Tudjman with substantial support from political émigrés. The HDZ won power in 1990 on the basis of its anticommunist expression of Croatian identity. It was viewed as the most serious alternative to the atheistic socialism of the ex-communists or the Party of Democratic Change (later renamed the Social Democratic Party [SDP]).[53] A majoritarian electoral system turned the HDZ's 46 percent of the popular vote into 67.5 percent of the seats in parliament. The losing Coalition of National Accord, composed of former communists and liberals, fragmented and formed a series of smaller parties. A majority of Serb SDP members chose to leave the evolving Croatian SDP. Regional parties in Istria have demonstrated considerable staying power. The war began in 1990 and 1991 with the refusal of the Serb Democratic Party (SDS) leadership to join the broad governing compact led by HDZ in 1990, which strengthened exclusivist tendencies within the HDZ as the most serious defender of Croatia against Serb aggressors. As long as Serbs occupied Croatian territory, Tudjman's HDZ was able to monopolize power in Croatia. It supported moderate Serb groups in Croatia in a demonstration of political openness, but its monopoly of power enabled the HDZ political and administrative elite to engage in corrupt practices.

With the return of all Serb-held territory and changes in the electoral laws, the diverse opposition to the HDZ made significant electoral gains on platforms of good governance and political change. After President Tudjman's death in the run-up to elections in early 2000, a moderate six-party opposition coalition headed by the SDP won control of parliament on a campaign that included accession to the EU. Its governing program included cutting the purse strings of the hard-line HDZ in Bosnia and cooperation with the ICTY. However, a governing coalition whose connecting bond lay mainly in beating the HDZ in power would not prove authoritative itself. Its inability to improve economic performance and its cooperation with The Hague's efforts to capture Croatian generals for trial led to its defeat in elections in 2004 by a more compact and reformed version of the HDZ. Following its loss of power in 2000, the HDZ had splintered and adapted its own electoral appeal to pursue integration into the EU. Its increased cooperation with the ICTY in 2006 helped convince EU leaders to begin talks on accession. The HDZ won another close election in late 2007 and formed a government with support from a broad range of parties, including those representing national minorities. It continued support of EU norms by appointing one deputy prime minister from the Independent Democratic Serbian Party (SDSS), committing to providing proportional Serb presence in public institutions, and encouraging the return of Serbian refugees to Croatia.[54] However, the HDZ government proved fragile: Prime Minister Ivo Sanader resigned under a cloud in July 2009 in favor of Jadranka Kosor, the first woman to serve as prime minister in Croatia since its independence in 1990.[55] Sanader was sentenced to ten years in prison for accepting bribes in 2011 and is the highest official to serve time for corruption in Central and Eastern Europe since 1990. This assuaged EU fears that Croatia would ignore corruption and enabled the HDZ to reconfigure itself over the medium term.

Kosor's government was short-lived. In January 2010, SDP candidate Ivo Josipovic was elected as the third president of Croatia since 1990. The SDP-led Kukuruku (Cock-a-Doodle-Do) coalition claimed victory over the HDZ-led coalition with 80 of the 151 seats in the Sabor and with the support of the eight seats set aside for ethnic minorities. Kukuruku's campaign focused on corruption scandals, high unemployment, and the poor economic performance of the previous HDZ government. Following this defeat, HDZ leadership passed from Kosor to Tomislav Karamarko, the former minister of the interior and director of security and intelligence, who appeared to be leading a resurgent party at the end of 2013.

Croatia joined the EU formally on July 1, 2013. On one hand, Brussels did not greet this accession with the same fanfare displayed at the 2004 induction of eight former socialist states. On the other hand, the Croatian public appears unenthusiastic about the EU: less than 21 percent of Croatian voters participated in the July 1 elections to the European Parliament won by the opposition HDZ. In elections held on May 25, 2014, a turnout of 25 percent of Croatian voters elected to the European Parliament six from the HDZ coalition, four from the Kukuruku coalition, and one from the Croatian Sustainable Development Party. Further, the EU threatened, in the fall of 2013, to sanction Croatia for passing a law three days before joining the EU that limits the execution of European arrest warrants to crimes committed after August 2002.[56]

Leaders in Bosnia-Herzegovina and Macedonia sensed the impending danger that the disintegration of Yugoslavia could lead to the dissolution of their own republics, and they attempted to forge compromises among competing political forces in their areas to respond to the designs of their more powerful and covetous neighbors. Electoral rules, social structure, and anticommunist sentiment worked to establish ethnic party systems.

Only the rejection of their compromise proposals in negotiations over Yugoslavia's future led Macedonian and Bosnian leaders to pursue independence. In both countries, external interventions drastically rewrote domestic political rules.

A 1990 court decision striking down Bosnia's ban on ethnic parties and an electoral rule mandating that election results not deviate more than 15 percent from the ethnic distribution in the census contributed to the victory of the ethnically based Muslim Party of Democratic Action (SDA) and Bosnian branches of the HDZ and SDS in the founding elections. During the campaign, all three party leaders committed to protecting ethnic interests and to interethnic cooperation.[57] Although twice jailed in socialist Yugoslavia (in 1946 and 1983) for Islamic activities, SDA leader and president of Bosnia-Herzegovina Alija Izetbegović continued Yugoslavia's socialist practice that Bosnia is a state of three constituent peoples and others, the latter representing a residual category for those citizens not declaring themselves Bosniac, Serb, or Croat. However, interparty cooperation deteriorated over the formula for the ethnic distribution of positions within the government administration. A majority of Bosnian citizens supported the referendum on independence, although Serbs boycotted the vote, just as they did in Croatia. Leaders in Serbia and Croatia egged on, radicalized, and armed their coethnic parties in Bosnia on the pretext that the republic was dominated by radical Muslims.

Ethnic cleansing, international intervention, and institutional engineering created a break with the Yugoslav tradition of brotherhood and unity. The Dayton Accords included an unwieldy constitution with ineffective state institutions that easily became dominated by the ethnically based SDA, HDZ, and SDS in the name of institutionalizing power sharing.[58] Electoralism—or the idea that holding elections will jump-start the democratic process—has heightened interethnic tensions in Bosnia.[59] Since ethnically based parties rarely win votes from other groups, party leaders have strong incentives to make radical appeals to ensure greater turnout of their own group.[60] Nonetheless, nationalists won increasingly narrow victories until the 2000 elections, when international officials convinced diverse social democratic forces to unite behind the Social Democratic Party–led Coalition for Change. The coalition's efforts at comprehensive reform failed due to internal bickering and opposition from exclusivist groups forged during the wars. The leading parties among the Bosniac, Croat, and Serb electorates in the mid-2000s reaffirmed their divergent objectives, which have strengthened the political deadlock in national-level politics and scuttled domestic initiatives in late 2008 and those of EU-US officials in October 2009 for constitutional changes that would both create a functional state and advance Bosnia's accession to the EU.

In the federation, the Party for Bosnia-Herzegovina has advocated for a more unified Bosnian state and has challenged the Republika Srpska's right to exist. Croat parties continue to advocate for increased Croatian collective rights. An expert group supported by the US embassy in spring 2013 formulated 188 recommendations to reconfigure the cumbersome federation structure. Among other recommendations, they advocated replacing the federation president and two vice presidents with the existing parliamentary presidency to reduce the number of deputies and lower salaries.[61] The cool reactions of major political leaders appear to emerge from their fear of damaging patronage networks.

Since 2006, the Republika Srpska's governing Party of Independent Social Democrats has acknowledged its lack of interest in a functioning central government and sought to enhance the RS's already substantial autonomy in politics, economy, and security, even explicitly advocating a referendum on secession. Following the 2010 parliamentary elections, it took sixteen months for the SDP to form a central government. In 2012, the EU declared that Bosnia's progress on the EU agenda had stalled because of failure to agree on functional state institutions, to amend the constitution to meet the European Court of Human Rights' ruling that individuals other than Bosniacs, Serbs, or Croats can run for the presidency and House of Peoples, and to strengthen the justice sector.[62]

International intervention has generally failed to build effective and self-sustaining domestic political institutions in Bosnia, and the EU's significant expenditure of resources has not deepened democratic reform.[63] Nor have international officials pursued a consistent strategy: they failed to act against ethnic extremists in the period just after Dayton and then significantly employed executive powers to override Bosnian institutions to pass legislation and remove domestic officials. In the period from December 1997 through September 2013, the High Representative employed this tool 923 times, a rate of almost five decisions per month. In the period from 1999 through 2005, the High Representative made 728 decisions at a rate of almost nine decisions per month.[64] International officials constrained this employment of executive authority after 2006 in response to internal disagreements within the Peace Implementation Council, the diminishing utility of international executive authority, and increasing calls for giving real authority to Bosnian officials. The self-interested policies of powerful domestic leaders and fragmentation of international approaches in Bosnia have revived pessimism over Bosnia's very viability and some fears that violence might follow the possible withdrawal of international forces from Bosnia.[65]

In Macedonia, nationalists and reformed communists (soon to form the Social Democratic Union of Macedonia [SDSM]) split the vote during the founding elections. Although the nationalist Internal Macedonian Revolutionary Organization (later called the VMRO-DPMNE) won the most parliamentary seats in 1990, its government fell in a vote of no confidence in 1991. The reformed communists then formed a four-party coalition government that included the Albanian party. The party's leader, Kiro Gligorov, was elected president by the parliament and served as a bridge between the communist past and pluralist future. The coalition supported interethnic cooperation by including four Albanian cabinet ministers in the government.[66]

All coalition governments—including those led by right-of-center VMRO-DPMNE—have been multiethnic. External pressure has enhanced multiethnic cooperation in Macedonia, as it has always ensured a European, US, or UN commitment to support some sort of power-sharing agreement. The Ohrid Framework Agreement, which ended the fighting in 2001, provided Macedonians with strong incentives to form an inclusive government and adopt ethnic power-sharing arrangements—albeit far less rigid ones than in Bosnia—in the constitution. Macedonia's first election following the violence resulted in a multiethnic coalition government led by the SDSM and other parties most committed to the peace agreement. Subsequent national-level elections have been won by a more centrist VMRO-DPMNE that has continued the SDSM-initiated reforms required for EU accession and NATO membership and the tradition of multiethnic governments. However, problems emerged over forming the 2008 multiethnic governing coalition, as the victorious VMRO-DPMNE initially reached out to its traditional coalition partner among the Albanians, the Democratic Party of Albanians, although it had won fewer votes than its rival Democratic Union for Integration (DUI). DUI successfully advocated for inclusion in the coalition government supported by European and American leaders. While Western organizations and leaders demanded a rerun of the 2008 elections in a number of hotly competitive Albanian-dominated municipalities where security services failed to prevent violence, they lauded peaceful presidential and municipal elections held in 2009 as a significant step forward toward EU membership.

Macedonia also faces serious problems with organized crime, ethnic separation, corruption, and economic development that cannot be so nimbly resolved. Greece scuttled Macedonia's membership bid for NATO in 2008 and is moving to do the same for its EU candidacy. With the stalled EU accession process and the increasing length of the VMRO-DPMNE's hold on power (it and DUI also won the 2011 and 2014 elections) have come increasing accusations of institutionalized corruption. The 2011 early elections were pushed by the SDSM's boycott of participation in the parliament. Small opposition parties joined the boycott that protested what SDSM characterized as the "undemocratic rule" of the governing coalition following arrests of executives from the largest independent television station, A1 TV. The 2011 elections were held under a controversial new electoral law pushed through by VMRO-DPMNE that allowed the Macedonian diaspora to vote for the first time for 3 of the 123 seats in parliament. The 2014 elections for both president and the parliament were criticized by the OSCE monitoring mission for failing to uphold international obligations for democratic elections due to inadequate separation between party and state activities.[67] Boycotts by opposition parties have continued, and it is not unusual for international mediators to spend weeks conducting "shuttle diplomacy" to convince the opposition and government parties to agree to keep the parliament in operation. These troubling developments reflect the recent backtracking on democratic reform.

Analyses of the accomplishments of the Ohrid Framework Agreement have been mixed, though significantly more positive than analyses of the Dayton Accords in Bosnia. One scholar has argued that it has "been able to remove some of the obvious inequalities of the system" and now meaningfully includes Albanians in the state. Yet Ohrid has been "unable to address the systemic problems," which include a deeply ethnically divided political system, segregationist practices in education, party patronage in the public sector, and neglect of smaller minorities.[68] The European Commission has nonetheless recommended several times that the European Council move Macedonia to the next stage in the accession process by opening negotiations, which it believes would consolidate the sustainability of reforms and create conditions conducive to finding a solution to the dispute between Greece and Macedonia over rights to the name "Macedonia."[69]

In Montenegro and Kosovo, personalistic parties remain firmly entrenched in power. The Democratic Party of Socialists (DPS) has dominated Montenegrin politics and government since it emerged from the League of Communists in 1991, and Milo Djukanovic has led the party since 1997 on a platform of increasing autonomy from a Serbian-dominated Yugoslavia. Djukanovic has served as president or prime minister with short breaks from 2006 to 2008 and 2010 to 2012. In elections in 2012, the DPS fell short of an absolute majority and formed a multiethnic coalition government with smaller parties, and DPS president Filip Vujanovic was reelected in April 2013 to serve his third term in office.

Photo 17.3. July 2006 rally in Macedonia held by the then ruling coalition led by the Social Democratic Alliance of Macedonia during the parliamentary elections campaign. (Paula Pickering)

With the start of EU accession negotiations in 2012, the Montenegrin government faces significant challenges in addressing the full menu of issues in the *acquis communautaire*.[70]

Kosovo's public life also remains dominated by wartime personalities. Since 2001, the late president Ibrahim Rugova's Democratic League of Kosovo (LDK) has steadily lost ground to parties that emerged from the Kosovo Liberation Army, including Prime Minister Hashim Thaqi's Democratic Party (PDK) and Ramush Haradinaj's Alliance for the Future of Kosovo (AAK). The PDK had succeeded in establishing its credibility throughout Kosovo while pursuing an agenda of European integration that includes negotiations with the government of Serbia and forming a governing coalition with minority parties even though it suffers from internal division. However, although the PDK won the most votes in elections held in June 2014, it appears, at this writing in August 2014, that the LDK will form a broad coalition with the AAK, minority parties, and others to form a government that will continue with a similar agenda. Kosovo's government must systematically address basic issues related to rule of law, corruption, organized crime, minority rights, and economic and political reform to take steps toward an SAA. Further, acquittals in The Hague of senior political figures in the leading parties suggests that the political system could benefit by opening up to newer groups, such as Self-Determination, in order to demonstrate domestically and externally a commitment to strengthening the stable, democratic, and normal state desired by ordinary citizens of Kosovo.[71]

In sum, there is uneven progress in the development and institutionalization of party systems across former Yugoslavia. In Slovenia and Croatia, movement parties that won the founding elections have dissipated and given way to party systems with solid conservative and social democratic parties and sets of parties with amorphous programs somewhere in the middle. The inclusion of minority parties in governing coalitions in Croatia, Macedonia, Serbia, and Kosovo is a positive sign, albeit one that partly comes from EU pressure, that enables right-center parties to squeeze moderate leftist parties, and that can allow these catchall coalition parties to divide the spoils. Bosnia-Herzegovina's rigid power sharing further entrenches its ethnic party system and encourages dysfunctional governance. The unfinished character of the second transitions means that these countries' political parties have not completely outgrown the zero-sum, constitutional dilemmas or moved more fully into interest-driven politics. Enduring regional parties, as well as smaller parties in these countries, may have little hope of winning elections, but they can facilitate the formation of coalitions in support of democratic reform. The durability of these smaller parties might demonstrate that, in the proper circumstances, the post-Yugoslav party systems can resemble those of more settled political systems that lack the daily drama and legacies of crisis and war.

Transitional Justice

The establishment of rule of law and justice systems has been significantly impeded by the wars and extended political transitions in the Yugoslav successor states. To be sure, there has been ample external assistance for development of legal codes in accordance with international norms and practice; physical reconstruction of courts, prisons, and police services; and training in the full repertoire of policing, case management, and good judicial practice. International deployments focusing on police and the rule of law have provided substantial numbers of international professionals to assist the governments of Bosnia-Herzegovina, Kosovo, and Macedonia in the relatively early stages of legal system development, especially in areas of interethnic and domestic war crimes. The governments of Croatia, Macedonia, Montenegro, and Serbia have received less assistance, and international officials have not had any executive authority in these states. Overall, this assistance has led to progress in formally developing legal systems and codes that are in accordance with international norms, although domestic practice often falls short.

There has been progress in addressing the grave crimes of the war. With some hesitation, the deepest and longest of which was exhibited by Serbia, all governments in the region have responded to external demands to cooperate with the ICTY. Domestic war crimes courts have been established in Croatia, Bosnia, and Kosovo, although these domestic courts have not always operated very effectively. The issue of war crimes remains highly divisive: amid routine commentary on the biased and political nature of the international court, governments in Croatia and Serbia have only reluctantly cooperated with the ICTY. Further, a number of relatively short sentences, deaths of prominent indictees during trial (e.g., Milošević), delayed acquittals, and reversals of convictions, as well as the clear conditionality of cooperation with the ICTY for accession to the EU—which has affected Serb, Croat, Bosniac, and Kosovar Albanian indictees—have strengthened a sense that the war crimes trials are not contributing to strengthening norms of rule of law and objectivity of the legal system. In addition, the contradiction between official compliance with the ICTY, on the one hand, and official support for the defense of coethnic indictees and lack of support for mechanisms (educational programs or truth commissions) that engage the region's populations in a serious discussion of responsibility for past crimes, on the other hand, hinders movement toward reconciliation.

There has also been some progress in high-profile corruption cases, as with former Croatian prime minister Sanader and several "tycoons" in Serbia. But domestic civil society organizations have pointed out that these high-profile cases have drawn attention to the more systematic corruption and sweetheart privatization deals from the 1990s for which few people have been held accountable and that these corrupt patronage systems remain intact.

It is also the case that minorities in all of these countries, including Slovenia, face a very uneven legal playing field in supporting their claims and winning protection and security. For example, the Slovene government views inhabitants from former Yugoslavia not as minorities but as "economic migrants" who have had difficulties in regularizing their status despite the fact many of them have long lived and worked in Slovenia.[72]

Civil Society

It is often held that voluntary organizations produce social capital that will strengthen democratization in the successor states. However, the actual impact of such organizations depends partly on the type of social capital they build and the rootedness of the organizations in local society. Advocacy organizations that link citizens to policy makers can help hold political leaders accountable. Those groups that disperse authority horizontally, rather than concentrate it, are best at cultivating the repeated interdependent interaction that builds interpersonal trust. Groups that look outward, beyond the interests of their own members toward benefiting the larger community, are better at solving broader social problems than those that focus only inward. Finally, those groups that link together people of different cultural backgrounds are better at helping integrate a diverse society than those that bring together and provide social support only to those of the same cultural background.[73]

The developments described in this chapter leave little doubt that many civil society organizations in the region are monoethnic. The many voluntary associations that focus on strengthening bonds within single ethnic groups contributed to conflict in Yugoslavia's multiethnic republics. For example, it is difficult to see how many of the religious organizations revived in the late 1980s could provide a basis for reconciliation and moderation when many religious leaders directly participated in exclusivist nationalist appeals.[74] Some monoethnic local organizations, which were linked to nationalist parties, crowded out a range of moderate groups that opposed violence.[75] Other organizations are inward looking, hierarchically structured, and willing to use violence to realize their exclusivist goals. These formerly included paramilitary groups such as Arkan's Tigers and Šešelj's Četniks in Serbia.[76] ICTY has indicted many leaders of such groups that display the "dark side" of social capital.

Some local, multiethnic organizations that grew out of the war produce social capital that bridges ethnic divisions. Medica Zenica, for example, is a voluntary organization formed by local women residents of all backgrounds in Zenica, Bosnia, to aid female victims of the war.[77] Other groups include displaced persons, veterans, and families of missing persons. Victims' groups in Bosnia and Kosovo can adopt different strategies: either to return as minorities to their homes in their places of origin or to rebuild new lives in areas where they are among the ethnic majority. Veterans associations, which are split along ethnic lines and are inward looking, resent their marginalization in the postconflict period and tend to support nationalist parties.[78]

Western agencies have generously supported nongovernmental agencies (NGOs) that produce "good" social capital that contributes to the democratization of postcommunist states, but they overlook NGOs that emerge from local traditions of informal mutual-help networks rooted in everyday life, such as in the neighborhood and the workplace.[79] From their own experiences, donors have favored NGOs that engage in advocacy—even where they have shallow roots in society—and whose formation is driven largely by donors' needs. A recent study of civil society in the Western Balkans found that civic organizations remain heavily dependent on foreign donors, with more than 50 percent of donations to social organizations in Kosovo coming from foreign donors, 35 percent of organizations in Bosnia admitting they depend wholly on foreign donors, and 75 percent of NGOs in Macedonia and in Serbia revealing that foreign donors are their main source of funding.[80] It is encouraging that leaders of advocacy groups, such as legal aid and human rights groups, are making progress in forming networks to monitor and influence government. For example, Sarajevo's Serb Civic Council cooperated with Bosniac and Croat opposition intellectual groups to ensure that Serbs, Croats, and Bosniacs were all legally constituent nations throughout Bosnia. In other examples, NGOs in Bosnia successfully lobbied for legislation providing for direct election of mayors, and NGOs in Serbia participated in developing the Law on Associations in Serbia. In general, however, NGOs tend to be sidelined in discussions of politically sensitive policies.[81] In diverse societies nationalist leaders tend to use conflict to discourage the formation of civic organizations that unite diverse peoples around common interests and thus help keep intercommunal peace.[82] More often, efforts to improve interethnic relations have been mounted by monoethnic groups committed to interethnic cooperation.

The long-term character of building tolerant civil societies in Yugoslavia's successor states is clearer to many local activists and some international implementers on the ground than to donor agencies that demand immediate results. Several studies concluded that many NGOs in southeastern Europe "have weak links with their communities" because of their orientation toward international donors.[83] Ordinary citizens remain disaffected and often view local NGOs as promoters of Western agendas and sources of support for opportunistic leaders. A nationally representative sample survey conducted in 2009 in Bosnia found that only 17.8 percent of the respondents reported participating in a nonparty organization.[84] In an example that fuels citizens' skepticism about NGOs, a 2013 investigative report on seven years of contracts awarded by Serbia's Ministry of Youth revealed that the party that controls the ministry awards the largest projects to organizations headed by fellow party members.[85] To be sure, some domestic activists have made progress in strengthening organizations that embrace civility, responsiveness, and democratic principles. And there are encouraging signs that a new generation of young, urban, highly educated, well-trained activists who played a role in the electoral revolutions or have worked with international NGOs is striving creatively and constructively to hold elected leaders accountable.[86] However, the successor states' civil societies remain dominated by organizations that promote narrow group interests rather than focusing on crosscutting problems, such as social integration or the political accountability of the government. International donors could be more successful in empowering domestic communities by learning to work in partnership with domestic groups that are well rooted in local communities and adopt agendas and timelines that reflect local needs and capacities.

Citizens and Politics

As in most postcommunist systems, the significant gap between elites and ordinary citizens that persists in most successor states is both a legacy of the one party system and a product of relatively weak party systems and corruption. The willingness of citizens to participate in politics has varied according to timing, political context, and economic situation. Voter turnout was high during the euphoria of the founding elections and then tapered off with the realization that the end of one-party rule would not solve problems with political responsiveness. Citizens also quickly discerned the self-serving behavior of political elites working in the new political institutions. In all countries, voter turnout for parliamentary elections declined from high rates in 1990 to stable but moderate rates two decades later, slipping from 84.5 percent in 1990 to 54.3 percent in 2011 in Croatia; from 71.5 percent in 1990 to 57.8 percent in 2012 for Serbia; from 80 percent in 1990 to 56.5 percent in 2010 in Bosnia; and from 78 percent in 1990 to 63.5 percent in 2011 in Macedonia.

Elections for the president of Serbia were invalidated three times when less than 50 percent of voters bothered to turn out in 2002 and 2003. Only amending the law allowed the elections to succeed. The heavy hand of the Office of the High Representative in Bosnia-Herzegovina has further depressed citizens' reported efficacy. Of those who did not vote in the last elections, 43 percent explained that they stayed home on election day because "Bosnia and Herzegovina's politicians cannot change anything."[87] It appears that modest levels of participation result from the general perception that parties do not offer meaningful political alternatives, are not responsive to citizens' concerns, or have little power compared to the High Representative.

It is interesting to note that levels of participation in a range of political activities in the former Yugoslav states are roughly the same as the modest level of political participation for the Central and East European region as a whole. Citizen mistrust of political organizations is widespread in postcommunist societies and also leads to low levels of membership in political parties.

During wartime, exclusivist leaders succeeded in deflecting the effect of citizen-initiated protests that had become common in the late 1980s through 1991 in Slovenia, Croatia, and Serbia. We saw above that Milošević used demonstrations of unemployed and embittered Serbs to change republic and provincial leaderships. Large nonviolent demonstrations for political reform in Belgrade in 1991 and peace in Sarajevo in 1992 met with violence by the JNA and SDS snipers, respectively. The Tudjman and Milošević governments easily deflected antiwar protests by committed activists—often women—and could enlist rural-based and nationalist victims groups in support of national goals. But from the mid-1990s onward, antiauthoritarian protests in Zagreb and Belgrade grew larger and bolder. An estimated one hundred thousand people protested their leaders' attempts to silence popular opposition radio stations in Croatia, for example.[88] Most significantly, the youth organization Otpor took advantage of low-key US aid and a weakened SPS to mobilize citizens successfully against Milošević in the fall of 2000. A relatively high percentage of respondents in Serbia reported participating in such demonstrations. In Bosnia and post-Milošević Serbia, citizens are more willing to engage in protests that involve economic rather than political issues.[89] In a rare example of civic activism, Bosnian citizens in June 2013 launched weeks of spontaneous protests in Sarajevo, Mostar, and Tuzla against political deadlock, spurred by the unwillingness of the Bosnian parliament to pass legislation on obtaining personal identification numbers needed for access to health care and travel.[90] This preference reflects the priority citizens in all of the former Yugoslav states give to economic concerns, as well as the continuing poor performance of the economies in the region.[91]

Nationalist protests continue to take place in Croatia, Kosovo, and Bosnia, sometimes with the assistance of ruling parties and the tacit support of local police. Developments that threaten entrenched nationalist leaders—returning refugees and internally displaced people, the normalization of relations in the divided communities of Mostar (Bosnia) and Mitrovica (Kosovo), campaign rallies by minorities, and (re)construction of religious institutions—have sometimes engendered violence, particularly through the mid-2000s. Two days of cross-Kosovo violence in March 2004 that saw Albanian extremists attack Serbs and Roma, as well as UN and NATO forces, were the most significant incidence of this. Soccer matches between ethnically based teams or with teams from outside the Balkans can also become explosive. Through 2010, intraethnic political competition for the spoils of political office was occasionally violent in Serbia, Kosovo, Bosnia, and Macedonia.

Political Values and Attitudes toward Politics

Some political scientists hold that the nations of former Yugoslavia tend to have "subject" political cultures, in which citizens sit back and expect the government to provide for them.[92] But it makes better sense to argue that citizens are rationally disaffected with a political system whose parties present them with few meaningful choices, especially when patronage networks do not deliver benefits to ordinary citizens. In deeply divided societies with ethnic party systems, citizens tend to vote for parties that represent ethnically defined interests. Reflecting constraints imposed by Bosnia's ethnically consociational political system, a mere 19 percent of respondents in a nationally representative survey in that country believed only monoethnic parties could protect their vital interests.[93] Ordinary citizens also avoid involvement in politics, which they consider dirty. Some citizens believe that political parties contribute to ethnic tension.[94]

Surveys indicate that citizens of most of successor countries lack confidence in their political institutions (see table 17.1). The low level of confidence in domestic political institutions runs against the general aspiration for a democratic political system. The percentage of respondents who agreed that "though democracy has its problems, it is the best political system" ranged from a high of 96 percent in Croatia to a low of 81 percent in Macedonia,[95] findings consistent with opinions across postcommunist Europe. When asked to identify elements of democracy they considered extremely important, citizens from Serbia, Vojvodina, Kosovo, Croatia, Bosnia, and Macedonia all ranked "a justice system treating everybody equally," "economic prosperity in the country," and "a government that guarantees meeting the basic economic needs of all the citizens" as their top three associations with democracy.[96] These priorities reflect concern about arbitrary rule, the absence of prosperity, and the prevalence of corruption during the periods of socialism and the wars of succession. They also indicate an enduring preference for the state to provide for basic needs. The low priority given to political elements of democracy, such as civil liberties and political pluralism, is consistent with the views of citizens in Romania and Bulgaria.[97] When asked in 2010 whether they were satisfied with the way democracy works in their country, only 14 percent of respondents in Slovenia and only 20 percent of respondents in Croatia answered yes.[98] This substantial dissatisfaction may partly reflect the respondents' interpretations of economic performance: throughout the successor states, citizens consistently identify unemployment as the most important problem facing

Table 17.1. Levels of Confidence in Political Institutions (percentage)

	Political Parties	National Government	Judicial Institutions	Religious Institutions	Police	Army
Bosnia	15.8	18.9	34.4	61.7	60.4	57.6
Croatia	24.6	31.1	31.8	51.3	63.4	68.4
Kosovo	31.8.	31.2	35.2	83.8	83.8	85.8
Macedonia	23.7	37.0	30.6	63.8	47.4	56.6
Montenegro	22.2	35.5	38.5	70.2	63.6	61.4
Serbia	16.0	22.3	26.3	56.4	53.5	63.1
Slovenia	9.0	15.0	29.9	34.3	39.4	64.5

Sources: Gallup's "Balkan Monitor: Insights and Perceptions, Voices of the Balkans," 2010 (http://www .balkan-monitor.eu), for public opinion data in Serbia, Croatia, Bosnia, Macedonia, Kosovo, and Montenegro on political parties (respondents who expressed some or a lot of confidence), national government (respondents who expressed confidence), religious institutions (respondents who expressed confidence), judicial institutions (respondents who expressed confidence), the police (respondents who expressed some or a lot of confidence), and the military (respondents who expressed some or a lot of confidence).
European Social Survey Dataset ESS5-2010, ed.3.0, Norwegian Social Science Data Services, http:// nesstar.ess.nsd.uib.no/webview, for public opinion in Slovenia on police (respondents who choose 5 to 10 on a 0-10 scale of trust, with 0 corresponding to no trust at all and 10 corresponding to complete trust); judicial institutions (respondents who choose 5 to 10 on a 0-10 scale of trust in the legal system, with 0 corresponding to no trust at all and 10 corresponding to complete trust). "Public Opinion in the European Union,"
Standard Eurobarometer 78, European Commission, December 2012, http://ec.europa.eu/public_opinion/ archives/eb/eb78/eb78_en.htm, for public opinion in Slovenia on political parties (respondents who tend to trust) and national government (respondents who tend to trust).
World Values Survey 2005 official data file v.20090901, 2009, World Values Survey Association, Aggregate File Producer: ASEP/JDS, Madrid, available at http://www.worldvaluessurvey.org, for public opinion in Slovenia on religious institution (respondents who tend to trust their religious institution).
Antonis Papacostas, "National and European Identity, European Elections, European Values, and Climate Change," Eurobarometer 6.82, ICPSR, March–May 2008, datafile, available at http://www.icpsr.umich. edu/icpsrweb/ICPSR/studies/25021, for public opinion in Slovenia on the military (respondents who tend to trust).

their countries.[99] Poverty and corruption vie for second place, with opinions about the latter contributing to dissatisfaction with judicial institutions and the functioning of the political system.

Citizens express moderate-to-low levels of tolerance for other ethnic groups. As expected in areas experiencing interethnic brutality, levels of tolerance toward other ethnic groups worsened during and in the immediate wake of violence. In Croatia, individuals who expressed high levels of religiosity expressed lower levels of ethnic tolerance than the less religious.[100] But this pattern varies. Although Bosnia experienced much higher levels of violence than Macedonia, Bosnian citizens express higher levels of tolerance than do Macedonian citizens. In 2007, only 8 percent of Bosnian respondents in a nationally representative sample survey expressed unwillingness to live next door to someone of another religion, whereas 12 percent of Macedonian respondents expressed such unwillingness.[101] As the memory of mass violence recedes, ethnic tolerance among citizens in Bosnia, Croatia, and Macedonia has significantly increased, which suggests that interethnic relations have made greater progress at the grass roots than at the elite level. Nationalist demonstrations against the use of the Cyrillic alphabet on signs in Vukovar, Croatia, throughout 2013 highlight the freshness of the psychological wounds of war.[102] Tolerance has not been restored to prewar levels, and ethnically motivated crimes continue.[103] As is consistent with prewar patterns in the region, Kosovo continues to display the lowest levels of ethnic tolerance, which have not increased since the end of the war. Only 20 percent of Kosovar Serbs and 29 percent of Kosovar Albanians agree to live on the same street with each other.[104] In response to policies primarily formulated by a dominant national group, ethnic minorities express significantly less pride in the nationality of their state and trust in political institutions than do members of the predominant group.[105]

The extent to which political values vary according to socioeconomic status depends partly on the political environment. For example, in the immediate wake of Milošević's ouster, voters in Serbia with some university education overwhelmingly (65 percent) supported the DOS opposition coalition, while only 5 percent supported SPS in 2001.[106] With the breakup of DOS, the difficult economic transition, and disputes with the EU over war crimes and Kosovo, there appeared no strong correlation between values and socioeconomic status by 2004.[107] However, generational differences in values are still reported. Relatively liberal young Bosnians have abstained from voting in larger percentages than older cohorts.[108] Surveys also reveal that urbanites resent rural residents—even within the same ethnonational group—who have fled their villages for cities because of violence and poverty.[109]

The transformation of values into support for democratic principles and processes is necessary for democratic institutions to take root and to prevent a reversion to authoritarianism. In particular, tolerance toward other ethnic groups is essential for transition toward more normal political competition and stable states that promote regional stability. The good news is that citizens express levels of confidence in new political institutions and values that are largely consistent with the rest of West-leaning Central and Eastern Europe. They are broadly supportive of democratic ideas but lack confidence in those political institutions that have often failed to function effectively, be responsive, or consistently deliver benefits to ordinary citizens.

Economic Transition and Social Change

Wars in Croatia and Bosnia in the early 1990s and in Serbia and Kosovo at the end of that decade entrenched corruption and inhibited substantial foreign investment. The economies suffered physical destruction of infrastructure and productive capacity, as well as the emigration of young, highly educated, and skilled labor. Serbia suffered under sanctions throughout the decade for its support of the Serb war effort in Bosnia. Macedonia suffered from a Greek boycott of its economy in the early 1990s and from the cutoff of Yugoslav markets that had been easily available before 1990.

Even the region's most developed country, Slovenia, has privatized its banking sector slowly and has been on "crisis watch" among observers in Western Europe.[110] The wars dramatically slowed the economic development of all successor states, particularly in the first half of the 1990s. In a period of increasing unemployment, these economies uniformly experienced great inflation and decreasing production and gross domestic product (GDP). These trends have been particularly significant in Kosovo, where unemployment is as high as 60 to 70 percent.[111]

The wars also significantly curtailed already decreasing interrepublican trade. Those countries with more advanced economies—Slovenia and Croatia—were more able than the less developed republics to capitalize relatively quickly on their advantageous status by better integrating into the European and global economy (see table 17.2). For Serbia, Montenegro, Bosnia, and Macedonia, trade tends to be split among former Yugoslav successors and the EU. Deepened political commitment to integration with the EU has accelerated the economic reform and improved the economic performance—albeit to varying degrees—of those countries still seeking entry into the EU.

The wars in Bosnia, Croatia, and Kosovo provided fertile soil for the development of gray economies and corruption—especially with the golden goose of international

Table 17.2.   Increasingly Divergent Economies in 2011 and 2012

	GNI per Capita, 2011 (Current US$)	GDP Growth, 2011 (Annual Percentage)	FDI Inflow, 2012 (Millions US$)	Unemployment, 2011 (as Percentage of Labor Force)
Slovenia	23,780	0.7	999.2	8.7
Croatia	13,830	0.0	1,500.0	14.3
Serbia	5,530	1.6	2,700.0	23.0
Montenegro	6,810	3.2	558.1	19.7
Macedonia	4,710	2.8	421.9	31.4
Bosnia	4,690	1.3	435.1	28.0

Sources: For gross national income (GNI) per capita, "GNI per Capita, Atlas Method (Current US$)," World Bank, http://data.worldbank.org/indicator/NY.GNP.PCAP.CD; for unemployment data in all but Slovenia and Croatia, Eurostat, http://epp.eurostat.ec.europa.eu/portal/page/portal/statistics/search_database; for unemployment data in Slovenia and Croatia, Eurostat, http://epp.eurostat .ec.europa.eu/portal/page/portal/statistics/search_database; for GDP growth in Bosnia and Montenegro, CEC 2012 Progress Reports, European Commission, http://ec.europa.eu/enlargement/pdf/ key_documents/2012/package/ba_rapport_2012_en.pdf and   http://ec.europa.eu/enlargement/ pdf/key_documents/2012/package/mn_rapport_2012_en.pdf; for GDP growth in Slovenia, Croatia, Serbia, and Macedonia, "Real GDP Growth Rate—Volume," Eurostat, http://epp.eurostat.ec.europa .eu/tgm/table.do?tab=table&init=1&plugin=1&language=en&pcode=tec00115.

reconstruction aid. Corruption significantly hampers economic development and democratization in all successor states but Slovenia. In terms of Freedom House's measure of corruption from 1 (least corrupt) to 7 (most corrupt), Slovenia scores 2.25, Croatia and Macedonia score 4, Serbia scores 4.25, Bosnia scores 4.75, Montenegro scores 5, and Kosovo brings up the rear at 6.[112] Of the postcommunist states, only the non-Baltic countries of the former Soviet Union score worse. Leadership circles around Serbian president Milošević and Croatian president Tudjman were especially prone to personalizing the public trust, but this phenomenon was also evident elsewhere.[113] Estimates of the size of Bosnia's gray economy range from 30 to 40 percent of unadjusted, official GDP.[114] Control over the gray market has also enabled the leading nationalist parties in Bosnia to maintain power and undermine implementation of the Dayton Accords. Attempts to prosecute war profiteers in Serbia cost Zoran Djindjić his life. Criminal networks among Macedonia's Albanians contributed to armed violence in 2001.[115] These phenomena are linked to transnational trafficking networks in people and commodities that will not be easily eradicated.

The wars significantly slowed economic reform and the privatization of property. The social implications of the wars are no less severe. A higher percentage of women than men are unemployed. Young adults are unemployed at higher levels than other age cohorts. This fact leads young and educated labor to emigrate, a brain drain that affects future economic development. In Kosovo, Bosnia, and Croatia, unemployment is higher for minorities than for majorities. Widespread poverty in Bosnia, Serbia, Montenegro, and Kosovo has led to social atomization and political demobilization.[116] In these countries, high un- and underemployment, coupled with severe cutbacks in the social safety net, results in many citizens living from day to day. These economies continue to wait to embark on the process of reform and modernization.

International agencies have attempted to address these problems as part of larger peace accords. They have donated over $14 billion to the Bosnian economy since the signing of the Dayton Accords, and donors' conferences have generated substantial income for Croatia and Kosovo. Although this aid contributed initially to the repair and reconstruction of housing and infrastructure, it was unevenly distributed and kept away from those groups—especially in Republika Srpska and among the Serb community in Kosovo—that did not explicitly support the implementation of the peace accords. A great deal of effort is needed to provide a proper legal framework for the economic transition that will enable these countries to benefit from trade and foreign investment. It will be no easy task for international agencies to find an effective balance among the goals of recovery, reconstruction, and reform. The global recession that began in 2008 made more difficult efforts of the region's governments to attract sufficient investment to help diminish unemployment and improve standards of living. Overall, a European Bank for Reconstruction and Development report argues that the Western Balkans, which suffered a decline in economic activity, weathered the crisis better than expected because of "mature policies by governments and strong financial support from international organizations, and the continued commitment of privately owned foreign companies and banks to the region."[117]

The combination of the 2008 recession and Eurozone crisis hit Slovenia particularly hard. Slovenia had a problem with corporations financing operations through debt rather than equity, with a lot of that debt going bad in 2008. Austerity programs enacted until early 2013 cut debt but also revenues. And because corporations took out such large quantities of debt and now are having trouble repaying it, banks are suffering too.[118]

Critical Issues

There is no shortage of critical issues facing governments in Yugoslavia's successor states. First, the governments of all post-Yugoslav successor states either aspire to EU membership or hope to maintain good standing in the EU.[119] However, EU membership requires a genuine break with past autarkic and undemocratic practices. The economic difficulties facing Slovenia and the possible EU sanctions on Croatia for the extradition law described above draw attention to the reality that EU membership is not a simple end point, after which national leaderships can revert to old habits as free riders on European largesse. EU membership requires opening up policy-making processes and content and presumes a genuine commitment to multilateral norms and rules over which no national leaders have much control. Domestic democratic advocacy groups and EU sanctions for backtracking can encourage the governments of Slovenia and Croatia to continue to strengthen rule of law, reduce corruption and insider dealing, genuinely treat citizens equally regardless of ethnicity, and provide an adequate social safety net.

The other successor states face even higher thresholds for addressing these issues as they seek entry from the outer circle of potential EU membership. For example, in recent years, the government of Serbia has made substantial progress in its cooperation with the ICTY and in a deeper, underlying political consensus that Serbia's best future is in the EU. As it moves forward, it will need to demonstrate progress in establishing security and the rule of law, finding durable solutions for internally displaced persons and refugees, eradicating public corruption and organized crime, and undertaking economic reform in order to expand employment. These are no small tasks.

Other governments must still resolve the basic issues of political status and the constitutional order. The continued implementation of the Ohrid Agreement could help create a better functioning political system in Macedonia that can prepare itself for EU membership. All legitimate political actors in Macedonia can demonstrate progress in adopting consensual rules of the game that move beyond narrow partisan and personal interests. Bosnia-Herzegovina has a far longer way to go to demonstrate its readiness for EU membership. Ineffective international efforts to integrate Republika Srpska into Bosnia, at the same time that RS institutions function more effectively than the more complex ones in the federation, continue to impede the wish of all Bosnians to enjoy a more hopeful future. Bosniac, Croat, and Serb political leaders have proven unable to agree on some minimal rules of the game that are necessary to strengthen the capacity of local, cantonal, and entity- and state-level institutions to govern and administer effectively. It has been difficult for the Macedonian and Bosnian governments to make real efforts to reduce party patronage and deep divisions in the political systems and to demonstrate progress in addressing organized crime, corruption, ethnic separation, and economic development.

A final settlement of differences among the governments of Kosovo and Serbia is far from imminent. However, the recent EU-brokered agreement provides a basis for building confidence and space for more conventional social, economic, and political development in both countries. The Serbian government faces a difficult test in employing its ongoing dialogue with the Kosovo authorities to ensure that Serbian cultural and historical interests are fully recognized in Kosovo and to influence Kosovo's Serbs to look both to Pristina and to the Association of Kosovo Serb Municipalities. Similarly, the Kosovo government must demonstrate its commitment to EU membership by following through on its commitment to better integrate minorities, establish effective rule-of-law institutions, and undertake the economic reforms that lead to the type of economic development that expands employment. These hopeful steps in relations between Serbia, Montenegro, and Kosovo could provide the basis for the emergence of normal politics in all three countries and strengthen their credibility in efforts to meet the conditions to join the EU.

There are clear limits to the capacity of the EU accession process to support democratization and develop normal politics and policy making in the post-Yugoslav successor governments. The EU's preaccession process has helped induce meaningful reform in Croatia in preparation for membership. The EU integration process has also initially spurred some positive reforms in Macedonia and Serbia but has been much less successful in Bosnia. Scholars have convincingly argued that the EU accession process works best in encouraging meaningful reforms among applicant countries that have already resolved fundamental state-building issues and with domestic leaders whose commitment to reform also brings personal political benefits.[120] The record of EU accession in spurring a process of self-sustaining reforms must also be judged by new member Croatia's decision to limit the execution of European arrest warrants and also by the assaults in Hungary, Romania, and Bulgaria on important components of the rule of law after those countries joined the EU. This could lead to an extended wait in the outer ring for Bosnia, Montenegro, and Kosovo. And the EU's own internal problems are likely to further blunt its ability to play a powerful, constructive role in post-Yugoslav governments in the outer ring and thus to lead to calls for greater US involvement, especially in deeper rule-of-law reforms, even against the fatigue of over two decades of strife and engagement in the region and the call of economic recession at home and instability in other regions.

Without a doubt, Yugoslavia's successor states have made tremendous progress since the dark days of the 1990s, but they continue to face multiple issues in building tolerant societies and effective and democratically accountable institutions at the same time that they continue their transition to market economies. The successor governments must find ways to increase employment for their citizens and to build cooperation and economies of scale with governments and businesses in the region. These difficult challenges are complicated by unconstructive conflicts among political and ethnic factions, which often act from narrow self-interest. With negative implications for the future, internationally endorsed power-sharing arrangements have allowed for ethnonational elites to institutionalize ethnic separation in educational systems. While domestic leaders bear the greater burden of addressing serious problems of governance, it remains unlikely that any solution to these constitutional problems will be found without constructive assistance from the international community, the same community that neither acted to preserve Yugoslavia nor intervened to end aggression. International agencies have been deeply involved in developments in Yugoslavia since 1991 and have overseen the often flawed implementation of peace accords throughout the region. Their greatest test will be how adroitly they assist governments in the successor states in managing the transition from war to sustainable, inclusive, and democratic peace.

Study Questions

1. What external and internal factors contributed to the violent disintegration of Yugoslavia?
2. What external and internal factors explain differences in the timing and pace of the democratization of the governments of the Yugoslav successor states?
3. What key social, economic, and political issues face the governments of the Yugoslav successor states?
4. How are relationships between political elites and ordinary citizens in the former Yugoslav states similar, and how do they differ during the postsocialist period?
5. How effectively has international intervention into the countries of former Yugoslavia promoted inclusive and stable democratization?

Suggested Readings

Bieber, Florian. *Post-war Bosnia: Ethnicity, Inequality and Public Sector Governance*. New York: Palgrave, 2006.

——, ed. "Unconditional Conditionality? The Impact of EU Conditionality in the Western Balkans." Special issue of *Europe-Asia Studies* 63, no. 10 (2011).

Brown, Keith, ed. *Transacting Transition: The Micropolitics of Democracy Assistance in the Former Yugoslavia*. Bloomfield, CT: Kumarian Press, 2006.

Burg, Steven L., and Paul S. Shoup. *The War in Bosnia-Herzegovina*. Armonk, NY: M. E. Sharpe, 1999.

Cohen, Lenard, and John Lampe. *Embracing Democracy in the Western Balkans*. Washington, DC: Woodrow Wilson Center Press, 2011.

Dauphinee, Elizabeth. *The Politics of Exile*. New York: Routledge, 2013.

Dawisha, Karen, and Bruce Parrott, eds. *Politics, Power, and the Struggle for Democracy in South-East Europe*. Cambridge: Cambridge University Press, 1997.

Demetrijević, Nenad, and Petra Kovacs, eds. *Managing Hatred and Distrust: The Prognosis for Post-conflict Settlement in Multiethnic Communities in the Former Yugoslavia*. Budapest: Open Society Institute, 2004.

Donais, Tim. *The Political Economy of Peacebuilding in Post-Dayton Bosnia*. New York: Frank Cass, 2005.

Gagnon, V. P. *The Myth of Ethnic War: Serbia and Croatia in the 1990s*. Ithaca, NY: Cornell University Press, 2004.

Gow, James. *Triumph of the Lack of Will: International Diplomacy and the Yugoslav War*. New York: Columbia University Press, 1997.

Judah, Tim. *Kosovo: War and Revenge*. New Haven, CT: Yale University Press, 2000.

Lampe, John. *Yugoslavia as History: Twice There Was a Country*. 2nd ed. Cambridge: Cambridge University Press, 2000.

Naimark, Norman, and Holly Case, eds. *Yugoslavia and Its Historians: Understanding the Balkan Wars of the 1990s*. Stanford, CA: Stanford University Press, 2003.

Ramet, Sabrina Petra. *Balkan Babel: The Disintegration of Yugoslavia from the Death of Tito to the Fall of Milošević*. 4th ed. Boulder, CO: Westview Press, 2002.

Ramet, Sabrina Petra, and Vjeran Pavlakovic, eds. *Serbia since 1989: Politics and Society under Milošević*. Seattle: University of Washington Press, 2005.

Subotic, Jelena. *Hijacked Justice: Dealing with the Past in the Balkans*. Ithaca, NY: Cornell University Press, 2009.

Woodward, Susan. *Balkan Tragedy*. Washington, DC: Brookings Institution, 1996.

Websites

Balkan Investigative Reporting Network (BIRN): http://birn.eu.com

European Commission, "Enlargement Package 2013: Strategy and Progress Reports": http://ec.europa.eu/enlargement/countries/strategy-and-progress-report/index_en.htm

European Stability Initiative: http://www.esiweb.org

International Crisis Group, "Balkans": http://www.crisisgroup.org/en/regions/europe/balkans.aspx

United Nations Secretary General, "Reports Submitted by/Transmitted by the Secretary-General to the Security Council": http://www.un.org/en/sc/documents/sgreports

BOSNIA-HERZEGOVINA

Government: http://www.vladars.net/eng/Pages/default.aspx; http://www.fbihvlada.gov.ba/

Office of the High Representative: http://www.ohr.int

Organization for Security and Co-operation in Europe, Mission to Bosnia and Herzegovina: http://www.oscebih.org/Default.aspx?id=0&lang=EN

Parliament: http://www.parliament.ba

United Nations Development Programme in Bosnia and Herzegovina: http://www.ba.undp.org/bosnia_and_herzegovina/en/home.html

USAID, "Bosnia and Herzegovina": http://www.usaid.gov/where-we-work/europe-and-eurasia/bosnia

World Bank, "Bosnia and Herzegovina": http://www.worldbank.org/en/country/bosniaandherzegovina

CROATIA

Government: https://vlada.gov.hr

Parliament: http://www.sabor.hr/English

United Nations Development Programme in Croatia: http://www.hr.undp.org/croatia/en/home.html

World Bank, "Croatia": http://www.worldbank.org/en/country/croatia

KOSOVO

EULEX Kosovo: http://www.eulex-kosovo.eu/en/front
Government: https://www.rks-gov.net/en-US/Pages/Fillimi.aspx
Kosovo Force (KFOR): http://www.aco.nato.int/kfor.aspx
Organization for Security and Co-operation in Europe, Mission to Kosovo: http://www
    .osce.org/kosovo
Parliament: http://www.kuvendikosoves.org/?cid=2,1
United Nations Development Programme in Kosovo: http://www.ks.undp.org/kosovo/
    en/home.html
USAID, "Kosovo": http://transition.usaid.gov/kosovo/eng
World Bank, "Kosovo": http://www.worldbank.org/en/country/kosovo

MACEDONIA

Government: http://www.vlada.mk/?language=en-gb
Organization for Security and Co-operation in Europe, Mission to Macedonia: http://
    www.osce.org/skopje
Parliament: http://www.sobranie.mk/en
USAID, "Macedonia": http://www.usaid.gov/where-we-work/europe-and-eurasia/mace
    donia
World Bank, "Macedonia": http://www.worldbank.org/en/country/macedonia

MONTENEGRO

Government: http://www.gov.me/en/homepage
Organization for Security and Co-operation in Europe, Mission to Montenegro: http://
    www.osce.org/montenegro
Parliament: http://www.skupstina.me/index.php/en/
United Nations Development Programme in Montenegro: http://www.me.undp.org/
    montenegro/en/home.html
USAID, "Montenegro": http://www.usaid.gov/where-we-work/europe-and-eurasia/
    montenegro
World Bank, "Montenegro": http://www.worldbank.org/en/country/montenegro

SERBIA

B-92: http://www.b92.net/eng
Government: http://www.srbija.gov.rs/?change_lang=en
Organization for Security and Co-operation in Europe, Mission to Serbia: http://www
    .osce.org/serbia

Parliament: http://www.parlament.gov.rs/national-assembly.467.html

United Nations Development Programme in Serbia: http://www.rs.undp.org/serbia/en/home.html

USAID, "Serbia": http://www.usaid.gov/where-we-work/europe-and-eurasia/serbia

World Bank, "Serbia": http://www.worldbank.org/en/country/serbia

SLOVENIA

Government: http://www.vlada.si/en

Parliament: http://www.slovenia.si/slovenia/state/parliament-the-national-assembly

World Bank, "Slovenia": http://www.worldbank.org/en/country/serbia

Notes

1. To get a sense of differences, see essays by Sabrina Ramet, *Thinking about Yugoslavia: Scholarly Debates on the Western Balkans and the Wars in Bosnia and Kosovo* (Cambridge: Cambridge University Press, 2005); Gale Stokes et al., "Instant History: Understanding the Wars of Yugoslav Succession," *Slavic Review* 55, no. 1 (1996): 136–60; Sarah Kent, "Writing the Yugoslav Wars," *American Historical Review* 102, no. 4 (1997): 1085–114; Ivo Banac, "Historiography of the Countries of Eastern Europe: Yugoslavia," *American Historical Review* 97, no. 4 (1992): 1084–102.

2. William Zimmerman, *Open Borders, Non-alignment and the Political Evolution of Yugoslavia* (Princeton, NJ: Princeton University Press, 1986).

3. It is impossible to do justice to the diverse cultural, social, economic, and political background of the lands of former Yugoslavia in so short a space. For a general introduction, see Ivo Banac, *The Yugoslav National Question* (Ithaca, NY: Cornell University Press, 1984); Barbara Jelavich, *History of the Balkans*, 2 vols. (New York: Cambridge University Press, 1983); Charles Jelavich and Barbara Jelavich, *The Establishment of the Balkan National States, 1804–1920* (Seattle: University of Washington Press, 1977); Joseph Rothschild, *East Central Europe between the Two World Wars* (Seattle: University of Washington Press, 1974); Jozo Tomasevich, *Peasants, Politics and Economic Change* (Stanford, CA: Stanford University Press, 1955); John Lampe, *Yugoslavia as History: Twice There Was a Country*, 2nd ed. (Cambridge: Cambridge University Press, 2000); Gale Stokes, *Three Eras of Political Change in Eastern Europe* (New York: Oxford University Press, 1997); Mark Mazower, *The Balkans: A Short History* (New York: Random House, 2002).

4. Banac, *The Yugoslav National Question*, 415–16.

5. Dennison Rusinow, *The Yugoslav Experiment, 1948–1974* (Berkeley: University of California Press, 1978).

6. See Ivo Banac, *With Stalin against Tito: Cominform Splits in Yugoslav Communism* (Ithaca, NY: Cornell University Press, 1988).

7. See Zimmerman, *Open Borders*; Alvin Z. Rubinstein, *Yugoslavia and the Nonaligned World* (Princeton, NJ: Princeton University Press, 1970).

8. Zimmerman nicely makes this argument. See also Susan Woodward, *Socialist Unemployment: The Political Economy of Yugoslavia, 1945–1990* (Princeton, NJ: Princeton University Press, 1995).

9. Woodward, *Socialist Unemployment*; Lampe, *Yugoslavia as History*.

10. Woodward, *Socialist Unemployment*, 384.

11. The term "Bosniac" is used to describe the Slavic Muslims who live mainly in Bosnia-Herzegovina, but also in Serbia, Montenegro, and Kosovo. They had been known as Muslims in a national sense since 1971, but the Congress of Bosniac Intellectuals officially adopted "Bosniac" as the name for the people in 1993, and it has been generally accepted among all Slavic Muslims. See Mustafa Imamović, *Istorija Bošnjaka* (Sarajevo: Preporod, 1998); Francine Friedman, *The Bosnian Muslims: Denial of a Nation* (Boulder, CO: Westview Press, 1995); and Banac, *The Yugoslav National Question*.

12. Radivoj Papic, "Sta je to 'Zajednistvo,'" *Komunist*, September 14, 1972, as cited in Mark Baskin, "National in Form, National in Content: Some Consequences of Consociationalism in Yugoslavia" (paper prepared for delivery at the American Political Science Association, August 30 to September 2, 1984).

13. Kosovo became an "autonomous province," in 1974 enjoying almost all of the perquisites of republican status, but with fewer representatives in the state presidency and without the formal right to secede. It had earlier been an "autonomous region" within Serbia. See Mark Baskin, "Crisis in Kosovo," *Problems of Communism* 32, no. 2 (March–April 1983): 61–74.

14. Arend Lijphart, *Democracy in Plural Societies* (New Haven, CT: Yale University Press, 1980); Paul Shoup, *Yugoslav Communism and the National Question* (New York: Columbia University Press, 1968); Pedro Ramet, *Nationalism and Federalism in Yugoslavia, 1963–1983* (Bloomington: Indiana University Press, 1984); Steven Burg, *Conflict and Cohesion in Socialist Yugoslavia: Political Decision Making since 1966* (Princeton, NJ: Princeton University Press, 1983).

15. Burg, *Conflict and Cohesion*, 346.

16. Lenard J. Cohen, *Serpent and Bosom: The Rise and Fall of Slobodan Milošević* (Boulder, CO: Westview Press, 2001).

17. Lenard J. Cohen, *Broken Bonds: Yugoslavia's Disintegration and Balkan Politics in Transition*, 2nd ed. (Boulder, CO: Westview Press, 1995), 47. See also Dijana Plještina, *Regional Development in Communist Yugoslavia* (Boulder, CO: Westview, 1992).

18. Lampe, *Yugoslavia as History*, 354–55; Sabrina Petra Ramet, *Balkan Babel: The Disintegration of Yugoslavia from the Death of Tito to the Fall of Milošević*, 4th ed. (Boulder, CO: Westview Press, 2002), 54–55.

19. Jacque Poos, Luxembourg's foreign minister at the time of Luxembourg's presidency of the European Community Council of Ministers in 1991, famously declared that "this is the hour of Europe" during his shuttle diplomacy between Belgrade, Zagreb, Ljubljana, and Brioni. See International Commission on the Balkans, *Unfinished Peace: Report of the International Commission on the Balkans* (Washington, DC: Carnegie Endowment for International Peace, 1996), 56; Dan Smith, "Europe's Peacebuilding Hour? Past Failures, Future Challenges," *Journal of International Affairs* 55, no. 2 (spring 2002): 441–60, quote on 442.

20. Lenard Cohen, "Prelates and Politicians in Bosnia: The Role of Religion in Nationalist Mobilisation," *Nationalities Papers* 25 (September 1997): 481–99; Ramet, *Thinking about Yugoslavia*; V. P. Gagnon, *The Myth of Ethnic War: Serbia and Croatia in the 1990s* (Ithaca, NY: Cornell University Press, 2004); Ramet, *Balkan Babel*; Cohen, *Broken Bonds*; Anthony Oberschall, "The Manipulation of Ethnicity: From Ethnic Cooperation to Violence and War in Yugoslavia," *Ethnic and Racial Studies* 23, no. 6 (2000): 994–95.

21. See the estimates for individual countries at "South-Eastern Europe: 2014 UNHCR Regional Operations Profile—South-Eastern Europe," United Nations High Commissioner for Refugees, South-Eastern Europe, http://www.unhcr.org/pages/49e45b906.html and "Serbia: 2014 UNHCR Regional Operations Profile—South-Eastern Europe," United Nations High Commissioner for Refugees, South-Eastern Europe, http://www.unhcr.org/pages/49e48d9f6.html.

22. Lampe, *Yugoslavia as History*, 370.

23. "The 2004 Enlargement: The Challenge of a 25-Member EU," European Union, http://europa.eu/legislation_summaries/enlargement/2004_and_2007_enlargement/e50017_en.htm; "Slovenia Joins the Euro Area," European Commission, http://ec.europa.eu/economy_finance/articles/euro/slovenia_joins_the_euro_area_en.htm; "Accession: Estonia, Israel and Slovenia Invited to Join OECD," OECD, http://www.oecd.org/estonia/accessionestoniaisraelandsloveniainvitedtojoinoecd.htm.

24. For basic information on the UN Protection Force (UNPROFOR), see "Former Yugoslavia—UNPROFOR," United Nations, http://www.un.org/Depts/dpko/dpko/co_mission/unprof_p.htm.

25. An estimated nine hundred Serbs were killed in the Croatian offensive against Serb-held Krajina in 1995. See "Croatia: Three Years since Operations Flash and Storm—Three Years of Justice and Dignity Denied," Amnesty International, EUR 64/05/98, August 4, 1998, http://www.amnesty.org/ar/library/asset/EUR64/005/1998/fr/c416cce8-d9d6-11dd-af2b-b1f6023af0c5/eur640051998en.pdf (accessed August 4, 2007).

26. Quoted in Branka Magaš, "Franjo Tudjman, an Obituary," *Independent*, December 13, 1999, reprinted in *Bosnia Report* (December 1999–February 2000), at http://www.bosnia.org.uk/bosrep/decfeb00/tudjman.cfm.

27. Ethnic cleansing is a campaign in which authorities, acting according to a premeditated plan, capture or consolidate control over territory by forcibly displacing or killing members of opposing ethnic groups. Human Rights Watch/Helsinki, *Bosnia and Herzegovina: Politics of Revenge—the Misuse of Authority in Bihac, Cazin, and Velika Kladua* (New York: Human Rights Watch/Helsinki, 1997), 6.

28. For example, the HVO destroyed the beautiful sixteenth-century bridge that united east and west Mostar, and Serb forces destroyed the Ferhadija Mosque in Banja Luka, the largest in Europe, among the many objects.

29. Mirsad Tokača, *Bosanske knjige mrtvih: Ljudski gubici u Bosni i Hercegovini 1991–1995* (Sarajevo: Istraživačko Dokumentacioni Centar, 2012).

30. For information on Operation EUFOR ALTHEA, see the European Military Force (EUFOR) website at http://www.euforbih.org; information on the NATO-led Stabilization Force can be found at http://www.nato.int/sfor/index.htm and http://www.nato.int/sfor/organisation/mission.htm (accessed August 19, 2014).

31. See "The Mandate of the OHR," Office of the High Representative, February 16, 2012, http://www.ohr.int/ohr-info/gen-info/default.asp?content_id=38612 (accessed September 22, 2013).

32. See, e.g., Tim Judah, *Kosovo: War and Revenge* (New Haven, CT: Yale University Press, 2000).

33. For the declaration of independence, see "Full Text: Kosovo Declaration," BBC News, February 17, 2008, http://news.bbc.co.uk/2/hi/europe/7249677.stm. On developments in Kosovo from 1999 to 2008, see, e.g., Mark Baskin, *Developing Local Democracy in Kosovo* (Stockholm: IDEA, 2005), http://www.idea.int/publications/dem_kosovo/index.cfm; Conflict Security and Development Group, *Kosovo Report* (London: International Policy Institute, 2003), http://ipi.sspp.kcl.ac.uk/rep005/index.html. See also Tim Judah, *Kosovo: What Everyone Needs to Know* (Oxford: Oxford University Press, 2008).

34. The ICJ ruled in July 2010 that Kosovo's declaration of independence did not violate international law. See the opinions at "Kosovo in International Court of Justice," Ministry of Foreign Affairs, Republic of Kosovo, http://www.mfa-ks.net/?page=2,61 (accessed September 22, 2013).

35. See United Nations Security Council, "Report of the Secretary General on the United Nations Interim Administration Mission in Kosovo," S/2013/444, July 26 2013. Among the other

issues are integrated border management, multiethnic policing, energy and telecommunications, the exchange of liaison officers, freedom of movement, civil registry, cadastral records, and acceptance of university diplomas. See "Serbia and Kosovo Reach Landmark Deal," European External Action Service, http://eeas.europa.eu/top_stories/2013/190413__eu-facilitated_dialogue_en.htm; "Serbia and Kosovo: The Path to Normalisation," International Crisis Group, February 19, 2003, http://www.crisisgroup.org/en/regions/europe/balkans/kosovo/223-serbia-and-kosovo-the-path-to-normalisation.aspx; "The Implementation of Kosovo-Serbia Political Dialogue," Policy Paper no. 4/13, KIPRED, July 2013, http://www.kipred.org/advCms/?id=5,1,1,1,e,299. Both governments have shown commitment to this process; see, e.g., "PM Strongly Condemns Killing of EULEX Member," *B-92*, September 19, 2013, http://www.b92.net/eng/news/politics.php?yyyy=2013&mm=09&dd=19&nav_id=87721.

36. See, e.g., Banac, *The Yugoslav National Question*, 307–28.

37. Republika Makedonija Državni zavod za statistika, *Popis 2002* (Skopje: Republic of Macedonia State Statistical Office, December 1, 2003), http://www.stat.gov.mk/PrikaziPoslednaPublikacija_en.aspx?id=54.

38. "Macedonia's Name: Why the Dispute Matters and How to Resolve It," Report No. 122, International Crisis Group Balkans, December 10, 2001, http://www.crisisgroup.org/~/media/Files/europe/Macedonia%2014.pdf, 12–13. See also "Macedonia's Name: Breaking the Deadlock," Europe Briefing No. 52, International Crisis Group, January 12, 2009, http://www.crisisgroup.org/~/media/Files/europe/b52_macedonias_name___breaking_the_deadlock.pdf.

39. See, e.g., "Macedonia: Not Out of the Woods Yet," International Crisis Group, February 25, 2005, http://www.crisisgroup.org/home/index.cfm?id-3295&l-1.

40. See Florian Bieber, "Montenegrin Politics since the Disintegration of Yugoslavia," in *Montenegro in Transition: Problems in Identity and Statehood*, ed. Florian Bieber (Baden-Baden: Nomos Verlagsgesellschaft, 2003), 11–42; "Montenegro's Independence Drive," International Crisis Group, December 7, 2005, http://www.crisisgroup.org/en/regions/europe/balkans/montenegro/169-montenegros-independence-drive.aspx.

41. Mary Kaldor, *New and Old Wars: Organized Violence in a Global Era* (Palo Alto, CA: Stanford University Press, 1999).

42. Mirjana Kasapovic, "Voting Rights, Electoral Systems, and Political Representation of Diaspora in Croatia," *East European Politics and Societies and Cultures* 26, no. 4 (2012): 777–91.

43. Center for Research and Policy Making, *Analysis of Internal Party Democracy in Macedonia* (Skopje: Konrad-Adenauer-Stiftung, 2013), http://www.crpm.org.mk; Georgi Karasimeonov, ed., *Organization Structures and Internal Party Democracy in South Eastern Europe* (Sofia: Goetex Press, 2005).

44. Valerie Bunce, "The Political Economy of Postsocialism," *Slavic Review* 58 (winter 1999): 756–93. See also Vernon Bogdanov, "Founding Elections and Regime Change," *Electoral Studies* 1 (1990): 288–94; Valerie Bunce, "Rethinking Recent Democratization: Lessons from the Postcommunist Experience," *World Politics* 55, no. 2 (January 2003): 189.

45. Sabrina Petra Ramet, "Democratization in Slovenia—the Second Stage," in *Politics, Power, and the Struggle for Democracy in South-East Europe*, ed. Karen Dawisha and Bruce Parrott, 189–217 (Cambridge: Cambridge University Press, 1997); Patrick Hyder Patterson, "On the Edge of Reason: The Boundaries of Balkanism in Slovenian, Austrian, and Italian Discourse," *Slavic Review* 62, no. 1 (spring 2003): 110–41.

46. See, e.g., Peter Spiegel, "The Day After: Digging Deeper into Slovenia," *Financial Times* Brussels blog, May 30, 2013, http://blogs.ft.com/brusselsblog/2013/05/the-day-after-digging-deeper-into-slovenia.

47. Eric Gordy, *The Culture of Power in Serbia* (University Park: Pennsylvania State University Press, 1999).

48. Gagnon, *The Myth of Ethnic War*, 92.

49. Gagnon, *The Myth of Ethnic War*; Gordy, *The Culture of Power*.

50. Vladimir Matić, *Serbia at the Crossroads Again* (Washington, DC: US Institute of Peace, 2004). Many observers regard Koštunica's DSS as merely more savvy, not less nationalistic, than SRS. See International Crisis Group, *Serbia's New Government: Turning from Europe* (Belgrade and Brussels: International Crisis Group, May 2007).

51. See the commentary by Prime Minister Ivica Dačić in the *Financial Times*: http://blogs .ft.com/beyond-brics/2013/09/17/guest-post-no-time-to-rest-as-serbia-moves-towards-europe. "Serbia: Narodna Skupstina: 2012 elections," Inter-parliamentary Union, Parline Database, http:// www.ipu.org/parline-e/reports/2355_E.htm (accessed August 9, 2013).

52. "European Commission Opinion on Serbia's Application for Membership of the European Union," Brussels, 12.10.2011 COM(2011) 668 final, European Commission, http://ec.europa.eu/ enlargement/pdf/key_documents/2011/package/sr_rapport_2011_en.pdf.

53. Ivan Šiber, "The Impact of Nationalism, Values, and Ideological Orientations on Multi-party Elections in Croatia," in *The Tragedy of Yugoslavia: The Failure of Democratic Transformation*, ed. Jim Seroka and Vukašin Pavlović, 141–71 (Armonk, NY: M. E. Sharpe, 1992); Mirjana Kasapovics, "Demokratska konsolidacija i izborna politika u Hrvatskoj 1990–2000," in *Hrvatska politika 1990–2000*, ed. Mirjana Kasapovics, 15–40 (Zagreb: Fakultet političkih znanosti, 2001); Paula M. Pickering and Mark Baskin, "What Is to Be Done: Succession from the League of Communists of Croatia," *Communist and Post-communist Studies* 41 (2008): 521–40.

54. Miljenko Antics and Maja Dodic Gruics, "The Parliamentary Election in Croatia, November 2007," *Electoral Studies* 27 (2008): 755.

55. Sanadar was ultimately sentenced to ten years in prison for accepting bribes in 2011. This relatively severe penalty for the highest-ranking executive in East Central Europe to be convicted of corruption since 1990 helped to quiet concerns that Croatia was soft on corruption on the eve of its accession to the EU.

56. "Perkovic Case Puts Croatia, EU in Conflict," *Southeast European Times*, September 25, 2013, http://www.setimes.com/cocoon/setimes/xhtml/en_GB/features/setimes/features/2013/09/25 /feature-01.

57. *The 1990 Elections in the Republics of Yugoslavia* (Washington, DC: International Republican Institute for International Affairs, 1991); Suad Arnautovics, *Izbori u Bosni i Hercegovini 1990* (Sarajevo: Promocult, 1996).

58. "Opinion on the Constitutional Situation in Bosnia and Herzegovina and the Powers of the High Representative," European Commission for Democracy through Law, March 2005, http:// www.venice.coe.int/webforms/documents/?pdf=CDL(2005)021-e.

59. Sumantra Bose, *Bosnia after Dayton: Nationalist Partition and International Intervention* (Oxford: Oxford University Press, 2002), 117.

60. Donald L. Horowitz, *Ethnic Groups in Conflict*, 2nd ed. (Berkeley: University of California Press, 2000); Paul Mitchell, "Party Competition in an Ethnic Dual Party System," *Ethnic and Racial Studies* 18 (October 1995): 773–96.

61. Daria Sito-Sucic, "Bosnian Experts Present U.S.-Backed Plan for Reform," Reuters, May 15, 2013.

62. CEC (2012) Bosnian and Herzegovina 2012 Progress Report, COM(2012) 600 final, Brussels, European Commission, October 10, 2012, http://ec.europa.eu/enlargement/pdf/key_docu ments/2012/package/ba_rapport_2012_en.pdf.

63. Elizabeth Cousens, "Missed Opportunities to Overcompensation: Implementing the Dayton Agreement on Bosnia," in *Ending Civil Wars: The Implementation of Peace Agreements*, ed. Stephen Stedman, Donald Rothchild, and Elizabeth M. Cousens, 531–66 (Boulder, CO: Lynne Rienner Publishers, 2002).

64. See "High Representative's Decisions by Topic," Office of the High Representative, http://www.ohr.int/decisions/archive.asp.

65. Patrice McMahon and Jon Western, "Bosnia on the Brink," *Foreign Affairs* 88, no. 5 (September–October 2009): 69–83.

66. Duncan Perry, "The Republic of Macedonia: Finding Its Way," in *Politics, Power, and the Struggle for Democracy in South-East Europe*, ed. Karen Dawisha and Bruce Parrott, 235 (Cambridge: Cambridge University Press, 1997).

67. OSCE, "The Former Yugoslav Republic of Macedonia Presidential and Early Parliamentary Elections 13 and 27 April 2014, OSCE/ODIHR Election Observation Mission Final Report" (Warsaw: OSCE/Office of Democratic Institutions and Human Rights, July 15, 2014), http://www.osce.org/odihr/elections/fyrom/121306.

68. Florian Bieber, "Assessing the Ohrid Framework Agreement," in *One Decade after the Ohrid Framework Agreement: Lessons (to Be) Learned from the Macedonian Experience*, ed. Marija Risteska and Zhidas Daskalovski (Skopje: Friedrich Ebert Stiftung and Centre for Research and Policy Making in Macedonia, 2011), 22.

69. CEC (2012) Enlargement Strategy and Main Challenges 2012–2013, COM(2012) 600 final, 35.

70. Daliborka Uljarevic and Stevo Muk, "Montengro," in *Nations in Transit 2013*, Freedom House, http://www.freedomhouse.org/report/nations-transit/2013/montenegro; Montenegro 2012 Progress Report, SWD (2012) 331 final, Brussels, European Commission, October, 10, 2012, http://ec.europa.eu/enlargement/pdf/key_documents/2012/package/mn_rapport_2012_en.pdf.

71. The European Union's Special Investigative Task Force (SITF) is continuing to explore allegations that senior officials were involved in organ trafficking. See Julian Border, "Senior Kosovo Figures Face Prosecution for Crimes against Humanity," *Guardian*, July 29, 2014, http://www.theguardian.com/world/2014/jul/29/senior-political-figures-kosovo-prosecution-crimes-humanity; "Statement by the Chief Prosecutor of the Special Investigative Task Force (SITF) on Investigative Findings," SITF, July 29, 2014, http://www.sitf.eu/index.php/en.

72. "Slovenia Overview," *World Directory of Minorities and Indigenous Peoples*, Minority Rights Group International, http://www.minorityrights.org/?lid=5168.

73. Robert D. Putnam, ed., *Democracies in Flux: The Evolution of Social Capital in Contemporary Society* (New York: Oxford University Press, 2002).

74. Cohen, "Prelates and Politicians in Bosnia."

75. Oberschall, "The Manipulation of Ethnicity," 994–95; Patrizia Poggi et al., *Bosnia and Herzegovina: Local Level Institutions and Social Capital Study*, vol. 1 (Washington, DC: World Bank, 2002).

76. Other groups—the Croatian Defense Forces (HOS) in Croatia, Muslim gangs operating in Sarajevo in 1992, the Kosovo Liberation Army in Kosovo, and the Albanian National Liberation Army and Macedonian Lions in Macedonia—have similar elements.

77. Cynthia Cockburn, *The Space between Us: Negotiating Gender and National Identities in Conflict* (London: Zed Books, 1998).

78. Poggi et al., *Bosnia and Herzegovina*, 83; Bose, *Bosnia after Dayton*, 127.

79. On NGOs, see Paul Stubbs, *Displaced Promises: Forced Migration, Refuge and Return in Croatia and Bosnia-Herzegovina* (Uppsala: Life and Peace Institute, 1999). On good neighborly relations, see Tone Bringa, *Being Muslim the Bosnian Way* (Princeton, NJ: Princeton University Press, 1995). On work, see Paula M. Pickering, "Generating Social Capital for Bridging Ethnic Divisions in the Balkans," *Ethnic and Racial Studies* 29, no. 1 (2006); David Chandler, *Faking Democracy after Dayton* (London: Pluto Press, 2000); Sevima Sali-Terzic, "Civil Society," in *Policies of International Support to South-Eastern European Countries: Lessons (Not) Learnt from Bosnia and Herzegovina*, ed. Žarko Papić (Sarajevo: Open Society Institute, 2001), 138–59.

80. Ivana Howard, "Unfinished Business: Civil Society," in *Unfinished Business: The Western Balkans and the International Community*, ed. Vedran Džihić and Daniel Hamilton (Washington DC: Center for Transatlantic Relations, 2012), 38–39.

81. Howard, "Unfinished Business," 40.

82. Ashutosh Varshney, *Ethnic Conflict and Civic Life: Hindus and Muslims in India* (New Haven, CT: Yale University Press, 2001).

83. Jennifer Stuart, ed., *The 2002 NGO Sustainability Index* (Washington, DC: US Agency for International Development, 2003); Howard, "Unfinished Business," 40.

84. Cynthia Nixon, *The Ties That Bind: Social Capital in Bosnia and Herzegovina* (Sarajevo: UN Development Programme Mission to Bosnia-Herzegovina, Human Development Report, 2009).

85. Aleksandar Djordjevic, BIRN Belgrade, "Party Ties Help NGOs Win Key Serbian Ministerial Deals," *Balkan Insight*, September 6, 2013, http://www.balkaninsight.com/en/article/party-ties-help-ngos-win-key-ministerial-deals (accessed September 14, 2013).

86. See, e.g., the Civil Society Organization, Open Parliament in Serbia at http://www.otvoreniparlament.rs.

87. UN Development Programme (UNDP), *Early Warning System in Bosnia-Herzegovina*, IV (2004, 52), http://www.undp.ba/index.aspx?PID-14 (accessed October 30, 2005).

88. Lenard J. Cohen, "Embattled Democracy: Post-communist Croatia in Transition," in *Politics, Power, and the Struggle for Democracy in South-East Europe*, ed. Karen Dawisha and Bruce Parrott (Cambridge: Cambridge University Press, 1997), 112.

89. UNDP, *Early Warning System in Bosnia-Herzegovina*, 70; UNDP, *Early Warning System Report, FYR Macedonia* (November 2004), 20, http://www.undp.org.mk/default.asp?where-publications (accessed October 30, 2005).

90. Bedrana Kaletović, "Struggle Continues over Personal ID Numbers in BiH" *Southeast European Times*, July 15, 2013, http://www.setimes.com/cocoon/setimes/xhtml/en_GB/features/setimes/features/2013/07/25/feature-03 (accessed September 14, 2013).

91. Mirjana Kasapović et al., *Hrvatska politika, 1990–2000* (Zagreb: Fakultet političkih znanosti Sveučilišta u Zagrebu, 2001), 301, 336; Institute for Democracy and Electoral Analysis (IDEA), "Survey Results: South Eastern Europe: New Means for Regional Analysis," IDEA, 2002, http://archive.idea.int/balkans/survey_detailed.cfm.

92. Gabriel Almond and Sidney Verba, *The Civic Culture* (Princeton, NJ: Princeton University Press, 1978).

93. UNDP, *Early Warning System in Bosnia-Herzegovina*, 180.

94. UNDP, *Early Warning System in Bosnia-Herzegovina*, 70; UNDP, *Early Warning System Report, FYR Macedonia*, 30.

95. European Values Study Group and World Values Survey Association, *European and World Values Surveys Integrated Data File*, 1999–2002, Release 1 (Computer file), 2nd ICPSR version, 2004.

96. IDEA, "Survey Results," http://archive.idea.int/balkans/survey_detailed.cfm. The total survey sample, which includes Romania and Bulgaria, is ten thousand.

97. IDEA, "Survey Results," http://archive.idea.int/balkans/survey_detailed.cfm. The other extremely important elements to have in a society in order to call it democratic include "at least two strong political parties competing in elections; a government that guarantees economic equality of its citizens; the freedom to criticize the government; and equal representation of men and women in elected positions."

98. "European Social Survey Data," ESS5-2010, ed. 3.0, Norwegian Social Science Data Services, http://nesstar.ess.nsd.uib.no/webview.

99. IDEA, "Survey Results." Numerous other studies corroborate these concerns, including Kasapović's *Hrvatska politika*.

100. Zan Strabac, "Social Distance and Ethnic Hierarchies in Croatia," in *The Aftermath of War: Experiences and Social Attitudes in the Western Balkans*, ed. Kristen Ringdal and Albert Simkus (Surrey, UK: Ashgate, 2012), 163.

101. Prism and Paula M. Pickering, *Back from the Brink in Bosnia*, database, 2007; Centre for Research and Policy Making and Paula M. Pickering, *Back from the Brink in Macedonia*, database, 2006. Surveys during the socialist period revealed greater levels of interethnic tolerance in Bosnia than in Macedonia. See Bjiljana Bačević et al., eds., *Jugoslavia na kriznoj prekretnici* (Belgrade: Institut društvenih nauka, 1991). Despite low levels of interethnic tolerance, groups in Macedonia are more resigned to coexisting in the same state than are groups in Bosnia.

102. "Croatian Anti-Cyrillic Protests Continue in Vukovar," *Balkan Insight*, September 4, 2013, http://www.balkaninsight.com/en/article/vukovar-protests-continued-violence-stopped.

103. Paula M. Pickering, *Peacebuilding in the Balkans: The View from the Ground Floor* (Ithaca, NY: Cornell University Press, 2007); Strabac, "Social Distance," 165–66.

104. Public Pulse Report 6, UN Development Programme–Kosovo, Prishina, August 2013, 18–19.

105. European Values Study Group and World Values Survey Association, *European and World Values Surveys*.

106. European Values Study Group and World Values Survey Association, *European and World Values Surveys*.

107. Matić, *Serbia at the Crossroads*, 17.

108. OSCE Democratization Department, *Public Opinion Research* (Sarajevo: OSCE Mission to Bosnia and Herzegovina, May 2004), http://www.oscebih.org/documents/741-eng.pdf.

109. Anis Dani et al., *A Social Assessment of Bosnia and Herzegovina* (Washington, DC: World Bank, Europe and Central Asia Region, Environmentally and Socially Sustainable Development Unit, ECSSD, April 1999).

110. Harriet Alexander, "Slovenia: The Next Crisis for the EU?" *Telegraph*, September 14, 2013, http://www.telegraph.co.uk/news/worldnews/europe/slovenia/10309237/Slovenia-The-next-crisis-for-the-EU.html.

111. International Commission on the Balkans, *The Balkans in Europe's Future* (Sofia: Secretariat Center for Liberal Strategies, 2005), 20.

112. *Nations in Transit 2013*, Freedom House, http://www.freedomhouse.org/report/nations-transit/nations-transit-2013. The corruption score includes a measure of government implementation of anticorruption measures, laws, and public perceptions.

113. Gagnon, *The Myth of Ethnic War*; Cohen, *Serpent and Bosom*, 90.

114. *Bosnia-Herzegovina: Selected Economic Issues*, IMF Country Report 5/198 (Washington, DC: International Monetary Fund, June 2005).

115. Robert Hislope, "Organized Crime in a Disorganized State: How Corruption Contributed to Macedonia's Mini-War," *Problems of Post-communism* 49, no. 3 (May–June 2002): 33–41.

116. Poggi et al., *Bosnia and Herzegovina*, appendix; Gordy, *The Culture of Power*, chap. 5.

117. Peter Sanfey, "South Eastern Europe: Lessons from the Global Economic Crisis," Working Paper No. 113, European Bank for Reconstruction and Development, February 2010, http://www.ebrd.com/downloads/research/economics/workingpapers/wp0113.pdf.

118. Dylan Matthews, "Move Over, Cyprus. Slovenia Is the New Tiny Country You Should Worry About," *Washington Post*, March 24, 2013.

119. The EU publishes annual reports on the progress made by the governments toward meeting the conditions. For example, see "Enlargement," European Commission, http://ec.europa.eu/enlargement/index_en.htm and http://ec.europa.eu/enlargement/countries/strategy-and-progress-report/index_en.htm.

120. Florian Bieber, "Building Impossible States? State-Building Strategies and EU Membership in the Western Balkans," in "Unconditional Conditionality? The Impact of EU Conditionality in the Western Balkans," special issue of *Europe-Asia Studies* 63, no 10 (2011): 1783–802.

Map 18.0.   Ukraine

CHAPTER 18

Ukraine

LEAVING THE CROSSROADS

Taras Kuzio

The year 2014 will prove to be a historical one for Ukraine. Not only did Ukraine leave the crossroads for Europe, but it also underwent a democratic revolution, the Crimea was annexed by Russia, it held two preterm elections and ousted president Viktor Yanukovych, and some members of the Party of Regions and Russia launched a counterrevolution that turned into a violent separatist conflict followed by Russia's invasion of Ukraine. These developments came alongside (weak) Western sanctions; the shooting down of a Malaysian airliner by Russian troops working alongside the separatists, killing three hundred innocent people; the deterioration of the West's relations with Russia, which has been described as a new cold war; an ineffectual and divided European Union (EU); a rejuvenated North Atlantic Treaty Organization (NATO) that called for higher defense spending; and Russian president Vladimir Putin's sabre rattling with his nuclear weapons. "Direct, unconcealed aggression has been launched against Ukraine from a neighboring country," president Petro Poroshenko said in a speech to a military academy in Kyiv in August 2014, believing this "radically changes the situation in the conflict area." US and UK security guarantees given to Ukraine in the 1994 Budapest Memorandum in exchange for giving up the world's third-largest nuclear weapon stockpile proved worthless with a third "guarantor," Russia, annexing one region of Ukraine and invading another. Putin has repeatedly stated that Ukrainians and Russians are "one people."

Elected four months earlier, Poroshenko had to deal with the above factors and a bankrupt country that he inherited from his predecessor, the violent kleptocrat Yanukovych, who fled from Ukraine in February. Poroshenko's options for dealing with the conflict in the Donbas (composed of Donetsk and Luhansk oblasts) were limited. His armed forces and National Guard were defeating the separatists, giving Putin the choice of accepting defeat or using his forces to invade and give direct (no longer covert) backing to separatists; he chose the latter. Putin aims to drive his armed forces and separatist proxies southwest along southern Ukraine towards Odessa to establish a NovoRossiya (New Russia), the tsarist name he uses for eastern and southern Ukraine, to provide a land bridge to the Crimea. Putin insists that this region be given "statehood"—that is, extensive autonomy that would create a frozen conflict inside Ukraine controlled by Moscow, giving Putin a veto over Ukraine's domestic and pro-European foreign policy. Poroshenko will be unable to accept this ultimatum, and therefore Ukraine will continue to be at war with Russia, and the ceasefire negotiated in Minsk remains tenuous; indeed, Putin warned the president of the European Commission José Manuel Durão Barroso that his forces could be in Kyiv in "two weeks." In fact, Putin failed to achieve his objective in Ukraine of creating a "New Russia" from eight Russian-speaking regions of Eastern and Southern Ukraine. He found support in only two (Donetsk, Luhansk), and even there his proxy forces were being defeated. The so-called Donetsk Peoples Republic and "Luhansk Peoples Republic" continue to exist because of Russian occupation forces but only control a third of the Donbas. Ukrainian forces control two-thirds of the Donbas, including most of Luhansk and Western and Southern Donetsk. The ceasefire was a recognition of stalemate whereby neither side had won by achieving its objective—defeat of the separatists (Poroshenko) or establishing a "New Russia" state inside Ukraine (Putin).[1]

The Donbas counterrevolution by the Yanukovych family clan and some members of the Party of Regions would have largely remained peaceful, except for street battles between pro-Ukrainian and pro-Russian supporters. The Donbas never had autonomy in Ukraine, and the Party of Regions centralized Ukraine even more during Yanukovych's presidency. The regions population has an ethnic Ukrainian majority, although the region is also Russian speaking and exhibits (like the Crimea) a strong Soviet identity. Donbas anger at the removal of Yanukovych and counterrevolution only became violent after Russia sent its special forces, provided military training to separatists and heavy and low level military equipment, and invaded with its own troops. Four years earlier the seeds of the conflict were sown with the election of Yanukovych, which ushered in a reversal of the three previous Ukrainian presidents' politics of promoting democratization, Ukrainian national identity, and European integration. Freedom House downgraded Ukraine in early 2011 to "partly free" because it held nondemocratic elections, reintroduced media censorship, and introduced selective use of justice against the political opposition. Yanukovych's term in office brought a return to Sovietophile and Russophile national identity policies last seen in the 1970s and first half of the 1980s. President Yanukovych removed membership in NATO as Ukraine's declared aim (one supported by all three previous Ukrainian presidents), although he continued negotiations with the EU for an association agreement until he abruptly pulled out on the eve of the November 2013 Vilnius Summit.

The ensuing mass protests, known as the Euromaidan, led to bloodshed and Yanukovych's overthrow. The chaotic regime change that resulted provided Russian president Putin with the opportunity to occupy and annex Crimea. The opposition leadership quickly signed the political component of the association agreement in March 2014 and held preterm presidential elections in May 2014. Signing of the Deep and Comprehensive Free Trade Agreement (DCFTA) with the European Union and preterm parliamentary elections took place in June. The European and Ukrainian parliaments simultaneously ratified the Association Agreement in September 2014. Russia's proxy war against and invasion of Ukraine has become the biggest conflict in Europe since the Kosovo crisis in the late 1990s.

Precommunist and Communist Ukraine

Ukraine entered the twentieth century divided between three states. In the eighteenth century, the tsarist Russian Empire annexed central, southern, and eastern Ukraine. Volhynia in western Ukraine was also part of that tsarist empire. Galicia and Transcarpathia were within the Austrian and Hungarian components of the Austro-Hungarian Empire, respectively. Northern Bukovina was part of Romania.

Between 1917 and 1920, western and eastern Ukrainians made various attempts to create an independent state, all of which failed. Ukraine declared independence from tsarist Russia on January 22, 1918, and united with western Ukraine a year later. The White Russian armies that supported the post-tsarist provisional government, the Bolsheviks, and the Poles fought against the independent Ukrainian state. In 1920 and 1921, Ukrainian lands were therefore divided up between four states. The largest portion of Ukrainian territory that had belonged to tsarist Russia became the Ukrainian Soviet Socialist Republic (SSR). Galicia and Volhynia were transferred to newly independent Poland, and Northern Bukovina went to Romania. Transcarpathia went first to the newly constituted Czechoslovakia and then, when Czechoslovakia was dismembered in 1938 and 1939, to Hungary, at the time an ally of Nazi Germany.

In the Soviet era, Ukraine's territory was enlarged on two occasions. The first occurred at the end of World War II with the annexation of western Ukraine (becoming the five oblasts (provinces) of Lviv, Ivano-Frankivsk, Ternopil, Volyn, and Rivne) from Poland, Transcarpathia from Czechoslovakia, and Northern Bukovina (becoming Chernivtsi oblast) from Romania. The second occurred in 1954 when the Crimea was transferred from the Russian Soviet Federative Socialist Republic (RSFSR) to the Ukrainian SSR. Ironically, therefore, the Soviet regime united territories with ethnic Ukrainian majorities into one state (with the exception of Crimea, where Ukrainians were in a minority). The successor state to the Ukrainian SSR declared independence from the USSR on August 24, 1991.

Soviet nationality policies bequeathed two important legacies for post-Soviet Ukraine. First, under Soviet rule, the non-Russian republics were designated as homelands for non-Russian peoples, whose Communist leaders, in return, were expected to keep nationalism in check in strategically important republics such as Ukraine. Soviet nationality policies also included as a central tenet a policy of Russification by encouraging Russians to settle, and Russian to be used, in non-Russian territories. This led to the growth of large numbers of ethnic Ukrainians who spoke Russian, as well as Ukrainians who were bilingual in Russian and Ukrainian. A large number of ethnic Russians also came to live in eastern and southern Ukraine, and ex-military personnel who retired in Crimea, together with the Black Sea Fleet, swelled the ranks of future Russian nationalist-separatist groups.

Paradoxically, Soviet nationality policies also reinforced loyalty to the republics, and non-Russians came increasingly to look on their republics as their homelands and the borders of those republics as sacrosanct. Public opinion polls in the post-Soviet era have reflected a high degree of support for maintaining these inherited borders, including in the Crimea. In post-Soviet Ukraine, separatism never became a major security threat in eastern Ukraine; in Crimea it was influential only in the first half of the 1990s and following the overthrow of Yanukovych in 2014, when a Russian invasion force supported it both covertly and overtly. In both instances, separatism never had majority support. In March 2014 Crimea was formally annexed by Russia in a landgrab unseen in Europe since the 1930s, legitimized by a fraudulent referendum that officially received 97 percent support—an impossible number, because the Tatars boycotted it. The real level of support was 15 percent in a turnout of only 30 percent, as inadvertently reported by the president of Russia's Council on Civil Society and Human Rights.[2]

In the 1920s, Soviet policies of indigenization (*korenizatsia*) supported the Ukrainianization of education, media, and cultural life in Ukraine. Indigenization in the 1920s led to the migration of Ukrainian-speaking peasants to growing urban centers that became home to industry. State institutions and educational facilities provided a Ukrainian language and cultural framework, and in urban centers, increasing numbers of people came to speak Ukrainian.

Soviet dictator Joseph Stalin deemed the continuation of indigenization to be too dangerous, fearing that it would eventually lead to political demands, such as for independence, propelled by a growing differentiation of Ukrainians from Russians. Stalin thus reversed early Soviet nationality policies in three areas. First, the Ukrainian Autocephalous (i.e., independent from Russian) Orthodox Church was destroyed. Second, there were widespread purges, arrests, imprisonments, and executions of the Ukrainian intelligentsia, nationalists, and national communists. Third, Russification replaced indigenization policies, and there was a return to Russian imperial-nationalist historiography. From the 1930s, eastern Ukrainian urban centers, although including increasingly large ethnic Ukrainian majorities, came to be dominated by the Russian language and Soviet/Russian culture, especially in the Donbas region. Soviet identity in the Donbas and Crimea is also Ukrainophobic and its political leaders routinely cooperated with Russian nationalists, fascists, neo-Nazis, imperialists, and Eurasianists who had become influential in Putin's presidency.

The most devastating example of the reversal of Ukrainianization policies was the 1933 artificial famine (*holodomor*, or terror famine) that claimed 4 million lives in Ukraine and the Ukrainian-populated region of Kuban in the North Caucasian region of the RSFSR. The Ukrainian nationally conscious peasantry based in private farms was decimated. Although widely publicized by the Ukrainian diaspora on its fiftieth anniversary in 1983, the *holodomor* only became a subject of public discussion in the USSR in the late 1980s as the result of Soviet leader Mikhail Gorbachev's policy of glasnost. The Communist Party of Ukraine (KPU) condemned the famine in moderate tones in 1990, but it took until 2006 for a law describing the mass murder as "genocide" to be adopted. The law was not supported by the Party of Regions or the Communist Party of Ukraine, both based in the east. After coming to power, Yanukovych adopted Russia's position that the famine affected the entire USSR, not just Ukraine—a viewpoint that infuriated Ukrainian patriots.

A fifth of Ukraine's current population comes from seven oblasts that historically existed outside tsarist Russia or the USSR. Four of these western Ukrainian oblasts (in Galicia and Northern Bukovina) underwent nation building under Austrian rule prior to 1918. After its incorporation into the USSR, nation building in western Ukraine was ironically further facilitated by the actions of the Soviet regime: populations in urban centers in western Ukraine became Ukrainian after the genocide of the Jews and the transfer of Poles to communist Poland. Industrialization and urbanization of Lviv (Lemberg in Austrian, Lwów in Polish) and western Ukraine further increased the numbers of Ukrainians who came to dominate the region's urban centers.

Transcarpathia also underwent ethnic Ukrainian nation building after its incorporation into the USSR. As a consequence of Hungarian assimilationist policies, the region had always been the least Ukrainian nationally conscious of any western Ukrainian region. By the late 1930s, two orientations competed for the allegiance of its eastern Slavic population: Ukrainian and Rusyn, the adherents of the latter claiming that theirs was a separate and fourth eastern Slavic nationality (a third pro-Russian orientation, influential until World War II, became marginalized after the Soviet annexation of the region). After 1945, Soviet nationality policies automatically designated all of the Ukrainian-Rusyn inhabitants of Transcarpathia as Ukrainians. Although a Rusyn revival developed in the late 1980s, it remained marginal in scope, unlike the Rusyn revivals in northeastern Slovakia and the Vojvodina region of Serbia. Ukrainians living in southeastern Poland were expelled in 1947 to former German territories incorporated into Poland under Akcja "Wisła" (Operation Vistula), with the aim of reducing local support for Ukrainian nationalist partisans.

Thus, the Soviet Union pursued contradictory policies in Ukraine. The modernization of Ukraine ensured that its urban centers came to be dominated by ethnic Ukrainians, as seen in the capital city of Kyiv, where the seventeen-day Orange Revolution in 2004 and four-month Euromaidan in 2013–2014 had overwhelming support. At the same time, the eastern and southern territories of Ukraine were exposed to Russification and bilingualism. In western Ukraine, national consciousness grew in Galicia and Volhynia, while in Transcarpathia Soviet power came down on the side of Ukrainian identity. Ethnic Ukrainians came to dominate the Communist Party in the Ukrainian SSR in the post-Stalin era. Nevertheless, the bulk of the republic's largest urban and industrial centers in eastern and southern Ukraine became Russophone or bilingually Ukrainian-Russian, rather than linguistically Ukrainian. Donetsk and Crimea, two regions with large Soviet identities, were the hardcore bases of the KPU and Party of Regions, which won first-place plurality in the 1998, 2006, 2007, and 2012 elections.

Divisions between eastern and western Ukraine continue to complicate national integration. These were starkly evident in the differing degrees of support for Viktor Yushchenko and his opponent, Yanukovych, in western-central and eastern-southern regions, respectively, in the 2004 elections following the Orange Revolution. In the Euromaidan, this east-west split was less stark, as widespread discontent with the Yanukovych regime had spread to eastern and southern Ukraine, and Yanukovych's supporters felt betrayed following his flight from power and the Party of Regions' denunciation of his policies. Crimea remained the only bastion of support for him, fueled by Russian anger at the alleged "Western-backed coup d'état," until he fled into exile in Russia. Criminal charges of mass murder and abuse of office were filed against him, and the EU and United States imposed sanctions and asset freezes on him and over thirty senior officials of his regime.

The End of Soviet Rule and Ukrainian Independence

The differences between the western and eastern parts of Ukraine have always influenced the development of the opposition and civil society. As in the three Baltic states, nationalist partisans (the Ukrainian Insurgent Army [UPA]) fought against Soviet power from 1942 until the early 1950s. Under communism, nationalist sentiment that built on a strong national consciousness influenced the creation of nationalist dissident groups in western Ukraine, such as the National Front, and the largest underground Greek Catholic Church in the world from the 1950s to the 1980s. At the same time, western Ukrainians backed national democrats rather than extreme right nationalists and did not produce an electorally popular nationalist party—Svoboda (Freedom)—until the 2012 elections. Svoboda and nationalist groups uniting in Pravyy Sektor (Right-Wing Sector) then provided volunteers for Euromaidan self-defense units and volunteer battalions for the National Guard sent to fight Russian-backed separatists in the Donbas.

Ukrainian prisoners of conscience were the largest ethnic group proportionate to their share of the population in the Soviet gulag, or system of forced-labor prison camps. Following this tradition, Ukraine was then home to a relatively large number of dissident movements in the post Stalin period. These included the Ukrainian Helsinki Group in the 1970s and 1980s. As in other non-Russian republics, Ukrainian dissidents promoted both national and democratic rights. The Ukrainian movements closely cooperated with Baltic, Georgian, and Jewish dissidents. Some groups (primarily based in western Ukraine) called for Ukraine's separation from the USSR; others (more often based in central and eastern Ukraine) demanded the transformation of the USSR into a loose confederation of sovereign republics. National communism was also never totally crushed and during periods of liberalization, such as the 1960s and the Gorbachev era, became influential within the Communist Party in Soviet Ukraine.

In 1990 and 1991, the Communist Party within the Ukrainian SSR divided into the Democratic Platform (close to the opposition and dominating the leadership of the Komsomol [All-Union Leninist Young Communist League]), sovereign (i.e., national) communism, and pro-Moscow imperial communism. The latter became discredited after it supported the hard-line coup d'état in August 1991. Sovereign communists coalesced around parliamentary speaker Leonid Kravchuk after republican semi-free elections in March 1990. For the first time, a noncommunist opposition, dominated by the Ukrainian Popular Movement for Restructuring (known as Rukh, or "Movement"), the core of what would be the democratic bloc, obtained a quarter of the seats within the Soviet Ukrainian parliament (known as the Supreme Soviet, or Rada).

Moderate Rukh and nationalist radicals began to demand Ukrainian independence in 1989 and 1990. Through a combination of pressure from the more moderate Rukh and sovereign communists, the Ukrainian SSR declared independence in August 1991 after the hard-line coup collapsed in Moscow. All shades of Ukrainian political life (Rukh, radical nationalists, liberal Communists in the Democratic Platform, and national communists) supported the drive to state independence in fall 1991 after the Moscow putsch failed. This movement toward independence was crowned by a December 1, 1991, referendum on independence supported overwhelmingly by 92 percent of Ukrainians. A week later Ukraine, Belarus, and Russia signed an agreement to transform the USSR into the Commonwealth of Independent States (CIS), and the USSR ceased to exist on December 26, 1991.

Political Institutions

In June 1996, Ukraine was the last former Soviet republic to adopt what political scientists describe as a semi-presidential constitution—where the government is controlled by the president, who is elected in a national vote. Not only do presidents dominate the government, but they also have the right to dismiss it.

In roundtable negotiations in the Orange Revolution, a compromise package was agreed on and voted through by parliament on December 8, 2004. The package amended the election law to reduce election fraud, adopted constitutional reforms to go into effect in 2006, and replaced the Central Election Commission chairman. The reformed constitution transformed Ukraine from a semi-presidential into a parliamentary system in which the government was responsible to a parliamentary coalition and the president was elected in a national vote (not by parliament, as in a full parliamentary system). The president continued to control foreign and defense policy, the National Security and Defense Council, the Security Service, and the prosecutor general's office and also appointed regional governors in consultation with the government. Four years later, after Yanukovych had been elected president, the Constitutional Court overturned this change and returned Ukraine to a presidential system. Then, as one of its first acts, the Euromaidan opposition leadership overturned the Constitutional Court's 2010 decision and reinstated parliamentary rule, because Yanukovych's four-year absolutist monopoly on power had thoroughly discredited presidentialism.

Electoral law has also shifted in response to popular demand and disgust with Yanukovych's authoritarian rule. In April 2004 the election law was changed, and all 450 seats were contested in a proportional system with a lower 3 percent threshold for a longer five-year term. This election system was used in the March 2006 and the preterm September 2007 elections. The election law was changed again for the 2012 elections, returning Ukraine to the mixed system used in 1998 and 2002, in which half of seats were elected proportionally under a 5 percent threshold and the other half in first-past-the-post single-mandate districts. Preterm parliamentary elections in October 2014 continued to use this mixed system.

The Yanukovych administration preferred the mixed system, because they could get a plurality of the seats allocated in the proportional representation half and then the support of a majority of deputies elected in single-member districts. The victors in this half of the election tended to be officials or businesspeople who aligned with the authorities, enabling the Party of Regions, when it held the presidency, to establish a parliamentary majority. This backfired after Yanukovych fled from office because the majoritarian deputies switched sides, giving the opposition a constitutional majority of more than three hundred, enabling it to adopt revolutionary changes, such as constitutional reforms, introduce criminal charges against Yanukovych and his entourage, and free political prisoners, such as Yulia Tymoshenko.

During Yanukovych's four years in power, the president took control over the judicial system and gave senior appointments on the Constitutional Court and Supreme Court to allies from his home region. The Supreme Court was marginalized by the July 2010 judicial reforms in revenge for its annulment of Yanukovych's second-round election in November 2004. The Constitutional Court made two rulings in 2010 that it had refused to countenance under President Yushchenko. The first decreed that individuals (not just factions as it had ruled in 2008) could join parliamentary coalitions. This increased political corruption in parliament when sums of $1 million to $5 million were paid to opposition deputies to encourage their defection. The second decreed that the

2004 constitutional reforms implemented after the 2006 elections were unconstitutional and returned Ukraine to the 1996 semi-presidential system.

Political Parties and Elections

On the same day as the referendum on independence in December 1991, parliamentary speaker and senior leader of the Soviet Ukrainian Communist Party, Kravchuk, was elected in Ukraine's first presidential election, winning in the first round with 61.59 percent. National democratic reformers grouped in Rukh supported the former political prisoner Vyacheslav Chornovil, who obtained a quarter of the vote. The main competition in the 1994 election was between two wings of the pre-1991 national communist camp: former prime minister Leonid Kuchma and incumbent Kravchuk, who was defeated by 52.1 to 45.1 percent. The Ukrainian parliament continued to be dominated by former communists until the March 1994 elections, when the results reflected the negative impact of economic reform and delays in the adoption of a post-Soviet constitution. National democrats won the 2004 presidential elections after the Orange Revolution and again in 2014 when Ukraine elected its first pro-European parliament, the first without a sizable pro-Russian lobby.

During the Kravchuk presidency (December 1991–July 1994), Ukraine's political landscape continued to be dominated by three groups. The KPU returned, after being banned from August 1991 to October 1993, as a new political party led by Petro Symonenko. Being required to register as a new Communist Party meant it legally had no connection to the pre–August 1991 party and no claim to Communist Party assets nationalized by the Ukrainian state after the party was banned. The newly registered KPU attracted less than 5 percent of the members of the pre-1991 Communist Party in Ukraine, which, at its peak in 1985, had 3.5 million members. The post-1993 membership of the KPU has never exceeded 150,000 members.

The KPU's high point of influence had been in the 1990s, when it was ostensibly the main opposition to the ruling authorities. In the 1994–1998 and 1998–2002 parliaments, the KPU had the largest factions, with 135 and 123 deputies, respectively. In the October–November 1999 presidential election, KPU leader Symonenko came in second in a field of thirteen candidates and then faced incumbent Kuchma in round two. Kuchma defeated Symonenko by a large margin, and the KPU's fortunes declined.

In the 2002–2006 parliament, the KPU faction was halved to sixty-six deputies. The KPU declined rapidly following the end of the Kuchma era, as many voters transferred their allegiance to the Party of Regions. In the 2006 and 2007 elections, the KPU obtained only 3.66 and 5.39 percent, respectively, of the vote. In 2012, some former communist voters returned from the Party of Regions, and it again came in fourth, with 13 percent. After the Euromaidan, the KPU came under legal scrutiny for supporting separatism, and its popularity plummeted. As a result, the party failed to enter parliament in the 2014 elections."

The Socialist Party of Ukraine (SPU), led by Oleksandr Moroz, became the only left-wing competitor to the KPU after its launch in October 1991. The SPU is a left-wing social democratic party committed to democratization and Ukrainian statehood but largely opposed to economic reform, especially land reform. The SPU was one of two Ukrainian members of the Socialist International until it was expelled in July 2011. The

SPU's membership grew to one hundred thousand, and its electoral support overtook that of the communists, surpassing them in the 2004 and 2006 elections. In 2004, Moroz came in third with 5.82 percent of the vote, followed by Symonenko with 4.97 percent. The SPU achieved fourth place in the 2006 elections with 5.69 percent and thirty-three seats, followed by the KPU with 3.66 percent and twenty-one deputies.

The SPU's fortunes declined after it defected from the Orange coalition in summer 2006 and joined the Party of Regions and KPU in the Anti-Crisis parliamentary coalition. The preterm September 2007 and 2010 presidential elections marginalized the SPU as a political force. Moroz, in refusing to step down as leader of the party, took the party down with him. In Ukraine political leaders treat parties as their private property and refuse to resign following election defeats. In the 2012 elections, the SPU continued its slide into oblivion, coming in tenth with 0.45 percent of the vote, and in 2014 Moroz did not stand as a candidate.

On the right, a plethora of national democratic parties grew out of Rukh. As in the Soviet era, these parties and movements combined national and democratic demands, such as affirmative action for the Ukrainian language, making them popular primarily in Ukrainian-speaking regions of western and central Ukraine. The 2002 elections proved to be a watershed for national democrats when Our Ukraine, with 23.57 percent of the vote, beat the KPU into second place. But after many voters defected to the Bloc of Yulia Tymoshenko (BYuT), Our Ukraine fared poorly in the March 2006 and September 2007 elections, coming in third with 13.95 and 14.15 percent of the vote, respectively, and then became marginalized after Yushchenko left office in 2010. In the 2006, 2007, and 2012 parliamentary elections, a pattern emerged whereby BYuT—which included Batkivshchina (Fatherland), the Social Democratic Party of Ukraine, and the Reforms and Order Party—took second place with between 24 and 31 percent of the vote; Our Ukraine and the Ukrainian Democratic Alliance for Reforms (UDAR) came in third, with a total of 14 percent. In effect, national democratic and liberal voters who did not wish to support Tymoshenko backed Our Ukraine and UDAR and also voted for the candidacies of Sergei Tigipko and Arseniy Yatseniuk in 2010. UDAR's leader, Vitaliy Klitschko, did not run for president in 2014, dropping out in favor of Poroshenko; instead, he ran for and won the election for Kyiv city mayor.

Centrist-liberal and social democratic parties emerged in Ukraine in the late Soviet and early post-Soviet era from two primary sources. The first was the Komsomol, whose members, as the youth elite of the Soviet Communist Party, used their connections to enter newly formed cooperatives under Gorbachev and formed banks and new businesses in the 1990s. The Komsomol supported the Democratic Platform inside the Communist Party in the late 1980s, which placed them ideologically close to moderate national democrats, with whom they cooperated in the 1990s. An early ex-Komsomol-led political force was the Party of Democratic Revival of Ukraine (PDVU), which merged in 1996 with two other parties to establish the People's Democratic Party (NDP). The PDVU and Interregional Bloc of Reforms created the New Ukraine bloc, which, together with the Union of Industrialists and Entrepreneurs, supported Kuchma's candidacy in the 1994 elections. In Dnipropetrovsk, former Komsomol leaders Viktor Pinchuk and Tigipko launched Labor Ukraine, while Pavlo Lazarenko took control of the Hromada (Community) party, on whose list Tymoshenko was elected to parliament in 1998.

A second source for so called centrist parties emerged in Crimea, Donetsk, and Odessa, the most violent cities and regions during Ukraine's 1990s transition to a market economy. In Donetsk a nexus of criminal figures, emerging tycoons, and former leaders of large Soviet plants (so-called Red Directors) played a major role. Violence and assassinations of senior criminal and business leaders were dramatic elements of politics throughout the 1990s, with the most famous being the murders of crime boss Akhat Bragin in the Donetsk football stadium in 1995 and of Yevhen Shcherban, then Ukraine's wealthiest oligarch, in the city's airport in 1996. Rinat Akhmetov, who established a close alliance with Yanukovych, whom he lobbied for the position of regional governor, eventually replaced Shcherban as Ukraine's wealthiest oligarch. Akhmetov was reportedly involved in criminal activities from the mid-1980s to early 1990s, when he was routinely seen in the company of more senior local criminal figures, such as his mentor, Bragin. In Donetsk, Red Directors established the Labor Party and the Party of Regional Revival, but they, together with another Donetsk party, the Liberals, failed to gain popularity in the 1990s. In Crimea, similar wide-scale violence decimated the Party of Economic Revival and others.

The breakthrough for that group in Donetsk came following the appointment of Yanukovych as regional governor in 1997, after which competing criminal groups and political leaders were eliminated and removed. Violence abated from 1999–2000, when victorious criminal groups, new tycoons, Red Directors, and regional elites came together and launched the Party of Regions. In return for de facto regional autonomy to pursue political consolidation and capital accumulation, the Donetsk clan, which had established a local monopoly of power in all facets of life, supported Kuchma in the 1999 and 2002 elections and were rewarded with the positions of prime minister and presidential candidate in 2002 and 2004, respectively. Yanukovych was a serial election "fraudster," abusing state administrative resources as Donetsk regional governor (1999, 2002), prime minister (2004), and president (2010, 2012). His misuse of power ended only when he disappeared into Russia, leaving a multi-million-dollar palace (Mezhyhirya) built with state monies.

The Party of Regions, which emerged from the nexus forged in the violent and criminal Donetsk region in the 1990s, had three attributes that were visible during the Euromaidan and Donbas separatist conflict. First, it was far more authoritarian than ex-Komsomol-led centrist parties. Second, with a more leftist populist ideology, it could readily cooperate with the KPU, with whom it shared home bases in Donetsk and Crimea, in contrast to anticommunist centrists. Third, its regional Sovietized culture facilitated an alliance with Russian nationalist-separatists in Crimea whom President Kuchma had fought and marginalized. These three characteristics meant the Yanukovych presidency and Party of Regions posed a greater threat to Ukraine's democracy than any other group in three ways. First, violence came naturally to them as seen through the imprisonment of opposition leaders, extensive use of violence in the Euromaidan, and widespread human rights abuses during the Donbas separatist conflict.[3] Second, corruption was rapacious, as witnessed by the palaces they occupied, which were opened to the public after their overthrow.[4] The Ukrainian prosecutor's office estimated the Yanukovych team had stolen upward of $100 billion during its four-year kleptocracy—nearly enough to trigger a national financial collapse on its own. Third, they were hostile to ethnic Ukrainian national identity, opposed to NATO membership, and lukewarm on EU integration—all of which inflamed nationalist and anti-Soviet sentiment.

In Donetsk, the 1990s-era disunity of regional elites was overcome when, with the support of regional governor Yanukovych, the Party of Regions was launched through a merger of five political parties ("Red Director" Labor Party, Party of Regional Revival, Poroshenko's Party of Solidarity, former Kyiv mayor Leonid Chernovetsky's Party of Beautiful Ukraine, and the Party of Ukrainian Pensioners). In the March 2002 elections, the Party of Regions joined the Party of Industrialists and Entrepreneurs, the Agrarians, the NDP, and Labor Ukraine in the pro-presidential For a United Ukraine (ZYU). With 11.77 percent of the vote, ZYU came in third in the proportional half of the elections but was able to control half of parliament by adding a large number of deputies elected in majoritarian districts. In the 2006 elections, the Party of Regions came in first with 32.14 percent and 186 seats; it was the only former pro-Kuchma party that succeeded in entering parliament in the next two elections. The Party of Regions won 34.37 percent in the 2007 elections but obtained fewer votes and eleven fewer seats than in the 2006 elections. In the 2012 elections, the Party of Regions again won a first-place plurality with 30 percent.

The Party of Regions became Ukraine's only political machine for a decade because it was never tied to a single leader. Instead, since its launch in 2001, it has had Nikolai Azarov (2001 and 2010–2014), Volodymyr Semynozhenko (2001–2003), and Yanukovych (2003–2010). The other parties that have played significant political roles in this period (Our Ukraine, Batkivshchina, SPU, KPU, and UDAR) cannot be divorced from their leaders, Yushchenko, Tymoshenko, Moroz, Symonenko, and Klitschko, respectively.

The Party of Regions will not remain a formidable political machine following the battles over control of Donbas and Russia's invasion, as well as the ouster of Yanukovych and criminal charges against government and party leaders. The meager vote (3 percent) for its candidate Mykhaylo Dobkin in the 2014 presidential elections represented a major defeat and undoubtedly influenced its decision to not put forward candidates and participate in that year's parliamentary elections.

Ukraine's electoral map changed in the October 2014 preterm parliamentary elections when Ukraine elected its first pro-European parliament. Ukraine's new political geography owes much to former president Yanukovych's four-year kleptocracy and Russian president Putin's annexation and invasion of Ukraine, which led to the disintegration of the pro-Russian camp. The OSCE, EU, and United States hailed the elections as having been held in a free and fair manner while European Commission president Jose Manuel Barroso described them as a result of the "victory of democracy and European reforms' agenda."

Political forces taking the top three places include the Petro Poroshenko bloc, Prime Minister Yatseniuk's Popular Front, and Lviv mayor Andriy Sadovyy's Samopomych (Self Reliance) who together with Tymoshenko's Fatherland party, which came in last, control 63 percent of seats. Yatseniuk continued as head of government after his hastily created new Popular Front received a similar vote to the Poroshenko bloc. A new political force elected to the Ukrainian parliament was Sadovyy's Self Reliance party, which attracted middle class businesspersons and professionals in Western and Central Ukraine, although one of its leading candidates was Russian-speaking Semen Semenchenko, commander of the Donbas volunteer battalion. Other new faces—journalists, civil society leaders, and military commanders—were elected inside established political forces.

Although Russian television continues to overwhelmingly portray Ukraine as a country run by "fascists" the two nationalist parties (Freedom and Right Sector) did not enter parliament. Ukraine's nationalists are decidedly pro-European, unlike their counterparts throughout the European Union (EU), and individuals elected in single mandate districts will join the pro-European coalition giving it a constitutional majority of over two-thirds of the seats.

Two of the three representatives of the former Yanukovych regime failed to enter parliament. The Communist Party had long ago given up being a party of the downtrodden proletariat and had become a satellite of the party of wealthy tycoons, which is for the first time no longer represented. It is highly likely Ukraine has seen the heyday of the Communist Party. Former Deputy Prime Minister Tigipko's Strong Ukraine also failed to cross the five percent threshold. Yanukovych's flight from Ukraine followed by Putin's military invasions led to the disintegration of the party's monopolization of power in Russian-speaking eastern and southern Ukraine. The Crimea and Donbas were the Party of Regions' two main strongholds and voting took place in thirteen out of thirty-two election districts in the Donbas controlled by Ukrainian security forces. Separatist insurgents threatened anybody attempting to vote in areas under their control. Reconstituted as the so-called Opposition Bloc but still led by the same discredited personalities, the old-new force came in fourth. The Radical Party that came in fifth is a populist protest party funded by Ukraine's gas lobby, created to take votes from Euromaidan parties.

President Poroshenko, speaking after the elections closed, called for a "purification of authorities" and said, "It's time to complete a full reset of power."[5] With the election of a pro-European president in May 2014 and the October 2014 election of a pro-European constitutional majority in parliament, there are no longer political obstacles to implementing long-overdue reforms and fighting high-level abuse of office and corruption. Ukraine's civil society, as witnessed in the four-month Euromaidan revolution, its massive support to the armed forces and National Guard, and election monitoring, is far more politically mature than the country's ruling elites.

Civil Society: The Orange Revolution and the Euromaidan

The Orange Revolution occurred when the authorities blatantly attempted to rig the presidential elections in 2004, while the Euromaidan exploded in response to Yanukovych's turning away from European integration and in reaction to his wide-scale abuse of office during his presidency. The Yushchenko team had a program, alternative candidates, and a process for change in 2004. The Euromaidan was a spontaneous response to Yanukovych's decision that had, initially, no leadership, alternative, or process for making change. As is clear from the choice of orange as an optimistic and neutral color to attract a broad constituency of voters, rather than using the national colors of the blue and yellow flag; the Orange Revolution was intended to be inclusionary. Participants in the Euromaidan carried a wide array of Ukrainian national (blue and yellow), nationalist (red and black), and party flags and did not produce its own colors and symbols.

The victory of Our Ukraine in the 2002 election ensured that Yushchenko would become the main alternative to the authorities' candidate in the 2004 election. The 2004 election, therefore, became a choice in the eyes of a large proportion of Ukrainian voters between democracy (Yushchenko) and authoritarianism (Yanukovych).[6]

Two factors provided momentum for civil society prior to the Orange Revolution. First, the Kuchmagate crisis, which began on November 28, 2000, arose after excerpts of tapes made illicitly in the president's office by Mykola Melnychenko, an officer of the Directorate on State Security (the Ukrainian equivalent of the US Secret Service), were released during a parliamentary session. Kuchma was heard on the tape ordering Interior Minister Yuriy Kravchenko to "deal with" opposition journalist Georgiy Gongadze, who had been kidnapped on September 16, 2000, and whose decapitated body was found on November 2, 2000, near Kyiv. The second factor was the mounting criticism of Prime Minister Yushchenko's anticorruption policies from oligarchs close to Kuchma who were threatened by anticorruption measures in the energy sector. Deputy Prime Minister Tymoshenko had reorganized the energy sector and targeted distribution companies owned by leading oligarch groups, which returned billions of dollars to the government budget that were used to pay wage and pension arrears. The Kuchmagate crisis and anticorruption government policies led to an April 2001 vote of no confidence in the Yushchenko government, pushing him into the opposition, where he never felt truly comfortable.

The Kuchmagate crisis had mobilized the largest opposition movement since the late Soviet era in Ukraine, the "Ukraine without Kuchma" movement based in Kyiv and dominated by the center-left SPU and BYuT. These anti-Kuchma protests in 2000 and 2001 were followed by "Arise, Ukraine!" protests in 2002 and 2003 just ahead of the Orange Revolution. The protests became an important source of experience for youth and election-observer nongovernmental organizations (NGOs) and political parties that was useful for the 2004 elections and the Orange Revolution.

State-administrative resources were massively deployed in support of Yanukovych in the 2004 elections. The state- and oligarch-controlled mass media, particularly television, gave widespread positive coverage to Yanukovych while covering Yushchenko largely in negative terms. Yanukovych used official and underground election campaign teams. The official campaign was headed by the chairman of the National Bank, Tigipko; the shadow campaign was led by Yanukovych's longtime ally, Andriy Kluyev, and Russian "political technologists" who were deeply involved in the use of dirty tricks. The most dramatic of these was the poisoning of Yushchenko with dioxin in September 2004, which removed him from the campaign trail for a month. Kluyev was implicated in police violence during the Euromaidan (specifically ordering Berkut to brutally attack students on the night of November 30 after Yanukovych had returned from Vilnius and gone hunting at Mezhyhirya; the president was very angry at his reception in Lithuania and wanted to see blood) and, as Yanukovych's last chief of staff, fled with him into hiding in Russia.

On October 31, 2004, Yushchenko won the first round of the election, followed by Yanukovych. Yanukovych's shadow campaign team and the presidential administration hacked into the Central Election Commission server, which allowed them to manipulate results as they were being sent in. Despite the government's manipulation and the poisoning, Yushchenko won round one, which was an important psychological boost to the opposition. His victory also influenced fence sitters among state officials, many of whom would swing to his side or stay neutral in the next two rounds of voting and the Orange Revolution.

The Yanukovych camp ratcheted up its efforts to deliver him the election by using more blatant fraud, whatever the actual vote. The Committee of Voters of Ukraine, an authoritative NGO, calculated that 2.8 million votes were fraudulently added to Yanukovych's tally in round two. Fraud was especially blatant in Donetsk and Luhansk, Yanukovych's home base. Ballot stuffing, massive abuse of absentee ballots, and voting at

Photo 18.1. In what would come to be known as the Orange Revolution, protesters take to the streets in Kyiv to protest fraudulent presidential election results in 2004. (This photo was taken through joint efforts of the UNIAN news agency [http://www .unian.net] and the International Renaissance Foundation/George Soros Foundation in Ukraine [http://www.irf.kiev.ua].)

Photo 18.2. Yushchenko and Yanukovych after Yushchenko won the rerun of the second round of the 2004 Ukrainian election, after the fraud in the second round triggered the Orange Revolution. Two years later Yanukovych's party won enough votes to dominate the parliament and make him prime minister from 2006 to 2007. In 2010 he won the presidential election. (This photo was taken through joint efforts of the UNIAN news agency [http://www.unian.net] and the International Renaissance Foundation/ George Soros Foundation in Ukraine [http://www.irf.kiev.ua].)

home were also used. Tapes made illicitly by the Security Service (SBU) in Yanukovych's election campaign headquarters recorded conversations organizing a fraudulent 3 percent election victory for Yanukovych.[7]

The Ukrainian parliament and the Supreme Court overturned the fraudulent election results that declared Yanukovych the victor in round two. Roundtable negotiations brokered by Poland, Lithuania, and the EU led to a compromise; the election law was revised so that many of the fraudulent acts committed in round two could not be repeated. The Supreme Court ordered a repeat election held on December 26, 2004. Yushchenko also agreed to support moving to a parliamentary system in 2006. After winning by 8 percent in the rerun of round two, Yushchenko was inaugurated on January 23, 2005, as Ukraine's third president.

Yushchenko's election victory came about as a consequence of a very broad political alliance that included center-leftists (SPU), center-left-liberals (BYuT), free market liberals (Party of Industrialists and Entrepreneurs), center-right national democrats (Our Ukraine), and nationalists (Congress of Ukrainian Nationalists). The divisions within this election alliance over political and institutional policies included support for parliamentary or presidential systems, whether to launch criminal investigations of former regime officials on charges of corruption and election fraud, the degree of reprivatization to be undertaken, types of economic reform, whether to pursue land privatization, and NATO membership.

Yulia Tymoshenko, who had partnered with him in the presidential campaign and the Orange coalition, became prime minister in February 2005. In Yushchenko's (and her) first one hundred days in office, divisions over economic policies brought about an oil crisis, continuing concerns over economic policies that focused on social issues, and a decline in the growth of the gross domestic product (GDP) by half. In September 2005, Yushchenko dismissed Tymoshenko's government and replaced her with Yuriy Yekhanurov, whose government lasted until after the March 2006 elections. It was replaced in August by a government led again by Yanukovych, who was to be the first prime minister to benefit from enhanced powers in the parliamentary constitution.

Dealing with reprivatizations was a major issue. The 2005 Tymoshenko government had supported investigating a large number of privatizations undertaken in the 1990s, while Yushchenko and the 2005–2006 government led by Our Ukraine leader Yekhanurov (who had been head of the State Property Fund in the 1990s, when most oligarchs emerged) opposed the investigations and subsequent reprivatizations in all but the most egregious of cases, such as the Kryvorizhstal steel plant. This, Ukraine's largest metallurgical plant, was privatized in June 2004 for $800,000 and sold to two Ukrainian oligarchs, one of whom was Kuchma's son-in-law, Viktor Pinchuk. It was reprivatized in October 2005 for six times this amount.

Elections from 2006 to 2014

Out of the multitude of parties and blocs that stood in elections in 2006, 2007,2012, and 2014 only five or six crossed the 3 to 5 percent threshold in each election. The 2006 elections brought three Orange parties to parliament (Our Ukraine, BYuT, and SPU), but the SPU defected to the Party of Regions and KPU, which established the Anti-Crisis parliamentary coalition. The 2007 elections brought Our Ukraine, BYuT, and two opposition political forces into parliament, with the Party of Regions the key winner, electing 186 deputies, a threefold increase in its support.

In the 2006 elections, BYuT also scored a remarkable success, tripling its support and becoming the second-largest faction, with 129 deputies. In the 2007 elections it dramatically increased its vote to receive 30.71 percent, and in 2012, when blocs were banned from participating, Batkivshchina (by then merged with the Reform and Order and Front for Change parties) received 25.54. Our Ukraine and Our Ukraine–People's Self-Defense (NUNS) received third place in the 2006 and 2007 preterm elections. Our Ukraine/NUNS center-right niche in Ukrainian politics was taken by UDAR (*udar* means "punch"), led by international boxing champion Klitschko.[8] Protesting Yanukovych's policies against Ukrainian national identity and the 2012 language law, some national democratic (Orange) voters backed the Svoboda party, which became the first nationalist party to enter parliament. Svoboda had been called the Social-National Party of Ukraine until 2004, when the charismatic Oleh Tyahnybok took over as leader and set it on a course of modernization into a European nationalist populist party. In the 2014 elections, the largest vote went to the vacuous Poroshenko bloc, an alliance of the president's third Solidarity party and UDAR that included the largest number of candidates with ties to the *ancien régime*, Oleh Lyashko's Radical Party, Yatseniuk's Popular Front (which split from Batkivshchina), Tigipko's revived Strong Ukraine party (the original had merged with the Party of Regions in 2012), Batkivshchina, Anatoliy Grytsenko's Civic Initiative (which includes the Democratic Alliance dominated by young activists), and Lviv mayor Andriy Sadovyy's Samopomych (Self-Help). These political forces included Euromaidan activists, middle class businesspersons, well-known independent journalists (such as Serhiy Leshchenko), and military and National Guard commanders.

The 2007 elections returned a slim Orange coalition that eventually agreed to put forward Tymoshenko as prime minister but faced by two major obstacles. The first was opposition from Yushchenko, who—as in 2005—sought to undermine the government at every turn. As Anders Aslund notes, "Yushchenko's behavior in 2008 was perplexing. Although he formed a coalition with Tymoshenko, he never gave her government a chance to work. His whole presidency has been marked by legislative stalemate."[9] Bizarrely, Yushchenko was opposing a government in which he had demanded and received cabinet positions. Second, from fall 2008, Ukraine was one of the five countries in Europe most affected by the global financial crisis. The government negotiated a $16.4 billion stand-by arrangement with the International Monetary Fund (IMF), without which it would have been impossible to stabilize the economy after GDP had decreased by 15 percent. But the government faced continued domestic obstruction from the president and a parliament often blocked by the Party of Regions.

In September 2008, the coalition collapsed after NUNS voted to withdraw. In December 2008, a new Orange coalition was established by BYuT, NUNS, and the Volodymyr Lytvyn bloc, and Lytvyn was offered the position of parliamentary speaker.

The January 17, 2010, presidential elections in many ways repeated the 2004 elections, with Yanukovych facing a main Orange opponent, this time Tymoshenko. These two candidates remained unchallenged and made it easily into the second round with 35 and 25 percent of the vote, respectively. In the second round, Tymoshenko greatly expanded her voter base from 25 to 45 percent by including a large number of negative votes against Yanukovych. But this proved insufficient, and she was defeated by 3.48 percent. Yanukovych became the first Ukrainian president not to receive 50 percent of the vote and not to win a majority of Ukrainian regions.

Tymoshenko was ultimately defeated by three factors. First, she was the incumbent prime minister during a global economic-financial crisis when Ukraine's economy had gone into recession. Second, voters were tired of Orange infighting between Yushchenko and Tymoshenko, which bred disillusionment and cynicism in politicians, and Yushchenko convinced some voters to vote against both candidates, thereby hurting Tymoshenko. Third, unlike in 2004, the former Orange camp was heavily divided between five candidates in the first round, making it impossible for Tymoshenko to win in that round.

Yatseniuk's popularity grew quickly, making it seem that a new face would emerge in Ukrainian politics (Yatseniuk only turned thirty-five, the minimum age to contest a presidential election, in 2009). Unfortunately, his election campaign was a disaster. It was led by Russian political technologists (combining dirty tricksters, election manipulation, and black PR consultants) who designed his messages that were characterized by unpopular military fatigue colors displayed on billboards. Yatseniuk received 7 percent of the vote, pushed into fourth place by Tigipko, who polled 13 percent. Together, the combined Yatseniuk-Tigipko 20 percent of the vote for third and fourth place represented a new middle-class voting phenomenon in Ukrainian elections that became an important factor in providing resources and supporters for the Euromaidan. Tigipko and Yatseniuk voters were urban professionals and businesspeople who disliked the second-round choice because it represented the old guard of Ukrainian politics.

The mass protests over the course of seventeen days in 2004 came to be known as the Orange Revolution, but they never became a genuine revolution, and the opaque manner in which politics and business were conducted in Ukraine never changed. The four-month-long Euromaidan was a genuine civil-society-driven revolution with its own pantheon of martyrs. The Euromaidan exploded spontaneously in November 2013 in protest at Yanukovych's abrupt decision to drop European integration. The passage of antidemocratic legislation on "Black Thursday" (January 16, 2014) and his refusal to compromise and negotiate with the opposition led to two explosions of violence that left over one hundred dead and more than one thousand wounded protesters.

Public outrage had been fueled by four years of attacks on democracy and ethnic Ukrainian national identity and the lawlessness rampant in the courts, police, and SBU and among the lawmakers from the ruling Party of Regions. Ukrainians felt their rulers were treating them with visible contempt as a conquered population and that there was no accountability or limit to what could be undertaken. The constitutional court was stacked with the president's cronies, the judiciary was corrupted, parliament had been turned into a rubber-stamp body through which legislation was railroaded without the votes, and opposition leaders were thrown into jail.

Meanwhile, the government headed by Party of Regions leader Azarov undertook incompetent policies that pushed Ukraine to the edge of default. While the standard of living of most Ukrainians was in decline, a small clique of oligarchs and the president's "Family" (a cabal of his family members and loyalists from his home region) continued to amass fortunes through rigged government tenders that became the subject of criminal investigations by the Euromaidan leaders. Together, these factors provided a combustible protest mood that united students, middle-class professionals, businesspeople,

Photo 18.3.   Euromaidan demonstrations with police facing off against demonstrators in 2014. (Corbis)

nationalists, farmers, and workers. The Euromaidan was anti-Soviet, nationalist, and pro-democratic—much like the protest movements in the late 1980s—and supported Ukraine's European integration. This anticommunist/Soviet revolution was witnessed in the Euromaidan and since then over four hundred monuments to Vladimir Lenin were dismantled, the most well-known being in Kyiv (December 2013) and the largest in Kharkiv (September 2014). Domestic and international outrage at the mass murder of protesters in February 2014, EU-targeted sanctions against officials and oligarchs, and EU assistance in brokering a peace agreement led to a short hiatus before Yanukovych and his close allies fled Kyiv, fearing for their lives. The opposition quickly took control of parliament, which began to rule the country, introduced reforms backed by a new IMF agreement and Western diplomatic support from the G7, and set preterm elections. The new government was led by Prime Minister Yatseniuk and included a wide range of civil society activists such as investigative journalist Tetyana Chornovol, who had been savagely beaten during the protests after she published a blog post on Interior Minister Vitaliy Zakharchenko's luxurious palace.

The May 2014 preterm presidential election campaign was shorter, relations between candidates were less antagonistic, and the mood, following the state of the economy and finances and Russian annexation of the Crimea, was more somber. A third of the Donbas controlled by pro-Russian separatists could not participate, and pro-European candidates and parties dominated both the 2014 presidential (Poroshenko and Tymoshenko) and parliamentary elections (the only moderate pro-Russian force entering parliament was Strong Ukraine).

The Economic Transition

Between 1989 and 1999 Ukraine's GDP collapsed by more than half, the deepest economic recession in the former USSR. The shadow (unofficial) economy has averaged 40 percent (official figure) to 50 percent (World Bank figure) of total economic activity, a factor that further reduced income to the state budget, facilitated corruption, and encouraged ties between business and corrupt figures and criminal structures. Billions of dollars have been sent to offshore zones in EU countries, including Cyprus, which accounted for a third of total "foreign" investment in Ukraine, Switzerland, and offshore tax havens such as the Virgin Islands, Monaco, and Lichtenstein.

Ukraine underwent two rapid periods of economic reform that established a market economy, the first between 1994 and 1996 after Kuchma was elected and signed an agreement with the IMF and the second in 2000 and 2001 during the Yushchenko government. Following the signing of IMF agreements, government policies have traditionally been successful with stabilizing the situation but then have stagnated without undertaking structural reforms. Ukraine has therefore been stuck at the crossroads in what economists have described as a "partially reformed equilibrium," where elites receive advantages from the still opaque nature of the economy and business and politics remain closely interwoven.[10] As the Heritage Foundation has shown in its annual rankings, Ukraine is defined as a "repressed economy," the least free in Europe and ranked toward the bottom of the fifteen former Soviet republics. The Ukrainian economy is still only three-quarters the size of the Soviet Ukrainian economy in 1989, and small and medium businesses only contribute 16 percent of Ukraine's GDP, less than anywhere in the EU, where the average is 57 percent.

Frequent changes of government were a major problem that plagued Ukraine's economic policies during the Kravchuk and Kuchma eras (1991–2004), when Ukraine had ten governments. Of these, the government led by Yushchenko (December 1999–April 2001) was the only one genuinely committed to economic reform and battling corruption. Yushchenko had also been chairman of the National Bank when Ukraine introduced its independent currency, the hryvnia, in 1996.

Economic reform under Kravchuk was never a priority; instead, he adopted nationalist protectionist policies directed against Russia. These policies proved to be disastrous, and in 1993 the country experienced hyperinflation and further economic collapse. Miners' strikes and social unrest deepened and led to preterm presidential elections. Kuchma introduced economic reform policies to stabilize the domestic economy after the IMF and World Bank began to provide assistance to Ukraine for the first time in return for a pledge to pursue reforms and relinquish nuclear weapons. However, on the whole, Kuchma's economic policies were similar to his policies in politics and foreign policy in that they lacked any clear direction. Privatization was undertaken in fits and starts from 1994, but it primarily benefited a small group of businessmen with good relations with the president. They became tycoons and oligarchs. The absence of structural reforms dragged out the transition from 1995 until 2000 when Ukraine's economic growth resumed. A small and medium-sized business class did develop, but not to the same extent as in Central and Eastern Europe, where this sector became the driving force of the postcommunist transitions. Ukraine's corruption, overregulation, and unfriendly business climate, however, discouraged large volumes of foreign investment from entering the country. The exception was in 2005–2007 when Ukraine received relatively high levels of foreign investment.

The Yushchenko administration had a high turnover of four governments, only one of which, led by Yekhanurov, had good relations with the president. The first, headed by Tymoshenko, lasted only eight months until President Yushchenko dismissed it during the September 2005 political crisis. Yushchenko loyalist Yekhanurov led a caretaker government until the March 2006 elections. A month after Yekhanurov became prime minister, he ended all speculation on reprivatization by calling a meeting of Ukraine's oligarchs to mend relations between the government and Ukraine's major businessmen, whom he described as Ukraine's "national bourgeoisie." Yushchenko continued to maintain close relations with Ukraine's oligarchs, many of whom saw him as an ally against the Party of Regions and BYuT. Gas tycoon Dmitri Firtash, behind a host of opaque gas intermediaries (Eural-Trans Gas, RosUkrEnergo [RUE], OstChem), provided an alternative source of funds for Yanukovych and the Party of Regions. Firtash was arrested in Vienna in March 2014 and is to be deported to the United States to stand trial.[11] The arrest of Firtash, one of the most pro-Russian oligarchs, was also a signal to Russian oligarchs that the West meant business as it came at the same time as Western limited sanctions over the annexation of Crimea.

Ukraine's economy began to grow in 2000 during the Yushchenko government with a 5.9 percent GDP increase, followed by 9.1 percent the next year, 4.8 percent in 2002, and 8.5 percent in 2003. The 12 percent GDP growth in 2004 was therefore exceptional rather than the norm. The Ukrainian economy never fully recovered from the 2008 global financial crisis, and by the end of 2013, following four years of mismanagement under Azarov and Yanukovych and rampant asset stripping, it came close to default. Euromaidan leaders inherited a bankrupt Ukraine.

Ukraine's energy dependency on Russia is two pronged, as Russia is also dependent on Ukrainian pipelines for the export of 60 percent of its gas and on gas storage in western Ukraine for delivery to European customers in winter. The January 2006 gas contract, following a gas crisis that affected gas supplies to Europe, was contested by BYuT and the then opposition Party of Regions in a parliamentary vote of no confidence in the Yekhanurov government, but the contract was backed by President Yushchenko and Our Ukraine. The contract permitted the opaque RUE to be given the right to transit Central Asian gas through Russia and Ukraine to Europe. Russia's strategic aim has always been to control a consortium over Ukraine's gas pipelines that Yanukovych promised in return for Russian assistance in December 2013. New legislation adopted in summer 2014 opened up Western investment in the pipelines while at the same time blocking Russian investment and control.

A second, longer gas crisis affected Europe in January 2009. On this occasion, the government was better prepared with stored gas that ensured Ukraine could survive a gas blockade by Russia. The ten-year gas contract signed between Prime Ministers Tymoshenko and Putin outlined a two-year shift to European prices, which had collapsed during the global crisis, and the removal of the RUE gas intermediary. The contract was used as the basis for criminal charges of abuse of office that led to Tymoshenko's imprisonment.

The election of Yanukovych returned Ukraine's energy policy to that of the Kuchma era, when Ukraine sought gas subsidies in exchange for granting Russia geopolitical advantages. On April 27, 2010, the Ukrainian parliament railroaded a twenty-five-year extension of the Sevastopol base for the Black Sea Fleet from 2017, when the twenty-year "temporary" lease was set to expire, in exchange for a 30 percent "discount" on Russian gas. The "discount" was flawed as it was based on the pricing formula used in the 2009 gas contract. More importantly, although Yanukovych gave many concessions to Russia in 2010, there was never any willingness by Putin to change the terms of the 2009 gas contract to reduce the price Ukraine paid, which was the highest in Europe. Relations between Ukraine and Russia over energy continue to be highly contentious because of Moscow's policies toward the Crimea and Donbas.

Social Change

Economic reforms, in particular privatization, coupled with a widespread tolerance of corruption, facilitated the rise of an oligarch class that survived due to close personal, economic, and corrupt ties to the president.[12] Instead of experiencing real social change, Ukraine became known as the "blackmail state,"[13] where corruption was tolerated and even encouraged by the president, even as it was diligently recorded by the law enforcement bodies. If the corrupt elites remained politically loyal to national leaders, their files were not acted on by the prosecutor general's office. Political loyalty, therefore, was exchanged for large incomes ("rents") obtained through corruption and insider privatization.

Corruption has remained a major problem in Ukraine that has contributed to a very poor business environment, holding back economic growth and foreign investment. As Transparency International, the anticorruption watchdog, has shown, Ukraine has a persistently high level of corruption and, of the fifteen former Soviet republics, ranks fifth from the bottom, alongside the Central Asian states. None of Ukraine's four presidents have possessed the political will to battle corruption, and the majority of political parties have paid lip service to the fight against it during election campaigns. Poroshenko, Ukraine's fifth president, will be under pressure from the Euromaidan and civil society not to permit business as usual by returning to the cozy relationship between business and politics. A major factor contributing to the flourishing of corruption is the lack of reform of key institutions such as the Interior Ministry (police), the SBU, and the prosecutor general's office, all of which are bloated and incompetent and remain essentially Soviet in their operating cultures (as seen with the imprisonment of opposition leaders and during their operations against Euromaidan protesters), and Ukrainians have very low levels of trust in them. Ukraine, with a smaller population than Britain, has three times the number of policemen, who are despised by the population.

Ukraine inherited a large number of social problems from the Soviet Union that were exacerbated during the transition to a market economy. From 1991, Ukraine's population declined from 51.6 to 45.6 million due to the death rate's exceeding the birthrate, deteriorating socioeconomic conditions, and out-migration. Ukraine is eighth out of the top ten countries with the highest death rate and has the highest death rate in Europe at 16.1 per thousand inhabitants, which is higher than its birthrate of 10.5 per thousand inhabitants. Every tenth Ukrainian dies before reaching the age of thirty-five because of health factors. Ukrainian men have a relatively short life span of 62 years, compared to women, with 73 (with a Ukrainian average of 69.5 compared to 78.6 in the EU). This situation is made worse by the decline in the Soviet health-care system, alcoholism, widespread tobacco smoking, and poor diet. Unhealthy *salo* (pork fat or lard) remains a highly popular ingredient in Ukrainian cuisine. Ukrainians, who drink on average 8 liters of alcohol a year, rank third in the world in the consumption of vodka after Russia (which comes first with 13.9 liters) and Belarus (second with 11.3 liters). Ukraine has the highest road-fatality death rate in Europe, with twenty deaths on average each day, arising partly from alcohol use and also from poorly maintained roads, from poor driving, and vehicle maintenance.[14]

Ukrainians drink the dirtiest water in Europe, partly a result of widespread pollution. In a ranking of forty-five Ukrainian cities, those in the bottom half (twenty-second through forty-fifth) are primarily in eastern and southern Ukraine, and the top half (first through twenty-first) are mainly in the less industrialized central and western Ukraine. A 2001 UN projection of future population trends calculated that Ukraine's population would continue to decline by as much as 40 percent by the middle of the twenty-first century. Ukrainian demographic experts believe the UN projection of a population decline to 33 million by 2050 is too low and project a figure of 36 million.[15] One factor that could contribute to Ukraine's further population decline is the AIDS epidemic, which is growing faster in the former USSR than anywhere else in the world, except Africa. Ukraine has the highest HIV infection in Europe and the fastest rate of infection, which the World Bank considers to be a national epidemic: 1.63 percent of Ukrainians between fifteen and forty-nine (or 360,000 people) are HIV positive.

Ukrainian coal mines are the second most dangerous in the world after China's, leading to nearly four thousand deaths from accidents. The Donbas conflict will inevitably damage the region's outdated coal-mining industry and could close it down. With 13 million Ukrainians living below the official poverty line, Ukraine is the second-poorest country in Europe after Moldova. The World Bank estimates that a quarter of Ukrainians live in poverty.

Women's rights have not greatly expanded since Ukraine became independent. Under the Soviet regime, women were theoretically accorded equality with men and allowed to enter many areas of traditional male employment, but usually for lower pay and at the bottom of the social spectrum. Meanwhile, they continued to remain subservient in the home and were regarded not as equals but as belonging in traditional roles as housewives and mothers. In the late 1980s and first half of the 1990s, some women became active in national democratic groups, such as Rukh, and formed offshoot NGOs, many funded by Western governments and international endowments. During the prioritization of nation and state building, national democratic groups looked on women engaged in politics in traditional nationalist terms as "guardians of the hearth" (*Berehynya*), protectors of the family and nation. Gender equality was not on their political agenda.

Tymoshenko has been the exception, rather than the rule, as a woman at the center of Ukraine's still male-dominated politics. She rose to prominence in the mid-1990s as chief executive officer of United Energy Systems of Ukraine and was elected to parliament in 1996 as an independent; two years later she was elected to parliament by Hromada. A year after that, she created her own political party, Batkivshchina, which joined the center-right European People's Party political group in the European Parliament. Tymoshenko's first taste of government was under Yushchenko in 2000 and 2001, when she earned the wrath of the oligarchs by undermining corrupt energy schemes. Her arrest and brief detention in 2001 failed to dampen her antiregime political activity and merely served to radicalize her further.

Gender undoubtedly played a role in Tymoshenko's defeat in 2010, although it is impossible to know to what degree. During the 2010 elections Yanukovych excused his refusal to debate with Tymoshenko on television by saying that a woman's place is not in politics but in the kitchen. Yushchenko's obsessive dislike for Tymoshenko also lay in his inability to deal with a very self-confident and ambitious woman. A psychological portrait of Yushchenko found him to hold a patriarchal, traditional view of women stemming from his rural background and rootedness in Ukrainian folk and village culture. His spouse's origins in the Ukrainian American diaspora gave her similar interests in Ukrainian culture and history. Ultimately, for Yushchenko, Tymoshenko's gender, self-confidence, and unwillingness to compromise with the ruling elites made her into a *protyvnyk* (mortal enemy) rather than a mere *oponent* (opponent) who could, like many Ukrainian politicians, such as Yushchenko, be bought and co-opted.

The victory of the Euromaidan led to the release of Tymoshenko and other political prisoners from jail, and she and Poroshenko were the leading candidates in the May 2014 preterm elections. Tymoshenko, one of Ukraine's most formidable political operators, will undoubtedly remain in politics, but the country she reentered had dramatically changed compared to the one she left behind on her imprisonment. As a *protyvnyk* Tymoshenko thrived when she faced enemies, whether Kuchma or especially Yanukovych, both of whom are gone. Ukraine's two elections in 2014 showed Tymoshenko's position in Ukrainian politics was in decline.

Ethnic Relations

Ukraine inherited a wide diversity of regions. This regionalism was compounded by weak statehood traditions and a population divided between those holding an exclusively ethnic Ukrainian (primarily Ukrainophone) identity and those with multiple Ukrainian-Russian (primarily Russophone) identities.[16] This division was complicated by nation and state building during a severe socioeconomic crisis in the 1990s. The annexation of the Crimea and Russian-backed separatism are increasing nationalism and patriotism among the former and latter identity groups respectively. At a time of crisis, invasion, and war, people are pressured to take sides, and a majority of Ukrainians who previously preferred to declare themselves as Ukrainian-Russian adopted a Ukrainian civic identity. This was especially noticeable in Kharkiv and Odesa where pro-Russian separatists attempted to ignite (but ultimately failed) civil strife in the spring of 2014. Nearly80 percent of Ukrainians view Putin in negative terms, and the decades-long Soviet propaganda claim of "Russian-Ukrainian fraternal brotherhood" is forever shattered. Support for NATO membership has massively grown to 50 percent.

Regionalism in Ukraine is not ethnically driven, and separatism remained muted, except in Crimea in the first half of the 1990s and since the Euromaidan crisis—in both cases supported by Russia. The central issue facing Ukraine is reconciling regional diversity between mutually exclusive and multiple identities through national integration and rebuilding center-Donbas relations.[17] The eastern and southern parts of Ukraine are overwhelmingly Russophone, while the western and central regions of the country are primarily Ukrainophone, but the majority of Ukrainians are bilingual, especially in the electoral swing region of central Ukraine.

The Crimea is unique because it is the only region with an ethnic Russian majority. Crimean elites sought to return to the status of autonomous republic permitted after a Crimean referendum overwhelmingly approved the decision in January 1991. Relations between Crimea and Ukraine were strained between 1992 and 1995 over the delegation of powers to Crimea. Two of Crimea's three political forces—centrists and the KPU—supported the maximum delegation of powers to Crimea but opposed separatism. Only Russian nationalist-separatists advocated Crimea's separation from Ukraine and union with Russia. A Russian nationalist-separatist, Yury Meshkov, won the newly created Crimean presidency in January 1994, and his allies took control of the Crimean Supreme Soviet, but this influence proved short-lived. In March 1995, Kuchma issued a presidential decree abolishing the Crimean presidency, an event that, together with infighting within the Russian nationalist coalition, progressively marginalized Russian nationalist-separatists. The KPU and centrists in Crimea were able to reach agreement with Kyiv on the parameters of a new Crimean constitution adopted in October by the Crimean parliament and ratified in December 1998 by the Ukrainian parliament. The constitution recognized Crimea as part of Ukraine. In 1998 and 1999 both houses of the Russian parliament also recognized Ukraine's borders after Crimea had adopted its constitution. This treaty and the Budapest Memorandum (see next section) were infringed by Russia when it annexed the Crimea.

Interethnic relations in Crimea were complicated because of strained relations between eastern Slavs and Muslim Tatars, who began returning in the late 1980s and now number 15 percent of the Crimean population. The 2001 Ukrainian census showed the progressive decline of ethnic Russians in Crimea to 58 percent, down from 65 percent in the 1989 Soviet census, due to out-migration of Russians and in-migration of Tatars. The issue of Crimean separatism was dealt a blow by President Kuchma, who successfully integrated the peninsula into Ukraine and marginalized nationalist-separatists.

But the Crimean question was reopened after 2006. A year after the Party of Regions signed a cooperation agreement with Putin's United Russia party, it established an alliance with Crimean Russian nationalists in regional elections. After being marginalized for a decade, Russian nationalists in Crimea received an infusion of life when the Party of Regions united with the Russia bloc and the Russian Community of Crimea in the 2006 Crimean elections. The US embassy in Kyiv reported, "Regions had given the Russia bloc undue political prominence in 2006 by forming a single Crimean electoral list, providing them with slots in the Crimean Rada they would not have won on their own."[18] These Russian nationalists, who went on to lead Russia's annexation of the Crimea, were led by Sergei Aksyonov, an organized crime leader in the 1990s with the nickname "Goblin."[19] Self-proclaimed Crimean prime minister Aksyonov, leader of the minuscule Party of Russian National Unity (which had only three out of one hundred seats in the Crimean parliament), received backing from the eighty-two deputies in the Party of Regions faction in the Crimean parliament.

Russia has long supported separatism and covert operations in Crimea and Odessa. Some of these policies were similar to those pursued in South Ossetia and Abkhazia prior to the 2008 invasion of Georgia, such as distributing Russian passports. The Party of Regions and Crimean Russian nationalists protested against Ukrainian exercises with NATO, derailing the exercises for the first time since Ukraine joined the Partnership for Peace program in 1994. In fall 2008, the Party of Regions, KPU, and Crimean Russian nationalists backed Russia's recognition of the independence of South Ossetia and Abkhazia. In summer 2009, two Russian diplomats were expelled, leading to a Russian storm of protest and President Dmitri Medvedev's undiplomatic open letter to Yushchenko.[20] Regime change in Kyiv during the Euromaidan led to a resumption of Russian covert and overt support for separatism, this time in the Donbas.

Foreign and Security Policy

Ukraine under Kravchuk placed greater emphasis on nation and state building and the security of the state, principally vis-à-vis Russia, than on economic and political reform. This influenced Ukraine's slow nuclear disarmament until 1996 and weak cooperation with transatlantic structures. From the mid-1990s, relations between the West and Ukraine improved dramatically. When Kuchma was elected president in 1994, he initially supported reforms and agreed to denuclearize Ukraine. In December 1994, Ukraine signed the Nuclear Non-Proliferation Treaty, which paved the way for denuclearization between 1994 and 1996. In return for nuclear disarmament, the United States, United Kingdom, and Russia signed the Budapest Memorandum guaranteeing Ukraine's territorial integrity and sovereignty—security guarantees that Russia overturned when it occupied the Crimea. The United Kingdom and United States, in refusing to provide military assistance to Ukraine, reneged on their security guarantees. In the second half of the 1990s, the United States sought to support Ukraine both bilaterally in a "strategic partnership" and multilaterally through NATO as a "keystone" of European security. During the Bill Clinton administration, Ukraine became the third-largest recipient of US assistance and was the most active CIS state within NATO's Partnership for Peace program, which it joined in January 1994.

In 2002, Ukraine officially declared its intention to seek NATO membership, but the government did little to pursue this objective. NATO membership could have been possible in 2005 and 2006 when it was promoted by the George W. Bush administration, but it was undermined by infighting in the Orange camp and after 2008 by strong opposition from Germany and other West European members.

In his first year in office, Yanukovych extended the Sevastopol Black Sea Fleet base and renounced the goal of NATO membership. Kuchma was neither pro or anti-Russian, but at the same time he supported close security cooperation with NATO and recognized that Russia could be a threat to Ukraine's territorial integrity, twin beliefs that Yanukovych never upheld (even though both were eastern Ukrainians). Yanukovych and the Party of Regions always opposed NATO membership. They cited low levels of popular support for NATO membership that had declined from a third in the 1990s to 20 percent in the Yushchenko era, with especially low levels of support in eastern-southern Ukraine. The high levels of cooperation between Ukraine and NATO that existed in the Kuchma and Yushchenko eras were reduced in the four years of the Yanukovych administration. The occupation of the Crimea and Russia's proxy war in the Donbas and invasion of Ukraine have dramatically increased support for NATO membership to 50 percent. Ukraine's new parliament will vote to replace Yanukovych's 2010 "nonbloc" foreign policy program with the program that existed previously, that of the goal of Trans-Atlantic and European integration.

Such cooperation assisted in reforming and democratizing the armed forces, which paid dividends when they refused to intervene against protesters in the Orange Revolution and the Euromaidan. Public trust in the military is relatively high, whereas trust in the police was already at rock bottom prior to the Euromaidan and has fallen even lower after incidents of police violence and murder. In 2013, prior to the Euromaidan, three police stations were stormed by angry Ukrainians in response to growing police mistreatment, torture, and rape of innocent victims. In a particularly disgusting case in summer 2013, two police officers and a taxi driver raped a local woman in a village in the southern Mykolayiv oblast.

The EU has never considered Ukraine or any other CIS state to be potential future members. The partnership and cooperation agreement signed by Ukraine and the EU in 1994 and ratified four years later never included membership prospects. A three-year action plan with the EU signed in 2005 as part of the European Neighborhood Policy was completed in 2007 and 2008. In 2007, Ukraine began negotiations with the EU for an association agreement, but unlike those signed in the 1990s with Central and East European countries, this agreement did not offer membership prospects. In fall 2008, after the Tymoshenko government took Ukraine into the World Trade Organization, Ukraine began negotiating the Deep and Comprehensive Free Trade Agreement as one of the components of the association agreement. The DCFTA and association agreement became part of the Eastern Partnership unveiled in 2009 by Sweden and Poland that provided the opportunity for deep levels of political and economic integration for six former Soviet republics: Ukraine, Moldova, Belarus (suspended), Georgia, Armenia (which opted out in 2013 when it joined the CIS Customs Union), and Azerbaijan. Russia was too geopolitically important and big to be included. The EU was offering what has been described as "enlargement-lite,"[21] with pro-enlargement countries in the EU (such as Poland, Sweden, and the United Kingdom) viewing it as a stepping-stone to full membership.

Negotiations for the association agreement were completed in fall 2011—at the same time as Tymoshenko was sentenced. The EU postponed the initialing of the agreement (signifying a completion of negotiations) from December 2011 until March 2012 and then froze the next two stages of signing and ratification while negotiations continued toward Ukraine fulfilling criteria, such as releasing Tymoshenko. The next two stages—the European Council's signing of the association agreement and its recommendation to the European Parliament and the twenty-eight member states to ratify it in their parliaments—would have gone ahead if the benchmarks had been fulfilled.[22]

Tymoshenko herself and the EU were inclined to sign the association agreement at the November 2013 Vilnius Summit, arguing that it was imperative to move Ukraine inside Europe, where it could be influenced to reform. Yanukovych, though, abruptly dropped EU integration because Russian financial assistance better suited his prospects of reelection in 2015. The opposition leaders who came to power following the ouster of Yanukovych quickly moved to sign the political component of the association agreement first—symbolically significant because it moved Ukraine from the crossroads and ended speculation about its joining Putin's Eurasian Union, and the DCFTA later that year. Georgia and Moldova joined Ukraine in signing the association agreement.

Critical Challenges

Ukraine faces three critical challenges: re-energizing national integration (particularly vis-à-vis the Donbas), deepening democratization, and facilitating the rule of law and fighting corruption. Extreme levels of violence, economic and civil destruction, human casualties, and human rights abuses will make it difficult for negotiations to be successful between Donetsk and Kyiv. Russia seeks to create a pro-Russian "state" structure inside Ukraine, and the front line between Ukrainian and separatist/Russian forces could become the de facto new "permanent" border.

During the nearly quarter century since Ukraine became an independent state, national integration progressed in the first decade, when national democrats and centrists were united, and has declined during the second and third decades. The Euromaidan gave the opposition a second chance after the Orange Revolution to de-Sovietize and Europeanize Ukraine through reforms laid out in the EU association agreement.

Confrontation between eastern and western Ukraine has dominated each election held since 2002, especially in presidential elections, in which the second round was inevitably a contest between candidates from both halves of Ukraine. The 2014 elections were an exception to this rule. Whereas President Kuchma sought to build bridges between eastern and western Ukraine, national-identity policies pursued by Presidents Yushchenko and Yanukovych (coupled with antidemocratic policies against the opposition by the latter) deepened regional divisions and undermined national integration. Weak national integration creates an "immobile state" and harms the pursuit of declared objectives, be they political and economic reforms or European integration. The Euromaidan leaders and newly elected president in 2014 face the major task of building bridges to the Donbas following the Russian annexation of Crimea and Russia's proxy war and invasion of Ukraine.

The second critical challenge is democratization. Ukraine's 2004 democratic revolution and the election of Yushchenko in January 2005 brought democratic gains for Ukraine in a number of key areas, such as media pluralism and the holding of free and fair elections, making Ukraine's transition different from that of Russia and Eurasian authoritarian states. Constitutional reforms transforming Ukraine from a presidential to a parliamentary system also reinforced Ukraine's democratic path both then and after the Euromaidan victory. Ukraine held four free elections in December 2004, 2006, 2007, and 2010, whereas elections under Yanukovych never met democratic standards. In 2014, Ukraine returned to a parliamentary system and held two free elections (presidential and parliamentary), last seen during the Yushchenko presidency. Central and East European and Baltic postcommunist states with parliamentary systems have progressed further in democratization. In Russia and the CIS, the dominant political system is superpresidential, with parliaments emasculated by overly powerful executives, opposition groups marginalized, and media muzzled.

Politicians, whether the ruling authorities or the opposition, continue to be viewed as distant from voters, out of touch, and corrupt. State institutions such as the judiciary, police, and parliament have little public trust. The strongest political party to emerge in

Ukraine was the Party of Regions, which, unlike national democratic parties, successfully consolidated eastern-southern Ukrainian voters into a powerful political and financial machine. The KPU could—and should—be banned as a party that supports totalitarian policies, as seen in the unveiling of monuments of Joseph Stalin during Yanukovych's presidency. Nearly a quarter century into Ukrainian independent statehood, the country has no strong political parties, which are required for parliamentary systems and to push through policies promoting European integration.

A third critical challenge is facilitating the rule of law, which forms the basis of a democratic state and market economy, and fighting corruption. Ukraine's judicial system has been tampered with through piecemeal reforms but has never been thoroughly de-Sovietized. This is especially the case within the bloated 20,000-strong prosecutor general's office, which continues to remain a neo-Soviet institution that would be best disbanded and replaced rather than reformed. Prosecutor General Viktor Pshonka fled with Yanukovych and also faces criminal charges. The Constitutional and Supreme courts, two of Ukraine's most important, were undermined and corrupted under Yanukovych.[23] In addition, European reforms of the Interior Ministry and SBU, including vast reductions in their manpower levels, are essential to prevent future potential authoritarians from dismantling democracy, as took place during Yanukovych's presidency. The Euromaidan opposition disbanded the Berkut police special forces responsible for much of the violence against the protesters. A new institution similar to the US Federal Bureau of Investigation (FBI) or Royal Canadian Mounted Police (RCMP) is being established to tackle domestic high-level corruption and ensure accountability of elites. In nearly a quarter century of statehood, Ukrainian leaders have not provided the political will to tackle corruption. High levels of graft and lack of elite accountability discourage the payment of taxes (as in Italy and Greece), encourage employment in the massive shadow economy, and lead to low levels of popular trust in state institutions.

Policies toward these three challenges taken together are more likely following the Euromaidan than they were after the Orange Revolution because of the desire to not repeat its failures and because of the strength of civil society, as well as the backing of the West in general, and reforms undertaken within the confines of the EU association agreement. As was the case in Ireland vis-à-vis colonialism and Spain, Portugal, and Greece vis-à-vis fascism, European integration represents the only manner in which Ukraine can overcome its totalitarian and colonial legacies. Integration into the Eurasian Union would have merely deepened Ukraine's Soviet legacy and kleptocratic system and revived Russification policies.

Study Questions

1. Why is national integration important for the success of reforms and European integration in Ukraine and more broadly in other countries with regional diversity?
2. Compare the Orange Revolution and Euromaidan. What factors made the Euromaidan revolution more violent, and will its aftermath produce more reforms and reduce corruption?
3. What in the Soviet experience makes Ukrainian political parties continue to be weak, as are parties throughout Eurasia?

4. Why have deep levels of corruption persisted in Ukraine, and how does this impact the rule of law, political system, and economy? What examples exist of successful policies implemented by similarly corrupt states?

5. What are the roots of the long-term poor relations between Russia and Ukraine, and why has Putin occupied the Crimea and invaded Ukraine? What were Putin's objectives in Ukraine, and has he achieved all of them?

6. Why has the EU's response to Putin's actions in Ukraine been divided and weak? Why do the far right and far left in the European Parliament align with Putin on Ukraine?

7. With Ukraine electing its first pro-European parliament in October 2014, reforms and the fight against corruption could become a new strategic priority. What are the obstacles to the fundamental change in Ukraine's political geography translating into concrete policies?

Suggested Readings

Alexeyeva, Lyudmilla. "Ukrainian National Movement," in *Soviet Dissent: Contemporary Movements for National, Religious, and Human Rights*. Middletown, CT: Wesleyan University Press, 1985.

Aslund, Anders. *How Ukraine Became a Market Economy and Democracy*. Washington, DC: Peterson Institute of International Relations, 2009.

D'Anieri, Paul, ed. *Orange Revolution and Aftermath: Mobilization, Apathy, and the State in Ukraine*. Washington, DC: Woodrow Wilson International Center Press; Baltimore: Johns Hopkins University Press, 2010.

———. *Understanding Ukrainian Politics: Power, Politics, and Institutional Design*. Armonk, NY: M. E. Sharpe, 2006.

D'Anieri, Paul, and Taras Kuzio, eds. "A Decade of Leonid Kuchma in Ukraine." Special issue of *Problems of Post-communism* 52 (September–October 2005).

Fournier, Anna. *Forging Rights in a New Democracy: Ukrainian Students between Freedom and Justice*. Philadelphia: University of Pennsylvania Press, 2012.

Kudelia, S., "Revolutionary Bargain: The Unmaking of Ukraine's Autocracy through Pacting." *Journal of Communist Studies and Transition Politics* 23, no. 1 (March 2007): 77–100.

Kudelia, Serhiy, and Taras Kuzio. "Nothing Personal: Explaining the Rise and Decline of Political Machines in Ukraine," *Post-Soviet Affairs* 30, no. 6 (December 2014): 1–29.

Kuzio, T. *The Crimea: Europe's Next Flashpoint?* (Washington DC: The Jamestown Foundation, November 2010).

———. "Crime, Politics and Business in 1990s Ukraine." *Communist and Post-communist Studies* 47, no. 2 (July 2014): 195–210.

———. "Impediments to the Emergence of Political Parties in Ukraine," *Politics* 34, no. 3 (September 2014): 1–15.

———. "Nationalism, Identity and Civil Society in Ukraine: Understanding the Orange Revolution." *Communist and Post-communist Studies* 43, no. 3 (September 2010): 285–96.

———. "Political Culture and Democracy: Ukraine as an Immobile State," *East European Politics and Societies* 25, no. 1 (February 2011): 88–113.

———. *Ukraine: Perestroika to Independence*. 2nd ed. London: Macmillan; New York: St. Martin's Press, 2000.

———. "Ukraine's *Relations* with the West since the Orange Revolution." *European Security* 21, no. 3 (September 2012): 395–413.

Magosci, Robert. *A History of Ukraine: The Land and Its Peoples* 2nd ed. Toronto: University of Toronto, 2010.

Motyl, Alexander J. "Ukraine, Europe and Bandera." Cicero Foundation Great Debate Paper 10/05, March 2010. http://www.cicerofoundation.org/lectures/Alexander_J_Motyl_UKRAINE_EUROPE_AND_BANDERA.pdf.

Shulman, Stephen. "National Identity and Public Support for Political and Economic Reform in Ukraine." *Slavic Review* 64, no. 1 (spring 2005): 59–87.

Way, Lucan A. "Authoritarian State-Building and the Sources of Political Liberalization in the Western Former Soviet Union, 1992–2004." *World Politics* 57 (January 2005): 231–61.

———. "The Sources and Dynamics of Competitive Authoritarianism in Ukraine." *Journal of Communist Studies and Transition Politics* 20 (March 2004): 143–61.

Wilson, Andrew. *Ukraine Crisis. What It Means for the West.* New Haven, CT: Yale University Press, 2014.

———. *Ukraine's Orange Revolution.* New Haven, CT: Yale University Press, 2005.

Wolczuk, Kataryna. *The Moulding of Ukraine: The Constitutional Politics of State Formation.* Budapest: Central European University Press, 2001.

Zimmer K., and Haran, Olexiy. "Unfriendly Takeover: Successor Parties in Ukraine." *Communist and Post-communist Studies* 41, no. 4 (December 2008): 541–61.

Zimmer, Kerstin. "The Comparative Failure of Machine Politics, Administrative Resources and Fraud." *Canadian Slavonic Papers* 47, nos. 3–4 (September–December 2005): 361–84.

Websites

Chesno (Honesty): http://www.chesno.org (Ukrainian NGO that monitors members of parliament)

Kyiv Post: http://www.kyivpost.com (Ukraine's only English-language newspaper)

OpenDemocracy, "Ukraine": http://www.opendemocracy.net/countries/ukraine (analysis of democracy questions in the world)

Opora: http://oporaua.org/en (Ukrainian civil network that grew out of the "black" wing of the Pora [Its Time] NGO and specializes in election monitoring)

Radio Free Europe/Radio Liberty, "Latest Ukraine News": http://www.rferl.org/section/ukraine/164.html

Transitions Online, "Ukraine": http://www.tol.org/client/search-by-country/26-ukraine.html

Ukraine's Orange Blues: http://www.worldaffairsjournal.org/blogs/alexander-j-motyl (Alexander Motyl's weekly *World Affairs* blog)

Ukrayinska Pravda: http://www.pravda.com.ua (Ukrainian- and Russian-language daily news, analysis, and blogs)

Notes

1. T. Kuzio, "Five reasons why Putin's objectives in Ukraine have backfired and failed," *Financial Times*, October 9, 2014. http://blogs.ft.com/beyond-brics/2014/10/09/five-reasons-why-putins-objectives-in-ukraine-have-backfired-and-failed/.

2. "Putin's 'Human Rights Council' Accidentally Posts Real Crimean Election Results," Forbes. Accessed November 10, 2014, http://www.forbes.com/sites/paulroderickgregory/2014/05/05/putins-human-rights-council-accidentally-posts-real-crimean-election-results-only-15-voted-for-annexation/.

3. "Ukraine: Mounting Evidence of Abduction and Torture," Amnesty International, July 10, 2014, http://www.amnesty.ca/news/news-releases/ukraine-mounting-evidence-of-abduction-and-torture; "Ukraine: Rebel Forces Detain, Torture Civilians," Human Rights Watch, August 28, 2014, http://www.hrw.org/news/2014/08/28/ukraine-rebel-forces-detain-torture-civilians; "Ukraine, Human Rights Assessment Mission: Report on the Human Rights and Minority Rights Situation, March–April 2014," Organization for Security and Cooperation in Europe, The Hague/Warsaw, May 12, 2014, http://www.osce.org/odihr/118476; "Report on the Human Rights Situation in Ukraine," Office of the United Nations High Commissioner for Human Rights, May 15, 2014, http://www.ohchr.org/Documents/Countries/UA/HRMMUReport15May2014.pdf. Report on the human rights situation in Ukraine, Office of the United Nations High Commissioner for Human Rights, 16 September 2014, http://www.ohchr.org/Documents/Countries/UA/OHCHR_sixth_report_on_Ukraine.pdf.

4. T. Kuzio, "Viktor Yanukovich—Mr 50 Per Cent," *Financial Times*, March 24, 2012, http://blogs.ft.com/beyond-brics/2014/03/24/guest-post-viktor-yanukovich-mr-50-percent/#axzz2wuxthxCI.

5. "Poroshenko: 'It's Time to Complete a Full Reset of Power,'" KyivPost, accessed November 10, 2014, http://www.kyivpost.com/content/politics/poroshenko-its-time-to-complete-a-full-reset-of-power-369409.html.

6. See articles on Ukraine's elections under "Elections," *Taras Kuzio*, http://taraskuzio.net/media_14_15_17_20_23.html.

7. T. Kuzio, "Yanukovych-Gate Unfolds after Ukrainian Elections," *Eurasian Daily Monitor* 1, no. 139 (December 3, 2004), http://www.jamestown.org/single/?no_cache=1&tx_ttnews[tt_news]=27241.

8. T. Kuzio, "UDAR—Our Ukraine Pragmatists in a Radical Opposition Era," *Eurasia Daily Monitor* 9, no. 197 (October 29, 2012), http://www.jamestown.org/single/?no_cache=1&tx_ttnews[tt_news]=40030#.UgACZaxvCSo.

9. Anders Aslund, *How Ukraine Became a Market Economy and Democracy* (Washington, DC: Peterson Institute of International Economics, 2009), 222–33.

10. Joel S. Hellman, "Winners Take All: The Politics of Partial Reform in Postcommunist Transitions," *World Politics* 50, no. 2 (January 1998): 203–34.

11. Office of Public Affairs, "Six Defendants Indicted in Alleged Conspiracy to Bribe Government Officials in India to Mine Titanium Minerals," Department of Justice, April 2, 2014, http://www.justice.gov/opa/pr/2014/April/14-crm-333.html.

12. Rosaria Puglisi, "The Rise of the Ukrainian Oligarchs," *Democratization* 10, no. 3 (August 2003): 99–123.

13. Keith Darden, "The Integrity of Corrupt States: Graft as an Informal State Institution," *Politics and Society* 36, no. 1 (March 2008): 35–59.

14. "Ukraine," World Bank, http://www.worldbank.org/en/country/ukraine; United Nations Development Programme in Ukraine at http://www.ua.undp.org/ukraine/en/home.html.

15. "До 2050 року українців залишиться 36 мільйонів," *Pravda*, July 10, 2013, http://www.pravda.com.ua/news/2013/07/10/6993962.

16. The argument was first developed by Paul R. Magocsi in his "The Ukrainian National Revival: A New Analytical Framework," *Canadian Review of Studies in Nationalism* 16, no. 102 (1989): 45–62.

17. T. Kuzio, "Ukraine: Coming to Terms with the Soviet Legacy," *Journal of Communist Studies and Transition Politics* 14, no. 4 (December 1998): 1–27.

18. US Embassy Kyiv, "Ukraine: Crimea Update—Less Tense Than in 2006: Interethnic, Russia, Land Factors Remain Central," WikiLeaks, June 8, 2007, http://wikileaks.org/cable/2007/06/07KYIV1418.html.

19. T. Kuzio, "Crime and Politics in Crimea," Open Democracy, March 14, 2014, http://www.opendemocracy.net/od-russia/taras-kuzio/crime-and-politics-in-crimea-Aksyonov-Goblin-Wikileaks-Cables.

20. The open letter is available in Russian at "Послание Президенту Украины Виктору Ющенко," August 11, 2009, http://www.kremlin.ru/news/5158. On the expulsions, see T. Kuzio, "SBU Challenges the FSB in Crimea," *Eurasia Daily Monitor* 6, no. 134 (July 14, 2009), http://www.jamestown.org/single/?no_cache=1&tx_ttnews%5Btt_news%5D=35261, and "Russia-Ukraine Diplomatic War," *Eurasia Daily Monitor* 6, no. 147 (July 31, 2009), http://www.jamestown.org/single/?no_cache=1&tx_ttnews[tt_news]=35347.

21. Nicu Popescu and Andrew Wilson, *The Limits of Enlargement-Lite: European and Russian Power in the Troubled Neighbourhood* (London: European Council on Foreign Relations, June 2009), http://ecfr.eu/page/-/ECFR14_The_Limits_of_Enlargement-Lite._European_and_Russian_Power_in_the_Troubled_Neighbourhood.pdf.

22. Slawomir Matuszak and Arkadiusz Sarna, *From Stabilisation to Stagnation: Viktor Yanukovych's Reforms*, Point of View 32 (Warsaw: Centre for Eastern Studies, March 2013), http://www.osw.waw.pl/en/publikacje/policy-briefs/2013-03-12/stabilisation-to-stagnation-viktor-yanukovychs-reforms.

23. Bohdan Vitvitsky, "Corruption, Rule of Law, and Ukraine," in *Open Ukraine: Changing Course towards a European Future*, ed. T. Kuzio and Daniel Hamilton (Washington DC: Center for Transatlantic Relations, Johns Hopkins University–SAIS, 2011), 45–49, http://transatlantic.sais-jhu.edu/publications/books/Open_Ukraine/03.Vivitsky.pdf.

Part IV

CONCLUSION

CHAPTER 19

Twenty-Five Years after 1989

A BALANCE SHEET

Sharon L. Wolchik and Jane Leftwich Curry

Twenty-five years after the fall of communism, as this volume was being completed, the miracle of the peaceful transformations of these states from inclusion in the Soviet bloc to, for most, full membership in North Atlantic Treaty Organization (NATO) and the European Union (EU) and from communism to democracy, remains. At the same time, while it is clear that most of these states, with the notable exceptions of Ukraine, Bosnia, and Kosovo, have firmly "returned to Europe," it is also clear that the legacies of their histories, particularly under communism, and their transitions keep them from being "just like Western Europe," even though they sport sparkling malls, high rises, and all the accouterments of democracy and capitalism—competitive elections, stock markets, critical media, and goods from Western Europe.

All of these changes seemed impossible dreams until 1989, when the collapse of communism and the disintegration of the Soviet bloc surprised almost everyone: the communist leaders and the opposition of Central and Eastern Europe, Western and Soviet politicians, and observers and scholars of the area. The daily headlines of the *New York Times* heralded the changes as "the Year of Freedom." US and West European foreign policy turned from fighting communism to "democracy promotion," which helped incipient democracies in the region make their transitions and established a model for Western assistance to those states elsewhere in the world that wanted to democratize.

The end of communism throughout this region was followed by efforts to create or re-create democracy, establish market economies, and earn recognition once again as part of Europe. All these Central and East European states have had bumps in the road to consolidating their democracies, but none has gone off the road. In part, these bumps reflect the legacies of their early histories and the communist period, whether they had "communism lite," as in Yugoslavia and for significant periods in Hungary and Poland, or the more draconian communism that Albania, Bulgaria, Czechoslovakia, East Germany, Romania, Ukraine, and the Baltic states experienced until after Mikhail Gorbachev came to power. They also reflect the complicated nature of the tasks leaders faced in simultaneously transforming their countries' politics, economies, social welfare systems, and foreign policies. In addition, ethnic divisions, papered over under communist rule, came to the fore with the transitions: Czechoslovakia split in a peaceful "Velvet Divorce," and Yugoslavia, following a series of wars and NATO intervention, broke up into seven separate states. The legacies of the Yugoslav wars persist and have slowed former Yugoslav states' entry into NATO and the European Union.

The international environment changed dramatically as well. The Soviet Union no longer existed. The foreign policies of these new states turned to the West. But the shifts of power in Europe that began in 1989 in most of Central and Eastern Europe and continued in 1991 with the collapse of the Soviet Union have proved not to be etched completely in stone. In the aftermath of the 2013–2014 Euromaidan demonstrations in Kyiv, the fragility of at least some parts of the new Europe was more than clear. Vladimir Putin's illegal annexation of Crimea, following what was, at best, a sham referendum held after Russians fomented separatist actions, challenged the turn from the East to the West. After this annexation, the first forcible change of European borders since World War II, Russian separatists, armed and trained by Russia and, as of late August 2014, joined by Russian troops, fought in eastern and southern Ukraine as additional Russian troops massed on the border. Putin's warning that he would, if necessary, intervene to protect Russians in other states put the Baltic states, which have significant Russian populations, on notice. NATO, the European Union, and the United States responded with a series of sanctions and warnings to Russia that as of this writing have had little impact on Putin's actions in Ukraine. It has thus become clear that Russia is now a player not just in the politics of Ukraine but in the security concerns of all of Central and East Europe, as well as NATO, Western Europe, and the United States, as Putin's actions have challenged the post–World War II international order.

The return of Russia as a significant player in this area has happened only recently. In 1989, the Soviet Union was too weak to hold back change in Central and Eastern Europe. Instead, with the implicit Soviet blessing of Gorbachev's Sinatra Doctrine, its former satellites simply ended communist rule and withdrew from the Warsaw Pact military alliance and the Comecon economic union, and the Baltic states began to reject Soviet control visibly. In the past quarter century, Russia has regained its economic footing by opening to Western trade and becoming a major source of oil and natural gas for the states from Ukraine to the west. As Russia's ruler, Putin, used this new wealth to strengthen his base in Russia, expand his control to weaker post-Soviet states, and increase Russia's presence in international bodies. He also sought to definitively put down mass mobilization and protest in Russia. Although he clearly cannot turn back the clock in the states that have become part of NATO and the European Union, Russia has been more and more bellicose.

Initial Gains and Later Setbacks

The euphoria of the men and women on the streets from Berlin to Bucharest and in the rest of the world was palpable in 1989 and 1991. Most thought creating or re-creating democracy would be a matter of shifting to life without the shackles and hardships of communism and would guarantee them prosperity and the "good life." In actuality, the change was not as easy as many expected. Prosperity did not necessarily follow for most in these populations, and democracy proved hard to make work. The resulting disappointments and memories of the communist past have continued to impact politics in the area for the last twenty-five years. As the chapters in this book illustrate, the improvisations and reversals that marked the democratization process have, in many cases, been surprising and even agonizing.

The governing political institutions of the countries included in this volume are, on the whole, now similar to those of more established, and particularly European, democracies. The rule of law and guarantees of civil and political liberties and human rights have been formally instituted. Popular support for democracy as a general concept, if not for current political leaders or even institutions, is high, and there is little desire to turn back to communism, although some look back nostalgically to the "good old days" of communist cradle-to-grave social support.

But it is also clear that these institutions and values are less stable than they are in most other European democracies. Although the radical right lost out in Poland after the 2007 parliamentary election in Hungary, the even more radically right-wing party FiDeSz (once a liberal youth movement that helped bring down communism) was voted into power in 2010. With a large majority of seats in the parliament, its leader, Viktor Orbán, as prime minister, pushed through limits on freedoms of the media and expression, as well as economic reforms that cut down on outside investment, and encouraged attacks on minority groups like Jews and Roma. Orbán's government also lamented the territorial losses Hungary suffered in the twentieth century. Continued public support for these challenges to democratic structures was undeniable in 2014 when FiDeSz won the election, keeping its supermajority, and an even more radical right-wing party, Jobbik, became a significant player as well. Even the Czech Republic, the postcommunist country that had the most successful experience with democracy before World War II and one of the smoothest economic transitions after the end of communism in 1989, has had periods of division that left it with months of failed attempts to form governments, then found itself mired in a corruption scandal that decreased the credibility of the government, as has often happened in Romania, Bulgaria, and Albania.

The shift to a market economy has been completed in almost all of these states. Private enterprises account for the largest share of gross national product, and previously neglected sectors of the economy, such as the service sector, continue to grow, as have most of these economies as a whole, with few exceptions. The worldwide economic crisis of 2008 to 2009 did reverberate throughout this area. As chapter 3 illustrates, the impact of this crisis and the severity of the resulting economic disruption varied within the region. It was most severe in Latvia, Hungary, and Ukraine, where gross domestic product (GDP) plummeted, international investment and credit dried up, and people found themselves owing more than their property was worth. By the time of this writing in 2014, most of the economies in the region—with the dramatic exception of Ukraine, which found itself deeply in debt and with empty state coffers in 2013—have largely recovered, although unemployment remains high especially among young people. Even prior to the global crisis, however, economic reform and progress had real costs: unemployment and rising inequality have caused hardship for less well-positioned groups in society and led to political backlash in some countries.

Most of the countries examined in this volume—with the notable exception of Ukraine and a number of the states formed after the dissolution of Yugoslavia and Albania in the case of the EU—have also succeeded in joining Euro-Atlantic institutions, most importantly the

North Atlantic Treaty Organization (NATO) and the European Union (EU). As members of these institutions, they have achieved their original goal of returning to Europe. They have asserted their independence in the international realm and moved from grateful recipients of European aid to become players with their own agendas in the European Union and, in some cases, providers of democracy assistance and other aid to countries to their east.

The successes of these states in achieving the major points in their political agendas following the end of communism raise new questions. Two of the most important of these concern how we should view these polities now. Are they really just European or are they still postcommunist? And what are the reasons for the pattern of two steps forward, one step back that seems to have emerged even in states that, in the first decade and a half, had been the most successful? These questions have been reflected in the scholarly debates over what frameworks are most useful in guiding the study of and research into politics in these countries now.

Postcommunist or "Normal" European Countries?

In the early years after the end of communism, as detailed in the introduction, the theoretical approaches that most frequently informed our study of these countries were based on the transitions from authoritarian rule in southern Europe and Latin America. These were used despite the many ways in which these transitions differed from those in the postcommunist world.[1]

As the transitions continued and democratic institutions and processes were established, some scholars of politics in this region came to rely on concepts drawn from studies of politics in more established democracies. These included studies of political values and attitudes, legislatures and their processes, the roles of presidents and other political actors, and electoral behavior. Other scholars used approaches developed in the rest of Europe and the United States to study the development of political parties. Studies of the intersection of politics and the economy, in turn, employed concepts and approaches used by students of political economy in other regions of the world. Increasingly, we became aware of the need to include international actors, such as international and regional organizations and transnational actors and networks, in our analyses of political change in the postcommunist world. To do this, scholars have drawn on the literature on norms in international politics and the role of international organizations, as well as on the democracy-promotion literature.

Many of the studies based on these frameworks, including those by contributors to this volume, have yielded valuable insights into the political process in these countries. At the same time, it soon became clear that use of these approaches based on transitions from authoritarianism and political systems in Western Europe and the United States was not always fruitful. These postcommunist societies had their own problems, and although Central and East European countries had much in common with their Western neighbors and countries that underwent democratization elsewhere, there were and are important differences to consider.

Simply put, these new systems remain products of their special histories. Communist rule was different from the authoritarianism in southern Europe and Latin America. The political systems in place in the postcommunist European states today also differ in certain ways from those of their more established European neighbors. Although there are many similarities in the institutions of both sets of countries, and the although leaders of Central and East European countries face many of the same problems evident elsewhere, it would still be a mistake to lump these systems together with the more established democracies in what we used to call "Western" Europe. Due in part to their particular histories and in part to the demands and opportunities created by the transition, institutions that look similar in the two parts of Europe sometimes operate quite differently if one looks more closely.

As the chapters in this book illustrate, the transition from communism seemed to be smoothest in Poland, Hungary, the Czech Republic, Slovenia, and the Baltic states for much of the first decade and a half. But these countries, like others in the region, continue to have weak political parties, fluid party systems, leaders who more often use office to enrich themselves than to serve the public good, and political cultures on the part of elites and citizens with elements at odds with democracy. They also suffer, as do most other countries in the region, from corruption in both the economic and political realms.

In all of these countries, to a greater or lesser extent, politics has also been affected by the economic disaffection of the population. That dissatisfaction has been mirrored by the demise of the political power of the old opposition; by a shift, particularly evident in Poland but also in other countries such as Hungary and Bulgaria, among many politicians and voters to radical, populist politics; and by the rise, a decade and a half later, of concerns about communist-era abuses and agents. It is ironic that this shift occurred after these countries joined the EU and at a time when their economies were growing faster than most in Europe, until the global economic crisis hit. Poland was the only country in the EU with a GDP that grew during this time period. In the process, its voters turned away from radical parties to a party that emphasized rational debate and efficient policy making. There and elsewhere, though, inequality remained high, and many people felt that their dreams for capitalism had been dashed.

In the other countries we have considered in this volume (Slovakia, Romania, Bulgaria, Albania, Ukraine the Baltic states, and the successors to former Yugoslavia), the shift of power in the late 1980s and early 1990s was not so clear. In many, communist leaders maintained power while claiming to be democrats or nationalists for at least the first set of elections. In others, the initial victory of the opposition was quickly followed by the election of "old forces," or a period of de-democratization. Ostensibly democratic political institutions in these states often did not function democratically, and democratically elected governments sometimes took actions that were decidedly not the norm in more established democracies. Efforts to account for this fact led scholars to describe many of these polities as "illiberal" or "hybrid" democracies.[2] Others termed these systems "semi-authoritarian" or "competitive authoritarian" systems.[3] Whatever term was used, the basic elements were the same: governments, some of whose leaders were elected in relatively free and fair elections, acted to restrict the freedom of action of their opponents; attempted to control the media and deny the opposition access; enacted legislation that disadvantaged minorities; worked to discourage the development of civil society; and reinforced values at variance with those supportive of democracy, such as compromise and tolerance.

As the period we examine in this book progressed, some of these states went through democratizing elections. Often termed "electoral" or "color revolutions" due to the tendency of their supporters and leaders to use certain colors as symbols, such as orange in the case of Ukraine, these events involved the mass mobilization of citizens by more unified oppositions in cooperation with nongovernmental organizations and campaigns to encourage citizens to participate in elections and, if necessary, protest in the streets if incumbents tried to steal the elections or failed to yield their offices if defeated. These events, which took place in Slovakia in 1998, Serbia and Croatia in 2000, and Ukraine in 2004, as well as in two countries not covered in this volume (Georgia in 2003 and Kyrgyzstan in 2005), have had different outcomes. With the exception of the latter two cases, the ouster of semi-authoritarian leaders was followed by initial movement, though not always linear or long term, in a less corrupt and more democratic direction.[4] In Ukraine, these gains were reversed under Viktor Yanukovych, who was fairly elected president in 2010 and turned the country into an even more kleptocratic state than before the Orange Revolution. His turn to Russia precipitated the events that resulted in the Euromaidan protests in 2013 and 2014 and, with the help of Russia, led to a violent struggle in the east and south of the country and to the Russian annexation of Crimea after what was, at best, a sham referendum there.

Understanding "Democracy" in Central and Eastern Europe

If we adopt a minimal definition of democracy,[5] which requires free and fair elections and the alternation in power of different political groups, then all of the states considered in this volume, with the exception of those parts of former Yugoslavia still under international rule, are democracies. If we adopt a definition of democracy that requires not only democratic political institutions and the rule of law, but also a well-articulated, dense civil society, a well-developed political society that includes political parties and movements that structure political choice for citizens by articulating different policy perspectives and link citizens to the political process, and a functioning market economy to provide resources for individuals and groups independent of the state and to keep the government in check,[6] many of the states under consideration in this volume still have a way to go.

The question that remains is how we can best understand politics in the region now, particularly in those countries that have become part of the EU and NATO. Is it still useful, for example, to see these states as postcommunist? Or, as some have suggested and others fear, have they become "normal, boring European countries"? Václav Havel, for example, once noted that we no longer talk about the United States as a postcolonial country. Why then, he asked, should we continue to talk about the countries of Central and Eastern Europe as postcommunist? We would argue that the term still makes sense, at least in certain areas. It is clear that the countries we have focused on in this book share certain characteristics and problems with the more established democracies of "Western" Europe. These similarities can, in fact, be expected to increase as these countries become more integrated into the EU and as generations of young people who have not had any meaningful experience with communism come of age politically.

However, at present, the countries analyzed in this book also face additional issues arising from their communist pasts and from the fact that they are newly established or reestablished democracies. Communism was a form of authoritarianism in which the state not only controlled politics but also the economy; communist leaders were not content merely to hold the reins of power but also wanted to transform their citizens into "new Socialist men (and women)," at least initially. Mobilizing citizens was important in these systems in which leaders used propaganda, mass political demonstrations, and police control to ensure that there were no public questions or alternatives to the march they claimed to be making to "socialism."

The experience of democratization and the transformation of the economy were often not what people had either hoped for or expected. The lessons they learned under communism and during the period immediately after its collapse have stayed with them. Citizens learned, for example, that the system did not work as it said it did, that they needed to be part of informal groups that helped each other get the goods and services they needed but could not get on the market, and that they could have little voice in politics. In their lives, much had happened behind the veil of the secret police and their informers or in a bureaucratic morass about which people had little information. Indeed, people often read the media not for what was said but for what was not. They assumed that democracy and prosperity would be instantly linked; they expected the remaking of the political system and the restructuring of the economy to bring about almost instant gains in their living standards. This improvement did not happen immediately or, for some groups of the population, at all. As a result, democratic institutions and traditions had to be built when people were disillusioned about what they were getting from their new governments. Political leaders also had to deal with citizens who had learned that politics was about appearing to support the top leadership's policies and not expressing their opinions or acting in groups to articulate interests or put pressure on political leaders to take action. Although many, if not most, citizens had seen through the claims of communism, they had also come, in some cases unconsciously, to expect the state to provide a wide array of services, however basic.

These legacies remain, with often high levels of popular alienation and anger at systems that did not meet their expectations, higher levels of corruption rooted in the lessons of surviving by "living outside the law," and high levels of distrust in politicians and "democratic institutions." Although alienation and a loss of faith in politicians and political institutions have appeared in other democratic systems, their roots are different and they have been less acute. These differences still make it difficult to simply use concepts and approaches borrowed from studies of political phenomena in more established democracies in some areas. And when these are used, differences often appear.

As the chapters in this volume indicate, even in states that were early democratizers, such as the Baltic states, Slovenia, Hungary, Poland, and the Czech Republic, the future is not entirely clear. To a greater or lesser degree, a gulf remains between the rulers and the ruled. Parties and party systems are still fluid in most states, and citizens have low levels of party identification and loyalty. They also tend to have lower levels of political efficacy than their counterparts in more established democracies.

Even prior to the recent economic crisis, when many of these economies had high growth rates, levels of economic performance and the functioning of social welfare systems did not please many citizens. This dissatisfaction has only increased as economic growth stopped or plummeted and governments struggled to stay afloat. Disenchantment with the "lived" democracy and capitalism that developed out of the transitions has led to a search, in most of these countries, for someone or something to blame. Ethnic conflicts are often more dramatic not only because they were allowed to fester by being papered over in the communist period but also because people search for the reason their systems are not doing what they hoped. Many citizens also question how best to deal with the past and puzzle about what to do about increasing inequality. The conflation of these two issues, egged on by the rhetoric of the right, has increased the sense among many that the systems are unfair and that punishing and lustrating former communists has not been done thoroughly enough. Other European governments also face a number of these questions, but they are particularly acute in the postcommunist region.

Membership in European and Euro-Atlantic institutions strengthened, at least initially, movement in a more democratic direction in many of these areas. Generational change may also accelerate this process, particularly as those young people who have made good use of the ample opportunities to travel and study abroad come into positions of political responsibility. There is no guarantee of this, however, given the high unemployment levels of youth in many countries and the decrease in the number of young people both because of out-migration and also the drop in the birthrate at the end of communism and during the first years of the transition.

EU membership itself also poses new issues and demands for leaders and citizens in these countries. As part of the broader community, political leaders in the postcommunist EU member states obviously will also face many of the same challenges as their counterparts in other advanced industrial societies. As the section to follow discusses more fully, the postcommunist states in particular also face challenges in the international realm.

Central and Eastern Europe in the World: New Roles and Concerns

Central and East European countries have, since 1989, shifted their sights and ties west and away from Russia. Even before communism collapsed in each of these states, European and American aid and trade with the states of the former Soviet bloc increased substantially. In 1990, those in the Warsaw Pact military alliance and Comecon deserted them. The goal of the new leaders was to go further and "return to Europe" by joining both NATO and the European Union. Achieving this goal required significant changes in everything from their military equipment and training to their laws regarding civil rights to their economies. To accomplish all this, the states seeking membership received significant aid from the European Union and NATO states. In the end, this created the incentives and resources for Central and East European states, as they entered, to meet West European standards and become full players in the politics of Europe and NATO. Yugoslavia, although it had, under Tito, the closest ties with the West, was not part of this process as it was mired in the wars of succession that ultimately, in the cases of Bosnia and Kosovo, resulted in a representative of the international community holding supreme power in Bosnia and NATO actions against the Serbs. These new states—with the exception of Slovenia, which joined the EU in 2004, and Croatia, which joined in 2013—are still in the process of preparing for EU membership. Slovenia and Croatia are also the only states of former Yugoslavia that are members of NATO. Of the states covered in this volume, only Ukraine remained outside even membership talks with the EU and NATO. Membership in the European Union, much less NATO, was not seriously contemplated for Ukraine because of its long border with Russia. But the European Union did provide aid and training to Ukraine and, after the Euromaidan protests, signed an agreement with Ukraine.

The states that have succeeded in joining Euro-Atlantic institutions, most importantly the EU and NATO, have achieved their original goal of returning to the European stage. Those that surrendered part of their sovereignty to an outside power, this time voluntarily, by joining the European Union and NATO were, by the turn of the century, beginning to play significant roles in both organizations. But the increasing strength of the Russian economy and Putin's control has begun to challenge a "new world order" in which the world is not divided between superpowers. The events in Ukraine and Russia's threat that it will protect Russians wherever they are have made clear that Russia can pose a real challenge to Europe and particularly to states like Ukraine and the Baltics, where there are significant Russian-speaking populations. The crisis in Ukraine has also pointed out the lack of viable responses to Russian power beyond sanctions—given the West's reluctance to engage directly in response to Russia's annexation of Crimea, fomenting of separatist unrest in eastern Ukraine, and invasion of Ukraine in 2014—due to the dependence of much of Europe, west and east, on Russian oil and natural gas, Europe's strong trade ties with Russia, and fear of the unpredictability of Russia's leaders, given Russia's status as a nuclear power.

Despite these challenges, membership in the EU has been a significant change in international relations for both those that have joined and others that have yet to accede or that are unlikely to become members in the near future. With membership, postcommunist European states, like earlier members, have voluntarily taken on obligations that impose certain limitations on their freedom of action.

Although the states of Central and East Europe that have joined the European Union hold fewer European Parliament seats than the older members, they have played a larger role in the politics of the European Union than their numbers would suggest. Initially, a number of states like Poland elected a significant proportion of Euroskeptic deputies who shifted the balance of power to the right. However, the EU remained committed to admitting more of the states covered in this volume, however costly doing so was. So, since the timetable for entrance had been set, Romania and Bulgaria were allowed to join in 2007, even though there remained huge gaps between the formal standards for EU accession and actual practice in areas such as transparency, control of corruption, and judicial reform. These countries were accepted but remain subject to continued monitoring in these realms. In Bulgaria, in fact, failure to address the corruption that pervades economic and political life led to the temporary suspension of EU funds in 2008. Not only have representatives been active in pushing their agendas, but Poland, particularly, took on the role of serving as the "bridge to the east," advocating for more support for former Soviet states like Ukraine. In addition, by now, six Central and East European states have held the presidency of the EU.

Within the EU, some of the poorer states were concerned with the cost of preparing these former communist states for entrance. In addition, there was initially a fear among many of the original members that the local labor markets of the original states would be flooded with workers from the new member states, where unemployment is far higher and wages are far lower. In France, in fact, this fear of "Polish plumbers" was one reason for the defeat of the European Union constitutional referendum in May 2005. A number of states were allowed to delay permanent work permits for those coming from Poland and elsewhere in Central and Eastern Europe for up to seven years. In the states that did not put restrictions on foreign workers—Ireland, England, and the Scandinavian countries—this influx occurred. Some stayed after the European recession took hold in 2008, but many others returned to their home countries with newfound skills.

On the other hand, countries that border on post-Soviet states other than the Baltics have created a porous border through which many desperate workers come from Ukraine and beyond. Although the EU funded one of the most secure border fences in the world between Poland and Ukraine, Poland has maintained a "good neighbor policy" with Ukraine and others. So Ukrainians and Belarusians can get visas to work in Poland for three months at a time at virtually at no cost. Once in Poland, since the Schengen Treaty allows for the free flow of peoples within the EU, those who do not find jobs in Poland or who want to go further west travel freely on to Germany and elsewhere in Europe since their passports are not checked at borders. In addition, the border trade in cheap goods between Poland and Ukraine or Belarus has continued to help the poor, less industrialized regions of Poland survive. This is the case, to a lesser degree, in Romania as well.

Even as they have succeeded in "returning to Europe," Central and East European states have been a key element of US foreign policy as well. Their transformation itself was a major issue in US foreign policy and also served as a platform and model for US aid to be used in democracy promotion. In the years immediately after 1989, non- and quasi-governmental organizations in the United States and Western Europe joined the US and European governments in providing funds and expertise related to many aspects of the transition. Activists from many of these countries, including but not limited to those that experienced early democratizing elections such as Slovakia and Serbia, have subsequently played important roles in supporting democratization in other semi-authoritarian countries by sharing their experiences, strategies, and techniques, in many cases with US funding. A number of countries in the region have committed their own resources to these efforts by targeting all or part of the development funds EU members are required to set aside for these efforts.

EU members, as well as those countries that still aspire to join that organization, also face the sometimes difficult task of reconciling their desire for, as many put it, "more Europe and more United States," or good relations both with other members of the EU and with the United States. A number of countries in the region sent troops or peacekeepers to Afghanistan; the governments of some also bucked both domestic public opinion and the attitudes of several other EU members, most notably France and Germany, by sending troops or otherwise supporting the US war in Iraq. Romania and Poland housed secret prisons where high-level terrorism subjects were tortured in the early years of the war on terrorism, and they were willing to house installations of the antimissile shield proposed by the George W. Bush administration in the United States, despite strong domestic as well as Russian opposition, until the plans were cancelled by the Barack Obama administration. The leaders of several postcommunist members of the EU have expressed a desire to strive for strong transatlantic relations, but this task can be expected to remain a difficult one when EU and US perspectives and objectives clash.

Although there is no way the clock will turn back for the states that are part of NATO and the European Union, Russia's increased involvement poses new dilemmas for member countries. It is clear Russia is now a player in the politics not just of Ukraine but in the security concerns of all of Central and East Europe, as well as NATO and the European Union.

What Next?

As illustrated by this brief overview of some of this volume's main conclusions and of the utility of various theoretical frameworks for the study of the region's politics, including the very designation "postcommunist," leaders and citizens of the formerly communist countries in Central and Eastern Europe have achieved both more and less than might have been expected in 1989 or 1991. Both postcommunist and European, the countries we have considered in this book face problems that are peculiar to postcommunist states and also those that are common to other European or, more broadly, democratic governments. Their success in achieving the main goals outlined at the beginning of the transition period testifies to the ingenuity, sacrifice, and vision of both leaders and citizens. But while the gains made since 1989 are impressive in many ways, these countries still differ in important ways from their European counterparts that did not have a communist past.

In 2010, we concluded that despite these differences, these countries had become or were on their way to becoming "normal" European countries. In 2014, this answer seems too optimistic, and their futures appear less clear. Although we would still argue that most of the countries in the region are on a trajectory to becoming "normal" European countries, the setbacks that have occurred in the recent past in some and the ongoing challenges all face suggest that their politics will be far from boring for some time to come.

Notes

1. For arguments that advocate this approach, see Philippe C. Schmitter with Terry Lynn Karl, "The Conceptual Travels of Transitologists and Consolidologists: How Far to the East Should They Attempt to Go?" *Slavic Review* 53, no. 1 (spring 1994): 173–85. For arguments against this approach, see Valerie J. Bunce, "Should Transitologists Be Grounded?" *Slavic Review* 54, no. 1 (spring 1995): 111–27. See also Juan J. Linz and Alfred Stepan, *Problems of Democratic Transition and Consolidation: Southern Europe, South America, and Post-communist Europe* (Baltimore: Johns Hopkins University Press, 1996); Adam Przeworski, *Democracy and the Market* (New York: Cambridge University Press, 1991).

2. See Fareed Zakaria, *The Future of Freedom: Illiberal Democracy at Home and Abroad* (New York: W. W. Norton & Co., 2004); Thomas Carothers, "The End of the Transition Paradigm," *Journal of Democracy* 13 (January 2002): 5–21; Larry Diamond, "Thinking about Hybrid Regimes," *Journal of Democracy* 13 (January 2002): 21–35; Andreas Schedler, "The Menu of Manipulation," *Journal of*

Democracy 13 (January 2002): 36–50; Steven Levitsky and Lucan A. Way, "The Rise of Competitive Authoritarianism," *Journal of Democracy* 13 (April 2002): 51–65.

3. See Levitsky and Way, "The Rise of Competitive Authoritarianism."

4. For examples of the growing literature on these elections, See Valerie J. Bunce and Sharon L. Wolchik, "Favorable Conditions and Electoral Revolutions," *Journal of Democracy* 17, no. 4 (October 2006): 5–18; Taras Kuzio, "Kuchma to Yushchenko: Ukraine's 2004 Elections and the Orange Revolution," *Problems of Post-communism* 52, no. 2 (April 2005): 117–30; Sharon Fisher, *Political Change in Post-communist Slovakia and Croatia: From Nationalist to Europeanist* (New York: Palgrave Macmillan, 2006).

5. See Adam Przeworski et al., *Democracy and Development: Political Institutions and Well-Being in the World, 1950–1990* (Cambridge: Cambridge University Press, 2000).

6. See Linz and Stepan, *Problems of Democratic Transition and Consolidation.*

Index

Note: Page numbers in italics indicate figures, photos, and tables.

About the Contributors

Federigo Argentieri received a degree in political science from the University of Rome and a PhD in history from Eötvös Loránd University in Budapest. He also attended the Harvard Ukrainian Summer Institute and has been a member of the Association for Slavic, East European, and Eurasian Studies since 1989. He serves as director of the Guarini Institute for Public Affairs at John Cabot University, teaching politics and history there and at Temple University (Rome Campus). Scholarship and research interests are mostly focused on Central and Eastern Europe and international communism after Stalin, transatlantic relations, postcommunist Hungary and Ukraine, and Western views of Eastern Europe. A regular commentator for various media on the region's current political events, he is an adviser to the Hungary Europe Society and a member of the editorial board of *Limes*, a monthly Italian journal of geopolitics. Recent publications include chapters in the books *Il mondo ci guarda* (2011), *Chi era János Kádár?* (2012), and *Il patto Ribbentrop-Molotov, l'Italia e l'Europa* (2013). He is currently working on a book about Palmiro Togliatti and international communism from 1949 to 1964.

Mark Baskin is research professor in the University at Albany's Department of Political Science and a senior fellow at the Center for International Development at the State University of New York. He has been a public policy scholar at the Woodrow Wilson International Center for Scholars in Washington, DC, and served as director of research at the Pearson Peacekeeping Centre in Canada from 2001 to 2002. From 1993 to 2000 he worked as a civil affairs and political officer for the United Nations Peace Operations in Croatia, Bosnia-Herzegovina, and Kosovo. He held Fulbright and IREX fellowships in Yugoslavia and Bulgaria in the 1970s and 1980s. His research has focused on ethnicity and nationalism in socialist Yugoslavia, the economic and political transitions in the Balkans, and institution building in conflict zones and developing countries. He recently coedited *Almost Pork: Distributive Politics in Developing Countries* (2014). He has published and lectured in North America and Europe. He received his PhD in political science from the University of Michigan.

Elez Biberaj is director of Voice of America's (VOA) Eurasia Division. He is responsible for VOA's radio, television, and Internet programming targeting Russia, Ukraine, Armenia, Georgia, and the Balkans. From 1986 to 2004, he served as chief of VOA's Albanian Service. He has authored three books on Albanian affairs, including *Albania in Transition: The Rocky Road to Democracy* (1998), and contributed chapters to several others. He has also published articles in the *World Today*, *Encyclopedia Britannica*, *Conflict Studies*, *Problems of Communism*, *Survey*, and *East European Quarterly*. Biberaj holds a PhD in political science from Columbia University. The views expressed herein are the author's and do not represent the views of Voice of America.

Daniel Brett studied at the University of the West of England, Bristol, and the University of London. His research deals with rural politics and the Agrarian movements in Europe and Latin America. He currently teaches at the Open University in the United Kingdom.

Janusz Bugajski is a senior fellow at the Center for European Policy Analysis in Washington, DC, and host of the television shows *Bugajski Hour*, on Albanian Screen in Tirana, Albania, and *Bugajski Time*, on Atlas TV, Podgorica, Montenegro. He is author of nineteen books on Europe, Russia, and transatlantic relations, contributor to various US and European newspapers and journals, and columnist for media outlets in Albania, Bosnia-Herzegovina, Bulgaria, Croatia, Georgia, Kosovo, and Ukraine. His newest book is titled *Conflict Zones: North Caucasus and Western Balkans Compared* (2014). Recent books include *Return of the Balkans: Challenges to European Integration and U.S. Disengagement* (2013), *Georgian Lessons: Conflicting Russian and Western Interests in the Wider Europe* (2010), *Dismantling the West: Russia's Atlantic Agenda* (2009), *America's New European Allies* (2009), and *Expanding Eurasia: Russia's European Ambitions* (2008).

Valerie Bunce is the Aaron Binenkorb Chair of International Studies and professor of government at Cornell University. Her research has addressed four issues, all involving comparisons among the postcommunist states: patterns of regime change, the relationship between democratization and economic reform, the impact of US democracy promotion, and the role of nationalism in democratic politics and the dissolution of states. She is author of over seventy articles and two single-authored books, most recently, *Subversive Institutions: The Design and the Destruction of Socialism and the State* (1999). She is also coeditor, with Kathryn Stoner-Weiss and Michael McFaul, of *Democracy and Authoritarianism in the Postcommunist World* (2009). Finally, she is coauthor with Sharon Wolchik of *Defeating Authoritarian Leaders in Postcommunist Countries* (2011). She received her PhD in political science from the University of Michigan.

Alfio Cerami was a research associate at the Centre d'études européennes at Sciences Po, Paris, and an international consultant for UNICEF. He held appointments as lecturer or visiting lecturer at the University of Erfurt (Germany), Sciences Po Paris, the Centre for German and European Studies of the State University of St. Petersburg (Russia), Schiller International University (Paris Campus), and Southern Methodist University (Paris Campus). He was also an assistant professor at the American Graduate School of International Relations and Diplomacy. His research concentrates on the way political, economic, and social transformations influence the process of democratization and the consolidation of democratic institutions. His most recent publications include *Permanent Emergency Welfare Regimes in Sub-Saharan Africa* (2013), *Migration and Welfare in the New Europe*, with E. Carmel and T. Papadopoulos (2011), *Post-communist Welfare Pathways*, with P. Vanhuysse (2009), and *Social Policy in Central and Eastern Europe* (2006).

Zsuzsa Csergő is associate professor of political studies and graduate chair at Queen's University in Kingston, Canada. She is also president of the Association for the Study of Nationalities. She specializes in the study of nationalism in contemporary European politics, with particular focus on postcommunist Central and Eastern Europe. Csergő obtained her undergraduate education at the Babeş-Bolyai University in Cluj, Romania, and her graduate education at The George Washington University in Washington, DC (MA in Russian and East European studies, PhD in political science). Before joining the Queen's faculty, she was assistant professor of political science and coordinator of the Women's Leadership Program in US and International Politics at The George Washington University. She was also a regular lecturer at the US Foreign Service Institute. Csergő is currently working on a comparative book about minority inclusion in the enlarged European Union. She is author of *Talk of the Nation* (2007) and articles in *Perspectives on Politics, Foreign Policy, Nations and Nationalism, Europe-Asia Studies*, and *East European Politics and Societies*. She has received the Fernand Braudel Senior Fellowship from the European University Institute in Florence, Italy (fall 2006); the 2005 Sherman Emerging Scholar Award from the University of North Carolina, Wilmington; and research grants from the Woodrow Wilson International Center for Scholars, the Institute for the Study of World Politics, the American Council of Learned Societies, the Social Science Research Council, the George Hoffman Foundation, and the Social Sciences and Humanities Research Council of Canada.

Jane Leftwich Curry is professor of political science at Santa Clara University. She is author of several books on Polish and Central and East European politics, including *Poland's Permanent Revolution* (1995), *Polish Journalists: Professionalism and Politics* (2011), *The Black Book of Polish Censorship* (1983), *The Left Transformed* (2004), and *Dissent in Eastern Europe* (1983). She has also written extensively on issues of civil society and pluralism in transitions, as well as transitional justice. In 2003 and 2004, she held the Fulbright–University of Warsaw Distinguished Chair in East European Politics. In 2006, she received a United States Institute of Peace grant to examine the dynamics of the colored revolutions in Serbia, Ukraine, and Georgia. She holds a PhD in political science from Columbia University.

Daina S. Eglitis is associate professor of sociology and international affairs at The George Washington University. Her research focuses on the social, economic, and cultural dimensions of postcommunist transformation in Central and Eastern Europe. Her articles have appeared in *Acta Sociologica, Cultural Sociology, East European Politics and Societies, Slavic Review*, and the *Journal of Baltic Studies*, among others. She is author of *Imagining the Nation: History, Modernity, and Revolution in Latvia* (2002) and coauthor of the introductory text *Discover Sociology* (2014). From 2007 to 2008, she was a Fulbright scholar in residence at the Latvian Academy of Culture in Riga, Latvia, and from 2011 to 2013, she was an international scholar with the Department of Sociology at Yerevan State University in Armenia. Her current work examines Soviet and post-Soviet collective memories of Latvian women in the Red Army in World War II. She received her PhD in sociology from the University of Michigan (1998).

Sharon Fisher is principal economist with IHS Global Insight in Washington, DC. In that role, she provides economic and political analysis, risk assessment, and forecasting on a number of countries in Central and Eastern Europe. During the mid-1990s, she worked as an analyst at the RFE/RL Research Institute in Munich and the Open Media Research Institute in Prague. Fisher has presented her work at numerous conferences and seminars in Europe and the United States, and her extensive list of publications includes *Political Change in Post-communist Slovakia and Croatia: From Nationalist to Europeanist* (2006). She holds a PhD from the School of Slavonic and East European Studies at University College London.

Brian Grodsky is associate professor of comparative politics at the University of Maryland, Baltimore County, and a graduate of University of Michigan, Ann Arbor (PhD, 2006). His research interests include human rights, transitional justice, democratization, global civil society, social movements, and US foreign policy. He is author of *The Costs of Justice* (2010) and *Social Movements and the New State: The Fate of Pro-Democracy Organizations When Democracy Is Won* (2012). His articles have appeared in journals including the *European Journal of International Relations, Journal of Peace Research, Journal of Human Rights, International Studies Review, Government and Opposition, Slavic Review, Europe-Asia Studies, Democratization, Human Rights Review, World Affairs, Problems of Post-communism, Central Asian Survey,* and *Journal of Central Asian Studies.*

Shane Killian is a PhD student in the Department of Political Science at the University of Pittsburgh, specializing in international organizations and international political economy. His dissertation focuses on the structure of the international financial system at both the global and European levels and the financial crisis of 2008.

Taras Kuzio is a research associate at the Centre for Political and Regional Studies, Canadian Institute of Ukrainian Studies, University of Alberta, and a nonresident fellow at the Center for Transatlantic Relations, School of Advanced International Studies, Johns Hopkins University. His latest book is *Commissars into Oligarchs: A Contemporary History of Ukraine* (2014). He is author and editor of fourteen books, including *Open Ukraine: Changing Course towards a European Future* (2011), five think tank monographs, twenty-five book chapters, and seventy-five scholarly articles on postcommunist and Ukrainian politics and European studies. He received a BA in economics from the University of Sussex, an MA in Soviet and East European studies from the University of London, and a PhD in political science from the University of Birmingham, England. He was a postdoctoral fellow at Yale University.

Ronald H. Linden is director of the EU Center of Excellence and the European Studies Center and professor of political science at the University of Pittsburgh (Pitt). A Princeton PhD (1976), he was director of the Center for Russian and East European Studies at Pitt from 1984 to 1989 and 1991 to 1998. From 1989 to 1991, Dr. Linden served as director of research for Radio Free Europe in Munich, Germany, with responsibility for observing and analyzing the extraordinary changes in Eastern Europe. Dr. Linden's research has focused on Central and southeastern Europe and, in recent years, on Turkey's foreign policy. His publications include *Turkey and Its Neighbors: Foreign Relations in Transition* (2012) and, with Yasemin Irepoğlu, "Turkey and the Balkans: New Forms of Political Community?" in *Turkish Studies* (2013). His publications on Eastern Europe include editing two special issues of *Problems of Post-communism*, titled "The Meaning of 1989 and After" (2009) and "The New Populism in Central and Southeast Europe" (2008). Dr. Linden is a contributing author to *The Berlin Wall: 20 Years Later* (2009), published by the US Department of State, commemorating twenty years since the fall of the Berlin Wall. He has received fellowships and research grants from the German Marshall Fund, the United States Institute of Peace, and the National Council for Eurasian and East European Research. He has been a Fulbright research scholar, a Fulbright distinguished lecturer, and a research scholar at the Kennan Institute for Advanced Russian Studies and a guest scholar of the East European Studies Program, both in the Woodrow Wilson International Center for Scholars.

Paula Pickering is associate professor of government at the College of William and Mary. Her research focuses on peace building, democratization aid, and ethnic politics in southeastern Europe. She is completing a project on the impact of foreign aid on local democratic governance in the Western Balkans. As part of her work with the AidData Research Consortium, she is working on a collaborative, cross-regional study of the impact of aid for subnational governance. She is author of *Peacebuilding in the Balkans: The View from the Ground Floor* (2007). Recent articles have been published in *Suedosteuropa*, *Problems of Post-communism*, *Democratization*, *Europe-Asia Studies*, *Communist and Post-communist Studies*, and *Ethnic and Racial Studies*. Between 1990 and 1994, she worked as the politico-military analyst for Eastern Europe at the US Department of State. She also worked as a human rights officer for the Organization for Security and Co-operation in Europe's Mission in Bosnia-Herzegovina (1996). She received her PhD in political science from the University of Michigan in 2001.

Peter Rožič, SJ, is the Jesuit Legacy Research Scholar and Postdoctoral Fellow in the Department of Political Science at Santa Clara University. His research focuses on democratization, conflict resolution, modern political philosophy, and transitional justice. His recent publications have been on transitional justice and electoral results in Bosnia.

Marilyn Rueschemeyer is professor of sociology at the Rhode Island School of Design and the Watson Institute for International Studies at Brown University, where she is chair of the European Politics Series. She is also an associate of the Davis Center for Russian Studies at Harvard University. Her research has focused on social and political life in Central and

Eastern Europe before and after the end of communism. Her books include *Professional Work and Marriage: An East-West Comparison* (1981); *Soviet Émigré Artists: Life and Work in the USSR and the United States*, with Igor Golomshtok and Janet Kennedy (1985); *The Quality of Life in the German Democratic Republic*, with Christiane Lemke (1989); *Participation and Democracy East and West*, edited with Dietrich Rueschemeyer and Bjorn Wittrock (1998); *Women in the Politics of Postcommunist Eastern Europe* (1994, 1998); *Left Parties and Social Policy in Postcommunist Europe*, edited with Linda Cook and Mitchell Orenstein (1999); *Art and the State: The Visual Arts in Comparative Perspective*, coauthored with Victoria Alexander (2005); and *Women in Power in Post-communist Parliaments*, edited with Sharon Wolchik (2009). She has been a fellow at the Stockholm Institute of Soviet and East European Economics, the Swedish Collegium for Advanced Study in the Social Sciences in Uppsala, and the Department of Sociology at the Hebrew University of Jerusalem. She has also been a guest of the Wissenschaftszentrum, Berlin, and the Academy of Sciences of the Czech Republic. In 1972, 1982, and 1997, she was a senior associate member of St. Antony's College, Oxford University. She holds a PhD from Brandeis University.

Joshua Spero is associate professor of international politics at Fitchburg State University, where he has taught since 2003, serves as the director of the university's Regional Economic Development Institute, and also coordinates the International Studies Minor Program and the Washington Center Internship Program. He focuses on international security, international relations, government decision making, and simulation crisis-management decision making. Before transitioning to academia, he served as senior civilian strategic planner for the Joint Chiefs of Staff's J-5 Strategic Plans and Policy Directorate in the Europe-NATO Division (1994–2000); national security analyst at the Institute for National Strategic Studies (1990–1994); and deputy assistant for Europe and the USSR at the Office of the Secretary of Defense (1988–1990). From 1988 to 1994, he also served as the US Army's Ft. Leavenworth, KS–based Soviet Army/Foreign Military Studies Office liaison officer in Washington, DC. He received his PhD from the Johns Hopkins University's School for Advanced International Studies and has authored, among numerous publications, *Bridging the European Divide: Middle Power Politics and Regional Security Dilemmas* (2004).

Sharon L. Wolchik is professor of political science and international affairs at The George Washington University. She has also served as adjunct chair (contractor) of the Advanced Area Studies Seminar on East Central Europe at the US Department of State's Foreign Service Institute. She has conducted research on the role of women in the transition to postcommunism in Central and Eastern Europe and the role of women leaders, as well as on ethnic issues and other aspects of politics. She is author of *Czechoslovakia in Transition: Politics, Economics, and Society* (1991) and coeditor of *Women in Power in Post-communist Parliaments*, with Marilyn Rueschemeyer (2009); *Women and Democracy: Latin America and Central and Eastern Europe*, with Jane S. Jaquette (1998); *Domestic and Foreign Policy in Eastern Europe in the 1980s*, with Michael Sodaro (1983); *Ukraine: In Search of a National Identity*, with Volodymyr Zviglyanich (2000); *The Social Legacy of Communism*, with James R. Millar (1994); and *Women, State and Party in Eastern Europe*, with Alfred G. Meyer (1985). She is coauthor with Valerie Bunce of *Defeating Authoritarian Leaders in Postcommunist Countries* (2011). She received her PhD in political science from the University of Michigan.